THE
VALLEY OF KASHMIR

PLATE I

Frontispiece.] [*Negative by Captain Allan*

VIEW OF CITY AND RIVER. TO THE LEFT THE SHRINE OF SHAH HAMADÁN. THE ARCHITECTURE OF THE SHRINE IS TYPICAL OF ALL KASHMÍRI ZIÁRATS

THE
VALLEY OF KASHMIR

WALTER R. LAWRENCE, I.C.S., C.I.E.

SETTLEMENT COMMISSIONER,
KASHMIR AND JAMMU STATE

WITH ILLUSTRATIONS

GYAN

Published by

Gyan Publishing House
5, Ansari Road
Daryaganj, New Delhi-110002
Phone: 011-47034999, 9811692060
E-mail: books@gyanbooks.com

Distribution Network
gyanbooks.com
India, USA, Canada, UK, Australia, France

ISBN : 978-81-212-4181-6 (PB)
First Published, London, 1895

2nd Impression 2020

Printed at: Gyan Press, Delhi.

The Valley of Kashmir
Author: Walter R. Lawrence

THE

VALLEY OF KASHMÍR

BY

WALTER R. LAWRENCE, I.C.S., C.I.E.

SETTLEMENT COMMISSIONER, KASHMÍR AND JAMMU STATE

WITH ILLUSTRATIONS

London

HENRY FROWDE

OXFORD UNIVERSITY PRESS WAREHOUSE

AMEN CORNER, E.C.

1895

Oxford
HORACE HART, PRINTER TO THE UNIVERSITY

CONTENTS

LIST OF PLATES

THE VALLEY OF KASHMÍR.

CHAPTER I.

INTRODUCTORY.

THIS report, which is written on the lines of the Punjab Gazetteers, deals with Kashmír proper. Though our Settlement operations have extended to Gilgit and to Jammu territory, it has been necessary to exclude information gathered in those countries, even though connected with Kashmír. It has been difficult to decide what facts should be recorded and what discarded, but so far as it has been possible I have avoided the repetition of information already presented to the State in the fifteen Assessment Reports of Kashmír which have been written by me. In them will be found the rates of assessment, the mode of classifying and valuing soils, and many facts bearing on the past revenue administration of Kashmír. In this report I shall deal with subjects of general interest. It has been written at odd hours, in the midst of much interruption, and I regret that I have not the leisure to use one half of the notes made by me during the six seasons I have worked in Kashmír. In this opening chapter I allude to matters which may help to elucidate points incidentally mentioned in other parts of the report, and I offer suggestions which may help the future administration of the country. Kashmír, as possessing a distinct nationality, character, language, dress, and body of customs, affords much that is interesting, while its unique history and curious administration are worth careful study. The beautiful valley has been for many years a pleasure resort of Europeans, and many books have been written on the subject of Kashmír. But even the best of these, Drew's *Jammu and Kashmír*, says little about the valley or its people, and most works which I have read do not add much to the information gathered by Vigne. Strange and hazy ideas have prevailed regarding the wealth of the country, the character of the people, and the system of administration— CHAP. I.

CHAP. I.

ideas which can only be confirmed or refuted by one whose life and work have brought him into close contact with the villagers and officials. From the first I have found the villagers communicative as they sat by the camp fire, while the officials are often well informed, and excellent talkers, by no means reticent.

Kashmír in 1887, when the Settlement commenced, may be described as an absolute monarchy. If an aristocracy of power ever existed, the tall poppies were cut down years ago, and the people looked to the Mahárájá as their direct lord and master. They yearn for personal rule centred in one man, and they are bewildered and disgusted when rule and power filter into many channels. In Kashmír the Mahárájá is represented by a Governor (Hákim-i-Alá), and it is of the highest importance that this official be a man of energy and experience, and that all departments, whether revenue, police, forests, &c., should be absolutely under his control. If this be borne in mind, the administration of Kashmír will be very easy. It is a small country, and an energetic Governor could visit any village in the valley in a day's ride.

Much has been written of the abuses which have prevailed in the administration of Kashmír. They were numerous and deplorable, and when I first came to Kashmír in 1889, I found the people sullen, desperate and suspicious. They had been taught for many years that they were serfs without any rights but with many disabilities. They were called *Zulm parast*, or worshippers of tyranny, and every facility was afforded to their cult. They were forced by soldiers to plough and sow, and the same soldiers attended at harvest time. They were dragged away from their houses to carry loads to Gilgit, and every official had a right to their labour and their property. Their simple proposition *yus Karih gonglu sui Karih Krao*[1] was ignored, and their position was infinitely worse than that of the Tiers État before the French Revolution. While the villagers were thus degraded, the people of the city were pampered and humoured, and the following passage from Hazlitt's *Life of Napoleon Bonaparte* gives a fair idea of Kashmír before the Settlement commenced :—

'The peasants were overworked, half-starved, treated with hard words and hard blows, subjected to unceasing exactions and every species of petty tyranny . . . while in the cities a number of unwholesome and useless professions, and a crowd of lazy menials, pampered the vices or administered to the pride and luxury of the great.'

It was no wonder that cultivation was bad, that the revenue was not paid, and that the peasants were roving from one village to another in the hope of finding some rest and freedom from oppression. The Kashmíri is

[1] He who ploughs shall reap.

made up of contradictions. He is timid yet persistent, degraded yet intellectual. Village life meant little to him. His one object was to escape the pressgang when carriage was wanted for Gilgit, and to secure some share of the autumn's grain when the tax collectors appeared. He would not hesitate to throw his burden on to his neighbour's shoulders, and if he failed he would depart to some other village under the aegis of a privileged person who would protect him from the *corvée*, and would allow no one but himself to oppress the wanderer. Pages might be written by me on facts which have come under my personal observation, but it will suffice to say that the system of administration had degraded the people and taken all heart out of them. The country was in confusion, the revenue was falling off, and those in authority were making hay while the sun shone. Strong personal government is, I believe, the only form of government possible in Kashmír for many years to come, but it is difficult for the Mahárájás to supervise the administration of the valley when they are away in their winter capital Jammu. The peasants, one and all, attributed their miseries to the deputies through whom the Mahárájás ruled, and they have always recognized that their rulers were sympathetic and anxious to secure their prosperity. But the officials of Kashmír would never allow their master to know the real condition of the people, or to find out that the revenue of the country was diminishing. If the Governor of Kashmír were not active and honest, dishonesty ran rampant through every grade of officialdom.

> 'There's not a crime
> But takes its proper change out still in crime
> If once rung on the counter of this world,'

and the slightest weakness or corruption on the part of the Governor had its echo in every corner of the valley. Not only were the officials corrupt but the peasants and their headmen were also dishonest, all joining to rob their master's treasury.

His Highness the Mahárájá Pratáb Singh, G.C.S.I., recognizing that it was impossible to check these abuses without records and statistics, resolved on effecting a land Revenue Settlement of his country. At first it was extremely difficult to persuade the people that the Settlement would be a reality, or to inspire them with a belief that there would be some continuity in the administration. Little by little, confidence has sprung up. Land which had no value in 1889 is now eagerly sought after by all classes. Cultivation has extended and improved. Houses have been rebuilt and repaired, fields fenced in, orchards planted, vegetable gardens well stocked, and new mills constructed. Women no longer are seen toiling in the fields, for their husbands are now at home to do the work, and the long journeys to Gilgit are a thing of the past. When the

CHAP. I. harvest is ripe the peasant reaps it at his own good time, and not a soldier ever enters the villages. The old saying—

> '*Batta, batta,*
> *Tah piyada patta,*'

which meant 'we are asking for food and the tax collector is after us,' is no longer heard, for the people are left with ample grain to feed their families. Before 1887 the peasants rarely tasted their beloved food rice. Now all eat rice, and enjoy salt, and the luxury of tea. Little shops are springing up in the villages, and whereas I never saw a metal vessel in any peasant's house three years ago, now a brass cooking-pot is by no means rare.

There has been a great change, but it is important that the State should remember that the change has been sudden, and every effort should be made to keep faith with the villagers. A few breaches of the promises made at Settlement would again plunge the country into confusion, and it is well to bear in mind that many hungry middlemen (the *fermiers*) driven out by the Settlement are waiting and watching. It is well too to remember that a people so broken and degraded as the Kashmíris do not in a few years harden into a resolute and self-respecting community. They are a soft, timid people, only too ready to avoid a citizen's responsibilities and to shelter themselves behind the plausible and fraudulent middleman. There is not a single middleman left in the villages at the present time, but if the State withdrew its vigilant watch some 40 per cent. of the peasants might again become the serfs of middlemen and officials.

Security of tenure has a magical effect, but I think that immunity from forced labour has been as efficacious in promoting confidence among the villages. The construction of the Gilgit road, and the organization of a transport service have done much to abolish the worst incidents of the *corvée*, but if the Mahárájá himself had not set the example of limiting the demands made by his camp-followers, 'Purveyance' would have lingered on for years. It was no uncommon thing for 300 sheep to be collected at one stage. Nothing would be paid for them. Now all supplies are paid for. If honest dealing continues for another ten years I believe that the Kashmíris, so hardly spoken of, will become honest. It should be remembered that from the point of view of the peasant, honesty has not hitherto been the best policy.

Kashmír is a very old country, and its people are very old-fashioned. Those who have studied the history of Kashmír say that the people have not changed much since the times of ancient Hindu kings. This is quite possible, but I think that many of the hard things said about the Kashmíris are due to the fact that the official interpreters of their character have been foreigners, often grasping and corrupt, always unsympathetic.

Mughal Subahs, Pathán Sirdars, Sikh and Dogra Governors dismissed all difficulties of administration, and all humane suggestions emanating from their masters, with the remark that the Kashmíris were dishonest, treacherous and *zulm parast*. It is the old tale of giving a dog a bad name, and I must confess that during my first year's work in the valley I shared these views. But I soon grew to understand that the Kashmíri, like other orientals, has two sides to his character as distinct as light and darkness. His great yearning is to be left alone—to till his fields and weave his woollen cloth. The official visit, which to us officials seems so pleasant to all concerned, sends the pulse of the village up many degrees. and those are happy who dwell far away from the beaten tracks. The dark side of the Kashmíri is revealed when he is in the presence of officials. He has had good reason to hate and distrust them, and his only weapon against them is deceit. His light side is seen when he is in his field or with his family in the house. Take as an instance the relations of a Kashmíri cultivator with the village shopkeepers. The shopkeeper (*wáni*) is a Musalmán and must not take *interest*. He lends money to the peasants on a system known as *wád*. A man borrows 50 rupees, and promises to pay this within the year in blankets, ghi, apples, grain, &c. The rate fixed by the *wáni* for blankets will be 3 rupees, whereas the market price at which the *wáni* will sell is 3 rupees 8 annas, or 4 rupees. No bond (*hujat*) is signed by the borrower, and the only record of the transaction is an entry in the daily ledger of the *wáni*. I have always made a point of talking with the *wánis* whenever I see a village shop, and they are unanimous in saying that they never make a bad debt and that they are never obliged to sue a debtor. This state of things does not argue that the Kashmíri peasants are dishonest.

In the statistical chapter, facts will be found which show that crime is almost non-existent in Kashmír. Crimes of dishonesty may be said to be absolutely non-existent among the peasants. Property is entirely safe, and during the six years which I have spent in the villages, I have never heard of crimes of theft, or burglary being committed by agriculturists. This surely points to the fact that the Kashmíris are not the dishonest people they are represented to be.

Since 1890 all suits connected with land, saving land situated within Srinagar and a few adjoining villages, have been removed from the ordinary courts and have been made over to me for decision. My procedure has been to hear and decide such suits in the village where the claim has arisen. Under a chenár tree in the presence of the assembled villagers the claimant prefers his suit and the defendant makes his reply. Then the old men of the village and the headmen of the neighbourhood give their opinion on the case. and a brief entry is made by me which finally settles the claim.

CHAP. I. This may seem a very rough and ready way of disposing of land suits, but so far no man has ever appealed against my decision. If a claimant went to the Courts in Srinagar, the dark side of his character would appear. Pleaders and Court attendants would adulterate his simple claim, and in the same way the defendant would throw off the candour and truthfulness inspired by the presence of his neighbours in the village, and would lie in the most ingenious and surprising manner. For five years this procedure of enquiry on the spot has gone on, and I attribute much of the quiet prosperity which is now growing in the villages, to the fact that money is not spent and bad blood is not engendered by litigation. My system is the old system of the village *pancháyat*. The commonest intellect can tell from the faces of the villagers whether the claim is just, and the 'genius loci' seems to keep both claimant and defendant to the point and to the truth. This system is easy and possible in Kashmír, for as I have already remarked, one can reach any village in the valley in a day's ride.

My object in alluding to this procedure is to add further testimony to the fact that the Kashmíri peasants are not dishonest. If they had been the hopeless liars they are reputed to be, I could never have disposed of the many suits which have arisen. A Kashmíri will rarely lie when he is confronted in his village by his fellow villagers; he will invariably lie when he enters the murky atmosphere of the Law Courts.

Perhaps this summary procedure would have been impossible if I had not in 1889 induced the State to withhold from the Kashmíris the power to alienate their land by sale or mortgage. If hereafter, when population increases and communications are improved, the State should unfortunately see fit to give the fatal gift of alienation to their Musalmán tenants, I trust that some portion of the holding (which should be two acres of irrigated and four acres of dry land) will be rendered absolutely inalienable. I hope too that the suggestion that pleaders should be allowed to intervene in suits connected with land will never be made again, or that if it is made that it will meet with the wise veto which was accorded to it in 1892. If litigation is fostered in Kashmír prosperity in the villages will be checked.

The work of Settlement has been anxious and difficult. Powerful interests were at work against us, and if it had not been for the loyal and consistent support rendered to me by His Highness the Mahárájá and his advisers, these interests would have made a Settlement impossible. These adverse interests were:

(1) The official classes and the Pandits who held land on privileged terms.

(2) The headmen of the villages.

(3) The city of Srinagar.

As regards the officials it is pleasant to be able to say that from active opposition they have now passed to friendly co-operation. The Tahsildars, on whom the Revenue Administration chiefly depends, have been reduced from fifteen to eleven. With one exception they are all men of the old officialdom of Kashmír, and at the present time only one of the eleven is a Pandit. It would have been easy to carry out *temporary* reforms in Kashmír, if trained Tahsildars had been imported from the Panjab as was at one time suggested. But apart from the unfairness and unpopularity of such a measure, I am not sure that reforms effected through so foreign an agency would have been permanent. By selecting the best of the Kashmíri officials as Tahsildars, by raising their pay and by treating them with the respect due to their office, I believe that the most important agents of the revenue administration have grown to look on the Settlement with favour. Of course numbers of superfluous officials who hovered round the carcass of the revenue have disappeared from the scene, and the *fermiers* and the soldiers have been obliged to seek other occupations. Happily, owing to the large influx of silver into the country, and to the briskness of internal trade, most of the drones have found a livelihood. As regards the privileged holders of land every effort has been made to treat them with indulgence, and for another ten years they will continue to be privileged, though their revenue will be somewhat higher than it used to be. The headmen of villages have on the whole accepted the change brought by the Settlement without any prolonged opposition. They have now to pay revenue for their land like other cultivators, but their social position is better, and they are paid five per cent. on Revenue Collections, whereas formerly they received nothing.

The interests of the city have from the earliest times been opposed to the interests of the villages. The city people want grain and other village produce at rates far below the cost of production. 'What the eye does not see the heart does not grieve'—and the authorities saw and heard the city, but the villagers were out of sight and out of mind. I have described in another chapter the facts connected with the collection of revenue in kind.

Low prices of the chief staple rice (lower this year, 1894, than they have been for years) coupled with difficulty in selling the State grain brought into Srinagar at the end of 1893, the opening of a cart road from Bárámúlá to Srinagar, the extraordinary increase in the amount of silver now in circulation in the city, and last, but not least, the growing desire of shawl-weavers and even Pandits to obtain labour, all point to the conclusion that a new era has dawned for Srinagar, and that before long honest industry will be the rule, and helpless and ignoble dependence on the State and its charities will be the exception.

I have urged on the authorities the establishment of Technical Schools;

CHAP. I. and the State which has unwittingly done so much to pauperize and emasculate the population of its summer capital, has splendid work now before it in raising the *Shahr-bash*[1] to the position of self-helping and industrious citizens.

In Chapter X, I have endeavoured to describe some of the most striking points of the national character, and it will be wise to bear these points in mind when further reforms or changes are contemplated. A feeling of impatience may be aroused when the reformer sees that the Kashmíris are opposed to changes which are obviously for their good. It should, however, be remembered that if it had not been for their essentially conservative nature the Kashmíris would have succumbed to the stern rules of social evolution, and would have been blotted out as a distinct nationality by their strong superiors the Mughals, Patháns, Sikhs, and Dogras. It is no exaggeration to say that these successive dynasties have left no impress on the national character—that there has been no progress in the ordinary sense of the word, and that the Kashmíris are now, in spite of many experiments in administration, very much what they were in the times before the Mughal conquest linked the valley with India. It is therefore necessary to be patient, and it is wrong to condemn the Kashmíri if he is sceptical regarding the advantages of progress. The people have a keen intellect, and this joined to their steady aversion to change makes them very difficult subjects for administrative experiments. Many changes have been introduced by the Settlement, but they have been made after a careful study of the character and ideas of the people. Old institutions have been adapted to new wants, and in the future reform will be futile unless it proceeds on these lines. But in order to understand old institutions it is essential to learn the customs of the people, and the shortcomings of past administrations are chiefly due to the fact that the authorities considered the Kashmíris and their usages unworthy of study. My experience is that in dealing with so peculiar a people nothing, however small, is unimportant if it gives a clue to the working of their minds. Take as instances the old practice of espionage, or the blind credence which the village people place in any news coming from Srinagar. The Kashmíris are well styled *Háwabín*[2], and it would save much trouble and disquietude if the State would endeavour to suppress the evil system which still lingers on of disseminating false rumours. The *Zaina-kadal*, or fourth bridge of the city, used to be the place where false rumours were hatched, but now the news makers have moved to the first bridge, the *Amiran-kadal*. Though the wise knew that *Khabar-i-Zaina-kadal*[3] was false, the majority are not wise, and much misery is caused to the villagers by the reports which

[1] City people. [2] Watchers of the wind.
[3] News from the *Zaina-kadal*.

emanate from the city. The Kashmíris are very unstable and very prone to give undue weight to rumours. They are emotional and ruled by sentiment. They will do excellent work on water-courses and embankments if coaxed, and praised, and encouraged with small presents of snuff. They will do little if paid a full daily wage. They like and admire stern determination in their ruler. All they ask is that they may have access and hearing on certain occasions. They are accomplished talkers, but have an instinctive dread of their words being committed to paper. Writing in their opinion is a trap and a fraud. While on the whole they like certainty in the revenue administration, and are not as some suppose enamoured of the elastic properties of a fluctuating assessment, they would hate our western ideas of justice and judicial procedure. I have done my utmost to leave the system of Kashmír alone where it was possible, and should deplore the introduction of elaborate rules and procedure. These Sibylline books, with officials as interpreters, would do no good to Kashmír. All that the State need now do for its agricultural population is to leave the villagers alone. Cholera and small-pox should be grappled with so that the population—at present inadequate—should increase and multiply. Kashmír is generations behind the Panjab, and what is good and necessary in the Panjab is dangerous and premature in this country. A wise Kashmíri with whom I was conversing on the subject of the alleged oppression of the police, said. in answer to a question of mine, 'Of course the police annoy us, and I presume that this is the purpose for which they are employed. There is no crime in the country, and the police must have something to do.' There is no doubt work for the police in the city and towns and on the road, but I doubt whether their presence is necessary in the villages. But police are necessary in the Panjab districts, and it has perhaps been argued that human nature being the same in all countries police are required in the districts of Kashmír. I merely mention the police as an instance to show that Kashmír is a peculiar country, which need not necessarily be administered at present by the strict pattern adopted in British India. While the object of administration should be to leave the people alone to recover from the atrophy which has been caused by over-government, much can be done by example and advice.

At the present time the Kashmíri is ruled by *Rawáj*[1] and is content to abide by the *Aín*[2] of the country. In some respects he is better off than his fellows in India, he has ample grazing for his sheep and cattle, fuel for the winter, good warm clothes, and sufficient manure for cultivation. He is not extravagant, and happily spends little on marriages and similar occasions. But it is possible as prosperity increases the Kashmíri

[1] Custom. [2] Code of Customs.

will follow the example of India and will increase the expenses of marriages. If the State will intervene and order that the old scale of marriage expenses shall be observed the people will gladly obey. They are docile and always ready to carry out orders which are conservative in their tendency. They understand that they are responsible for the maintenance of irrigation, channels, and of communications between villages, and it would be a great mistake if the State ever relieved them of this responsibility.

Apart from the work of settling the villages and assisting in the revenue administration of Kashmír, I have held charge of Viticulture, Hops, Horticulture, and Sericulture. These subjects will be discussed elsewhere, but here I wish to state that although the last three have been worked with a fair profit they will never become of real importance until the State makes them over to private capitalists. I think that whereas no Europeans could live and thrive as ordinary agricultural colonists in Kashmír, they could do good to themselves and to the State if they settled in Kashmír and devoted capital and labour to the production of wine, hops, canned and dried fruits, vegetables and silk. The cultivation of vines could be enormously extended in the immediate neighbourhood of Srinagar; there is a vast area of land admirably suited to hops. Horticulture can practically take care of itself, while the countless mulberry trees and the ease with which the tree can be propagated open out a wide field for sericulture. An amateur's experiences, though extending over six years, may not be worth much, but the opinions I now express are founded on the views held by men who are practical experts in viticulture, wine-making, and sericulture. As regards hops I can appeal to the best criterion, financial results. If private enterprise were allowed in these special industries, the good which would result to the State would be a perceptible increase in the revenue, and what is of greater importance an increased field of labour and employment for the people of Srinagar.

My best thanks are due to His Highness the Maháráját Pratáb Singh, G.C.S.I., and his brother Rájá Sir Amar Singh, K.C.S.I., for the help and encouragement which they have always extended to me. They and the Revenue Adviser to the State, Rai Bahádur Pandit Suráj koul, C.I.E., have, by their knowledge of the country and by their insight into oriental character, been able to protect me from falling into errors arising from ignorance and haste. By the interest which they have shown in the Settlement and by their personal kindness and sympathy they have made my work easy and pleasant, and I can never sufficiently acknowledge my gratitude nor bear fitting testimony to the fact that the Dogra rulers of Kashmír mean well and kindly by their subjects.

My warmest thanks are also due to Colonel Parry Nisbet, C.I.E.,

Colonel Prideaux, and Colonel Barr, who have held the office of Resident in Kashmír while the Settlement was in progress. They never failed to help me by advice, and the interest which they have taken in a work which is somewhat monotonous and technical has assisted my operations in many ways.

I have further to acknowledge the friendly assistance of Dr. W. King, Director of the Geological Survey of India, for perusing and revising the chapter on Geology. In the chapter on the Flora of Kashmír Dr. Aitchison, C.I.E., F.R.S., London and Edinburgh, has helped me in the kindest manner, while Mr. Duthie, Director of the Botanical Survey of Northern India, has contributed a list of plants which will form an admirable basis for further investigation. In the chapter on Fauna all that is valuable regarding mammals is due to Colonel A. Ward, while the splendid list of Birds has been compiled at a moment's notice with great labour by Colonel Unwin [1]. The chapter on Political History has been revised by the Sanskrit scholar, Dr. Stein.

For the illustrations I am indebted to Major Hepburn, Captain Allan, Captain Godfrey, and to Alam Chand, the State photographer. Many friends have read through my chapters on Social Life, Tribes and Castes, and Agriculture, and have helped me with their advice. Written as this report has been without books of reference, and at odd hours snatched from other more urgent work, it will appear clumsy and disjointed. I have probably left out much which would have been useful and interesting, but I have done my best to bring information regarding Kashmír up to date. When English words are printed in italics their Kashmíri equivalents will be found in the glossary.

[1] This list has been most kindly revised by Dr. Bowdler Sharpe, of the British Museum.

CHAPTER II.

DESCRIPTIVE.

CHAP. II.

General.

IF one looks at the map of the territories of His Highness the Mahárájá of Jammu and Kashmír one sees a white foot-print set in a mass of black mountains. This is the valley of Kashmír, known to its inhabitants as *Kashir*. Perched securely among the Himáláyás at an average height of about 6,000 feet above the sea, it is approximately eighty-four miles in length, and twenty to twenty-five miles in breadth. North, east, and west, range after range of mountains guard the valley from the outer world, while on the south it is cut off from the Panjab by rocky barriers fifty to seventy-five miles in width.

The valley is a resting-place for adventurous traders who seek the distant markets of Yarkand and Central Asia, and it furnishes a base whence military operations have been in recent years directed against the wild and turbulent tribes of the Shináki country to the north and north-east. More to the east lie the peaceful valleys of Báltistan or Little Thibet, where the gentle Báltis lead their harmless lives in a high, dry climate. Between Kashmír and Skardu (8.873 feet), the chief stronghold of the Báltis, are the great mountain plains of Devsai (13,400 feet), and to the east lies the high valley of Drás, through which runs the road to Leh and Yarkand. A journey of a few days from Kashmír carries one into countries of new languages, customs and religions, and the ethnologist and philologist would find much of interest in the primitive Shins, who live along the spurs of the mighty Nanga Parbat, in the Mongolian Báltis of Little Thibet, and in the simple Ladákhis,—Buddhists and polyandrists. South of the valley of Kashmír amidst the great mountains, the ethnologist would find the pleasant pastoral Gaddis, and might, if native historians are to be believed, discover in the customs of the old-fashioned Hindús of Kishtwár the ancient manners and usages of the Kashmíris as they were before the dwellers of the valley were converted to Islam.

The mountain ranges rising to a height of 18,000 feet on the north-east, dip down to something over 9,000 feet in the south, where the Bánihál pass affords an exit from the valley. Up to the end of May and sometimes by the beginning of October there is a continuous ring of snows around the valley. The winter snows disappear in summer, and with the spring and summer rains drain into the Jhelum river which rises within Kashmír. The catchment area of the valley has been calculated to be 116 miles long, with a width that varies from forty to seventy-five miles. So that the great artery of Kashmír receives the rainfall of some 3,900 square miles.

The only outlet for this from the valley is the narrow gorge at Bárámúlá where the placid river leaves the smooth grassy banks, and hurries headlong down its rocky course to the plains of the Panjab.

It has been the custom to describe the valley as an oval plain girt with a chain of mountains. But no figure can give a true idea of the splendid variety in the trend of the ranges, in the midst of which lie other vales rivalling in beauty the main valley of Kashmír[1]. Much has been written by Europeans on the subject of this beautiful country since Bernier told the world of 'Cachemire, the Paradise of the Indies[2],' and even the languid orientals, supposed by some to be incapable of appreciating beauty of scenery, are moved to admiration when they see Kashmír. In their language the valley is an emerald set in pearls, a land of lakes, clear streams, green turf, magnificent trees and mighty mountains—where the air is cool and the water sweet, where men are strong and women vie with the soil in fruitfulness. In the words of the Kashmíris the valley was a rock-bound prison from which in past time escape was difficult. The great snow mountains suggested nothing to them beyond the hopelessness of flight from tyranny. In the brief delineation of the valley, which I shall attempt, a comparison of Kashmír with other well-known countries would have been of great assistance. But its high elevation, its dry climate and curious flora, in which east blends with the west, render this impossible. In latitude Kashmír corresponds with Peshawar, Baghdád, and Damascus in Asia: with Fez in Morocco: and South Carolina in America, but it presents none of the characteristics of those countries. Persons have likened the climate of the valley to that of Switzerland until the end of May, and of Southern France in July and August. But as I shall explain, it is impossible to speak of Kashmír as possessing any one climate or group of characteristics. Every hundred feet of elevation brings some new phase of climate and of vegetation, and in a short ride of thirty miles

[1] An excellent account of Kashmír is given in the *Aín Akbari*. With the exceptions that the inhabitants no longer 'go upon the lakes in small boats to enjoy the diversion of hawking,' and no longer 'train leopards to hunt the elk,' the description is absolutely accurate at the present time.

[2] In his introduction to the Rajtarangini Kulan or Kalhána, Pandit says of the valley: 'It is a country where the sun shines mildly, being the place created by Kashayapa as if for his glory. High school-houses, the saffron, iced-water and grapes, which are rare even in heaven, are common here. Kailásá is the best place in the three worlds, Himáláyá the best part of Kailásá, and Kashmír the best place in Himáláyá.'

CHAP. II. one can pass from overpowering heat to a climate delightfully cool, or can escape from wearisome wet weather to a dry and sunny atmosphere. Though this report on Kashmír is written for the State administration with the object of recording the statistics and resources of the valley, it may not be out of place in this chapter to touch briefly on certain points which possess an interest for Europeans as well as for the rulers of Kashmír. I allude to these facts with the less hesitation, firstly because the country benefits to some extent by the visits of Europeans, and secondly because it has long been the ambition of the Mahárájás of Kashmír to accord hospitality and assistance to all who travel in their dependencies. In no country in the world are the officials more courteous and helpful than in Kashmír, and the old saying of Mahárájá Guláb Singh to the effect that the British subaltern was in his eyes equal to a king is still remembered and acted on. From an English point of view the valley contains nearly everything which should make life enjoyable. There is sport varied and excellent, there is scenery for the artist and layman, mountains for the mountaineer, flowers for the botanist, a vast field for the geologist, and magnificent ruins for the archaeologist. The epicure will find dainty fruits and vegetables cheaper here than perhaps in any part of the world, while the lounger can pass delightful days of *dolce far niente* in the mat house-boats moored under the shady chenár tree. And last, but not least, the invalid must find somewhere in the varied climate of Kashmír the change of 'air and water' which will restore him to the health of which the heat of the Indian plains have robbed him. Some authorities say that the valley is good for consumptive people. There are sulphur springs at Wean, within easy reach of Srinagar, and I imagine that the day will come when Kashmír will be a health resort not only of Anglo-Indians, but also of people from all parts of the world. Neither the natural beauty nor the delicious climate of the valley has been exaggerated in the books which I have read, and every year's residence in the valley discloses some new charm and new interest.

Mountains. The mountains which surround Kashmír are never monotonous. Infinitely varied in form and colour, they are such as an artist might picture in his dreams. Looking to the north one sees a veritable sea of mountains, broken into white crested waves, hastening in wild confusion to the great promontory of Nanga Parbat (26,620 feet). To the east stands Harámukh (16,903 feet), the grim mountain which guards the valley of the Sind. On it the legend says the snow only ceases to fall for one week in July, and men believe that the gleam from the vein of green emerald in the summit of the mountain renders all poisonous snakes harmless. Further south is Mahadeo, very sacred to the Hindús, which seems to almost look down on Srinagar, and south again are the lofty range of Gwásh Brári

(17,800 feet), and the peak of Amarnáth (17,321 feet), the mountain of the pilgrim, very beautiful in the evening sun. On the south-west is the Pánjál range with peaks of 15,000 feet, well-known to travellers from the Panjáb—further north the great rolling downs of the Tosh Maidan (14,000 feet) over which men pass to the Poonch country, and in the north-west corner rises the snowy Kazi Nág (12,125 feet) the home of the Márkhor. Every mile reveals some exquisite peak, around which cling curious legends of battles, demigods, and elephants. As the time draws on for the harvesting of the rice, the *pir* or *pantsál*[1], as it is called in the Kashmír language, possesses a painful interest for the cultivators, since early snows on the mountain tops carry a chill air to the valley which will do considerable injury to their crops. On the west, and wherever the mountain sides are sheltered from the hot breezes of the Panjáb plains, which blow across mountains fifty to seventy miles in breadth, there are grand forests of pines and firs. Down through these forests dash mountain streams[2] white with foam, passing in their course through pools of the purest cobalt. When the great dark forests cease, and the brighter woodland begins, the banks of the streams are ablaze with clematis, honeysuckle, jasmine and wild roses, which remind one of azaleas. The green smooth turf of the woodland glades is like a well-kept lawn dotted with clumps of hawthorn and other beautiful trees and bushes. It would be difficult to describe the colours which are seen on the Kashmír mountains. In early morning they are often a delicate semi-transparent violet relieved against a saffron sky, and with light vapours clinging round their crests. Then the rising sun deepens shadows, and produces sharp outlines and strong passages of purple and indigo in the deep ravines. Later on it is nearly all blue and lavender, with white snow peaks and ridges under a vertical sun, and as the afternoon wears on these become richer violet and pale bronze, gradually changing to rose and pink with yellow or orange snow, till the last rays of the sun have gone, leaving the mountains dyed a ruddy crimson with the snows showing a pale creamy green by contrast. Looking downward from the mountains the valley in the sunshine has the hues of the opal, the pale reds of the karéwá, the vivid light greens of the young rice, and the darker shades of the groves of trees relieved by sunlit sheets, gleams of water, and soft blue haze give a combination of tints reminding one irresistibly of the changing hues of that gem. It is impossible in the scope of this report to do justice to the beauty and grandeur of the mountains of Kashmír, or to enumerate the lovely glades and forests, visited by so few.

[1] *Pir* is the Dogri word for a mountain peak. *Pantsál* the Kashmíri word. Pir Pánjál, which is a corruption of Pir Pantsal, is a reduplication of terms.

[2] A mountain stream flowing noisily over stones is called by the Kashmíris *Arnáh*. When the stream reaches the flat country and flows gently it is known as a *Chóp*.

CHAP. II. Excellent guide-books tell of the magnificent scenery of the Sind and Liddar valleys and of the gentler charms of the Loláb, but none have described the equal beauties of the western side of Kashmír. Few countries can offer anything grander than the deep green mountain tarn Konsa Nág in the Pánjál range, the waters of which make a wild entrance into the valley over the splendid cataract of Arabal, while the rolling grass mountain called Tosh Maidán—the springy downs of Raiyár looking over the Suk Nág river as it twines, foaming down from the mountains—the long winding park known as Yusumárg,—and lower down still the little hills, which remind one of Surrey, and Nilnág with its pretty lake[1] screened by the dense forests, are worthy to be seen. Apart from their beauty and variety of temperature the mountains of Kashmír are of great importance to the country. They supply water for irrigation, timber, fuel, and the grazing upon which so much of the agricultural prosperity of the valley depends. As the summer draws on the sheep and cattle are driven up from the valley to the woodland *glades*, and as the sun grows hotter they pass on to the *Margs*[2] those beautiful stretches of turf which, ringed round with great forests, lie at an elevation of from 7,000 to 9,000 feet above the sea. But the best of the grazing is found even higher up, when the forests of pines and firs cease, and the birch trees appear. This high country is known as *Ílák*[3], and is the summer home of the shepherds and graziers. Many of the Margs are visited every year by Europeans, and Gulmarg, Sonamarg, and Nágmarg are charming places for a summer holiday. Perhaps Pahlgám, the village of the shepherds which stands at the head of the Liddar valley with its healthy forest of pines, and Gurais which lies at a distance of thirty-five miles from Bandipura, the port of the Wular lake, will before long rival in popularity the other Margs. Gurais is a lovely valley five miles in length lying at an elevation of about 8,000 feet above the sea. The Kishnganga river flows through it, and on either side tower mountain scarps of indescribable grandeur. Perhaps one of the most beautiful scenes in the whole of Kashmír is the grove of huge poplars through which the traveller enters the Gurais valley. The climate is dry and mild, excellent English vegetables can be grown, and the wild raspberries and currants are delicious.

The lateral valleys. As one descends the mountains and leaves the woodland glades cultivation commences immediately, and right up to the fringe of the forests the useful maize is grown and walnut trees abound. A little

[1] 'This is also held sacred, and many fanatics consume themselves with fire on its border.'—*Ain Akbari.*

[2] There is a Persian word (*Margh*) signifying a garden abounding in plants, but the Kashmíris use the word to denote land lying at a distance from the abode of men.

[3] The summer quarters of the Persian nomad tribes are known as Ílák.

PLATE II

To face page 17]

Negative by Captain Allan

A TYPICAL VIEW OF MOUNTAIN SCENERY. HIGH ELEVATION WITH BIRCH-TREES IN FOREGROUND

lower down, at an elevation of about 7,000 feet, rice of a hardy and stunted growth is found and the shady plane tree appears. Lower still superior rices are grown, and the water-courses are edged with willows. The side valleys which lead off from the vale of Kashmír, though possessing distinctive charms of their own, have certain features in common. At the mouth of the valley there is the wide delta of fertile soil on which the rice with its varying colours, the plane trees, mulberries and willows grow luxuriantly, a little higher up the land is terraced and rice still grows, and the slopes are ablaze with the aniline blooms of a wild indigo, till at about 7,000 feet the plane tree gives place to the walnut and the rice to the millets. On the left bank of the mountain river endless forests stretch from the bottom of the valley to the peaks, and on the right bank, where there is a nook or corner which is sheltered from the sun and the hot breezes of India, the pines and firs establish themselves. Then further up the valley the river, already a roaring torrent, becomes a veritable waterfall dashing down between lofty cliffs, whose bases are fringed with maples and horse chestnuts, white and pink, and the millets are replaced by the buckwheat and Tibetan barley. Soon after this the useful birch tree appears, and then come grass and glaciers—the country of the shepherds.

The valley. As regards the formation of the vale itself, perhaps the theory of its lake origin will best explain the slopes and ledges which render the configuration of Kashmír striking and unique.

Where the mountains cease to be steep, fan-like projections, with flat arid tops and bare of trees, run out towards the valley. These are known as *Karéwa*. Sometimes these dry table lands stand up isolated in the middle of the valley, but whether isolated or attached to the mountains the karéwa present the same sterile appearance and offer the same abrupt walls to the valley. The karéwa are pierced by mountain torrents and seamed with ravines. It has been suggested that 'a plane, not indeed an even one joining the tops of all the remaining plateaus, would represent the position and form of the lake bottom at the last.' Bearing in mind that Kashmír was once a lake, which dried up when nature afforded an outlet at Bárámula, it is easy to recognize in the karéwa the shelving shores of a great inland sea, and to realize that the inhabitants of the old cities, the traces of which can be seen on high bluffs and on the slope of the mountains, had no other choice of sites, since in those days the present fertile valley was buried beneath a waste of water.

The river and mountain streams. Leaving the karéwa one drops down to the alluvial soil which slopes gently towards Jhelum, the great river. The Hydaspes of the ancients, the Vedasta of the Hindus, it is known to the Kashmíris as the Veth. When it leaves Kashmír at Bárámula it is called the Káshur Darya, and after joining the Kishnganga, it is spoken of as the Jhelum river. This river is navigable without a single lock from Baramula to Kanabal, the port of Islamabad, a distance of 102 miles[1]. Up to the present by far the larger part of the traffic of the country is carried along it in the flat-bottomed boats which are towed up stream or drop gently down at the speed of about 1½ miles an hour. The lazy river and the absence of roads and wheeled carriage have had their influence on native character, and time seems to be no object to a Kashmíri. The great Wular lake may be regarded as the delta of the Jhelum in Kashmír. In its course from Kanabal to the Delta the fall of the river is 165 feet in the first 30 miles, and 55 feet in the next 24 miles. From the Wular to Baramula the fall is very slight. In December, when the river is at its lowest, the average breadth is 210 feet and its mean depth is 9 feet. To the ordinary observer it would seem evident that the river arose from the grand spring of deep blue water at Vernág which bubbles up underneath a steep scarp of rock clothed with pines, but the Hindus maintain that a spring a little below Vernág, known as Vethvatru, has the honour of being the source of the great Kashmír river.

Above Kanabal the mountain streams from the south, the Sándrin, the Brang, the Arpat from Kotahár, the Kokarnág and the Achibal springs, join the river, and just below Kanabal on its right bank the Jhelum receives one of its most important tributaries, the Liddar or Lambodri, which comes down from the everlasting snows which overhang the head of the Liddar valley and from the lake of Tarsar. Further down on its right bank the Jhelum receives the water of the great Arpal Nág spring and the drainage from the Wástarwan and the mountains above Trahal, and at Pámpur a small amount of overflow from irrigation channels falls into the river. The Sind river, the most important of all the tributaries of the Jhelum, joins it at Shadipur, the place of marriage of the two rivers, and after passing through the Wular lake the Jhelum receives only one more tributary on its right bank before it reaches Baramula, the Pohru stream which drains the Loláb valley and enters the main river at Dubgám.

On its left bank the Jhelum receives the drainage of the western mountains, but none of the streams possesses the same importance as the Liddar and Sind rivers. The chief tributaries on the left bank are the Vishau, the Rembiára, the Rámshi and the Dudganga, which last joins the Jhelum at the lower end of the Srinagár city, the Suknág and

[1] From Vernág to Kichhháma, the point below Baramula where the Jhelum may be said to leave the valley, the distance is 122 miles.

the Ferozepura, which lose themselves in the large marshes under the banks of the Jhelum, and the Ningl which flows into the Wular lake and affords a secure haven to wind-bound boats. Of these streams[1] the Pohru, Sind and Vishau are navigable for a short distance.

In ordinary times the Jhelum river flows gently between high stable banks of deep soil, and until the stream shrinks in November, navigation, in spite of the absence of a proper tow-path, is easy. But in the winter the river above Srinagár is blocked by shoals, and the boatmen often have to dig out a channel for the heavy grain barges. In times of flood the river overtops its natural banks, and when the flood is high the water pours over the artificial embankments which have been constructed on either side of the river. Great damage is then caused to the crops of maize and linseed, and sometimes stacks of wheat, barley, and rape-seed are swept away. The loss caused by floods is always greatest below Srinagár, as the fall of the country is slight and the flood-water remains on the land rotting the crops. Above Srinagár the fall of the river and the slope of the country cause the flood-water to run down quickly and the crops often recover.

In former times the villages lying along the river were obliged to keep the artificial embankments in repair, and flood-gates existed which let out the water of the mountain streams, and protected the country against the floods of the Jhelum. For many years this obligation had not been enforced, and under my supervision the embankments below Srinagár were repaired, and the normal floods of 1892 were kept in check. Above Srinagár the question of repairing embankments is complicated by the presence of the city, the safety of which must not be endangered. It is unfortunate that Srinagár should have been built on its present site. It is not only exposed to constant danger from floods, but is itself the cause of floods, because it checks the drainage of the country. The old Hindus were wise for they chose high land for their cities, and ancient Srinagár stood on ground secure from floods. Akbar, the first of the Mughal rulers, selected the slopes of the Hari-Parbat for his city Nagar, but his successors, without thought for the future, closed the Dal lake to the floods of the Jhelum, and thereby robbed the river of one of the escapes for its flood-water. Later the Pathans built their palace on the left bank of the Jhelum and prevented the river from escaping to the west, and now all the flood-water from the south of the valley must pass through the narrow waterway of Srinagár. There the channel of the river is narrowed by stone embankments, by the piles of encroaching city magnates, and the flow is further

[1] Among the streams the Ningl, the Suknág and the Sind are considered to give the best drinking-water. Abdullah Khán the Pathan governor had his drinking-water brought daily from the Ningl to Srinagár.

CHAP. II. arrested by the cumbrous though picturesque piers of the seven bridges. Below Srinagár the old system of embankments has led to the usual result, and the river is now above the level of the country on its left bank. The consequence is that there is a series of swamps into which the drainage from the mountains of the west pours, and from which there is no outlet to the Jhelum, except in the winter months or in years of drought. The situation is further complicated by the fact that the Wular lake—the Delta of the river—is silting up. When the great king Zain-ul-abadin made the island on the lake the waters of the Wular stretched south to Asham and Sumbal, and the island was in the centre of the lake. Now the island is in one corner, and Asham and Sumbal are high and dry. Men who know the Wular well declare that within the last twenty-six years a strip of land over three miles in breadth has emerged from the lake, and I believe that the silting-up process is going on rapidly, and that it will probably lead to difficulties in the future. The question of floods will be dealt with in the chapter on Physical History, and it need only be remarked here that the placid Jhelum, useful as it is to the people as a waterway, is looked upon by them as a sleeping lion.

The lakes. Kashmír abounds in mountain tarns, lovely lakes, and swampy lagoons. Of the lakes the Wular, the Dal, and the Manasbal are the most beautiful, owing to the varied scenery given by the mountains which surround them. The Wular lake is the largest in India, being about 12½ miles by 5 miles in extent, and is almost surrounded by the lofty mountains which tower over the north and north-east of the valley. The Bohnar, Madmati, and Erin streams flow into the lake, while from the south the Jhelum seeks a passage through the Wular to Baramula. The lands around the Wular are never safe when the floods come down, and 24 hours of rain over the valley with melting snows will spread the lake over many miles of country[1]. The natives say that the Pohru stream when in flood is the cause of the inundation effected by the Wular and the Jhelum river, and that the Pohru forms a bar checking the overflow waters of the lake. In the north-east corner is an island made by the great Kashmíri king Zain-ul-abadin, and the ruins on it show that it must have been a place of great beauty. It

[1] The following details regarding the Kashmíri lakes may be useful :—

In normal years the Wular lake is 12.90 miles in length, 6.07 miles in breadth, and has an area of 78.3030 square miles. In years of flood, such as 1893, its length is 13.30 miles, breadth 7.81 miles, and its area is 103.8730 square miles.

The Manasbal lake is 2.40 miles long and 0.47 miles broad. It covers an area of 1.1280 square miles.

The Dal lake is 3.87 miles in length and 2.58 miles in breadth. It covers an area of 9.9846 square miles. Of this area 1890 acres consist of demb or fixed cultivation, so the total area of the Dal under water and floating gardens is 7.0346 square miles.

The Ánchár Dal is 3.51 miles in length and 2.15 miles in breadth. It covers an area of 7.5465 square miles.

is said that the good king built the island as a storm-refuge for boats. The Wular has a bad reputation among the boatmen of Kashmír, for when the winds come down the mountain gorges of Erin and Bandipura, and the gale blows from Shukr Din hill over the deep water, the quiet surface of the lake changes into a sea of rolling waves most dangerous to the flat-bottomed craft of the country. It is said that where the blue waters of the Wular now rest there was once a great and wicked city which was swallowed up in an earthquake, and the floods completed its destruction. The meaning of the word 'Wular' is cave[1], and legends say that the remains of the wicked city have been seen by boatmen.

The charm of Manasbal chiefly consists in its deep clear water and its pink lilies, but it has behind it a grand mountain which forms an effective contrast to the gentle beauty of the lake. The waters of Manasbal flow out through a canal to the Jhelum river. The Srinagár people visit the lake in boats, but it does not possess the same importance in Kashmír as the Wular and the Dal lakes, which are rich in natural products. It has some hot springs which never freeze even in the coldest winters.

The Dal lake, measuring about 4 miles by 2½, lies close to Srinagár, and is perhaps one of the most beautiful spots in the world. The mountain ridges which are reflected in its waters, as in a mirror, are grand and varied, the trees and vegetation on the shores of the Dal being of exquisite beauty. It is difficult to say when the Dal is most beautiful. In the spring the fresh green tints of the trees and the mountain sides are refreshing to the eye, but it is perhaps in October that the colours of the lake are most charming. The willows change from green to silver grey and delicate russet, with a red tone on the stems and branches, casting colours on the clear water of the lake which contrast most beautifully with the rich olives and yellow greens of the floating masses of water weed. The chenárs are warm with crimson, and the poplars stand up like golden poles to the sky. On the mountain sides the trees are red and gold, and the scene is one of unequalled loveliness. Perhaps in the whole world there is no corner so pleasant as the Dal lake. If one looks at the mountains, the shapes and shadows are wonderful in their boldness; citywards from the lake stands the famous hill, the Takht-i-Suliman to the left; and to the right the hill of Hari-Parbat, with its picturesque fort full of recollections of the grandeur of past times. Between these hills lies Srinagár, and away to the west are the snow-capped mountains of Kashmír. The water of the Dal is clear and soft as silk, and the people say that the shawls of Kashmír owe much of their excellence to being washed in the soft waters of the lake. Those who can afford to fetch a good drinking-water will go to Gagribal, the south-east quarter of the Dal, and will eschew in cholera times the polluted liquid of

[1] Dr. Bühler states that the Sanskrit name is 'Ullola,' (the lake) with 'high going waves.'

CHAP. II. the Jhelum. Nature has done much for the Dal, but the Mughal emperors have in their time nobly exerted themselves to enhance the natural beauties of the lake, and though the terraced gardens of Jehangir and Shah Jehan, with the prim rows of cypress through which formal cascades tumble down to the edge of the Dal, may not please the European landscape gardener, the magnificent plane trees[1], which the great Mughals bequeathed to posterity, have added a distinctive charm to the lovely Dal lake, the lake *par excellence* of Kashmír. The park of plane trees known as the Nasim Bagh, the garden of breezes, which was planted in Akbar's time, is the most beautiful of all the pleasure places of the royal gardeners of old times, but wherever one looks the Dal lake has some new view of beauty, and nothing is perhaps more striking than the ruined Pari Mahal, standing grandly on a spur of the Zebanwan mountain, a memorial of the Mughal love for letters. The Pari Mahal or fairies' palace was built by Prince Dara Shikoh for his tutor Mulla Shah. Mulla Shah's tomb is at Mulshahi Bagh, near the entrance of the Sind valley. Strange tales are told of the Pari Mahal, of the wicked magician who spirited away kings' daughters in their sleep, how an Indian princess by the order of her father brought away a chenár leaf to indicate the abode of her seducer, and how all the outraged kings of India seized the magician.

People say that the lake is silting up, and there can be no doubt that as years pass by the deposit of the Arrah river which feeds the Dal must result in the lake becoming even more shallow than it now is, as its only real outlet is through the narrow gate, the Dal Darwaza at Drogjun, which lets out the lake water and prevents the inroad of the Jhelum floods. Unless great vigilance is shown the floating gardens of the lake will be extended, and the already narrow waterways to the Mughal gardens will become blocked to boat traffic.

Springs.

Kashmír is rich in springs, all associated with the quaint old snake-worship. The people recognize the springs of great sanctity by the fact that their water is cold in the summer and warm in the winter, and curious legends are told of intermittent fountains and of other hydraulic phenomena. The springs are useful auxiliaries to the mountain-streams in irrigation, and are sometimes the sole sources of water, as in the case of Achábal, Vernág and Kokarnág on the south, and Arpal in the east.

Perhaps the most beautiful of all the springs is Achábal, which gushes out of the Sosanwar hill, and was at once enlisted by the emperor Jehangir in the service of beauty and pleasure. It is said that the Brang river which disappears at Dewalgam in the fissures of the limestone is the real

[1] There is mention of plane trees in the *Ain Akbari*. 'Shaebeddempoor is situated on the Behut, whose banks are planted with plane trees. At this town the rivers of Behut and Sind unite their streams.' Bernier, who visited Kashmír in 1664, does not notice the plane trees.

source of the Achibal spring. Vernág on the road to Jammu is another spring of great importance and beauty, with deep blue water which also issues from the bottom of a high scarp of a mountain spur, and here again Jehangir built a pleasure garden and a summer house. Islamabad or Anantnág, 'the place of the countless springs,' sends out numerous streams. One of the springs, the Maliknág, is sulphurous and its water is highly prized for garden cultivation. All these springs are full of sacred fish, a kind of carp. The Kashmíris are judges[1] of water and will discriminate between the properties of the various springs, but all seem to give to Kokarnág[2] the first place as a source of drinking water, though Chashma Shahi above the Dal lake, from which the richer citizens of Srinagár procure their water, stands high in order of merit. CHAP. II.

Roads. One of the points which at once strikes a visitor to Kashmír is the absence of roads fit for wheeled carriage. In the flat country around the Wular lake, low *trollies* resting on wheels roughly fashioned from the round trunks of trees are used for carrying crops, but at the time when I write, there is no other wheeled carriage in Kashmír. There are roads along which ponies and bullocks can pass in fair weather, but roads as understood in other countries do not exist. The main roads at present connect Srinagár with Islamabad, Vernág and Jammu via the Banihal pass (9,200 feet) with Shupiyon, Bhimber and Gujrát in the Panjáb via the Pir Panjál pass (11,400 feet) with Gandarbal at the mouth of the Sind valley, and Ladákh via the Zojila pass (11,300 feet) with Bandipura and Gilgit via the Rajdiangan (11,700 feet) and Burzil (13,500 feet) or Kamri (13,101 feet) passes and with Baramula, whence a cart road runs down the Jhelum valley to the Panjáb. In fair weather these roads, so far as the valley is concerned, are easy for the traveller, but heavy rains and snow render them difficult; and the frail bridges over the side streams are often carried away by floods. There are no real difficulties in road-making in the valley, and when the cart-road now being constructed from Baramula to Srinagár is completed, it is hoped that other cart-roads will be made. They will prove of the greatest benefit not only to the villagers, but also to the people of Srinagar, who will be no longer at the mercy of the boatmen, so clever in adulterating grain when it reaches the barges. Besides the main routes already mentioned, there are other tracks leading to the headquarters of tahsils, and each village is connected with its neighbour by a path which is intersected by irrigation channels, and is wearisome and sometimes dangerous to equestrians.

[1] A people who drink nothing but water are naturally connoisseurs. They always consider the weight of the water as the point of chief importance. A heavy (hard) water suits some dispositions, a light (soft) others.

[2] 'Here is another spring called Kokarnág, whose water satisfies both hunger and thirst, and it is also a remedy for indigestion' (*Aín Akbari*). The author of the *Aín Akbari* notices that touchstone is found in Kokarnág.

CHAP. II. Some of the roads and tracks are well shaded by trees, and the traveller can always find rest underneath the shady planes and walnuts, and delicious water from the innumerable springs. And at present he need not want for food as mulberries, apricots, apples, pears, and walnuts abound along the roads, and no one grudges them to the traveller. This will change as time goes on, and the Kashmíris will find that fruits have their value.

Trees. The trees of Kashmír will be dealt with in another chapter, but here it may be said that the trees of the valley form one of its greatest charms. The delightful plane trees, the magnificent walnuts; the endless willows, the poplars and the elms, the countless orchards of apples, pears, and apricots give the valley the appearance of a well-wooded park. There is a curious mixture of the East and West. The crops are eastern, but the rounded forms of the trees, the rivers and the streams with their banks of green turf, and willows recall the West, and the Loláb with its villages rich in fruit trees through which pass lanes shaded by elms and overshadowed by hills covered with the graceful Deodars, presents a scene which has nothing eastern in it.

Climate. In many books remarks have been made regarding the climate of Kashmír, and as opinions on the subject seem to differ I have obtained from Mr. John Eliot, Meteorological Reporter to the Government of India, notes and data not only for Kashmír, but also for places surrounding the valley. So far meteorological observations are only made in Srinagár, which is in latitude 34° 5′ north and longitude 74° 48′ east, and lies about the centre of the valley. The south and south-west limits of the valley are separated from the plains of the Panjáb by a wall of mountains ranging from 50 to 70 miles in breadth. The mountains on the west of the valley seem to catch the tail of the monsoon of India, but the valley itself is apparently beyond its full influence, and heavy rain in the hills on the Panjáb side of the Himalayas does not necessarily connote rainfall in the Kashmír valley. In the *Ain Akbari* it is said, 'It rains and snows here at the same seasons as in Tartary and Persia, and during the periodical rains in Hindustan here also fall light showers.' In considering the data available for Srinagár it should be remembered that a day's journey from the capital will bring one into a wholly different climate, and I have known constant rains in the southern end of the valley while Srinagar and the northern part of Kashmír were parched with drought.

The rains may be either partial or may be what the Kashmíris call *alamgír* or world-embracing. When the clouds gather over the Konsanág lake on the south-west mountains and over the Wular lake on the north, the Kashmíri can predict[1] with some degree of certainty that there will

[1] The Kashmíris are weather-wise, and do not, like the people of India, consider it presumptuous to make prophecies regarding rain. They believe in our proverb—

PLATE III

To face page 25]

[Negative by Captain Allan

WINTER IN KASHMÍR. SHOWS PART OF THE EUROPEAN QUARTERS IN SRÍNAGAR
THE HILL CROWNED WITH A TEMPLE IS THE TAKHT-I-SULIMÁN

be a general rain over the valley, and 24 hours of rain will cause heavy floods on the river. The fords of the mountain streams become impassable and the frail bridges are swept away. But happily rain of 24 hours' duration is a rare occurrence, and, as a rule, 12 hours' rain is followed by pleasant sunshine which soon dries up the soil. In the spring months showers are frequent, and when the summer heat becomes excessive in June a heavy thunderstorm will cool the air for days, and in July and August the peasant expects showers every fortnight, though he sometimes expects them in vain. Showers sometimes fall in the beginning of September, known to the people as *kámbarka*, of great importance to the spring crops of the next year. September, October, and November should be and usually are dry months, but in December the sky becomes overcast with clouds and haze, and by Christmas the snows set in. This may be said to be the normal year in Kashmír, but unfortunately the rains often behave in a very abnormal manner, being excessive in the spring and deficient in the summer, or vice versa. Thus in 1889 the spring rains were very heavy and protracted, followed by a drought in the summer months. The winter was clear and sunny, the snowfall being below the average. In 1890 the spring rains were moderate, the summer rains good, the climate cool, and the winter snowfall, which commenced on Christmas Day, the heaviest that had been known for fifty years. In 1891 the spring rains were deficient, the summer rains badly distributed and protracted, and the winter snowfall very deficient. In 1892 the spring rains failed, but the summer rain was in excess and saved the rice crop. The first snow fell on December 17, the winter being one of unusual severity. In 1893 the spring rains were moderate, but the summer rains of unusual heaviness causing the disastrous floods.

The old men of the valley declare that the climate is changing, and they are very positive that there are now no such winters as they remembered as boys. In Maharájá Gulab Singh's time the snow was up to a man's shoulders, in Maharájá Ranbir Singh's time up to his knees, but now winters pass without any fall of snow. Nearly every man who talks on the subject holds to this belief, and they all say that much less water comes into the valley than of yore. They point to villages which once grew rice, and to old canals which are now dry, and they maintain that the mountain springs are decreasing and that the climate of Kashmír is becoming milder and more like that of the Panjáb. The Hindus attribute

'Red in the night the shepherd's delight,
Red in the morning the shepherd's warning.'

Obras ketun nár, that is, the clouds have caught fire in the evening, is a sure prelude to fine weather; *Níhdau*, which is red in the morning, presages rain. White clouds are certain to bring heavy rain; dark clouds mean no rain or light showers.

CHAP. II. the falling off in water and the diminished productiveness of the land to the fact that we are living in the Kaliyug. I do not know how much truth there is in this, but the cold season of 1890–91, when the snow was four feet deep in the valley and the thermometer fell below zero, shows that King Winter does visit Kashmír still, and the intense cold of January and February, 1893, when it was possible to skate all over the Dal, will not be soon forgotten. Winter is a hard time for men and animals in Kashmír, and when wood and charcoal are dear the poorer citizens of Srinagár are much to be pitied. After the winter the smell of the warm eager earth, which glows with sudden and beautiful colours, is very pleasant, and it is no wonder that the Kashmíris of the city hail the spring with joy, and flock to the almond-gardens and pay pilgrimages to the sweet lilacs. It is not mere love of beauty and colour that impels them, but a spirit of thanksgiving that the winter with its miseries of cold and its dreary monotony of white snow has passed, and that the earth has come to life again with all her bright flowers and promise of kindly fruits. Directly spring appears the days become warm and sunny, in June, July, and August if the rain keeps off the temperature rises to a considerable heat over 90° in the shade, and the climate of Srinagár in the last two months becomes muggy and unwholesome, and mosquitos swarm. As the temperature rises the valley is covered with a haze, said by the people to be dust from the plains of the Panjáb, which hides the mountains from view. The sun is bright, and seems as powerful just after sunrise and before sunset as it is at noon. The dryness of the air and the glare from the flooded fields make work in the valley very trying to the eyes. In September the temperature begins to fall, the nights become cool, and by the end of September the evenings are almost cold. I have seen autumnal tints on walnut trees as early as August 25. October and November are bracing months with a bright, pleasant sun and cold nights, and October, which is so unhealthy in India, is perhaps the healthiest and most delightful of all months in Kashmír. As in the case of rainfall, so in the case of temperature, a short ride will take one from heat unpleasant to Europeans to a perfect climate, and a journey of 30 miles from Srinagár will enable a traveller to reach a height of over 8,000 feet where the mean temperature never rises above 60°. In severe winters the cold of Kashmír becomes very intense and the Jhelum river sometimes freezes, causing great distress to the people of Srinagár whose chief highway is thus blocked to traffic. But a greater calamity than this is the occurrence of the *Kot Kushu*, which seems to freeze the damp moisture of the air and destroys trees and even congeals eggs. Walled in by snows, with frozen lakes and freezing rivers, Kashmír in a hard winter is like a huge refrigerator. I append the notes and data which have been kindly supplied by Mr. John Eliot. The remarks on Murree and Leh are taken from Mr. Blandford's book on the Climate and Weather of India. The remainder of the notes are written by Mr. Eliot, and are based on the observations made at Srinagár during 1892 and 1893. CHAP. II.

'Murree.—This is the chief sanatorium of the Western as Simla is of the Eastern Panjáb. It is situated on the summit of the ridge that divides the Jhelum Valley from the Patwar (the tableland above the Salt range), and commands an extensive view of mountain and plain. The hills around are well wooded except in the direction of the plains. None of those in the vicinity of Murree are of much greater elevation than the station itself, which stands nearly 7,500 feet above the sea. The observatory, which was established on its present footing in 1875, is at the Lawrence Asylum, the military school, and fully 1,000 feet lower than the station, on the crest of a spur that runs down towards the plains, and has a somewhat higher mean temperature than the station itself, while it is screened from northerly winds by the main ridge.

'Being thus situated on the crest of one of the outermost spurs of the Himalayas, its climate, like that of other Himalayan sanatoria, is of a very different type from that of Leh and Quetta. Although drier than that of stations such as Mussooree and Naini Tal, similarly situated but further to the south-east, its atmosphere is much damper than that of the plains immediately below, and subject to smaller variations of temperature both annual and diurnal. The mean temperature of the observatory is 56°, in January and February 39°, and in June 71°. From this time it falls gradually to 65° in September, and then rapidly to the end of the year. The lowest temperature is generally reached in February, when the mean minimum reading is 34°. The lowest yet recorded, in 1886, is 16·7°. Owing to the comparative lightness of the summer rainfall, the temperature from June to September is higher than at the most easterly hill stations. Notwithstanding the elevation the shaded thermometer not unfrequently rises above 90° in June, and in 1880, a very dry year, registered as high as 98·7°. The diurnal range varies but little in the course of the year. It is rather smaller in the winter and in August, when it amounts to 14°, than at other times of the year, and is greatest in the driest months, viz. from April to June, when, however, it does not much exceed 17°. These figures, it must be remarked, represent the conditions of the observatory only, and it is probable that the amounts would be found to differ considerably, with differences of position and aspect, in different parts of the station, but those general characters which distinguish the climate from those of other hill stations are doubtless shared by all parts of the site.

'From June to November the air is much drier than that of Simla or any other hill station of the outer Himalayas, but in February it is apparently damper, and in the remaining months of the winter and spring of about the same character. The humidity is highest in August, when it amounts to about 80 per cent. of saturation. In March the skies are as cloudy as during the rains. In the spring months, from March to May, it rains on an average about one day in three, most frequently in April. The rainfall on each rainy day averaging about one-fourteenth of an inch. Rain is less frequent in June, but increases again in July and August, when about half the days are more or less rainy and the falls heavier than in the spring, averaging three-quarters of an inch on each day of rain. The number of rainy days has varied from 74 only in the dry year 1880, to 123 in 1885, and the total quantity from 39·1 inches in the former to 71·8 inches in the latter year.

'October and November are the clearest months, but even these, and every month up to May, are more cloudy than at Simla or on the plains. On the other hand, in July and August there is less cloud than at Simla or other more easterly stations, as might be expected from the smaller frequency of rain.

'Leh.—Situated 4° further north than Quetta, and 6,000 feet higher, this station in the leading characteristics of its climate represents that of Western Tibet. Its observatory, 11,500 feet above the sea, is the most elevated in Asia, and has now furnished a register for twelve years.

'Leh, the chief town of the province of Ladákh, is situated in the upper valley of the Indus, which is here from six to eight miles across for a distance of forty or fifty miles, and shut in on both sides by portions of the Tibetan plateau, averaging 16,000 feet above sea-level, and bearing some of the loftiest ranges of the Himalayas. The flats and terraces along the banks of the river are all cultivated, and dotted with numerous villages, but for a mile on each side, between the fields and the foot of the hills, is a waste of sand, gravel, and large boulders, similar to that which fringes the much lower hill ranges of Baluchistan, but on a larger scale. The town of Leh nestles under the hills north of the valley, at a distance of some four miles from the river, up a long gentle, gravelly slope.

'The atmosphere of the valley is remarkably clear and transparent, and the heat of the sun very great. There is generally a difference of more than 60° between the reading of the exposed sun thermometer in vacuo and the air temperature in the shade, and this difference has occasionally exceeded 90°. It has been mentioned on a former page that Dr. Cayley succeeded in making water boil by simply exposing it to the sun in a small bottle blackened on the outside, and shielded from the air by inserting it in a larger phial of transparent glass. Owing to the diminished pressure of the atmosphere at the elevation of Leh, this would, however, take place at about 191° or 192°, or about 20° below the normal boiling-point at the sea-level.

'The mean annual temperature of Leh is 40°, that of the coldest months (January and February) only 18° and 19°; but it rises rapidly from February to July, in which month it reaches 62°, with a mean diurnal maximum of 80°, both in that month and August, and an average difference of 29° or 30° between the early morning and afternoon. The mean highest temperature of the year is 90°, varying between 84° and 93° in the last twelve years. On the other hand, in the winter the minimum thermometer falls occasionally below 0° Fahrenheit, and in 1878 reached as low as 17° below zero. The extreme range of recorded temperature is, therefore, not less than 110°.

'The air is as dry as at Quetta, and rather more uniformly so. In the driest month (June) the mean humidity is but 37 per cent. of saturation, and in the dampest months (January and February) only 61 per cent. But the skies are more cloudy than these circumstances would lead one to expect, and in no month does the mean cloud-proportion fall much below four-tenths of the expanse. The amounts of rain and snow are, however, insignificant. The average rain (and snow) fall is only 2·7 inches in the year, and twice that amount is the greatest yet recorded in any one year (1879), while in one year (1876) it was less than half an inch. It snows most frequently in January and February, but the falls are very light in the valley and soon disappear. Rain is most frequent in July and August, but even then it occurs, on an average, only on one day in ten, between one and two-tenths of an inch being the average fall of each rainy day. Agriculture is, therefore, almost entirely dependent on irrigation.

'The winds are generally light, and depend on the local direction of the valleys. At Leh, which stands at the entrance of the valley leading to the Khardong Pass, the most common directions are between south and west in the daytime and summer, and from north-east in the night, especially in the later months of the year.

'In January and February the air is generally calm, and April and May are the most windy months of the year.

'Srinagar is situated in the Kashmír Valley, at an elevation of about 5,200 feet. The valley is enclosed on all sides by mountains rising to an elevation of 15,000 feet and upwards, and is hence completely shut in, so that it does not share in the general air circulation of the Panjáb or Western Himalayan area. The winds are, in fact, chiefly from south and south-east, and appear to be mainly determined by the general direction of the river valley. The observatory was established in 1891, and hence the observations are too few in number to give more than the broad features of the climate of the Kashmír Valley. The mean annual temperature is probably 55°. The coldest months are January and February, when the mean temperature is 36° or 37°. It increases until the months of July and August, when it is 72°, and then decreases rapidly to the end of the year. It is probably slightly cooler than Murree throughout the year, except in the months of July, August and September. As might be expected, the diurnal range of temperature is in clear weather much greater than at Murree. In the cloudy weather of January and February it averages 15°, and is nearly the same as at Murree. It then increases to an average of 25° in April, May and June, when it is 8° more than at Murree. It decreases slightly to an average of 21° during the next three months of July to September. In the clear months of October and November it rises to 32°, when the diurnal range is twice as great as at Murree, and nearly as great as on the plains of India. With the return of cloudy weather in December it falls to a mean of 19°.

'The air is much damper at Srinagar than at Murree. The mean pressure of aqueous vapour for the year is about ·34″, or 30 per cent. greater than at Murree. The mean humidity of the two years 1893–4 was 84°, whereas at Murree it was only 57°. The greater humidity of Srinagar is, of course, mainly due to its position in a closed-in valley on the shores of a large body of water. There is also more cloud at Srinagar than at Murree. The average cloud amount of the past two years at Srinagar is 4·6, whereas at Murree it is only 3·7. The climate by its humidity and greater cloud hence approaches more nearly to that of England than Murree. The most remarkable feature at Srinagar is the calmness of the air. Thus out of 731 observations of wind taken at Srinagar at 8 a.m. during the years 1893–4, 345 are recorded as calms, out of the remaining 386 observations 198 were from south or south-east directions, and eighty-one from the opposite or north or north-west direction.

'In the Western Himalayan mountain area the precipitation is chiefly received during two periods, and under very different conditions. The chief periods are the cold weather period from December to March or April, and the south-west Monsoon period from July to September. During the intervening period, April to June, thundershowers are of occasional occurrence, and give what might be termed hot weather rainfall; but it is of comparatively little importance. The cold weather rainfall is chiefly due to storms of a somewhat peculiar character, their chief feature being that the precipitation increases with elevation up to 20,000 feet at least, and probably higher. On the other hand, the south-west Monsoon rainfall is heaviest at the foot of the Kashmír hills facing the Panjáb, and decreases with elevation, and also in proceeding into the interior, and is of little importance in Ladákh, Gilgit, &c. Hence, although all parts of Kashmír receive rainfall during each of these two periods, the south-west Monsoon is the predominant feature in Jammu and Kishtwar, whilst in Ladákh, Gilgit, and the higher ranges the cold weather precipitation is the heaviest and most important. It occurs chiefly as snow in the Kashmír Valley and mountains, and on the higher ranges as much as forty to sixty feet of snow falls in a severe winter season. In the intermediate regions of the Kashmír Valley the rainfall is fairly distributed throughout the whole year.

'In Jammu the chief rainfall is the summer rainfall. In Kishtwar it is also probably the chief period, but the fall is more equally divided than in Jammu.

'In the Indus Valley the rainfall is always very small at Leh, but appears to increase in descending the valley, as the average rainfall at Iskardo (as far as is indicated by two years' data) is four times as much as at Leh. The rainfall at Leh and Iskardo in the Upper Indus Valley occurs almost solely during the cold weather, which there extends from December to April or May, and as a rule little or no rain falls in the period June to December. The rainfall at Gilgit is similar to that of Leh in amount, but, so far as can be judged, it is remarkable for the non-occurrence of rain in the cold weather, and its chief rain is due to scattered showers from April to September. The neighbouring mountains have frequent snow in the cold weather, and the melting of these snows probably enables cultivation to be carried on. At Srinagar the rainfall appears to be divided over the whole year. It has a good winter rainfall from December to March, light to moderate rain, probably from thunderstorms, in May and June, and occasional rain during the height of the Monsoon from July to the middle of September.'

CHAP. II.

The following data will give some idea of the climates of the countries by which the valley is surrounded, and show all that is known accurately about Srinagár itself.

SRINAGAR.—RAINFALL.

Year.	Inches of Rainfall.												
	Jan.	Feb.	Mar.	April.	May.	June.	July.	Aug.	Sept.	Oct.	Nov.	Dec.	Total.
*1891						—	1·46	0·80	0·04	3·02	0·40	0·04	
1892	0·95	0·98	2·13	0·13	2·55	2·05	4·16	3·56	0·50	0·01	0·05	1·25	18·32
1893	2·14	15·34	2·19	2·97	3·67	1·55	6·31	0·28	1·52	0·09	—	0·26	36·32

	Average of seven years.		Average of seven years.
Leh (Ladákh)	3·12	Jhelum	30·6857
Skardu (Baltistan)	28·305	Gujrat	28·4585
Gilgit	3·67	Sialkot	38·3157
Kishtwar	35·595	Murree	62·8114

SRINAGAR.—MEAN TEMPERATURE.

Year.	Jan.	Feb.	Mar.	April.	May.	June.	July.	Aug.	Sept.	Oct.	Nov.	Dec.	Total.
*1891	?	?	?	?	?	?	?	?	?	52·0	46·9	40·3	?
1892	40·5	42·0	51·4	61·4	64·8	67·1	74·2	73·6	66·1	54·2	44·4	37·7	56·4
1893	33·1	25·9	43·6	56·5	64·7	74·2	70·7	70·6	66·8	54·8	43·0	39·1	53·6

	Average of seven years.
Leh (Ladákh)	43·17
Gilgit	63·05
Sialkot	74·74
Murree	57·64

*Record began in June.

SRINAGAR.—MEAN MAXIMUM.

Year.	Jan.	Feb.	Mar.	April.	May.	June.	July.	Aug.	Sept.	Oct.	Nov.	Dec.	Year.	Highest.	Date.
*1891										62·1	59·3	53·0	?		
1892	49·2	50·2	62·9	75·6	77·8	79·6	85·0	82·5	77·8	72·0	59·4	46·7	68·2	95·4	July 9.
1893	8·8	33·5	53·3	67·1	76·4	81·8	81·7	81·4	76·9	70·4	59·7	49·8	64·2	91·3	June 22. July 15.

	Average of seven years. Year.	Highest.
Leh (Ladákh)	56·04	87·8
Gilgit	74·05	113·2
Sialkot	87·21	118·0
Murree	65·3	95·0

SRINAGAR.—MEAN MINIMUM.

Year.	Jan.	Feb.	Mar.	April.	May.	June.	July.	Aug.	Sept.	Oct.	Nov.	Dec.	Year.	Lowest.	Date.
*1891										41·8	34·5	27·6			
1892	31·7	33·8	39·9	47·1	51·8	54·5	63·3	64·6	54·3	36·4	29·3	28·7	44·6	21·1	December 11
1893	27·4	18·2	33·8	45·9	52·9	66·6	59·7	59·7	56·7	39·1	26·3	28·4	42·9	4·1	February 2.

	Average of seven years. Year.	Lowest.
Leh (Ladákh)	30·25	17·0
Gilgit	52·0	17·7
Sialkot	62·5	29·3
Murree	50·0	16·7

* Observations available from October.

CHAP. II.

Health.

For people who can travel the valley offers a climate perhaps unsurpassed by that of any country, but in July and August, Srinagar, surrounded as it is by swamps, is apt to prove unhealthy and depressing. Speaking generally the valley may be said to be fairly free from disease. Malarial fever, liver complaints, consumption and dysentery are rare, and typhoid fever is said to be unknown. But certain diseases are unfortunately very common. In October and throughout the winter small-pox is very prevalent and causes great mortality among children. Vaccination has not yet been introduced, and in the winter of 1892 the ravages of small-pox among the children of the valley and the city probably caused greater mortality than the cholera epidemic of the same year[1]. Goitre is frequent and is especially common in villages where drinking-water comes from limestone or magnesian limestone rocks. In one group of villages in the Cherat tahsíl, known as the *Gadaru* or goitre circle, nearly all the peasants are afflicted with this disease. Among the cultivators who work stooping in the cold water on the rice-fields lumbago is a very common complaint, and coughs are very prevalent. The Kashmíri is much given to clearing his throat by spitting, and he is evidently a man of a delicate throat for he will not eat 'ghi,' the butter of India, and he considers the use of tea and of snuff as essential for clearing his head and throat. Scald head is a very frequent and unpleasant complaint among the Musalmáns; and the children seem to suffer from ophthalmia.

But the great scourge of Kashmír is the cholera, for when once this terrible epidemic enters the valley the mortality is very heavy. The epidemic finds a congenial soil in the alluvial parts of the valley, but its nursery is the filthy city of Srinagar, a sad and striking illustration of the saying that 'God made the country and man made the town.' Cholera has visited the valley ten times since 1824, but probably the worst epidemic within the memory of man occurred in the summer of 1892 when, according to the report of the Chief Medical Officer of Kashmír, 11,712 persons died in the city and in the valley. The panic was so great and the registration of deaths so imperfect, that it is quite possible this figure does not represent the total mortality; my own impression is that the mortality in the villages, which is given as 5,931, was far greater, and that not less than 18,000 people died of cholera in 1892 in the whole valley. I was in camp in the villages during the cholera, and have never seen anything so awful as the helplessness and despair of the people. All work was suspended, and silent groups of villagers would sit all day long in the graveyards. They mistrusted all remedies, but seemed to believe in the efficacy of sour green grapes, and in blood-letting by the village

[1] The State has now taken up the question of vaccination, and an excellent beginning was made at the end of 1893. Marked progress was made in 1894.

barber. Much has been written by experts on the subject of cholera in Srinagar, and all are agreed that something should be done[1]. But it should be remembered that the towns of Kashmír and the larger villages equally call for sanitary reform.

Before concluding this very inadequate description of the valley it is necessary to attempt some account of the great city known to most as Srinagar[2], the city of the sun or the blessed city, also known to the cultivators of the valley as 'Kashmír.' Srinagar became the capital of Kashmír about A.D. 960. Considering its unhealthy surroundings of lakes and swamps and its low lying position, it is a matter for regret that some higher and more healthy site was not chosen. The city consists of 22,448 houses crowded together in utter confusion on either side of the Jhelum river, which winds through Srinagar with an average width of eighty yards. These houses occupy a length of about three miles and a breadth of about one-and-a-half miles on either side of the river, but the greater part of the city lies on the right bank. The houses vary in size from the large and spacious burnt-brick palaces of the Pandit aristocrat and his 500 retainers, warmed in the winter by *hammáms*, to the doll house of three stories, and three rooms of wood and sun-dried bricks, where the poor shawl-weaver lives his squalid cramped life and shivers in the frosty weather. Frail as most of the houses seem with their walls of single bricks held together in wooden frames, their very frailness is perhaps a protection against earthquake, but their wooden walls and their thatched roofs make them an easy victim to the fires which sweep at steady intervals through the city. After a conflagration the houses are built up again in the same confused jumble and with the same want of plan and arrangement. In these 22,448 houses, 118,960 persons eat and sleep and die. Writing on the cholera epidemic of 1892, the Chief Medical Officer of Kashmír, a Bengali gentleman, who has worked for many years in the city, makes the following remarks on its insanitary condition, and I can vouch from personal observation that the description is in no way exaggerated:—

'The Kashmíris are notoriously filthy and negligent of personal cleanliness. Within an area of six square miles live a population of

[1] Since this was written the work of sanitary improvements in Srinagar has commenced. Much opposition was shown at first, but thanks to the energy and tact shown by those in charge of the work, this opposition is diminishing, and the people who live near the new road on the right bank of the city, most clamorous at first, are now congratulating themselves on the transformation wrought in their lives. An excellent street, airy and well drained, has replaced the filthy tortuous kennel which formerly existed. Surgeon-Colonel Harvey, who visited Srinagar during the epidemic of cholera in 1892, writes, 'It is not too much to say that the inhabitants eat filth, drink filth, breathe filth, sleep on it, and are steeped in it and surrounded by it on every side.'

[2] Kashmíris pronounce Śrinagar with palatal Ś – Sh.

CHAP. II. 118,960 in houses low and dirty, built irregularly and without any method, on narrow tortuous paths. Ventilation in the town is therefore very imperfect. Few houses have latrines, and small lanes and alleys are used as such. Two hundred sweepers are now engaged by the municipality, but the number is too microscopic compared with the requirements of such a vast population. There is no drainage. Slush, filth and ordure are washed by storm-water into the river and the Nalla Már which supply the city with drinking-water. On account of absence of snow in winter and rain in spring, the river was dry and low and the bed of the Nalla Már canal was converted into a string of cesspools. People were immersed in a polluted atmosphere caused by the products of putrefactive and fermentable matter accumulated in houses and numerous narrow lanes, passages, nooks, and crevices which intersect the town. This produced an epidemic constitution in the people fitted for the reception and fostering of cholera-germs.'

This is the city of the sun exposed with the scalpel of the Sanitary Officer, but when the river runs high between the raised banks formed by a Musalmán king from the stone sculptures and plinths of Hindu temples, when the seven wood bridges which knit the city into one almost touch the water, and the earth-roofs of the houses are covered with green herbage and flowers, Srinagar in spite of its internal squalor is one of the most picturesque places in the world. The hill of Takht-i-Sulimán, which rises abruptly to a height of 1,000 feet, and the Hari-Parbat ridge with the fort of Akbar surmounting it, form an appropriate frame to the scenery, and beyond these near hills the great mountains seem to tower over the city as one passes up the river highway. The very absence of order in the location of houses and their tumbled-down appearance add a peculiar charm to the scenery, and Srinagar possesses at once the attraction of a city full of life and of a city of ruins. The fashionable sites for houses are the banks of the river and the Nalla Már, the snake canal. This is the most important of the many canals which intersect the city. It connects Srinagar with the Anchár lake and the Sind valley. Its curious stone bridges and shady waterway are most picturesque, but the canal is choked with filth, and the dreadful odours make one oblivious of the beauties of the Nalla Már. From the riverside windows the city people can see life—busy, picturesque, and various. Boats of all sizes are to be seen, from the great grain barges which lie moored to the *gháts* to the little shell in which the Dal lake cultivator paddles his vegetables and lake-produce to market, and up and down the river paddled with many strong arms go the *dungas* of officials, merchants and travellers. Perhaps the daily boat up to

Islamabad or down to Baramula is at last starting, if sufficient passengers have taken seats, the boat is low down in the water and each man is sitting in his neighbour's lap; or a pleasure party is starting to Mánasbal, or a pilgrim boat is setting off for some shrine. The topsey-turvey bathing-boxes are full of people leisurely bathing, chattering, and gesticulating. In the winter the scene changes, the river narrows and falls, the lattice windows are covered with paper, and no one stirs out on the river except on urgent business. High up the river, below the first bridge, 'Amiran Kadal,' stands on the left bank the Sher Garhi, where the palaces of His Highness the Mahárájá and the offices of the Government are situated. The picturesque palace which stands next to the golden temple was built by Mahárájá Ranbir Singh, and is a reminiscence of the Dogra country. New palaces of another style are springing up, and before long the Sher Garhi will be a mass of large buildings. Across the river is the finest *ghát* in Srinagar, the Basant Bagh, with grand stone steps pillaged from the mosque of Hassanabad. In the old days a rope was stretched from Basant Bagh to the palace and petitions were hauled up from the river to Mahárájá Gulab Singh's hall of audience. Hindú temples glistening like silver are dotted along the banks, and below the third bridge, the Fatteh Kadal, on the right bank, is the beautiful wooden mosque of Shah Hamdán. Beneath it on the river is a large bathing-house, where the Musalmáns perform their ablutions before they go to their prayers. Nearly opposite is a grand stone mosque which rigid Musalmáns rejected because they despised its foundress, and the Patr Masjid is now the chief of the State granaries. Below the fourth bridge, the Zaina Kadal, is the tomb of Kashmír's great king, Zain-ul-abadin, and on the right bank is the Mahárá j Ganj, where the art wares of the city are exposed for sale. Below the sixth bridge, the Nawa Kadal, is the temple built by the well-known and respected Pandit Ramju, and last of all comes the Safr Kadal or bridge of departure. These bridges are cheap, effective, and picturesque, and their construction ingenious. Old boats filled with stones were sunk at the sites chosen for pier foundations. Piles were then driven and more boats sunk. When a height above the low-water level was reached wooden trestles of deodár were constructed by placing rough-hewn logs at right angles. As the structure approached the requisite elevation to admit of chakwáris (house-boats) passing beneath, the deodár logs were cantilevered. This reduced the span, and huge trees were made to serve as girders to support the roadway. The foundations of loose stones and piles have been protected on the up-stream by planking, and a rough but effective cut-water made. The secret of the stability of these old bridges may perhaps be attributed to the skeleton piers offering little or no resistance to the large volume of water brought down at flood-time. It is true that the heavy floods of 1893 swept away six out of the seven city bridges, and that the cumbrous piers tend to narrow the waterway, but it should be remembered that the old bridges had weathered many a serious flood. Not long ago two of the bridges, the Habba Kadal and the Zaina Kadal, had rows of shops on them, reminding one of old London, but these have now been cleared away. At close intervals the river is approached by ruined steps; up and down these the people pass to bathe, to wash their clothes, and to fetch drinking-water. The *ghâts* are known as *Yárabal*, 'the meeting-place of friends.' In the summer, when the vines and other trees are in full leaf, climbing over trellis and falling down the sculptured stones which line the river bank, when the people are splashing about in the water, the highway of the city is a very pretty and lively scene, but its chief beauty is derived from the peeps of the hills and the snow mountains which are caught between the narrow winding alleys running from the river banks. East and south of the city run magnificent poplar avenues, but the oldest and finest was planted by the Ata Mahomad Khan, one of the Pathan governors, and leads almost to the foot of the Takht-i-Sulimán. It is showing signs of decay, and the people are hurrying on the work of destruction by barking the old poplars. A longer but more recent poplar avenue, planted by Wazir Punnu in 1864, runs for about seven miles along the Shupiyon road. There is also a fine avenue leading from the Sher Garhi to the bridge over the Dudganga river. Between the Takht-i-Sulimán and the right bank of the river lies the Munshi Bagh, an orchard planted many years ago by Munshi Tilok Chand, and it is there that the European community chiefly lives. West of the Munshi Bagh is the Residency, and further west still are the Post Office and the provision shops for the supply of Europeans. On the left bank of the river are gardens of the Rájas; between them and the Amiran Kadal lie the Lál Mandi and the State Hospital. The Lál Mandi is a fine building used for State banquets and other public purposes. Across the Amiran Kadal, in an angle formed by the poplar avenues which run to the Dudganga river, and along the Shupiyon road, is the cantonment of the Kashmír troops, and across the Dudganga river lies the great parade ground. Scattered about within the limits of Srinagar there are numerous gardens and open spaces, and at survey we measured 1,624 acres of orchards and cultivated land, most of which is under tobacco and garden crops. In this short account of Srinagar I have for want of space had to discard much that is of interest to the historian or archaeologist, but Srinagar has been so well and minutely described that it becomes unnecessary to give the numerous interesting details of the canals, temples, and mosques which all deserve mention. I shall attempt in other chapters to discuss the occupations of the city people and their condition. It must, however, be borne in mind that the name Kashmír given by the villagers to the city carries with it a deep meaning, that for many generations Srinagar has monopolized the attention of the rulers of Kashmír, and that the interest of the cultivators and the country have been jealously subserved to the well-being and comfort of the city. In short, Srinagar was 'Kashmír' in fact as well as in phrase.

CHAPTER III.

GEOLOGICAL.

CHAP. III.

THE geological facts of the Kashmír valley have been recorded in a memoir[1] written by Richard Lydekker. His treatise represents the labour of seven long seasons spent in Kashmír and the neighbouring regions, while to his own personal knowledge, Mr. Lydekker has added the observations of many other geologists who have visited the valley. Mr. Lydekker's great work deals with an enormous mountain country of about 68,000 square miles, of which the valley of Kashmír forms a small, but from a geological point of view, not an unimportant part. For the purpose of easy reference I shall in this chapter give the more important extracts, from Mr. Lydekker's memoir, which refer to the valley of Kashmír.

Physical Features.

Lakes.

The lakes or tarns, which occur in the mountains surrounding the valley, mostly lie in what are generally considered to be true rock basins, but it is difficult to say whether the lakes in the valley itself are real rock basins. The depth of Mánasbal suggests that its bottom is below the level of the rock gorge at Bárámúlá, but Lydekker shows that the real rock entrance to the Kashmír valley is blocked by alluvium, so that the level of its base is unknown, and therefore the rock basin theory cannot be proved in the case of Mánasbal. As regards the other lakes of the valley they are so covered by alluvium that no conclusion can be drawn as to the nature of their basins.

Caverns.

Mr. Lydekker only notices the well-known caverns near Bawan in the Liddar valley. One of these has its opening about forty feet above the ground and may be traversed for a length of about 210 feet, but seems to extend farther. The entrance to the second is nearly 100 feet above the ground, and the cavern itself is about 48 feet in length. A thick coat of stalagmite forms the floor of these caverns.

[1] *The Geology of the Kashmír and Chamba Territories and the British District of Khágán*, by Richard Lydekker, B.A. (Cantab.), F.G.S., F.Z.S.; late Geological Survey of India. Extracts are given in inverted commas.

Glaciation.

Mr. Lydekker gives facts which show that the glaciers of the Kashmír Himáláyá were formerly of vastly greater proportions than they are at present, although the existing ones include the second largest in the world. He points out that glaciers existed at levels and in districts where there are none at the present day. Mr. Drew thought that a very fine impalpable buff sand occurring among the alluvial deposits (karéwá) was glacier mud, and Prof. Leith Adams considered some of the gravels at Bárámúlá to be of glacial origin, which would point to the existence of glaciers in the valley at a level of 5,000 feet, but Mr. Lydekker is doubtful. He says:—

'Leaving these more or less doubtful instances, cases may now be noticed where there is no question of the validity of the evidence. On the Pír-Pánjál range Mr. Drew has recorded that at heights where mountain tarns are numerous there are abundant and unequivocal signs of former glaciation; both in the form of rock-groovings and polishings, moraines, and scratched stones. On the Kashmír side of the range the numerous small valleys running parallel with the strike of the rocks, and known by the local name of *Margs*, are generally surrounded by rounded masses of detrital matter, which, in the opinion of the present writer, are unquestionably of glacial origin. These moraines are well exhibited at the summer station of Gulmarg, and extend downwards to an elevation of about 7,000 feet. In the Sind valley, on the north side of the Kashmír valley, Mr. Drew has observed a well marked *roche moutonnée* near the village of *Kulan*, at an elevation of about 6,500 feet above the sea level, or 1,500 feet above Srinagar. Other similar traces of extinct glaciers have been observed near the same place; while higher up the Sind valley, at and in the neighbourhood of the summer station of *Sonámarg*, at an elevation of some 9,000 feet there are undulating valleys which are entirely made up of old moraines. Small glaciers are now found at Sonámarg at a level of some 2,000 feet above these old moraines.'

In connexion with glaciation the sacred cave of *Amar Náth* is described, although this cave and its form need not necessarily be attributed to glaciation.

'This cave, which is situated at an elevation of some 16,000 feet, is a large hemispherical hollow in the side of a cliff of white mesozoic dolomite. At the back of the cave there issue from the rock several frozen springs, the ice from which juts forth in spirals which subsequently reunite and form a solid dome-shaped mass of ice at the foot of the back wall of the cave: the size of this mass of ice, which is esteemed sacred by the Hindús, varies according to the season.

CHAP. III.

Evidences of igneous action.

'In palaeozoic and again in eocene times, as will be fully shown in the sequel, there is abundant evidence that igneous, or volcanic agencies were actively at work in the Kashmír Himáláyá, as is proved by the outpouring of vast quantities of volcanic rocks. Remains of volcanoes themselves have not, however, been hitherto detected among any of the volcanic rocks; and none of the latter are known to have been erupted since the eocene period. The persistence of subterraneous thermal action is, however, indicated by the prevalence of numerous thermal springs [1], some of which are of relatively large size, and show evidence of having formerly been still larger.'

I may add that there are sulphurous springs in the valley, and that the Kashmíris claim that all the real Nágs or springs possess the characteristics of the Thed spring, and are hot in winter and cold in summer.

The phenomenon noticed by the late Dr. Hugh Falconer, and quoted by Lydekker, occurred I imagine at Soiyam in the north-west of the valley:—

'A very remarkable manifestation of some form of igneous, or volcanic action is briefly recorded by the late Dr. Hugh Falconer. He states: "I have met with a most remarkable volcanic tract in Kashmír, and so far as my reading goes, without example elsewhere, a tract of alluvium with the strata elevated at a slight angle, and torrefied up to the surface to the condition of a well-burnt brick; but there is no outpouring of lava, and the tract is very circumscribed. Thirty-three years ago [this passage was written in 1837, which would make the date referred to 1804] the ground was so hot that the Hindús of Kashmír, simply by digging a few inches, were enabled to boil rice by the heat of the under strata. There must have been a layer of incandescent matter underneath; but strange, is it not, that it nowhere reached the surface?" From the mention of the inclined alluvial strata in this passage, it is evident that the locality alluded to must be somewhere along the fringe of the Pír-Pánjál range, although the present writer has not been able to identify the precise spot. There can be no question that, as stated by Dr. Falconer, the phenomenon was due to subterranean volcanic action.'

Soiyam is a tract of land situated in the village of Nichhámá, Machipurá. The soil became heated in 1875, and for thirteen months the heat was so great that the Hindús who flocked to see the miracle were enabled to cook their food over the burning ground. The soil

[1] *Thed.* A spring hot in winter and cold in summer, situated at the village of Thed on the Dal lake.

Wian. At Wean, south-east of Srinagar and north of Pámpur, there are three sulphurous springs with a high temperature issuing from the limestone rocks; they are called *phúk nág*.

Islámábád. Two sulphurous springs issue from the limestone rock at the back of the town.

has been burnt to a hard red brick, in which are perfect impressions of leaves. Some thirty-six years before 1875 the soil became hot, but the phenomenon only lasted for two months. The people believe that the occurrence is a *Karan*, that is, an abnormal display of the powers of nature manifested at certain fixed periods. And they are quite certain that Soiyam will again boil up in the year 1911. Dr. W. King, the Director of the Geological Survey of India, who has kindly read through my notes, remarks with reference to Dr. Hugh Falconer's observations :— CHAP. III.

'It must not be forgotten, however, particularly as the locality is doubtful, that there are reported instances in the Kashmír region of hidden seams of tertiary coal having taken fire and produced the burnt appearance of outcrop described above. The case quoted answers very well to such a phenomenon.'

Mr. Lydekker, writing in 1883, alludes to the present rarity of earthquakes, which pointed to the conclusion that subterraneous igneous action was slowly dying out. Two years later one of the most violent earthquakes, ever experienced in Kashmír shook the valley, destroying countless houses and cattle, and killing some 3,000 people. Since 1885 hardly a year has passed without distinct shocks of earthquakes, so it is possible that subterraneous igneous action is either not dying out or else the fact of any necessary direct connexion between earthquakes and igneous action is questionable. Again, if the natives of Kashmír are to be believed there are numerous thermal springs besides those mentioned. The position of the meizoseismal and first isoseismal areas of the earthquake of 1885 is of interest. The isoseismal area was an ellipse with Srinagar as its eastern and Bárámúlá as its western focus, and the fact that the subterraneous force was extremely violent at Bárámúlá would seem to confirm the view that the desiccation of the valley was caused by an earthquake which created an outlet for the lake waters through the Bárámúlá gorge.

The earthquake of 1885 was accompanied by loud noises. Large fissures were formed, from which water and fine sand smelling strongly of sulphur were thrown out. Many irrigation springs disappeared and a large landslip occurred to the south of Bárámúlá. This landslip, which took place on sloping ground at Larridura, about 1,500 feet above the level of the Wular lake, has left behind it a hardened clay in which I have found many perfect specimens of Singhárá nut. This would indicate, perhaps, that in former times the waters of the lake of Kashmír rested over Larridura, and suggests that the climate of the country was

CHAP. III.

milder than it now is, as I doubt whether Singhárá nuts could be grown at the present elevation of Larridura.

Geological formations.

Among the many interesting geological facts connected with the Kashmír valley none are of greater interest than those which support, or refute, the tradition that Kashmír was once covered by the waters of a vast lake. Mr. Lydekker has discussed this question in his memoir, and as the system within which it falls stands first in his table[1] of geological formations, I quote extracts from the chapter on the alluvial system or prehistoric and pleistocene rocks.

Alluvial system.

'It may be observed in the first place that the Kashmír valley is distinctly basin-shaped, and that it has a length of about eighty-four, and a width varying from twenty to twenty-five miles. The lowest point in the valley has an elevation of 5,200 feet, and the mean elevation is 6,000 feet above the sea. The lowest (Banihál) pass in the Pír-Pánjál range, forming its outer boundary, is 3,000 feet above the level of the valley.

'In its course the river Jhelum, below the town of Islámábád, flows through a plain of low level recent alluvium: the width of this plain varies from two to fifteen miles. It appears level to the eye, having in the first thirty miles a fall of 165 feet, but only fifty-five feet in the lower four-and-twenty miles. There is no doubt but that this alluvium has been formed by the river in flood, and its formation may still be locally observed, though the operations of natural agencies have been greatly impeded by artificial embankments.

'It is chiefly composed of *loam* and *clay*, and it would be difficult to distinguish it from the deposits now forming in the lakes of the valley, though the latter may be more distinctly stratified. There is no evidence

[1] The following table of geological systems, in descending order, is given by Mr. Lydekker for the whole of the Kashmír territory:—

Kashmír territory.			European equivalents.
Alluvial system	Low level alluvia, &c.		Prehistoric
	High level alluvia, glacial, lacustrine, and Karéwá series		Pleistocene
Tertiary system	Siwalik series	outer	Pliocene
		inner	
	Sirmúr series	Murree group	Miocene
		Subáthú group, Indus tertiaries	Eocene
Zánskár system	Chikkim series		Cretaceous
	Supra-Kuling series		Jura and Trias
	Kuling series		Carboniferous
Pánjál system (not generally subdivided)			Silurian, Cambrian
Metamorphic system	Metamorphosed Pánjáls, &c.		Palaeozoic and
	Central gneiss		Archaean

to show that any change of level has taken place since the deposition of this alluvium, which contains in many cases pottery and other works of art, of a comparatively modern date.

'On the borders of this great plain of recent alluvium, or forming islands within it, there occur extensive elevated plateaus of alluvial or lacustrine material, which occupy a great portion of the valley, and to which the local name *Karéwá* is applied, a name which has been generally adopted for the deposits. From their elevated position these karéwás cannot generally be brought under irrigation, and are, therefore, in summer easily distinguished from the plain of the river alluvium, which in most part is densely covered with rice crops. In the central parts of the valley the karéwás consist chiefly of loam, or loamy clay, with but faint indications of stratification and with level surfaces.

'They are divided from each other, sometimes cut into stripes, so to say, by ravines of from 100 to 300 feet in depth; occasionally they are surrounded altogether by lower ground, but more generally they connect on to some of the mountains that bound the valley. Karéwás, and their dividing ravines, occupy a width varying from eight to sixteen miles, along the south-western side of the valley, for a length of about fifty miles, from near Shupiyon to the river flat between Sopur and Bárámúlá. Beyond Sopur again, the north-western end of the valley is mostly karéwá ground. Lastly, on the north-east side of the valley across the river, on its right bank, are spaces of karéwás; in some cases these are in recesses made by retiring hills, in others they project out from spurs. The karéwás adjoining the mountains have their surfaces inclined from the latter with decreasing slopes. On the south-eastern side of the valley, the karéwás reach upwards to an elevation of about 6,500 feet, or 1,300 feet above the lowest part of the plain of the river alluvium.

'The flat-topped karéwás always consist of horizontal beds, and in the neighbourhood of Islámábád attain a thickness of 300 feet. A characteristic section of a portion of a karéwá near that town is given by Mr. Drew, and is as follows, viz.:—

	Feet.
Rather coarse drab or brown sand, with some small pebbles .	20
Fine soft brown sand	3
Hard, very fine grained, sand	15
Blue sandy clay	5
Fine soft sand	5
Coarse sand like the uppermost bed	2

'The coarse sand is occasionally hardened to stone; and in some places there occurs a fine impalpable buff sand, which Mr. Drew thinks may have been formed by the grinding action of glaciers on silicious rocks.

CHAP. III.

'The sloping karéwás are best studied along the flanks of the Pír-Pánjál range, where they form a continuous series reaching from Shalúrá in the north-west to below Shupiyon in the south-east. In the neighbourhood of Bárámúlá these beds are composed of yellowish clays, sands, gravels, and conglomerates with an average dip of 10° to the north-east; the pebbles in the conglomerates seldom exceed three or four inches in diameter, and consist of the rocks of the old formations of the Pír-Pánjál: the dip varies from 5° to 20°, and to the south-east stiff blue clays are frequently intercalated among the yellow beds. Colonel Godwin-Austin[1] estimates the thickness of these beds at upwards of 1,400 feet, and has obtained from them many species of land and fresh-water shells all apparently of living forms, together with plant remains and minute fish scales. Old land surfaces are indicated by anthracitic and lignitic layers of from one to three inches in thickness. In a later memoir[2] the same author terms these tilted beds the Hirpur series, from a village of that name near Shupiyon, on the Pír-Pánjál road; this name will not, however, be adopted here. To the south-east of Bárámúlá, almost as far as Shupiyon the lowest beds of these deposits consist of the above-mentioned stiff blue clays, but the conglomerates reappear at Hirpur.

'A section across the strike of these beds, towards the centre of the valleys, such as may be seen along the road from the summer station of Gulmarg to the capital, shows that as the distance from the Pír-Pánjál increases, the dip of the beds gradually lessens until it is scarcely perceptible: at the same time the blue clays and conglomerates disappear and give place to the brown loamy clays and sands of the flat-topped karéwás of the centre of the valley. There does not seem to be the least sign of unconformity between any of the beds of the series, although false bedding is frequent, and there would seem to be no doubt but that they all belong to one continuous formation, the lower beds of which are tilted and either conglomeritic or clayey, while the higher beds are undisturbed and clayey or sandy. The lower tilted beds may be called the "lower karéwás," and the undisturbed the "upper karéwás."

'Reverting once again to the upper karéwás in the neighbourhood of Islámábád, Mr. Drew observes that "behind the town, below the level of most of the beds we have been looking at [the upper karéwás], there are beds of conglomerate of rounded pebbles of the [mesozoic] limestone, of all sizes, and upon these is an accumulation of large angular blocks. These beds lie sloping on the sloping face of rock, their angle with the horizon varies from 7° to 15°, there is sand and calcareous mud mixed up with the limestone pebbles." The relation of these beds to the upper karéwás is not apparent.

[1] *Quar. Jour. Geol. Soc.*, vol. xx. p. 383.

[2] *Brit. Assoc. Rep.*, loc. cit.

'At the mouth of the Sind valley, on the north-eastern side of Kashmír, there are thick deposits of conglomerate, sand, and gravel, with a slight inclination towards the centre of the valley of Kashmír, but whose relations to the upper karéwás are likewise not apparent.

'From the similarity of the conglomerates of Islámábád and the Sind valley to those of the Pír-Pánjál it would seem highly probable that these also belong to the lower karéwá group.

'Before considering the manner in which these deposits were formed, two points in connexion with them must be noticed. In the first place it appears that the great development of the conglomerates exists on the present lines of drainage; thus they are in great force at Hirpur, on the stream flowing from the Pír-Pánjál pass; again at Báránúlá, on the Jhelum, where it flows out of the valley at the mouth of the Sind river, and at Islámábád on the Liddar. Minor developments occur on the smaller Pánjál streams, as below Gulmarg. It would therefore seem pretty certain that the conglomerates are, at all events in part, stream deposits.

'The second point is the lower boundary of the valley of Kashmír. At the present time the Jhelum makes its exit from the valley through a narrow rocky gorge a short distance below the fort of Bárámúlá. This, however, does not appear to have been the original exit from the valley, since to the left (south-east) of the present gorge there is first a hill of slate and then a long high ridge of tilted lower karéwá deposits, over which the road passes, which blocks another gap and forms the present boundary of the valley. The bottom of these deposits is not seen, but it is probable that if they were removed the rocky bottom would be lower than the present gorge of the Jhelum. The open plain which occurs below this ridge of lower karéwás would, in the absence of the latter, form a part of Kashmír proper. There are traces of the same deposit for some miles below the Bárámúlá ridge. It will be at once apparent from the foregoing remarks that until the depth of the lower karéwás of the Bárámúlá ridge is known, it is impossible to say whether the valley of Kashmír is a true rock-basin, or a blocked river-valley, but in the opinion of the author it is most probably the latter.

'The question as to the manner in which the karéwá deposits were formed, may now be taken into consideration. From the great similarity in the petrological characters of the lower karéwás (which have only been detected along the sides of the valley, fringing the mountain ranges, and probably do not extend across the valley) to the higher Siwáliks of the Outer Hills, it is highly probable that the two series have been deposited in an analogous matter. In the case of the Siwáliks it has been proved that these beds are not of lacustrine origin, but have been laid down by the action of rivers, torrents, and rains, and they may conveniently be designated as "wash deposits." In the karéwás as already said, the presence of thick beds of conglomerate near the present valley of the Jhelum at Báramúlá, has led to the inference that these beds were probably deposited by the river itself, which must then have flowed out from the valley in a course not very far removed from its present one; if this be correct no lake could have existed here at that time.

'With regard to the upper karéwás, it seems difficult to imagine how a series of fine clayey and sandy deposits, perfectly horizontal, and extending completely across a wide and open river valley, and attaining a height of more than 200 feet above the level of that valley, could have been accumulated without the aid of a dam lower down the valley by which its waters have been ponded back. Accordingly, the only explanation of the mode of formation of the upper karéwás that presents itself is that Kashmír was formerly occupied by a vast lake, of which the existing lakes are remnants. Mr. Drew estimates that at one period of its existence this old lake must have reached a level of nearly 2,000 feet above the present level of the valley. This estimate is, however, probably far too high, as it is made to include the sloping karéwás of the Pír-Pánjál, which are probably not of lacustrine origin at all; and, even if they are, they were probably horizontal when deposited, and far below their present level.

'The question as to the nature of the barrier which dammed this old lake cannot be certainly determined, until it is finally decided whether the lower karéwás of Báramúlá are true lacustrine, or "wash deposits." If they are the former, the old lake must have continued below the Báramúlá ridge; but if, as seems probably the case, they are the latter, this ridge may have formed the boundary of the lake. On the latter hypothesis it may be that the tilting of the lower karéwás of Báramúlá, which was probably connected with a general rise of the country along the whole length of the Pír-Pánjál range, may have caused the valley of Kashmír, which was previously an open river valley, to have become elevated and blocked at its tower end in the neighbourhood of Báramúlá, and that in the basin thus formed the upper karéwás may have been deposited, with their southern edges resting apparently conformably on the tilted beds of the lower karéwás. This basin may have been subsequently drained by the river cutting down the present rock-gorge at Báramúlá. Should this explanation be the true one, traces of the "overlap" of the upper karéwás on the lower beds of the same series ought to be detected.

'Should it be that the lower karéwás are in part of lacustrine origin, then it will be necessary to assume that the barrier existed below Báramúlá, and the most likely place of its occurrence would be the narrow gorge for Rámpur, some distance below Naushehra. As, however, it is highly probable that the former solution may be the correct one, it would be idle to discuss what might have been the nature of a barrier at Rámpur, which may never have existed.

'The whole question, however, requires further light thrown upon it by an observer well versed in the study of similar deposits, before there can be any hope of arriving at any very satisfactory conclusions, as to the barrier which dammed the old Kashmír lake, and the relative period of its existence.

'With regard to the age of the karéwás, their considerable geological age is indicated by the tilting which their lower beds have undergone, and by the amount of denudation which they have suffered, as well as by their relations to the low-level alluvium of the Jhelum. The lower karéwás bear, as already said, a very marked and striking resemblance to the topmost Siwáliks of the Outer Hills, which are likewise tilted, and have a similar north-westerly strike. In the Outer Hills, the period of disturbance did not extend down to the post-Siwálik deposits (? higher pleistocene) and it seems, therefore, highly probable that the same disturbance may have acted on the upper Siwáliks of the Outer Hills, and the lower karéwás of Kashmír. If this be so, the age of the later must be either lower pleistocene, or the very highest pliocene, whichever the topmost Siwáliks may be; while the upper karéwás may belong to some part of the pleistocene period. It would seem likely, as already said, that the elevation of the Pír-Pánjál, which probably caused the tilting of the karéwás, took place during the later part of the lower karéwá period, and that the upper karéwás were deposited in apparent conformity on the inner border of the tilted lower beds.

'The glacial period presents the usual difficulties and perplexities in connexion with these lacustrine and wash deposits. If, as seems probable, they are in great part of pre-glacial age (although, from the presence of what has been supposed to be glacial mud, their upper beds, as Mr. Drew suggests, may be of glacial age), it is difficult to see how they were preserved, if the Kashmír valley ever filled with ice. This difficulty may perhaps be solved if it be considered that, although glaciers descended to the level of the Kashmír valley, yet they never filled it with ice; and this may really be the clue to the problem. This view, of course, involves the conclusion that the glacial period in these regions was not so intense as has sometimes been supposed.'

The latest summing-up of the evidence regarding the formation of the Kashmír valley, and of its deposits is given by Mr. R. D. Oldham in the second edition of the *Manual of the Geology of India* (1893).

'The best published description of these beds (*karéwás*) are those of Colonel Godwin-Austin and Mr. Drew, by both of whom they are regarded as of lacustrine origin, an opinion also adopted by Mr. Lydekker, but difficult to accept in its entirety. It is very probable that some of the finely-bedded fine-grained deposits described by Colonel Godwin-Austin were deposited in still water, but the frequent alternations of beds of shingle with sand and the layers of lignite from one to three inches in thickness, point to subaërial conditions of formation. Even the presence of true lacustrine deposits does not prove that the whole of the Kashmír lake basin was ever occupied by a lake. This rock basin was probably gradually formed by a deformation of the earth's crust, and the hollow so produced was filled up almost, if not quite, as soon as formed. At the present day true lacustrine deposits are being formed in those places on the northern limit of the valley where, owing to a deficiency of deposition, hollows have been left in which water has accumulated, and it is probable that the conditions have been much the same as at present, throughout the geological history of the Kashmír valley, and that a minor area of true lacustrine deposits has been accompanied by a greater area where subaërial accumulation of sediment has been in progress.

'It is possible that some of the older beds of the karéwás may be contemporaneous with part of the upper Siwáliks, but the only fossils yet found, besides undetermined fish-scales and plant remains, have been land and fresh-water shells, all apparently belonging to living species.'

Zánskár system.

The Zánskár system (Mesozoic and Carboniferous rocks) plays the next important part in the geology of the valley. As regards the designation *Zánskár* and its correlation in the above list with the European names, Cretaceous, Jura, Trias, and Carboniferous, Mr. Lydekker warns his readers that this correlation must be regarded only in the most general sense.

'It can only imply that the general relative order of the succession of organic forms has been in the main the same, but it cannot be strictly considered, even in the homotaxial sense, that one Himáláyán formation is the exact equivalent of its European namesake. Thus since, as will be shown below, in the Kashmír valley no break has been detected between strata containing fossils characteristic of the lower carboniferous (mountain limestone) of Europe, and the overlying and underlying strata which have respectively been referred to the silurian and the trias, it is quite evident that these cannot really exactly correspond to the European formations after which they are named, but must rather collectively correspond, in a homotaxial sense, to the whole of the silurian, devonian, upper and lower carboniferous, permian, and trias of Europe. Again, the carboniferous of Kashmír, which contains fossils characteristic of the lower part of that period, is only a few feet in thickness, and cannot, therefore, contain divisions corresponding to the European divisions of that great system, nor can it represent anything like a period of time corresponding to the enormous carboniferous epoch of Europe. CHAP. III.

'At the mouth of a narrow gorge situated at the village of Khunmú (Khoonmoo), on the north-western side of the Vihú valley, some five miles north of Pámpur, the following series of rocks are found overlying the older palaeozoic trappean rocks which form the great bulk of the neighbouring mountains.

		Feet.	
Supra-Kuling series.	1. Limestones	2,200	(?)
Kuling series.	2. Bed with shells and *Athyris*	2	43.
	3. Grey limestone	6	
	4. Limestone with *Productus* and *Spirifer*	3	
	5. Hard limestone with *Orthoceras*	10	
	6. Sandy calcareous and shaly beds	10	
	7. Compact quartzite	12	

'Another section also modified from Colonel Godwin-Austin's memoir, taken near the village of Barus, on the right bank of the Jhelum, under Wastarwán peak, to the south-east of the Vihú district, is as follows:—

		Feet.	
Supra-Kuling series.	1. Hard grey compact limestone (denuded)	150	(remaining).
Kuling series.	2. Micaceous sandy calcareous beds with *Spirifer*, *Productus* and *Chonetes*	60	300.
	3. Calcareous slate or shale	30	
	4. Compact limestone with obscure fossils	100	
	5. Shaly limestone with *Fenestella* and *Streptorhynchus*	50	
	6. Hard compact limestone with *Productus*, *Terebratula* and *Athyris*	40	
	7. Compact quartzite	20	

'The fossils occurring in the beds marked two to six of the foregoing section, which have been named the Zewan, or Ziawan beds, by Messrs. Godwin-Austin and Verchere, are all of carboniferous forms, and will be further discussed below. They indicate that these beds, with the underlying quartzite, which vary in thickness from a little over 40 feet to upwards of 300 feet, must be referred to the carboniferous, and it will be subsequently shown that they correspond to the Kuling series of Dr. Stoliczka. In the Khunmú ravine, from some of the limestones marked 1 in the above section, the present writer obtained a specimen

CHAP. III. of a large triassic species of *Megalodon*, indicating the triassic age of some of these limestones; and from the same great series Colonel Godwin-Austin has obtained a cephalopod referred to the genus *Goniatites*, while numerous other fossils, noticed below, were obtained by Dr. Verchere. It is difficult to assign any very fixed boundaries to the Kuling and the supra-Kuling series in this district, as the two pass insensibly one into another. As, however, in the upper Sind valley a characteristic triassic fossil has been found at the base of limestones and dolomites corresponding to No. 1 in the above section. It has been deemed advisable for the present to class as Kuling only such beds as contain characteristic carboniferous fossils, all the higher beds being provisionally referred to the supra-Kuling series.

'The Kuling rocks, as already observed, in the Vihú district are generally underlain by massive amygdaloidal and other traps, which frequently, when the bottom quartzitic bed is less strongly developed, pass insensibly upwards into the fossiliferous beds, and it is accordingly probable that some of these traps with their associated shales may really be of carboniferous age. From the remarks already made as to the propriety (when there is no strong palaeological evidence to the contrary) of restricting the European geological terms to accord with the petrological conditions of the rocks of other countries to which they are applied, it will be inferred that it is considered best to confine the lower extent of the Kuling, or carboniferous, to the proper beds of the fossiliferous series: all the traps in this district are, therefore, referred to the older palaeozoics. The carboniferous rocks of Vihú may be traced to the northward into the Árráh valley, to the north-east of Srinagar, where they bend round to take a north-easterly direction below the survey station of Mahádeo: fossils have, however, not been generally found in the Árráh valley, and the upper boundaries of the Kuling series are consequently given somewhat approximately. The whole series is here inverted on the northern side, the supra-Kuling rocks underlying the Kuling series, and the latter the older palaeozoic rocks, which are more generally sedimentary in their character. The eastern boundary of this area of Zánskár rocks runs across the western side of the upper Trál valley, thence cutting again into Vihú on the northern side of the peak above Awantipurá (Wastarwán peak). Along this boundary line the characteristic carboniferous fossils are to be found in great abundance, especially on the high ridge to the north-east of Prongám, and also to the south-east of Mandakpál. The Kuling rocks on this side generally consist of black and brown highly carbonaceous shales, cherts and blue limestones, in varying proportions. The shales, when freshly split, omit a strong fetid odour, and are frequently crowded with fenestellae and other fossils. Near Mandakpál the cherty beds often pass into a highly siliceous blue or white rock closely resembling flint or chalcedony. From south to north along this border, the underlying rocks change considerably in character, becoming entirely trappean on Wastarwán peak. The Kuling series, overlain here and there by supra-Kuling beds, may be traced round the north-western flanks of the same peak. On the south side of this peak, to the north-west of Awantipurá, there is a small outlier of the Kuling series occupying a spur projecting from the underlying traps, the rocks of which are crowded with the characteristic fossils. The connexion existing here between the sedimentary Kuling rocks, and the underlying traps is extremely intimate, and fossils are frequently found in juxtaposition with the traps; so that on splitting open the rock it will not unfrequently be found that a fossiliferous layer divides so as to leave one portion adhering to the underlying trap, and the other to the overlying shales. Occasionally the fossils are found entirely in beds which cannot be well distinguished from the traps, though doubtless consisting in part either of contemporaneously altered sedimentary detrital rocks, or of those mingled with ashes. This intimate connexion of the Zánskár and Pánjál systems will be subsequently referred to. The limestone rocks of Vihú and other parts of the Kashmír valley form a very striking feature in the landscape, their light blue and white tints standing out in marked contrast to the sombre hues of the older slates and traps. The limestones are usually thin-bedded; narrow partings of shale dividing the different layers, and causing the sides of the cliffs of these rocks to present a very characteristic banded appearance, which in Vihú is rendered still more picturesque by the numerous graceful folds and waves into which these strata have been thrown. From the base of cliffs of these rocks in various parts of the south-eastern end of the valley of Kashmír, burst the numerous springs of water which form the sources of the Jhelum. The largest of these occur at the villages of Bawan, Islámábád, Achábal, and Verinág. The water is remarkable for its transparency, and frequently gushes out in great volumes: it is generally somewhat higher in temperature than the surface water.

'The next development of Zánskár rocks to be noticed occurs in the Liddar valley, where these rocks are to be found at the village of Pahlgám, and again lower down half-way between that place and Islámábád. The latter outliers of these rocks commence at the village of Aishmákám, where they occur in three ellipses, situated on the strike of the Vihú rocks, thickest on the line of the river, and gradually dying out on either side. Their relations will be best made clear by a brief description of the whole section from Pahlgám to the mouth of the Liddar valley. At Pahlgám itself there occur the characteristic thin-bedded limestones and dolomites of the supra-Kuling series, underlain by a thin band of the Kuling shales

CHAP. III. and limestones in which the characteristic fossils are of not uncommon occurrence: these rocks gradually pass downwards into a great mass of amygdoloidal traps of the Pánjál system, which show some signs of stratification in their higher beds, but lower down are extremely massive. Some eight miles down the valley, below the village of Bhatkot, these trappean rocks are underlain by a band of Kuling rocks with their characteristic fossils; among which the caudal part of a specimen of a trilobite of the genus *Phillipsia*, not improbably identical with *P. semenifera* of the carboniferous of Europe, was obtained in 1880 by the writer. These Kuling rocks are in their turn underlain by dark slates and light coloured quartzites of the Pánjál system, and the latter by a band of Kuling rocks, which is followed by the Pánjál slates and quartzites. Approaching Aishmákám these Pánjál rocks are again underlain by a band of the Kuling shales and calcareous rocks, followed inferiorly by limestones, dolomites, and green and purple shaly slates, some of which are evidently the representatives of the supra-Kuling series, and below which there again occur the rocks of the Kuling series with their characteristic fossils. Below Aishmákám there is once more a series of the sedimentary Pánjál rocks, which to the south are inverted upon the rocks of the Zánskár system of Islámábád. Some further inferences from the Liddar section will be drawn in the subsequent chapter, but it will suffice here to say that the section indicates a vast inversion of a great part of the series coupled with complex folding, the original extent of which is approximately indicated in the accompanying section.

'The Zánskár rocks of Pahlgám which on their south and south-western border consist of Kuling series, overlain by supra-Kuling series, form a sub-oval-shaped mass, of some eight miles in length, extending up the two branches of the Liddar river. It is probable that the Kuling rocks also occur along the north-eastern border of this oval, since on the eastern branch of the river, on the road to *Sheshnág*, the strata have a northerly strike and a westerly dip, and the rocks of the Zánskár system are underlain by the traps of the Pánjál system. The Kuling series on this line seems, however, to have been obliterated by the traps, as will be shown to be the case elsewhere, and it has consequently been found necessary on the map to place the rocks of the supra-Kuling series, in direct contact with the Pánjál rocks.

'Turning now to the great truncated ellipse of Zánskár rocks occupying the axis of the south-eastern extremity of the valley of Kashmír, it has been already stated that these rocks first occur at Islámábád, where they form the high isolated rock at the back of the town, having a low north-easterly dip, and consisting chiefly of thin-bedded limestones and dolomites with shaly partings. A band of karéwá deposit conceals the northern part of these rocks, beyond which they reappear at the village of Bawan, where they are inverted under the older palaeozoic. rocks of the lower Liddar valley. To the south-east of Bawan the boundary of these rocks runs close to the village of Naubug, where there is a considerable flexure, and thence across the Márbal pass to a point some six miles on the eastern side, where the writer obtained characteristic Kuling brachiopods in a hard grey shaly slate. At this south-eastern extremity of the ellipse the Kuling rocks, which are here the only representatives of the Zánskár system, are almost indistinguishable from the underlying slaty Pánjáls, and would not have been recognized to the eastward of the pass, had it not been for the above-mentioned fossils. Along the inverted Naubug boundary. fossils may here and there be detected in the normal Kuling shales.

'Towards the south-west the rocks of the Zánskár system extend as far as the northern flanks of the Pír-Pánjál range at Bánihál, whence their boundary probably runs to meet the point to the eastward of the Márbal pass where the above-mentioned fossils were obtained. On the road leading up to the Bánihál pass, as far as can be seen through the dense forest which covers the mountain side, the Zánskár rocks consist of dolomites and limestones of the supra-Kuling series, having a south-westerly dip towards the older Pánjál rocks; the dip of the latter, as recorded in a section taken some years ago, being in the opposite (north-east) direction.

'The rocks in the centre of this great eclipse of the Zánskár system belong mainly to the supra-Kuling series, and are characterized by the prevalence of light-coloured and thin-bedded dolomites and limestones. On the line from the Márbal pass to Ságám, however, there occurs an anticlinal axis, in which the cherts and shales of the Kuling series, crowded with various species of *Productus*, *Spirifer*, and *Fenestella* are well exposed. Owing, however, to the variation in the petrological characters of the beds themselves, as well as the absence of fossils at Ságám itself, the precise boundaries of the Kuling series are difficult to determine, and it is possible that rocks of the Pánjál system may be exposed.

'Passing to the north-western side of the valley, two small outcrops of supra-Kuling limestone appear on the flanks of the Pír-Pánjál range, at and near the village of Berwá (Berú). These limestones have a low north-easterly dip, and protrude through the karéwá formation; they are on the strike of the Shahábád ellipse, and it is probable they are connected below the karéwá formation with lower Zánskár rocks, overlying the older palaeozoics of the Pánjál range.

'On the opposite side of the valley three small patches of Zánskár rocks occur in the neighbourhood of the Wular lake. The first of these

CHAP. III. is situated at the village of Mánasbal, forming the shore of the small lake there, and running in two projections high up on the sides of the adjoining mountains. Near the mouth of the Sind valley these rocks consist of pale-blue banded limestones overlying the blackish amygdaloidal trap, with a north-easterly dip: they extend a little distance to the south of the Safápur trigonometrical station, to the west of which the trappean rocks again project into the middle of the Zánskár rocks; the latter having a quaquaversal dip around the former. To the south of the lake another small dome-shaped mass of amygdaloidal trap underlies the calcareous rocks. Near this spot, at the village of Kándarbal, the Zánskár rocks consist mainly of nearly pure white thick-bedded dolomitic limestones, which are largely quarried for the manufacture of cement.

'Remains of crinoids and obscure shells are very common in these rocks, but the only well-preserved fossil that has been obtained from them is part of the shell of a specifically indeterminable *Orthoceras*, which was collected by Mr. W. Theobald. The Mánasbal rocks are much contorted, and are characterized by the usual banded appearance, which, with their light colour, forms a striking contrast to the underlying unstratified traps. These rocks are the same as the supra-Kuling series of other parts of Kashmír, but no traces of the fossiliferous carbonaceous shales and cherts of the underlying Kuling series have hitherto been detected at their base resting upon the traps. The most probable explanation of this apparent anomaly, here and elsewhere, seems to be that the trap, which, from its showing no signs of intrusion into the overlying limestones, must be of contemporaneous origin with the rocks with which it is associated, was outpoured during the deposition of the Kuling series, and has, so to speak, absorbed these deposits, and altered them out of all recognition. On this theory the upper trap here, and in other localities where similar conditions prevail, must really belong to the Zánskár system, but, as already said, it is found more convenient to class the whole of it with the underlying Pánjál system.

'To the northward of Mánasbal another small patch of Zánskár rocks occurs near the village of Háján, and there are other patches in the neighbourhood. These small patches lead on to the larger mass which occurs at the village of Bándipura, at the north-western extremity of the Wular lake. At this spot the rocks of the Zánskár system occupy a rudely triangular area on the left bank of the Bándipura stream; having a low and regular north-easterly dip, or one towards the older rocks. From this dip, and from the fact that there is evidently no inversion of the rocks at Mánasbal, it would seem probable that the junction between the Zánskár and Pánjál systems is here a disturbed one. The lower beds (assuming the absence of inversion) consist of cherty sandstones, and blue limestones, with occasional shaly bands, while the higher beds consist of thin-bedded, light-coloured, and frequently dolomitic limestones; the lowest exposed beds contain numerous crinoids and corals. The greater part of these rocks certainly belong to the supra-Kuling series, but whether the Kuling series may not also be represented at the base of the series must remain uncertain until it be definitely determined whether the beds are in their normal position, or inverted.

'At the extreme north-western end of the valley of Kashmír, rocks belonging to the Zánskár system are met with at the village of Tregám. These rocks consist mainly of the usual limestones and dolomites, the former being generally of a dark blue colour, and frequently occurring in beds of some two feet in thickness, they apparently rest in a synclinal of the Pánjál rocks; and do not extend across the ridge into the valley of the Kishngangá. The greater part of these rocks certainly belongs to the supra-Kuling series, but on their northerly and easterly borders they are underlain by some greenish and black shaly and slaty beds mixed with earthy limestones, which must probably be regarded as the representatives of the Kuling series, although fossils have not hitherto been obtained from them. On the western border of the exposure, the basement beds are in great part concealed by alluvium and debris.

'The mode of occurrence of the Zánskár rocks in the valley of Kashmír, will lead to the conclusion that this valley is formed on the line of a synclinal axis of newer palaeozoic and mesozoic rocks, the original symmetry of which has been partially destroyed by faulting or other movements. It is probable that the area now covered by alluvial and karéwá deposits is mainly underlain by the rocks of the Zánskár system.'

The Pánjál system.

The name Pánjál is a local term, like Zánskár, employed to denote all the rocks below the Kuling (lower carboniferous) and above the metamorphics. These rocks consist mainly of dark slates, sandstones, quartzites, conglomerates and volcanic rocks. It is noticeable that the strata of the Pánjál system are totally devoid of organic remains.

'Underlying the Zánskár rocks in the neighbourhood of Srinagar and Mánasbal, the amygdaloidal rocks of the Pír-Pánjál attain a great development, and, as already stated, in some instances entirely obliterate the characteristic rocks of the Kuling series. These rocks form almost the whole of the small isolated hill on which the fort of Hari-Párbat near Srinagar is built, and also the conspicuous hill at the back of the town so well known to all visitors as the Takht-i-Sulimán. On the north-eastern side of the latter, on the road from the Munshi-bágh to the Dal lake, fine

CHAP. III. splintery black and green slates are partly interstratified with the amygdaloidal rocks, but in great part appear to underlie them. These slates form a considerable part of the higher hills to the north-east of the gap behind the Tákht through which the road passes, while on the north-eastern side of the Dal lake the high ridge forming the outer boundary of the Árráh valley, consists mainly of the massive amygdaloidal rocks. At the foot of this ridge, near the Nishát Bágh, there occur some calcareous sandstones, dark cherts and slates, occasionally containing obscure impressions of fossils, and dipping towards the ridge, which may be the representatives of the Kuling series. The amygdaloidal traps of the above-mentioned ridge are continuous with those at the mouth of the Sind valley, Mánasbal, and the shores of the Wular lake.

'The amygdaloidal and allied rocks in this neighbourhood are generally of a greenish, or blackish colour, sometimes containing numerous amygdules; but at other times are homogeneous, fine-grained rocks like greenstone. The latter rock not unfrequently contains large isolated pear-shaped amygdules of chalcedony, reaching to two or three inches in length. The whole formation is generally devoid of any visible signs of stratification, and forms bold, massive cliffs, from which cuboidal fragments disintegrate. In many parts of the Pír-Pánjál, and, as already mentioned, in the neighbourhood of Awantipura, these rocks pass insensibly downwards into the argillaceous and arenaceous rocks with which they are interstratified.

'A very characteristic rock of not unfrequent occurrence among the traps of the Kashmír valley, is a dark compact trap, having at intervals clusters of small white (? felspar) crystals diverging from a central point in the form of a many-rayed star, to which Dr. Verchere applied the name of *Suláimánite*, from its common occurrence in the Takht-i-Sulimán. One of the most common varieties may be described as a felspar-porphyry, or perhaps rather as a porphyritic trap, since the base appears to be basaltic; and accordingly these rocks may generally be alluded to as altered basalts.

'From the foregoing observations it may be taken as certain that the amygdaloidal rocks of Kashmír are of volcanic[1] origin, and that they are mingled with what are probably trap-ashes and other rocks, which from their mode of deposition, and from the effects of subsequent metamorphic action, have become so fused with detrital sedimentary rocks, that it is now frequently impossible to distinguish the one from the other. With regard to their geological age and mode of origin, it will in the first place be apparent from the descriptions given in an earlier chapter, that these rocks cannot be intrusive, since they underlie the rocks of the Zánskár system

[1] The term volcanic is employed here as analogous to igneous, and does not necessarily imply any connexion with a true volcano.

without penetrating them by dykes: and as they are interstratified with those rocks, and also with the slates of the Pánjál system, it is evident that they must be of contemporaneous origin with the rocks with which they are associated.

'From the extremely intimate connexion existing between the traps of the valley of Kashmír and the rocks of Kuling series, which are certainly of submarine origin, there would seem to be little or no doubt that the traps were likewise poured forth beneath the surface of the ocean. In regard to submarine lavas it is remarked by Professor Geikie that these rocks differ from lavas poured forth on land only "in their more distinct and originally less inclined bedding, and in their tendency to the admixture of non-volcanic or ordinary mechanical sediment with the volcanic dust and stones. No appreciable difference either in external aspect or in internal structure seems yet to have been established between subaërial and submarine lavas. Some undoubtedly submarine lavas are highly scoriaceous. There is no reason, indeed, why slaggy lava and loose non-buoyant scoriae should not accumulate under the pressure of a deep column of the ocean." In their great intermixture with what are apparently materials of non-volcanic origin, the traps of Kashmír agree well with the above-mentioned characteristics of submarine and volcanic rocks.

'In their mode of occurrence these partially altered volcanic rocks of Kashmír appear to present considerable resemblances to certain still more altered amygdaloidal and tufaceous volcanic rocks occurring in the devonian of Devonshire, beneath the carboniferous. The metamorphism of the latter has, however, been so great as to produce a schistose structure in the amygdaloids, which is wanting in those of Kashmír. In Devonshire rocks, which are partly lavas, partly tuffs, and partly tufaceous sediments, are mingled together in a manner very similar to the mode of occurrence of the palaeozoic volcanic rocks of Kashmír.

'Summing up the general conclusions to be derived from the study of these rocks, it appears probable that during the Pánjál period, which immediately preceded that of the lower carboniferous, very extensive submarine eruptions of lava and ashes were emitted, probably from volcanoes: these eruptions probably took their origin from several distinct points, and at several distinct intervals of time. Throughout the whole period, during which these eruptions were continued, uninterrupted deposition of ordinary sedimentary detrital material appears to have continued at the sea-bottom, the strata resulting from which became at once so intimately mingled with the volcanic products as to render it now difficult to distinguish between the original factors of the deposit; while subsequent metamorphic action has served to obliterate still more completely their original distinction. In certain spots, as at Mánasbal,

CHAP. III.

the Kashmír valley, the eruption of volcanic matter appears to have continued, during a part or the whole, of the Kuling, or lower carboniferous period, and to have rendered the distinctive sedimentary rocks of that period in many places totally unrecognizable.'

Metamorphic system.

In the chapter describing the Pánjál system, Mr. Lydekker notices the occurrence of a considerable thickness of coarse gneiss, associated with grey sandstones and beds of limestone, some of which is white and highly crystalline, and some blue and scarcely altered. These rocks are found at Kángan in the Sind valley, and on either side of the mouth of the Wángat valley which runs off from the main valley. Mr. Lydekker writes:—

'The age of the Kángan gneiss is not easy of determination; if the sequence be uninterrupted from its relation to the traps, it would appear to occupy a place high in the Pánjál system, but no such rocks are found in a similar position in the neighbourhood, and it may, therefore, be that the junction of the rocks is not really undisturbed, and that the gneiss may be below the great mass of the Pánjáls as in the Pánjál range itself.'

This is the only instance of the crystalline and metamorphic system in the valley of Kashmír, but it is impossible to determine whether these rocks correspond to the central gneiss of Mr. Lydekker's table:—

'If it should prove to be the same, it would seem probable that there must either exist considerable dislocation between the granitoid gneiss and Pánjál rocks, or that the higher beds of the latter overlap the former, because the Pánjál rocks adjoining the gneiss belong to the higher volcanic portion of that system.'

Economic geology.

Although there has been no organized exploration, Mr. Lydekker is of opinion that the Kashmír Himáláyá is not likely to be an important producer of the precious metals. But the chance discovery of valuable sapphires in the Padar country in 1882 leads one to hope that other sources of mineral wealth may still be found in the territories of His Highness the Mahárájá of Jammu and Kashmír, and I do not think that in a state like Kashmír it is correct to infer that the natives of the country would be prompt to disclose the existence of rich lodes, or that they would prove energetic miners. The people are engaged in agricultural or pastoral pursuits, and their experience in the past teaches them that the discovery of mineral wealth is attended with drawbacks in the shape of forced labour and the presence of a large number of officials who have to be fed. Mr. La Touche in his note on the sapphire mines of Kashmír agrees with Mr. Lydekker. Mr. La Touche writes:—

'So much has been said lately about the great mineral resources of Kashmír, that it may perhaps be well, in conclusion, to say a few words on the subject. In speaking of the mineral wealth that might be brought to light by properly-conducted prospecting, it does not seem to be generally taken into consideration that the natives of the country have for ages had good opportunities of discovering what minerals the hills contain, and that as a rule they have shown themselves fully capable of making use of their opportunities. I think that I am not far wrong in saying that in very few instances in India have useful minerals been discovered in localities that were unknown to the natives, and in which the ores had not been worked by them at one time or another. Even the more uncivilized hill tribes are more or less well acquainted with the minerals their hills contain, and are by no means in the condition of the blacks of Australia or the bushmen of Southern Africa, in whose country the European prospector has found so great a field for his energies. To take a single instance, the Khasis of Assam, who till the beginning of the present century had hardly felt the influence of Western civilization, have for ages obtained their iron from an ore which occurs as minute grains of magnetite disseminated in the granite of their hills. Many a highly-trained European geologist might justly have been sceptical as to the possibility of obtaining a productive iron ore from granite, and would very possibly have passed the rock over as being utterly useless for such a purpose. Yet the Khasis discovered the mineral, and in all parts of the hills ancient heaps of slag testify to the use they made of their discovery; moreover, they obtained the ore by a process which was ingenious and even scientific, in fact a kind of hydraulic mining somewhat similar to the latest process devised for obtaining gold in California. Can it be doubted that if any other useful minerals existed in their hills, the Khasis would not have found and worked them long ago? Similarly, in Kashmír any mineral deposits that exist are probably well known to the natives, and, if useful, are already worked, and these are not of any great importance. Even the common minerals, coal and iron, are not found in any large quantity, and where they do occur are poor in quality. Accident may bring to light the presence of some of the rarer minerals, as in the case of the sapphires, but even the most energetic and intelligent prospector might spend years among the mountains before making such another discovery.'

With great diffidence I still maintain that there are special reasons in Kashmír, which would lead the natives of the country to look upon the discovery of the valuable minerals as a calamity to their neighbourhood. I have often discussed the question of iron-mining with the villagers who

CHAP. III. live near Sof, and if their views on the subject of mineral wealth represent the general ideas of the people, it is not an exaggeration to say that the Kashmíris detest the very name of mining. I have heard the same views expressed in other parts of the valley, where iron has been found, and have noticed that the Kashmíris, who are ready to talk with me on all subjects relating to their country and its products, are strangely reticent on the subject of minerals. It may therefore prove in the future that organized exploration will reveal mineral wealth. Men who were in charge of the sapphire mines in Padar have told me of other valuable minerals being found in that direction, and there are persons still alive who tell stories of the discoveries of mineral wealth in Gwásh brári and in the mountains below Harámak. There are reasons perhaps unknown to Messrs. Lydekker and La Touche which cause both State and people to view the exploitation of minerals with disfavour.

Coal. Mr. Lydekker notices that some of the Zánskár rocks of the Kashmír valley have here and there almost a coaly nature, but he remarks that there does not appear to be the slightest probability that workable coal will ever be found in the Kashmír territories. I have seen the blacksmiths of Kashmír using a black substance like fossil peat, and they say that it gives a great heat.

Peat. Peat is extracted from the low-lying ground which lies on both sides of the Jhelum river below Srinagar. Potters use it, and if the peat is cut in the dry weather and stacked it is an excellent fuel. I have used it regularly for two winters in Kashmír, and mixed with wood it is at once a cheap and effective fuel. It is formed of the remains of water-plants, and at present it could be obtained in enormous quantities. It is known to the Kashmíris as *demb tsak*.

Sulphur. There are several strong sulphur springs in Kashmír at Wean, Islámábád, Sadarkat, and elsewhere. Specimens of native sulphur from the Kashmír valley were shown to Mr. Lydekker, but at present no sulphur is produced in the valley, and the supply comes from Púgá in Ladákh.

Gold. Kashmíris who reside in distant parts of the valley affirm that gold has been found in the Wastarwán mountain. This may be a legend like the widespread belief that there is an emerald mine in the crest of the Harámak mountain.

Copper. It is said that copper was once extracted from the mountain on which Aishmákám in the Liddar valley stands. In old history it is stated that the great king Zain-ul-abadin defrayed all his private expenditure from the proceeds of a copper mine which he discovered in Kashmír.

Iron. Iron has been discovered and worked in several places in the valley, and there are extensive workings of iron ore in the neighbourhood of

Sof. In 1892 an Englishman spent some time in exploring the resources of Sof. He held that the supply of ore was practicably inexhaustible, and that owing to the presence of pine forests iron smelting could be carried on with profit. He had a good opinion of the iron, which he described as being equal to mild steel, and his preliminary operations led him to hold most sanguine ideas as to the future of an iron industry in Kashmír. The Kashmíris regard the Sof iron as superior to the iron imported from India for the purposes of agricultural implements, and the blacksmiths always speak of it most favourably. No iron is at present extracted from Sof or the other mines, and the experience of past years points to the fact that the State cannot work its iron mines with profit. The heavy cost of carriage on imported iron might perhaps allow of the Kashmír mines being worked with success if they were placed under proper management. The cost of fuel would not seriously hamper the industry. Mr. La Touche, however, writing in 1889, says of the Sof mines:—

'I also paid a visit to the ironworks of Sof in the Kashmír valley, the ore for which is obtained from a bed of impure calcareous limonite intercalated in the limestone and rocks to the east of Achabal. The bed is only one or two feet in thickness, and dips at an angle of 35° into the hill, but its outcrop extends for a distance of at least two miles along the hillside, and there must be sufficient ore here to keep the small native furnaces supplied for many years to come, so long as there is any demand for the iron, but it would certainly not be advisable to start large blast furnaces on the English plan, and moreover the ore seems to be very poor in quality.'

No salt is found in the valley, but certain salt licks exist to which the stags resort in the spring. Salt.

Small nests of saltpetre (potassic-nitrate) are found occasionally in some of the upper karéwás of the Kashmír valley. Saltpetre.

This is known to the Kashmíris as *Gach*. It is obtained in large quantities from a place below Bárámúlá on the right bank of the Jhelum, and also from the lime mountain, Ahak Tang, which overlooks the Mánasbal lake. Gypsum.

Up to the present the chief source of limestone has been the Ahak Tang or lime mountain. Lime is also extracted at Ajas on the Wular lake, and used to be burnt at Birú Other more convenient sources have recently been discovered on the shores of the Dal lake, and on the banks of the Jhelum. There is Kankar in most of the karéwás, all of which makes good hydraulic lime. An excellent chalk similar to tailors' chalk is Limestone.

CHAP. III. obtained from a karéwá near Srinagar, and is known as *Sipar*. It is used for wall plaster and for writing on slates.

Building stones. Blue limestones belonging to some part of the Zánskár system are, according to Mr. Lydekker, the chief materials both of the ancient and modern buildings of Kashmír.

'These limestones can be worked as a freestone, are very durable, and have been quarried in blocks of great length. The largest buildings in which they are employed are the old temples dotted over the valley, the chief of which are situated at Martand near Islámábád, at Awantipurá, at Pandratan near Srinagar, and at Payech. The old building at the summit of the Takht-i-Sulimán at Srinagar is also built of the same stone. In the city itself the modern temples and the handsome flights of steps and embankments on the river in the neighbourhood of the Mahárájá's palace are constructed of the same stone. The buildings of the Mughal period on the borders of the Dal lake are largely built of these limestones, the supports of the pavilion in the Shálámár gardens consisting of handsome columns of black and grey fossiliferous marble.

'The Zánskár rocks of Vihú are probably the source of most of the limestone employed in the buildings of Srinagar, but it is to be regretted that much of the material used in the construction of the modern erections is obtained from the demolition of the ancient buildings rather than from the quarries. The distribution of Zánskár rocks in the valley of Kashmír is such as to render them peculiarly convenient for the construction of buildings in any part that may be desired.'

Slate. Slates are obtained from Bárámúlá, and recently a slate quarry has been opened near the village of Brain on the shores of the Dal lake. The Bárámúlá slates are much used for the floors of Hammáms, and are known as *Sang-i-farash*.

Clay. The Kashmír valley is rich in a variety of clays most suitable for potters' purposes. Some rude attempts have been made in the ceramic art, and it is believed that some of the clays are admirably adapted for the manufacture of a superior pottery. An Englishman acquainted with some well-known potteries in England pronounced certain clays which I sent to him to be of considerable value. Special localities in the south of the valley are famous for their superior clays, but at present the Kashmíri potters aim at nothing higher than turning out water- and cooking-vessels of the simplest description. I have pointed out in another chapter that metal is very rarely used for domestic purposes, and rough earthenware supplies all the wants of the Kashmíri peasants.

Mill stones. These are made from sandstones and grits of the Pánjál system.

Lapidaries. The lapidaries (Hakák) import all their more valuable stones, such as agate, bloodstone, cornelian, cat's-eye, garnet, lapis-lazuli, onyx, opal, rock crystal, and turquoise, from Badakhshán, Bukhárá, and Yarkand. There are, however, certain local stones for ornaments and buttons. These stones are soft, and are incapable of a high polish. Among the more common may be mentioned :—

Vernacular name.	Colour.	Locality.
Takht-i-Sulimán	black with white streaks	Wastarwán Mountain.
Sang-i-Musá	black	Krihu.
Bilor	white crystal	Wángat.
Sang-i-Sumák	blue or purple with green spots	,,
Sang-i-Shalamar	green	,,
Sang-i-Ratel	chocolate	,,
Sang-i-Nadid	dark coffee colour	,,

Besides these a kind of jade, which used to be employed for flint locks, is brought from the Wastarwán mountain, and from the same locality a kind of moss agate is procured.

Cups and plates are made of a stone known as *Sang-i-Nalchan*. The stone is so soft that it can be cut like wood. It is a kind of soap-stone, grey, yellow and green in colour.

Sang-i-dálam is obtained from a place near Vernág, and is used by goldsmiths. *Sang-i-baswatri* is a yellow stone used in medicine.

CHAPTER IV.

FLORA.

CHAP. IV.

General.

IN this chapter I shall only attempt to enumerate the plants and trees of the Kashmír valley and its mountains which possess some well-known economical value for the people, and even this limitation would not be sufficient to keep the chapter within the bounds required by this report, for the Kashmírís turn nearly every plant and tree to some use, and attribute medicinal properties to every growing thing. At the outset I am met with the difficulty of classification. In the first place it is not easy to decide whether certain plants should be noticed under agriculture or under the heading attached to this chapter.

Thus I have dealt with walnuts and with the water-chestnut in the chapter on agriculture, because these plants are subject to certain operations which are akin to cultivation. Next I have been uncertain as to whether the plants of Kashmír should not be classified according to their habitat or environment, and I thought that the valley might be divided into mountains, hilly country, plain, lakes and lagoons. But perhaps the easiest classification, and the one most ready for reference, will be found in grouping the various indigenous plants and trees under their several economic uses and properties, and in the following remarks I shall endeavour to adhere to this classification. Where possible their scientific nomenclature with their European and Kashmír synonyms will be given, the last in italics :—

1. Condiments.
2. Drugs.
3. Dyes and tans.
4. Fibres.
5. Fodders.
6. Foods and Fruits.
7. Hair-washes.
8. Medicines.
9. Poisons.
10. Scents.
11. Soap and Alkali.
12. Timber.
13. Yeast.
14. Adulterants.

Carraway seeds.

1. CONDIMENTS.—The most important of the condiments is Carum sp., the *zirah siyah*. This plant grows on the karéwás of Kashmír when the land is cultivated with wheat and barley. It is a peculiar circumstance that the *zirah siyah* is not produced in any quantity unless the land is ploughed for cultivation. In former days *zirah siyah* was taxed, and the tax was farmed out to a contractor. The seeds of another umbelliferous plant (Daucus Carota), known in Kashmír as the *mor mujh*, are used as an adulterant for the real carraway of the *zirah siyah*. No attempt has ever been made to cultivate the *zirah siyah*.

Hemp.

2. DRUGS. Cannabis indica (*Bhang*).—This plant grows in great profusion along the banks of the Jhelum and the Vishau, and not long ago it was the custom to reserve the land on the river banks, for a distance of 15 yards on either side, for the growth of the *bhang*, and occasionally hemp seed was sown. The farm of the right to collect hemp drugs and hemp fibre once realized as much as Rs. 25,000, but at the present time the amount of hemp drugs made in Kashmír is very small, and the revenue from the hemp plant for the last five years has averaged Rs. 6,200. The Kashmírís usually speak of the drug manufactured in the valley from the hemp plant as *charras*, and it has been stated that *ganja* is not produced in Kashmír. It is also said that though the *charras* of the valley is inferior to the drug of Yárkand it is superior to the *charras* of Bukhára and Kábul. But recent inquiries show that in the south of the valley the drug known as *gard bhang* or *churu charras*, is extracted from the female plant, and Indians who consume it declare that it is real *ganja* and utterly distinct from the Yárkandi *charras*, which is also procurable in Srínagar. It is stated that the annual production of this so-called *ganja* is about 70 maunds, and that about 400 maunds of fibre are collected every year. Below Srínagar the hemp plant does not yield any drug and is only used for its fibre. About 600 maunds of fibre are annually collected in the country below Srínagar. The consumption of hemp drugs in Kashmír is about equal to the local production. The Kashmírís do not use the hemp-plant leaves for smoking or drinking, but the preparation known as *majun* is eaten to some extent. If the Kashmírí drug is *ganja* and not *charras* it is somewhat surprising, and I have taken some pains to verify the statement made by the official who investigated the subject of hemp drugs. He and the men employed in the trade maintain that the drug made in Kashmír is *ganja*. I had always understood that *ganja* could not be obtained from the female plant after impregnation, but the female plant in Kashmír is impregnated and the hemp seeds yield an oil which, like *charras*, is used for intoxicating purposes. Artemisia (*Tetwan*).—This is a very common plant in Kashmír, and from its leaves is distilled a drug known as *ibsántin*, a name no doubt

CHAP. IV. derived through the Arabic from the Greek *absintha*. Large quantities are exported to the Panjab. *Assafoetida* is not produced within the limits of Kashmír, but I found Narthex Assafoetida below Doian in the Astor Tahsil. I have procured plants for Dr. Aitchison with a view to experimental cultivation in Kashmír. As far as I know the *assafoetida* of commerce is not manufactured in Astor, but the natives use the fresh plant in cooking, and the milky juice which exudes from it gives forth the well-known odour of *assafoetida*, wholly unlike the pleasant celery smell of Ferula Jaeschkeana.

3. DYES AND TANS.—The people are somewhat reticent on the subject of the dyes used in the arts. In the days when the shawl trade flourished every factory employed a skilled dyer, who, by mixing the vegetable dyes of the country, produced colours of the softest tints. Datisca cannabina, *waft tanj* or *pát*, gives a yellow dye which was mixed with all colours save red and dark blue; Rubia cordifolia and its more common substitute Geranium nepalense, both known as *Mazait*, were mixed with rose, gold, and cream; *Pamb tsallan*, the wild rhubarb, was mixed for orange and gold; the pomegranate flowers and rind were mixed with red, gold, and black; *Ruhil*, mixed with other dyes, furnished a Kháki and black colour; *Mowwin* was mixed with an ashy grey. Mallotus philippinensis, *Kamila*, is said to be a product of Kashmír.

Brown dyes are obtained from the outer rind of the walnut and from the bark of a species of Cotoneaster. The fruits of the apricot and mulberry give characteristic dyes.

Among tanning materials may be mentioned the deodar, spruce, apricot, bark of alder and rind of pomegranate.

4. FIBRES.—Kashmír is very rich in fibres, and the natives make great use of them. It is possible that as communications with India improve a trade in fibres may be developed, as every year sees a great waste of valuable fibre-yielding plants. The boatmen of Kashmír require ropes of good quality, and it is stated that for towing-ropes the cotton fibre is the best material. The following indigenous plants yield fibre for ropes and other purposes :—

Iris ensata	*Krishm.*	Carex sp.	*Fikal.*
Cannabis sativa.	*Bhang.*	Ulmus Wallichiana . . .	*Bren.*
Abutilon Avicennae . . .	*Yechkar.*	Celtis australis	*Brimij.*
Rush	*Vandil.*	Indigofera heterantha . .	*Kats.*
Typha sp.	*Pits.*	Cotoneaster sp.	*Lun.*
Betula utilis	*Burza.*	Parrotia Jacquemontiana .	*Poh.*
Carex nubigena	*Koin.*	Salix sp.	*Vir.*

The *krishm*, or river bank iris, grows in great quantities along the river banks, and at a distance its mass of blue flowers resembles water in colour.

The fibres are used for the manufacture of ropes which serve many purposes in agriculture. The fibre is not very durable.

The *bhang* furnishes an excellent fibre, from which strong and durable ropes are made. The stems of the plant are used for wattled fences around gardens, and in the winter the open ends of the tops of the houses are shut in with *bhang* stems. In former days Kashmír was famous for its paper. For Koráns and for superior paper the pulp of the *bhang* fibre was always used.

The *yechkár* grows in low, damp, rich soil, and is an excellent fibre for ropes, mats, beds and *kiltas*. It is superior in some ways to the *bhang* fibre as it resists the action of water. The fibre of Abutilon Avicennae is pronounced superior to Indian jute and finer than Manilla hemp.

The *vandil* (literally grocer's rush) is used for the manufacture of twine, and is used by shopkeepers to tie up parcels.

The *pits* is the swamp plant from which the excellent matting (*waggu*) of Kashmír is made. The Anchar lagoon, to the north of Srínagar, is the great home of the *pits*, though it is found in most of the swamps of Kashmír. All boats are roofed with the *pits* matting, and the mats are employed as coverings for floors and in numerous other ways. The industry of mat-making gives employment to a large number of the people. The villagers of Lasjan to the south of Srínagar are perhaps the best mat-makers in the valley.

The *burza*, or paper birch, grows at high elevations from 9,000 to 13,000 feet, and is of great importance to the Kashmírís. The bark, known as *bhoj pattar*, is used to perform the duties of rough paper, and the roofs of all the better class of houses and of shrines are formed of birch bark on which a thick layer of earth is laid. The stems of *hookahs* are lined with it. Village shopkeepers always use it for writing-paper. Snuff, sugar and tea are wrapped up in *bhoj pattar*. Many of the old manuscripts are written on birch bark. Art-ware sent down to India is usually packed in this useful substance, which is at once strong and impervious to water. This last quality renders it an admirable material for roofing, and it is much to be regretted that this useful tree is not protected from the destructive herdsmen. For extracting the bark an instrument like a tin opener is used. The operator cuts a vertical line in the tree which pierces seven coatings of bark, then two horizontal rings are cut and the bark is stripped off. It is said that if the incision is limited to seven layers the tree recovers and will again make new bark.

Koin grows along the banks of rice fields, and provides an excellent rope for agricultural purposes and also fibre for *chaplis*. The *koin* grass forms the bed on which the Kashmírí Hindú is ushered into the world and on which he dies.

CHAP. IV. *Fikal* is chiefly used for interlacing the stakes of irrigation weirs. It is able to stand the action of water.

The *bren*, or elm, gives from its young shoots an excellent fibre, rough but very strong and used for ropes.

The *kats* which flourishes in all parts of the valley, together with the *lun* and the *poh*, furnish in their pliant branches materials for the useful and universal *kilta* or creel and for wattle fences. The outer covering of the *kangar* or chauffemain of Kashmír is frequently made of *poh* or *luni*.

The *vir*, or willow, grows in every village of Kashmír where there is water or moisture, and its reproduction is very simple. There is an enormous waste of withies every year, as the young wands are cut down for fodder and after being stripped of their leaves are burnt for fuel. I have suggested that a Kashmírí should be sent to England to learn the basket industry. There is ample material in the valley to supply the whole of India with excellent baskets and chairs.

5. FODDERS.—The people of Kashmír depend very much for their comfort on milk and wool, and in the severe winter plough- and milk-cattle and sheep are penned in the byres which form the lower story of the Kashmír house. The straw of rice and the stalks of maize furnish a portion of the fodder required for the winter months, but this has to be supplemented, and nature has been very bountiful in supplying food for cattle and sheep. In September one sees various kinds of maimed trees bearing in their forks the fodder which has been cut for winter use. Of the trees used for fodder the chief are as follows:—

Salix (*Vir*). This is the best of sheep fodders, and the willow is cultivated almost entirely with a view to providing food for sheep. There are varieties of willows, and the mountain willow is much prized as a cattle fodder. The Indian chestnut, Aesculus indica (*Dán*), the Cotoneaster sp. *lun*, the hawthorn *ring*, poplars, *phrast*, are always lopped to provide cattle-fodder in the winter. In the spring the tender shoots of Ulmus Wallichiana form a favourite food of the buffalo.

Kashmír is rich in grasses, and the boundaries of the rice fields furnish a fine crop of hay every year. This hay is twisted into long ropes, which are suspended from trees. This protects the hay from the weather. In the higher villages fields are set apart for hay (*lao*), and the hay is made and stacked in the English fashion. The best grasses are the *beran*, *lundr*, *jab*, *bataklut* (clover) and *methi* (Trigonella Foenum-graecum). There is a poisonous clover which is very deadly to cattle before flowering, though innocuous to horses, and there is a grass known as *kungi* (Stipa sibirica) which produces a curious intoxicating effect on horses and other cattle, and unless remedies are applied the *kungi* often proves fatal.

(Two remedies are employed: the animal's head is placed over dense smoke, and, if this fails, acid fruit and vinegar administered internally sometimes give relief.) The cattle of the country seem aware of its poisonous effects and do not touch it. The swamps of Kashmír produce some valuable fodder plants, and in the summer one sees ponies deep in the water grazing upon the marsh plants. The most valuable of the swamp fodders is the *nari*, a kind of reed, which is either eaten green or is stored away for the winter. It is considered an excellent food for horses, and the State stables use no other.

The *khur* (Limnanthemum nymphoides) is a round-leafed swamp plant, much valued as a food for cows. It is said to increase the yield of milk.

The *tari* grass is also a valuable fodder for horses, and the *kabbal* grass (the *dub* grass of India) is very common and much prized as a fodder. Among other grasses should be mentioned the spurious rice, *háma* (Panicum colonum), which is alluded to in the chapter on agriculture. This is one of the most fattening horse foods in the country.

The *durháma* (Sorghum halepense) is regarded as poisonous till it comes into flower, but its poisonous properties then depart and it is one of the best cattle fodders.

Rye (Secale cereale) grows wild in the wheat fields and is used as a fodder. It is sometimes cultivated for thatching purposes. No rats will go near it. The Kashmírís call it French wheat.

6. FOODS AND FRUITS.—Under this head I have decided to eliminate the important water-chestnut and the walnut, and they will be described in the chapter on agriculture. In that chapter I have also mentioned the wonderful wealth of food given by the wild plants of the Dal lake. But as these plants occur on other lakes and swamps I shall at the risk of repetition enumerate them here. I should further preface my remarks on the foods and fruits yielded by indigenous plants in Kashmír by the observation that it is impossible to mention all plants that are used for food. I can only mention those plants which are in common use, and cannot find space for the numerous products of the swamps and forests which were eagerly devoured in the famine time. There is a superstition in Kashmír that plants like the *kámbe* (Solanum nigrum), *trer*, *kuna* and *kreri*, which were largely eaten in 1877-79, only appear when famine is imminent, and from all accounts experiments were made in that awful calamity with nearly every plant in the valley. One plant known as *brári* caused many deaths. *Krála mundu* (Capsella Bursa-pastoris); *bera muji* (Umbellifer); *koi kok*, a turnip-rooted Umbellifer; *throh* (Barbarea sp.), and many others which cannot be identified, were greedily eaten by the starving. On the lakes and swamps we find the following food plants growing wild :—

CHAP. IV.

Water-chestnut . . .	Trapa bispinosa	*Singhára* and *gari.*
„ . . .	Euryale ferox	*Jewár.*
„ . . .	Nymphaea stellata	*Bumposh.*
Water-lily	Nymphaea alba.	
Sacred lotus	Nelumbium speciosum . .	*Pamposh or Pambach.*
Sweet flag	Acorus Calamus.	
Reed mace	Typha sp.	*Pits.*

The *singhára* will be described in the chapter on agriculture. The *jewár* gives a soft, sweet seed which is eaten raw or roasted. The *bumposh* provides from its fragrant white flowers a pleasant *sharbat*, and from its stem a relishable vegetable. The *pamposh* gives a sweet nut, while its stem is the white *nadru* which the Kashmírís stew with meat. From the pollen of the *pits* the *dal nabád* or lake sweetmeat is made, and the root of the *pits* is also eaten.

In the streams the familiar watercress (Nasturtium officinale) *nág bubr* is found.

In every field the bright blue flower of the Cichorium Intybus (*handiposh*) is seen, and people value it as a vegetable. The plant is often cultivated in the gardens. Phytolacca acinosa and Megacarpaea polyandra (*chattr*) form useful potherbs, while Nepeta raphanorhiza furnishes an excellent root which would rival the radish if it were cultivated. The outer skin comes off easily and has the flavour of a radish. The inner part is milk-white, delicious to eat, somewhat like a good almond.

Rheum (*pombahak*) grows at high elevations, and gives a rhubarb which is, in my opinion, far more delicate and delicious than the cultivated rhubarb. *Sehbargi* (Oxalis corniculata) mixed with mint makes a delicious, somewhat acid chutney.

Polygonum polystachyum (*tsok laddar*) and Polygonum rumicifolium (*rumach*) provide a vegetable quite equal to the finest English rhubarb, and not so acid. Rumex (*aibij*) is picked and dried for winter use, and is much valued as a potherb. Another Rumex, probably R. acetosa (*kakutari*), is employed as an acid vegetable. The young leaves of the red poppy (*gulala*) are much esteemed as a vegetable. They are known as *tanyal*. Chaerophyllum sp. (*Kev*) is looked upon as an excellent substitute for carrots both by the herdsmen and by the red bears. Wild onions (*prán*), the *wolikot*, which resembles the national vegetable (the *karam ság*), the *hopal* (Dipsacus inermis), the *pamsal*, and the leaves of the *zwan ruhan* are largely eaten. *Wata krim* (Lychnis sp.) makes an excellent sweet potherb. The roots of the *zergogal*, a turnip-rooted Umbellifer, give a warm food. *Chaun-charu*, the adder's tongue, is said to be extremely pungent as a vegetable. *Drab* (Polygonum sp.) is eaten boiled with milk. *Chari hak* (Campanula sp.) is a warm potherb. The bark of the yew, Taxus baccata (*posthil*), not long ago, when tea was a luxury only enjoyed by the few, was regularly used by the Kashmíris in the place of tea, and was largely exported to Ladákh. In the famine the bark was ground into flour and consumed by the people. *Venna* (Mentha) is a sweet herb somewhat like peppermint, and is sometimes used by the Hindus as a substitute for the *tulsi*. The valley or rather the mountains of the valley are rich in fungi, and the people assure me that the English distrust of the huge, coral-like excrescences which cover the forest trees is uncalled for, and numerous fungi are eaten by the Kashmíris with no evil results. Our mushroom, Agaricus sp. (*hedur*), is common, and the morel (Morchella sp., *kanaguchi*) abounds in the mountains and forms an important export to India. It is an excellent addition to a stew, and it is surprising that it is not more frequently used by the European visitors. Hydnum coralloides and Agaricus flammans, known to the people respectively as *káho khur* and *silri* or *sírlri*, are highly thought of by the natives. Agaricus flammans is only found on the bark of the elm, while Hydnum coralloides affects rotten wood and the burnt-out hollows of Picea Morinda. *Mazkhel*, which is found on the walnut, pine and mulberry, sometimes weighs two pounds and is an excellent fungus. Of the ferns the *ded* is dried and eaten in the winter. It is like bracken in appearance and is considered a good and healthy food. Of the fruits of Kashmír, the following are indigenous and are found in all parts of the valley. Their fruit is not so good as that of the cultivated trees, but it is by no means to be despised, and though the Kashmíris always speak of the wild fruit as bears' food (*hapat kheun*), I notice that they do not scorn to eat the apples and pears :—

Mulberry	Morus sp.	*Tul.*
Bitter cherry	Prunus Cerasus	*Alucha.*
Plum	Prunus communis	*Ar.*
Apple	Pyrus Malus	*Tsunt.*
Pear	Pyrus communis	*Tang.*
Vine	Vitis vinifera	*Dach.*
Walnut	Juglans regia	*Dún.*
Pomegranate	Punica Granatum	*Dán.*

The following list contains the chief indigenous plants which grow wild in Kashmír and yield an edible fruit :—

Raspberry	Rubus niveus	*Chánch.*
Blackberry	Rubus fruticosus	*Dhán chánch.*
Bramble	Rubus lasiocarpus	*Sur chánch.*
,,	Rubus saxatilis	*Popai.*
Strawberry	Fragaria vesca	*Ingra.*
Gooseberry	Ribes Grossularia.	
Red currant	Ribes rubrum.	
Black currant	Ribes nigrum	*Hárgil.*

CHAP. IV.

Bird cherry . .	Prunus Padus . . .	*Zúmb.*	
Barberry . . .	Berberis Lycium . .	*Kdodách.*	
"	"	*Chukiphal.*	Like the *kdodách* but with red berries.
Elaeagnus . . .	Elaeagnus parvifolia .	*Gaun.*	
Beam tree . . .	Pyrus lanata	*Maillang.*	
"	"	*Chirain*	Tree found at high elevation with a slightly acid berry.
Hazel	Corylus Colurna . .	*Virin.*	
Guelder	Viburnum foetens . .	*Kulmanch* (honey flower).	

As regards these fruits, I would only say that the raspberry and the currants are, in my opinion, equal to the cultivated varieties of Europe. The black currant is identical with our English black currant. The red currant is similar in flavour, but there is a difference in the arrangement of the berries. I have only seen hazel-nuts of a small size, but travellers say that on the slopes of the Pír Panjál they have met with excellent filberts.

7. HAIR-WASHES.—The Kashmírís take some pains with their hair, and besides using butter and oil they employ the following plants:—To strengthen the hair they use the powdered roots of a plant known as *zonír*, mixed with butter. To destroy insects they use washes made from Euphorbia Thomsoniana (*hirbi*) and from Aconitum sp. (*manirah dág*). To induce a curliness in the hair they employ a wash made from Corydalis Falconeri (*át níl*).

8. MEDICINES.—The hakíms of Kashmír, the native physicians, attribute some property to every plant, and when I have made inquiries as to the various herbs which I have seen in the valley and on the hill-sides, I am always told that they are hot and good for cold humours, cold and good for hot humours, dry and beneficial to damp humours, damp and beneficial to dry humours. The Panjabís employed in my department, usually inclined to despise all Kashmírí methods, show great respect for the hakíms, and have told me of wonderful cures effected by the herbs of the valley. I give below a list of the more common medicinal herbs:—

Scientific name.	Kashmírí.	Uses.
Aconitum heterophyllum .	*Patis* or *Nar-Máda* .	Root, tonic. Much exported. Regarded by Kashmiris as an excellent substitute for quinine. Fetches one rupee per seer.
Hyoscyamus niger . . .	*Bagar bhang* . . .	Leaves and seeds exported.
Macrotomia Benthami .	*Gáo zabán*	Used for the heart.
Viola serpens	*Banafsha*	Also called *nuna posh* or salt flowers, as they used to be exchanged for their weight in salt.

Scientific name.	Kashmírí.	Uses.
Artemisia	*Telwán*	Largely exported.
Peganum Harmala	*Isband*	Employed in rheumatism and colds, also to avert the evil eye.
Euphorbia Thomsoniana	*Hirbi*	Roots, purgative.
Pichorhiza Kurrooa	*Chob-i-kor*	Much exported, a bitter root and tonic used in Kashmír for horses.
Berberis Lycium	*Káodách*	A remedy for cholera, is astringent.
Senecio Jacquemontiana	*Khalar.*	
Salvia sp.	*Sholra*	Used for bringing boils to a head.

Podophyllum emodi, Colchicum luteum, and Atropa Belladonna are common in Kashmír, but they are not used in medicine. The following list contains the most important of the indigenous medicines of Kashmír not already mentioned. I give the Kashmírí names and where possible the scientific names, together with the property of each plant :—

Kashmírí.	Scientific name.	Action.
Abási	Mirabilis Jalapa spread from cultivation	Seeds used as astringent.
Hamesha bahar		Used internally as antiphlogistic.
Wan prán	Allium sp.	Stimulant, expectorant.
Krits	Dioscorea deltoidea	Diuretic, dose 1 dram. Poison in large dose.
Kakilipot	Cuscuta sp.	Laxative.
Bobuna	Cotula anthelmintica	Stomachic, considered good for rheumatism.
Soi	Urtica dioica	Diuretic.
Sosan	Iris sp.	Stimulant, expectorant.
Brari gasa	Labiate	Anthelmintic.
Kalawini		Antineuralgic.
Mantsaran		Antidysenteric, used in menorrhagia.
Gewthir	Adiantum Capillus Veneris	Expectorant.
Wedang		Anthelmintic.
Mowal		Seeds used as demulcent.
Nunar		Styptic internally.
Lisa		Expectorant.
Janiádam	Salvia sp.	Diuretic.
Zadibabr		Expectorant.
Rangarichh		Seeds emetic.
Taritus		Diuretic.
Pahand		Do.
Maniphal		Emetic.
Krotha		Used in renal calculus.
Pala mánz		Internally used in herpes.
Mitsari Kund		Diuretic.
Abuj		Astringent.
Hunak dun	Aesculus indica	Cathartic.
Sutsal	Malva rotundifolia	Expectorant.

CHAP. IV.

Kashmíri.	Scientific name.	Action.
Tsari latshaj . . .	. . . .	Antiperiodic.
Saza posh	. . . .	Internally as antiphlogistic.
Tromba	Fagopyrum esculentum . .	Anodyne.
Boin	Platanus orientalis	Capsules used internally in ophthalmia.
Kawa dachh mul .	. . . .	Used as gargle in toothache.
Tsoka ladar . . .	. . . .	Astringent.
Ziri gogul	. . . .	Diuretic.
Most	. . . .	Stomachic.
Bamtsunt	Pyrus Cydonia	Demulcent.
Bola jal	. . . .	Stomachic.
Shahtarr	Fumaria officinalis	Used internally in skin diseases; cooling sharbat for fevers.
Gulala	Papaver Rhoeas	Cardiac tonic.
Mora kachh . . .	. . . .	Soporific.
Jugi padshah . . .	. . . .	Internally as antiphlogistic.
Zakhmi hayat . . .	. . . .	Internally in ulcer.
Bombiposh	Nymphaea stellata	Antiperiodic.
Pambachh	Nelumbium speciosum . .	Nervine tonic.
Kambai	Solanum nigrum	Antiperiodic.
Gula	. . . .	Styptic internally.
Punda nást . . .	Rhododendron campanulatum	Used as snuff for headache.
Mangal	. . . .	Internally in skin diseases.
Sooi	. . . .	Stomachic.
Gugar Kund . . .	Astragalus sp.	Root used for toothache, also for tooth-brushes.
Sulai	Labiate	Used as an eyewash.
Gurgás	Gramen	Leaves pounded applied externally for snake bites or panther wounds.
Butvir	Salix sp.	Leaves bitter, employed as a cooling remedy for fevers, as a local application to the feet.
Gandalinu	Daphne oleoides	Good for colic in horses and tumours.
Dand lidar . . .	Berberis sp.	Root good for horses.
Sarpang	Euphorbia sp.	Good for scurvy and skin diseases, used both internally and externally.
Wan bubr	Mentha sp..	Dried powdered leaves good for wounds inflicted by the bear.
Pahlmund	Pyrethrum sp.	Root good for toothache.
Halkagás	Polyganum sp.	Good for saddle sores.
Panchpatri	Geranium sp.	Good for burn wounds.
Sheoramgás . . .	Mentha sp..	Good for sword wounds.
Suru Krilu . . .	Rubus sp.	Good for dropsy.

9. POISONS.—Among the poisons may be mentioned :—

Impatiens Roylei	*Trul.*
Aconitum Napellus	*Mohundguji.*
Datura Stramonium	*Dátur.*
Hyoscyamus niger	*Bágar bang.*
Atropa lutescens.	
Rhus acuminata	*Arkhor.*

The seeds of the Datura Stramonium of Kashmír have been largely exported of late years, and Panjábi dealers give Rs. 5 per maund. I have not been able to ascertain for what purpose they are exported.

10. SCENTS.—The following plants are valued as scents:—The sweet-scented lousewort, Pedicularis brevifolia (*kasturi*), grows at an elevation of 11,000 feet and has a delicious odour, but not of musk.

The roots of Jurinea macrocephala (*gogal dhup*) are largely exported to India, where they are used by Hindús, and the dried plants and roots of Morina longifolia (*kandcher* or *khandij*) are esteemed by the Ladákhís as an incense.

The most important of the aromatic plants of Kashmír is the Saussurea Lappa (*kut*). This plant grows at high elevations from 8,000 to 9 000 feet, and is more especially abundant on the mountains of the northern end of the valley. The root, which has a scent like orris with a slight blend of violets, is extracted in the summer by the shepherds and herdsmen. Every year a large amount of the roots of the Saussurea Lappa is demanded by the State, and the villagers are obliged to bring a certain weight, for which they receive Rs. 4 per kharwár from the State. The root, which is known as *chob-i-kot*, is exported to India, and at present the monopoly in *chob-i-kot* is farmed out to a contractor for Rs. 45,000 per annum. The root loses weight by drying, but it is believed that the price obtained in Bombay, whence the *chob-i-kot* is exported to China, allows of a very handsome profit. In China the root is used for incense in the Joss houses, and is also used in India for clearing wells. It is an excellent remedy for preserving clothes from insects, and is much used in perfumery. As a medicine it has many properties, tonic, aromatic and stimulant, and it is useful in cough, asthma, fever, dyspepsia and skin disease. It has also been used as an ingredient in a stimulating mixture for cholera, and has been applied in cases of toothache and rheumatism. From Bombay and Calcutta the root finds its way to China and the Red Sea. It is very easy to adulterate *chob-i-kot*, and its perfume is so strong that 20 seers of the real drug will flavour 100 seers of spurious root. It is stated that in 1864 the Kashmír State obtained nearly Rs. 90,000 from the sale of *chob-i-kot*. The present revenue of Rs. 45,000 compares unfavourably with the revenue of 1864, but it is believed that prices have fallen, that a large quantity of the root is now imported into India from Afghánistán, and that undue exploitation of the *chob-i-kot* has led to a diminution in the supply of the plant in Kashmír. No attempts have as yet been made to cultivate the Saussurea Lappa, but experts believe that cultivation would be at once easy and profitable.

Salix caprea (*bed mushk*) from its flowers yields an essential oil or *attar* much used in perfumery. The roses of Kashmír were formerly used for

CHAP. IV. the manufacture of *attar*, and in the Mughal times the roses and willows in the gardens on the Dal lake yielded a revenue of one lakh of rupees per annum. On certain occasions, such as the recitation of a Saint's texts (*khatm*), or at the funeral pyre of a wealthy Hindu, sandal-wood (*tsandum*) is burnt. Many Kashmíris say that the sandal-wood grows in Kashmír, but this is impossible, and the sandal-wood used in the valley is imported.

11. SOAP AND ALKALI.—The roots of the Aster diplostephioides (*sahour*) and of Dioscorea deltoidea (*krits*) are much used in the washing of wools, while in the manufacture of soap the alkaline ashes of the pine, elm (*bren*) and the amarantus (*ganhar*) are much employed. These ashes furnish a substance known as *saz*, which, when mixed with mutton fat and the flour of a kind of pulse known as *mah*, constitutes the soap of Kashmír. Sopur was once famous for its manufacture of soap. The red beans of the *lobia* are also much used in the washing and in the preparation of woollen fabrics.

12. TIMBER.—Kashmír is rich in grand forests, which produce a great variety of timbers. The most valuable timber, that of the deodar, is not very widely spread, and with the exception of a few small cedar patches along the west of the valley all the deodar forests are located in the north-west corner of Kashmír. The system of farming out timber to contractors resulted in the destruction of many fine forests in the vicinity of rivers, and tracts which the contractor has spared have suffered at the hands of the ubiquitous Gujar, who with his small axe cuts down trees partly for the sake of fodder and partly from a kind of natural instinct which impels him to make forest clearings for the sake of grass. It is a melancholy sight to see huge trees felled and left to rot, and the past administration of forests in Kashmír has been reckless and short-sighted. Dry timber is harder to cut up than green trees, and the contractor, instead of using trees which have been felled, prefers to cut down fresh ones. A department has now been formed under the supervision of a European Forest Officer, and it is to be hoped that the indiscriminate and wanton destruction of forests will cease. In a country like Kashmír, where the houses are chiefly constructed of timber, and where the greater part of the fuel consists of wood, forests must always be of great importance, and it is a matter for congratulation that the danger of scarcity of timber and fuel threatened by the thoughtless and self-interested action of temporary contractors will now, perhaps, be averted by the introduction of some system of forest conservancy. It should, however, be borne in mind that forests are subservient to the wants of the agricultural community, and any system of conservancy which would tend to make timber and fuel expensive to the agricultural classes is to be deprecated in a country like Kashmír.

The following is a list of the more common trees in Kashmír. It is a curious fact that no oaks occur in the valley and its mountain sides, and I have never seen the holly or the Himalayan rhododendron :—

No.	Scientific name.	Kashmiri.	English.
1	Cedrus Libani, var. Deodara	*Deodár* or *Diár* . .	Deodar.
2	Pinus excelsa	*Kairu* or *yár* . . .	Himalayan blue pine.
3	Picea Morinda	*Kachil*	Himalayan spruce.
4	Abies Webbiana	*Budal* or *Sungal* .	Himalayan silver fir.
5	Taxus baccata	*Posthal*	Yew.
6	Alnus nitida	*Sarul* or *Kanzal* .	Alder.
7	Ulmus sp.	*Brenn*	Elm.
8	„ Wallichiana . .		
9	Prunus Padus	*Zonb*.	Bird-cherry.
10	Fraxinus floribunda . .	*Hom*.	Ash.
11	„ Moorcroftiana .		
12	Juglans regia	*Dún*	Walnut.
13	Aesculus indica	*Hán*	Indian horse-chestnut.
14	Corylus Colurna	*Virin*	Hazel.
15	Celtis australis	*Brimij.*	
16	Crataegus Oxyacantha . .	*Ring*.	Hawthorn.
17	Populus nigra	*Phrast*	Italian poplar.
18	„ alba	*Dudh Phrast* . . .	White poplar.
19	Acer sp.	*Kanar*	Maple.
20	Salix tetrasperma	*Vir*	Willow.
21	Viburnum foetens	*Kulmánch*	Guelder.
22	Betula utilis	*Burza*	Birch.
23	Parrotia Jacquemontiana .	*Poh*	Witch Hazel.
24	Platanus orientalis	*Boin*	Plane.
25	Morus sp.	*Tul*	Mulberry.
26	Pyrus Malus	*Tsunt*	Apple.
27	„ communis	*Tang*	Pear.
28	Cotoneaster bacillaris . .	*Lun.*	
29	Euonymus sp.	*Chol*	Spindle tree.
30	Zizyphus vulgaris	*Bre*	Jujube.
31	Rhus Wallichii	*Arkhor.*	
32	„	*Wutil.*	
33	Juniperus excelsa.		

1. The best of all timber is that produced by the deodar. It is much in request for houses, boats and bridges, and it seems to be impervious to water. The old shrines, some of great age, are made of deodar, and the great Juma Masjid of Srínagar, with its lofty shafts of cedar, is said to have been constructed of timber cut from the Tashawán Forest. The Tashawán Forest is now part of the city lying on the left bank of the river between the Fatteh and Zaina bridges. It is interesting to notice that isolated deodars are found at low elevations in many parts of the valley, where they resemble in growth the cedar of Lebanon. It is probable that in old days the deodar was spread all over the valley, but the building requirements of Srinagar soon exhausted the deodar forests in the vicinity of the city. At present, with the single exception of the forests of the north-west of the valley, there are no deodars within reach of the streams ; they have all been cut either for export to the Panjab or for local use. Young deodar poles (*hamatola*) are much sought after by boatmen for poling purposes, and in former days the hop gardens were supplied

with deodar poles. From the roots of deodar a resin is distilled, used by the herdsmen as an ointment for buffaloes. The mortars (*kanz*) in which paddy is husked are usually made of deodar.

2. The blue pine (*yár* or *kairu*) is much valued as a timber for house building. It lasts for a long time. The white resin of the pine (*kanglan*) is used by the natives as an application to wounds and for medical purposes, and from the roots of the tree a kind of black pitch is distilled known as *kilam*. Men who work in the rice fields anoint their legs and arms with *kilam* in order to protect themselves against the *kirza*, or water insects, which are troublesome. Sheep are marked with the *kilam*. The *yár* furnishes the people of the higher villages with light, and every house stores up a quantity of pine shavings which are made into excellent torches (*lashi*). Many a pine tree is hacked into for torches, and if it does not contain sufficient oil is left to die. The *yár* yields an excellent charcoal much esteemed by the blacksmiths of Kashmír.

3. The Himalayan spruce (*rayil* or *kachil*) furnishes a timber much used in house building. The wood, although largely employed for shingles, is not durable when exposed to wet. Excellent planks for indoor work are obtained from the spruce. The young cones of the spruce are used in the manufacture of a drug known as *gaz pipal*.

4. The silver fir (*budal*) is preferred by the Kashmíris to the spruce. It is easier to work, as it is free from knots, and it is more durable than the spruce. It is very suitable for joists. Both the spruce and the silver firs grow to an enormous height. Trees have been measured 110 feet long with a girth of 16 feet. The people have an idea that land on which the silver fir has grown will never repay cultivation.

5. Yew (*posthal*) is not valued as a timber for house building. I imagine that it does not lend itself to the Kashmíri methods of cutting all timber with the axe, but for small work like the legs of a bed, &c., the yew is useful.

6. The alder grows by river banks up to 7,000 feet. As a timber the alder is valued for furniture and ploughs and it yields an excellent fuel. Its twigs are used for rope bridges and its bark is employed in dyeing and tanning.

7, 8. The elm is found at all elevations up to 9,000 feet and is a favourite tree for shrines. It attains a great height and girth. In one village, Raháma of Hamal, I measured two elms. At 5 feet from the ground one had a circumference of 33 feet 6 inches, the other 35 feet 1 inch. The Hindus regard the elm as sacred to Ganpati, but the Musalmáns use the tree for making trays (*tattul*), ploughs, for building, for fuel. The ashes of burnt elm have alkaline properties. The young shoots of the tree are much esteemed as a food for buffaloes. The elm abounds in the Loláb valley.

9. The bird-cherry is used for spinning-wheels.

10, 11. The ash furnishes a strong, useful timber much prized by agriculturists for implements, more especially the handles of ploughs. Boatmen esteem the wood for paddles.

12. The timber of the walnut is in great demand for furniture, gunstocks, ploughs and spinning-wheels, but it is difficult to procure the dark-grained wood. Walnuts are to be found in every village, from an elevation of 5,500 to 7,500, but in many places the old trees are showing signs of decay, and in few cases do the people make any effort towards reproduction. Some account of the walnut will be found in the chapter on agriculture, but it may be mentioned here that the wild and

indigenous walnut of the forests yields a nut which by boiling is made to yield oil. Kashmír is well suited to the culture of walnuts, and steady pressure should be brought to bear on the people to replace their old trees. The mistletoe (*ahalu*) attaches itself to the walnut and the people make no attempt to remove it. They say that it would be cruel to rob the bulbul of its favourite food. The walnut tree attains a great size. Three trees in the village of Tikar, at 5 feet from the ground, had a circumference respectively of 14 feet 11 inches, 15 feet 2 inches and 16 feet 4 inches. One tree which I measured at Goglusa had a circumference of 18 feet 10 inches.

13. The timber of the Indian horse-chestnut is much used for furniture, for pattens and spoons.

14. The hazel is used for making spinning-wheels and for spoons. The large spoon in which tea is ladled out is always made of hazel.

15. The *brimij* is usually found in graveyards and in the vicinity of shrines, where it sometimes grows to a magnificent tree. I measured one tree in Andrháma (Loláb); at 5 feet from the ground it had a circumference of 9 feet 3 inches. When *brimij* can be obtained from places not consecrated it is always used for the yokes (*yiput*) of plough cattle, as it is a soft, cool wood.

16. The hawthorn is chiefly used for the roller employed in oil presses, and for the pestle with which paddy is husked. The wood is very hard.

17, 18. The poplar is not esteemed for its timber. Poor people however use it for house building, more especially in the city. The poplar grows at all elevations from 5,000 to 7,500 feet. It is spoken of by the Kashmírís as the minister of the kingly plane tree. There are several varieties in Kashmír, and the *Kabuli phrast* is a very beautiful tree with white bark and silvery leaves. There are fine avenues of poplar near Srínagar, Islámabad and Báramula, and it is usually stated that the Mughals introduced the poplar. Near shrines the beautiful *Kabuli phrast* is always found, and one of the most charming objects in Kashmír is the grand grove of poplars at the entrance to Gurais valley. The Gurais poplar is Populus alba and attains to a great height, one having been measured 127 feet in height with a girth of 14½ feet.

19. The maple grows at high elevations. Its wood is valued for making ploughs. Maple yields an excellent fuel, but so far no saccharine matter has ever been extracted from this tree. I shall allude elsewhere to the question of introducing the sugar maple in Kashmír. The golden foliage of the maple makes a charming contrast to the dark green of the firs and other trees of high altitudes.

20. The willow is not valued for its timber, but good light pattens are made of it. As a fuel it is not esteemed highly, but it is cheap and plentiful. The valuable withies of the willow are practically wasted in Kashmír, and there is an abundance of material ready for chair and basket making.

22. The birch grows at such a distance from the habitations of man that hitherto its elastic timber has not been much used. It gives an excellent fuel.

23. *Poh* supplies a good hard wood for the pestles (*mohl*) with which rice is husked. Poh poles are also used for the rafters of houses, and in the absence of deodar poles I have used poh in the hop-garden. Poh is, however, very inferior to deodar as a hop-pole.

24. The *boin* or chenar is a royal tree, and, like the walnut, belongs to the State. Its reproduction by cuttings is a very simple matter, and of late years I am glad to say that people have planted many chenars in the villages. As a shade tree the chenar is unrivalled, and when the soil is suitable and water is near its roots it

CHAP. IV. attains a magnificent size. In their old age the chenars decay, and many fine trees in the Nasim Bágh are hollowed out. The Kashmírís consider 300 years to be the age limit of the chenar, but long after the tree goes at the top vigorous growth is seen from the buttress of boles with which the chenar surrounds itself. The finest tree is said to be the Langar boin in the Chenar Bágh. One boled giant I measured in the Loláb had a circumference of 63 feet 5 inches at a height of about 5 feet from the ground. The chenar is especially valued for making oil presses, and its fine-grained wood is used for small boxes. It would be suitable for furniture. Its wood and charcoal are considered the best fuel in Kashmír. The seeds of the chenar seem to be in most instances sterile, but I know of a few trees which give good seed. On the banks of the Jhelum river, for two marches below Báramula, may be seen numerous chenars banking up the river, originating from the seed that is carried down by the streams. A similar phenomenon may be seen on the Srínagar-Gulmarg road between Magám and Rerum. Like the poplar the chenar is said to have been introduced by the Mughals.

25. The mulberry wood is chiefly used by the natives for the doors of shrines and for ploughs. Europeans have employed it in boat-making, and its pliability would make it suitable for bent-wood furniture. It yields an excellent fuel, but the mulberry may not be cut down, as the tree is preserved for the purposes of sericulture. This prohibition is wise, as apart from its potential value in sericulture, the mulberry yields an enormous amount of food to the people and to cattle and sheep. The leaves are especially valued as a sheep fodder. The mulberry lives to a great age and attains fine dimensions. One measured by me in Andrháma (Loláb) at 5 feet from the ground had a circumference of 23 feet.

26. The *apple* gives a good timber for ploughs. It yields a first-rate fuel.

28. The *lun* furnishes excellent alpenstocks.

29. The *chol* is now a somewhat rare tree, growing at high elevations from 6,000 to 7,000 feet, and its wood is highly valued as a material for the famous pen boxes of Kashmír and for tablets in lieu of slates at school.

30. The *bre* gives a hard red-coloured wood, and the richer people of Kashmír esteem the bre for chairs, lintels and hair combs. In many of the shrines the lintels are made of bre. The tree grows at Drogjan near Srínagar, but is not common.

31. No carpenter in Kashmír will meddle with the poisonous *arkhor*. The sap of the green wood is said to cause terrible weals or blisters if touched. Wax for candles is said to be made from the berries of this tree in Japan, but the Kashmírís make no use of the seed.

32. The *wutil* is a tree with red berries. Its wood is used for spoons and combs.

13. YEAST.—The *jawen* or wild thyme is commonly employed for *khamir* or leaven. The Kashmírís use other plants for *khamir*, and the celebrated bread of Pampur is made from a leaven which is kept a strict secret.

14. ADULTERANTS.—The bark of the yew and the roots of the strawberry are used as a substitute for, or adulterant of tea.

The dried leaves of the Rhododendron campanulatum (*yung patr*) are mixed with snuff to increase the sternutatory action.

The seeds of Daucus Carota (*mor mujh*) are used as an adulterant of carraway seeds. Many roots are used as adulterants of the valuable *chob-i-kot* (Saussurea Lappa). The chief are the roots of Salvia lanata, Ligularia sp. and Aconitum sp.

These lists of plants possessing some economical uses are by no means exhaustive, and I have only mentioned the plants which have been pointed out to me by the villagers. There are many other plants which would be of interest to the economical botanist.

Most books on Kashmír mention the great variety of the Flora of the valley, but so far as I know no list of plants has yet been published. By the kindness of my friend Mr. J. F. Duthie, the Director of the Botanical Survey of Northern India, I am enabled to furnish a list of the plants which may be found in the neighbourhood of Gulmarg. The list omits perhaps some of the more common plants which occur at Gulmarg and at many of the other margs of Kashmír, but it will be of use and interest to visitors who come to ramble in the beautiful dells and mountain lawns which surround Gulmarg, and may serve as a good basis for future investigation. The plants marked A have been added by Dr. Aitchison, C.I.E.

CHAP. IV.

Botanical Name.	English Name.	Elevation in feet.	Tree or Shrub, &c.	Colour of flowers.	Locality.	Further particulars.
Ranunculaceae:—						
Clematis montana, Ham.	. . . . . .	5–7,000	Woody climber	White	Amongst scrub	A.
„ orientalis, L.	. . . . . .	6–7,000	. . .	Yellow	Amongst bushes	
Thalictrum foliolosum, DC.	Meadow rue	8–9,000	H.	White	Forest	
„ minus, L.	„	8–9,000	H.	Dingy purple	Stony ground	
„ pedunculatum, Edgew.	„	8–9,000	H.	White	Forest	
„ alpinum, L.	. . . . . .	9–11,000	H.	Greenish	Above forest	A.
Anemone Falconeri, Thoms.	. . . . . .	8–9,000	H.	White	Forest	A small insignificant-looking plant, and very local.
„ obtusiloba, D. Don	. . . . . .	8–12,000	H.	Blue, yellow and white	Marg	Abundant, becoming more dwarf at the higher elevations.
„ rupicola, Camb.	. . . . . .	11–13,000	H.	Fls. woolly	Rocks	Very handsome, and showy. A.
„ tetrasepala, Royle	. . . . . .	11–12,000	H.	White	Birch forest	Tall, handsome, with large white flowers, worthy of cultivation.
Adonis Chrysoscyathus, Hook. f. & T.	Pheasant's eye	11–12,000	H.	Yellow	High margs	Very handsome.
Ranunculus laetus, Wall.	. . . . . .	. . . .	H.	. . . .	Damp ground	Closely allied to one of the English Buttercups (R. acris).
„ aquatilis, L., var. trichophyllus	. . . . . .	. . . .	H.	. . . .	Still water	Common in England.
„ diffusus, DC.	. . . . . .	. . . .	H.	. . . .	Forest	
„ hirtellus, Royle	. . . . . .	8–12,000	H.	. . . .	Margs	A characteristic marg plant at Gulmarg.
„ hyperboreus, Rotlb.	. . . . . .	10–12,000	H.	Yellow	Wet rocks	
„ pensylvanicus, L.	. . . . . .	. . . .	H.	Yellow		
Caltha palustris, L., var. alba	Marsh marigold	8–10,000	H.	White	Water-courses	
Trollius acaulis, Lindl.	. . . . . .	10–12,000	H.	Yellow	High margs	Very showy.
Aquilegia vulgaris, L., and varieties	Columbine	8–10,000	H.	Lilac, white and yellow		
Delphinium denudatum, Wall.	Larkspur	. . . .	H.	Light blue		
„ cashmerianum, Royle	. . . . . .	11,000	. . .	Purplish with deeper-coloured veins	. . .	A.

Aconitum heterophyllum, Wall. . . .	Aconite	8-11,000	H.	Blue or greenish blue	Margs	The root called 'atis' is medicinal.
„ Napellus, L.	„	8-10,000	H.	Bright blue	Forest and margs	With varieties, A.
„ „ var. multifidum, A.	. . . . . .	13,000	. . .	. . . . .	Gulmarg	Profuse.
„ „ var. rotundifolium, A.	. . . . . .	11-14,000	. . .	. . . . .	Margs	
„ Lycoctonum, L.	. . . . . .	7-9,000	H.	Purple and yellow	Forest	
Actaea spicata, L.	Baneberry	9-11,000	H.			
Paeonia Emodi, Wall.	. . . . . .	8,000	H.	White	Forest	A.
Berberideae:—						
Berberis vulgaris, L.	Barberry	. . . . .	Shrub	Yellow	Forest	
„ Lycium, Royle	. . . . . .	6,000	Shrub	„	Open ground	A.
Epimedium elatum, Morr. & Dcne. . .	. . . . . .	. . . . .	H.	White	Forest	
Podophyllum Emodi, Wall.	. . . . . .	8-10,000	H.	White	Forest	
Nymphaeaceae:—						
Nymphaea pygmaea, Ait.	Small water-lily	8-9,000	H.	White	Water-holes at Gulmarg	A very interesting plant, known only here and on the Khasia hills in India. Also in China.
Papaveraceae:—						
Papaver dubium, L.	Poppy	5-6,000	H.	Crimson	. . .	Common in the valley.
Fumariaceae:—						
Corydalis Falconeri, H. f. & T. . . .	. . . . . .	8-11,000	H.	Yellow	Rocks	A.
„ rutaefolia, DC.	. . . . . .	6-9,000	H.	Purplish	Under trees	A.
Cruciferae:—						
Barbarea vulgaris, R. Br.	Winter cress	9-10,000	H.	Yellow	Near water	
Arabis amplexicaulis, Edgew.	Rock cress	8-9,000	H.	White		
„ alpina, L.	. . . . . .	9,000	H.	White		
Cardamine impatiens, L.	Bitter cress	9,000	H.	White		
„ macrophylla, Willd. . . .	. . . . . .	8-9,000	H.	Lilac	Damp ground	
Draba fladnizensis, Wulf., var. homotricha	. . . . . .	13,000	H.	White	Rocks	A.
Sisymbrium Thalianum, J. Gay . . .	Thale cress	8-9,000	H.	White	. . .	A common English weed.
„ himalaicum, Hook. f. & T.	. . . . . .	9-12,000	H.	Purple or white	Margs	

Botanical Name.	English Name.	Elevation in feet.	Tree or Shrub, &c.	Colour of flowers.	Locality.	Further particulars.
Sisymbrium mollissimum, C. A. Mey.	. . . . . .	11–12,000	H.	Purple or white	Margs	
Erysimum altaicum, C. A. Mey.	. . . . . .	8–9,000	H.	Pale yellow	Rocks	Habit of Wallflower.
Capsella Bursa-pastoris, Medic.	Shepherd's purse	. . . .	H.	White	. . .	Plentiful, especially on sheep-runs and near habitations.
Megacarpaea polyandra, Benth.	. . . . . .	11–12,000	H.	Light yellow	Open rocky ground	Leaves used as *ság*. Vern. *Chattr*.
Thlaspi arvense, L.	. . . . . .	. . . .	H.	White		
,, alpestre, L.	. . . . . .	8–12,000	H.	White	. . .	Becomes more dwarf at high elevations.
Violaceae:—						
Viola arenaria, DC.	Violet	10–12,000	H.	Purple	Open	
,, biflora, L.	. . . . . .	. . . .	H.	Yellow		
,, serpens, Wall.	. . . . . .	. . . .	H.	Lilac	Forest	Used medicinally.
,, canina, var. sylvatica, Fries	. . . . . .	7–11,000	H.	,,	,,	A.
Polygaleae:—						
Polygala sibirica, L.	Milkwort	7–8,000	H.	. . . .	Open	
Caryophylleae:—						
Tunica stricta, Bunge	. . . . . .	8–9,000	H.	White	Open	
Gypsophila cerastioides, D. Don.	. . . . . .	9–10,000	H.	White with lilac veins	Open rocky	
Silene inflata, Sm.	Bladder campion	. . . .	H.	White	Forest	
,, Moorcroftiana, Wall.	. . . . . .	. . . .	H.	Lilac	Rocks	
Cucubalus baccifer, L.	. . . . . .	8–9,000	H.	Greenish white	Forest	
Lychnis cashmeriana, Royle	. . . . . .	8–9,000	H.	White or pale lilac		
,, coronaria, Desr.	. . . . . .	. . . .	H.	Reddish purple	Dry banks	Below Gulmarg.
,, indica, Benth.	. . . . . .	. . . .	H.	White, outside purple		
Cerastium davuricum, Fisch.	. . . . . .	8–9,000	H.	White	Forest	A tall weak plant, with glaucous stems and foliage, and large pure white flowers.

Cerastium trigynum, Vill.	. . . . . .	. . . .	H.	White	Margs	A conspicuous and characteristic plant at Gulmarg during May and June.
„ vulgatum, L.	Mouse-ear chickweed	. . . .	H.	White	Sunny banks	
Stellaria aquatica, Scop.	Water starwort	. . . .	H.	White	Forest	
„ bulbosa, Wulf.	. . . . . .	10-11,000	H.	White	Shady rocks	
„ subumbellata, Edgew.	. . . . . .	11,000	H.	. . . .	Rocks, grassy places	A.
Arenaria orbiculata, Royle	. . . . . .	8-9,000	H.	White		
„ serpyllifolia, L.	Thyme-leaved sandwort	. . . .	H.	White	. . .	Abundant.
Sagina procumbens, L.	Pearlwort	. . . .	H.	. . . .	Damp ground	Flowers inconspicuous.
Hypericineae:—						
Hypericum perforatum, L.	St. John's wort	. . . .	H.	Yellow	Open hillsides	
Malvaceae:—						
Malva rotundifolia, L.	Dwarf mallow	. . . .	H.	Lilac	Waste ground	
Geraniaceae:—						
Geranium nepalense, Sweet	Crane's-bill	8-9,000	H.	Lilac		
„ palustre, L.	. . . . . .	8-9,000	H.	Purple		
„ pratense, L.	. . . . . .	. . . .	H.	Reddish purple	Margs	
„ Wallichianum, D. Don	. . . . . .	. . . .	H.	Purple	Margs	
Oxalis corniculata, L.	. . . . . .	. . . .	H.	Yellow		
„ Acetosella, L.	Wood-sorrel	. . . .	H.	White		
Impatiens brachycentra, Kar. & Kir.	Balsam	. . . .	H.			
„ Roylei, Walp.	. . . . . .	. . . .	H.	Reddish purple	Damp forest	Tall, with stout stems and large handsome flowers.
„ scabrida, DC.	. . . . . .	. . . .	H.	Yellow		
„ sulcata, Wall.	. . . . . .	. . . .	H.	Light purple		
Rutaceae:—						
Boenninghausenia albiflora, Reichb.	. . . . . .	8-9,000	H.	White		
Skimmia Laureola, Sieb. & Zucc.	. . . . . .	. . . .	Shrub	Pale yellow	Forest	Strongly scented evergreen shrub, with scarlet berries.
Celastrineae:—						
Euonymus Hamiltonianus, Wall.	Spindle tree	8-9,000	Small tree	Greenish white	Forest	

Botanical Name.	English Name.	Elevation in feet.	Tree or Shrub &c.	Colour of flowers.	Locality.	Further particulars.
Rhamneae:—						
Rhamnus purpurea, Edgew.	Buckthorn	8-9,000	Small tree	Pale green	Forest	
„ dahurica, Pall.	. . . . . .	. . . .	Small tree	Pale green	Forest	
Ampelideae:—						
Vitis lanata, Roxb.	Vine	. . . .	Climbing shrub	Greenish	Forest	Leaves cordate-ovate, with rusty or reddish tomentum underneath.
Sapindaceae:—						
Aesculus indica, Coleb.	Himalayan horse-chestnut	. . . .	Tree	White and yellow	Forest	
Acer caesium, Wall.	Maple	8-10,000	Tree	White	Forest	
Staphylea Emodi, Wall.	. . . . . .	. . . .	Tree	White	Forest	Vern. *Marchob.*
Leguminosae:—						
Trigonella pubescens, Edgew.	. . . . . .	. . . .	H.	Yellow		
Medicago denticulata, Willd.	Medick	. . . .	H.	Yellow		
Trifolium pratense, L.	Clover	. . . .	H.	Purple	Margs	
„ repens, L.	Dutch clover	. . . .	H.	White		
Lotus corniculatus, L.	Bird's-foot trefoil	. . . .	H.	Yellow	Margs	
Indigofera atropurpurea, Buch.-Ham.	Indigo	. . . .	Shrub	Dark red-purple	Forest	
„ Gerardiana, R.-Grah.	. . . . . .	. . . .	Shrub	Red-purple	Edges of forest	
„ linifolia, Retz.	. . . . . .	. . . .	H.	Red		
Caragana brevispina, Benth.	. . . . . .	8-9,000	Shrub	Yellow	Forest	
Astragalus Candolleanus, Royle	. . . . . .	. . . .	Small shrub	Yellow	Rocky ground	
„ rhizanthus, Royle	. . . . . .	8-9,000	Small shrub	Yellow		
„ sikkimensis, Benth.	. . . . . .	10,000	Small shrub	Purple	Rocky slopes	A.
„ tibetanus, Benth.	. . . . . .	9-10,000	. . .	Purple		
Oxytropis mollis, Benth.	. . . . . .	9-10,000	H.			
Desmodium tiliaefolium, G. Don	. . . . . .	8-9,000	. . .	Lilac	Outskirts of forest	
Vicia sepium, L.	Bush vetch	. . . .	. . .	Light purple		

Vicia tenuifolia, Roth.	...	...	...	Blue		
Lathyrus altaicus, Ledeb.	Vetchling	10–11,000	...	Purple		
„ pratensis, L.	...	...	...	Yellow		
„ luteus, Baker	...	8–10,000	...	Yellow	Forest	
Rosaceae:—						
Prunus Padus, L.	Bird cherry	8–10,000	Tree	White	Forest	
Spiraea bella, Sims	...	8–9,000	Shrub	Red	Forest	
„ canescens, D. Don	...	8–9,000	Shrub	White	Open forest	
„ sorbifolia, L.	...	...	Shrub	White		
„ vestita, Wall.	...	...	H.	White	Forest	Similar in habit to the English 'meadow-sweet' (S. Ulmaria).
Rubus pungens, Camb.	...	8–9,000	Shrub			
„ purpureus, Bunge	...	8–9,000	Shrub	White	Forest	
„ lasiocarpus, Smith	...	5–6,500	Shrub	White	Sides of fields, &c.	A.
„ niveus, Wall.	...	...	Shrub	Pink	Forest	There are many varieties. Leaves usually white beneath, fruit red and of good flavour.
„ fruticosus, L., var.	Bramble	5–6,500	Shrub	Pinkish	Sides of fields, &c.	A.
Geum elatum, Wall.	Avens	8–12,000	H.	Yellow	Margs	Like a Potentilla, with large bright yellow flowers.
„ urbanum, L.	...	8–9,000	H.	Yellow		
Fragaria indica, Andr.	...	...	H.	Yellow		
„ vesca, L.	Strawberry	7–10,000	H.	White		
Potentilla argyrophylla, Wall.	...	8–11,000	H.	Crimson, orange and yellow	Margs	
„ var. leucochroa	...	11–12,000	H.	Yellow	Margs	
„ Doubjouneana, Camb.	...	10–11,000	H.	Yellow	Margs	
„ gelida, C. A. Mey.	...	10–11,000	H.	Yellow	Margs	
„ nepalensis, Hook.	...	7–9,000	H.	Crimson	Forest and margs	
„ Sibbaldi, Haller f.	...	10–12,000	H.	Yellow	Margs	
Alchemilla vulgaris, L.	...	...	H.	Yellow-green		
Agrimonia pilosa, Ledeb.	Agrimony	...	H.	Yellow	Forest	
Rosa anserinaefolia, Boiss.	...	9–10,000	Shrub	...	Forest	
„ macrophylla, Lindl.	...	8–11,000	Shrub	Red	Forest	
„ moschata, Herrm.	...	...	Climbing shrub	White	...	Common in the valleys, and the flowers are very sweet-scented.

CHAP. IV.

Botanical Name.	English Name.	Elevation in feet.	Tree or Shrub, &c.	Colour of flowers.	Locality.	Further particulars.
Rosa Webbiana, Wall.			Shrub	Pink to white	Open rocky ground	This rose is abundant in Baltistan.
Pyrus Aucuparia, Ehrh.	Rowan, or mountain ash		Tree	White	Forest	
,, Pashia, Buch.-Ham.			Tree	White	Forest	Fruit eaten overripe like that of the medlar.
,, Malus, L.	Apple		Tree	White and red		
,, lanata, D. Don			Tree	White	Forest	
,, microphylla, Wall.			Small tree	White	Forest	Found first by Aitchison in Kashmír, since Webb found it in Sirmore, A.
Crataegus Oxyacantha, L.	Hawthorn		Tree	White		
Cotoneaster bacillaris, Wall.			Tree	White	Forest	Vern. *rauns.* Wood used for walking-sticks.
,, microphylla, Wall.			Shrub	White	Rocky ground	
,, nummularia, F. & M.		10–11,000	Shrub	White or pink		
Saxifragaceae:—						
Saxifraga diversifolia, Wall.		8–11,000	H.	Yellow	Near water	A.
,, ligulata, Wall., var. ciliata	Saxifrage	7–9,000	H.	White or pink	Rocks	Conspicuous at all times by its large fleshy leaves.
,, Hirculus, L.		10–12,000	H.	Green-yellow	Grassy banks	A.
,, sibirica, L.		11–12,000	H.	White		
,, Stracheyi, Hook. f. & T.		11–12,000	H.	White or pink		Similar in habit to S. ligulata, but it is found at much higher elevations.
Parnassia ovata, Ledeb.	Grass of Parnassus	8–10,000	H.	White	Margs, wet ground	
Ribes rubrum, L.	Red currant		Shrub	Greenish yellow	Forest	
,, glaciale, Wall.		11–12,000	Shrub	Green	Forest	
Crassulaceae:—						
Sedum quadrifidum, Pall.	Stonecrop	11–12,000		Red	Rocks	
,, linearifolium, Royle		11–12,000		White	Rocks	

Sedum tibeticum, Hook. f. & T.	. . .	11-12,000	. . .	Red	Rocks	
,, adenotrichum, Wall.	. . .	. . .	. . .	White with pink stripes	Rocks	
,, Rhodiola, DC.	. . .	10-12,000	. . .	Yellow	Rocks	
,, Ewersii, Ledeb.	. . .	8-10,000	. . .	Red	Rocks	
Datiscaceae:—						
Datisca cannabina, L.	. . .	7,000	. . .	. . .	Plains near water	A.
Hamamelideae:—						
Parrotia Jacquemontiana, Dcne.	. . .	8,000	Tree	White	Forest	The twigs are much used for making bridges, and the close-grained wood is used for a variety of purposes. When in fruit it is sometimes mistaken for the hazel. Vern., *pusser* or *po*. The medicine known as hazeline is prepared from a species of an allied genus, Hamamelis.
Halorageae:—						
Hippuris vulgaris, L.	Mare's tail	. . .	H.	Green	Water	
Myriophyllum spicatum, L.	Water milfoil	. . .	H.	Green	Water	
Callitriche verna, L.	Water starwort	. . .	H.	Green	Water	
Onagraceae:—						
Epilobium angustifolium, L.	Bay, or French willow	. . .	H.	Rose purple	Banks of streams	
,, roseum, Schreb.	. . .	. . .	H.	Pink		
Circaea alpina, L.	. . .	. . .	H.	White	Forest	
,, lutetiana, L.	Enchanter's nightshade	. . .	H.	White	Forest	
Umbelliferae:—						
Eryngium caeruleum, Bieb.	. . .	6-7,000	H.	. . .	. . .	A.
Bupleurum falcatum, L.	Hare's ear	. . .	H.	Yellow	Rocks	
,, longicaule, Wall.	,,	. . .	H.	Dark brown	High margs	
,, lanceolatum, Wall.	,,	. . .	H.	Yellow	Forest	
,, Candollii, Wall.	,,	. . .	H.	Yellow	Forest	
Pimpinella Saxifraga, L., var. dissectifolia	Burnet saxifrage	11-12,000	H.	White	High margs	
,, diversifolia, DC.	. . .	. . .	H.	White	Forest	

CHAP. IV.

Botanical Name.	English Name.	Elevation in feet.	Tree or Shrub, &c	Colour of flowers.	Locality.	Further particulars.
Chaerophyllum villosum, Wall.	Chervil	9-10,000	H.	White	Forest	
Anthriscus nemorosa, Spreng.	Beaked parsley	8-9,000	H.	White	Forest	
Selinum tenuifolium, Wall.	...	9-11,000	H.	White	Grassy spots	A.
Pleurospermum angelicoides, Benth.	...	9,000	H.	White	Shady streams	A tall handsome species.
Archangelica officinalis, Hoffm.	...	9,000	...	...	"	A. Very handsome.
Ferula Jaeschkeana, Vatke	...	8-9,000	H.	Yellow	Open	
Heracleum candicans, Wall.	Cow parsnip	8 9,000	H.	White	Open	
Araliaceae:—						
Aralia cachemirica, Dcne.	...	...	Small shrub			
Hedera Helix, L.	Ivy	8-9,000	...	...	On trees and rocks	
Caprifoliaceae:—						
Adoxa Moschatellina, var. inodora, L.	Moschatel	...	H.	...	Forest	
Sambucus Ebulus, L.	Dwarf elder	6-10,000	Shrub	White	Waste ground	Abundant near villages.
Viburnum cotinifolium, Don	...	10 12,000	Tree	White or pink	Forest	Allied to the English Wayfaring tree, V. Lantana.
" foetens, Dcne.	...	...	Shrub	White or pink	Outskirts of forest	Branches foetid. The sweet fruit is much eaten by the Kashmíris. Vern., *Kílmich*.
" nervosum, Don	...	9-12,000	Shrub	Rose	High forest	The flowers often open before the leaves have expanded.
Lonicera quinquelocularis, Hardw.	Honeysuckle	9-10,000	Shrub or small tree	Yellow	Forest	
" hispida, Pall.	"	10-11,000	Shrub	Pink		
" orientalis, Lam.	"	7-8,000	Small tree	Pink	Forest	
" purpurascens, Walp.	"	8-12,000	Shrub	Purple	Forest	
" obovata, Royle	"	11-12,000	Shrub	Cream		
" spinosa, Jacquem.	"	11-12,000	Shrub	White		
" alpigena, L.	"	9,000	Small tree	Pink		
Rubiaceae:—						
Rubia cordifolia, L.	Indian madder	...	H.	Red	...	Climbing over shrubs.

Galium triflorum, Michx.	. . . . . .	. . . .	H.	White	Forest	Habit of Sweet Woodruff.
„ verum, L.	Yellow bedstraw	. . . .	H.	Yellow		
„ boreale, L.	Northern bed-straw	. . . .	H.	White		
Valerianeae :—						
Valeriana Hardwickii, Wall.	Valerian	. . . .	H.	White	. . . .	Yields a perfume.
„ var. acuminata	. . . . . .	7–8,000	H.	White		
„ Wallichii, DC.	„	10,000	H.	White	Forest	Yields a perfume.
„ pyrolaefolia, Dcne.	„	10–11,000	H.	White or pink		
Dipsaceae :—						
Morina Coulteriana, Royle	Whorl-flower	8–9,000	H.	Yellow	Open	
„ longifolia, Wall.	Long-leaved whorl-flower	8–9,000	H.	Red	Open	
Dipsacus strictus, D. Don	Teasle	9–10,000	H.	Pale yellow	Margs	Flowers in compact globular heads.
Scabiosa speciosa, Royle	Scabious	8–9,000	H.	Mauve, rarely white	Margs	
Compositae :—						
Solidago Virgaurea, L	Golden-rod	. . . .	H.	Yellow	Forest	
Aster diplostephioides, Benth. & Hook. f.	Starwort	11–13,000	H.	Blue	High margs	Flowers large and handsome.
„ asperulus, Wall.	„	8–9,000	H.	Lilac	Forest	
Erigeron multiradiatus, Benth. & Hook. f	Flea-bane	10–12,000	H.	Blue	High margs	
„ alpinus, L.	Alpine flea-bane	8–13,000	H.	Blue, lilac, or white	Open	A very variable plant.
Leontopodium alpinum, Cass.	'Edelweiss'	8–13,000	H.	. . . .	Open	Very variable as to habit and size.
Anaphalis cuneifolia, Hook. f.	. . . . . .	11–12,000	H.	. . . .	. . . .	Habit of an Everlasting.
Gnaphalium luteo-album, L.	. . . . . .	. . . .	H.	Yellow		
Inula racemosa, Hook. f.	. . . . . .	. . . .	H.	Yellow	Bushy places	A tall handsome plant, with large heads of flowers in racemes.
„ Royleana, DC.	. . . . . .	. . . .	H.	Yellow	Bushy places	Heads of flowers solitary, and very handsome. Aitchison says that the root of this plant is used for adulterating *Kut*.
Achillea Millefolium, L.	Milfoil	. . . .	H.	White		
Tanacetum longifolium, Wall.	Tansy	10–13,000	H.	Yellow	Open	
„ robustum, Hook. f. & T.	. . . . . .	10–12,000	H.	Yellow	Open	
Artemisia vulgaris, L.	Wormwood or mug-wort	. . . .	H.	. . . .	. . . .	Other species probably occur at Gulmarg.
Cremanthodium reniforme, Benth.	. . . . . .	11–13,000	H.	Yellow	Open ground	A.

Botanical Name.	English Name.	Elevation in feet.	Tree or Shrub, &c.	Colour of flowers.	Locality.	Further particulars.
Doronicum Roylei, DC.	Leopard's bane	10–12,000	H.	Yellow		
Senecio chenopodifolius, DC.	Rag-weed	8–9,000	H.	. . . . .	Forest	
„ Ligularia, Hook. f.	. . . . . .	8–9,000	H.	Yellow	Wet ground in shade	
„ Jacquemontianus, Benth. . .	. . . . . .	12–13,000	H.	Yellow		
„ Thomsoni, C. B. Clarke . . .	. . . . . .	. . . .	H.	Yellow		
„ chrysanthemoides, DC. . . .	. . . . . .	8–12,000	H.	Yellow or orange	Open	Abundant on the margs, especially where cattle are in the habit of grazing.
Carduus nutans, L.	Musk, or Scotch thistle	. . . .	H.	Purple		
Cnicus arvensis, Hoffm.	Plume thistle	. . . .	H.	Dull purple	Margs	
„ Falconeri, Hookf.	. . . . . .	. . . .	H.	Pale yellow	Margs	A tall handsome thistle.
Saussurea Atkinsoni, C. B. Clarke . .	. . . . . .	10–13,000	H.	Purple	Rocks	Close-growing, on stony ground. A.
„ Kunthiana, C. B. Clarke . .	. . . . . .	11–13,500	H.	. . . . .	Rocks	„ „
„ Lappa, C. B. Clarke . . .	. . . . . .	9–12,000	H.	Bluish purple	Amongst much shrubs	An important article of commerce, the root stalk. Vern., *Kút*. A.
Jurinea ceratocarpa, Benth. & Hook. f. .	. . . . . .	. . . .	H.	Light purple	Rocks	
„ macrocephala, Benth. . . .	. . . . . .	9–12,000	. . .	. . . . .	Rocky ground	A.
Serratula pallida, DC.	Saw-wort	. . . .	H.			
Ainsliaea aptera, DC.	. . . . . .	8–9,000	H.	White	Forest	
Lapsana communis, L.	Nipple-wort	. . . .	H.	Yellow		
Pterotheca Falconeri, Hook. f. . . .	. . . . . .	. . . .	H.	Yellow		
Taraxacum officinale, Weber	Dandelion	8–12,000	H.	Yellow	Open	The leaves are eaten as *ság*, and the plant is also used medicinally by Kashmíris.
Lactuca dissecta, D. Don	Lettuce	8–9,000	H.	Blue	Banks and paths	
„ Lessertiana, C. B. Clarke . .	„	10–12,000	H.	Blue	High margs	
„ decipiens, C. B. Clarke . . .	„	8–10,000	H.	Blue	Forest	
Prenanthes Brunoniana, Wall. . . .	. . . . . .	8–9,000	H.	Rose purple	Forest	
Campanulaceae :—						
Codonopsis rotundifolia, Royle . . .	. . . .	9–12,000	H.	Grey-blue		

Codonopsis ovata, Benth.	. . . . . .	10-11,000	H.	Blue	Rocks	
Phyteuma Thomsoni, C. B. Clarke	. . . . . .	8-9,000	H.	Blue	Forest	
Campanula argyrotricha, Wall.	Bell-flower	. . . .	H.	. . . .	Rocks	
,, latifolia, L.	. . . . . .	. . . .	H.	Purple	Forest	
,, aristata, Wall.	. . . . . .	11-12,000	H.	Dark blue, or white	High margs	
Ericaceae :—						
Cassiope fastigiata, D. Don	. . . . . .	13,000	Small shrub	White	Open	
Rhododendron campanulatum, D. Don.	. . . . . .	13,000	Shrub	Lilac	Birch forests	
,, lepidotum, Wall.	. . . . . .	11-12,000	Shrub	Yellow	Open	
,, Anthopogon, D. Don	. . . . . .	12,000	Shrub	Pink and whitish	Amongst juniper	
Monotropeae :—						
Hypopithys lanuginosa, Rafin.	. . . . . .	8-9,000	H.	Pale yellow	Forest	A leafless fleshy parasite, common about Gulmarg under pine trees.
Primulaceae :—						
Primula denticulata, Sm.	. . . . . .	10-12,000	H.	Purple	Open	
,, var. erosioides	. . . . . .	8-9,000	H.	Lilac	Open	
,, elliptica, Royle	. . . . . .	12-13,000	H.	Purple	Open	A.
,, Stuartii, var. purpurea, Wall.	. . . . . .	10-13,000	H.	Purple	Wet ground	
,, rosea, Royle	. . . . . .	8 13,000	H.	Deep rose	Wet ground	
Androsace rotundifolia, Hardw.	. . . . . .	8-10,000	H.	Lilac	Rocks	
,, var. glandulosa	. . . . . .	8-9,000	H.	White	Rocks	
,, sempervivoides, Jacquem.	. . . . . .	10-12,000	H.	Lilac	High margs	
,, villosa, L.	. . . . . .	12-13,000	H.	Lilac with yellow eye	Open	
,, sarmentosa, var. primuloides, Wall.	. . . . . .	. . . .	H.	Rose purple, with yellow eye	Open	
Cortusa Matthioli, L.	Bear's-ear sanicle	8-12,000	H.	Purple	Shady slopes	
Oleaceae :—						
Jasminum humile, L.	. . . . . .	8-11,000	Shrub	Yellow	Forest	
Syringa Emodi, Wall.	Himalayan lilac	9-12,000	Small tree or shrub	White	Forest	
Fraxinus excelsior, L.	Ash	8-9,000	Tree	Green	Forest	

CHAP. IV.

Botanical Name.	English Name.	Elevation in feet.	Tree or Shrub, &c.	Colour of flowers.	Locality.	Further particulars.
Fraxinus xanthoxyloides, Wall. . . .	. . . . . .	8–9,000	Tree	Green	Forest	
Asclepiadeae:—						
Cynanchum Vincetoxicum, Pers. . . .	. . . . . .	8–9,000	H.	Green	Sunny slopes	
Gentianaceae:—						
Gentiana decumbens, L. f.	Gentian	8–9,000	H.	Purple	Rocky ground	
" venusta, Wall.	. . . . . .	11–12,000	H.	Blue	Rocks	A.
" tenella, Rottb.	. . . . . .	9–13,000	H.	Blue	Stony grassy ground	A.
" carinata, var. marginata, Griseb.	"	8–12,000	H.	Blue	Open grassy ground	Common at Gulmarg.
Jaeschkea latisepala, C. B. Clarke . .	. . . . . .	. . . .	H.	Blue	Rocky ground	Root very bitter.
Swertia petiolata, Royle	. . . . . .	. . . .	H.	Whitish with blue green nerves	Wet ground	
Polemoniaceae:—						
Polemonium caeruleum, L.	Jacob's ladder	8–10,000	H.	Blue	Margs	Very common at Gulmarg.
Boragineae:—						
Heliotropium strigosum, Willd. . . .	. . . . . .	. . . .	H.	White		
Trichodesma indicum, Br.	. . . . . .	. . . .	H.	Blue		
Cynoglossum denticulatum, A. DC. . .	Hound's tongue	8–9,000	H.	Blue		
Lindelofia spectabilis, Lehm.	. . . . . .	8–9,000	H.	Blue		
Solenanthus circinatus, Ledeb. . . .	. . . . . .	. . . .	H.	Yellow		
Paracaryum glochidiatum, Benth. & Hook. f.	. . . . . .	8–9,000	H.	Deep blue		
Lycopsis arvensis, L.	Small bugloss	. . . .	H.	Blue, purple, or white		
Mertensia primuloides, C. B. Clarke .	. . . . . .	11–13,000	. . .	Sky blue	Stony ground	South and west exposure. A.
Moltkia parviflora, C. B. Clarke . . .	. . . . . .	8,000	H.	. . . .	Under trees	A.

Myosotis sylvatica, Hoffm.	Wood forget-me-not	8-13,000	II.	Deep blue or white	Open	
Macrotomia Benthami, DC.	. . . . . .	9-11,000	II.	Pink to purple		
Convolvulaceae:—						
Cuscuta reflexa, Roxb.	Dodder	. . . .	II.	White	. . . .	A leafless parasite climbing over bushes.
Solanaceae:—						
Solanum nigrum, L.	Garden night-shade	. . . .	II.	White		
Atropa Belladonna, L.	Deadly night-shade	. . . .	II.	Violet or yellow		
Physochlaina praealta, Miers	. . . . . .	. . . .	II.	Yellow		
Scrophularineae:—						
Verbascum Thapsus, L.	Mullein	9,000	II.	Yellow	. . . .	A tall plant with flowers on a thick spike.
Scrophularia calycina, Benth.	Fig-wort	9-10,000	II.	Green		
" lucida, L.	"	8-12,000	II.	Purple		
" variegata, Bieb.	"	. . . .	II.	Purple		
Picrorhiza Kurroa, Royle	. . . . . .	10-12,000	II.	Dark blue	Open	Flowers dimorphic, the form with long stamens has greenish flowers. The root is used as a medicine
Wulfenia Amherstiana, Benth.	. . . . . .	8-9,000	II.	Blue	Shady banks and rocks	
Veronica ciliata, Fisch.	Speedwell	10-13,000	II.	Blue	Open	
" laxa, Benth.	. . . . . .	9,000	II.	Blue		
" serpyllifolia, L.	Thyme-leaved speedwell	. . . .	II.	Blue and white	Open ground	A very characteristic plant on the margs, and conspicuous in the month of May.
" capitata, Benth.	. . . . . .	11-12,000	II.	Blue	Open	
" deltigera, Wall.	. . . . . .	. . . .	II.	Blue	Rocks	
" Anagallis, L.	Water speedwell	6-8,000	II.	Pink or purplish	Near water	
" Beccabunga, L.	Brooklime	9-12,000	II.	Blue or pink	Near water	
Euphrasia officinalis, L.	Eye-bright	8 12,000	II.	White or lilac with purple veins	Open	
Pedicularis siphonantha, D. Don	Louse-wort	8-10,000	II.	Red	Near water	
" brevifolia, D. Don	. . . . . .	11,000	II.	Pink	Amongst grass	Noted for its scented flowers. A.

Botanical Name.	English Name.	Elevation in feet.	Tree or Shrub, &c.	Colour of flowers.	Locality.	Further particulars.
Pedicularis rhinanthoides, Schrenk . .	Louse-wort	9–10,000	H.	Pink	Near water	
„ versicolor, Wahlb.	. . . . . .	11–13,000	H.	Yellow	Grassy ground	A.
„ pectinata, Wall.	„	12–13,000	H.	Red	Forest	
„ bicornuta, Klotzsch . . .	„	10–11,000	H.	Yellow	Open	A very handsome species.
„ Oederi, Vahl.	. . . . . .	11–12,000	H.	Cream and purple	High margs	
Orobanchaceae:—						
Orobanche Epithymum, DC.	. . . . . .	8,000	H.	. . . . .	. . .	On thyme and other herbs. A.
Boschniakia himalaica, Hook. f. & T. .	. . . . . .	8,000	. . .	. . . . .	. . .	On Rhododendron campanulatum at Ban-bul-nag. A.
Selagineae:—						
Lagotis glauca, J. Gaertn.	. . . . . .	8–13,000	H.	Hyacinth blue	Stony ground	A.
Lentibularieae:—						
Utricularia flexuosa, Vahl.	. . . . . .	9,000	H.	Fls. yellow	In water	A.
Verbenaceae:—						
Verbena officinalis, L.	Common vervain	8–9,000	H.	Blue		
Labiatae:—						
Plectranthus rugosus, Wall.	. . . . . .	7–8,000	Small shrub	White with purple spots	Outskirts of forest	
Mentha sylvestris, L.	Horse-mint	. . . .	H.	Lilac	. . .	Called *podina* by the natives.
Origanum vulgare, L.	Wild marjoram	. . . .	H.	Purple	Open ground	
Thymus Serpyllum, L.	Wild thyme	8–12,000	H.	Purple	Open ground	
Calamintha umbrosa, F. & M. . . .	Calamint	. . . .	H.	Purple		
„ Clinopodium, Benth. . .	Wild basil	. . . .	H.	Purple		
Salvia glutinosa, L.	Jupiter's distall	7–9,000	H.	Yellow	Forest	
„ plebeja, R. Br.	. . . . . .	. . . .	H.			
„ hians, Royle	Kashmír sage	8–12,000	H.	Dark blue	Open ground	A characteristic marg plant, and very handsome.
Nepeta linearis, Royle	Cat-mint	8–9,000	H.	Lilac	Open	
„ spicata, Benth.	„	. . . .	H.	Pale blue		
„ Govaniana, Benth.	„	. . . .	H.	Yellow	Forest	

Nepeta erecta, Benth.	Cat-mint	8-9,000	H.	Blue		
„ connata, Royle	„	11-13,000	H.	Blue or white	Open	
„ ciliaris, Benth.	„	. . . .	H.	Lilac		
„ raphanorhiza, Benth.	. . . . . .	6 8,000	H.	Lilac	. . .	A.
Scutellaria prostrata, Jacquem. . . .	Skull-cap	. . . .	H.	Yellow tipped with lilac	Gravelly banks	
Prunella vulgaris, L.	Self-heal	. . . .	H.	Purple or white	Open	Also called 'Prunella.'
Stachys sylvatica, L.	Archangel	7-8,000	H.	Pink		
„ sericea, Wall.	. . . . . .	8-11,000	H.	Pink, spotted with purple		
Leonurus Cardiaca, L.	Mother-wort	. . . .	H.	Rose or white		
Lamium album, L.	White dead nettle	. . . .	H.	White		
Phlomis bracteosa, Royle	. . . . . .	8-12,000	H.	Purple	Open	Common on the margs.
Plantagineae:—						
Plantago lanceolata, L.	Rib-grass	. . . .	H.			
„ brachyphylla, Edgew. . . .	. . . . . .	10-11,000	H.	. . . .	Open stony ground	
„ major, L.	Greater plantain	. . . .	H.			
Amarantaceae:—						
Amaranthus paniculatus, L.	. . . . . .	9,000	H.	Yellow or red	. . .	Cultivated for its grain.
Chenopodiaceae:—						
Chenopodium Blitum, F. Muell. . . .	Strawberry spinach	8-9,000	H.	. . . .	. . .	Fruit bright red, and somewhat like that of the strawberry.
Phytolaceaceae:—						
Phytolacca acinosa, Roxb.	Indian poke	9,000	H.	. . . .	. . .	Leaves used as a pot-herb.
Polygonaceae:—						
Polygonum alpinum, All.	Alpine knot-weed	6-7,000	H.	. . . .	Forest	
„ polystachyum, Wall. . .	. . . . . .	8-10,000	H.	. . . .	Grassy land	A.

Botanical Name.	English Name.	Elevation in feet.	Tree or Shrub, &c.	Colour of flowers.	Locality.	Further particulars.
Polygonum amplexicaule, D. Don . .	. . . . . .	8-9,000	H.	Crimson or white	Forest	
„ rumicifolium, Royle . . .	. . . . . .	11,000	H.	. . . .	Open grassy spots	A.
„ affine, D. Don	. . . . . .	10-13,000	H.	Crimson	High open	
„ Hydropiper, L.	Water pepper	8-9,000	H.	. . . .	Wet ground	
Rheum Webbianum, Royle	Rhubarb	11-13,000	H.	. . . .	High open rocky ground	
Oxyria digyna, Hill	Mountain sorrel	9-13,000	H.	. . . .	Sides of streams	
Rumex Acetosa, L.	Sheep's sorrel	11-12,000	H.			
„ hastatus, D. Don	. . . . . .	8-10,000	H.	. . . .	Rocky ground	
„ nepalensis, Spreng.	. . . . . .	. . . .	H.	. . . .	Sheep pastures	
Thymelaeaceae:—						
Daphne cannabina, Wall.	. . . . . .	7-11,000	Shrub	Yellow-green	Hillsides	Forms most of under-scrub at Gulmarg. Leaves yield a charming colour. Fibre not used in Kashmír. A.
„ oleoides, Schreb.	Olive-leaved daphne	7,000	Shrub	. . . .	. . .	Used medicinally.
Elaeagnaceae:—						
Elaeagnus umbellata, Thunb.	. . . . . .	6,000	Shrub	. . . .	Amongst scrub	
Loranthaceae:—						
Arceuthobium minutissimum, Hook. f..	. . . . . .	8-11,000	Small shrub	Yellow-green	Branches of Pinus excelsa	A minute parasite, abundant at Gulmarg, where it does considerable damage to the trees. First discovered in Western Nepal in 1884.
Euphorbiaceae:—						
Euphorbia pilosa, L..	Hairy spurge	7-9,000	H.	. . . .	Margs	
„ var. cognata	. . . . . .	8-11,000	H.	. . . .	Margs	
„ thyrsoidea, Boiss.	. . . . . .	8-9,000	H.			

Euphorbia Stracheyi, Boiss.	. . . . . .	12,000	H.	. . . .	High open ground	
" Wallichii, Hook. f.	. . . . . .	8,500-11,000	H.	. . . .	Margs	Very handsome and showy. A.
Sarcococca pruniformis, Lindl.	. . . . . .	8-9,000	Shrub	Green	Forest	
Urticaceae:—						
Urtica dioica, L.	Stinging-nettle	. . . .	H.	Green	Waste ground	
Ulmus Wallichiana	Elm	6-9,000	Tree	. . . .	Forest	Very handsome tree. A.
Juglandeae:—						
Juglans regia, L.	Walnut	. . . .	Tree	Green	Forest	
Cupuliferae:—						
Betula utilis, D. Don	Indian birch	9-12,000	Tree	Greenish yellow	Upper forest level	In addition to the well-known paper bark, the foliage is largely used for feeding sheep.
Corylus Colurna, L.	Constantinople hazel	9-11,000	Tree	. . . .	. . .	The nuts, which are smaller than those of the European hazel, are much eaten.
Salicineae:—						
Salix Wallichiana, Anderss.	Willow	. . . .	Shrub			
" hastata, L.	"	. . . .	Shrub			
" flabellaris, Anderss.	"	12,000	Shrub			
" elegans, Wall.	"	9-10,000	Shrub			
Coniferae:—						
Juniperus recurva, Buch.-Ham.	Drooping Indian juniper	10-11,000	Shrub			
Taxus baccata, L.	Yew	. . . .	Tree	. . . .	Forest	
Pinus excelsa, Wall.	Blue pine	7-11,000	Tree	. . . .	Forest	
Cedrus Libani, Barrel. var. Deodara	Deodar	8,000	Tree	. . . .	Forest	
Picea Morinda, Link	Himalayan spruce	10-11,000	Tree	. . . .	Forest	
Abies Webbiana, Lindl.	Himalayan silver fir	8-11,000	Tree	. . . .	Forest	
Orchideae:—						
Microstylis muscifera, Rid.	. . . . . .	8-9,000	H.	. . . .	Forest	
Neottia listeroides, Lindl.	Bird's-nest orchis	. . . .	H.	Green	Under trees	
Cephalanthera ensifolia, Rich.	. . . .	8-9,000	H.	White	Forest	

Botanical Name.	English Name.	Elevation in feet.	Tree or Shrub, &c.	Colour of flowers.	Locality.	Further particulars.
Goodyera fusca, Lindl.	. . . . . .	7–9,000	H.	. . . .	Forest	
Epipactis latifolia, All.	Helleborine	. . . .	H.	Green tinged with purple	Forest	
Herminium pugioniforme, Lindl.	. . . . . .	12,000	H.	. . . .	. . .	A.
Orchis latifolia, L.	Marsh orchis	8–9,000	H.	Red-purple	Wet ground	
Cypripedium cordigerum, D. Don	Lady's slipper	8–9,000	H.	White	Forest	
Haemodoraceae:—						
Ophiopogon intermedius, D. Don	. . . . . .	. . . .	H.	White	Forest	The flowers resemble 'Lily of the Valley.'
Irideae:—						
Iris kamaonensis, Wall.	. . . . . .	. . . .	H.	Red-purple	Open	
Amaryllideae:—						
Hypoxis aurea, Lour.	. . . . . .	. . . .	H.	Yellow		
Dioscoreaceae:—						
Dioscorea sp.	. . . . . .	7–8,000				
Liliaceae:—						
Polygonatum verticillatum, All.	Whorled Solomon's-seal	8–9,000	H.	White	Forest	
Eremurus himalaicus, Baker	. . . . . .	8–9,000	H.	White	Open hillsides	Very handsome, with its tall dense spikes of flowers.
Allium Govanianum, Wall.	. . . . . .	10–11,000	H.	White	High open	
Lilium polyphyllum, D. Don	Himalayan white lily	9,000	H.	White within, with purple streaks	Forest	Flowers sweet-scented.
Fritillaria Roylei, Hook.	Fritillary	9–11,000	. . .	Greenish yellow, with purple spots		
Gagea lutea, Ker-Gawl.	Star of Bethlehem	12,000	H.	Yellow	Open grassy ground	

Lloydia serotina, Sweet	Mountain spider-wort	10–11,000	H.	White	Rocks	
Trillium Govanianum, Wall.	Wood-lily	10,000	H.	Reddish brown	Forest	
Juncaceae :—						
Juncus glaucus, Sibth.	Hard rush	7,000	H.	. . . .	Near water	
„ bufonius, L.	Toad rush	. . . .	H.	. . . .	Near water	
„ himalensis, Klotzsch	. . . . . .	8–9,000	H.			
„ membranaceus, Royle	. . . . . .	9–10,000	H.			
„ concinnus, D. Don	. . . . . .	11,000	H.	. . . .	. . .	A.
Luzula sp.	Wood rush	8–9,000	H.			
Naiadaceae :—						
Potamogeton natans, L.	Broad pond-weed	. . . .	H.	Green	Water	
Cyperaceae :—						
Eleocharis palustris, R. Br.	Spike rush	8–9,000	H.	. . . .	Near water	
Kobresia capillifolia, C. B Clarke	. . . . . .	11–12,000	H.	. . . .	High open	
Carex obscura, Nees	Sedge	9–10,000	H.			
„ psychrophila, Nees	. . . . . .	8–9,000	H.			
„ inanis, Kunth	. . . . . .	8–9,000	H.			
„ cruenta, Nees	. . . . . .	10–11,000	H.	. . . .	High open	
Gramineae :—						
Pennisetum triflorum, Nees	. . . . . .	7–9,000	H.			
Rottboellia speciosa, Hack.	. . . . . .	8–9,000	H.			
Andropogon Gryllus, L.	. . . . . .	8 9,000	H.	. . . .	Margs	
Hierochloë laxa, R. Br.	Holygrass	11–12,000	H.	. . . .	High open	Emits during the process of drying a sweet odour due to the presence of *cumarin*, a substance found also in Sweet Woodruff.
Alopecurus pratensis, L.	Meadow foxtail	8–9,000	H.	. . . .	Margs	A good pasture grass in England.
Stipa sibirica, Lam.	. . . . . .	7–9,000	H.	. . . .	Forest	This is what is known as the poisonous grass of Kashmir.
Oryzopsis sp.	. . . . . .	. . . .	H.			
Milium effusum, L.	. . . . . .	8–9,000	H.	. . . .	Forest	
Muehlenbergia sp.	. . . . . .	8·9,000	H.			
Phleum alpinum, L.	. . . . . .	. . . .	H.	. . . .	High margs	
Agrostis spp.	. . . . . .	. . . .	H.			
Calamagrostis sp.	Small reed	. . . .	H.			

Botanical Name.	English Name.	Elevation in feet.	Tree or Shrub, &c.	Colour of flowers.	Locality.	Further particulars.
Deschampsia caespitosa, Beauv.	......	10-12,000	H.	.....	High open	
Trisetum subspicatum, Beauv.	......	10-12,000	H.	.....	High open	
Koeleria cristata, Pers.	......	8-12,000	H.	.....	Margs	
Eragrostis poacoides, Beauv.	......	.....	H.			
Melica nutans, L.	Mountain melick	.....	H.			
Dactylis glomerata, L.	Cock's-foot grass	.....	H.	.....	Margs	
Briza media, L.	Common Quaker-grass	.....	H.	.....	Margs	
Poa pratensis, L.	Meadow poa	.....	H.	.....	Margs	
,, trivialis, L.	Roughish poa	.....	H.	.....	Margs and forest	
,, laxa, Haenke	......	10-12,000	H.	.....	High open	
,, annua, L.	Annual poa	.....	H.	.....	Margs	
,, alpina, L.	Alpine poa	10 12.000	H.	.....	High open	
Festuca ovina, L.	Sheep's fescue	.....	H.	.....	Margs	A good grazing grass for sheep.
Bromus spp.	Brome grass	.....	H.	.....	Forest	
Brachypodium sylvaticum, Beauv.	Slender false-brome	.....	H.	.....	Forest	
Filices:—						
Cystopteris fragilis, Bernh.	Brittle bladder-fern	.....	H.	.....	Rocks	
,, montana, Link	......	9,000	H.	.....	Rocks	A.
Adiantum venustum, Don	......	.....	H.	.....	Shady banks	Used as a medicine.
Cheilanthes fragrans, Webb and Berth.	......	.....	H.	.....	Rocks	
Onychium multisectum, F. Henders.	......	8-9,000	H.	.....	Forest	
Cryptogramme crispa, R. Br.	Parsley fern	8 12,000	H.	.....	Open	
,, Brunonianum, Wall.	......	11-12,000	H.	.....	Rocks	A.
Pellaea gracilis, Hook.	......	11-12,000	H.	.....	Shady rocks	
,, nitidula, Wall.	......	.....	H.	.....	Dry rocks	
Pteris cretica, L.	......	.....	H.			
,, quadriaurita, Retz.	......	.....	H.			
,, aquilina, L.	Bracken fern	.....	H.	.....	Open and forest	
Botrychium Lunaria, Sev.	Moon-wort	8,000	H.	.....	In forest	

Ophioglossum vulgatum, L.	Adder's tongue	5 8,000	II.	. . . .	Grassy land	
Asplenium alternans, Wall.	. . . . . .	. . . .	II.	. . . .	Shady banks	
,, septentrionale, Hoffm. . . .	Forked spleen-wort	. . . .	II.	. . . .	Rock crevices	
,, fontanum, Bernh.	Rock spleenwort	8-9,000	II.	. . . .	Rock crevices	
,, viride, Huds.	Green spleenwort	9-11,000	II.	. . . .	Rock crevices	
,, Trichomanes, L.	Maidenhair spleenwort	8-9,000	II.	. . . .	Shady rocks	
,, varians, HK. and Grev. . .	. . . . . .	8-9,000	II.	. . . .	Shady rocks	
,, Filix-foemina, Bernh. . . .	Lady fern	8 9,000	II.	. . . .	Forest	
,, thelypteroides, Michx. . .	. . . . . .	. . . .	II.	. . . .	Near water	
Aspidium Prescottianum, Hook. . . .	. . . . .	11-12,000	II.	. . . .	High open	
,, Lonchitis, Swartz.	Holly fern	8-9,000	II.	. . . .	Forest	
,, aculeatum, Swartz.	Prickly shield fern	8-9,000	II.	. . . .	Forest	
Nephrodium nemorale, Hope, M. S. .	. . . . . .	. . . .	II.	. . . .	Forest	
,, pungahense, Hope, M. S. .	. . . . . .	8-9,000	II.	. . . .	Forest	
,, Filix-mas., Rich	Male fern	. . . .	II.	. . . .	Forest	
,, var. parallelogramma . .	. . . . . .	8-9,000	II.	. . . .	Rocks in forest	
,, barbigerum, Hook. . . .	. . . . . .	10 12,000	II.	. . . .	High open	
,, Brunonianum, Hook. . .	. . . . . .	10-12,000	II.	. . . .	High open	
Polypodium clathratum, C. B. Clarke .	. . . . . .	12-13,000	II.	. . . .	Rock crevices	
,, Phegopteris, L.	Beech fern	8-9,000	II.	. . . .	Shady banks	
,, Dryopteris, L.	Oak fern	8-9,000	II.	. . . .	Shady banks	= P. Robertianum, Hoffm.
Gymnogramma Levingei, Baker . . .	. . . . . .	. . . .	II.			
Osmunda Claytoniana, L.	. . . . . .	8-12,000	II.	. . . .	Forest and high open	
Lygodium japonicum, Swartz	. . . . . .	. . . .	II.	. . . .	. . .	A climbing fern.

CHAPTER V.

FAUNA.

CHAP. V.

THE valley of Kashmír offers great attractions to sportsmen, and, for its size, possesses a large and varied animal kingdom. Facilities of communication, and a rapid increase in the number of visitors who come to the valley for the purposes of sport, have had their natural result, and those who wish to make large bags must seek the distant corners of His Highness the Maháràja's territories. In 1890, the diminution in the big game of Kashmír, led the State to re-introduce rules for the preservation of bara-singh, ibex, and musk deer, which had fallen into abeyance after the death of Maháràja Ranbir Singh, and it is believed that these rules have already had a beneficial effect. The State maintains a few preserves, in which the public are not allowed to shoot without special permission, and these preserves may have tended to retard the rapid extinction of game. But the chief cause of the diminution of game, may be traced to the wholesale slaughter of hinds in the winter. When the snow lies deep, the hinds, in their stress, would approach the villages, in the hope of finding food, and the Kashmíri, in his greed for venison, would cut their throats with little scruple. Europeans, who ought to have known better, have occasionally disgraced themselves by stag-driving in the snow, and one case was reported, a few years ago, when a person killed fourteen stags, which were driven through the deep snow, past the chair on which he was comfortably seated. Driving is now prohibited, and there is every hope that the splendid stags of Kashmír will be saved from extermination. The musk deer were harried by natives and others, for the sake of their valuable musk bags, and were usually driven and caught in nets. They, too, will be protected by the rules recently framed by the Kashmír State. But, though the State is anxious to co-operate in the interests of game preservation, and recognizes that it is the sport of Kashmír which chiefly attracts the European visitors whom His Highness the Maháràja welcomes so hospitably, I do not think that game preservation will be placed on a satisfactory basis until an association is formed for the purpose of controlling sport in Kashmír. If some association were formed, a healthy public opinion would be created, which would soon check wholesale slaughter of game, and all unsportsmanlike behaviour. The question is of considerable importance, as Kashmír and its neighbouring mountains have afforded health and excitement to British officers serving in India, and it would be a matter of serious regret if game were exterminated by the selfish and ignorant conduct of the 'fin de siècle' sportsman, and if the grand stalking of the Kashmír mountains, so congenial a relaxation to the soldier, became a thing of the past.

The same remarks apply equally to the chikor (partridge), and the natives always quote the year in which a wholesale destroyer of chikor visited Kashmír, as the time from which they became scarce. It is, however, fair to add that, as in the case of big game, so in the case of chikor, the native shikári and the poaching herdsmen from Poonch are to blame for the diminution in sport. In the winter. the chikor are driven on to the soft snow, and caught in blankets, and a common practice is to attract the birds by spreading grain, and then firing into the middle of them, killing some and wounding many. It would be well, however, if shooting commenced on September 1. At present, sportsmen begin about August 12 or 15, when the birds are in the ripening corn. The hen bird gets up, and is shot: the cheepers hide and temporarily escape. But they cannot take care of themselves, and fall an easy prey to foxes. In sport, as in other affairs, posterity should be considered. Game preservation may be regarded from another point of view, and, from this point of view, too, it is most important that the extermination of stags and other animals should be prevented. At present, the forests of Kashmír and the neighbouring countries bring no revenue to the State, so far as game is concerned. But, as time goes on, and as improved communications bring Kashmír nearer to India and Europe, it is possible that a 'nullah' in Kashmír will command a rent, as readily as a moor in Scotland. At present, nothing could be further from the mind of the ruler of Kashmír, and his one idea is that Europeans should enjoy themselves as cheaply and as freely as possible, while they are in his country. But the increased number of sportsmen and the decreased stock of game may reduce the happy hunting-grounds of Kashmír to the business level of 'a shooting to let.' It should, however, be noticed that a 'nullah,' under existing circumstances, would not be a very safe or satisfactory investment, as the goatherd drives his flocks all over the glens where the stags want to summer, and it is said by careful observers that the barasingh is working towards Kishtwar, Badrawar, and even to distant Chamba. If an association, for the preservation of game and the regulation of sport in Kashmír, were formed, something might be done towards bringing the shikáris under control. At present, the old and experienced shikáris are being shouldered out by young impostors, who obtain service by feeing the native agents and bankers in Srinagar. Any man, now, who dons pattis and wears a waist-band, can borrow a bundle of certificates and obtain service as a shikári. These new-fashioned shikáris are a plague to the country. They rob their masters, and rob the villagers, to whom they rarely pay anything for supplies. It is a mere chance if they show their employer sport. I have discussed this question with shikáris, European and native, and all are agreed that shikáris should be passed by a committee and registered. As regards the preservation of game, nothing can be simpler, for every Kashmíri will give information regarding his neighbour. The sight of a fellow-villager enjoying a feast of venison, would send off the rest in hot haste to give intelligence to the police. The cost of such an association would not be heavy, and a large income might be made by the State, if a battue of musk deer were allowed every three years, the musk pods being sold.

I give, below, a list of the mammals of Kashmír. As elsewhere in this report, Kashmír includes only the main valley, and the side valleys draining into the Jhelum river above Baramula. For the notes in inverted commas I am indebted to Colonel A. Ward, a well-known authority on Kashmír and mountain sport.

Order PRIMATIS.

Genus *Macacus.*

1. 'The Bengal Monkey, *Innuus rhesus* (Blyth and Jerdon), *Macacus rhesus* (Kashmíri, *Ponz*). ascends to an elevation of 8,000 to 9,000 feet, but is more frequently met with at about 6,000 feet and under. Blandford gives *wándar* as the Kashmíri for this monkey, but most of the shikáris call the langúr by that name.'

The *Ponz* is very common in the north-west of the valley, where great damage is caused to the crops by the troops of monkeys. They are quite fearless.

2. 'The Himalayan Langúr, *Semnopithecus Schistaceus* (*Langúr*). Probably this monkey never descends even in the outer Himalayas below 6,000 feet, unless by stress of weather it is forced to do so. It differs little from *Entellus,* and by many is considered only a variety. I have seen large numbers of the Himalayan langúr in the Sind, Liddar, and in Dandwar during the winter.'

The langúrs which I have seen in the Sind valley are of a brighter and more reddish colour than the langúrs which are seen in Simla. The natives always speak of them as wándar, and tell tales of their ferocity, often stating that two or more will attack a solitary man. CHAP. V.

Order CARNIVORA.

Family FELIDAE.

1. '*Felis pardus* (*Suh*, Kashmíri), the Leopard. It is seldom that the leopard takes to man-eating in these hills, but two instances have occurred within my knowledge: one, a most determined brute, killed many people in the Liddar, and the second was in the Sind.

2. '*Felis uncia*, the Ounce or Snow Leopard. The Kashmíris call it the Safed Chetah. Sah is a name given by some.

'The ounce is rare in the territory to which these remarks are confined. In Brariangan, and high up the Sind, are the only places I actually know of its occurrence, but a skin was brought to me in Lidarwat; this specimen was said to have been shot near Tar-Sár.

'It now and again kills sheep, but is not nearly so destructive as the leopard. A couple of ounces frequent the hills above Narastan and evidently hunt the few ibexes that are left in Brariangan.

'The male measures about 4 feet and has a tail 3 feet long.

'*Felis bengalensis* is represented by a variety, the *F. partichra* of Hodgson. I have only seen one or two specimens, and most of the skins sold in Srinagar do not come from Kashmír proper.

'The Jungle Cat, *Felis chaus*, is found in the valley, and the skins are sold in Srinagar; it varies greatly in size, weighs from 12 lbs. to 18 lbs.

'The Waved Cat, *Felis torquata*. The only specimen I know of was found by Sir O. St. John. The colouring is greyish-brown above, and buff below, but Blandford tells us it is variable.'

Family VIVERRIDAE.

The small Indian Mungoose, *Herpestes auropunctatus* (*Nul*, Kashmíri). Common in the main valley.

Family CANIDAE.

The Wolf, *Canis Lupus*. Colonel Ward has never seen a wolf in Kashmír, but believes that wolves are found[1]. Several Englishmen have

[1] Colonel Unwin writes: 'I saw a fine wolf (*Canis pallipes*) at the foot of the hills near Pandrátan in February, 1887. About a foot of snow was lying, and he had killed a sheep within a hundred

CHAP. V. told me that they have met with wolves, and the shepherds have often described to me an animal answering to the wolf and known to the Kashmíris as *Ráma hun*. They are rare, but they cause great loss when they attack flocks of sheep on the mountain sides.

'*Canis laniger* is common in Tibet and Ladákh. It is most likely a variety of *C. lupus*. A black variety is not rare.

'Jackal, *Canis aureus* (*Shál*, Kashmíri). Common in Kashmír; very large specimens are met with and many sheep are killed by these animals. I have had sheep killed at Gandar-bal, Shadipur, and Bij Bihara, also at Kotsoo (Liddar).

'Wild dog (*Cuon rutilans*, of Blyth and Jerdon), *Cyon dukhunensis* (*Ram-hun*, Kashmíri). I have seen one near the hop-garden, others in Hammel, and have little doubt that they are in most of the western valleys. They are common in the more distant nullahs.

'The ordinary weight is from 25 lbs. to 30 lbs. I have known a single one kill a sheep, and rode after it a short distance but was soon pulled up by ravines.

'The Common Fox (*Vulpes montana*, Blyth). *V. montana* is a variety of *V. alopex*. Foxes are now scarcer in Kashmír than they were a few years ago. They are the most inveterate poachers and destroy large numbers of chikor. Length of body, 24 in.; tail with hair, 19 in.'

The fox is known to the Kashmíris as *Loh*. It has a fine skin and carries a good brush. It eats fruits, berries, birds, and small animals.

Order ARCTOIDEA.

Family MUSTELIDAE.

'The Indian Marten, *Mustela flavigula* (*Grán*). The pine-marten is very active and a great tree-climber; it is very destructive. I have seen them hunting musk-deer, once in the Kaj-Nag and another time in Garhwal.

'The Beech Marten (*Mustela foina*). I have not actually seen this marten in Kashmír, but have seen skins which were said to have been obtained in Kashmír. It is widely distributed and is found in Ladákh, Baltistan, Kumaon, &c.; there is no reason to suppose it is not found in the immediate neighbourhood of the "Vale."

'The White-nosed Weasel (*Putorius canigula*). I have obtained it in the Musjid nullah above Aroo, and seen other specimens.'

yards of a hamlet in open day. I fired three long shots at him, all misses. The villagers thought it was a leopard, but the tracks in the snow, and a good view through my telescope at 400 yards, showed him to be an undoubted wolf.'

Sub-Family LUTRINAE.

'The Otter (*Lutra vulgaris*). The skin is highly prized, and prices in the bazár are more than double those of Mussorree; not often seen, but the tracks are fairly plentiful in some places. The *otter* is known to the Kashmíris as *wudar*.'

Family URSIDAE.

'Black Bear, *Ursus torquatus* (*Hapat*, Kashmíri). The old name, *U. tibetanus*, was misleading as the black bear does not occur in Tibet.

'The length of the largest I have seen is 6½ feet. Perhaps this bear is not so much "shot out" as many people believe. It has taken to cliffs and secluded spots, and many of the old males are met with at high elevations. I shot one in April, 1892, above Lidarwat'

The Black Bear (*Bomba Hapat*) is very common, especially in the Loláb valley. It is more formidable than the red bear, and often attacks villagers in the fields of Indian corn. Like the red bear, it is partly carnivorous, but it is a large consumer of maize and rice, walnuts, mulberries, roots, and the berries of the *Viburnum foetens*. The Kashmíris have many proverbs about the bear, all founded on the supposed stupidity of the animal (*Hapat Yáraz*); or the friendship of a bear always leads a man into trouble through the blundering of his friend. There has, apparently, been little diminution in the number of black bears, and their depredations cause serious injury to the crops. In 1871, four officers of one regiment carried away eighty skins, of which nearly half fell to one man's rifle. Most of the bears of Kashmír have been fired at, and near the villages their temper is not of the best. The people believe that black bears sometimes carry off women into the forests, and they speak of their wonderful ingenuity—how they tie up bushes to form a shady bower, and how sometimes they tie up female bears.

'The Brown or Red Bear, *Ursus arctus*, or *Isabellinus* (*Lal Hápat* of Kashmíri shikáris). Greatly diminished in numbers but still far from uncommon. The old bears are shy and seldom appear until nearly dusk. Length of a large male, 7 feet.'

This animal is fairly common in Kashmír, and is known as *Koin Hápat*. The red bear is keen of scent, but short-sighted. It is partly herbivorous, and partly carnivorous, and many cattle are killed every year by red bears. Length, up to and slightly over 7 feet. Height, 3 ft. 4 in. It is said that the red and black bears interbreed.

Order INSECTIVORA.

Family SORIRIDAE.

'The Brown Musk Shrew (*Crocidura murina*). The musk-rat or shrew, *C. coeruleae*, and a water-shrew which is found in some of the side valleys. I killed one in the Aroo river, but unfortunately the coolie lost it or threw it away. Jerdon mentions the Himalayan water-shrew as coming from Darjeeling (*Crassopus himalaicus*), and Blandford gives the habitat south-eastern Himalayas. I have seen water-shrews in many parts of Kashmír.'

Order CHIROPTERA.

Family PTEROPODIDAE.

The Flying Fox. I have only seen this bat on the outer ranges. The native name is *wutsgagar*, and it is common in the Sind valley. It gives a very soft light fur which is made into rugs.

'There are doubtless many insectivorous bats in Kashmír, but I have never studied them. The Kashmíri cave-bat or Theobald's bat, the common bat of Europe (*Vespertilio murinus*), and others are especially mentioned in the Fauna of British India as coming from Kashmír, but on the bats I can write nothing except what I could get from books, and those anxious for further information can study Jerdon and Blandford.'

Order RODENTIA.

Family SCIURIDAE.

'The Red Flying Squirrel (*Pteromys inornatus*). The Kashmíri Flying Squirrel (*Sciuropterus fimbricatus*). Both these are very common and are easily shot in the wild walnut trees and amongst the hazels in October.

'In the Pir Panjál I obtained an almost black flying squirrel, it was too large to have been *S. alboniger*.'

Family MURIDAE.

'Kashmír is overrun with rats and mice.

'The Common Indian Rat, the Brown Rat (*Mus decumanus*). I have only seen this near Baramula. The common house mouse is everywhere. The sides of every bank are full of rat holes.'

The water-rat is common, and the musk-rat occurs. At Gulmarg, I have seen huge bandikots. All rats are known as *gagur*; mice are known as *krints*. They cause great damage to crops of wheat and barley.

'Royle's Vole (*Microtus Roylei*), commonly known as the Common Himalayan Vole. As far as I am aware the other Himalayan voles are only found over the passes. To travellers in Ladákh, Blyth's vole must be well known.'

Family HYSTRICIDAE.

'The Porcupine (*Hystrix leucura*), not common. I have found the quills, but have never seen a live specimen in Kashmír.'

Family LEPORIDAE.

'I have seen the common hare near Domel; the Ladákh hare is a different species.'

There are no hares in the valley. Perhaps this is due to the prevalence of irrigation.

Order UNGULATA.

Family BOVIDAE.

Genus *Capra*.

'We now come to the most interesting of the mammals which attract a considerable portion of the visitors to the hills of Kashmír and its neighbouring districts.

'The Markhor (*Capra Falconeri*). The Pir Panjal is sadly "shot out," and the Kaj-Nag is in the same category.

'In 1884 heads of 59 in. and 54 in. were bagged. The weight of a full grown male shot on Malamgan cliffs was 240 lbs., but this was exceptional, and few of the Kashmír markhor attain that weight.

'The Kutai and other nullahs are much driven with dogs by the natives, and there is no doubt that the numbers of these magnificent goats are fast being diminished. In winter the markhor is grey, in summer a brownish red.

'The female is an insignificant creature, with horns of 10 to 11 in.; under no circumstances should one be shot. The Kashmíri markhor has from two to three complete turns in the spirals. The Astor animal has one turn or almost one and a half. The markhor ruts in December, and the kids are born in June.

'*Habitat*—the Pir Panjal, the Kaj-Nag and Shamsibri mountains.'

CHAP. V. The best ground for markhor is the well-known Kaj-Nag mountain north-west of the valley. The markhor (i.e. snake-eater) is an enormous goat with two turns, sometimes nearly three, in the spiral of the horns. In one nullah on the Kaj-Nag a sportsman bagged three markhor with horns of 52, 55, and 59 inches long in the course of a few days. A good cragsman is wanted for the successful pursuit of markhor, as they generally choose dangerous and inaccessible ground. The markhor keep in herds, the old males go in with the females and young males in December and separate again in the spring. The finest horn on record is said to be 61 inches. The markhor is found on the Pir Panjal, but the heads on that range are not so fine as the heads on the Kaj-Nág.

'The Ibex, *Capra sibirica* (*Kail*, Kashmíri). There are still ibex to be found in Kashmír, though they are seldom sought for, as most men go to the far-off shooting grounds. I picked up a 50-in. horn on the Zogila hill in 1881, and I have never heard of a larger head. I am of course alluding to the near shooting grounds, as 54 in. and 56 in. are on record for elsewhere.

'Sadly has the sport deteriorated of late years, but rifles have been improved and the game suffers.

'Dimensions of a large buck from the Wardwán:

	Height at shoulder.	Length of body.	Tail.	Weight.
Male.	38 inches.	54 inches.	8 inches.	188 lbs.
Female.	32 inches.			104 lbs.

'Unlike the markhor, the ibex faces the winter at considerable elevations but the green grass of the spring-time tempts them down. I saw a herd of small ibex within two miles of Aroo village in 1892.'

The ibex (*kel*) is said to be found on the northern side of the Loláb and in the Sind and Liddar valleys, but of late years sportsmen have to seek the ibex in the more distant mountains of Ladákh, Baltistan, and Wardwán. In the winter and spring it is easy to find the ibex, but in the summer it goes to great heights and roves over a large area of country. The ibex is a gregarious animal. The breeding season commences in November, and the young are generally born towards the end of June. The *kel* is said to be larger than the European ibex, its horns are longer, more curved and more tapering. In Baltistan an excellent homespun is made from the under hair of the ibex (*kel famb*).

Genus *Hemitragus*.

'*Hemitragus jemlaicus* (the *Tahr jagla*, Kashmíri). The Pir Panjal is the only ground within the limits of this book. I have seen no good specimens from those parts, but other nullahs in the Mahárájá's dominions give very fine heads. An old male standing out on a cliff is a very fine sight. He is a wary creature, hard to stalk, and frequents bad walking ground. Weight, 200 lbs.; maximum length of horns, 14 in. Kashmír is not *the* shooting ground for this game. Rutting season, December.'

Genus *Nemorhaedus.*

'*Nemorhaedus bubalerius* (the *Serow ramu*, Kashmíri). Fairly plentiful, but difficult to obtain. I have no measurements of the few specimens killed in Kashmír, but give those of the finest animals I have killed in the Ganges valley and the vicinity of Dehra.

	Height at shoulder.	Weight.	Horn.
Male.	37 inches.	190 lbs.	12 inches.
Female.	33 „	120 „	10 „

'Above Shalamár there are still serow.

'Under genus *Cemas* or, according to Blyth and Jerdon, *Nemorhaedus*, comes the Goral (*Cemas* or *Nemorhaedus goral*, *Pij*, Kashmíri), uncommon in Kashmír except in the Pir range; is recorded from the Sind and Dandwar, &c.

Height at shoulder.	Weight.	Length of horn.
28 inches.	55 to 65 lbs.	6 in., maximum 8 in.

'The female has thin horns of sometimes 5 in. long. Sexes much alike and difficult to distinguish when standing on the hill side. Although to a certain extent solitary in its habit, others are generally found on the same hill.'

Family CERVIDAE.

Genus *Cervulus.*

'*Cervulus aureus* or (to follow Blandford), *Cervulus muntjac*. I have only seen one specimen in Kashmír, this was driven out of the Achibal preserve in 1885—how it got there I cannot say. It is found on the outer slopes of the Pir Panjál. I give measurements of the rib-faced or barking deer from those shot in Garhwal and elsewhere.

Height at shoulder.	Weight.	Length of horn.
Maximum, 26 inches.	38 to 42 lbs.	5 to 8 inches.

'There is very great difference in the size of this animal. Those found in the Siwaliks are generally small. Blandford gives height 22 in.; this is decidedly very small.'

CHAP. V.

Genus *Cervus*.

The Barasingh. This fine stag may be seen in the Sind valley, in the Loláb, and, as winter comes on, may be found in most parts of the valley, where it joins the mountains. The barasingh sheds its horns about the end of March and makes its way to the high mountains above the forest line, and does not return till its horns are renewed in autumn. Then the calling season commences, and in September and October the sportsman has his best chance. Stags are always to be found in the State preserves in the Wangat, at Khunmu and Trahal, and later in the winter they descend to the State forest above Achibal. The barasingh is known to the Kashmíri as Hangal, a name said to have been given on account of the barasingh's love for horse chestnuts. Native shikáris tell me that stags are very fond of water-cress. The flesh of the barasingh is much esteemed by the Kashmíris, and the horns are used for a variety of purposes. In the State palaces the antlers are employed as candelabra. Pieces of horn are used for the pommels of country saddles.

'At one time we might almost have said that it was nearly extinct, but if the game laws are only strictly upheld we may still see this magnificent beast fairly plentiful in Kashmír. As long as the goat-herd roams the hills and penetrates into the recesses of the mountains where the hornless stag loves to dwell in seclusion, we shall never see the same numbers that formerly existed.

'The rutting season is from September 20 to about October 20. Stags are generally shot when calling, or else in February and March when down on the green grass. The horns of nearly all the large animals are cast in April, and when one hears of them carrying horns in May and June it is very exceptional. The largest measurements I have are:

Height at shoulder.	Weight.	Length of horns.
94½ inches.	400 lbs.	47 inches.

'Ten tines is the common number. Good royals are scarce. The fairest way to test a head is to weigh it.'

Genus *Moschus*.

'The Musk Deer (*Moschus moschiferus*, *Rass* or *Rous* of Kashmíris). This little animal was becoming very scarce, and even now is seldom met with near the main valley. They breed at a very early age, and should multiply quickly, if only the game laws are not allowed to be a dead letter.

'The pod (*Náfa*) contains a soft, brownish matter which is the much-coveted musk; about 2 tolas is the limit of the weight, and the price rules high, consequently the Kashmíri will risk a good deal to secure it. This deer grazes chiefly on leaves in the summer. The musk-deer is found at altitudes varying from 6,000 to 13,000 feet or more.

'The musk-deer of Kashmír is generally smaller than those of our own Himalayas. It is higher in the croup than at the shoulder.

Height.	Weight.
22 inches.	20 to 25 lbs.

'The young are spotted on the back and sides. They are pretty pets and become quite tame, but require considerable variety in food, hence they are difficult to keep in the winter.'

Order SUINA.

Family SUIDAE.

'The Indian Wild Boar (*Sus cristatus*) is common in many parts of Kashmír. In winter it is generally found below 6,000 feet, but in summer ascends to 8,000 and over.'

The Wild Pig is known to the Kashmíris as *Bad.* and is said to have been introduced in the time of Mahárája Gulab Singh. It is common in the State preserves and along the foot of the mountains on the eastern side of the valley. Pigs attain a great size, and do much injury to the crops. The Dogras and Sikhs consider the flesh of the wild pig to be a great delicacy.

The Marmot (*Arctomys hemachalanus*). The marmot is found among the rocks on the high passes leading from Kashmír to Gilgit and Ladákh. It is known as *Drin*, and has a handsome fur of a reddish-yellow colour from which excellent rugs can be made. The marmot on the approach of a traveller utters a shrill, bird-like sound. It is very quick, and disappears rapidly into holes in the rocks.

The Mouse hare, *Lagomys roylei*, is found in Gulmarg.

BIRDS.

The Kashmíri knows little about birds. He speaks of them all as *Janwar*, and though he takes considerable interest in the song birds he is ignorant of the habits of the feathered kingdom. He knows that the Swallow, *Katij* (No. 207) and the Golden Oriole, *Poshnal* (No. 119), are harbingers of spring, but he has never noticed the altruistic habits of the Cuckoo. The Kashmíris are kind to birds, and up to the present time the hateful plumage hunter, so common in India, has not made his way to

CHAP. V. the valley. The Kashmíri boy does not collect eggs, and on the whole the birds have a happy and careless existence in this beautiful country. The blue Heron, *Breg* (No. 39), is very common in the valley, and there are fine heronries at Palhalan, Narabal, Kulgám, and at other places. In the old days every man of position wore a plume of herons' feathers (*gund*), and on marriage occasions the bridegroom dons the plume. The feathers are carefully kept in round boxes and are handed down as heirlooms. The fashion is passing away. The right to collect herons' feathers is farmed out. In 1893 the farmer paid Rs. 268 and 2,999 feathers to the State, but there is little competition for the farm. One old man once begged hard to be released from his contract, and deplored his wretched fate, paddling about in a boat with a decoy heron which he had to feed with live fish. He proved to me that there was no profit in herons' feathers, and asked to be allowed to adopt agricultural pursuits.

The classification here adopted is that of Dr. Bowdler Sharpe, communicated to the Second Ornithological Congress at Budapest in 1891. His nomenclature and that of Mr. E. W. Oates have also been followed.

Order GALLIFORMES. Game-Birds.

Sub-Order PHASIANI.

Family PHASIANIDAE. Pheasants.

1. *Lerwa lerwa.* The Snow Partridge (in Gilgit, *Koreish*). I have only seen this partridge in Gilgit at about 14,500 feet elevation on a rocky ridge. There was a pair of old birds with their brood of six or seven chicks. Dr. Adams, however, found it on the mountains between the Wardwán and the Liddar valley, so I include it in this list.

2. *Tetraogallus himalayensis.* The Himalayan Snow Cock (*Ram chikor* of sportsmen; *Gurka-kao* in Kashmír). Is found on most of the higher ridges in Kashmír among crags and rocky ground near the snow-line, generally in coveys of ten to twenty. Has a loud, clear, long whistle, uttered while the bird is seated, which is intensified and repeated more rapidly when it flies. It also utters a chuckling note something like that of the chikor, but not so rapid, when on the ground. I have caught the young in July, and once, when following a wounded ibex, I found the nest placed under a stone on the margin of a boulder-strewn glacier. It contained eight eggs, of a pale olive-brown colour, tinged light bluish, slightly dotted at the lower end, with light brown spots; length $2\frac{1}{1}\frac{3}{8}$ inches, width $1\frac{7}{8}$ inches. The old bird sat very close, and I almost caught her as she flew off.

3. *Caccabis chukar*. The Chikor Partridge (Kashmíri, *kak*). The chikor belongs to the genus of 'rock' or 'sand' partridges, and is the only example of the true partridges in Kashmír. It is exceedingly common, every rocky hill and slope round the valley being more or less frequented by them. Favourable ground is to be found in rocky, bushy slopes, with a backing of steep cliffs above them to which the birds can retire for security and shelter; dense bushy cover is generally unlikely for birds unless they have been driven into it when disturbed from their usual haunts. I have seen them in rice fields after the crop has been cut, picking up stray grains left by the reapers, and in millet fields near the foot of hills are a favourite resort while the crop is standing. Pairing commences early in March, when many birds retire up hill for the season; and during summer, and even in October, chikor may be seen up to over 9,000 feet elevation. Many, however, seem to breed near their usual winter haunts, and these birds form the stock which supplies sport in early September.

There has been a great falling off in the number of chikor recently, due to the severe winters of late years, to poaching by natives in the breeding season, encouraged by some English visitors who buy the birds for the table, and to indiscriminate shooting by sportsmen of the class who care for nothing but the 'bag.' The Game Laws passed this year by the Kashmír Government will do much to rectify this state of affairs, if properly enforced. The chikor is both hardy and prolific, and with ordinary fair play will soon be as numerous as ever.

4. *Coturnix communis*. The Large Grey Quail. Visits Kashmír in small numbers in April and May, remaining throughout July and August. I have heard it calling in these months in the valley, and in August, 1888, in the trúmba (buckwheat) crops at Sonamarg. It probably breeds here to some small extent. The best seasons I know of were 1887 and 1894, when from eight to ten brace were shot at a time. In ordinary seasons half that number would be a good bag.

5. *Lophophorus refulgens*. The Monaul Pheasant (Kashmíri, male *Sunal* or *Suna 'Murg'*; female *Haum*). The Monaul is well distributed in the upper forests, but one never sees any great number; though twelve to fifteen may be flushed in some places in the course of a day's walk, oftener not half that number will be seen. Formerly they were much more plentiful. In October, 1864, while following a wounded stag on the southern slope of the Lashkot spur between the Bonár and Búnzar glens, I put up quantities of Monaul, chiefly hens. They rose at every step from the dry grass and bracken, perching on the pine trees around, and ten or fifteen brace might have been bagged by simply shooting them as they sat. A recent visit to this spur showed only three or four birds.

6. *Tragopan melanocephalum.* The Simla Horned Pheasant (*Rang Ráwul* of some Kashmíris; *Riar* in Hazara). Rare in Kashmír. I have never seen or heard of it on the Sind-Liddar side of the valley. A few exist on Dandwár, where the shikáris know it, and it is probably sparingly distributed on the wooded slopes on the south and east sides of Kashmír. One was shot near Hai Háma, Loláb, on May 20, 1894, by a Pathán Zemindar. The people round said they had never seen the bird before. It was probably a wanderer from the Kaj-Nag or Shamsibri hills, where the bird is more common.

7. *Pucrasia biddulphi.* The Kashmír Pucras Pheasant. Commonly called *Koklas.* To be found in all Kashmír forests singly or in scattered parties, and when numerous, its short hoarse crowing call is one of the earliest bird-sounds heard at daybreak. Like the Monaul it is never found in sufficient number to afford a 'bag.' It comes lower down than the Monaul, though generally seen at much the same elevation. While chikor shooting near Lár, in November, 1893, one was flushed by the beaters in thorny scrub. It had probably been driven down by a hawk from the steep hills above.

Dr. Jerdon considers that *Pucrasia castanea* (of Gould) may possibly be found in Kashmír limits (*Birds of India,* vol. iii. pp. 526, 527). I know of no other pheasants in. Kashmír proper; though the adjacent outer ranges contain the 'Chic' (*Catreus Wallichii*), and white-crested 'Kalij' (*Gennaeus albocristatus*) in addition to the Monaul and 'Koklas.'

Order PTEROCLETES. Sand-Grouse.

Family PTEROCLIDAE.

8. *Pterocles arenarius.* The Large Sand-Grouse. Can hardly be called a Kashmír visitant, but stragglers are occasionally seen. I saw the bird, after being attracted by hearing the call, on the high dry karewás near Pampur in late November, 1889, on more than one occasion, but could never get within shot.

Order COLUMBIFORMES. Pigeons.

Family COLUMBIDAE. True Pigeons.

9. *Columba Hodgsoni.* The Speckled Wood-pigeon. This splendid pigeon is fairly numerous in the Kashmír forests at from 7,000 to 9,000 feet generally, though I have seen it at fully 11,000. Male. Above dark vinaceous purple, with white spots on median wing-coverts; head ashy-

grey, tinged ruddy, nape vinous grey, with pointed pearl grey tips; rump ashy, neck and under surface warm grey, with a ruddy mesial streak to each feather, especially on the breast; abdomen dark vinous; tail ashy black; bill purple black; irides grey, orbital skin livid; feet blackish, green in front, yellow behind; length 15 inches, extent 26 inches.

The female is smaller, the grey on the head darker and very slightly ruddy in parts; general plumage as seen flying almost as dark as a jack-daw. I have seen this pigeon in various parts of Kashmír, most numerously in Wángat Nála, where I shot a number as the birds came down to a salt-lick in the forest. I was well concealed in a birch thicket, and the salt mud must have been a great attraction or I should never have got a succession of shots at these most wary birds.

10. *Palumbus casiotis.* The Himalayan Wood-pigeon. This pigeon, though very numerous in Poonch, is rare in Kashmír, and I have only seen one or two on the Dandwár side of the valley. It differs from the English wood-pigeon in being less blue-grey and more brownish dove-colour on the upper plumage, and in having the neck-patch buff or fulvous instead of white. Length 17 inches; bill orange at tip, whitish at the base; feet red.

11. *Columba intermedia.* The Blue Rock-Pigeon. Is too well known to require description. Fairly common in Kashmír, though not so abundant as in India. Large flocks are sometimes seen about cultivation, especially in autumn. It should be noted that in the British Museum Catalogue *C. rupestris* and *C. livia* are included from Kashmír.

12. *Columba leuconota.* The White-bellied Pigeon. The 'Snow-Pigeon' of sportsmen. Generally seen at high elevations, in upland glens and plateaux above the forest-line, generally in parties, sometimes in immense flocks, feeding on the turf and about sheep-folds. I have seen it low down after stormy weather in spring and autumn, but *never* in the valley in winter; whether it migrates at that season or remains aloft in the snows remains to be solved. I have not found it very shy, and it is far less wary than the wood-pigeons. Bill black; irides yellow; legs red. Length 13 inches to 14 inches.

Sub-Family TURTURINAE. Turtle-Doves.

13. *Turtur ferrago.* The Rufous Turtle-Dove. Excessively common in the side glens, but less so in the valley of Kashmír: found round cultivation and glades and clearings in the forests and near villages. Ascends to

CHAP. V. 9,000 or 10,000 feet. Is seen singly or in small parties, and sometimes in flocks of fifty or sixty, especially when feeding in the fields. General colour rufescent above, head bluish grey; wing coverts and scapulars dusky, broadly-edged rufous, beneath vinaceous; under tail coverts white; bill blackish-crimson; irides orange; feet dull red. Length 11½ inches to 12½ inches.

14. *Turtur douraca.* The Indian Ring-dove. General colour pale grey, brownish on the back; a narrow black ring on neck; bill black; irides crimson; feet dull red; length 12 inches to 13 inches. The common dove of India summers in the Kashmír valley, but never ascends beyond it; arrives in April, leaving in autumn. I have seen stragglers lingering till November, chiefly at the east end of the valley.

Order RALLIFORMES. Rails.

Family RALLIDAE.

15. *Fulica atra.* The Bald Coot (Kashmíri, *Kolar*). Common on the Wular lake and adjacent lagoons in winter, and generally distributed throughout the valley. I once watched a flock of coots diving for some favourite weed near the shore of the Wular and being robbed of their morsels as they came to the surface by Gadwall, which swam about among the coots, snatching the weeds from their bills, to the great annoyance of this latter. The Gadwall being one of the non-diving ducks were unable to procure the weeds for themselves, but their greater activity on the surface enabled them to rob the coots with impunity.

16. *Gallinula chloropus* The Water-hen (Kashmíri, *Téch*). Is fairly common on lakes and in reed beds in summer. The general colour is as described by Jerdon (vol. iii. p. 718), but (in the females particularly) the head is black, not dusky grey, and the wings bronze olive, not dusky. The general dark plumage, the red shield over the forehead, and the light green legs with an orange garter above the knee make this bird easy to recognize Length of a female 13½ inches; of a male 12¾ inches. This is one of the few birds in which the female is larger and more richly coloured than the male.

17. *Porzana pusilla.* The Eastern Crake. Found in sedges and reed beds, &c. It lies close and is difficult to find.

Order PODICEPIDIDIFORMES. Grebes.

18. *Tachybaptes albipennis* (Kashmíri. *Pind*). Indian Little Grebe. Very common in lakes and swamps, and occasionally seen on the open waters of the Jhelum in hard winters. In summer it betakes itself to the thicker sedges and reed beds where it breeds. and at this time it assumes a darker plumage than in winter. It is a quaint little bird, with a strong element of curiosity; when duck-shooting over decoys, myself well concealed, I have seen it swim up and examine the ducks that had fallen, and I once saw one peck vigorously at a decoy.

Order LARIFORMES. Gulls.

Family LARIDAE.

19. *Larus ridibundus*. The Laughing Gull (Kashmíri. *Krind*). Found in considerable numbers on jheels and lakes in the winter, and a good many may always be seen off the rocky shore of the Wular near Watlab at that season. Head and under surface white; back and general upper plumage pale ashy: first four primaries tipped black: bill and legs deep red; length 15 to 16 inches. In summer the head and upper neck become deep reddish-brown. Adams states that it breeds on the lakes in Ladákh. It is only a winter visitant to Kashmír.

20. *Hydrochelidon hybrida*. This Tern is very abundant on the swampy lagoons and marshes in Kashmír in summer. Jerdon notes it as very common in India, and as breeding in large churrs on the Ganges, and probably on some other large rivers.

· 21. *Sterna hirundo*. The European Common Tern (Kashmíri, *Kreu*). Is found on swamps and marshes in summer and breeds here, not as common as the last species. The eggs are quite as good as plovers' eggs. Head and nape black; plumage above pale grey, beneath white; bill red; irides brown. Length 12½ inches. Adams observed it in Kashmír.

Order CHARADRIIFORMES. Plovers and Snipes.

Family OEDICNEMIDAE. Thick-Knees.

22. *Oedicnemus crepitans*. The Common Thick-Knee. I saw a pair of this species on a stony beach of the Veshau river, near Nihánia, in August,

 1889, but was unable to secure a specimen. I have never seen the bird since in Kashmír. It is a permanent resident in India.

Family CHARADRIIDAE. Plovers.

I have never seen either the Grey or Golden Plovers in Kashmír, although they might be expected to visit the country, being found in India during the cold season.

23. *Aegialitis dubius.* The Lesser Ringed Plover. Found on the stony beaches and boulder-strewn sandy turf bordering the Sind river near Gandarbal, and also on the Pohra river. Plumage as in Jerdon, vol. ii. pp. 641, 642, but the legs are *yellowish-ashy*, not *yellow*. I failed to find the nest. Has a low piping note, constantly repeated, and also a louder call, chiefly uttered at night. It no doubt breeds here, as I obtained a specimen on June 2, 1894.

24. *Vanellus vanellus.* The Crested Lapwing. Very common in autumn and winter. I have no evidence of its breeding here; it frequents marshes and wet pastures, and is often seen in large flocks.

25. *Sarciophorus indicus.* The Red-wattled Lapwing. Better known as the 'Did he do it.' Very common, I have seen it in nearly every month in the year; no doubt it breeds here. Eggs large, rich olive yellow, blotched grey and brown.

Family PARRIDAE. Jacanas.

26. *Hydrophasianus chirurgus.* The Pheasant-tailed Jacana. This handsome bird is a well-known feature of Kashmír lakes and swamps in summer. It has very long thin toes and claws. General plumage—brown above with a gold-coloured patch on back of neck; beneath and wings and tail, black. It may be seen running over the broad leaves of aquatic plants and feeding in parties on marshy ground. The cry, like that of a hound or beagle, may be heard both by day and night. I found the flesh (called 'excellent' by Jerdon) to be black, dry, and insipid.

27. *Numenius arquata.* The Curlew (Kashmíri, *Golar*). The Kashmíris say that this bird is common, but such is not my experience. I have seen it in winter about Ninghel and the shores of the Wular, and in September, 1893, I shot one out of a party of three on the Veshau river near Korwyn.

28. *Ibidorynchus struthersii* The Red-billed Curlew. This handsome curlew is seldom seen. It is found on the pebbly strands where mountain rivers widen out and are fringed with willow bushes and scrub, generally singly. although two or three may frequent the same locality. Has a wild whistling cry, uttered when it takes wing. I saw it at Inshin in the Wardwan, and a pair frequented the bifurcations of the Liddar below Pahlgam during a summer I was there; they were no doubt breeding. though I failed to find their nest. General plumage—above ashy olive; beneath white; head. and a broad gorget on breast, black; a white wing-bar; bill crimson; irides red; legs blood-red. Length 16½ inches.

29. *Machetes pugnax.* The Ruff. Seen in flocks in March, frequenting grass lands and the edges of marshes. Have only seen it in its winter plumage, when the males are without their characteristic ruff. Not very common.

30. *Totanus glareola.* The Wood Sandpiper. This and the next two species are common throughout the winter, and individuals may be found in summer. Most probably breeds here.

31. *Totanus glottis.* The Green-shanks. Very common in autumn and winter. Arrives about September and stays till April. It is capital eating.

32. *Actitis hypoleucos.* The Common Sandpiper. Is not so common as the two last species.

Family SCOLOPACIDAE. Snipes.

33. *Scolopax rusticula.* The Woodcock. Breeds in the forests all round Kashmír in considerable numbers, and at dusk may be seen flying over glades and open spaces during the summer months. At this time it utters a short. metallic whistle, heard at a considerable distance, and preceded by a low, croaking note, not audible till the bird is close at hand. Kashmíri name, *Zár batchi.* The majority of the woodcock bred here must migrate in the winter. I once shot one in January in the Awantipura 'chikor' ground. and have also shot them in Wangat, and near Bringan lamar, but have never seen or heard of sufficient numbers being shot in winter to account for a tithe of the number bred here in the summer months; a few may remain near warm springs in the forests, but where the great majority go is at present a mystery.

34. *Gallinago solitaria.* The Himalayan Solitary Snipe. Is sparsely

distributed in Kashmír. I once shot three in late November along the course of a small stream at Kotsoo in the Liddar valley, and have seen it in other localities. The cry is somewhat like that of the common snipe, but shorter and more husky.

35. *Gallinago scolopacinus.* The Common Snipe. Very common, and often seen in great numbers from September till the end of March. A good day's sport with snipe is, however, seldom obtained, as after the first few shots the birds generally betake themselves to swamps and quagmires, where it is impossible to follow them either on foot or in a boat. The Kashmíris catch them in horsehair nooses, and I found a man who had shot a few along the marshy channel of the Sind river, using his long poking punt-gun charged with fine gravel!

36. *Lymnocryptes gallinula.* The Jack-snipe. Common in Kashmír. Found in marshes, &c., together with the common snipe.

37. *Rhynchaea bengalensis.* The Painted Snipe. Is not very common, but exists in Kashmír, and is flushed in ordinary snipe ground, and among rice fields; most probably breeds here.

Order GRUIFORMES. Cranes.

Family GRUIDAE.

38. *Grus lilfordi.* Lord Lilford's Crane (*Kulang* in India; *Kunj* in the Punjab). Is a regular winter visitant to Kashmír, and chiefly frequents the flat country around the Wular, the cultivated plain of Kamraj near Sopur, and is seen more rarely between Shadipur and Srinagar. In an open season it remains the whole winter, but as I have never seen it after severe weather has set in, I conclude that a heavy snowfall drives it southward. They collect in large flocks for migration in late February and early March, where I have seen 150 or more together, wheeling upward in circles above Sodnor and Ajus till they were level with the mountain tops, and then flying off straight northward. It is remarkable that their arrival in, and departure from, Kashmír, should be respectively later and earlier than their migratory movements to and from India.

Order PELARGIFORMES. Herons.

Family ARDEIDAE.

39. *Ardea cinerea.* The Blue Heron (Kashmíri, *Breg*). Very common all over the valley, and ascends mountain rivers to over 7,000 feet, generally,

however, passing downward in the evening to roost. Heronries exist at Koolgam and many other places, the chenar tree being chosen by the birds for their nests. The trees selected are much damaged by their droppings. The heron is a royal bird in Kashmír, and the right to collect the head feathers is farmed out to men who watch the heronries in the moulting season. These men also keep tame herons, using them to attract wild birds, which are caught in nooses set round where the tame birds stand tethered leg-deep in water. This heron farming is said to be on the wane now, there being little demand for the feathers.

40. *Herodias egrettoides.* The Smaller Egret. Frequents, in large flocks, the shores of the Wular lake and the wet mud-flats in winter.

41. *Ardeola leucoptera.* The Pond Heron ; the Paddy Bird. Seen about rice fields, groves of trees, &c., in summer. It must migrate to India in the winter, for it seems to disappear from Kashmír at that season.

42. *Ardetta sinensis.* The Yellow Bittern. Common in the reeds and sedges mixed with willow plantings on the Dal lake and similar localities. Hides among the reeds or perches on the willows. I have only seen it in summer, i. e. May to September. Length 14 to 15 inches.

43. *Ardetta minuta.* The Little Bittern of Europe. Found, together with the Yellow Bittern, in similar places. May be distinguished by its black head, back, scapulars, and tail. Length 14 inches.

44. *Botaurus stellaris.* The Bittern. Seldom seen in Kashmír, possibly partly owing to its nocturnal habits, and partly to the inaccessible nature of the swamps to which it resorts. I saw a very fine one in one of the jheels near Ajus in November, 1893, but it was out of shot.

Family CICONIIDAE. Storks.

45. I have seen Storks at various times in Kashmír, but never had a chance of identifying them. In March, 1886, I saw a flock of what looked like the White-necked Stork, *Ciconia leucocephala*, hovering close over the Takht-i-Suliman, and some alighting on the ridge of the hill. They were evidently migrating. I examined them through a telescope and believe them to have been the above species, but had no means of shooting a specimen.

Order ANSERIFORMES. Ducks and Geese.

Family ANATIDAE.

Sub-Family ANSERINAE. True Geese.

46. *Anser cinereus.* The Grey Goose (Kashmíri, *Ans*). Found in vast flocks on the Wular in the winter months, arriving in the latter half of October and leaving for its northern resorts in March. This is the only wild goose I have been able to identify in Kashmír, although I think that I once saw the white-fronted species (*A. albifrons*) on the Wular. The grey geese spend the greater part of their time about the shores of the great lake, sleeping and feeding on the dry mud flats left by the receding waters in the autumn. Large numbers also pass the day on the lake itself, where they are incessantly persecuted by native punt-gunners. On the mud flats they are practically secure, although I have managed to bag a few by getting on to the flats after sunset and waiting for parties of geese to pass overhead where it was too dark for them to see me. Hard weather and heavy gales drive them inland, where they may be found hovering over jheels and marshes, but always with a careful eye to their own safety; nowhere does the wild goose better maintain his character for wariness than in Kashmír. Solitary birds and small parties sometimes pass within easy shot even on the open lake, but generally choose a time when you do not expect them. On one occasion I shot one out of a small flock from my tent door at Míni-marg on the Astor road, while heavy snow was falling. This was in early November, and the geese were no doubt migrating. Length 30 to 32 inches. Dr. Jerdon gives the weight at from 9 to 12 lbs., but in Kashmír I have never found one much over 7 lbs., and many are less. Probably the food here in winter is much inferior to what they find in India.

Sub-Family ANATINAE. Ducks.

47. *Casarca rutila.* The Ruddy Shieldrake (Hindi, *Chakwa, Chakwi*; *Tsakdo* in Kashmíri). The 'Brahminy Duck' is not very common; most often seen at the end of winter and in early spring during its migration. Breeds in Ladákh.

48. *Spatula clypeata.* The Shoveller. Common in winter, and can be easily distinguished by the large spoon-shaped bill. The male has a very handsome plumage. The call is a quiet 'chook-chook,' not heard at a distance. Kashmíri name, *Honk*.

49. *Anas boscas.* The Mallard. In Kashmíri, *Nilij.* The female, called *Thuj*, arrives in late October and leaves in March. I once shot a female in May near Sumbal, and it is possible that a few pairs remain to breed here, but the majority certainly migrate, and I can find no evidence to support the statement in *The Game Birds of India* that this bird breeds extensively in Kashmír, and that the eggs are sold in large numbers in Srinagar. The four curled central feathers of the tail of the male have a saleable value, and are always stolen by the boatman after a day's shooting unless looked after. Women are said to use them as ornaments in their hair.

50. *Chaulelasmus streperus.* The Gadwall (Kashmíri, *Búdan*). Very numerous in some winters and more scarce in others. Is one of the best ducks, both for sport and the table, and the season which produces large flocks of Gadwall is sure to be a good one for duck-shooting.

51. *Dafila acuta.* The Pintail Duck (Kashmíri, *Sok pachin*). This very handsome duck is seldom seen (except here and there a few) in Kashmír till the winter is well advanced, and it is towards the latter part of February that large numbers arrive, probably halting on their northward migration from India; at this time the jheels are often full of them, and they afford excellent sport. The call is soft and not often heard, and the drakes have also a short whistle not unlike that of the male teal (*Q. crecca*), but deeper and fuller. This whistle is constantly repeated when the birds are collected in large flocks. Migrates in the spring and does not breed here.

52. *Mareca penelope.* The Widgeon (Kashmíri, *Shicwrni Búdan*). Not common, and rarely shot, but may be found every winter mixed up with other wild-fowl on the Wular, and adjacent jheels. The whistling call ('whee-oh') of the males and the 'pur-r' of the females at once proclaims the presence of widgeon in a flock of wild duck. Male—forehead and crown light buff; head and neck chestnut; back grey, in fine lines of black and white; wing-bar green, edged black; beneath white, neck and breast tinged ruddy; bill leaden blue; feet leaden grey. Female—generally fulvous brown: speculum without the green lustre; beneath as in male; bill and legs blackish grey; length 18½ inches. Does not breed here.

53. *Querquedula crecca.* The Common Teal (Kashmíri, *Keus*). Very great numbers frequent the Kashmír lakes and jheels in winter. The birds begin to arrive in the end of August and remain till spring has commenced. I have observed that early in the season the flocks consist

almost entirely of females of small size, probably young birds, while, later on, the males predominate in every flock. The call is a husky 'quack,' and the male has a short piping whistle chiefly heard when the bird is flying. Does not breed here.

54. *Querquedula circia.* The Blue-winged Teal, or Garganey (Kashmíri, *Kulkilar*). Comparatively rare, although flocks of considerable size may be seen in March and well on into April. I have shot stragglers in February. This teal may be known by the brown head, with white eyebrow prolonged down the sides of the neck, the French-grey wing coverts, and greyish green speculum. Length 15½ inches against 14½ inches in the common teal.

Sub-Family FULIGULINAE. Diving Ducks (with hind toe bordered by a web).

55 *Branta rufina.* The Red-crested Pochard (Kashmíri, *Tur*). This splendid duck is found in large flocks in winter, spending the day on the Wular and visiting favourite jheels at night, remaining there, if not disturbed, till nearly mid-day. The flocks swim in compact order and afford good chances to the punt-gunner. They seem to affect certain jheels where some favourite weed is to be obtained, for which they may be observed diving in rapid succession. Head and silky crest bright chestnut; back brown; beneath black; bill red, the tip white; irides red.

56. *Aythya ferina.* The Red-headed Pochard. Very rare in Kashmír, and I have only shot one or two. *Description*: Male—head and neck chestnut-red, *deeper* than in the *red-crested species*; back, wing-coverts and scapulars white, with numerous fine black lines, giving a general silver-grey effect; rump and tail black; beneath black; abdomen with whitish undulations; bill leaden-grey, tip and base black; irides orange-yellow; legs bluish-grey. Length 19 inches; bill at front 2 inches; tarsus 1½ inches. The female has the head, neck, and upper back reddish-brown; back as in the male, but the lines less distinct; throat and fore-neck white, mixed with reddish; breast reddish-brown, mottled white (Jerdon, vol. iii. p. 812).

57. *Aythya nyroca.* The White-eyed Duck (Kashmíri, *Hárwat*). Very common, and certainly breeds here in considerable numbers. I have seen this duck at all seasons and shot the flappers in August, and also observed old birds, flying with dry grass in their bills, in May, among the sedges near Naidkhai. Flies well and affords very sporting shots, but is generally inferior to the other ducks. Has a rather subdued call. Length 16 inches;

general colour deep brown; wing-bar and abdomen white; bill bluish-grey; irides white; in the young, pale brown.

58. *Fuligula cristata.* The Tufted Duck. Found on the Wular lake and in jheels in winter, generally in small parties and towards the end of the season. I have never observed it in the breeding months. General plumage black above and on neck; breast and belly white: a long, pendant, black crest on the head of the male (generally imperfect in winter): irides yellow; bill leaden.

59. *Erismatura leucocephala.* The White-faced Stiff-tailed Duck. Very rare; six specimens were shot on or near the Wular lake by a sportsman in the hard winter of 1890–1891. Is characterized by the stiff, pointed tail-feathers. Has been shot in the Panjab on one or two occasions.

Family MERGIDAE. Mergansers.

60. *Mergus castor.* The Goosander. I have only seen this handsome bird on the Wular in pairs or small parties in winter. Male—head, crest, and upper neck glossy blackish-green; lower neck white; upper back black; lower back and tail-coverts ashy; tail ashy-grey; breast and abdomen white, glossed orange-buff or salmon-colour; wing-coverts and outer scapulars rich buff-orange; bill deep red, black on the culmen; irides red; feet orange-red: length 26 inches. Female—head and neck reddish-brown; above ashy; throat white; beneath fulvous-white (Jerdon, vol. iii. p. 817).

61. *Mergellus albellus,* The Smew (Kashmíri, *Gagur*). Exists in considerable numbers on the Wular in winter, particularly affecting the bay of Watlab, at the foot of the rocky hill on which the Shukr Din shrine stands, where smews may be seen in scattered flocks. Male—head and occipital crest white, a black patch round the eyes and at base of bill, and another longitudinal one on the occiput; back, lesser wing-coverts and primaries black; beneath all white, with two narrow bands of black across the breast; bill bluish-grey; irides brown; legs leaden; length 16 to 17 inches. Female—head, crest, and occiput reddish-brown; back and tail grey; throat, neck, and abdomen white; bill and legs dark grey; much smaller than the male.

CHAP. V.

Order PELICANIFORMES. Pelicans.

Sub-Order PHALACROCORACES.

Family PHALACROCORAEIDAE. Cormorants.

62. *Graculus sinensis*. The Lesser Cormorant (Kashmíri, *Mung*). Does not breed in Kashmír and is most frequently seen in the migratory seasons, i. e. spring and autumn, either flying in flocks up and down the rivers, sunning itself on some mud-bank or beach, or sitting on trees.

Order ACCIPITRIFORMES. Birds of Prey.

Sub-Order FALCONES.

Family VULTURIDAE. Falcons, Vultures.

63. *Gyps fulvescens*. The Bay Vulture. Common on the mountains, and less so in the valley, unless attracted there by carcases, &c. Vultures are not so common in Kashmír as in India, and this is the species most generally seen.

64. *Gyps indicus*. The Long-billed Brown Vulture. I have observed this vulture occasionally in Kashmír and generally in the neighbourhood of Srinagar. It is not common.

65. *Neophron ginginianus*. The Indian Scavenger Vulture. Tolerably common at Srinagar and the riparian towns of the Jhelum ; rare in the hills and upper glens.

Family FALCONIDAE. Hawks and Falcons.

Sub-Family ACCIPITRINAE.

66. *Circus cyaneus*. The Hen Harrier. Occurs in Kashmír ; it is not so common as in India. The female is much more common than the male.

67. *Circus aeruginosus*. The Marsh Harrier. Is very numerous in winter, generally frequenting lagoons and swamps, where it is a persistent scourge to the wild-fowl, one or two keeping a whole jheel disturbed, teal rising in flocks and suddenly dropping into the reeds for shelter, and mallard being driven hither and thither by the ruthless persecutor. Wounded ducks, lost by sportsmen, are hunted out and devoured, and I have sometimes found this harrier useful in showing where a wounded bird was hidden. The cry is a shrill scream, often uttered when on the wing.

68. *Accipiter nisus.* The European Sparrow Hawk. I have seen a good many of this species from time to time in Kashmír. The female is the 'Básha' of India, and is trained to kill partridges by the natives. Some of the best partridge-ground in Hazara has been spoiled by this sport. Fortunately for the chikor, the Kashmíris are still ignorant of this use of the *Basha*.

Sub-Family BUTEONINAE. Buzzards.

69. *Buteo vulgaris.* The Common Buzzard. I feel to blame for not having put the existence of this bird in Kashmír beyond a doubt. I have constantly seen at Gulmarg and elsewhere in summer a buzzard which may be *B. plumipes.* It nests there, and its peculiar screaming call may often be heard in the pine-forests.

70. *Buteo ferox.* The Long-legged Buzzard, in all stages of plumage, may be found about the valley in October to December. I have not noticed it after the winter snow has fallen.

Sub-Family AQUILINAE. Eagles.

71. *Gypaetus barbatus.* The Laemmergeier. Often seen in the mountains, and in winter among the lower hills, searching for carcases or bones, of which latter it is a great consumer. The Ghoorkhas call it *Haddi Phor*, i.e. 'bone-breaker,' from his habit of carrying a large bone up to a height and then dropping it on rocks to break it. I have seen one do this, but it must be a large bone that the bird cannot dispose of summarily. In the stomach of one that I examined was the entire knee-joint of a large goat, with parts of the tibia and humeral bones, the joint itself *doubled up*, and also several entire good-sized beef-bones: while a young nestling swallowed mutton-chop bones with ease and only choked a little over a leg of mutton-bone garnished with hard gristle. The bright plumage and the magnificent even sweep of its flight make it a feature in any landscape, but, grand as it looks, the bird is a veritable carrion-eater, and its cousinship to the Scavenger *Neophron* is shown in its habit of using rags or old bits of cloth, if obtainable, for its nest, and in the reddish-yellow lining membrane of the egg. The darker specimens are the young birds.

72. *Aquila chrysaetus.* The Golden Eagle. This king of eagles may certainly be included among the Kashmír *Raptores.* It is not common; indeed it is common nowhere, but I have seen it two or three times in the valley in winter and late autumn. It also inhabits Ladákh, and I saw one in the Rupal Nála seated on a rock devouring a Snow-cock (*Tetraogallus*

himalayensis). A season's search among the forest-clad precipices in the mountains would surely show that it breeds here. I have taken the nest in Hazara. It preys on lambs, kids, pheasants and wild-fowl, and small deer would fall easy victims. No other eagle save the Harpy Eagle of America can rival it in strength, size of talons. and destructive power.

73. *Aquila heliaca*. The Imperial Eagle. Is occasionally seen in Kashmír in autumn and winter.

74. *Aquila bifasciata*. The Steppe-Eagle. Is to be seen everywhere, sitting on stocks and trees all over the valley in early winter. I take *A. bifasciata* to be far the most common eagle in Kashmír. It preys on rats. &c., and will not refuse carrion. It is of sluggish habits, and I once saw one pursue a cat, but give up the chase after missing its first stoop. allowing the cat to escape over open ground to its village. I may mention a large, dark coloured eagle I have seen wheeling round cliffs at a great height above me. and which may have been *Neopus malayensis*.

75. *Haliaetus leucoryphus*. Pallas' Sea Eagle. Is pretty common in spring, summer, autumn and winter on the Jhelum and country near the Wular lake. On Christmas Day, 1889, I shot one at Hajun. It was seated on a high chenár-tree, and the plumage indicated that of a young bird. Dr. Leith Adams also noticed the species in Kashmír.

76. *Milvus govinda*. The Common Pariah Kite. Very common at all seasons, and found at all elevations up to 15,000 feet. It devours scraps and refuse, which it often snatches upon the wing, and in spring the village women and children may be heard shouting to scare it from the young chickens. Hume separates, under the name of *M. major*, a large variety found in jungles and lonely spots, and I believe he is right. I have seen this latter kite in Kashmír, generally in the mountains.

Family FALCONIDAE. True Falcons.

77. *Falco peregrinus*. The Peregrine Falcon. I have no facts as to the breeding of this fine falcon in Kashmír, but as I have seen it at all seasons from spring to winter, it may be concluded that it does breed here. I shot a specimen in the Dal lake in November, 1886; he was perched on one of the poles used for fixing the so-called floating garden in its place. This falcon is the 'Bhyri' of India. *F. peregrinator*. the 'Shaheen' of Indian falconers, I have never seen in Kashmír.

78. *Hypotriorchis subbuteo*. The Hobby. I have shot this falcon in

the Wardwán, and seen it in many parts of the country; I fancy that it certainly breeds here, visiting India in the winter.

79. *Hypotriorchis severus.* The Indian Hobby. The only specimen I have seen here was an adult at Sumbal, November 30, 1893, in full autumn plumage.

80. *Cerchneis tinnunculus.* The Kestrel. Is seen occasionally, but not nearly as commonly as in the northern Panjab. Preys on grasshoppers, locusts, field-rats, mice, and lizards.

Sub-Order PANDIONES. Ospreys.

81. *Pandion haliaetus.* The Osprey. Is to be found in Kashmír at various elevations; I have seen it in the Dal lake, on the Jhelum and Sind rivers, and on the Aru branch of the Liddar above Pahlgám. On the Jhelum I saw one opposite Hari Singh Bagh at Srinagar dashing repeatedly at fish in the water, regardless of passing boats.

Sub Order STRIGES. Owls.

Family BUBONIDAE. True Owls.

82. *Bubo bengalensis.* The Rock Horned Owl. Found in the lower rocky hills, such as the Takht-i-Suliman at Srinagar and similar localities throughout the valley, where its deep-toned hoot 'tu-whoo' may be heard at dusk uttered at intervals. Perches on rocks and more rarely on trees. Nests in crannies and on ledges among rocks, laying two or three white eggs: its large size and conspicuous ears often make it look when sitting motionless, more like a large cat than a bird. Eyes very large, bright orange-yellow.

83. *Glaucidium Brodiei.* The Pigmy Collared Owlet. This quaint little owlet, scarcely larger than the silver 'owls' used as 'muffineers' at a dinner table, is, though not so common as in the Indian hills, to be included in the Kashmír Avi-fauna. It is chiefly found on the Pir Panjal side of the valley. It inhabits thick forests and is rarely seen by day; at night its note, a short, deep-toned whistle, repeated twice at intervals, like the words 'tink-tink,' may be heard in the forests.

84. *Asio otus.* The Long-eared Owl. Is rare in Kashmír according to Dr. Jerdon.

85. *Syrnium nivicolum* (perhaps *S. biddulphi*). The Himalayan Wood

Owl. This owl, or one closely resembling it, is found throughout the Kashmír forests from 6,000 to 10,000 feet elevation; it is seldom seen by day, but is everywhere audible at night, and in some places a dozen or more may be heard close to each other. The hooting is varied by a hoarse screeching note, which the shikáris declare to be uttered by the female.

Order CORACIIFORMES. Rollers, Kingfishers, &c.

Sub-Order CORACIAE. Rollers.

86. *Coracias garrula.* The European Roller (Kashmíri, *Nilakraish*). Is fairly common from April to the end of September. I have chiefly noticed it near Islamabad, Kulgám, and in the lower parts of the Sind and Liddar, and in the Loláb and Kamraj. I have never seen *C. indica*, the so-called 'Blue Jay' of India, in Kashmír.

Sub-Order HALCYONES. Kingfishers.

87. *Alcedo bengalensis.* The Common Indian Kingfisher. Very common in all rivers and streams in Kashmír, very tame in its habits, perching on the roofs and prows of boats, often within a few feet of the boat people. Stays all the year round, breeding in holes in river banks. Plumage—head and neck dusky, the feathers edged pale blue; a white patch on the sides of the neck; whole back bright turquoise-blue; wings and tail dusky greenish-blue; some light blue specks on the wing-coverts; beneath bright orange-brown; bill blackish above, orange below; feet orange-red. Length about 6½ to 7 inches.

88. *Ceryle rudis.* The Pied Kingfisher. Common at all seasons in Kashmír. This kingfisher searches for prey on the wing, hovering over the water and then darting down on a fish; other species watch from some fixed station, and drop obliquely on any fish they espy.

Sub-Order UPUPAE. Hoopoes.

89. *Upupa epops.* The European Hoopoe. Exceedingly common in spring and summer; breeds in holes in walls and trees. The nest emits a most abominable, carrion-like stench. The bird is said by Dr. Jerdon to be venerated by Muhammadans on account of its having been a favourite bird of king Solomon, who is said to have employed one as a messenger. The bulk of the hoopoes disappear from Kashmír in autumn, but some certainly hibernate here. I have seen one tempted out by mild

weather which preceded snow in January, and during the severe winter of 1891 I heard one calling faintly at 2 a.m. while a snowstorm was going on; the call seemed to come from some hollow in a neighbouring chenar tree.

Sub-Order MEROPES. Bee-eaters.

90. *Merops apiaster.* The European Bee-eater. Appears in great numbers in the valley in April. After keeping together in flocks and holding counsel for a day or two, they separate to breed, which they do in holes in banks. In August the birds again congregate, and may be seen sitting on telegraph wires. &c., in long lines. The migration commences almost immediately, and by September scarcely a bee-eater is left in the valley. In early September, 1891, I saw a large flock crossing Gulmarg and passing south-west.

Sub-Order CAPRIMULGI. Night-jars.

Apparently no species of Night-jar has been found in the valley up to the present date, and the Hume collection does not contain a specimen. *Caprimulgus unwini* may perhaps be discovered in Kashmír some day.

Sub-Order CYPSELI. Swifts.

91. *Chaetura nudipes.* Hodgson's Spine-tailed Swift. I have several times seen this splendid swift in the mountains, at from 8,000 to 10,000 feet elevation, generally in scattered flocks, wheeling and circling over some high ridge or plateau. Its flight is extraordinarily swift and powerful, and I believe that no other bird can equal the velocity it maintains in the air. One instant the flock is dashing round your head. and the next it is out of sight beyond some distant peak: suddenly again you hear the rush of wings. and the birds are wheeling round you again, and a quick—very quick—shot may secure a specimen. To prevent confusion with the next species, found in similar places but not equalling it in flight, I note plumage as follows:—head, nape, upper tail-coverts, rump, wings and tail black, with a blue-green gloss; back whity-brown, palest in the middle; chin, throat and neck white; lower neck, breast and belly sooty-brown; bill black; feet livid purple; irides brown. Length 8½ inches; expanse of wings 20 to 21 inches; tail feathers ending in rigid spines.

92. *Cypselus melba.* The Alpine Swift. Found on the Kashmír mountains. Of fast and powerful flight, but not equalling *C. nudipes.* Above wood-brown, glossed purple; beneath white; a wide pectoral band of brown. Length 9 inches; expanse 19 inches.

93. *Cypselus pekinensis.* The Pallid Swift. Adams says this swift is common in Kashmír, frequenting rocky streams, and I have seen it myself in various localities. Other swifts likely to occur in Kashmír are:—

C. affinis. The Common Indian Swift.

C. leuconyx. The White-clawed Swift.

Collocalia brevirostris. The Indian Edible-nest Swiftlet.

All these have been obtained in Hazara, and may be found at any time to visit Kashmír—a good problem to work out!

Order COCCYGES. Cuckoos.

In treating of this Family the following excerpt from Dr. Jerdon's famous work may be of interest. Speaking of their well-known habit of laying their eggs in the nests of other birds, and of the young Cuckoo ejecting his foster-brethren from the nest, he remarks:—

'The cause of this peculiar habit is supposed to be that the eggs of the cuckoo are matured very slowly, and that she requires an interval of several days to elapse between the laying of each egg, and the young too require to be fed longer than the young of other birds, which circumstances combined would make it difficult for her to incubate her own eggs and rear the brood. It may be that from want of intelligence she is unable to construct a nest. The low development of the parts subservient to generation, the small eggs of some, and a weakening of the parental impulses which is likely to accompany this, have been supposed to afford an explanation of their peculiar habits.'

94. *Cuculus canorus.* The European Cuckoo (Kashmíri, *Shakuk* or *Kuku*). Is a regular visitant to Kashmír, arriving in May, though rarely seen in the valley proper; the side valleys, lower slopes, and forests, shelter great numbers, while they ascend to a considerable elevation, and I have seen them in numbers on the crest of a pass over 13,000 feet high, with nought but snow and rock around, calling and answering each other as they flew and perched among the crags.

The cuckoo seems to take some little time to find his voice after arriving in the spring. and I have watched one practising and only able to utter a hoarse monosyllabic note.

95. A cuckoo which I have never shot, but which I believe belongs to the genus *Hicrococcyx*, is common in May, June and July, and in all the mountain Nalas. I have seen it in the Sind, Liddar, Wardwan, and elsewhere. The general colour is a brownish-ashy, and M. H. Dauvergne, who shot one many years ago, describes the head and back as fulvous;

wings umber-brown, beneath white; tail barred black and white in ovate stripes.

It is a very noisy bird, calling day and night, and the cry becomes a great nuisance in camp. The call is composed of six notes, running up in crescendo and down again, each group of six notes being repeated four or five times in a low key rising to a high one, and then falling to a lower tone at the end, thus 'chap, chap, chap, chap, chap, chap, cheep, cheep, cheep. cheep, cheep, cheep, choop, choop, choop, choop, choop, choop.' I shall take the first opportunity of identifying this species. It may possibly prove to be *Cuculus intermedius*, of which a specimen from Ruttun Pir is in the Hume collection.

96. *Coccystes jacobinus*. The Pied Crested Cuckoo. This cuckoo is found, though not very commonly, in the valley in summer. It does not ascend to high elevations. Its loud, whistling call is most often heard at the commencement of the rainy season in July.

Order SCANSORES. Climbing Birds.

Sub-Order CAPITONES. Barbets.

I have often been surprised at never finding a single representative of the Barbets in Kashmír.

Order PICIFORMES. Woodpeckers.

Sub-Family PICINAE. True Woodpeckers.

97. *Dendrocopus himalayensis*. The Himalayan Pied Woodpecker. Pretty common in all Kashmír forests up to 9,000 feet elevation. Adams mentions a woodpecker in Kashmír, which had the head white, neck and breast bluish-black, belly and vent red (possibly the 'White-cheeked Nuthatch,' *Sitta leucopsis*). *D. himalayensis* is the only one of the pied woodpeckers I have seen here. *D. brunneifrons* must also occur in the valley, and *Jyngipicus nanus* has been procured by Capt. Stackhouse Pimrill at Dharmzala.

98. *Gecinus squamatus*. The Scaly-bellied Green Woodpecker. Seen at various elevations from the mountain forests to the groves near Srinagar; has a loud, cackling call. This is the only *Gecinus* that I have observed, but its relation, *G. occipitalis*, the Black-naped Green Woodpecker, is also doubtless to be found in the Kashmír forests.

Sub-Family JYNGINAE. Wrynecks.

99. *Jynx torquilla.* The Common Wryneck. Is pretty frequent in Kashmír in spring and summer. I have seen it in the Munshi bagh, in many parts of the valley, and in several of the side Nalas, though never at any great elevation.

Order PSITTACIFORMES. Parrots.

100. *Palacornis schisticeps.* The Slaty-headed Parrakeet. This is the only parrot I have seen in Kashmír, and it is not very common. The Pir-Panjal side of the valley probably holds most, but I have seen it in the Sind and Liddar glens, and in autumn it plunders the walnut groves at Atawat, and it has been shot in the Loḷáb. Breeds in holes in trees and has a cheerful, pleasant note, enlivening the woodland corries it frequents. The slaty blue on the head comes after the first moult. It is easily tamed and is gentle and affectionate; one I brought up would follow me round the garden, climb up my clothes, and sit on my shoulder. He learnt to talk in a few months, practising when alone. and it was only by accident I found out the proficiency at which he had arrived. I have never seen it in Kashmír later than October. General plumage green, tail blue and yellow.

Order PASSERIFORMES. Perching Birds.

Family CORVIDAE. Crows.

101. *Corvus corax.* The European Raven. True ravens are rare in Kashmír, and I conclude that the few seen must be of this species. I had always thought that *C. tibetanus*, the Tibet Raven, must be the one we see here; but I am now informed on good authority that the Tibet Raven only arrives at Leh during the autumn, from the high plateaux of Tibet (where it breeds and passes the summer), and that it is never known to come from the direction of Kashmír. The bird we have here, therefore, must be *C. corax*, which is very common in the north Panjab in winter.

102. *Corone Corone.* The European Carrion Crow. May be seen on the 'jheels' near the Wular lake in the winter, together with his poaching *confrère* the Hooded Crow, *C. sharpii*, both, probably, on the look out for wounded wild-fowl.

103. *Corone sharpii.* The Eastern Hooded Crow. Is found as above stated. Both species are more common in Kashmír than in the Panjab, where they are looked on as a great prize by collectors. Dr. Bowdler

Sharpe, of the British Museum, states that in Scotland and other places in Europe the two species of crows interbreed, and the young are patterned like the Hooded Crow, but are smudged with black on the mantles and breast. Both have the same peculiar, rather shrill 'caw.'

104. *Corone macrorhyncha.* The Jungle Crow. Very common in the forests and mountain margs. Round one's camp his hoarse voice is ever present, he is always 'in at the death' of a stag or bear, and I believe he will follow a stalk in hope of profiting by the result. In the cooler months he may be found round towns and villages in the valley. One once carried off out of a cage a young blackbird (*Merula castanea*), which I had found away from its nest, and was trying to rear. *Corvus intermedius*, Adams, has been described as 'smaller than *C. corone* and not larger than the Indian Jackdaw (*C. splendens*), abundant on the mountains round the valley of Kashmír.' I have not observed it in Kashmír myself, and Oates unites *C. intermedius* with *C. macrorhynchus.*

105. *Corone splendens.* The Indian House-Crow. This well-known pest, with his thoroughly inappropriate Latin title, is, unfortunately, much more common at Srinagar and the towns on the Jhelum now than formerly, and has thus obtained a right to a place among the birds of Kashmír.

106. *Trypanocorax frugilegus.* The Rook. May generally be seen feeding in flocks in the fields in autumn and early winter. Later on it makes its way to Hazara and the Northern Panjab, where immense numbers congregate in winter. I do not believe that it breeds here.

107. *Colocus collaris.* The White-necked Jackdaw. Very common indeed all over the valley. Breeds in holes in trees, walls, &c. The eggs are pale blue-green, with dark brown spots, and are capital eating. I have seen them served in mistake for plover's eggs at a garden-party in Srinagar. Roosts in great numbers in the palace at Srinagar, the island on the Wular lake, and elsewhere. Some must migrate to the North Panjab, where large flocks are seen in the winter.

108. *Nucifraga multipunctata.* The Many Spotted Nutcracker. Is very common in the Kashmíri forests, generally seen singly, but sometimes in groups of two or three; has a loud, harsh, grating cry, constantly repeated; frequents the tops of pine trees. It seems to have a good deal of curiosity in its composition, hanging round the spot where it sees any one sitting quietly in the forest, watching, and uttering its discordant cry.

Oates records the Himalayan Jay (*Garrulus bispecularis*) from Eastern

CHAP. V. Kashmír, but neither of the two species of jays found in the Himalayas have ever, to my knowledge, been seen in Kashmír. I will therefore pass on to the genus *Urocissa*, which is allied to them.

109. *Urocissa cucullata.* The Yellow-billed Blue Magpie. This handsome bird, with its blue and white plumage, and long tail-feathers, is pretty common in the Kashmír forests, up to 7,000 or 8,000 feet elevation. It has a loud, ringing call, often repeated. Once when I was waiting over a goat that had been killed by a bear, two blue magpies kept up an incessant chattering over a thicket close by, from which, when it grew darker, the bear walked out straight up to the carcase. No doubt the magpies had watched him from the first.

110. *Pica Pica.* The Magpie. 'Said by Biddulph to be at all times common in Kashmír.' He found its nest on two occasions (cf. Oates, *Faun. Brit. Ind. Birds*, i. p. 25).

111. *Dendrocitta rufa.* The Common Indian Magpie. Is fairly common in the valley, frequenting groves and gardens. I have generally seen it in autumn. It has a great variety of notes, some harsh, and others softer, clear, and metallic.

Sub-Family FREGILINAE. Choughs.

112. *Graculus Graculus.* The Red-billed Chough. Is common on the higher mountains, generally above the forest line, in flocks and detached parties; has a clear resonant call. Plumage black; bill and feet bright red, which characters distinguish it from the next species. Some migrate to the plains in winter.

113. *Pyrrhocorax Pyrrhocorax.* The Alpine Chough. Is found in similar localities to the above species, and the two may be seen on the same hill-side. It occasionally descends to the lower valleys, and the natives say that it eats mulberries; but as a rule it remains at high elevations. Is found in Europe on the Alps and Apennines (Jerdon, vol. ii. p. 370). Glossy black; bill yellow; feet bright red. Call, much the same as that of the Red-billed species. Kashmír shikáris say that these two choughs are 'Halál' as food.

Family STURNIDAE. Starlings.

114. *Sturnus humii.* The Himalayan Starling (Kashmíri, *Tsinihagoor*). Found all over the valley, breeding in holes of trees, buildings, &c. Eggs pale azure blue. Out of the breeding season large flocks congregate to

roost in trees near swamps. A number remain in the winter, but there is a large migration to India at that season. Plumage glossy black with a pale whity-brown tip to each feather; feathers of back lanceolate. Young bird dull brown; bill brown at first, changing to yellow in the breeding season. Legs yellow-brown. Length about 9 inches, wings 5 inches, tail 3 inches.

115. *Sturnus porphyronotus.* The Central-Asian Starling. Has the rump reddish like the back. The wing is coppery bronze, and is over five inches in length. A specimen is in the British Museum from Kashmír, and doubtless the species migrates to India through the valley, with other species of starlings (cf. Oates, *Faun. Brit. Ind. Birds*, i. p. 521).

116. *Sturnus menzbieri.* The Common Indian Starling. Distinguished by having a purple head, purple ear-coverts, and a purple throat. Breeds in Siberia, and winters plentifully in India. Hume believes that it breeds also in Kashmír, and specimens in his collection from our country show that it either nests or at least passes through on migration.

117. *Acridotheres tristis.* The Common Myna. Very common in the valley, not ascending the higher glens.

Family DICRURIDAE. Drongos.

118. *Dicrurus longicaudatus.* The Indian Ashy-Drongo. Dr. Adams says that this species is common in Kashmír, where he has often found the nest. It is not, in my opinion, very common, and is rare in the valley proper. The side valleys and lower forests contain a good many. It may be known by its close general resemblance to the well-known King-crow (*Dicrurus ater*) of India, from which it differs in not having the white spot at the gape.

Family ORIOLIDAE. Orioles.

119. *Oriolus kundoo.* The Indian Oriole, 'Mango bird' of India, *Poshnal* of Kashmír. Arrives here at the end of April and remains throughout the summer. Its rich yellow and black colouring, and pleasant, mellow whistle are easily recognizable. I have seen it up to about 7,000 feet elevation. Builds in trees, suspending or binding its nest in a fork; eggs, three or four, white with dark spots. The nest is most ingeniously fixed with strips of rag, long grass, and twine, &c., worked in and out and bound round the supporting branch.

Family FRINGILLIDAE. Finches.

120. *Pycnorhamphus icterioides.* The Black and Yellow Grosbeak. Common in the forests up to 9,000 feet or higher. Has a short sharp twittering call, often repeated. Male—head, neck, wings, and tail black, rest of plumage bright yellow. Female—olivaceous grey, rump. quills, and tail black; bill pale greenish-yellow, thick and massive, 1 inch long at front. Length 9 inches.

121. *Mycerobas melanoxanthus.* The Spotted-winged Grosbeak. Male—head and entire upper parts dull slaty black, beneath pale yellow, a conspicuous white wing-spot. Female—smaller, upper parts as in the male, but a yellow eyebrow and some pale yellow on head and back, also on cheeks; beneath yellow spotted with black; general appearance, more spotted than in the male.

The bill is enormously thick. as deep as long, plumbeous in colour. Length of bird 8½ inches. Is found in our Kashmír forests, but much rarer than the last species. Frequents the tops of the highest trees, and has a plaintive clear whistle, audible from a considerable distance, and also a sort of chattering note. Is very fond of the fruit of the bird-cherry, the stones of which it cracks.

122. *Pyrrhula aurantiaca.* The Orange Bullfinch. This charming bird is well represented in some parts of Kashmír. I have seen it in the Wardwan, in Wangat, in the Bandipura glen, in woods just across the Sát Saran Pass, and most numerously at Sonamarg. Male—reddish orange, with black wings, face, and tail, white tail-coverts. Female—ashy and black. Has a sweet soft whistle, also a pleasant chirrup. Is very tame, sitting close to one on a tree, and feeding at the door of one's tent. On one occasion, while having a 'chota hazari' before sunrise, two or three quite entered my tent and hopped about close to my feet.

123. *Pyrrhula erythrocephala.* The Red-headed Bullfinch. Found in Southern Kashmír (cf. Oates, *Faun. Brit. Ind. Birds*, i. p. 205).

124. *Propasser rhodochrous.* The Pink-browed Rose Finch. Has been found at Dharmsála (cf. Oates, t. c. p. 217). Breeds at high altitudes, and descends in winter to lower elevations.

125. *Carpodacus erythrinus.* The Common Rose Finch. Is not uncommon in Kashmír, frequenting fields, groves, and cultivation. General plumage brown, tinged ruddy; head, *throat, breast, and rump*, rosy crimson.

126. *Carduelis caniceps.* The Himalayan Goldfinch (Kashmíri, *Séra*). Found in flocks in the valley in spring and winter, and in the higher glens in summer. I found the nest on the Takht-i-Suliman in May, placed on the ground under the edge of a stone. It was made of grass and moss, lined with fine grass and hair, and contained five eggs, ashy-white, lined and mottled with purplish-dusky. Has a pleasant note and is easily tamed.

127. *Hypacanthis spinoides.* The Himalayan Greenfinch. Plumage yellow and olive-brown. Is seen in flocks in all mountain glens, and near woods and cultivation. Is not so common in the valley proper as the Goldfinch.

128 *Collacanthis Burtoni.* The Red-browed Finch. I have seen this species at Gulmarg, in the Sind valley, Bandipura, and elsewhere, always in fir forests, and at from 8,000 to 10,000 feet elevation, and have examined it carefully through a glass at from 10 to 50 yards' distance, on several occasions, and seen it feeding on the ground within a few feet of my tent door. It is a bird of quiet habits, and I have not heard its note; it associates in small flocks of four to six, but is sometimes seen in pairs. Found in June, July, August, and October. The Kashmíris say that it comes lower down in winter, but I have never seen it out of the upper forests.

129. *Metoponia pusilla.* The Gold-fronted Finch. Breeds in Kashmír at heights of from 5,000 to 10,000 feet, according to season (cf. Oates, t. c. p. 231). It may be found in the valley in winter.

130. *Passer indicus.* The Indian House-Sparrow. Very common and familiar all over the valley. Differs only from the European house-sparrow in its purer colours.

131. *Passer cinnamomeus.* The Cinnamon Tree-Sparrow. Found round mountain hamlets, in tree copses, and forest glades up to quite 9,000 feet elevation, and often quite away from the haunts of man. It is much quieter than *P. indicus.* and is seen in fewer numbers. General plumage above cinnamon rufous; some dark marks on back; a black patch on throat; beneath yellowish light-grey. Length 5¼ inches.

Sub-Family EMBERIZINAE. Buntings.

132. *Emberiza leucocephala.* The Pine Bunting. Found in Kashmír in winter. but not so common as the next species: elevation 6,000 to

9,000 feet. The top of the head is white in the male, greyish in the female. Jerdon gives the length at 6 to 6½ inches. I found a male to measure 7½ inches.

133. *Emberiza Stracheyi.* The Eastern Meadow Bunting. Very common in Kashmír. Frequents open bushy ground, edges of woods, and cultivation, &c.; elevation 5,500 to 9,000 feet.

134. *Emberiza Stewarti.* The White-capped Bunting. Common in the valley, about fields and bushes, and in the mountains up to 9,000 feet.

135. *Emberiza arcuata.* The Kashmír Grey-headed Bunting. Frequents bushes, fields, and open lands. I obtained it in the Nowboog Valley, and have seen it elsewhere in Kashmír.

Family ALAUDIDAE. Larks.

136. *Ammomanes phaenicuroides.* The Desert Finch Lark. Is found in the Kashmír Valley and on open slopes at the base of the hills. Length about 6 inches. Feet yellow-brown. Theobald records it.

137. *Melanocorypha bimaculata.* The Eastern Calandra Lark. (*Jall* in Kashmíri.) Bill convex, very stout; length about 7½ inches, wing 4¾ inches, tail 4½ inches (Jerdon's *Birds of India*, vol. ii. p. 427). General plumage lark-like, lighter underneath, with a conspicuous black-brown crescent-shaped mark on the upper breast. Has a very sweet song, and is kept caged by natives as a song-bird. Stated to be numerous in the valley in winter, when the natives catch them in snow-time by placing a piece of matting on the snow with some rice spread on it. The larks descend to eat the rice, and are caught in horsehair nooses which are secured to the matting. A newly-caught bird sells for two to four annas, but a well-trained songster will fetch ten or twelve British rupees. My informant mentioned a Pathan who refused fifty shillings for a 'Jall' he had brought from Ghuznee. The bird's voice is improved by feeding him on a pulse pounded up in 'ghee.' In summer the birds retire to more northern localities to breed.

138. *Otocoris longirostris.* The Long-billed Horned Lark. I have not myself noticed this lark in Kashmír, but it is found on the higher elevations.

139. *Alauda gulgula.* The Indian Skylark (*Dedar* of Kashmír). Very abundant in the valley in spring, summer, and autumn. Its general aspect

and song are well known. Is kept by the natives as a song-bird. I once timed a lark as it sprang from the ground and soared singing upward till almost out of sight. From the start till the return to the ground the time occupied was fifteen minutes; a wonderful muscular and vocal effort for such a small bird.

Family MOTACILLIDAE. Wagtails.

140. *Motacilla Hodgsoni.* Hodgson's Pied Wagtail. This I believe to be the species which is very common in Kashmír both in summer and winter. In the latter season they collect in small flocks to rout in the grass and reeds of some quiet swamp or pool. *M. personata* and *M. alba* doubtless pass through on migration.

141. *Motacilla melanope.* The Grey Wagtail. More common in the hills than the last species. I have seen it up to 8,000 feet, and also in the valley.

142. *Motacilla beema.* The Indian Blue-headed Wagtail. Passes through Kashmír on migration (cf. Oates, t. c. p. 297).

143. *Motacilla citeoloides.* Hodgson's Yellow-headed Wagtail. Very common on the weedy lakes and swamps in Kashmír, where it may be seen running over the water-lily leaves, &c.: also frequents marshy streams and ditches. Its yellow and black summer plumage makes it easily distinguishable.

144. *Anthus similis.* The Brown Rock Pipit. Obtained on the open slopes at the foot of the hills near Pandratan on May 23, 1894. The general colouring and dimensions, the arrangement of the quills, and the oblique tipping of the outermost tail-feathers, together with the well-curved hind claw, correspond almost exactly with Jerdon's description of *A. sordida* (*Birds of India*, vol. ii. p. 236), but the bill seemed to be one-fifth to one-fourth of an inch longer. Blyth got it in the N.W. Himalayas, and Mr. Theobald found it in the Alpine Panjáb, and we may now assign it a place among Kashmír birds. Shot at about 5,300 feet elevation. Length 8 in., wing $3\frac{3}{4}$ in., tail $3\frac{1}{4}$ in., bill at front $\frac{1}{2}$ in. to $\frac{5}{8}$ in., tarsus $1\frac{1}{4}$ in., hind toe and claw $\frac{15}{16}$ in., first primary minute, second, third, fourth and fifth quills subequal and longest.

145. *Anthus rosaceus.* Hodgson's Pipit. Found on the lower slopes of the Himalayas from Kashmír to Assam (cf. Oates, t. c. p. 311).

CHAP. V.

Family CERTHIIDAE. Creepers.

146. *Certhia himalayana*. The Himalayan Tree-creeper. Is common in the forests, and in spring and autumn may be seen in groves and orchards in the valley and in the higher forests.

147. *Certhia Hodgsoni*. Hodgson's Tree-creeper. Occurs sparingly in the pine-woods near the snows (cf. Oates, op. cit. i. p. 330).

148. *Tichodroma muraria*. The Wall-creeper. Is often seen in Kashmír in autumn and winter. I have not observed it in summer. Frequents rocky hill sides, clay banks and cliffs. Its bright crimson wing-patch, only seen when the bird is flying, makes it very beautiful as it flits from rock to rock. Feeds on insects.

149. *Sitta leucopsis*. The White-cheeked Nuthatch. Is very common in the mountain forests, frequenting the tops of the highest firs and pines. Its cry, resembling the bleat of a small kid, is one of the commonest sounds in a Kashmír forest.

150. *Sitta cashmiriensis*. Brooks' Nuthatch. Is also found in Kashmír, though not so often as the species above noted.

Family PARIDAE. Titmice.

151. *Lophophanes dichrous*. The Crested Brown Tit. Adams obtained it and entered it in his list of the Birds of Kashmír.

152. *Lophophanes melanolophus*. The Crested Black Tit. Adams records it, and I have seen it myself in the Kashmír forests.

153. *Parus atriceps*. The Indian Grey Tit. Common; is sometimes very tame. While staying at Gulmarg in 1890 with a friend, one frequented our mess-tent, coming close to the breakfast-table and eating small crumbs, and roosting at night under the fringe of the pardah, inside the tent, without minding the lamps, talking at dinner, &c.

154. *Parus monticola*. The Green-backed Tit. Throughout the Himalayas from Kashmír to Bhutan (cf. Oates, op. cit. i. p. 50).

155. *Aegithaliscus niveigularis*. The White-throated Tit. 'I have examined specimens obtained at Gulmarg' (Oates, t. c. p. 52).

156. *Sylviparus modestus*. The Yellow-browed Tit. 'Throughout the Himalayas from Kashmír to Bhutan' (Oates, t. c. p. 54).

Sub-Family LANIIDAE. True Shrikes.

157. *Lanius erythronotus.* The Rufous-backed Shrike. Is the only true shrike I have seen here. It arrives at the end of March, disappearing again in autumn; ascends to about 6,500 feet. It is a wonderful mocking bird; I have heard it imitate the Black Partridge, Kestrel, Reed-Warbler, Wattled Lapwing, and Skylark most successfully.

Family SYLVIIDAE.

158. *Acrocephalus stentoreus.* The Indian Great Reed-Warbler (Kashmíri, *Karkat*). Is very numerous in the long reeds in the lakes, and along the banks of rivers where tall grass or weeds exist, from April to August; has a harsh note, 'Prit, Prit, Pritik,' continually repeated.

159. *Tribura major.* The Large-billed Bush-Warbler. In summer this species is found throughout Kashmír (cf. Oates, op. cit. i. p. 363).

160. *Sylvia althaea.* Hume's Lesser White-throated Warbler. Breeds in Kashmír at an elevation of 9,000 feet, and winters in the plains of India.

161. *Sylvia affinis.* The Indian Lesser White-throated Warbler. Brooks found this Warbler breeding in Kashmír at a height of from 5,500 to 6,000 feet amongst small bushes in May by the side of rivers (cf. Oates, t. c. p. 398).

162. *Phylloscopus Tytleri.* Tytler's Willow-Warbler. Summers in the higher elevations of the Himalayas, from Kashmír to Kumaon. Winters in the lower portions of the same mountains, and also descends into the Peninsula (cf. Oates, t. c. p. 402).

163. *Phylloscopus tristis.* The Brown Willow-Warbler. Summers in the higher portions of the Himalayas in Kashmír (cf. Oates, t. c. p. 403).

164. *Phylloscopus indicus.* The Olivaceous Willow-Warbler. Breeds in Kashmír, visiting the plains in winter (cf. Oates, t. c. p. 404).

165. *Phylloscopus subviridis.* Brooks' Willow-Warbler. Breeds in Kashmír (cf. Oates, t. c. p. 409).

166. *Acanthopneuste nitida.* The Green Willow-Warbler. Probably breeds in Kashmír. Winters in the Indian Peninsula (cf. Oates, t. c. p. 413).

167. *Acanthopneuste trochiloides.* Blyth's Crowned Willow-Warbler. Observed in summer in the Himalayas from Kashmír to Sikhim, and probably wintering in the lower valleys (cf. Oates, t. c. p. 419).

168. *Cryptolopha xanthoschista.* Hodgson's Grey-headed Flycatcher Warbler. From Nepal to Kashmír (cf. Oates, t. c. p. 425). Pretty common in woods and copses in the forests up to 8,000 feet.

169. *Horornis pallidus.* The Pale Bush-Warbler. Breeds in Kashmír (cf. Oates, t. c. p. 437).

170. *Suya crinigera.* The Brown Hill-Warbler. Occurs throughout the Himalayas from Kashmír to Bhutan (cf. Oates, t. c. p. 445).

171. *Prinia inornata.* The Indian Wren-Warbler. Is said to occur in the valley.

Family TURDIDAE. Thrushes.

172. *Henicurus maculatus.* The Spotted Fork-tail. Is pretty common on smaller hill streams in Kashmír, particularly on those with wooded banks and occasional waterfalls. General plumage spotted black and white. Very conspicuous as it flits in front of you up the bed of a watercourse, uttering its pleasant, clear, metallic whistle of one note. Length 10 inches.

173. *Microcichla Scouleri.* The Little Fork-tail. Seen on the larger streams; not so common as *H. maculatus.* Jerdon states that it often contends with the Plumbeous Water-Robin, *Rhyacornis fuliginosa*, for a choice perch on a rock, and is generally vanquished by the latter. I can vouch for this from personal observation.

174. *Pratincola maura.* The India Bush-Chat. Common in spring and summer in the valley, and on the lower slopes; goes to India in winter.

175. *Saxicola montana.* Gould's Wheatear. Found in summer on open plateaux, at from 7,000 to 9,000 feet elevation; not very common.

176. *Rhyacornis fuliginosa.* The Plumbeous Redstart. The name explains the colour of this little fellow. He has a rusty red tail which he expands and flirts while sitting on a rock in some roaring hill torrent. He is common on all mountain streams up to 7,000 feet elevation, and is very pugnacious in defending a favourite rock against other intruders.

177. *Chimorrornis leucocephala.* The White-capped Redstart. Also

very universal on Kashmír streams and torrents. The handsome plumage of black and rich chestnut with the white cap make it easily identified. It is very restless, flitting from rock to rock over the water and constantly uttering a short, clear, metallic whistle.

178. *Ruticilla frontalis.* The Blue-fronted Redstart. From Gilgit and Kashmír to Assam (cf. Oates, t. c. p. 92).

179. *Ruticilla erythronota.* Eversmann's Redstart. A winter visitor to every portion of Kashmír (cf. Oates, t. c. p. 94).

180. *Ianthia rufilata.* The Red-flanked Bush-Robin. Found in the forests up to 7,000 or 8,000 feet. Blue above, bright rufous beneath, with white eyebrow. Not very common.

181. *Cyanecula suecica.* The Indian Bluethroat. I have seen this bird at the end of March and in April. Its quiet, pale brown plumage is prettily relieved by the bright sky-blue on the throat and upper breast; it frequents low shrubs and bushes at the foot of the lower hills. The female has the breast dull white with some darkish spots edging it.

182. *Tharrhaleus Jerdoni.* Jerdon's Accentor. Has been found breeding near Sonamarg by Capt. Cock, and is probably found in many districts of Kashmír.

There are doubtless other species of Accentors to be found in Kashmír, as several occur in Gilgit.

183. *Petrophila cyanus.* The Blue Rock Thrush. I have seen this rock thrush pretty often on low rocky hills in summer. A pair or two are generally to be seen on the Takht-i-Suliman at Srínagar, where I am certain that they breed, though I never, after patient watching, was able to find their nest. Disappears from Kashmír in winter.

184. *Petrophila cinclorhyncha.* The Blue-headed Rock Thrush. I have only seen this thrush at Palgám in the Liddar valley, where it frequented a pine wood in which I was camped during May, June, and July.

185. *Merula unicolor.* The Dusky Ground Thrush ('The Song Thrush of Kashmír,' Adams; Kashmíri, *Kao kumr*). Is very common all over the valley, frequenting chenar groves, gardens, &c. The song may be heard from April till July, and the bird seen hopping on the turf in search of worms, &c. It sings at all hours of the day, and particularly in the morning and evening, and on cloudy days with rain impending. Adams

 compares the note to that of the blackbird but it is far more like that of the English thrush (*Turdus musicus*), though less full and varied.

186. *Merula maxima.* The Central Asian Blackbird. 'I have examined specimens of this blackbird from Kashmír' (Oates, t. c. p. 124).

187. *Merula boulboul.* The Grey-winged Blackbird. Is rare in Kashmír: called *Kastura* by natives. It has a full rich melodious song, very like that of the English blackbird, to which it has a great resemblance, excepting in the grey bar it possesses on the quills and greater wing-coverts; it fetches a high price as a song-bird.

188. *Merula castanea.* The Grey-headed Ouzel. This handsome thrush is fairly common, especially in the hills on the south and south-east side of the valley. The song is uttered generally in the evening, as the bird sits on the summit of some tall fir-tree, and is very charming, being the nearest Himalayan resemblance to the note of our English song-thrush. The bird being apparently little known to Englishmen in Kashmír, I give a short description. Male—head ashy white, darker on crown, lighter on throat and neck; general colour light chestnut or rufous, darker on back and brighter below; wings and tail blackish. The female has colours less intense and more brownish, chin and throat nearly white; bill, eyelids, and legs yellow; length 10½ inches. Is found in summer at Gulmarg, and I have heard it singing at Dandwár in early April, while the snow yet lay deep in the forests. Breeds in May and June, often placing the nest in the lower branches of a (Budil) fir-tree (*Abies Webbiana*). Lays four or five eggs, greenish blue, thickly mottled with brown.

189. *Merula atrogularis.* The Black-throated Ouzel. Quite common in early spring, in the valley and willow groves and orchards, and again in late autumn about low hills with bushy jungle. Also in early autumn in the upper hill forests. I have never seen it in summer, and know not where it breeds. I have seen it occasionally in winter.

190. *Turdus pilaris.* The Fieldfare. Is tolerably common in the forests, and I have seen it, in flocks of twenty or more, above the forest level, perching on rocks, also round the skirts of open 'margs' and forest clearings. Is generally shy and wary, and may be known by its low, husky note, 'Tirr–r,' repeated as it flies from tree to tree. It is very good eating. Adams records it in Kashmír. I have only seen it in summer and autumn in the hills.

191. *Myiophonus Temminckii.* The Yellow-billed Whistling Thrush.

Common on hill streams, and about copses and gardens, &c. Has a loud, clear, musical whistle, and shares with *Merula boulboul* the name of *Kastura* among the natives. It is sometimes called 'Blackbird' by Englishmen. Colour black, with a smalt-blue gloss. Nests on rocks overhanging some roaring torrent, and under bridges, breeding in May and June. Migrates to the lower Indian hills in winter. I have heard it sing at all seasons of the year.

Family CINCLIDAE. Dippers.

192. *Cinclus asiaticus*. The Brown Dipper. Found along running streams, flying along their courses. It plunges into the water or sometimes walks in deliberately and remains below the surface for some time searching for larvae and water insects. Is found at lower elevations than the next species.

193. *Cinclus kashmiriensis*. The White-breasted Asiatic Dipper. Jerdon writes: 'This bird is only found in the streams of the higher mountain ranges in Kashmír, whence it was brought by Dr. Adams.' I have seen it in such localities. Once, on reaching the edge of a small tarn lying at the eastern foot of the 'Kotwal' peak, over 14,000 feet elevation, I saw the water circling as if a fish had just risen, and while I was watching for another rise, a Dipper emerged and, seeing me, flew off down the little stream which runs from the lake down-hill towards Boorphrao in the Sind valley.

Family TROGLODYTIDAE. Wrens.

194. *Anorthura neglecta*. The Kashmír Wren. Adams saw this species 'among stony places, in glens, and round the margins of avalanches on the Kashmír ranges; common.' I have seen the bird in lower localities, in bushes and low scrub, &c. It is very like the English wren in its ways.

Family TIMELIIDAE. Babbling Thrushes.

195. *Trochalopteron simile*. The Western Variegated Laughing Thrush. It is tolerably common up to 7,000 or 8,000 feet, frequenting bushy coverts and copses on the edges of forests. Has a noisy but cheerful whistling note, often repeated.

196. *Ianthocincla rufogularis*. The Rufous-chinned Laughing Thrush. Found in hill-side thickets and woods in Kashmír up to 8,000 or 9,000 feet. Has a low chattering note, much uttered just before it roosts for the night.

197. *Trochalopteron lineatum*. The Streaked Laughing Thrush.

 Common in Kashmír, in gardens, &c., and in bushy hill-sides. Remains here in winter.

Family PYCNONOTIDAE. Bulbuls.

198. *Otocompsa leucogenys.* The White-cheeked Crested Bulbul. A permanent resident in the valley. but not ascending the higher glens. Very common and exceedingly tame and impudent, entering boats and houses freely. I have seen one perch on the sugar-basin and steal the sugar within a couple of feet of me. Nests in low trees or bushes; eggs white, with purplish speckles. It is a great pest in gardens and orchards, destroying buds and fruit.

Family CAMPOPHAGIDAE. Cuckoo-Shrikes.

199. *Pericrocotus brevirostris.* The Short-billed Minivet ('Raja bird' of Europeans in India). It is often seen in the hill forests, and sometimes at lower elevations, flying from tree to tree in flocks, where the bright scarlet and black of the males and yellow and grey of the females show most brilliantly in the sunlight. Has a pleasant, low-toned, twittering note. Migrates to the plains and lower hills in winter.

Family MUSCICAPIDAE. Flycatchers.

200. *Stoparola melanops.* The Verditer Flycatcher. Is found occasionally in wooded glens and groves. Its light blue colouring is very conspicuous.

201. *Hemichelidon sibirica.* The Sooty Flycatcher. Permanent resident in Kashmír, breeding in June.

202. *Siphia hyperythra.* The Indian Red-breasted Flycatcher. Spends the summer in Kashmír, and winters in Ceylon.

203. *Cyornis leucomelanurus.* The Slaty-blue Flycatcher. Breeds in Kashmír in the beginning of June, when the nest was found by Brooks.

204. *Cyornis superciliaris.* The White-browed Blue Flycatcher. Is by no means common, generally seen in woods and copses, at about 6,000 to 8,000 feet elevation; it is inclined to be tame, sitting close to one's tent on a branch, from which it darts at insects, returning each time to its perch. Adàms noted it in Kashmír.

205. *Alseonax ruficauda.* The Rufous-tailed Flycatcher. Inhabits Kashmír in summer.

206. *Terpsiphone paradisi.* The Indian Paradise Flycatcher. Common

in the valley, side glens and lower wooded slopes in summer, arriving in April. The male, during his first two years, is bright chestnut above and white below, assuming the pure white plumage in his third season. I have seen them chestnut, with the long tail-feathers white; and white, with one tail-feather chestnut. The female is smaller, chestnut above, smoky white beneath, and the long tail-feathers are wanting. The nest is beautifully made of cobweb and grey moss, lined with hair, placed in a forked branch. Eggs five or six, white with reddish streaks.

Family HIRUNDINIDAE. Swallows.

207. *Hirundo rustica.* The Common Swallow. Called 'Katij' by the Kashmíris. Arrives as early as latter part of February, and is fully established in the country early in April.

208. *Chelidon kashmiriensis.* The Kashmír House-Martin. Above black, with steel-blue reflections; tail brownish-black; throat, under surface, and rump, pure white; brownish on flanks; axillaries and beneath the shoulder dark brown. Dr. Adams found it abundant in Kashmír on the rocky banks of rivers.

The Common House-Martin also probably occurs in Kashmír, but I cannot at present identify several of the species of swallows. *Ptyonoprogne rupestris* and *Hirundo nepalensis* breed, in all probability.

REPTILES.

Snakes are known in Kashmír as *Sarraf*, and I have met with snakes in every part of the valley. It is universally said that no poisonous snakes exist in parts of the valley from which the peak of Harámak can be seen. There are two poisonous snakes: one is called *Gunas*, and is found in the Sind valley, the other is known as *Pohur*, and is met with on the east of the Liddar valley. The natives say that when the *Pohur* is old hairs appear on its back. The bite of the *Gunas* and *Pohur* is said to be usually fatal [1],

[1] Colonel Unwin writes: 'I have only seen one "Pohur" since I have known Kashmír, and this was on a spur above "Kollur," in the Liddar valley. He tried to bite my shikári, who, however, killed him. The man was very agitated, saying that he had escaped the bite of the most deadly snake in Kashmír. It was about two feet long, thick, and of a dark brown colour, with long poison fangs. The Kashmíris tell wonderful stories of the Pohur, saying he springs on you from a distance, &c. I believe it to be deadly. Natives in Hazara have died from the bite of a snake exactly resembling the Pohur I saw at Kollur. The "Gunas" is common, and varies from twelve or fifteen to thirty inches in length. General colour: above dusky grey, with a brownish angular pattern along the back; beneath dark grey. Natives say they grow to three or four "traks" in weight. The bite of a large one *may* be deadly; but I have seen several cases of terriers bitten by small Gunas, which all recovered, the dogs not seeming to suffer much. The bite was attended by a great deal of swelling about the head and neck in every case.'

and I lost one of my surveyors who was bitten by a *Gunas* at Sonamarg. Dr. Elmslie writes of the *Gunas*:—'It is a poisonous, round-headed, short, thick serpent found on the mountains of Kashmír. It is said to be black on the back and yellowish on the belly. It is a foot and a half long and ash-coloured according to some natives. Its bite is often fatal. When a person is stung on the arm or leg a ligature is applied between the heart and the wound, which is besmeared with foam. The patient has arrack and conserve of roses given him to eat, while music is played to cheer him up. This is the native treatment of serpent-bites. The *Gunas* is said to be numerous in the Lar pargana. Serpents are seldom seen on the southern side of the valley.'

Lizards (*kauklat*) and frogs (*ningi mundak*) are common, and on the slopes of the mountains the scorpion (*bich*) is frequently found. The Kashmíri scorpions are not very venomous, and the people look on the sting of a scorpion with indifference. Centipedes up to five inches long are found.

INSECTS.

Flies and sandflies abound, but the great pest of the low-lying parts of the valley is the mosquito. I have never seen mosquitoes in India so abundant as they are on the Jhelum river below Srinagar and on the lakes. They swarm, and in the evenings, in camp, it is necessary to sit in the fumes of dung fires if one wishes to escape the persistent mosquito (*muh*). Though they seem to be more numerous in Kashmír than in India, I think that they are less venomous, and the bite of the mosquito of the valley is not so irritating as the bite of its Indian brother. Mosquitoes occur sometimes at a high elevation. and on the Rajdiangan pass, 11,800 feet, they often appear, and seem more vigorous and aggressive than they are in the more enervating climate of the valley. Fleas (*pish*), bugs (*tsar*) and other unpleasant insects are common, and the Kashmíris say that though their native doctors have found a remedy for all diseases they have failed to discover any specific for fleas. Ticks are very numerous, especially in the upper forests after the snow has melted, and the large green-headed gadfly is, in some upland margs, in July and August, most numerous and aggressive.

Locusts (*halu*) occasionally find their way to Kashmír, and in the year 1868 considerable damage was done to the rice crops by the locusts. Large swarms appeared at the beginning of the summer of 1891, but were happily diverted to the side valleys and perished on the snows, where their frozen bodies were greedily devoured by the bears. No damage was caused in 1891 to crops.

There is a caterpillar, known as *Moru* to the Kashmíris, which causes considerable loss to trees, especially to the Wych Hazel. In a few days the Moru will leave a forest bare of leaves, but the damage caused is not permanent and the trees recover.

Among vegetable pests may be mentioned snails (*hangi*), leeches (*drik*), and a fish-like insect known as *Dádu*. These cause injury to the rice-plant. The leech used for blood-letting is imported from the Panjáb.

The *darz* is a darkish grub which injures the roots of maize and cotton, and is one of the worst of our vegetable pests.

FISH.

Fish forms an important item in the food of the Kashmíris, and those who dwell near the lakes; and the floating population of boatmen depend for a considerable part of their sustenance on the prey of their nets or lines. Fish are eaten fresh with oil or are dried without salt and kept for the winter. It has been suggested that the fecundity of the Kashmíri women is due to the fish and oil diet. At present it does not seem necessary to take any measures for the conservancy of fish, and the malpractices so common in India, such as the use of dynamite, are as far as I know unknown in Kashmír. I have heard no complaints of the diminution in the fish supply, and although prices have slightly increased the rate of 9 pice per seer, which is about one penny for 2 pounds, is not excessive. On the death of Mahárája Guláb Singh the killing of fish was strictly prohibited for about six years, and even now no man may catch fish between the Amiran Kadal and the Zaina Kadal (the first and second of the city bridges). The right to fish is leased annually. The average amount realized by the State for the last three years is Rs. 2,000. The Rainbow trout of Canada, used to snow-water, might very easily be introduced into Kashmír, and the Telbal valley, when the waterworks reservoir is completed, would be a very suitable place for the experiment. Colonel Unwin also suggests that pike might be tried in the Dal and Manasbal lakes[1].

The following notes give the names of the principal fishes and much information on the subject.

Charri Gad.—The average weight of this fish seems to be from 2 to 3 lbs.; it is sold for 3 pice a seer. It has one dorsal and five ventral fins, a large mouth, dark spotted back, silver belly and a line along the side

[1] I would suggest that the 'Rainbow' trout of Canada and America would be more suitable than the English trout, as being more used to snow-water. The ova of the 'Rainbow' is now, I believe, to be obtained in England. Pike might also be tried in the Dal and Manasbal lakes, and in the small detached lakes near Sumbal.—W. H. U.

CHAP. V. from near the eye to the tail; it has a soft scaleless skin. The *Charri Gad* is caught during the months of October and November.

Sattar Gad.—The average weight of this is said to be half a seer, and it is sold at the same price as the Charri Gad, of which it seems to be a small variety. It has one dorsal and five ventral fins, silvery sides and mottled back, with a soft, scaleless skin. This fish is very plentiful, and caught at all seasons of the year.

Krout Gad.—Average weight from half to three-quarters, of a seer, same price. It has one dorsal and five ventral fins, which are of a pink colour, a dark back, yellowish-white belly and soft skin. This fish is said to live under stones and rocks, and is caught throughout the year; it seems to be of the same species as the Charri and Sattar Gads.

Pikút or *Pekri Gad.*—Averages from 8 to 16 seers and is sold at the same price. It has a large mouth and is covered with scales, colour white; a scarce fish. in season from November to July.

Chash Gad.—Average weight half to one seer; same price. This fish has a pointed head and small mouth, soft scaleless skin, white colour. It is caught from December until March, but is very scarce.

Harj.—Average weight half a seer or less; same price. One dorsal and five ventral fins, small mouth, dark back, silver belly, firm scales. In season October until May.

Ramah Gad.—Average weight, a chittak; sold at 2 pice a seer, colour dark green This fish is taken in the Jhelum in June; when the water becomes cold, it retires to the lakes and morasses.

Unyour.— Average weight, a chittak; sold at 2 pice a seer, colour black; season and habits the same as the Ramah Gad.

Tet Gad.—Average weight, one chittak or less; sold at 2 pice a seer, dark colour; in season from August until October, when very small is known as 'tet Gardu.' When the river falls this fish is caught in shallow basins and channels which are made in the sands on the banks of the stream.

Dras.—Sold at a pice a seer; this fish is taken in August and September, it is doubtful if it is a separate species, being more probably a name given to any fry that comes to the net.

Ait Gad.—A small white fish; sold at 2 pice per seer; it inhabits the smaller streams flowing into the Jhelum and is carried into the river when the waters are high.

All the fish enumerated in the above list are said to be caught in their seasons throughout the entire course of the Jhelum, between Islamabad and Baramula. In the month of June the Mahsir (Pairim Gad, or the Panjab fish) is taken at various places in the Jhelum below Srinagar. A small fish called the *Gúran* inhabits the streams and morasses. In the Dal lake the Sattar Gad is taken with net and hook, and the Charri Gad and Ait Gad with hook only; all the fish inhabiting this lake are said to become of a dark green colour, which is attributed to the mass of vegetation, grass and weeds amid which they live. CHAP. V.

In the Wular lake the Sattar Gad and Charri Gad are taken in nets and also with hooks, the Pikút Gad with net only, and the Chash Gad and Harj with hook. Fish are also frequently speared in the waters of this and other lakes.

In the Sind river, which also abounds with fish below Gandarbal. are found the Sattar Gad, Chash Gad and Charri Gad, the latter species attaining a very great size. Consequent on the low temperature of the water of this river, the fish do not take readily except during the height of summer, the takes are then so plentiful that during the mulberry season the fishermen are not uncommonly attracted from the Jhelum to its waters. The tame fish which fill the sacred pools at Mattanji, Vernag and elsewhere seem to have no generic name, they are called Nág.

The month of March and the early spring is the most favourable fishing season in the Jhelum; in the winter months, from December until February, when the river is at its lowest, the fish betake themselves to Wular. Fishermen using the net (*zail bans*) form a distinct class from those getting a living by hook and line (*wail bans*). These latter use a long line, said to measure more than 1,000 yards, to which the hooks are attached at short intervals of less than a yard, and between each hook the line is weighted with a small stone or pebble.

During the months of December, January and February worms are used as bait, and at other seasons of the year a paste which is usually made of barley flour.

The lines are immersed throughout their entire length, being fished up with a hooked pole; in the summer months the fisherman in a small boat under-runs his line about every four hours, but in the winter, when the fish are sluggish and do not bite readily, they are usually placed at night and taken up in the morning. The hooks, which are very neatly manufactured by the fishermen themselves, differ in substance and shape from those used in Europe. Iron being found to be too brittle they are made of brass, the end of the hook is carried straight down from the barb and bent back abruptly to the shank instead of being curved. It is claimed for this shape that it renders the escape of a fish that has once taken bait impossible.

From two to three traks a day seems to be an average take for a successful fisherman; fish, however, are sold at eight seers[1] to the trak.

Vigne in his notice of the fish of Kashmír remarks:—

'I am aware of only six different kinds, of which by far the most

[1] The retail sellers of fish, however, give six seers to the trak, which is the ordinary trak weight.

common is Himalaya trout, and it varies so much in colour and appearance, according to its age and season and feeding-ground, that the natives would seem justified in trying to make me believe that there were several species instead of one. Unlike the true trout it rises rarely and very sluggishly at the fly. I tried fly-fishing in Kashmír until I found it an unprofitable employment. I remember that at Islamabad some fish were brought to me that in colour more resembled the real trout than any I had seen, but I believe that they were only fish of the above-mentioned species. They vary also in size from one, two or three pounds in weight; and I was informed that there were a few in the lake far larger than any I saw. I have seen fish of a yellowish copper-colour, blotched with dark spots, caught in the lake of Kashmír when out of season. The fish from the river are much better than those from the lake, but they are insipid when compared with the real European trout; this fish is also called the Sattar Gad; Gad signifies fish.

'I have seen what I believe to be the white mullet of India in the stream at Sopur Nagri on the Karywali of Zyn-i-gyr; but it is most probably found also in the Jhelum. There is also a little white fish, bluish on the hook, and somewhat resembling a bleak, called Chotur; its length is about six inches. There is another, I believe called the Tatur Gad, in the lake and river about five inches long. There is also a fish much resembling the American cat-fish in shape and called the Aumur, its general colour is dusky olive, inclined to reddish at the tail, it has three ventral and two dorsal fins, the eyes are nearly on the top of the head; a horny plate shaped like a horseshoe is continued between the gills to the mouth, and from it two feelers are projected at right angles, and there are also two worm-like appendages under the chin. Those I saw were very small, but it grows, I was informed, to three or four pounds' weight. Lastly comes the Ram Gad, or fish of Ramah, which has been already mentioned as being caught at the village of Sopur Nagri. The ground colour of this I believe new and singular fish is a reddish gold, fins reddish, its sides are covered with broad stripes of a very dark, dull, bottle-green colour; two worm-like appendages are pendant from the horn of the upper lip; a small, sharp spur, which it can erect and use as a weapon of offence, is situated close in front of the eye, and between it and the mouth, its curve being backwards and downwards, so that a straight line, if continued from its point, would cut the centre of the tail. It grows to about three-quarters of a pound. Fish forms a great proportion of the food of the poorer classes in the valley, or at least of those living near the lakes.'

CHAPTER VI.

ARCHAEOLOGY.

THE Valley of Kashmír is the 'holy land' of the Hindus, and I have rarely been in any village which cannot show some relic of antiquity. Curious stone miniatures of the old Kashmíri temples (*Kulr-Muru*), huge stone seats of Mahadeo (*Badrpith*) inverted by pious Musalmáns, Phallic emblems innumerable, and carved images heaped in grotesque confusion by some clear spring, have met me at every turn. The villagers can give no information as to the history of these remains, save the vague guess that they were the works of the Buddhists or of the Pandus. The Pandits of the city care nothing for archaeological research, and know little about the past glories of their country in the old Hindu times. When one comes to the more recent period of the Mughals tradition becomes more definite, and I have seen curious mosques built in a style unlike the present, of wooden beams with stones between, mostly raised by Aurangzeb. He built religious edifices, while the other Mughals devoted themselves to stately pleasure-domes, gardens, terraces, waterfalls, and pretty summer-houses. While the old Hindu buildings defy time and weather the Musalmán shrines and mosques crumble away and have little now of their pristine grandeur. Here and there the excellent masonry of Jehangir has withstood the great destroyer, but unless money is spent quickly and judiciously there will be little left, save the wild roses of the valley, to remind posterity of the pleasure-haunts of Selim and Naurmahal. It is to be hoped that the Kashmír State will never allow the beautiful pleasaunces of Achabal and Vernag, Shalamár and Nishat to pass away, but unless early steps are taken these fair places will become sad and unsightly ruins. As regards the older buildings of ancient Kashmír it is hard to say whether it would be possible to protect these monuments from further damage. I have often looked at Martand and noticed with sorrow that the temple to the north, supposed by Cunningham to be the fane of Ranesa, is sloping away from the main temple, and the push of an earthquake would send it crashing into the mass of mighty stones beneath. But if Martand—'precious specimen of ancient art, deserving a foremost place among the remains of antiquity'—is to be preserved, not only money but artistic skill would be required. A brick buttress would be an act of desecration. If the State ever takes up the work of conservation of ancient monuments, I think that the two relics of the old Hindus most worthy of preservation would be Martand and Payech. The former is the grandest of the ancient buildings, the latter the most perfect. Earthquakes will always render the future of the Kashmír temples uncertain, and the shock of 1885 caused great damage to the buildings at Pattan. I have made extracts from the greatest authority on the archaeology of Kashmír, and have quoted descriptions of the most important of the buildings of the old Hindus, but a rich field awaits explorers in the valley. Chance excavations, for irrigation and other works, reveal curious sculptures and interesting relics of ancient history, and any one with money and leisure might find profitable employment in tracing the old cities on the hill slopes and the karewas of Kashmír. In 1882 Mr. Garrick, late of the Archaeological Survey of India, carried out extensive excavations at Ushkpur near Barámula. He excavated a tope or stupa of squared stones, held together with iron clamps, in the hope of finding certain copper plates which, according to the Chinese pilgrim, Hwen Thsang, were deposited therein. On the copper plates were engraved the proceedings of a Buddhist synod held in the reign of Kanishka. Mr. Garrick's excavations were thorough, but unsuccessful. It was at Ushkpur that Lalitaditya is said to have built an image of the Mukhtswami and a large monastery with a stupa for the Buddhists. Along the eastern side of the valley one sees everywhere on the slopes of the mountains remains of ancient cities. I do not know how far these have been examined, but am under the impression that explorers, owing to the short time of their stay in the valley, have chiefly confined their attention to the well-known temples. I am also under the impression, founded on what the people say, that many valuable relics have been carried away from Kashmír, while the State itself has removed several sculptures and thousands of lingams from their old sites to Srinagar. The island on the Wulár is a notable example of this. To the explorer I would recommend the eastern side of the valley. Tradition assigns Sumbal, on the Jhelum, as the site of the ancient Jayapurá, and the people say that excavation at Sumbal would reveal great treasures. Hardly a year passes without rumours of fabulous treasure being discovered in Kashmír. Official measures are at once taken to secure the State's interests, but since I have been in the valley all such rumours have proved to be unfounded. It is quite possible, however, that treasure is found, and it is very possible that systematic exploration might discover some of the wealth with which Lalitaditya and other conquerors endowed the valley.

My duties left me no leisure to investigate the history of the ruined forts and the little palaces (kutráj) which occur so frequently on the western side of the valley. The forts are recent, of Mughal or Pathan times, but the little palaces carry one back to the prehistoric ages when Kashmír was parcelled out among a number of princelings. The forts and palaces are now mere heaps of stones, the abode of snakes and jackals, 'the populous city is deserted, and thorns and briers have come up upon the land.' A curious antiquity known as Ráman Kán, not described in previous accounts of the valley, may be mentioned here.

On the Kutraj karewa, near the village of Khushipura, the arrows of Ram Chandr and Lachman are to be found. The arrows are of cut stone, octagonal in section, stand about four feet out of the ground, and the depth to which they have penetrated the soil after their long flight is unknown. The karewá also has a number of depressions, varying in size and depth and containing water and weeds. This table-land was once the abode of the Rakshas, devils in human form, who lessened the tediousness of time by wrestling-matches among themselves and by devouring men. The depressions were made by the rubbing of giant elbows and knees against the ground during the wrestling-bouts. The avatars at last took compassion on the people thus oppressed, and preyed upon, and fired arrows from Ram Koond and Lachman Koond, sacred places in Machipura, where Hindus go to bathe, and the Rakshas were slain. The legend is interesting in that it points to a time when the Kutraj country was inhabited by a lawless people who made periodical inroads on the peace-loving and better-favoured lowlander. I have visited all the buildings which are now to be described, and have debated with myself whether anything of interest could be added by me to the excellent and accurate descriptions which expert writers have already given. I have decided that it would be presumptuous and useless, and just as in the chapter on geology I have availed myself of Lydekker's researches, so in this chapter I repeat the words of the greatest of Indian antiquarians, the late Sir Alexander Cunningham. I first give his general remarks on the architectural remains of Kashmír, and in the detailed description of each temple I reproduce the notices contained in Bates' *Gazetteer*.

'The architectural remains of Kashmír are perhaps the most remarkable of the existing monuments of India, as they exhibit undoubted traces of the influence of Grecian art. The Hindu temple is generally a sort of architectural pasty, a huge collection of ornamental fritters huddled together, either with or without keeping, while the Jain temple is usually

CHAP. VI. a vast forest of pillars, made to look as unlike one another as possible by some paltry differences in their petty details. On the other hand the Kashmírian fanes are distinguished by the graceful elegance of their outlines, by the massive boldness of their parts, and by the happy propriety of their decorations. They cannot, indeed, vie with the severe simplicity of the Parthenon nor with the luxuriant gracefulness of the monument of Lysicrates, but they possess great beauty, different indeed, yet quite their own.

'The characteristic features of the Kashmírian architecture are its lofty pyramidal roofs, its trefoiled doorways, covered by pyramidal pediments, and the great width of its intercolumniations. The Grecian pediment is very low, and its roof exceedingly flat, the Kashmírian pediment, on the contrary, is extremely lofty, and its roof high. The former is adapted for a sunny and almost rainless climate, while the latter is equally well suited to a rainy and snowy climate. But besides the difference of climate, there was perhaps another reason for the form of roofing peculiar to the two countries in the kind of material most readily procurable for buildings. In Greece it was stone, in Kashmír it was timber. The former imposed low flat roofs with small intercolumniations, the latter suggested lofty roofs and wide intercolumniations.

'In the Kashmírian architecture the great width of the interval between the columns (which is constant) is perhaps the most characteristic feature of the order. Indeed I have suspicion that the distinctive mark of the Kashmírian style was well known to the Greeks; for an intercolumniation of four diameters, an interval seldom, if ever, used by themselves, was called *Araiostyle*, a name which would appear to refer to the intercolumniation common amongst the Hindus or Eastern Aryas, the 'APEIOI of Herodotus. The vulgar etymology of Araiostyle from 'ΑΡΑΙΟΣ, "rare," seems extremely far-fetched if not absurd; while the etymology of the "*Arian columnar interval*" appears both natural and appropriate, as the intercolumniation followed by the Aryas of Kashmír was never less than four diameters.

'Now the interval between the Kashmírian pillars being always Araiostyle, I feel inclined to call the style of architecture used by the Aryas of Kashmír the "Arian Order." This name it fully merits, for it is as much a distinct order of architecture as any one of the more celebrated classic orders. Like them it is subject to known rules, which confine the genius of its architects within certain limits. A Kashmírian pillar is indeed distinguished from all Indian pillars by having a base, a shaft, and a capital, and each, besides, bearing a certain proportion to the diameter. How unlike is this to the columnar vagaries of the Hindus, which are of all shapes and of all dimensions A favourite Hindu pillar has the lowest fourth of its height square, the next eight-sided, and the third sixteen-sided, and the upper part round; another has a double capital with a low flat base; whilst a third has a shaft of only one-fourth of its height, the remaining three-fourths being all base and capital, and yet these three pillars may be neighbouring columns of the same temple.

'The superiority of the Kashmírian architecture over all other Indian buildings would appear to have been known to the Hindus themselves, for one of their names for the people of Kashmír is *Shastra-Shilpina*, or "architects," a term which could only have been applied to them on account of their well-known skill in building. Even now the Kashmíris are the most expert handicraftsmen of the East; and it is not difficult to believe that the same people, who at present excel all other orientals as weavers, gun-smiths, and as calligraphers, must once have been the most eminent of the Indian architects.

'Before entering upon any details of the Arian order of architecture, and upon the comparisons naturally suggested between it and some of the classical orders, I will first describe the present state and appearance of the principal buildings that still exist in Kashmír, all of which were accurately measured by myself in November, 1847. They are entirely composed of a blue limestone, which is capable of taking the highest polish, a property to which I mainly attribute the present beautiful state of preservation of most of the Kashmírian buildings; not one of these temples has a name, excepting that of Martand, which is called in the corrupt Kashmírian pronunciation, *Matan*, but they are all known by the general name of Pandavanki lari or "Pandus-house," a title to which they have no claim whatever, unless indeed the statement of Ptolemy can be considered of sufficient authority upon such a subject. He says "circa autem Bidaspum Pandovorum regio"—*the Kingdom of the Pandus is upon the Betasta* or (Behat), that is, it corresponded with Kashmír. This passage would seem to prove that the Pandavas still inhabited Kashmír so late as the second century of our era. Granting the correctness of this point there may be some truth in the universal attribution of the Kashmírian temples to the race of Pandus, for some of these buildings date as high as the end of the fifth century, and there are others that must undoubtedly be much more ancient, perhaps even as old as the beginning of the Christian era. One of them dates from 220 B. C.

'Most of the Kashmírian temples are more or less injured, but more particularly those at Awantipura, which are mere heaps of ruins. Speaking of these temples, Trebeck[1] says, "It is scarcely possible to imagine that the state of ruin to which they have been reduced has been the work of time or even of men, as their solidity is fully equal to that of the most massive monuments of Egypt; earthquakes must have been the chief agents in

[1] *Travels*, vol. ii. p. 245.

CHAP. VI. their overthrow." I have quoted this passage to show the utter confusion that characterizes the ruins of the Awantipura temples. In my opinion their overthrow is too complete to have been the result of an earthquake, which would have simply prostrated the buildings in large masses. But the whole of the superstructure of these temples is now lying in one confused heap of stones totally disjoined from one another. I believe, therefore, that I am fully justified in saying, from my own experience, that such a complete and disruptive overturn could only have been produced by gunpowder. I have myself blown up a fort, besides several buildings, both of stone and of brick, and I have observed that the result has always been the entire sundering of all parts one from another, and the capsizing or *bouleversement* of many of them. Neither of these effects can be produced by an earthquake. It seems also that Trebeck and Moorcroft would most likely have attributed their destruction to the same agency, had they not believed that the use of gunpowder was unknown at the time; for in speaking of a traditional attempt made by Shah Hamdan to destroy Martand, they say, "It is fortunate he was not acquainted with the use of gunpowder." I admit that this destructive agent was most probably unheard of in Kashmír so early as the reign of Shah Mirshah of Hamdan; but the destruction of the Kashmírian temples is universally attributed, both by history and by tradition, to the bigotted Sikander, whose idol-breaking zeal procured him the title of *But-Shikan*, or "Iconoclast." He was reigning at the period of Timur's invasion of India, with whom he exchanged friendly presents, and from whom I suppose he may have received a present of the "villanous saltpetre." This is not at all unlikely, for the furious Tamerlane was as great an idol-breaker as Sikandar himself. Gibbon, it is true, denies that either the Mughals or Ottomans in 1402 were acquainted with gunpowder, but as he points out that the Turks had metal cannon at the siege of Constantinople in A. D. 1422[1], I think it is no great stretch of probability to suppose that gunpowder itself had been carried into the East, even as far as Kashmír, at least ten or twenty years earlier, that is about A. D. 1400 to 1420, or certainly during the reign of Sikandar, who died in 1416.

'Even if this be not admitted, I still adhere to my opinion that the complete ruin of Awantipura temples could only have been effected by gunpowder, and I would then ascribe their overthrow to the bigotted Aurangzeb. Ferishta[2] attributed to Sikandar the demolition of all the Kashmírian temples save one, which was dedicated to Mahádeo, and which only escaped "in consequence of its foundation being below the surface of the neighbouring water." In A. D. 1580–90, however, Abulfazal[3]

[1] *Decline and Fall.* c. 65, note 93. [2] Briggs, vol. iv. p. 465.
[3] *Ain Akbari*, vol. ii. p. 124.

mentions that some of the idolatrous temples were in "perfect preservation;" and Ferishta himself describes many of these edifices as being in existence in his own time, or about A. D. 1600[1]. Besides, as several of them are still standing, although more or less injured, it is quite certain that Sikandar could not have destroyed them all. He most likely gave orders that they should all be overturned; and I have no doubt that many of the principal temples were thrown down during his reign. For instance, the tomb of his own queen in Srinagar is built upon the foundation, and with the materials of a Hindu temple; likewise the wall which surrounds the tomb of his son, Zain-ul-Ab-ul-din, was once the enclosure of a Hindu temple; and lastly, the entrance of a Masjid in Nawashahra[2] of Srinagar, which, according to its inscription, was built during the reign of his son Zain-ul-Ab-ul-din, is formed of two fluted pillars of a Hindu peristyle. These instances prove that at least three different temples, in the capital alone, must have been overthrown either by Sikandar or by one of his predecessors. But as the demolition of idol temples is not attributed to any one of the earlier kings, we may safely ascribe the destruction of the three above mentioned to Sikandar himself. But besides the ruthless hand of the destroyer. another agency, less immediate, but equally certain in its ultimate effects, must have been at work upon the large temples of Kashmír. The silent ravages of the destroyer who carries away pillars and stones for the erection of other edifices have been going on for centuries. Pillars from which the architraves have been thus removed have been thrown down by earthquakes, ready to be set up again for the decoration of the first masjid or tomb that might be erected in their neighbourhood. Thus every Muhammadan building in Kashmír is constructed either entirely or in part of the ruins of Hindu temples.

CHAP. VI.

. . . .

'Even at first sight, one is immediately struck by the strong resemblance which the Kashmírian colonnades bear to the classical peristyle of Greece. This first impression is undoubtedly due to the distinct division of the pillars into the three members—base, shaft and capital, as well as to the fluting of the shafts. On further inspection the first impression is confirmed by the recognition that some of the principal mouldings are also peculiar to the Grecian orders, but more especially to the Doric. Thus the echinos, which is the leading feature of the Kashmírian capital, is also the chief member of the Doric capital. A still closer examination reveals the fact that the width of the capital

[1] Briggs, vol. iv. p. 445.

[2] Cf. Fergusson, *History of Indian and Eastern Architecture*, pp. 281, 282.

is subject exactly to the same rules as that of all the classical orders excepting the Corinthian.

'Even the temples themselves, with their porches and pediments, remind one more of Greece than of India: and it is difficult to believe that a style of architecture which differs so much from all Indian examples, and which has so much in common with those of Greece, could have been indebted to chance alone for this striking resemblance. Professor Willis admits the probability that the Kashmírian pediments may have been borrowed from those of the Syrian Greeks, and he founds his opinion upon the fact that the trefoiled arch of the Kashmírian temple rises high into the tympanum of the pediment; a practice which was not introduced into the classical architecture until after the commencement of the Christian era. But the Professor had not, I believe, seen any examples of the older Kashmírian buildings, such as the enclosing walls of the temple on the Takht-i-Suliman and of the tomb of Zain-ul-Ab-ul-din, as well as the perfect little cave temple of Bhumju. Of these specimens the first dates as early as 220 B.C., at which time the Kabul valley, and even the western Panjáb, were occupied by the Bactrian Greeks, under Euthydemus and his son Demetrius. If, therefore, it is admitted that the Kashmírian architects have been indebted to those of Greece for their pediments, for their fluted columns, or even for any of their minor details, I think that they must certainly have borrowed them from the temples of their immediate neighbours the Bactrian Greeks, and not from the buildings of distant Syrian Greeks; I think also that had these pediments been imitated from the later Romanized examples the copyist would scarcely have overlooked the structural arches which occupy their pediments. In fact the forms of the principal Kashmírian mouldings, which are all *quirked ovolos*, or *echini*, could only have been borrowed from the pure Greek style of an earlier period than the Roman innovation of circular segmental mouldings.

'Another striking resemblance between the Kashmírian architecture and that of the various Grecian orders is its stereotyped style, which during the long flourishing period of several centuries remained unchanged. In this respect it is so widely different from the ever-varying forms and plastic vagaries of the Hindu architecture, that it is impossible to conceive their evolution from a common origin. I feel convinced myself that several of the Kashmírian forms, and many of the details, were borrowed from the temples of the Kabulian Greeks, while the arrangement of the interior, and the relative proportions of the different parts, were of Hindu origin. Such, in fact, must necessarily have been the case with imitations by Indian workmen, which would naturally have been engrafted upon the indigenous architecture. The general arrangement would therefore still remain Indian, while many of the details, and even some of the larger forms, might be of foreign origin.

'As a whole, I think that the Kashmírian architecture, with its noble fluted pillars, its vast colonnades, its lofty pediments and its elegant trefoiled arches, is fully entitled to be classed as a distinct style. I have therefore ventured to call it the "Arian order," a name to which it has a double right; firstly, because it was the style of the Aryas, or Arians of Kashmír; and secondly, because its intercolumniations are always of four diameters, an interval which the Greeks called Araiostyle.'

Bhumju or Bumzu or Bhaumajo lies at the mouth of the Liddar valley, and is easily reached from Islamabad.

'These caves are situated on the left bank of the Liddar river about a mile north of the village of Bawan, the largest is dedicated to Kaladeva. The cave-temple stands at the far end of a natural but artificially enlarged fissure in the limestone cliff. The entrance to the cavern, which is more than 60 feet above the level of the river, is carved into an architectural doorway, and a gloomy passage, 50 feet in length, leads from it to the door of the temple. It is a simple cella, 10 feet square, exterior dimensions, raised on a badly moulded plinth, and approached by a short flight of steps. The square doorway is flanked by two round-headed niches despoiled of their statues, and is surmounted by a high, triangular pediment, reaching to the apex of the roof, with a trefoiled tympanum. There is no record[1] nor tradition as to the time of erection; but from absence of all ornamentation, and the simple character of the roof, which appears to be a rudimentary copy in stone of the ordinary sloping timber roof of the country, it may with great probability be inferred that this is the earliest perfect specimen of a Kashmír temple, and dates from the first or second century of the Christian era. Close by is another cave of still greater extent, but with no architectural accessories; and about half a mile further up the valley, at the foot of the cliff, are two temples, the larger of which has been converted into a Muhammadan tomb. Both are, to a considerable extent, copies of the cave-temple, but may be of much later date.

'The shrine of Bábá Ramdin Rishi and the tomb of his disciple Rúkú din Rishi are also close by. Hugel states that the Bhumju caves occupy a very conspicuous place in the fables of the timid Kashmíris. and are supposed to have originated from the following causes. In the year Kali 2108 (993 B.C.) Raja Nara succeeded his father, Vibishána; during his reign a certain Brahman espoused Chandrasahá, the daughter of Susravas,

[1] Dr. Stein believes that the temple is the same as the Bhimakeśava temple mentioned by Kalhana. It was built by king Bhimaśáhi, who ruled in the Kabul valley in the first half of the tenth century.

CHAP. VI. a serpent-god, whose place was in a lake near the Vitusta, and near a city built and inhabited by Nara. One day, as Raja Nara beheld the beautiful daughter of the serpent on the shore of the lake, moving gracefully through the calm waters, he was struck with the deepest admiration, and endeavoured vainly to inspire the same sentiments he himself felt. At length he resolved to carry her off from her husband, but the plan failed, and the enraged Brahman called on her father to avenge the insult. A storm was accordingly called up, and the earth opened and swallowed up the king and his whole court. The sister of the serpent-god assisted him, and hurled on the city huge stones from the Bawan mountain. The caverns of Bhumju are said to be on the spot where these rocks were uptorn (Hugel, Growse).'

Awantipura lies on the right bank of the Jhelum and is distant about 18 miles by land from Srinagar.

'The ancient capital of Awantipura was called after its founder, the famous king Awanti-Varma, who reigned from A.D. 854 to 883. The whole neighbourhood is strewn with ruins, but the only traces that remain of its former greatness are the two temples which he founded—one before his accession to the throne, and the other and larger one subsequently. Both were dedicated to Mahadevá, the former under the title of Awanti-Swami, the latter under that of Awantiswara. These two temples are situated on the bank of the river, one at Awantipura and the other about three-quarters of a mile to the north, near the village of Janbior. They are now shapeless masses of ruins, but the gateways of both are standing, and the colonnade of the smaller temple, which had been completely buried underground, has recently been partially excavated. The style corresponds with that of the Martand quadrangle; but the semi-attached pillars of the arched recesses are enriched with elaborate carving of very varied character, while the large detached columns are somewhat less elegantly proportioned.

'The writer in the *Calcutta Review*, from whose description the above account has been extracted, is of opinion that the silting up of the Awantipura quadrangle can only be explained by the supposition that all the Kashmíri temples were originally surrounded by artificial lakes[1]. Forster, who visited Awantipura in May, 1783, calls the place Bhyteepour.'

Martand lies on the karewa above Islamabad, and is easily reached from Islamabad, Bawan and Achabal.

'The ruins of the Hindu temple of Martand, or, as it is commonly called, the Pandu-Koru, or the house of the Pandus and Korus—the cyclopes of the East—are situated on the highest part of a karewa, where it commences to rise to its juncture with the mountains, about

[1] Cp. Dr. Stein's remarks, p. 175.

3 miles east of Islamabad. Occupying, undoubtedly, the finest position in Kashmír, this noble ruin is the most striking in size and situation of all the existing remains of Kashmír grandeur. The temple itself is not now more than 40 feet in height, but its solid walls and bold outlines, towering over the fluted pillars of the surrounding colonnade, give it a most imposing appearance. There are no petty confused details, but all are distinct and massive, and most admirably suited to the general character of the building. Many vain speculations have been hazarded regarding the date of erection of this temple, and the worship to which it was appropriated. It is usually called the House of the Pandus by the Brahmins, and by the people "Martand," or the sun, to which the temple was dedicated. The true date of the erection of this temple—the wonder of Kashmír—is a disputed point of chronology; but the period of its foundation can be determined within the limits of one century, or between A. D. 370 and 500. The mass of building now known by the name of Martand consists of one lofty central edifice, with a small detached wing on each side of the entrance, the whole standing in a large quadrangle, surrounded by a colonnade of fluted pillars with intervening, trefoil-headed recesses. The length of the outer side of the wall, which is blank, is about 90 yards; that of the front is about 56. There are in all eighty-four columns—a singularly appropriate number in a temple of the sun, if, as is supposed, the number eighty-four is accounted sacred by the Hindus in consequence of its being the multiple of the number of days in the week with the number of signs in the zodiac. The colonnade is recorded in the Rajatarangini as the work of the famous king Laltaditya, who reigned from A.D. 693 to 729. From the same authority we gather—though the interpretation of the verses is considerably disputed—that the temple itself was built by Ranaditya, and the side chapels, or at least one of them, by his queen, Amritaprakha. The date[1] of Ranaditya's reign is involved in some obscurity, but it may safely be conjectured that he died in the first half of the fifth century after Christ. The remains of three gateways opening into the court are now standing. The principal of these fronts due west towards Islamabad. It is also rectangular in its details and built with enormous blocks of limestone, 6 or 8 feet in length, and one of 9, and of proportionate solidity, cemented with an excellent mortar.

'The central building is 63 feet in length by 36 in width, and, alone of all the temples of Kashmír possesses, in addition to the cella or sanctuary, a choir and nave, termed in Sanskrit the *antarála* and *arddhamandapa*; the nave is 18 feet square. The sanctuary alone is left entirely bare, the two other compartments being lined with rich panellings

[1] Fergusson gives the date of Martand as A. D. 750, and fixes the reign of Ranaditya as A. D. 578–594.

CHAP. VI. and sculptured niches. As the main building is at present entirely uncovered, the original form of the roof can only be determined by a reference to other temples and to the general form and character of the various parts of the Martand temple itself. It has been conjectured that the roof was of pyramidal form, and that the entrance chamber and wings were similarly covered. There would thus have been four distinct pyramids, of which that over the inner chamber must have been the loftiest, the height of its pinnacle above the ground being about 75 feet.

'The interior must have been as imposing as the exterior. On ascending the flight of steps, now covered by ruins, the votary of the sun entered a highly decorated chamber, with a doorway on each side covered by a pediment, with a trefoil-headed niche containing a bust of the Hindu triad, and on the flanks of the main entrance, as well as on those of the side doorways, were pointed and trefoil niches, each of which held a statue of a Hindu deity. The interior decorations of the roof can only be conjecturally determined, as there do not appear to be any ornamented stones that could with certainty be assigned to it. Baron Hugel doubts that Martand ever had a roof, but as the walls of the temple are still standing the numerous heaps of large stones that are scattered about on all sides can only have belonged to the roof[1].

'Cunningham thinks that the erection of this sun-temple was suggested by the magnificent sunny prospect which its position commands. It overlooks the finest view in Kashmír, and perhaps in the known world. Beneath it lies the paradise of the east, with its sacred streams and glens, its orchards and green fields, surrounded on all sides by vast snowy mountains, whose lofty peaks seem to smile upon the beautiful valley below. The vast extent of the scene makes it sublime; for this magnificent view of Kashmír is no petty peer in a half-mile glen, but the full display of a valley 60 miles in breadth and upwards of 100 miles in length, the whole of which lies beneath the "ken of the wonderful Martand."'

Narastan. In the east of the valley about 35 miles from Srinagar, via Trahat.

'This is one of the most interesting ruins in Kashmír. Its situation is very picturesque, looking down the narrow valley, while behind it the ground slopes up towards the lofty mountains of the Brariangan range. The cella stands in a walled enclosure about 65 feet square. This wall, which is about 5 feet thick and 8 feet high to the top of the coping-stone, has in some places fallen to the ground. The main entrance is on the west side, through an imposing portico; the outer portal is arched, the pediment possessing the usual characteristics of the Arian order of

[1] Fergusson thinks that the roof was of wood.

PLATE IV

To face page 172

Negative by Alam Chand, G.C.

THE OLD TEMPLE OF NARASTAN. IN THE BACKGROUND IS A PEASANT'S HOUSE

architecture. It was supported by two columns about 8 feet high, the width of the entrance between the pillars being about 4½ feet. The outer vestibule measured about 8 feet by 4; in the middle is a square gateway opening into a second vestibule of rather larger dimensions.

'In the middle of each of the other three sides of the wall within the enclosure there is a blank arched recess, and on the north side there is also a small square postern. measuring about 3 feet by 2, and a similar one on the west side seems to have led into a square chamber which occupied the south-west corner of the enclosure; this chamber was lighted by a small arched window. Projecting into the enclosure from the southern wall is a small cell about 5 feet square, with a pyramidal roof.

'The cella of the temple which occupies the centre of the enclosure is similar in general appearance to those of Payech and Pandrathan, but more imposing in its proportion and elaborate in its details. Each side measures about 15 feet above the plinth. The porch, which is on the west side, projects rather more than 3 feet from the face of the wall.

'In the middle of each of the other three sides is a blank trefoil archway corresponding in proportions to the portal. On either side of the vestibule the figure of a Hindu god is carved in bold relief on the panel contained within a trefoil-arched recess.

'The inner entrance is a square gateway about 6½ feet high by 3½ wide supported by pillars; both this and the middle gateway of the north seem to have been fitted with stone doors. The inside chamber is about 8½ feet square, the walls are blank, with the exception of a small arched recess on the south side of the entrance. The flooring is of stone, which has given way in the centre, where probably the lingam stood. About 8½ feet from the ground there is a cornice, from which the roof seems to have tapered to a point; the walls are now standing to a height of about 24 feet, and the pinnacle was probably about 10 feet higher. In each side of the roof was a lancet.'

Pandrathan lies on the Srinagar-Islamábád road, and is easily reached from Srinagar.

'The place is remarkable for a very old and interesting Hindu temple, standing in the middle of the tank, about 50 yards from the river bank, surrounded by a grove of willows and chenars. The tank is about 40 yards square, and in ordinary seasons 4 feet deep; it is filled with reeds growing in a bed of soft mud; the water is derived from small springs on its northern side.

'Access to the interior is therefore a matter of some difficulty, which is unfortunate, since the domed roof is well worth inspection, being covered with sculpture of such purely classic design that any uninitiated person

CHAP. VI. who saw a copy of it on paper would at once take it for a sketch from a Greek or Roman original.

'The temple is 18 feet square, with a projecting portico on each side, and displays in a confused exuberance of decoration, more especially the repetition of pediment within pediment and trefoil within trefoil, clear indications of having been built at a later date than other existing ruins; it is probably the most modern example of the true Kashmír style extant. It was erected during the reign of king Partha, who governed Kashmír from A.D. 921 to 931, by his prime minister, Meru, who dedicated it to Mahadeva under the title of Meru Vardhamá Swámi.

'The ground about it was then occupied by the original city of Srinagar, the modern name of Pandrathan being a corruption of the Sanskrit Puranadhishthana, i.e. "the old capital." Dr. Elmslie, however, supposes the name to be derived from Pandu and Durendun, the father of the Pandus. The seat of government had been transferred to the present site by king Pravarasena II nearly 500 years before the foundation of this temple; but the old city was not entirely deserted until its destruction by fire in the reign of Abhimanyu, about the year A.D. 960. The conflagration was so violent that, excepting the temple which was protected by the water about it, no other building escaped. There are in the neighbourhood some few fragmentary remains, consisting of two large lingams, one 6 feet high, erect and entire, the other broken into three pieces, the lower part polygonal, the upper round with conical top, which together made up a height of 16 feet. Near these, which are separated from each other by a short interval, is a huge mass of stone, being the feet and legs as high as the knees of a colossal seated figure, probably a Buddhist image. At some little distance beyond this an isolated crag has been cut, as it stood, into some sculptured form, apparently a Chaumukhi, i.e. a square pillar with a figure on each face. But the rock has been overthrown, broken into three pieces, and so defaced by the action of fire that it is impossible to speak positively as to the original design. Of three fragments, one the base is still attached to and forms part of the natural rock. Baron Hugel calls the Pandrathan edifice a "Buddhist temple," and states that there are some well-preserved Buddhist figures in the interior. But he is doubly mistaken, for the temple was dedicated to Mahadeva, and the figures in the inside have no connexion with Buddhism.

'Trebeck, Moorcroft's companion, swam into the interior, and could discover no figures of any kind; but as the whole ceiling was formerly hidden by a coating of plaster, his statement was at that time perfectly correct.

'The object of erecting the temples in the midst of water was doubtless to place them immediately under the protection of the Nagas or human-bodied and snake-tailed gods who were zealously worshipped for ages throughout Kashmír (Moorcroft, Hugel, Vigne, Cunningham, Growse). Dr. Stein in his "Tours Archaeological and Topographical in and about Kashmír"—read before the Royal Asiatic Society, London, November 13, 1894—speaking of his recent examination of ruins in Kashmír says, "In every case where a thorough examination of the ruins is still possible, I have found the Naga in a separate, larger or smaller walled basin in front or by the side of the temple. Irrespective of Pandrathan, which now stands in a morass, I have come across nowhere a trace of that arrangement, according to which, as has been frequently assumed, all Kashmírian temples were placed in the middle of tanks."'

Patan lies on the Srinagar-Baramula road, about half-way between these places.

'It is recorded in the Rajatarangini that Sankaravarma, who succeeded Awantivarma, and reigned from A.D. 883 to 901, in conjunction with his queen, Sugandha, dedicated to Mahadeva, under the title of Sankara Gauresa and Sugandhesvara, two temples at his new capital of Sankarapura. This town is identified with the modern Patan, where beside the highway on the south-east side of the village two stately temples are still standing. Each is a simple cella; but in the larger one, the projection of the closed porches at the sides is so considerable that they form deep niches, or rather shallow chambers, in each of which was once a lingam. In both the architecture is of the same character as at Martand, and of equal excellence. Here and there the carving is as sharp and fresh as if executed yesterday, but there are many ominous cracks in the walls, and if the forest trees which have taken root in these crevices are allowed to remain and spread, the destruction of both buildings is imminent.

'By the wayside to the north of the village, near the hamlet of Gasipur, are two very curious stone pillars which the natives call Gurmat, and believe to have been mortals who for their misdeeds suffered a fate similar to that which befell Lot's wife. These pillars are, however, nothing more than the miniature models of temples which occur here and there throughout the country, but they possess this peculiarity that they are not hollowed out in the interior, the place of the open doorway being occupied by a sculptured panel [1].

'A few letters also remain of an old inscription which Vigne copied and sent to Calcutta, but they were found to be illegible, although bearing some resemblance to Sanskrit (Vigne, Growse).'

Páyech lies about 19 miles from Srinagar, under the Naunagri karewa, about 6 miles from the Jhelum river.

[1] I have seen many of these miniature temples. The people call them *kulr-muru*. Dr. Stein says that they are in all probability funeral monuments.

CHAP. VI.

'On the south side of this village, situated in a small green space near the bank of the stream, surrounded by a few walnut and willow trees, is an ancient temple, which in intrinsic beauty and elegance of outline is superior to all the existing remains in Kashmír of similar dimensions. Its excellent preservation may probably be explained by its retired situation at the foot of the high table-land, which separates it by an interval of 5 or 6 miles from the bank of the Jhelum, and by the marvellous solidity of its construction. The cella, which is 8 feet square, and has an open doorway on each of the four sides is composed of only ten stones, the four corners being each a single stone, the sculptured tympanums over the doorways four others, while two more compose the pyramid roof, the lower of these being an enormous mass 8 feet square by 4 feet in height. It has been ascribed by General Cunningham, on grounds which, in the absence of any positive authority either way, may be taken as adequate, to king Narendraditya, who reigned from A.D. 483 to 490[1]. The sculptures over the doorways are coarsely executed in comparison with the artistic finish of the purely architectural details, and are much defaced, but apparently represent Brahma, Vishnu, Siva and the goddess Durga. The building is said to be dedicated to Vishnu as Surya or the sun-god.

'Inside the cupola is radiated so as to represent the sun, and at each corner of the square the space intervening between the angle and the line of the circle is filled up with a gin or attendant, who seems to be sporting at the edge of its rays. It will be observed that the roof has been partly displaced, which is said to have been the result of an attempt made by the Patans to take it down and remove it to the city.

'The interior is still occupied by a large stone lingam, and from the water-drain and the bulls carved on the smaller pilasters of the doorways it is evident that this was the original intention (Vigne, Growse).

'Takht-i-Suliman. The temple crowning the Takht-i-Suliman is stated to be the earliest of all the temples in Kashmír. Baron Hugel records that its erection is ascribed to Gopiditya of the Gonerdya dynasty, 370 B.C., but later authorities seem to agree that the first religious edifice on this commanding site was built by Jaloka, the son of the great Buddhist convert Asoka, about 200 B.C. In all probability there is not a fragment of this now remaining. The temple was subsequently rebuilt and dedicated to Jyeshtesvara, a title of Mahadeva, by Raja Gopiditya, who reigned from A.D. 253 to 328[2]. To this date may be

[1] Fergusson considers that Payech belongs to the thirteenth century of our era.

[2] Takht-i-Sulimán. Dr. Bühler, referring to speculations by which the Takht and its temples are connected with Sandhimati, or are regarded as identical with Gopadri, and as due to Gopaditya, writes, 'It seems to me that in neither story have we to deal with a genuine tradition, but with the speculations of the learned, and that the real name of the Takht, as well as the name of the builder of its temples, have still to be discovered.'

To face page 176] *Negative by Alam Chand, G.C.*

THE OLD TEMPLE OF PAYECH. THE INTERIOR IS OCCUPIED BY THE LINGA OR PHALLIC EMBLEM

ascribed the low enclosing wall and the plinth of the existing temple, but all the superstructure is evidently modern or greatly modernized. Its summit has been damaged, but its general figure has been that of a cone, with four sides formed by the rectangular adjustment of eight gable-shaped slabs of masonry, the surface of the outer slab being much less than that of the inner one. The cone, which is about 25 feet in height with proportionate base, rests upon an octagonal raised platform, whose wall is about 10 or 12 feet above the rock on which it is built, and whose circumference may be about 100 feet. A handsome flight of steps, formed, as the whole building is, of limestone, leads from the ground to the door of the temple. At a little distance below the latter building, which rises on the very summit of the Takht, are some ruins that indicate the existence of another edifice of the same material.

'The interior is circular, and 14 feet in diameter; the roof is flat and 11 feet high; the walls, which are 8 feet thick, are covered with white plaster composed of gypsum, and the roof is supported by four octagonal limestone pillars. In the centre of the floor there is a quadrangular stone platform; it supports a lingam of black stone, around which is carved a coiled serpent. Upon the hinder of the two pillars on the left there are two Persian inscriptions; that upon the front of it states that the *bút* or idol was made by Haji Hushti, a Soukár, in the year 54 of the Samvat or Hindu era, or about 1,870 years ago, while that at the foot of the back part of the same pillar states that "he who raised up this idol was Kwaja Rukm, son of Mír Jan, in the year . . ." The remainder of the inscription is below the pavement, and cannot be made out.' Fergusson is convinced that the temple as it now stands was commenced by some nameless Hindus in honour of Siva, during the tolerant reign of Jehangir, and that the building was stopped at the date engraved on the staircase, A.H. 1069 (A.D. 1659), the first year of the reign of the bigot Aurungzeb.

'Wangat. About three miles north of Wangat, at the head of the glen, far from all human habitations, are some ruined temples. They are situated high up on the precipitous mountain side, in the midst of dense jungle and towering pine-trees, which lend a more than religious gloom to their crumbling walls.

'In antiquity these ruins are supposed to rank next after those on the Takht-i-Suliman, at Bhumju and at Payech. They are in two groups, situated at a distance of a hundred yards from each other, and consisting respectively of six and eleven distinct buildings. The luxuriant forest growth has overthrown and buried almost completely several of the smaller temples; on the summit of the largest a tall pine has taken root and rises straight from the centre, in rivalry of the original finial. The architecture is of a slightly more advanced type than at Payech, the most striking feature being the bold projection and lofty trefoiled arches of the lateral porches.

'In close proximity is a sacred spring called Nagbal, and by it the footpath leads up the height of Haramak to the mountain lake of Gangabal, a celebrated place of pilgrimage. A great festival is held annually about August 20, which is attended by thousands of Hindus from all parts of Kashmír. By this footpath the Tilail valley may also be reached.

'It is probable that the Wangat temples were erected at different times by returning pilgrims as votive offerings after successful accomplishment of the hazardous ascent.'

CHAPTER VII.

POLITICAL HISTORY.

CHAP. VII.

THE Kashmíris divide their history into four periods: the early period of the Hindu kings chronicled in the famous Rájataranginí; the period of the Kashmír Musalmáns, known as the Salátíni Kashmír; the period of the Mughals, known as the Pádsháhi-i-Chagatai or Shahán-i-Mughlia, and the period of the Pathans, known as the Sháhan-i-Duráni. Each of these periods if dealt with in detail would furnish much of historical interest, but I can only attempt a brief sketch of the history of Kashmír.

I have endeavoured to reproduce the events which seem best remembered by the people—events which even now are common talk of the country side. I do not mean to imply that there is a survival of a genuine popular tradition in Kashmír, although there are some remarkable instances of local traditions of great age surviving in particular places. It is probable that the history of the country as I have gleaned it from the villagers may all be traced to literary sources. Most headmen of villages can read and write, and have had access to translations of the Rájataranginí. These headmen repeat the stories of Kalhana's Chronicle, and the uneducated villagers have thus acquired a general idea of the history of their country. It is vague and often contradictory, but the names and events mentioned in my brief abstract rarely fail to arouse recognition as one talks with the villagers by the camp-fire. The following note by Dr. Stein indicates the sources available for the study of Kashmír history, and furnishes some excuse for my not attempting anything more than a popular account of the historical events of the country.

'Kashmír can claim the distinction of being the only region of India which possesses an uninterrupted series of written records of its history, reaching back beyond the period of the Muhammadan conquest and deserving the name of real chronicles. In other parts of India the historical student is obliged to reconstruct the general outlines of the country's history with the help of the scanty and frequently uncertain data

CHAP. VII. which a patient examination of inscriptions, coins, and occasional references in literary works may reveal, and he can scarcely ever hope to recover a continuous account of the leading events even for a couple of centuries. If the student of Kashmírian history finds himself in a far better position, this is due to the preservation of the documents alluded to; they testify to the continued existence among the population of the valley of that genuine historical sense in which the Indian mind on the whole is so conspicuously deficient.

'These Chronicles have, on account of the striking contrast they offer to the scantiness of historical traditions in India proper, attracted early the attention of those European scholars who began the critical study of Indian antiquities. It was in consequence of the steady search made for these interesting documents by Colebrooke and other pioneers that Dr. Horace Hayman Wilson was able to publish in the Bengal Asiatic Society's Transactions of 1825 his famous "Essay on the Hindu History of Kashmír," in which the materials available for the study of Kashmírian history were analyzed for the first time, and in a manner truly admirable considering the condition of Indian philology of those days. Dr. Wilson showed that the Sanskrit History of Kashmír called the Rájatarangini, for which Sir William Jones had looked out in vain, was not one entire composition, as had till then been thought, but a series of four Chronicles, written by different authors, the last three being intended to serve as successive continuations of the first and most important work of the series.

'This is the Rájatarangini of the Kashmírian poet Kalhana. It comprises in eight cantos of Sanskrit verse the history of the various dynasties which ruled Kashmír from the earliest period down to the time of the author, who began to write this work A.D. 1148, in the reign of king Jayasimha. Although Kalhana himself mentions several historians as his predecessors, none of their works have come down to us. The Rájatarangini has thus become the most direct source of information on the ancient history of Kashmír. Allowing for the legendary character of much that is related in the first three cantos regarding the earliest dynasties and discarding the artificial chronology of these portions, we retain in Kalhana's work a connected account of Kashmírian history which has well stood the test of historical criticism. It can be accepted as a reliable record from the seventh century onwards, and steadily increases in detail and interest as we approach the time of the author.

'Kalhana's work was continued by Pandit Jonarája, who, writing in professed imitation of his predecessor's style and method, brought down the history of the valley through the troubled times of the last Hindu dynasties and the first Muhammadan rulers to the time of Sultan Zain-ul-Ab-ul-din, who ascended the throne in A.D. 1417.

'Śrívara's Jaina-Rájatarangini takes up the account of Zain-ul-Ab-ul-din's rule and continues the history of his descendants down to the accession of Fatteh Shah (A.D. 1486). The series of Sanskrit Chronicles is closed by Prájyabhatta's Rájávalípatáká, which records the history of the valley till its conquest by Akbar (A.D. 1586).

'For the period of Moghul rule we can utilize, besides general works of Muhammadan historians of India, the existing Persian histories of Kashmír written by Haidar Malik, Mohammad Azim, Narayan Kul, and other authors, most of whom seem to have lived in the early part of the eighteenth century. Though these works also contain more or less garbled accounts of the periods of Kashmírian history previous to Akbar's conquest, it is yet very doubtful whether their authors possessed any materials for this purpose besides the Sanskrit Chronicles, which are still accessible to us.

'That the interest in historical events has not ceased to exercise the minds of educated Kashmírians in more recent times, is amply proved by numerous Persian works like the Tawárikh of Bírabal Káchерí, the Gulzár-i-Kashmír of the late Diwán Kirpa Ram, which besides embodying the accounts found in earlier narratives describe also the history of the valley in the times of the Sikh and Dogra dominion.

'We have already noted that Dr. Wilson was the first who attempted to utilize the contents of Kalhana's Rájatarangini for a critical study of the early history and antiquities of Kashmír. His abstract embraced the first six cantos only, and was based on manuscripts so imperfect as to render a close translation quite impracticable. Ten years later the first edition of the work was published in Calcutta from a complete copy which had been obtained through the energy and zeal of Mr. Moorcroft, who had visited Srinagar in 1823 on his ill-fated expedition to Turkestan. This copy, though transcribed from the Codex which has proved the original of all existing manuscripts, was still so imperfect as to render the text of the Calcutta edition which was based on it, unintelligible in many important passages. With the help of the same insufficient materials Mr. Troyer undertook in 1840, under the auspices of the French Asiatic Society, an edition and translation of the work. The former was never completed, and the very limited value of the latter has long ago been pointed out by competent scholars.

'Subsequently researches of General Cunningham, Professor Lassen and others, have brought to light valuable results regarding the chronology of the Hindu dynasties and their connexions with territories outside Kashmír. Still, when in 1877 one of the most distinguished of living Indologists, Professor Bühler, had to review the work done up to that time for the elucidation of the Chronicle, his opinion was recorded in terms by no means reassuring to the general student of Kashmírian history: "It may

CHAP. VII. seem scarcely credible that a book which has engaged the attention of so many Sanskritists, and of some of the first rank, is, after all the labour expended, not in a satisfactory condition, and that its explanation leaves a great deal to desire[1]."

'Professor Bühler attributed rightly the scantiness of these results to the great deficiency of the materials on which European and Indian scholars had worked up to that time, and showed that close study on the spot of the old geography and antiquities of Kashmír was an indispensable condition for the further elucidation of that difficult work. The English translation published by Mr. Jugesh Chandra Dutta, soon after Professor Bühler's Report, has only tended to confirm the above opinion. Based on the corrupt text of the Calcutta edition, and made without corresponding researches in Kashmír itself, this translation can be used only with caution by the student to whom the original text is not accessible, however much commendation the translator may rightly deserve for his industry and devotion to the task. In 1892 a new edition of Kalhana's work was published by Dr. Stein, under the auspices of the Kashmír State Council. In this the correct text of the Chronicle was restored for the first time, on the ground of the *Codex Archetypus*, to which the editor had secured access. The second volume of this publication, which is to bring the results of researches carried on in the valley itself with regard to the interpretation of the work, has not yet appeared.

'As regards the later Sanskrit continuations of Kalhana's Rájataranginí, it need only be noted that no translation has hitherto been attempted, and that the corrupt state of the text in the only available Calcutta edition would render at present such an undertaking practically impossible.

'Reference has already been made to the fact that the Persian Chronicles cannot claim any independent authority for the earlier periods of Kashmírian history. As they are almost all of recent date, it is necessary in each case to inquire carefully into the question of their respective sources before they can be used with confidence even for the study of the Muhammadan epochs. None of these Chronicles have been printed, nor is there any translation or abstract which would make their contents conveniently accessible to the European student.'

The above remarks will suffice to show the wide range of research which a systematic study of the whole of Kashmírian history would have to embrace, and also the peculiar difficulties which beset this study at present, notwithstanding the ampleness of the materials. Under these circumstances no attempt can be made within the limited space of this chapter to take up the authentic history of the valley for each of the main periods.

[1] Detailed Report of a Tour in search of Sanskrit Manuscripts made in Kashmír, *Journal of the Bombay Branch, Royal Asiatic Society*, 1877, p. 53.

I shall only allude to the chief events which to this day are common talk of the country-side. One cannot look at the grand buildings of old Hindu Kashmír, or see the traces of the great cities on the hill-sides and the table-lands without wishing to know something of those men of large ideas who once lived in the valley. The buildings are in ruins, and are dismissed by the Kashmíris of the present day with the remark that they were *Pándavlari*—the houses of the Pandus. It is nothing to them that Kashmír was the birthplace of the fair-faced Pandu race, and 'furnished sovereigns to the plains of Hindustán [1].' CHAP. VII.

Again, it is interesting to hear Kashmíri villagers talking of the power and grandeur of China. They assert with confidence that Kashmír was once under the sway of Tartar princes from China, and Hushka, Jushka, and Kanishka [2], who flourished about the beginning of our era, are spoken of as Tartars and Buddhists. It would be of equal interest to trace the beginnings of Brahmanism, to watch it displacing and absorbing local cults, and fiercely combating the Buddhist heresy [3]. These are subjects for

[1] An Essay on the Hindu History of Kashmír, by H. H. Wilson, Esq.: 'It appears very evident that Kashmír has been a regular kingdom for a period that transcends the limits of legitimate history, and even if we feel disposed to contest the accounts of our author and to dispute his s.ries of dynasties and princes, we must still rest satisfied with the proof of its existence either under the names of Caspapyrus or Abisarius as early as the days of Herodotus and Alexander. There can be no doubt, however, of the regular organization of this state at a period much antecedent, and it is probable that in remote times it exercised a more decided interference in the concerns of India than it has done for many centuries past; it seems highly probable also that it was the original dominion of the Pandava princes, and that it furnished in them soverεigns to the plains of Hindustan.' Dr. Stein remarks: 'There is nothing to prove any special connexion of the *Pandu* family with Kashmir The name of this ancient clan has spread *through the Hindu Epics* over the whole of North-Western India, and its localization in any particular part of the country is beyond the hopes of legitimate historical research.'

[2] Dr. Stein remarks: 'It would be very interesting to record the survival of this tradition if its genuine character could be *authenticated*. The names of Hushka, Jushka, and Kanishka are found in Kalhana's first Book, and it would not be astonishing if a knowledge of these names has reached directly or indirectly also half-educated persons. I have met with so numerous cases of quasi-traditions of this kind which could be traced back to artificial sources of information, that I should hesitate to accept the tradition regarding these particular names, unless established by special inquiry. Kanishka's date has been fixed with something approaching certainty. The year of his accession is used as the beginning of an era in his and his successors' inscriptions, and is now identified by almost all Indologists as A. D. 78, the initial year of the Śaka (Indo-Scythian) era.'

[3] An Essay on the Hindu History of Kashmír, by H. H. Wilson: 'It appears that the Buddha schism was known in Kashmír at a very early period and possibly preceded the introduction of a fully organized Brahmanical priesthood, it probably, in short, preceded the introduction of the Brahmanical *caste*.' With reference to this Dr. Stein writes: 'Modern research has given up all theories relating to a forcible extermination of Buddhism in India proper, and there is no proof whatever for the assumption of real antagonism between Brahmanical *cult* and Buddhist *creed* in Kashmír. The two existed, as far as our evidence goes, peaceably together in Kashmír as they did elsewhere in India. Buddhism had a foothold in Kashmír, as e. g. the old tradition of Kanishka having held a "Council" there shows. But the Chinese pilgrims (e. g. Hwen Thseng about 638 A. D.) found the mass of the population addicted to the Devas, and the monasteries few and partly deserted. There is very good historical reason to believe that the Kashmirians were from the

CHAP. VII. the Sanskrit scholars. I must follow more humble paths, and base my sketch on the ideas of the Kashmíris of the present day. For chronology in the Hindu period I use Mr. J. C. Dutta's table in his translation of the Rájatarangini. For chronology in the later periods I use the dates given in certain vernacular histories. These dates are only approximately accurate, but they will serve my purpose, which is to give a popular account of the history of the valley as accepted by the people. To the real historian the facts on which the people dwell may seem insignificant as compared with other facts which literature reveals.

Every educated Hindu and most Musalmáns in Kashmír believe that the valley was once a vast lake on which the goddess Párvatí sailed in a pleasure-boat from her mountain home on Haramak in the north to Konsa Nág lake in the south. In her honour the lake was known as Satísar, the tarn of the chaste woman. But there dwelt in the lake a cruel demon Jaldeo[1], whose patron was Brahma, and this demon destroyed all life on the shores and rendered the country waste. By chance Kashaf, a grandson of Brahma, found his way to the lake, and distressed at the havoc wrought by Jaldeo resolved to overcome the demon. For 1,000 years Kashaf gave himself up to religious exercises and then braced himself up for a struggle with Jaldeo, but the demon eluded him and hid under the water. Then Vishnu came to the help of Kashaf and struck the mountains at Bárámúlá with his trident, and the waters of the lake rushed out. But Jaldeo entrenched himself in low ground near the Hari-Parbat, and though the gods searched for him with the sun in one hand and the moon in the other the demon baffled them. But at last the goddess Párvatí dropped a mountain on top of him, crushing his life out, and the mountain is now known as Hari-Parbat[2], and on it is a great shrine in honour of Devi. After this the valley was known as Kashafmar, the home of Kashaf, and it is now corrupted to Kashmír. Other legends say that Kashaf was a mighty wrestler, who becoming suddenly religious was smitten with a desire to worship at the one thousand temples which were hidden under the waters of the lake. He pierced the mountains at Bárámúlá with a tunnel and so dried up the valley.

When Jaldeo was crushed to death the smaller demons lost heart, and men began to visit the valley in the summer, as winter came on

earliest period accessible to us chiefly *Śaivas*, what their Brahman castes have remained to this day. Buddhism seems to have lingered on in Kashmír till the time of the Muhammadan conquest.'

[1] Dr. Stein notes: 'This name is an instance of "popular etymology" for the old Jalodbhava of the Nilamata Purána and other Kashmírian texts.'

[2] Dr. Stein remarks: 'Kashmíri, Hára-Parvat: Hari-Parbat is a Dogra "popular etymology." The name has nothing to do with the name Hari = Śiva. Har is the modern form of the name Śariká. Párvatí has been worshipped under this name since ancient times on the slope of the hill. Every *ś* of Sanskrit becomes *h* in Kashmíri.'

withdrawing to the warmer and drier regions of Kishtwar and leaving Kashmír to the demons. But by chance an old Brahman, who was unable to walk, spent the winter in the valley and went to Nílanág, and the deity of the fountain gave to him the Nilamata Purán. By studying the precepts of the Purán the Brahmans were enabled to rout the demons, and Kashmír became permanently inhabited about the twentieth century [1] before the Christian era. At first the country was split up into numerous little kingdoms known as Kutraj, the remains of which may even now be seen, but the little kings of these little kingdoms began to fight among themselves, and those who were worsted called in a Rajput from the Jammu country. So the Kashmíris say, and it is worthy of notice that the neighbouring countries of Kishtwar and Jammu always play a prominent part in the history of the valley. Whether Gonanda the First was the Rajput in question, and whether he lived B.C. 2448 or B.C. 1400 or B.C. 1260, as affirmed by Mr. R. C. Dutta, are points immaterial to me, for Gonanda's name is no longer remembered in the valley. Of the early kings who lived at the beginning of the Christian era, Asoka, the man who followed Buddha, is well known, and it is known that his son Jaloka reverted to the worship of Siva and was the lover of the Nága maidens. But a little later the Buddhists again waxed strong, under the auspices of the Turushka kings, Hushka, Jushka, and Kanishka. The Nágas took offence, and destroyed many of the Buddhists by rolling down boulders of ice from the mountains. At last Chandra Deva, a descendant of Kasaf or Kasyapa, interposed, and restored the rites of the Nílamata Purán. The next name remembered in the legends of the people is that of the wicked Mihirakula (515 A.D.), the prince 'cruel as death.' The people [2] point to a high pass in the south-west of the valley, and relate how the king, crossing the mountain with his army, was amused by the agonies and cries of an elephant which had fallen down a ravine. The king's amusement was so keen that he ordered a hundred more elephants to be forced down the precipice. Another tale is told of this tyrant. It was necessary to remove a stone from the Chandra Kulyá river, and the king was told in a dream that the stone

[1] Dr. Stein writes: 'The chronology of the Rájatarangini, previous to the Kárkota dynasty, is avowedly artificial and must be set aside entirely. Only a few dates (like that of Asoka, Mihirakula, Kanishka) can be fixed by independent evidence and with reference to contemporary Indian history. Under these circumstances I should suggest the advisability of omitting all dates earlier than the seventh century after Christ.'

[2] Dr. Stein writes: 'Mihirakula's date is known from reliable sources (inscriptions, Chinese travellers' accounts, &c.) as about 515 A.D. The legend recorded below has been localized on the Pír Panjál Pass, where the ridge to the south of Aliábád Serái bears to this day the name of *Hasti Vañj* (ascertained by local inquiry, 1891). The form in which the legends regarding Mihirakula are told, clearly indicates a literary source, i.e. derivation from the Rájatar. or one of its Persian renderings.'

CHAP. VII. could only be moved by a chaste woman—'many a citizen's wife tried to move the stone in vain till Chandravatí, wife of a potter, accomplished the feat. The king was enraged to find so many women unchaste, he ordered them to be killed, together with their husbands and brothers, three millions in all.'

Good king Gopaditya forms a pleasant contrast to bad Mihirakula. He did much to purify the Brahmans of Kashmír and to advance their interests. The legend of the great famine of king Tunjína's reign is remembered. The famine was averted by the miraculous arrival of countless pigeons. The name of Matrigupta is of interest, as it would appear that he was appointed to be king of Kashmír by the great monarch Vikramaditya of Ujain. Matrigupta was a gentle prince, and the story of his submission to Raja Pravarasena shows a chivalrous courtesy and nobility of character which speak well for the manners of the age.

Raja Pravarasena is said to have founded Srinagar, in the centre of which was the hill of recreation, from whose top the whole city could be seen.

But the name best remembered by the Kashmíris is that of Lalatádit, the famous king Lalatáditya, 697–738 A.D. He was the son of Raja Pratápáditya, king of Kashmír. His mother was the mistress of a magnificent merchant, and her beauty had attracted the notice of Pratápáditya. Shortly after his succession Lalatádit set off on a tour of conquest through India. After subduing the kings of India he turned his attention to central Asia, and everywhere victorious returned, after twelve years, to Kashmír by way of Tibet. He brought with him learned men and skilled artisans from all countries and devoted himself to great public works. He built grand temples and ornamented them with the gold which he had acquired in India. He raised a mighty column at Paraspur, and built [1] the temples in Mártand. He made fine canals, and reclaimed by drainage large areas of swamp land. He constructed a large cauldron from which 100,000 men could be fed daily. He was just and magnificent, but at times, when intoxicated, he issued cruel orders and did not always keep faith. After a time he yearned for more conquests and left Kashmír for central Asia (Uttara Kuru). The Kashmíris besought him to return, but he died in Turkestan after a reign of thirty-seven years. Before he left Kashmír he gave his subjects wise advice, some of which sounds like a gloss [2] of latter-day chroniclers. He commences by warning

[1] Dr. Stein writes: 'The Rájatar. distinctly attributes the building of the Mártand temple to Lalatáditya. The notion that he merely repaired an older temple (of Ranáditya) rests on a misunderstanding of another Rájatar. passage, and can be traced back to a paper of Gen. Cunningham, (*Journal Asiatic Society of Bengal*, 1848).'

[2] These are quoted from the Rájatar. iv. 347.

them against internal feuds, and says that if the forts are kept in repair and provisioned they need fear no enemies. He lays down the rule that in a mountainous country discipline must be strict, and that the cultivators must not be left with grain more than sufficient for the year's requirements. Cultivators should not be allowed to have more ploughs or cattle than absolutely necessary, or they will trespass on their neighbours' fields. Cultivators must be repressed and their style of living must be lower than that of the city people or the latter will suffer. Finally Lalatáditya orders that offices should not be held by family cliques. 'When the Kayasths are united to one another by marriage; when kings see their officers behaving like Kayasths, then you will know for certain that the people's lot is going to be changed for the worse.' Lalatáditya was a glorious conqueror, and his advice to his people has a ring of prophecy. It is true that in a fit of drunken madness he ordered Pravarasena's beautiful city to be set on fire and that he laughed as he watched the flames. But posterity pardons him for this. King Avantivarma, 855–883 A.D., was no conqueror, but during his reign attention seems to have been paid to the drainage of the valley. A curious story is told of Suyya[1], a sage. Owing to the waterlogged condition of Kashmír cultivation had declined and famine appeared. Suyya was consulted and he replied, oracularly, 'I have intellect, but no money.' The king placed the treasury at his disposal. The sage took the money in boats to the place where the course of the Jhelum (Vitastá) was obstructed by rocks and proceeded to fling handfuls of coins into the river. All said that the sage was mad, but the 'villagers, who were suffering from scarcity, began to search for the dinnáras (coins) and in so doing removed the rocks which were in the bed of the river and cleared the passage of the water.' Things have not changed much since Suyya's time, for the valley is still in some places waterlogged, and the Kashmíris of the present day would work harder if paid by Suyya's system than they do on a daily wage. Avantivarma is said to have had a leaning towards Vaishnavism, from which it may be inferred that in those days the Hindus as a body worshipped Siva as they do now. Avantivarma's son, Shankaravarman, was a great conqueror. Though Kashmír had fallen off in population 'he was able to set out with nine hundred thousand foot, three hundred elephants, and one hundred thousand horse.' The question arises as to whence this great army was recruited. There is mention of the warlike Tantris and Dámaras of Kashmír—tribes which exist to the present day, but

[1] Dr. Stein writes: 'Kalhana's story of Suyya records clearly historical facts, but in the form which they had assumed in the popular tradition of his own day. Accurate details are given by Kalhana regarding the dams, canals and villages built by Suyya, and these can be verified by actual inspection, even at the present time. Suyya's name survives in the modern *Sopur* = *Suyyapura*.'

CHAP. VII. the point of interest is whether the ever-victorious soldiers of Lalatáditya and Shankaravarman were natives of the valley or mercenaries from the Panjab. It is hardly possible to believe that a country which once bred splendid soldiers should, even after centuries of oppression, now contain no fighting men [1].

Shankaravarman is remembered by the temples of Pattan. Though a great conqueror, he was an avaricious tyrant, a gambler, and debauchee. Signs now appear of dissension in the kingdom of Kashmír. The Brahmans had already been thorns in the side of the kings. The Brahmans of Tulamul, powerful then as now[2], had brought king Jayapída to death in 782 A. D. King Yashaskara, 939–948 A. D., began by keeping the Brahmans at a distance, and ended by bestowing his wealth upon them. Mention is frequently made in the Rajátarangini of the rising power of the Pálas, Dámaras, Tantris [3], Diviras, Lavangas, Khashas, and Thakhurs, and it would seem that when the kings of Kashmír no longer invaded India their soldiers, sick of inaction, turned to civil war.

In the succeeding period the rule of queen Diddá possesses special interest. This remarkable woman, a granddaughter of king Bhíma of the Kábul Sháhi dynasty, was the wife of king Kshemagupta, in whose reign she already exercised much influence on the affairs of the State. After his death (958 A. D.) Diddá ruled Kashmír as the guardian of her minor son Abhimanyu. Subsequently she seems to have been concerned in his early death, and disposing, by equally doubtful means, or open murder, of three grandsons in succession, she at last assumed government in her own name in 980 A.D. Her rule lasted for twenty-three years longer, and appears to

[1] 'As late as Akbar's time it would appear (*Ain Akbari*) that the valley furnished 6,420 cavalry and 50,530 infantry. It would be interesting to know how the cavalry were mounted. Did they ride the little Kashmiri ponies or were remounts imported from the Panjab?' Regarding this Dr. Stein writes: 'The figures given by Kalhana for Sankaravarman's army (reproduced in the text) scarcely deserve close examination. The question as to the composition of Kashmírian armies under the later Hindu kings is very justly raised. From the detailed accounts which Kalhana gives of the feuds in his own time and in the preceding rules, it is quite clear that foreign adventurers from the hill-country to the south of Kashmír (Parnotsa = Punch, Rájapurí = Rajaori, Baddivása = Budil, &c.) played the main part in the fighting. Some of their leaders, true condottieri, rose to great power, e.g. Tunga under Didola. There is reason to believe that the conditions were not very different in the earlier centuries. The Dámaras and Tantrinis are represented as "great warriors" only in the civil wars, and are not credited with conquests outside the valley. It is characteristic that where Kalhana describes the contest of Tunga with Hammira (Mahmud of Ghazni), vii. 57 39, he takes care to describe the cowardly behaviour of the Kashmírian troops in contrast to that of their allies.'

[2] Dr. Stein writes: 'I am afraid the Báchbhaṭṭs of Tulamul have no better position nowadays than the rest of the fraternity at other sacred springs of the valley. Even in Kalhana's time the Purohitas at Tírthas were a body receiving but scant respect from the rest of their Brahman caste-fellows.'

[3] The Pálas, Damaras, Tantris, Khashas, and Thakhurs still exist in Kashmír. As regards the Diviras, Dr. Stein suggests that they may be recognized in the modern Dyór.

have been comparatively free from disturbing influences during this later period. The peace which Kashmír seems to have enjoyed under this strong queen soon gave way to protracted periods of internal strife under her adopted son Sangrámadeva and his descendants. CHAP. VII.

In Vchchala's reign, A. D. 1101–1111, it is said that 'his ministers and petty chieftains acted like highwaymen; his brother wished a civil war in the kingdom, and his treasury was empty.' From 1101 to 1149 A. D., when Kalhana Pandit ends his history, there was little else than civil war, and the Dámaras, 'well-skilled in burning, plundering, and fighting,' were a terror to the country. Central authority was at an end, and the kings seemed to grow more and more helpless and incapable. It is doubtful whether king Vchchala's policy of discarding the Kayasthas was wise, if one judges by the weakness of the subsequent administrations. It is said of the king that he held the view 'that besides spasmodic cholera, colic, and the disease which ends in sudden death, the Kayastha officers are the sources of the speedy destruction of the subjects.' All things point to a breaking up of the Hindu kingdom, which had lasted for so many centuries, and in 1305 A. D. when Raja Simha Deva was king, Kashmír was a country of drunkards and gamblers, and the women were no better than they should be. In this reign Zulkadar Khan, the Tartar, invaded Kashmír, and helpless Simha Deva fled to Kishtwar. The Tartar Zulzu [1], as he is commonly known, slaughtered the people, took slaves, and set fire to the city Srinagár. After an occupation of eight months, Zulzu, who had depopulated the valley, found provisions scarce, and tried to get out of Kashmír by the passes leading from the south through the Kuli Nárawáo Valley, but snow overtook him, and he and his army and his Kashmíri captives perished. Meanwhile, Ram Chand, the commander-in-chief of Simha Deva, had been trying to keep up some semblance of authority in the valley, and when Zulzu departed he moved down to Indrkot [2] and drove out the Gaddis who had come in from Kishtwar on a raid. Ram Chand had with him two men who, like other foreigners before, were destined to play an important part in the history of Kashmír. One was Shah Mirza from Swát, at whose birth it was prophesied that he would become king of Kashmír; the other was Rainchan Shah, who, having quarrelled with his father the king of Tibet, came as an adventurer to the valley. Before many days had passed Rainchan Shah broke with Ram Chand, and with the assistance of mercenaries from Tibet, attacked and killed him [3]. He

[1] Jonarája calls the Khan Dalcha.

[2] Perhaps the village called Andarkot, on the Nuru canal, is meant here: it marks the site of the town Antara Kotta, founded by king Jayapída.

[3] Dr. Stein writes: 'Jonarája mentions as the place of this event Lahara Kotta, i.e. the fort of Lahara = Lár. As the attacking force is described as Bhauṭṭas = Ladákhis, the locality seems correctly indicated.'

CHAP. VII. then married Kutá Ráni, Ram Chand's daughter, and proclaimed himself king, 1323 A. D. At this time it would appear that there was much confusion in the matter of religion in Kashmír, and Rainchan Shah, who had no strong convictions, found it necessary to adopt one or other of the various forms of faith which existed in the country. He could not become a Hindu because none of the Hindu castes would admit him to their brotherhood, so he determined to leave his religion to chance. One morning he saw Bulbul Shah at his prayers, and admiring that form of devotion, he decided on Islam, and taking the name of Sadr-ud-din, built the Jama Masjid and a great shrine for Bulbul Shah, known still by the name of 'Bulbul Lankar.' After a short reign of two-and-a-half years Rainchan Shah, the first of the Musalmán kings, died. At this juncture Udayanadeva, brother of Simha Deva, appeared on the scene, and married Kutá Ráni, the widow of Rainchan Shah. Urwan, a Turki, just then invaded Kashmír, and Udayanadeva, who like his brother was lacking in courage, fled, but his wife collected an army and sent it, under the command of Shah Mirza, against the foe. Urwan was defeated and Udayanadeva returned and reigned for fifteen years. On his death Kutá Ráni assumed power, but only wielded it for fifty days, as Shah Mirza (or Shah Mir as he is usually known) declared himself king (1343 A. D.). In order to consolidate his power Shah Mir proposed marriage to Kutá Ráni, and she, seeing that she was in his power, tried to temporize. At last she was forced to accept his advances, but as he entered the bridal chamber, she, the last representative of Hindu royalty, stabbed herself to death. Shah Mir then became king of Kashmír, under the name of Shams-ud-din, and was the first of the Salátin-i-Kashmír. In 1394 A. D. Sultan Sikandar came to the throne, and soon earned the nickname of Butshikan or Iconoclast, from the intense zeal he showed in destroying the grand old temples which the Hindu Rájás had bequeathed to Kashmír. Sikandar was brave and cultured, but all his good qualities were warped by his gloomy fanaticism. He attracted learned Musalmáns to his court, amongst others Muhamad Khan Hamadání, the successor of the famous Shah Hamadán, who added fuel to the fire of the king's fierce zeal. Hindu temples were felled to the ground, and for one year a large establishment was maintained for the demolition of the grand Martand temples. The massive masonry resisted all efforts, and finally fire [1] was applied, and the noble buildings were cruelly defaced. It is said that in certain temples stones were found prophesying that these buildings would be destroyed by

[1] In an essay on the Arian order of architecture as exhibited in the temples of Kashmír, Captain Cunningham believes that the complete and disruptive overturn of the temples could only have been produced by gunpowder. Dr. Stein, however, remarks: 'This early use of gunpowder in Kashmir has been doubted by others, and I believe rightly. Earthquakes and the imperfect fitting of the stones, observable in all Kashmírian temples, are sufficient to explain the complete ruin, notwithstanding the massive character of the materials.'

Sikandar, and he grimly remarked that if he had known of these inscriptions he would have spared the noble piles, for he had no wish to fulfil the predictions of an idolatrous people. There was a certain method in the mad zeal of Sikandar, for he used the plinths and friezes of the old temples for the embankments of the city and for the foundation of the Jama Masjid. Having glutted his vengeance on Hindu temples, Sikandar turned his attention to the people who had worshipped in them, and he offered them three choices, death, conversion, or exile. Many fled, many were converted, and many were killed, and it is said that this thorough monarch burnt seven maunds of sacred threads of the murdered Brahmans. All books of Hindu learning which he could lay his hands on were sunk in the Dal lake, and Sikandar flattered himself that he had extirpated Hinduism from the valley. In this gloomy reign wine, gambling, and music were strictly prohibited, and during Sikandar's twenty-five years of power Kashmír must have been a dolorous country. It is pleasant to turn to the more enlightened reign of Zain-ul-Ab-ul-din, who succeeded to the throne of Kashmír in 1417 A. D.; he is known in Kashmír as the great king, and his long reign of fifty-two years is even now quoted by the Kashmíris as the happiest period of their history. He was virtuous in his private life, self-controlled and frugal, paying all the expenses of his establishment from the income of a copper mine which he had discovered. He wisely entrusted the details of government to his brother, Muhammad Khan, while he devoted himself to bigger questions of policy. His accession was marked by acts of liberality, such as the release of prisoners taken by former kings, and he set himself to the task of regulating the profits of middlemen. He built a magnificent palace, twelve stories high, each story containing fifty rooms, and in each room five hundred men could sit. This building, known as Zaina Dab, was supplied with water from the Sind river. The great king was a staunch friend of the cultivators, and built many bridges and constructed many canals. In his time the waters of the Dal lake flowed into the Jhelum past the Haba Kadl, but the king closed this channel and forced the water into the Nalla Már, which he spanned with seven bridges of masonry. He was fond of sport, and wherever he went he planted gardens, but his favourite pastime was boating on the Wular lake, where he made an island, and on it reared a magnificent. three-storied palace and a mosque. He raised a grand causeway from Andarkot to Sopur, and carried out many other useful works. But the chief glory of the great king's reign was his tolerance[1] towards the Brahmans[2], and regarding this

[1] According to the *Aín Akbari* he forbade oxen being slain.

[2] Dr. Stein writes: 'It is most probable that by the time of Zain-ul-Ab-ul-din all Hindu inhabitants, except the Brahmans, had adopted Islám. It would seem more exact to use henceforth the term *Brahman* instead of the too general "Hindu."'

CHAP. VII. a curious tale is told. It is said that the king was on the point of death when a Hindu Jogi volunteered to give his soul for the dying monarch on condition that his body should be preserved in some safe place, the king took the Jogi's soul but burnt the body, and thenceforward the real king of Kashmír was not Zain-ul-Ab-ul-din but the Hindu ascetic. Whatever may have been the cause it is true that from the time of this illness the king manifested every desire to repair the wrongs inflicted on the Hindus by Sikandar. He remitted the Jazia or poll-tax on Hindus, taught them Persian, and encouraged them by grants of land and in many other ways. He repaired some of the Hindu temples, among others the temple on the Takht-i-Suliman, and he revived Hindu learning. The result of this religious tolerance was the return of the exiled Pandits, and in their train came many Brahmans from the south. Previous to this the official language of the country was Sanskrit [1], and it was fortunate for the Pandits, and to their credit that they quickly adapted themselves to the use of Persian, in the writing of which their descendants are now most proficient. It was from this time that the Brahmans of Kashmír split up into three divisions. Those who took to the use of Persian and entered official life were known as the Karkun Brahmans, those who adopted the functions of priests were known as Báchbaṭṭ Pandits, while those who devoted themselves to Sanskrit learning formed the class known as the Pandits.

The great king was the patron of letters, of the fine arts and of pyrotechnics. He introduced many art manufactures from foreign countries, and his court was thronged by poets, musicians and singers. An amusing story is told of a quarrel between the poet Mulla Ahmad Kashmíri and the king. The poet was expelled from Kashmír, but on his writing a panegyric in praise of the king he was speedily recalled. It was not, however, all peace in this reign, and the king had his warlike side. He conquered Tibet and the Panjab and established his kingdom from Peshawar to Sirhind, and in Kashmír he had serious difficulty with the mischievous Chaks who had sprung into sudden notoriety. They set fire to the grand Zaina Dab and gave much trouble until the king drove them back to the country of the Dards. Having secured the person of their leader, Pandu Chak, the king flogged him to death, but with characteristic generosity took his son Hussain Chak into favour. Sultan Zain-ul-Ab-ul-din died at the age of sixty-nine, having ruled Kashmír well for fifty-two years, and he has left behind him the reputation of a mild, generous and accomplished prince. Unfortunately he bequeathed no permanent system of government to his

[1] Dr. Stein observes: '*Sáradá* is the name of the character in which Sanskrit is written in Kashmír, an older sister of Devanágarí. We possess handbooks teaching the drafting of *official* documents (grants, judgements, police reports, &c., *in Sanskrit*, which were undoubtedly composed under Muhammadan rule.'

successors, and his son Haji Khan, who succeeded to the throne about 1469 A.D. under the name of Haidar Shah, was a drunkard whose weakness gave the Chaks the opportunity for the aggrandizement of power. Little is known about the origin of the Chaks, but their pluck and patience suggest that they were not of the same blood as the Kashmíris, and it is said that they came from the country of the Dards. Legends point to the fact that the Chaks came from the north. In Uttar Machipura the lovely pool of Trigám, one of the most beautiful scenes in Kashmír, is said to have been constructed by Maddan Chak. At Regipura, in the same neighbourhood, are the remains of an old Chak city. The stone arrows in Khushipura, also in the north-west, known as Ráman Kán, are said to have been aimed by the gods at the turbulent Chaks who had a fort at Khushipura. In the south of the valley there are no places connected with the Chaks. One of the leading men in Raja Simha Deva's reign was Langar Chak, and Pando Chak, Halmat Chak and Shams Chak, all seem to have been men of renown. A fable says that Pando Chak sprang from a father who was the offspring of a Kashmíri woman and an amorous demon, and that this branch of the Chaks, who lived at Trigám, were of enormous stature. The Chaks were Shias, and for the first half of the sixteenth century they gradually increased their power, subduing their rivals the Magris and Rainas, and at last, in 1556 A.D., Ghazi Khan, son of Kazi Chak, was practically king, the nominal kings of the line of Shams-ud-din being mere puppets. These Chaks, brave as they may have been, were not the men to found a stable dynasty. Ghazi Khan was a tyrant to the Sunnis, while Yusaf Khan, who came into power in 1580 A.D., married a peasant woman and gave himself up to pleasure. He was the first ruler of Kashmír who discovered the charms of Gulmarg, the summer retreat of the valley. He was an unwise man and quarrelled with his minister Saiad Mubarak Khan, who promptly turned him out of Kashmír. Yusaf Khan's son, Yakub Khan, was a different stamp of man, and in 1582 A.D., when Akbar[1] made his first attempt on Kashmír, he got together a force of the Bombas and Kukas who lived in the Jhelum valley and defeated the Mughals with great loss, though it is right to add that scarcity of food in the invading army, and heavy rains which made the country impassable, helped to the rout of Akbar's troops. Yusaf Khan had from the first wished to acknowledge Akbar, and it is to the credit of

CHAP. VII.

[1] Previous to this, according to the *Ain Akbari*, the Mughals had attempted the conquest of Kashmír. Baber's generals were at first victorious but were forced to leave the valley. In Humayun's reign 'Mehrum Kowkeh' subdued Kashmír. 'This Kowkeh exercising great tyranny the people rose against him, and the Mughal chiefs were obliged to sue for quarter and to return to their own country. Later, Humayun sent Mirza Hyder. He subdued the whole country, prevailed upon the Kashmírians to read the Kutbah and strike the coin in the name of the emperor Humayun instead of that of Nazek Shah.'

CHAP. VII. Yakub Khan that he withstood his father's weakness and declined to yield Kashmír to the Mughal. After his temporary success Yakub Khan became very cruel to the Hindus and Sunnis, and they sent representations to Akbar, who promised them religious tolerance and the abolition of the slave trade. Mirza Kasim was despatched with a force to Kashmír via Rajauri in 1585 A.D. Yakub Khan moved out to meet him with an army largely composed of malcontents who soon deserted to the Mughal side. A brisk contest ensued but Yakub Khan had to give way, retreating to the south of the valley. Mirza Kasim and the Mughal force reached Srinagar 1586 A.D., but were again attacked by Yakub Khan, who took up a position on the Takht-i-Suliman, and by Shamsi Chak, who moved up from the south. The Mughals were very nearly defeated, and for some time desultory fighting went on, but Kashmír was lost when the army of Akbar passed Hirpur, and from the year 1586–87 the valley passed from the period of the Sultans of Kashmír into the period of the Mughal Emperors.

The emperor Akbar apparently visited Kashmír three times. In 1587 he brought with him his revenue minister Todar Mal, who, with more speed than precision, settled the revenue arrangements of the valley from his camp at Patan. It is said that he omitted the villages around Patan from his records by an oversight. On the occasion of his third visit Akbar built the great fort on the Hari-Parbat hill at an enormous cost, and in the vicinity of the fort[1] he raised the town of Nagar Nagar, where his nobles built gardens and houses. It is said that the fort and the Hari-Parbat hill was commenced with the view of attracting the Kashmíris back to Kashmír, whence they had fled in the troublous times of the Chaks. High wages were given to men and women, married women receiving 6 annas and single women 4 annas per diem. It is probable that Akbar had not the leisure or inclination to spend much of his time in the delightful valley, and saving the Hari-Parbat fort and the rapid work of Todar Mal the great emperor has left little behind him. His successor Jehangir loved Kashmír[2], and when he was asked on his death-bed at Bahrámgalla whether he wanted anything he replied 'only Kashmír.' His numerous visits to Kashmír were marked by the construction of lovely pleasure gardens, and he set a fashion which was followed by his nobles. Magnificent chenar trees planted throughout the valley, with the ruins of cascades and summer-houses, all owe their origin to the Mughal vogue, and though it has been said of the emperors

[1] Akbar's fort known as the Sangín Darwáza fort or Nágar Nagar fort surrounds the slopes of the Hari-Parbat hill. The wall is of great strength and has numerous bastions. The fort on the top of the hill is of later construction and was built by Atta Muhamad Khan the Pathan governor.

[2] According to his autobiography he married a Kashmíri. 'After him, by the daughter of the prince of Kashmír who was of the society of the Jouggies, I had another daughter who died a year old.'

that they were stage kings, so far as Kashmír was concerned, they would be entitled to the gratitude of posterity if only for the sake of the beautiful and shady plane-tree. In the vicinity of the Dal lake there were 777 gardens in the Mughal times, and the roses and the bed-musk brought in a revenue of one lakh of rupees per annum. With an enormous empire to control, it was impossible for the Mughals to leave any strong personal mark on the administration of Kashmír, and everything depended on the character of the subah or pro-consul left in charge of the country. These subahs varied in character, but on the whole it would appear that the rule of the Mughal emperors was fairly just and enlightened, and their laws and ordinances were excellent in spirit. Itikád Khan, one of Jehangir's subahs, was a cruel ruler, but he was energetic, for he finally crushed the Chaks. The emperor Shah Jehan was also a great builder of pleasure-places, but he was fortunate in his subahs, Zaffr Khan and Ali Mardan, who are still spoken of with affection as kind and just rulers. Zaffr Khan abolished many of the severe taxes imposed by Itikád Khan, and reformed the system under which the revenue, on account of saffron, was collected. He reduced the poll-tax on boatmen and the taxes on wood and sheep, and put down with a firm hand the practice of seizing all the best fruits for the use of officials, which had led to the people cutting down their trees.

Alimardan Khan was credited with the possession of the philosopher's stone, and it was believed that it was through this he was enabled to build the splendid Serais on the Pir Pánjal route to India. In his time there was a severe famine in Kashmír, and he distinguished himself by the energy with which he imported grain from the Punjáb.

The name of Aurangzeb is execrated by the Brahmans of Kashmír, and though he only visited the valley once his fierce zeal against the unbelievers made itself felt in Kashmír. A legend is told of his persecution of the famous Rishi Pir Pandit Padshah, a Hindu ascetic. A messenger was sent citing the Rishi to appear before the emperor at his court in India. The Rishi travelled in one night through the air to India, and appeared in a terrible form, mounted on a lion, as the emperor lay asleep. Aurangzeb, in his fear, agreed to the Rishi's retaining his title of Padshah, but the legend does not say that the emperor relaxed from that time in his persecution of the Hindus. As the Mughal empire began to decay, the subahs in Kashmír became independent and high-handed, and in the reign of the emperor Muhamad Shah the Hindus were greatly oppressed by Abdul Ganni and Mulla Sharf-ud-din. Kaláshpura, a Hindu ward of the city, was set on fire, and the Hindus were forbidden to wear turbans. In this reign the subahs fought among themselves, and Kashmír fell into wild disorder. By the year

CHAP. VII. A.D. 1751, the office of subah of Kashmír appears to have become hereditary and practically independent of Delhi. Then the unfortunate valley passed into the hands of new masters, and from 1752–54 Kashmír became subject to the Pathan rule, the cruellest and worst of all. Before briefly sketching the chief events of the Shaháni Durani period, it will be well to consider some of the characteristics of the preceding periods. The Hindu period must from certain points of view have been one of great magnificence. With the plunder of conquest splendid temples and fine public works were constructed, and their ruins show that Kashmír in those days was endowed with noble buildings, while the potsherds of ancient cities on the karéwas and elsewhere suggest that the valley must have been very thickly populated. About the condition of the people little is known, but as Hindus living under Hindu kings their lot must have been fairly happy, and irrigation canals testify that the Rajas did not spend all their wealth on temples, but had some thought for the cultivators. Whether they were a brave, warlike people is equally unknown, for it is possible that the fighting-men of the State were mercenaries from the Panjáb. In the next period, that of the Salatín-i-Kashmír, there is the bright period of Zain-ul-Ab-ul-din's reign, but there is little else that is healthy or pleasant. The rise of the Chaks to power cannot be regarded as the brave struggle of a national party, for they were in all probability as much foreigners as the Mughals or Pathans, and in civilization they were the inferiors of both. The Mughal period, if the bad times of one or two cruel subahs be excluded, must have possessed many elements of happiness for the people. The magnificent courts of the emperors, though perhaps inflicting hardship on the people in the way of purveyance and forced carriage [1], must have introduced wealth into the country, while their civilization and splendour could not fail to have an effect on the ideas and life of the Kashmíris, for they, like all orientals, appreciated the outward display of imperial splendour, and were no doubt willing to pay for it. One hears so much of the junkettings and picnics of Jehangir and his lovely consort, the 'light of the world,' of the courtiers vieing with one another and with

[1] Bernier informs us that on the occasion of the visit of Aurangzeb to Kashmír 30,000 porters were employed to carry the luggage of the camp from Bhimbar to Kashmír, 'an enormous number when it is considered that the king and the omrahs have been sending forward baggage and the tradespeople articles of every sort for the last month.' In those days, however, the porters received ten crowns for every hundred pounds weight carried from Bhimbar to Kashmír. I have alluded to the high wages paid by Akbar to the coolies who worked on the construction of the Hari-Parbat fort, and the inscription on the Káthi Darwáza expressly states that no one was impressed and that all were paid. 'Mah karda ba kas begár nya.' Another couplet on the same inscription says that the emperor furnished one crore and nine lakhs of rupees and 200 Indian artisans for the work. The very durability of some of the buildings of the Mughals suggests that the work was paid for. Buildings constructed by forced and unpaid labour do not last long.

their royal masters in the construction of splendid gardens, that one is apt to think that the Mughal rule in Kashmír was one continuous pageant of pleasure, and that the real work of administration was set aside during the Kashmír recess. But public works were not neglected, and Todar Mal's revenue arrangements, though hasty, had much of permanence in them. The institution of village officers[1] dates from the times of the Mughals.

When, however, we pass from the Mughal period to the period of the Shaháni Durani, we pass to a time of brutal tyranny, unrelieved by good works, chivalry and honour. Men with interest were appointed as governors, who wrung as much money as they could out of the wretched people of the valley. Wealth had to be accumulated rapidly, as no one knew how many days would elapse before he was recalled to Kabul, to make room for some new needy favourite of the hour[2]. Amir Khan Jawán Sher was perhaps the best of Pathan rulers, for at least he built the Amiran Kadal, the bridge which stands at the entrance of Srinagar, and constructed the palace of the Shergarhi, but, on the other hand, he showed petty spite in destroying the Mughal gardens on the Dal. The other Pathan rulers are now only remembered for their brutality and cruelty, and it is said of them that they thought no more of cutting off heads than of plucking a flower.

'Sir buridan pesh in sangin dilan gulchidan ast.'

The victims of these fiends were the Pandits. the Shias, and the Bombas of the Jhelum valley. First in the rank of oppressors comes Asad Khan, who boasted that the savage Nadir Shah was his prototype. It was his practice to tie up the Pandits, two and two, in grass sacks and sink them in the Dal lake. As an amusement, a pitcher filled with ordure would be placed on a Pandit's head and Musalmáns would pelt the pitcher with stones till it broke, the unfortunate Hindu being blinded with filth.

The Pandits. who formerly wore moustaches, were forced to grow beards, turbans and shoes were forbidden, and the 'tika' or forehead mark was interdicted. It is said that the exaggerated forehead marks and the absurdly long turbans now affected by the Pandits, still serve to keep alive the memories of the tyranny of Pathan times.

The jazia or poll-tax on Hindus was revived, and many Brahmans either fled the country, were killed or were converted to Islam. Asad Khan was

[1] Dr. Stein, however, remarks: 'A regular system of village administration is alluded to in more than one passage of the Rájataranginí, which also knows of an intricate system of *bégár* dependent on the other. The same is proved for the time of the early Muhammadan rulers by the Sanskrit handbooks for "Office Correspondence" mentioned before. The Mughals may have introduced changes, but village officers were certainly known long before their time.'

[2] Azim Khan made a fortune of two crores of rupees in six years.

CHAP. VII. succeeded by Madad Khan, and there is a well-known proverb 'Zulm-i-Asad ra rasid madad,' which means that Madad out-Heroded Asad. Mir Hazar was another fiend who used leather bags instead of grass sacks for the drowning of Brahmans. He drowned Shias and Brahmans indiscriminately. Atta Muhamad Khan was a ferocious libertine, and his agent, an old woman named Koshib, was the terror of Brahman parents, who rather than allow the degradation of their daughters destroyed their beauty by shaving their heads or cutting their noses. In those days any Musalmán who met a Pandit, would jump on his back, and take a ride, and the saying 'Buta chuk ta khosa dita,' which means in Kashmíri, 'You are a Brahman and I will mount you,' is still quoted. It would be wearisome to recount instances of the brutal cruelty of the Pathans, but, at last, the oppression became so unendurable that Kashmír turned with hope to the rising power of Ranjit Singh, the Lion of the Panjáb. It would seem that Fatteh Khan Barakzai had been negotiating with Ranjit Singh, and had promised him eight lakhs of rupees per annum if he would take Kashmír. A force was sent up to Kashmír by the Pir Pánjal route, and the libertine governor Atta Muhamad Khan, though he made some show of resistance, yielded Kashmír. Fatteh Khan paid eight lakhs of rupees to Ranjit Singh and left his brother Muhamad Azim Khan to govern the country. Muhamad Azim failed to pay the annual tribute to Ranjit Singh, though he managed to accumulate two crores of rupees for himself, and in A.D. 1814 a Sikh army advanced by the Pir Pánjal, Ranjit Singh himself watching operations from Poonch. A false rumour was started by the Raja of Rajauri that the van of the Sikh army had been routed by Muhamad Azim at Hirpur, and the whole Sikh army fell back in orderly retreat. Elated by this success, Muhamad Azim now gave himself up to the delights of torturing Brahmans, and Pandit Birbal Dar, one of the leading men of Srinagar, escaped by stealth and got out of Kashmír by the Kulli Narwáo valley, with his son Rajkak. They repaired to Lahore, and begged Ranjit Singh to come to the assistance of Kashmír. Muhamad Azim, hearing of this, sent for the ladies of Birbal Dar's family. Birbal's wife committed suicide, but Rajkak's young bride was made a Musalmáni and sent to Kabul, where she was living until quite recently. Muhamad Azim became alarmed when he heard of the success of Birbal's mission to Lahore, and departed hurriedly for Kabul, leaving his brother Jabar Khan as governor. In A.D. 1819 Misr Diwan Chand, Ranjit Singh's great general, accompanied by Raja Gulab Singh of Jammu, defeated the governor with little difficulty, and entered Shupiyon. Thus Kashmír, after five generations of Musalmán rule, passed again into the hands of the Hindus. It must have been an intense relief to all classes in Kashmír to see the downfall of the evil rule of the Pathans, and to none was the relief greater than to the peasants, who had been cruelly fleeced by the rapacious sirdars of Kabul. I do not mean to suggest that the Sikh rule was benign or good, but it was at any rate better than that of the Pathans. The following extracts from Moorcroft (Part III. chapter ii. p. 235 and pp. 293, 294) show that the revenue system left much to be desired, and that the Kashmíris met with little mercy at the hands of the Sikhs.

'The village where we stopped was half deserted, and the few inhabitants that remained wore the semblance of extreme wretchedness; without some relief or change of system, it seems probable that this part of the country will soon be without inhabitants. Yet the soil seemed favourable for rice cultivation, and the crop appeared to have been a good one. The poor people, however, were likely to reap little advantage from their labours, for a troop of tax-gatherers were in the village, who had sequestered nine-tenths of the grain for their employer, Jawahir Mal, the farmer of the revenue.

. . . .

'The number of Kashmírians who were to accompany us over the mountains proved here to be no exaggeration, and their appearance, half naked, and miserably emaciated, presented a ghastly picture of poverty and starvation. Yet wretched as they were, the relentless Sikhs would have levied a pice a head for permission to pass the post had we not interfered. The Sikhs seem to look upon the Kashmírians as little better than cattle. The murder of a native by a Sikh is punished by a fine to the government of from sixteen to twenty rupees, of which four rupees are paid to the family of the deceased if a Hindu, two rupees if he was a Muhamedan. The body of a stout young man, whose throat had been cut, was lying close to the road on one part of this day's journey, and the only notice taken of it was by Mardan Ali, the Malik, who ordered it to be covered with grass, that our porters might not be frightened by the sight. Three other bodies were met with on the route; those were some of the followers of Jawahir Mal, who, to the number of forty-five, it was asserted, had perished in crossing the pass lately, in rough and cold weather, against which they were ill defended by clothing or shelter. Some of the people accompanying us were seized by our Sikhs as unpaid porters, and were not only driven along the road by a cord tying them together by the arms, but their legs were bound with ropes at night to prevent their escape.'

Moti Ram was the first Sikh governor; Hari Singh and Pandit Birbal were associated with him in the government. Hari Singh quickly brought Bombas and Kukas to their senses, and Moti Ram by his just and humane conduct restored confidence in the valley. In A. D. 1825 Kirpa Ram was governor. He was a mild, self-indulgent man, fond of boating and boat-

CHAP. VII. women, and nicknamed Kirpa Shroin, 'Shroin,' being the Kashmíri word for the sound of the boat-paddle. In 1827 there was a severe earthquake, and the city was almost destroyed, this was followed by cholera. In this year three Brahman women were burnt as Satis. After an easy rule of five years Kirpa Ram, in the midst of a pleasure party on the Dal lake, was recalled to Lahore, and there being disgraced, retired to Hardwar, where he lived an ascetic life. It is said in jest by the Kashmíris that Kirpa Ram introduced crows into Kashmír, considering that they were necessary to the due performance of funeral rites, as it is the custom in the Panjáb to feed crows on such occasions, and this valuable contribution to the fauna of Kashmír forms perhaps the most important act of Kirpa Shroin's idle rule. Sher Singh, the reputed son of Ranjit Singh, became nominal governor in 1831, but he amused himself, and left all business to Baisakha Singh. A serious famine occurred, and Jamadar Khushal Singh was sent up from Lahore to watch events. He by unwise interference deepened the famine, and numbers of Kashmíris fled to the Panjáb. The famine of Sher Singh is still a great mark in Kashmír history. In 1833 Colonel Mian Singh, the best of all the Sikh governors, came to Kashmír, and by importing grain and eggs from the Panjáb he restored some measure of prosperity to the villagers who had lost their grain seed and fowls in the awful famine. Mian Singh, with a view to stimulating population, remitted the tax upon marriages, and set to work to bring some order into the administration. Revenue divisions were made, and the villages were either farmed out to contractors or leased on the principle that the State took half of the produce in kind. Agricultural advances were made free of interest, proper weights were introduced, and fraudulent middlemen were punished. Colonel Mian Singh decided cases justly and quickly[1], and won a great reputation in Kashmír. But his useful life was cut short by mutinous soldiers, and the remainder of the Sikh rule was disorder and anarchy. To punish the murder of Mian Singh Raja Gulab Singh came up to Kashmír with a force, and having effected his object he returned to the Panjáb, leaving Shek Ghulam Muhiuddin as governor, A.D. 1842. In A.D. 1843 the Jhelum valley was thrown into confusion by the restless Bombas. These Bombas still live in the Jhelum valley and in the country known as Karnáo. They claim a Turkish origin, and before the Pax Britannica were a brave and troublesome tribe. Their leader, Sultan Zabardast Khan, had been entrapped by the authorities and imprisoned in Srinagar. To avenge this Sher Ahmad, the most daring of the Bombas, destroyed 7,000 men of the Sikh army at Kahori, and after raiding the country marched with 8,000 matchlocks against Kashmír. At Shilhál, in the north-west of Kashmír, the

[1] 'Sikha Shahi' is an expression used very commonly in the valley to denote 'summary justice,' as distinguished from a decision made after regular inquiry.

governor's son, Imamuddin, with a force of 12,000 men was defeated. Snow fell, the Sikh leaders were forced to retreat, and Zabardast Khan was given back to his friends. In the same year, 1843, Shekh Ghulam Muhiuddin opened the Jama Masjid, the gates of which had been closed since A.D. 1819. In A.D. 1845 Imamuddin became governor, and the next year, on March 16, 1846, Kashmír, and all the hilly and mountainous country situated eastward of the river Indus and westward of the river Ravi, which had been ceded by the Sikhs to the British Government in lieu of indemnity, was made over to Mahárájá Gulab Singh, and the heirs male of his body, for the sum of seventy-five lakhs of rupees. But Imamuddin, although believed to be well affected towards Mahárájá Gulab Singh, did not give up Kashmír without a struggle, and for some time fighting went on in Srinagar. He called in brave Sher Ahmad and his Bombas, and invested the Hari-Parbat fort for forty days. Mahárájá Gulab Singh's troops were defeated, and his representative, Lakpat Rai, was killed. The Bombas and Kukas raided the valley and plundered the city. At this juncture a British force moved into Jammu territory and Imamuddin surrendered.

Mahárájá Gulab Singh, the first of the Dogra[1] rulers, was a man of great vigour, foresight and determination. His first care was to safeguard his new property against the restless Bombas, and with this view he established forts which commanded the Koi Watawan, a pass of evil repute, and completely held the road over the Nastachhana mountain. Sher Ahmad struggled on for seven years. retreating to Kaghan whenever pursuit became too warm. Mahárájá Gulab Singh treated him with liberality, and he died not long since on his estate in the Deosar Tahsil. Next the Mahárájá looked carefully into the revenue administration of Kashmír. Gazing at the valley from a hill, he said that one part was mountain, one part under water, while the remaining third was in the hands of Jagirdars. He very soon altered this, and, by dint of untiring industry and by strict supervision of his officials, made the most of the revenues of the valley. Exaggerated reports state that the purchase-money paid for Kashmír was recouped in a few years, but this is not correct. Mahárájá Gulab Singh took care that the revenue reached the treasury, and he also took care that there should be no unnecessary expenditure. He repressed opposition and crime with a stern hand, and was universally feared and respected by his subjects and

[1] 'Dogra' is the name given to the country around Jammu, and is said to be derived from a word meaning the 'two lakes,' as the original home of the Dogra people was cradled between the lakes of Siroensar and Mánsar. There are numerous castes in the Dogra-country, and the Hindu, Musalmán, and Sikh religions are represented. All, whether Hindus or Musalmáns, whether high-born Rajputs of the Maharájá's caste or low-born menials, are known as Dogras. At the time of the first Sikh war the Dogras had a great reputation as soldiers. This has been worthily maintained and increased by the gallant conduct of the Dogra troops in the Hunza Nagar expedition, and in the affair at Chilás.

CHAP. VII. servants. He brought the principle of a personal rule to perfection, and showed the people that he could stand by himself. If he wanted their services he would have them, without resorting to the old-fashioned device of paying for them by the alienation of State revenues. The State was Mahárájá Gulab Singh, and as he spent much of his time in Kashmír, and was an able, just and active ruler, and a fairly wise landlord, the condition of the people improved, and after many years some confidence was inspired in the permanence of administration. He was a good friend to the British Government in the troublous time of 1857, and died in that year. The day of his death was marked by an earthquake. His cenotaph is built on the banks of the Dúdh-Ganga river. He was succeeded by his third son Mahárájá Ranbir Singh, who was a model Hindu prince, devoted to his religion and to Sanskrit learning, but kind and tolerant to the Musalmáns, to whom he allowed the free exercise of their religion. He was extremely hospitable to the Europeans, and his efforts to introduce dispensaries and schools in his state showed that he was an admirer of the institutions of the British Government. In 1872 there was an outbreak between the Sunnis and Shias, and the Mahárájá evinced his spirit of justice by granting three lakhs of rupees as compensation to the Shias. Mahárájá Ranbir Singh made great efforts to introduce new staples into Kashmír, and money was freely spent on sericulture, vines and wine-making and hops. He was an enlightened prince, who would have done much towards the development of the valley if he had possessed the stern determination of his father, and could have kept his servants in hand. The latter part of Mahárájá Ranbir Singh's life was darkened by the occurrence of the ghastly famine of 1877-79, and by a disease from which he never recovered. In September, 1885, he was succeeded by his eldest son, Mahárájá Pratáb Singh, who was created a Grand Commander of the Star of India in 1892. Like his father he is intensely devoted to his religion, and though his tastes are conservative, he has done much to change and improve the position of his subjects. His kindness to all classes in Kashmír has won him the affection of his people.

It is difficult to realize the change which has come over Kashmír in the short period of Dogra rule—a period of less than fifty years. Anarchy and constant warfare have been succeeded by complete peace, and the annual inroads of foreign troops, who pillaged the country and rendered the forlorn condition of the Kashmíris more and more desperate, has given place to the welcome invasion of European visitors, who spend large sums of money in the happy valley, and give employment to all classes of the population. In no part of India, perhaps, has the Pax Britannica effected such changes as in Kashmír, and, next to the immunity from foreign conquest and a constant change of rulers, the most important incident of the Dogra administration is the completion of the cart road from India to Baramula, by which the railway can now be reached in two days. CHAP. VII.

The isolation of Kashmír, which in former days was practically cut off from communication with India in the winter, has, from the days when the valley passed into the hands of the Mughals, been an important factor in the history of the people. It placed them at the mercy of shortlived governors, ignorant of their language and customs, who worked their will on the Kashmíris regardless of the policy of the courts of Delhi, Kabul and Lahore, and looked upon Kashmír in the same light as that in which the Roman proconsuls regarded Africa. The dependence on the whims and idiosyncrasies of foreigners of brief authority, coupled with the fact that the Kashmíris never knew how long the rule from which these strange governors drew their power would last, has had a powerful influence on the character of the people, and there is a strong and hereditary disbelief in the permanence of institutions and in the benevolence of rulers. Perhaps no country furnishes so curious a record of constant change as Kashmír, and it is a matter for surprise that under rapid transition of governments, varying in race, religion and language, the people of the valley should have retained their peculiar nationality unimpaired. The isolation of Kashmír accounts in a great measure for this, and it is quite possible that the Jhelum valley road will effect a change in the customs and ideas of the Kashmíris which Mughals, Pathans, Sikhs and Dogras could never have accomplished. As will be seen in the chapter on the social aspect of the people, there is much room for change; but the revolution which will follow the more rapid communication with India is one which will require wise guidance and most careful watching.

CHAPTER VIII.

PHYSICAL HISTORY.

CHAP. VIII.

As will be seen in the chapter on the Political History of Kashmír, the frequent changes of rulers and the absence of continuity in the administration have had a powerful effect on the character of the Kashmíris, but the incidents of the Physical History of the valley have also done much to unsettle the people and to make them suspicious and incredulous. Among the incidents of the physical history I shall include *fires*, *floods*, *earthquakes*, *famines* and *cholera*, and it is hardly to be wondered at that a people constantly liable to these calamities should be sceptical and doubtful as to whether things are ordered for the best. The Kashmíri always gives me the idea that he has just recovered from a fright or that he is daily expecting some great disaster, and hardly a day passes without reference being made to the curse under which the people have fallen and to the sin which gave rise to the curse.

Fires.

The ravages of fires are chiefly felt in Srinagar, where the wood houses and their thatch roof fall an easy prey to the flames, and when once a fire has commenced it is very difficult to arrest it. Accepting the fact that a fire is an incident of the curse, and therefore inevitable, the wretched people will make no effort to extinguish the flames, and it devolves on the authorities and the troops to prevent their spreading. There are no roads in the city along which fire-engines could be brought, and small pitchers of water are of very little effect when the conflagration has once commenced. Twice in the time of Maháréjá Ranbir Singh the greater part of Srinagar was burnt down, and before his accession the city had been destroyed by fire sixteen times. Every man, woman and child carries a potential instrument for a conflagration in the *Kángar*, and the beds of straw very quickly start a fire. I have never seen a city so liable to destruction by fire as Srinagar, nor have I ever seen a place in which it was so difficult to stop a fire, in spite of the fact that the water of the Jhelum river is so near at hand. Probably city roads, waterworks and the use of tiles in lieu of thatch will some day give immunity from fire, but at present every spell of fine, dry weather is sure to be followed by a conflagration, which inflicts misery and sometimes ruin on the helpless citizens. In the villages houses are not crowded together, and though fires often occur the damage done is quickly repaired.

Floods.

Many disastrous floods are noticed in the vernacular histories, but the greatest was the terrible inundation which followed the slipping of the Khadanyar mountain below Baramula in A.D. 879. The channel of the Jhelum river was blocked and a large part of the valley was submerged.

In 1841 there was a serious flood, which caused much damage to life and property; but though old men have shown me marks which suggest that the flood of 1841 equalled or surpassed the disaster of 1893, I cannot ascertain any accurate facts regarding the flood level in 1841. Some marks shown to me suggest that the flood of 1841 rose some nine feet higher on the Dal lake than it rose in 1893, but thanks to the strong embankments around the Dal the flood level in 1893 never rose on the lake to the level of the floods on the Jhelum.

The flood of 1893 was a great calamity, but it has had the good effect of warning the State that valuable house property in Srinagar was inadequately protected, and works are now in progress which may eventually render Srinagar secure from inundation. But the security of the city unfortunately means loss to cultivation on the banks of the river above Srinagar, for all the flood waters of the South must pass the city in their course to the outlet at Bárámula. The more, therefore, that Srinagar is protected the more obstruction will there be to the passage of waters from the south through the city. All things point to the fact that the founders of Srinagar have bequeathed a serious engineering problem to their successors, and some say that the only way out of the difficulty is to lower the bed of the river at Bárámula, regulating the water level of the valley by gates. Others talk of providing an alternative channel to the Jhelum which would run in a north-westerly direction above Srinagar, but this scheme is rendered difficult by the fact that the Dudh-Ganga river, the bed of which is higher than that of the Jhelum, must be crossed. Perhaps a solution of the difficulty might be found in dredging. I have pointed out in the second chapter of this Report how generation after generation has hemmed in the river as it passes Srinagar, and have shown that the Wular lake, which is the natural delta of the river, is gradually filling up from silt. The whole question is one of the first importance. Naturally Srinagar is the first consideration, but from the point of view of land revenue it is of equal importance to protect the crops from constant loss by inundation. In 1893 the floods cost the State Rs. 64,804 in land revenue alone, 25,426 acres under crops were submerged, 2,225 houses were wrecked and 329 cattle killed. Floods in Kashmír are caused by

CHAP. VIII. warm and continuous rains on the mountains which melt the snows or precipitate them down the hill-sides into the streams. Melting snows alone will not cause a flood; nor will heavy rains unless they are assisted by the melting snow. My observations show that rain rarely falls for more than twelve hours and that twelve hours of rain is followed by pleasant sunshine. Rain which lasts for twenty-four hours, if it is widespread, causes high water on the river, but not serious floods. In 1893 the rain which commenced on the morning of July 18, and continued without a break for fifty-two hours, was warm, and it was very noticeable when the clouds cleared away that the great mountains were denuded of snow. There was only one meteorological station in Kashmír when the flood occurred at Srinagar and five inches of rain were registered before the station was destroyed by the inundation. Warning was received by telegraph from Islamabad that a heavy flood was coming down, but unfortunately we do not know any facts about the rainfall in the south of the valley. However, we know that the rainfall was heavy and abnormal, and the simple fact that in the Deosar Tahsil a bear and a panther were found drowned side by side, while in Uttar Machipura a huge python was carried down to the plains, shows that the mountain torrents must have been very huge and violent. Large trees torn up by the roots and carried into the midst of cultivation, the Wular lake dotted with ricks of oilseed and barley, rising ground strewn with the fragments of the city bridges and the wooden ruins of dwelling-houses, and here and there corpses of men and cattle tossing on the stream indicated a great and sudden calamity. Mercifully the flood reached its climax in the day-time and the people were prepared. In the low villages around Panjinará the people hurried off to the higher villages with their children and cattle, and there was little loss of life. Those who stayed on spent the night in trees and begged hard for help from passing boatmen. But in too many cases the boatmen were grasping and heartless, and from information gathered in Srinagar and in the villages, I believe that the *Hanjis*, as a body, behaved in a brutal and disgraceful manner. In the city itself there was wild confusion. The second bridge, one of recent construction, succumbed to the flood and apparently swept away the other five bridges, not by collision but by piston-like pressure. All communication between the two sides of the city was at an end, for the Amiran Kadal, the first bridge, though it stood the shock of the flood, was under water and impassable. So reports were at once started that men whose work lay on one side of the river and whose homes were on the other were drowned, and the night of July 21 was one of anxiety and uncertainty. Marvellous escapes from drowning are recounted, and considering the size of the flood and the low level of the Rahnáwári Mohallá, it is at once a matter for surprise and congratulation that out of a population of 118,960 people, only seventeen were killed, sixteen from drowning and one from the falling of a house. In the villages the mortality was on the whole very light. In the low-lying country, where the crops had been destroyed, there was hardly any loss of life, for the people are always on the look-out for floods. But in the hilly country loss of life did occur, and men, cattle and sheep were carried off by rapid torrents which coursed down the ravines. One or two sad cases came to my notice in which men left their houses and sought refuge in trees, but the trees fell and the unfortunate creatures were carried off by the hill torrents. The chief victims to the floods were the herdsmen and shepherds who at night-time gather their cattle and sheep near the streams. They were taken by surprise and their mangled bodies were hurled down the steep ravines. But, as in the case of the city, it is a matter for congratulation that out of a total rural population of 670,988 only thirty-two perished in the great flood of 1893. Of these thirty-two men, twenty-one were drowned, five were killed by the falling of a tree in the forest above Gulmarg, and six were killed by the falling of houses. The loss of stock was not as great as might have been expected. There was no accurate estimate of the loss of sheep and goats, which in July are away grazing in the mountain pastures, but report said that many sheep were destroyed. The total loss of horned cattle was 329, and this figure may be accepted as correct, though it should be remembered that by the middle of July all plough-cattle and cows not in milk have been driven up to the high grazing grounds. But though I heard of sheep being drowned far away in the mountains, I did not hear any reports of cattle being drowned by the floods. The river is to a certain extent a truthful witness, and few carcasses of cattle were seen floating down towards Baramula.

In Kashmír proper 2,225 houses were destroyed by the floods, and these houses varied, from the frail huts of poplar wood in which the half-amphibious cultivators of the Dal lake live, to the larger and more substantial houses of the ordinary description found in the valley. Near the forests these houses are often real log huts, but further from the forests, where timber is more expensive, the buildings are of unburnt bricks set in wooden frames or are made of panels fitted into grooved beams. It is a noteworthy fact that this latter style of building showed a great power of resistance to the floods. It is difficult to assign a money value to the ordinary house of an average Kashmír cultivator, as the work of building is done by the villagers working in co-operation. Food is given to the friends who assist in bringing timber from the forest and in erecting the house, and regular fees are paid to the skilled carpenter and mason. In normal times there is no difficulty, and the Kashmíri likes to linger over the work. But

CHAP. VIII. unfortunately, owing to the disastrous fire which destroyed so many houses in Srinagar in 1892, there had been a great demand for carpenters and masons and wages had gone up. This rise in wages spread to the villages, and although the State showed its sympathy with the people who suffered from the floods by allowing the free felling of timber in the forests for two months, still the cost of building new houses was very heavy. And the winter was near and in many villages it was feared that the cultivators who had lost their houses would be forced to seek shelter with their friends and relations, as it was impossible to rebuild so many houses in so short a time. In order to prevent wandering, and to attach the people to their villages, I did my utmost to persuade them to lose no time in rebuilding their houses, but the great demand for carpenters, both in the city and villages, delayed the work, and some time would elapse before the once prosperous hamlets in the neighbourhood of Panjinara would recover from their former condition.

Above Srinagar the damage to crops was small. This was due to the formation of the country, which drains rapidly into the Jhelum, and to the fact that from Islamabád to Srinagar the fall of the river is of appreciable extent. Around Srinagar the damage was considerable, but the greatest loss occurred below the city. At the time when the great flood occurred, the spring crops of wheat, barley and rape-seed had been harvested, but for the most part had not been threshed or removed from the threshing-floor. The autumn crops of rice were either in flower or coming into ear. The maize was in ear, and other crops such as pulse, cotton and sesamum (*til*) were well forward and gave promise of an excellent harvest. When the torrents of the mountains of the south reached Kanabal, the port of Islamabád, their speed relaxed and the Jhelum came down slowly though in enormous volume. Along the Jhelum, on either side of the banks which the river has itself made, are erected embankments known as *Sathu*, and as has already been explained efforts were made in 1892 to repair these embankments and to raise them to a height sufficient to resist a normal flood as far as Pampur and Kakarpura. But at certain points the hill drainage comes into the Jhelum, and at these points in old days flood-gates were erected, which let out the hill drainage but kept back the water of the Jhelum when it came down in flood. It was the intention of the Director, Public Works Department, to restore these gates, but for some reason or other they were not put up. So that when the river came down in flood the water poured in at the entrances which should have been closed by gates, and in many places either over-topped the embankment or made large breaches in it. But I am of opinion that even if the flood-gates had been erected in time the floods would have still forced their way through or over the embankments which lie above Srinagar. Spring crops lying on the threshing-floor were damaged, and in low-lying tracts, where the water stood for some days, were destroyed. In the same way the standing crops of rice and maize were destroyed where the water stood for some time, and in many places the embankments built with the object of keeping the flood water out served to keep the water from flowing back into the river.

As the floods approached Srinagar the city and its bridges undoubtedly held up the water and converted the country to the south of Srinagar into a vast, almost stagnant, lake. The river embankment of the Munshi Bagh for the most part withstood the flood, but the back embankment breached, and at the same time the water rose over the river embankment. The European visitors were all prepared, and, thanks to the foresight and energy of Raja Sir Amar Singh, boats were provided for all. Had the climax come in the night instead of at noon there might have been great loss of life. Much discomfort was caused to the European visitors and others who live along the right bank of the Jhelum above Srinagar, and the officials of the Telegraph and Postal Departments suffered greatly. Communication with India and Gulmarg was at once cut off, and all business was at a standstill. There was no dry land anywhere within reach save the slopes of the Takht-i-Suliman. Ponies and cattle climbed into verandahs, and many men spent the night of July 21 in trees. The boatmen took advantage of the situation and charged exorbitant prices for taking people from trees and housetops, and in the city itself these harpies refused to ferry persons across the river unless they paid extravagant fares. In the city there was great alarm. The houses on the banks on either side of the river were never reached by the floods, but the crash of falling bridges, and the sight of the people struggling in the water filled the citizens with terror, and wild rumours were spread as to the loss of life. Women at once jumped to the conclusion that their husbands who were at work on the other side of the river were drowned, and for some days exaggerated reports were abroad as to the mortality caused by the floods.

The river had broken through the gate which protects the Dal lake from floods, and had submerged the lake gardens, destroying the melons, cucumbers, vegetable marrows and tomatoes, which form an important part of the citizens' diet in the month of July. All roads to the city were closed, water-mills had been washed away in the villages and prices at once began to rise. Rice, the staple food, rose from 26 seers to 18 seers per rupee, wheat rose from Rs. 4 to Rs. 5 per kharwar. Oil rose from Rs. $1\frac{1}{2}$ to Rs. 2 per 6 seers, and salt rose from 7 seers to 6 seers per rupee. This rise in prices was, however, only temporary, except in the case of oil and salt. As regards the former, though the price fell from Rs. 2 to Rs. 1.11.0, rates

CHAP. VIII. continued high, as great damage had been done to rape seed, and some loss had been caused to linseed. As regards salt prices continued high until the road to Kohala was again opened. In the low-lying suburbs of the city, notably Rahnáwári, several houses were destroyed, but I was surprised when I visited Rahnáwári and the other low-lying parts of the city to find that there had been so little damage. For though the gate of the Dal lake had been swept away, and though the great Sathu Kazi, which banks out the Jhelum floods, had been severely breached, still the level of the Dal waters never rose to the level of the river floods.

Below Srinagar the river runs with a very slight fall towards the Wular, and to the north the Anchar Dal was brimful of water from the Sind river, while on the right bank of the Jhelum the embankments had been carried away, and the floods of the Sind and the Jhelum rivers were mingling. The whole of the Achan Ilaka on the right bank was hopelessly submerged, and speaking generally the country as far as the Wular was a vast lake, beneath which grand crops of rice and maize lay rotting. Houses and fine ricks of wheat, barley and rape-seed were carried off, and the country presented a pitiable sight. Directly the rain had ceased, on July 20, a bright, hot sunshine followed, and this had the effect of rotting all crops standing in water. Rice as an aquatic plant has a greater power of resistance than maize, but the floods below Srinagar were so persistent that only a very little of the rice submerged survived. The smell of the rotting maize and rice was very pungent, and the villages were for the most part deserted, as the cultivators had fled with their cattle to the uplands. Here and there on the karewa cliffs cattle were collected, and the people were bivouacking in the open air. Up from Shadipur to the Sind valley great damage had been done by the floods, and in the delta of the Sind the fields were strewn with timber, and still worse with deep, white sand, which destroyed the rice for the year and rendered the fields unfertile for some years to come. Men were dancing and weeping in their ruined fields, and in all directions there was wailing and despair. Marvellous tales were told of the efficacy of the flags of saints which had been set up to arrest the floods, and the people believe that the rice-fields of Tulamula and the bridge of Sumbal were saved by the presence of these flags, which were taken from the shrines as a last resort. The worst havoc was wrought in the neighbourhood of Panjinara. In the times of the Mughals enormous embankments were erected to reclaim land from the Wular, and these embankments still preserve the memory of Jehangir and Shah Jahan. The core of the embankments is of heavy blocks of stone, for experience has shown that banks of earth are not sufficient when the foundation is on the peaty soil which is found in the neighbourhood of the Wular. Where stone is not available it has been the custom to drive piles in the ground, in order to consolidate the earth and to provide a firm foundation. I do not know whether this practice is justifiable from an engineering point of view, but all officials and cultivators in Kashmír believe that no embankment on the river-side is sound unless it has a foundation of piles. The land enclosed in the old Mughal embankments is known by the name of *gund*, and in one or two instances some of these *gund* were saved from the floods by dint of working day and night at strengthening the weak points. The people near Panjinara always live in expectation of a flood, but in 1893 they were lulled to a false security by two circumstances. In the first place the Wular lake, owing to the short snows of 1891–92, had dried up in an unusual manner, and its wide shores were dry and thirsty. The people argued that any ordinary flood would find ample room in the Wular. Next there had been a heavy flood on the Jhelum about a month previous to the flood of July 21, and having escaped without damage the people calculated that in all probability there would be no second flood. So wheat, barley, and rape seed were lazily left on the threshing-floors. and when the floods came these splendid crops were absolutely destroyed. The maize crop, which was the finest that had been known for many years, was utterly submerged, and apart from the loss of the grain there was the further loss of fodder. For in this tract cattle are very numerous, and their one food is the stalks of the maize. The whole tract consists of low, peaty soil. reclaimed at various times from swamp, and in many parts it was doubtful whether the land would be fit for cultivation for some years. For the land lies below the level of the Jhelum bed, and it would require a succession of dry years, and careful embankment against the Suknag river and the swamps to the south, in order to bring the land under cultivation again.

Towards the Wular the people who had lost their maize crops devoted their attention to the harvesting of the singhara nut, and it luckily happens that in years of heavy floods the outturn of singhara nut is always large. But the villages further away from the Wular had no such resources, and the State promptly started the construction of the road from Baramula to Srinagar as a famine relief measure.

For those who had lost their year's crops in the neighbourhood of Srinagar ample work was provided on the repairs of embankments and on the construction of the waterworks. In every way the State acted with the greatest liberality and consideration, and though 1893 will be remembered as a year of calamity, the calamity was tempered by the humane action of the Durbar.

CHAP. VIII.

The following diagram shows the rise and fall of the river in 1893, and also the extraordinary and unexpected flood which again visited Srinagar in June, 1894.

RISE AND FALL OF RIVER JHELUM AT SHERGARHI PALACE, 1893, 1894.

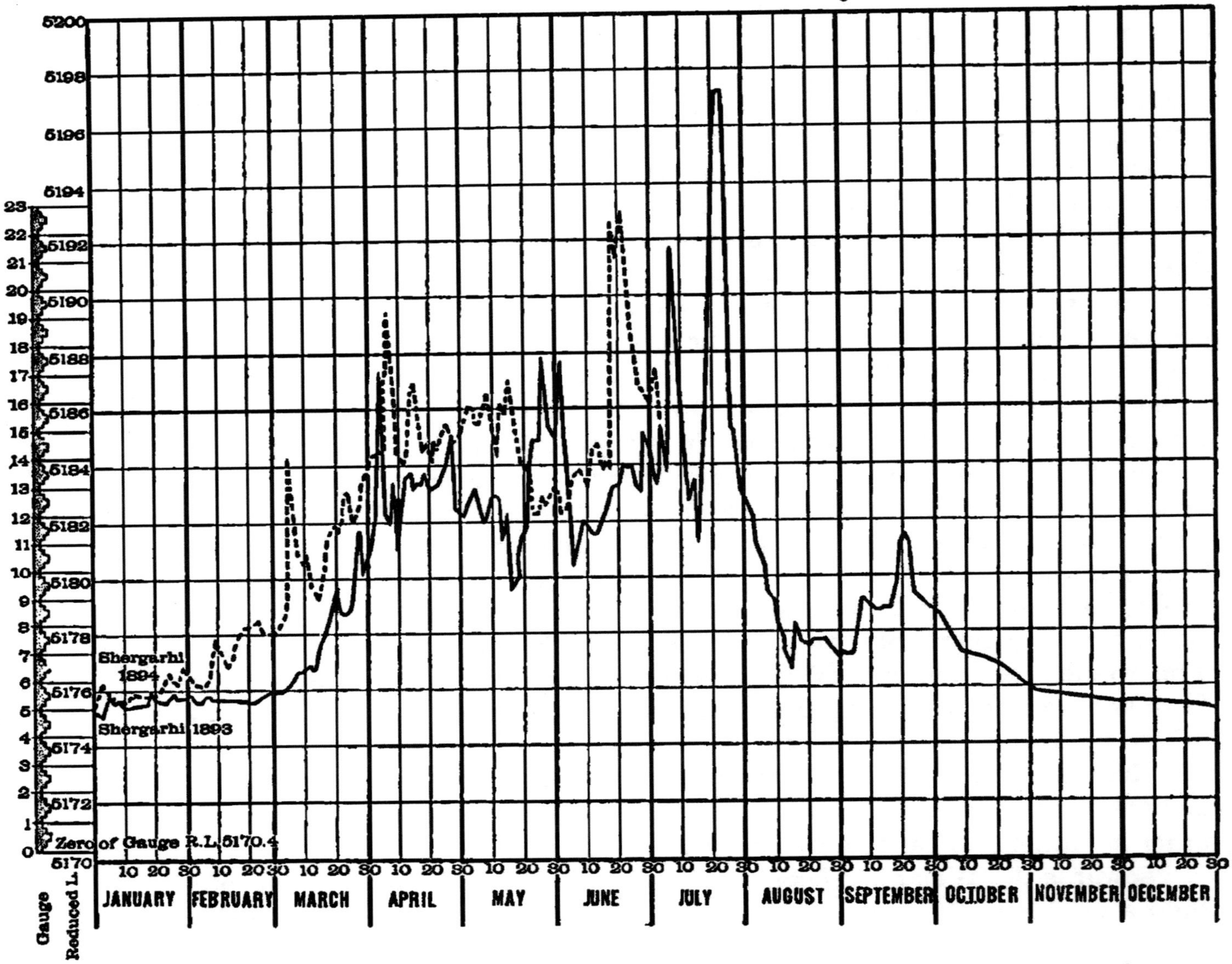

Earthquakes.

Fires and flood, however, sink into insignificance when compared with earthquakes, famines, and cholera. Since the fifteenth century eleven great earthquakes have occurred, all of long duration and accompanied by great loss of life. In the present century there have been four severe earthquakes, and it is worthy of notice that in the last two, of 1864 and 1885, the most violent shocks were felt in an elliptical area whose focuses were Srinagar and Baramula[1]. The earthquake of 1885

[1] The fact that Baramula is a focus of the seismal ellipse supports the theory that the dessication of the valley was caused by earthquake action.

commenced on May 30, and shocks more or less violent were felt up to August 16. Houses were destroyed and there was a general panic, people sleeping for many days out of doors. It is said that some 3,500 persons were killed, and the number of cattle, ponies and other domestic animals crushed by falling buildings was enormous. Baramula and Patan seem to have suffered the most. and large earth fissures were caused, from which it is reported that sulphur fumes and inflammable gases were emitted. Many old water-springs disappeared and landslips occurred, one of which, at Lari Dura in the Krihun Tahsil, revealed fossil singhara nuts at an elevation of about 1,500 feet above the level of the Wular lake. It has been suggested that the style of architecture in Kashmír is not calculated to withstand the shocks of an earthquake, but the inhabitants of the valley claim that the apparently frail structures escape when heavier and more massive buildings would succumb, and it must be remembered that the temples of Patan and the palace of Srinagar suffered in 1885. Even now I have noticed in the courtyards of many villagers' houses a temporary wigwam, which is always kept in readiness for shelter in times of shocks, and the dread of another earthquake is always present.

Famines.

Native historians record nineteen great famines, regarding which they give gruesome details, but the important fact on which they are all agreed is that the famines were caused by early snows or heavy rain occurring at the time when the autumn harvest was ripening. In this century there have been two terrible famines, one known by the name of Sher Singh which was caused by the early, heavy autumn snow of 1831, and the other, more recent disaster, which was similarly caused by continuous rains which fell from October, 1877, till January, 1878. It has been calculated that the population of Kashmír was reduced from 800,000 to 200,000 by the famine of Sher Singh, and a flood which followed the famine destroyed many important irrigation works and permanently submerged large areas of valuable cultivation. In the famine of 1877–79 there was an enormous loss of life. One authority has stated that the population of Srinagar was reduced from 127,400 to 00,000, and others say that of the total population of the valley only two-fifths survived. Years have now passed since the last famine, but the Kashmíri proverb 'Drag tsalih ta dág tsalih na,' which means that 'the famine goes but its stains remain,' is true in all senses, and the country has not yet recovered from the awful visitation of 1877. As the great famine is still fresh in men's minds, and forms a constant topic of conversation with the villagers in camp, I will notice a few of the more important facts connected with it. for there are certain lessons to be learnt which may be of use should famine again

CHAP. VIII. unhappily visit the valley. In the first place, it must be remembered that the one circumstance which can lead to a real famine in Kashmír is the occurrence of rain or snow when the rice and maize is being harvested, and this is a circumstance which cannot be met by any preventive works. Intense drought may cause a slight scarcity, but Kashmír is so amply provided with irrigation that drought cannot do much harm to the great staple food, rice. In 1877 much rice might have been saved if the people had been allowed to cut their crops and carry them. The old system, which delayed reaping operations for revenue purposes, has now been abolished, and the cultivators can cut their crops when they like and place them under cover. If this had been the case in 1877 the crops which had been reaped before the rain commenced would have been saved. It has often struck me that if the villagers would erect temporary thatched sheds at the time of the autumn harvest, rice and maize might be cut and placed under cover, for even when the rain is continuous, lasting for over three months as was the case in 1877, some portion of the crop could be saved, while in years when the rain is intermittent, and the weather catchy, the rice would be harvested in much better condition if temporary sheds were built. In 1877 the autumn crops were good, but as the rain went on they were beaten to the ground. The rice and maize which had been cut were stacked wet. Combustion set in and the grain became black and rotten. When it was evident that there would be no rice or maize for food, an order was issued to sell the State stocks of barley at Rs. 1.4.0 per kharwar to the city people. Middlemen at once bought up barley and wheat at this rate and afterwards retailed it at Rs. 19. As the winter drew on the plough-cattle began to die from want of food, and in the spring of 1878 the authorities turned their attention too late to the problem of obtaining seed for the autumn crops. Unfortunately an order was given to search houses for seed grain, and by this time the people were utterly demoralized, and rather than make over their scanty stocks to greedy and unprincipled officials they hid their grain in the damp earth or sunk it in the river. The one hope at the beginning of 1878 lay in the spring crops of barley and wheat, but heavy rain injured the harvest, and of the poor remnant very little was allowed to go to the cultivators. The same heavy rain had damaged the fruit trees, and when the hungry people had devoured the blossoms of the apples and pears, and the unripe fruit of the mulberries, they turned to the grasses and roots of the swamps and forests. The bark of the elm and the yew was ground into flour. Those near the forests lived on herbs while the skim milk lasted, but herbs without milk soon proved fatal, and by the summer of 1878 famine was raging. Then that awful sign of demoralization and helplessness, manifested by the non-burial of corpses, appeared: wells and holes were choked with bodies, and prowling dogs began to prey on human carcases. The Gujars of the mountains were the heaviest sufferers, and many orphan girls were sold to the city *Amjis*. Terror spread through the country, and men never thought of sharing their scanty stock of food with their relations, but greedily devoured all they could lay hands on. In ordinary times a seer of rice is sufficient for a day's food, but men ate twice and thrice this quantity and still remained hungry. There was a Jin or demon in every one's body, and the Jin had to be fed. Many attempted to escape to the Punjab, but at the barriers troops were stationed to prevent the migration of the people, and harrowing tales are told of the fathers of families getting past the barrier by bribing the guardians of the passes, while the wives and children were left to die in Kashmír. When the vegetables were finished the gaunt people took to oilcake and rice-chaff, and this diet soon hastened the work of death. Then, too late, half-hearted and feeble attempts were made to organize famine relief. A few almshouses were established and grain was imported from the Punjab; but the agency for its distribution was often corrupt, and the grain was adulterated with dirt and embezzled by officials, who retailed it to the wealthy at Rs. 25 per kharwar. At the end of 1878 the old system, *Rahdári*, under which no man could leave the valley without permission, was given up, and the weak survivors tottered over the passes to the Punjab, many dying on the way. The mortality was greatest among the villagers. In the city the unfortunate shawl-weavers were the chief victims of the famine. It is worthy of notice that there was little mortality among the Hindus from starvation. The Musalmáns attribute the immunity of the Pandits to the fact that they were a privileged class, whose official power enabled them to seize all available grain. But in justice it should be mentioned that the Hindus of Kashmír are daintier feeders than the Musalmáns and that they are accustomed to fasts. It is undesirable for many reasons to recount the horrors of the year 1878, or to comment on the apathy and wickedness of certain officials, who looked on the awful suffering of the people merely as an opportunity for making money. The Mahárájá Ranbir Singh did his utmost to save his people, but he never knew the real extent of the disaster until the end of 1878, and false reports were sent to him denying that there had been any deaths from starvation. When the Mahárájá knew that his subjects were perishing in thousands he spared no money, and if the grain, brought with great difficulty over the long, bad roads, had been fairly distributed to the people, even at that late hour, great mortality could have been prevented.

CHAP. VIII. But unfortunately the officials of Kashmír could not be trusted, and the Mahárájá's charity was turned by them into a source of profit. Even the turnip seed, which was wisely despatched to Kashmír, was intercepted by unscrupulous men and in its place rape-seed was sold to the villagers. Until October, 1879, all the horrors of famine prevailed, though many lives had been saved by the imports of grain and by the good fruit harvest. In June cholera had appeared to aggravate the miseries of the country, and great anxiety prevailed up to August as to the condition of the rice crop, which was mercifully saved by timely rains. It is impossible to say whether the estimate that only two-fifths of the population of the valley survived the famine is accurate, but it is correct to say that when I commenced the work of inspecting villages in 1889, there was hardly a village where I did not see deserted houses and abandoned fields, the owners of which had perished in the great famine of 1878. It is a great landmark in their history and in my settlement operations, and by the orders of the Durbar the greatest consideration has been shown to the unhappy fugitives of 1878 who have returned, after the lapse of more than ten years, to claim their ancestral holdings.

Though untimely rains and snow may again fall when the rice and maize are ripe for the sickle, I do not think that it is possible that so awful a famine can revisit Kashmír. In the first place, the policy of the State towards the city on the one hand and the cultivators on the other has greatly changed, and it has been recognized that it is bad economy to sacrifice the interests of 695,281 cultivators to the welfare of the 118,960 residents of Srinagar. But it was different in 1878, and the one preoccupation of the responsible officials was to save the city at all costs from the horrors of famine, and little mercy or consideration was shown to the cultivators. An active and sensible tahsildar, if he had not been hampered by requisitions for the city, might have kept his villagers together, might have exploited the wild foods of the forests and the swamps, and might have induced the people to let the fruit trees bring their fruit to maturity. But the villagers fell into a panic, and there was no one to guide them; and orders such as those for searching the houses for grain made every one suspect that the city alone was to be helped. Then when the spring crops of barley and wheat ripened it would have been politic, as well as merciful, to have encouraged the cultivators by a liberal division of the crops; but never was the number of State watchers so great or their greed so keen as in 1878, when they sat day and night watching for the crops to ripen, and eventually gave the starving cultivators a bare fourth of the harvest. It is no wonder that men surrounded by the dying and the dead should have lost heart, that crime should break out, and that they should make desperate efforts to get out of the charnel-house of the valley and escape to the Punjab. In the second place, there was no organization, and no attempt to start relief-works nor to constitute relief-circles was made till too late; and in this fertile country, where everything can be grown—where potatoes, turnips, carrots can be raised quickly and with ease—the people were prostrate and helpless merely from the failure of one harvest. It is all the more sad to reflect on the waste of life and the waste of energy when one considers how many excellent famine relief-works there are at hand in Kashmír—of the roads that might have been made, and of the irrigation channels which might have been restored and repaired in that horrible 1878, when thousands sat listlessly waiting for death. When famine next threatens the valley it may be safely said that there will be some organization to meet and arrest it. In the third place, the old system, under which no one was allowed to cut or carry his crops without official permission, has been abolished, and every cultivator can now keep his sheaves dry in his own house. And lastly, there is now a cart-road to India, along which grain for the relief of scarcity can be imported; and this alone, in my opinion, would be sufficient to prevent a recurrence of the disaster of 1878. But it must be remembered that it is a long way from Baramúlá to Rawalpindi, and, though rigid political economists would condemn the policy of preventing export, I venture to hold that until Kashmír is linked to India by the railway, the State is justified in prohibiting the export from the valley of the great staple, rice. Among other lessons to be learnt from the famine of 1878, is that it is fatal to issue an order for the searching of houses; and in the numerous conversations which I have had with all classes of Kashmíris I have always been impressed with the stress which they lay on the fact that the searching of houses for grain, in the spring of 1878, was the chief cause of scarcity deepening into famine. One other fact must be mentioned which will greatly modify the effect of the next real famine. In 1877 it was the fixed policy of the State to leave no surplus grain with the villagers. Everything which could be taken from them was carried into Srinagar, and was placed in large, leaky storehouses, where the grain very quickly became unfit for food purposes. Under the new Settlement a considerable surplus of food-stocks remain every year with the villagers, and there are already signs of an incipient thrift and a desire to save which were formerly unknown. If this thrift is encouraged I believe that when the next famine occurs it will be found that villages will hold together, and that there will be sufficient food and fodder to support the life of men and cattle till the spring crops are harvested, and that wandering will not commence before relief-works can be started and food and stocks be obtained from the Punjab.

Finally, it may be said that in a country like Kashmír, in spite of its

CHAP. VIII. isolation from India and the railroad, a famine ought to be impossible, if the administration is prepared and makes full use of the resources of the valley. Even leaving out of consideration the enormous mass of food which is provided by fish, horned water-nut, and other products of the lakes and swamps, by the roots and other edible products of the forests which fringe Kashmír, and by the teeming fruit-orchards which are dotted all over the valley, much can be done to save life by increasing the cultivation of the potato, turnip and carrot. In the chapter on agriculture it will be seen that the Kashmíris are fully alive to the importance of vegetables; but the State could do much to improve the vegetable gardens of the villages by starting a small seed-farm in the neighbourhood of Srinagar. Preparation and a fixed policy for meeting scarcity are all that is wanted to prevent Kashmír from ever again being depopulated by famine. In 1877–9 all estimates regarding the food stocks of the country, of the cultivated area and probable outturn of crops, and of the population, were mere guesswork. This is all changed, and the State now possesses accurate information on all these points. In the absence of any trustworthy statistics it is impossible to say whether the population is now as great as it was before the famine of 1878; but it is safe to say that for proper cultivation the population is still far too small, and in the interests of the land revenue alone every effort should be made to remove causes which lead to such awful and lamentable mortality as occurred in the famine. It has been noticed by many that the Kashmíri women are extraordinarily prolific, and one observer has accepted the statement that every woman has on an average ten to fourteen children.

Cholera. There is no doubt that children are very numerous, and if it were not for famine, smallpox, and the last of the incidents of physical history with which I shall deal—namely cholera, the population of Kashmír would soon be sufficient for the soil. In talking over the question of population many Kashmíris, while admitting the fecundity of their women, always remark that 'God takes his share,' and this is unfortunately true. This question will be discussed elsewhere, and though there are many other causes for infantile mortality, such as smallpox and cold weather, I think that the gigantic proportions of the cholera epidemics of Kashmír entitle them to a place in the physical history of Kashmír. As far as I can ascertain the first mention of cholera is in A. D. 1598, and before that time the disease was unknown or was known by a name different to that now used, 'Waba.' In the present century there have been ten epidemics of cholera, all more or less disastrous to the people of Kashmír, and of these perhaps the worst was the last, which occurred in A. D. 1892. It is stated by the chief medical officer of Kashmír that 5,781 persons died in Srinagar, and 5,931 in the villages. I was in camp during the epidemic, and moved through some of the most infected centres, and I believe that owing to the panic which set in the registration in the districts was not so careful as it may have been in the city, and that 5,931 deaths does not represent nearly the total mortality from cholera in the villages. Terrible gaps have been left in many families and villages which I know, and though it was not necessary to remit land revenue on account of cholera, the epidemic has thrown back the prosperity of many villages for years. It is generally agreed that the centre and nursery of cholera in Kashmír is the foul and squalid capital, Srinagar; but when it is once established there it soon spreads to the dirty towns and to the villages; no medicine or medical organization seems to avail, and the people sit silent and resigned to wait till the plague exhausts itself. It is a curious fact, which I noticed in my tours, that the villages on the karéwa plateaus seemed free from cholera, and that the disease was most rampant in the alluvial parts of the valley. The question of cholera in Kashmír has been discussed exhaustively by competent authorities, and all hold that something must be done to change and clean Srinagar. Some say that unless drastic measures are adopted cholera will become endemic; and now that Srinagar is joined to India by a road there is a twofold necessity for sanitary reform. For if cholera becomes endemic the Punjab and the great military cantonment of Rawalpindi will always be threatened, while, on the other hand, the occurrence of an epidemic in India is sure to be followed by cholera in Kashmír, for cholera, like trade, travels by roads. Before the road from Bárámúlá to the Punjab was opened cholera might occur in India while Kashmír was healthy, and whereas there were twelve epidemics of cholera in the Punjab between 1867 and 1890, there were only five outbreaks in Kashmír during the same period. Now it is almost certain that if cholera reaches the Punjab it will find its way along the crowded road and the narrow valley to Srinagar. I have stated above that if the disease is once established in the congenial filth of Srinagar it soon spreads to the villages, causing heavy mortality among the revenue-paying cultivators of the State, and just as I urge that, even in the interests of the land revenue alone, it is politic to prevent famine, and the utter disorganization and financial ruin which attend on famines, so do I urge that it is financially wise to clean Srinagar, and to remove the ever present danger of cholera. I would add that it is equally necessary to clean Bárámúlá and Sopur, the dirty towns which stand on the line of communication between India and Srinagar. There are higher considerations than those of land revenue which will doubtless move the State to put their house in order both in the matter of famine and of cholera. The horrors of the former are known to me only by hearsay and by the vivid evidence given by ruined villages and abandoned cultivation, but I have been an eyewitness of the ravages and demoralization caused by cholera. Defoe's *Plague of London* shows how

CHAP. VIII. even the strong English character fails in an awful pestilence, and it is not to be wondered at if the less stable orientals become unhinged in a visitation such as that of 1892. All business was stopped, and the only shops which remained open were those of the sellers of white cloth for winding sheets. Men would not lend money, and in the villages the people would sit all day long in the graveyards absolutely silent. In the city the people would go out at dawn to the gardens and parks in the suburbs, returning at night to hear that more of their relatives and friends had perished. The long lines of coffins borne to the graveyards resembled an endless regiment on the march, while on the river a sad procession of boats floated down to the burning-ghats, and living passengers in other boats passed by with averted faces. Men telling me how they had lost all the members of their family would break into hysterical laughter, and I have never seen such utter despair and helplessness as I saw in 1892.

Conclusion. When it is remembered that these calamities are not rare events, and that in one generation, fires, floods, earthquakes, famines and cholera may occur and are always expected, one should deal leniently with the Kashmíri character[1]. I have no means of ascertaining whether the inhabitants of other countries that re specially liable to earthquakes and other disasters are less stable in character than the people of countries happily free from such visitations. But I think that much that is to be regretted in the disposition of the Kashmíris arises from the constant fears and doubts which they feel regarding the terrible forces of nature. The valley is full of superstitions, which the religions of the country foster and accentuate; the administrations of the past have shaken all faith in the honesty and benevolence of rulers, and when on the top of this calamities recur again and again, which make men lose all confidence in the order of the universe, we have a chain of circumstances not conducive to the formation of a vigorous and reliant national character. Superstition has made the Kashmíri timid. Tyranny has made him a liar, while physical disasters have made him selfish and incredulous of the existence of good. Fires, floods, famines, and cholera can all be prevented, and the consideration that efforts devoted to the removal of these evils will eventually result in the moral amelioration of the much abused and little pitied inhabitant of Kashmír, should excite the State to grapple with them regardless of cost and labour.

[1] Take the instance of Patan, a village which lies about halfway between Srinagar and Barámula. It has a population of about 165 families. In 1885 seventy persons perished in the earthquake. In 1892 fifty-five persons were carried off by cholera. This is a terrible record for seven years, but it is by no means an unusual record in Kashmír.

CHAPTER IX.

STATISTICAL.

THERE are several reasons rendering it difficult, if not impossible, to give statistics for the Kashmír valley which would convey any accurate idea of the condition of the country previous to the operations of the Land Revenue Settlement and of the census of 1891. Akbar's great statistician in the *Ain Akbari* gives rough figures for the Subah of Kashmír, of which the valley formed a small and imperfectly defined part. Subsequent histories and notes give vague statistics, founded on no systematic inquiry, and while the figures of population and area are mere guesswork, they are further complicated by the fact that no accurate explanation is given of the country comprised in the geographical name Kashmír. As regards the figures which have been made public from time to time on the subject of the revenue of Kashmír, it is necessary to remember that each succeeding dynasty has done its utmost to exaggerate the financial resources of the valley, and to collect the revenue in accordance with exaggerated estimates. It should also be remembered that it is an old-established custom of the officials of Kashmír to manipulate accounts in such a way as to conceal from their masters the fact that the revenue was nominal, and that the real collections fell far short of the handsome income which existed only on paper. It is a curious fact that while individuals in the East modestly underrate their incomes, oriental States are prone to magnify their resources; and the hard-headed accountant, who declines to recognize in figures an elasticity by which the half is equal to the whole, would have met with small favour at the hands of the magnificent Akbar. The glory which attaches to huge areas, large populations, and enormous revenue is dear to the oriental ruler, and I believe that many of the exaggerated ideas regarding the financial capacity of the Kashmír valley are due to this sentiment. Again, the officials of Kashmír look upon averages as a sordid and contemptible method of calculating the resources of a country, and if in one year of extraordinary harvest a vigorous governor collected an astonishing revenue,

CHAP. IX. they would look upon that as the standard, and would omit from their calculations years of famine, flood and pestilence. It is good to be sanguine and to view one's country on the sunny side, but in statistics the average inevitably presents itself. Just as Akbar's statistician included Kabul and Kandahar in the Subah of Kashmír, so more recent notices of Kashmír include parts of Jammu territory, and it is very difficult to ascertain from rough estimates, which are to be found in scattered notices, how much of these estimates should be credited to the Valley of Kashmír. In order to prevent any mistake in future I must explain that the Valley of Kashmír treated of in this Report, and in this chapter, consists of the three wazárats or districts of Khás, Anantnág, and Sopur, and excludes the wazárat or district of Muzzafarabad, which lies below Bárámula. When I commenced work in Kashmír there were three wazárats in the valley—Khás, Anantnág and Sopur, and there were fifteen tahsils distributed as follows:—

	Tahsils.
1. Khás Wazárat	1. Khás. 2. Ich Nagám. 3. Donsu Mancháma. 4. Wular Vihu. 5. Cherat.
2. Anantnág Wazárat	6. Anantnág. 7. Sri Ranbir Singhpura. 8. Deosar. 9. Dachanpára. 10. Shupiyon.
3. Sopur or Kámráj	11. Lál. 12. Hamalzainigir. 13. Uttar Machipura. 14. Biru Magam. 15. Krihun.

I have maintained three wazárats, as before, but have reduced the tahsils to eleven. They are as follows:—

1. Khás Wazárat	1. Lál-Phák. 2. Srinagar. 3. Sri Partáb Singhpura. 4. Nagám.
2. Anantnág Wazárat	5. Wantipura. 6. Anantnág. 7. Haripura. 8. Sri Ranbir Singhpura.
3. Sopur Wazárat	9. Uttar Machipura. 10. Sopur. 11. Patan.

It should be explained that the Gurais valley, which, previous to Settlement, formed part of the Gilgit province, has been surveyed and assessed and is now part of the new Sopur Tahsil. The changes in the administrative divisions made by me were based on two principles, one, that so far as possible each irrigation system of the country should be under the jurisdiction of one tahsildar, the other that the river Jhelum should be utilized as the boundary of the tahsil.

The local divisions of Kashmír have varied considerably. In old days the country was divided into two parts, Maráj, the south, and Kámráj, the north. Tradition says that two brothers, Marhan and Kaman, fought for the crown, and that all the country below Srinagar fell to Kaman and was known as Kamanráj, and that all above became the territory of Marhan and was known as Marhanráj. These local divisions are still recognized by the people, and the *patois* of Maráj differs from that of Kámráj, and both differ from that of Yámráj which is the old name for Srinagar. In these divisions were thirty-four subdivisions, still recognized by the people, and though the State may for administrative purposes make changes in boundaries and in designation, the old names will linger on, and the people of Ranbir Singhpura Tahsil will style themselves residents of Shahabad and Brang for many years to come. In 1871 we find that the country was divided into five wazárats or districts, Srinagar, Patan, Anantnág, Kámráj. and Shupiyon. These were again subdivided into thirty-seven tahsils. In 1887, that is just before the Settlement commenced, there were four districts, Srinagar, Haripur or Shupiyon, Kámráj, and Anantnág. These districts contained twenty-eight tahsils and were said to contain 2,487 villages.

The Kashmír valley, with its three wazárats and its eleven tahsils, is under the executive charge of the Hákim-i-Ala, or Governor of Kashmír. This officer is also the executive head of the districts of Gilgit, Astor and Muzzafarabad. Ladakh and Skardu districts are under the charge of the Hákim-i-Ala or Governor of Jammu. As before explained, the statistics contained in this chapter refer to the Valley of Kashmír as comprised in the three districts of Khás, Anantnág, and Sopur, with eleven tahsils, and *do not include* Muzzafarabad, Gilgit, or Astor.

Population.

In 1835 it was stated that the population of the valley did not exceed 200,000 persons, 'to which number it had been in twenty years reduced from 800,000 by oppression and the awful dispensation of earthquake, pestilence, and famine.'

In 1868 a census was taken of the population of Srinagar, but its accuracy was doubted. The census gave a population of 112,715 persons, of whom 24,945 were Hindus and 87,770 Muhammadans. The number of houses was stated to be 20,304.

CHAP. IX.

In 1873 another census was taken, which returned the total population of Kashmír, including the Muzzafarabad district, as 491,846. Later, some time before the terrible famine of 1877–79, Dr. Elmslie, who had resided in the valley for six years as a medical missionary, calculated the population of the valley to be 402,700, of these 75,000 were Hindus and the rest Musalmáns. The city of Srinagar accounted for 127,400, and the rural population amounted to 275,300.

No accurate idea can be formed of the extent of the mortality caused by the famine, but my impression—gained from constant conversation with the villagers on the subject—is that the following description, written in 1879, is in no wise exaggerated:—

'No European who carefully examined the city this summer (1879), with a view to guessing its population, ever put the people at over 60,000 souls, but nothing can be exactly known. A number of the chief valleys to the north were entirely deserted, whole villages lay in ruins, some suburbs of the city were tenantless, the city itself half destroyed, the graveyards were filled to overflowing, the river had been full of corpses thrown into it. It is not likely that more than two-fifths of the people of the valley now survive.'

If, therefore, Dr. Elmslie's figures were approximately correct the famine removed 67,400 persons from the city, and 174,220 persons from the villages. Many of these escaped with their lives to the Punjab, and many have since returned to Kashmír. It is stated on the authority of a French shawl-merchant, long resident in Srinagar, that whereas in former times there were from 30,000 to 40,000 weavers in Srinagar only 4,000 remained after the famine.

Census of 1891.

The census of 1891 supplies statistics of population which may be taken as accurate. It shows that the Kashmír valley contains a population of 814,241, of which Srinagar accounts for 118,960, that is to say in twelve years the population of Srinagar has nearly doubled, while the rural population, which was supposed to have fallen to 101,080 in 1879, has risen to 695,281 in 1891. This would indicate great powers of recuperation and would bear out the observations of Major Montgomery, who remarks in his notes on the survey operations in Kashmír: 'It is said that every woman has at an average ten to fourteen children.'

I should, however, be inclined to think that Dr. Elmslie's calculation was under the mark, and in this I am supported by old and intelligent Kashmíris, who maintain that the population in 1891 was almost exactly equal to the population of the valley at the beginning of 1887, before the famine occurred. It is useless, therefore, to attempt any comparison between the population as determined by the census of 1891 and the population as estimated by Dr. Elmslie and others. Thus the census shows that out of a total population of 814,241 only 52,576 are Hindus. By Dr. Elmslie's calculation there were 75,000 Hindus before the famine, and it is a notorious fact that the Hindus of Kashmír did not suffer heavily in the famine. One important matter can, however, be elicited from these figures. I believe that although the census taken of Srinagar in 1868 may have been inaccurate as to the number of persons, it was probably accurate as regards the number of houses. In 1868 there were 20,304 houses, in 1891 there were 22,448. This increase is due to the fact that a large number of villagers migrated to the city after the famine of 1877–79, in order to escape from forced labour and to obtain cheap food. CHAP. IX.

Religions. The following table shows the division of the people according to religion :—

Hindus.	Sikhs.	Muhammadans.	Christians.	Parsis.
52,576	4,092	757,433	132	8

That is to say the Muhammadans form over 93 per cent. of the total population, while the Hindus represent less than 7 per cent.

Urban population. The census recognizes four towns in Kashmír. Their population is as follows :—

Srinagar	118,960
Anantnág	10,227
Sopur	8,410
Baramula	5,656
Total	143,253

The population of Srinagar may be fairly regarded as urban, but in the other three towns a large proportion of the people are agriculturists. The small towns of Shupiyon, Bij Behára, Pampur, and Bandipur, contain, however, a non-agricultural population, and if they be included they will balance the agricultural population of Anantnág, Sopur, and Baramula, which has been classed in the census as urban. It may therefore be said that the urban population forms about 17 per cent. of the total population of Kashmír, and it has been the policy of the rulers of the valley from time immemorial to sacrifice the interests of the agricultural population to the care and comfort of the people of Srinagar.

Rural population according to districts. The following table shows the division of the rural population according to districts :—

Name of District.	No. of Villages.	No. of Houses.	No. of Houses per Village.	Total Population.	No. of Persons per House.
Khás	847	28,330	33	190,825	7
Anantnág	796	32,536	41	214,331	6
Sopur or Kámráj	1,111	34,904	31	241,498	7
Jagirs of the Rájás	116	3,620	31	24,334	7

CHAP. IX.

The average number of persons per house is thus seven. But Major Montgomery, in his notes on the survey operations of Kashmír, writes: 'In the country generally the number of inhabitants in each house, including every living soul, ranges from ten to thirty; in twenty-three different villages in which special inquiries were made the average was found to be eighteen.' Assuming that the census figures are correct, we find that the patriarchal system is disappearing and that there is a tendency on the part of the agriculturists to leave the paternal roof and to set up for themselves. This tendency undoubtedly exists, and our Settlement operations brought it daily to my notice. It is a healthy tendency so far, because the holdings of the various members of a family are still too large for high cultivation.

Sex of population.

Of the total population 429,464 are males, 384,777 are females. In Srinagar itself and the towns there are 817 female Hindus for every 1,000 Hindu-males, and 916 Muhammadan females for every 1,000 Muhammadan males. In the villages there are only 721 Hindu women to every 1,000 Hindu men, but the Muhammadan agriculturists are better provided, since for every 1,000 men there are 895 Muhammadan women. The rates of females to males among the Muhammadan agriculturists is perhaps higher than it should be, for at the time of the final enumeration, viz. February 26, 1891, a considerable number of Muhammadan males were away in the Punjab. The deficiency of females is, however, sufficient to account for the fact that both among Hindus and Musalmáns polygamy is extremely rare.

Births and infantile mortality.

The census of 1891 fully confirms the remarks of Major Montgomery and other observers on the subject of the prolific character of the Kashmíris. The proportion of children to the total population is, among the agricultural classes, 4,463 per ten thousand. For the whole of India the proportion is 3,888 per ten thousand. The census reveals other facts which are of interest besides the fact that births are more numerous in Kashmír than in other Indian provinces. Deaths of children under two years are more frequent than they are in India, but from the age of two to four there appears to be greater vitality in Kashmír than there is in India. The chief victims of early mortality are female children, who succumb to smallpox, and who perhaps do not receive the same care which is bestowed on male children. It is a sad fact that in Kashmír about one-half of the children die after birth, and nearly one-third die after attaining one year, and it is especially to be regretted that though there are more females born than males, the ratio of females to males should be so small for the whole population. I have elsewhere discussed the enormous importance of introducing a vigorous system of vaccination. Kashmír requires a much larger agricultural population than it possesses at present, and self-interest and humanity alike demand that the baby girls should be protected against smallpox. Cholera is deadly, but it has not the same results on the population as smallpox. CHAP. IX.

Longevity. It has often been remarked that the valley is so healthy that men, like crows, have only one ailment to dread—old age. I have met with many old men in the valley, but my impression is that fifty years would be considered a ripe old age, and I have often noticed white-haired men of forty years. In one village, Wana kari (Hamal), I found a striking instance of longevity, due it is said to the purity of the water-spring (*gangaji*). Krishn Das is 95 and has four sons, aged respectively 70, 60, 40, 30. Krishn Das' father died at the age of 105, and his uncle died recently aged 114. Krishn Das' wife died at 90, Krishn Das can walk 30 miles with ease. His memory is excellent, and he attributes his vigour to goats' milk. He has never used tea, tobacco, or liquor.

According to the census, the life expectancy or average duration of life in Kashmír is as follows:—

	Rural.	*Urban.*
Males	20·11 years.	21·30 years.
Females	19·19 "	20·35 "

The easy life of the citizens gives them an extra year in which to enjoy the blessings of cheap food and security from exertion. The hard life of the agriculturists and exposure to damp and cold remove them from the valley one year sooner than the well-fed citizens. Our Kashmíri life expectancy contrasts unfavourably with the English average.

Crime. Gaols. Kashmír is happily very free from crime, and one gaol, in Srinagar, is sufficient for the valley. In the year 1891–92, which may be taken as a year of normal conditions, 243 convicts were admitted to gaol, and of these some were not inhabitants of the valley, but came from the Muzzafar-abad district. Of these convicts only two were women; and the agricultural population of 670,989 only contributed forty-one men. At the beginning of the year 1891–92 there were 121 convicts in gaol, but by the end of the year, including the new admissions, there were only 127 convicts in custody, and the daily average of strength of prisoners was 129. Taking, however, 243 as representing the average number of convicts in Kashmír in any one year, we find that whereas in England convicts form ·070[1] of the total population, in Kashmír they represent only ·029. The small number of convicts is due to no leniency on the part of the executive nor to want of zeal on the part of the police. In no country is secret espionage more keen than in Kashmír, and the absence of crime is due, in my belief, partly to the non-criminal character of the people, and

[1] *Secrets of the Prison House*, by Arthur Griffiths, vol. i. p. 356.

CHAP. IX. partly to the fact that, as every one is a potential spy, men on the brink of crime are kept back by the knowledge that their friends and relations will betray them. The total expenditure in 1891–92 on gaols in Kashmír amounted to Rs. 9,185, and the income was Rs. 1,708.

Apart from the fact that crime is rare in Kashmír, it is satisfactory to notice that the offences are chiefly against property and not against persons. Thus in 1891–92 of 543 cases reported only thirty-five were offences against the person, and no case of burglary occurred. Within the last ten years there have been only five capital punishments inflicted in Srinagar, and of the men hanged only one was a native of the valley. It is also satisfactory to notice that juvenile criminals are rare. Thus out of 243 convicts only two were boys under sixteen years of age.

Police. To control crime in Kashmír, and to watch 814,241 persons, a police force of 436 officers, rank and file, costing Rs. 58,312 per annum, is sufficient. The police officers are assisted, however, by the village watchmen or chaukidars, who are a numerous, vigilant, and inquisitorial body, numbering over 1,000 men. They are mostly of the Dúm class, and have keen detective faculties and an excellent system of transmission of intelligence. Everything of the slightest interest which occurs in a village is promptly reported by the watchman to the police. The watchman receives no pay from the State, and lives on the contributions of the villages within his beat. Even his uniform of blue and red and his official spear are provided by the villagers. The system works well, in that Kashmír is extraordinarily free from crime. It has been suggested that the watchmen should be paid by the State, but I hold that neither the State nor the villagers would benefit from the change. At present the watchman is a village institution, taking a lively interest in the one great event of village life—the outturn of the harvest. If the harvest is good the watchman's share of the crops is sufficient. If the outturn is bad the watchman suffers like the villagers. At present it is to the watchman's interest that the villagers should attend to agriculture and should eschew pursuits which would bring them into trouble. If he were a paid servant of the State he would soon strive to gain promotion by official zeal, and as an official he would soon cease to be one of the village community, and would thus lose his usefulness.

Education. In most countries drink is considered to be a pregnant source of crime, education a powerful check. In Kashmír drink and drugs do not enter into the life of the people, but the absence of crime cannot be in any way connected with the spread of education. The following table will show the extent of educational operations in the valley, so far as the State is concerned. I again take the year 1891–92 as representing the normal condition of the country:—

No. of boys on roll	1.585
Average daily attendance	1,228
No. of scholars learning—	
English	299
Vernacular only	1,541
Sanskrit only	44
Religion—	
Hindus	1,327
Sikhs	21
Muhammadans	233
Others	4

That is to say, out of a population of 52,576 Hindus only 1,327 are receiving State instruction, while out of a population of 757,433 Muhammadans only 233 obtain any benefit from the State schools. These figures also show that though the Hindus form less than 7 per cent. of the population, they monopolize over 83 per cent. of the education bestowed by the State. A further fact should be noticed, which is that of the 1,585 boys on the roll of the State schools 1,220 attend schools in Srinagar. These figures would justify the opinion that education is backward in Kashmír, and it might be urged that the State ought to establish more schools. Considering the enormous sums and the vast labour which have been expended in India on State education, it is only natural to ask why the Kashmír State, which is always so apt to borrow institutions from India, has not followed the example of giving a practically free education to the people of the valley. The answer is that the more affluent of the villagers prefer the mosque schools, or the system of private tuition, to the instruction given by the State, and it is a surprising fact that a large number of rural Muhammadans can read and write Persian with ease. The rural population does not at present want assistance from the State, and fathers have the old-fashioned idea that homely morals are better than the scholarship and advanced thought which is born of the State schools. The State is also old-fashioned and recognizes that the supply of educated Pandits is already far greater than the demand, and that the manufacture at State expense of a number of hungry students, for whom there is no employment, would be likely to cause discontent. If the Kashmíri Pandits would leave their country in search of work it might be well to extend education, but they prefer to stay in Srinagar. As regards the rural classes the State holds the view that those who want education will obtain it at their own expense, and that it is doubtful whether in the present circumstances of the agricultural population it would be wise to educate the masses at the cost of the exchequer. I think that the best policy will be to leave the rural classes alone at present, and to use every effort to introduce technical education in Srinagar.

CHAP. IX. The Kashmíris have artistic instincts and are famous for their skill in art manufactures. Nature has been bountiful in furnishing raw material for arts and manufactures, but owing to the want of technical instruction the excellent fibres, willow-withies, leather, and clay of the valley are practically wasted. I know of no place where technical education would succeed better than in Srinagar. The artistic faculty is always present—all that is needed is skilled direction, and perhaps at the outset State encouragement and patronage. There are many considerations which call for effort in the direction of technical education. The huge city population, already a burden to the State, is becoming every year more helpless and more degraded. The terrible system of pauperization by which the city people receive food-grain at half rates has removed the great incentive to industry and progress. Wages have no honour, and are a mere token representing so much rice and so many days' food. The Kashmíri artisan does not grumble at the small wage and has no quarrel with his employer, the middleman, who openly avows a profit of 50 per cent. But the Kashmíri artisan would very soon grumble if the State allowed prices of grain to be regulated by the laws of supply and demand. The fact is that the artisans of Srinagar have not yet discovered that the old conditions, under which they were practically slaves of the State, have disappeared. As I have shown elsewhere, in the good days of the shawl trade it was financially expedient to feed the shawl-weavers with cheap grain, for the loss to the State was handsomely recouped by the large and easily collected tax on shawls. But now the shawl trade is dead, the artisans contribute nothing to the exchequer, and the State might in fairness withdraw from its former position, and might allow prices to follow natural laws and wages to follow prices. The change has commenced, and I believe that directly some part of the middleman's profit finds its way into wages, and wages become a reality, there will be a marked improvement in the quality of the manufactures of Srinagar. Work and wages have their dignity in most countries, but in Kashmír there is no feeling of honest independence, and all realize that they are paupers—existing at the will of His Highness the Mahárájá. The change must come, for the State has recognized the fact that the only class which benefits from the old system of pauperization is the middleman class. Another consideration which urges the introduction of technical instruction is that the Musalmáns, who now practically derive no benefit from the educational institutions of the State, would gladly avail themselves of the chance of learning new handicrafts.

Medical aid. The State has always done its best to afford medical help to the people, and maintains one excellent hospital in Srinagar and six dispensaries, three of which are situated in the districts. The following table shows the extent to which the people availed themselves of State help in the normal year 1891–92:— CHAP. IX.

Total number of in-door patients	615
Total number of out-door patients	122,960
Total	123,575

2,188 surgical operations were performed, of which 283 were major operations. Eight cases of double amputation of legs were performed, in Srinagar, for gangrene after frostbite, all of which ended in recovery. In a country like Kashmír, where travellers are liable to frostbite on the passes, and where mountain accidents and injuries from wild beasts are frequent, the Srinagar hospital is a great boon. It is noticed that venereal diseases form fully 25 per cent. of the surgical cases. Of the diseases treated in the State hospital and dispensaries the following are the most common: fevers, syphilitic diseases, rheumatic affections, nervous system diseases, eye diseases, respiratory diseases, dyspepsia, diseases of digestive system, connective tissue and skin diseases. It is interesting to compare the working of the splendid Medical Mission.

'Kashmír Medical Mission, 1893. (These figures are about the average of last five years.)

'Hospital Srinagar, eighty beds—

In-patients	853
Out-patients	8,688
Total visits	20,606

'Temporary winter branch, two months only—

New patients	1,469
Total . . .	2,022

'Villages, number of days' work ninety—

Number of patients seen . . .	5,167

'Surgical operations—

Major	503
Minor	2,086

'Average income Rs.10,000 from voluntary sources.

'Villagers have apparently great faith in European medicines, e.g. at Hanjipore, Tahsil Deosar, 2,500 patients came for treatment in eight days, and at the opposite end of the valley, e.g. Tragam, the numbers have been almost equally great. But in the city and larger towns Kashmíris usually resort to their own *Hakíms*, in the first instance, for ordinary medical (non-surgical) diseases, and only consult Europeans for surgical complaints, or when *in extremis*. With regard to remoter parts, such as Drás, Kargil, the Wardwan and Skardu, the conditions seem similar to those of Kashmír villages.'

CHAP. IX.

Lepers and lunatics.

The census gives no figures showing the number of lepers or lunatics in Kashmír. It appears that in 1891–92, 103, and in 1892–93, 260 lepers were treated. From an inquiry made in 1890 it seems that there were 133 lepers in the valley. A large number of lepers are to be found among the nomad herdsmen who visit Kashmír in the summer. The State has shown great liberality in dealing with leprosy, and there is a State leper hospital which is under the charge of the Kashmír Medical Mission. In 1892–93, 146 lunatics were treated at the asylum connected with the Srinagar gaol. This is not an asylum in the English sense, but is a place where medicinal treatment for insomnia and attacks of intense excitement is given. Dr. Mitra Rai Bahadur estimates the number of lunatics at 250, and he notices that they are chiefly Hindus. It is unfortunate that we possess no statistics regarding lunacy, but my frequent tours through every village in the valley have acquainted me with the sad fact that lunatics are common. Some are lunatics from their birth, some have gone mad from the excessive use of charras, others have lost their senses through some calamity. The lunatics are a harmless people, and are well treated by the villagers. I have discussed the question of establishing a lunatic asylum, but the villagers think that the lunatics are happier as they are, and that captivity would do more harm than good. They regard them much as the Swiss regard the *cretins*. Suicide is very rare in the valley, but I have known cases which, in unscientific language, might be styled death from a broken heart. The Kashmíris are a nervous people, and cannot stand sudden and great misfortunes. They are very demonstrative, and when overtaken by calamity gesticulate in so frenzied a manner that one wonders that their mind regains its balance. Compared with the ordinary Kashmíri, the natives of India would seem cool and phlegmatic.

Goitre is common. In 1891–92, 520 cases were treated.

Blindness is very frequent, and is chiefly caused by smallpox. The number of deaf persons is also great, but we have no statistics on the subject of these infirmities.

It is only of late years that the Kashmíris have begun to recognize the benefits of the Western system of treatment, and the growing belief in the efficacy of the European methods is due to the devotion and skill of the medical missionaries of Kashmír. Even now the mass of the people believe in their own doctors, many of whom are men of considerable ability and experience. There are 300 *Hakíms* or doctors in Kashmír, and as a rule the profession is hereditary. Their system is based on the Greek system of medicine, and I have known cases in which some of my subordinates have derived great benefit from the skill of the Kashmíri *Ḥakím*. Once, when I was in great anxiety, a deputation of Kashmíris begged me to allow a well-known *Hakím* to treat my son. They urged that this *Hakím* had never failed to cure the disease. The *Hakíms* have a considerable knowledge of herbs, and their herb-collectors are the shepherds, who spend the summer on the high mountains where the most valued plants are found. The *Hakím* charges a wealthy patient eight annas a visit, but he makes some money by compounding medicines. He does not dabble in surgery. He will mark with a pen the vein which is to be opened, but a barber must be called in to operate. There are over 1,900 barbers in the valley. If leeches are to be applied a special man is sent for. Such simples as the *Hakím* does not obtain from the shepherds are bought from the druggists, of whom there are 159 in Kashmír. The *Hakím* never attends *midwifery* cases; special women, of whom there are seventy-four, dispose of these cases. Besides the professional *Hakíms* there are many 'wise women' in the villages who have considerable knowledge of the properties of herbs, and it is a remarkable fact that nearly every peasant seems to know something about the medicinal powers of plants. The sovereign remedy of the *Hakíms* for all very serious cases is the chob-i-chin (Smilax China), a kind of root brought from China and administered internally. Inoculation for smallpox, so common in Astor and elsewhere, is unknown in Kashmír, save to the Gujars of the mountains, and apparently the only help in smallpox is the reading of the Koran by a Pir. The people believe greatly in the efficacy of amulets given by Pirs. They cure all diseases. The amulet is either fastened on the right[1] arm, neck or turban, or is put in water and the water and ink of the writing drunk by the patient, or is burnt and the smoke inhaled by the sick man. This inhalation brings dreams, and the dreams must be told to the Pir, who at once knows what is to be done. The chief principle in the treatment of the Pir fraternity is that illness is caused by evil spirits (*jin*), and that a talisman suitably prepared, with the name of the patient's mother on it, will drive out any devil.

Priests, beggars, and buffoons.

There are many Pirs in Kashmír. They and others engaged in religious occupations number 4,005, and with their dependants make up a total population of 15,712. These are all fed at the expense of the working-classes. Beggars, with their dependants, number 24,673, while buffoons, actors, singers and dancers contribute 1,421 persons to the population. That is to say, over 5 per cent. of the population lives on the work of others, and adds nothing to the wealth of the country. In these figures are not included the lazy hordes of faqirs or beggars who wander up from the Panjab every summer like hungry locusts.

[1] The Jewish phylactery is worn on the left arm.

CHAP. IX. The term *faqir* in Kashmír does not imply a religious habit. A recluse who gives himself up to religious meditation is known as *Darvesh.* I have alluded to beggars in the chapter on races and tribes. Begging is regarded as an honourable calling in Kashmír.

Revenue. We learn from the *Ain Akbari* that the total revenue of Kashmír was 30,11,619 kharwars, worth 6,21,13,040 dams. From this it may be inferred that the value ascribed to the kharwar was 8 annas 3 pies. But unfortunately there are inaccuracies in the *Ain Akbari* which are incapable of explanation. Thus of the 30,11,619 kharwars stated to be the revenue demand, 9,43,507 kharwars, valued at 12,10,18,880 dams, were to be collected in cash. This gives a rate of 5 annas 2 pies per kharwar. In other places in the *Ain Akbari* the value of the kharwar works out to 8 annas 4 pies and 5 annas 9 pies. For the purpose of calculation I have adopted the rate of 8 annas 3 pies as representing the money value of the kharwar in the Mughal times. Not only are there discrepancies in the *Ain Akbari* as regards rates of commutation, but even in the total of the revenue demand there are differences which are not explained. Thus, when I add up the detailed revenue demand according to pargannas, I find that the total revenue demand of the valley of Kashmír (Sirkár Kashmír) was 28,61,468 kharwars, or in rupees 14,75,445; of this 9,28,780 kharwars, representing a money value of Rs. 4,78,902, were to be collected in cash. I can identify all the pargannas with pargannas now existing in the valley with the exception of Der, Dachan Khawra, and Banihál. Dachan Khawra now forms a part of the Muzzafarabad district. Banihál belongs to the Udampur district of Jammu, while Der cannot be traced. According to the *Ain Akbari* the revenue demand of these three pargannas amounted to Rs. 28,331. The city of Srinagar contributed Rs. 1,77,733 towards the total revenue demand, so that to find out the land revenue demand from the valley, as it is now constituted, we must deduct the amounts Rs. 28,331 and Rs. 1,77,733 from the total revenue demand. The land revenue demand of the valley would then be Rs. 12,69,281. But unfortunately there is no detailed account of the items of this revenue demand. We find in the *Parganna Super Saman* mention that 4,130 kharwars are included as a tax on firewood, and it may be inferred that the Rs. 12,69,381, which I have taken as representing the taxation on land in Akbar's time, really included other taxes, such as taxes on towns, grazing fees, forest dues, taxes on village servants, and a host of other imposts, which cannot fairly be included in land revenue. It is still more unfortunate that we have no evidence to show how much of the revenue demand was realized. One history states that the Mughal occupation of the valley was not successful from a financial point of view, and it is quite possible that the demand of Rs. 12,69,381 was not collected in full. We know that the condition of the villagers of Kashmír in the time of Akbar was not prosperous, whereas Srinagar was in its heyday[1].

For purposes of comparison with the revenue statistics of later times we may assume that the revenue demand of the Kashmír valley, excluding the city of Srinagar, was Rs. 12,69,381, and that the total revenue demand was Rs. 14,47,114.

It is, therefore, somewhat startling to learn from vernacular histories that the revenue of Kashmír was estimated at sixty lakhs of rupees in the time of the Pathans. We do not know what the value of the rupee was, but I think it may be safely said that not even the Pathans could have squeezed sixty lakhs of imperial rupees from the valley. Probably the word Kashmír included other territory besides the valley, but as the statement that sixty lakhs were collected rests on no trustworthy evidence it is unnecessary to pursue the subject.

In the Sikh times it is stated that the revenue demand was twenty-eight lakhs and that Ghulam Muhi-ud-din farmed the revenue for twenty-six lakhs of rupees. But here, again, it is not stated what rupee was meant. It may be that the rupee used in Kashmír in the time of the Sikhs was the Hari Singh rupee of eight annas. If, therefore, it is correct to surmise that the twenty-six lakhs of rupees offered by Ghulam Muhi-ud-din were Hari Singh rupees[2], we arrive at a sum of thirteen lakhs of imperial rupees, or about one-and-a-half lakhs less than the demand in the Mughal times. It should be added that Ghulam Muhi-ud-din's farm included the district of Muzzafarabad. About 1861 it would appear from Mr. Bowring's *Eastern Experiences* that the land revenue of Kashmír was not more than £150,000, while the total revenue was £250,000. Mr. Bowring calculated the rupee at two shillings, so that if his estimate was correct the land revenue was Rs. 15,00,000.

Ten years later an estimate is forthcoming of the receipts for 1871–72, but unfortunately nothing is known as to whether the estimate was ever realized. The person responsible for the budget was of a sanguine disposition, for he estimates the receipts at Rs. 41,79,152. He was equally sanguine as to economy in expenditure, for his estimate of civil expenditure amounted to only Rs. 4,50,600. I give the heads of receipts. Most of them refer to the valley alone, but some, such as town duties and

[1] 'This city has for ages been in a flourishing state, and abounding with workmen of every denomination.'—*Ain Akbari*.

[2] Moorcroft wrote in 1823: 'At the time of our visit the sum paid by the farmer was thirty-eight lakhs of Panjab rupees, equal to twenty-nine lakhs of Sicca rupees, or about £290,000.' Mr. H. H. Wilson adds a note to the effect that in 1835 scarcely any revenue could be raised. In 1836 twenty-three lakhs were demanded, but, according to Baron Hügel, it was not likely to be raised. In 1837 it was stated that Ranjit Singh reduced the demand to eighteen lakhs, but even this could not be collected.

CHAP. IX. customs, opium and mint, obviously include revenue of Jammu territory. The details of taxes on shops and artifices, which I also give, are of interest. They have mostly disappeared, like the once considerable income from the monopoly on shawls, but they present some idea of the universality of taxation in Kashmír. *The Chilki rupee equals ten annas.*

ESTIMATE OF RECEIPTS, 1871–72. CHILKI RS.

Item	Rs.	Item	Rs.
Value of Government's share of rice crop	29,44,844	Receipts from the Dal lake	20,792
Revenue in cash	14,96,741	Singhara	35,615
Receipts from the Shawl Department	6,00,000	Government ponies hired	51,178
Tribute from petty Chiefs	37,163	Zar-i-kazaya (fines on petty quarrels and wedding fees)	17,250
Town duties and customs	5,76,000	Mint	12,600
Timber	1,14,210	Stamps	9,600
Sheep and goats	1,07,311	Miscellaneous fines	17,230
Opium	1,56,000	Post Office	5,312
Offerings of pious Hindus	98,647	Sale of wild fruit	1,350
Cows and buffaloes	18,265	Sale of Government horses	67,500
Ferries	15,599	Sale of chenar leaves	25
Tobacco	40,840	Fruit of Government gardens	3,708
Courts of Justice	18,692	Taxes on shops, artificers and others	1,13,916
Churrus (or hemp drugs)	21,000		
Saffron	34,656		
Silk	50,000	Total	66,86,644
Khateenah (circumcision)	600	or, Imperial Rs.	41,79,152

DETAILS OF TAXES ON SHOPS, ARTIFICERS, AND OTHERS.

Item	Rs.	Item	Rs.
Sugar-makers	8,110	Soap-boilers	1,442
Fruiterers, makers of pickles and sweetmeats	8,891	Polishers of arms	160
Bakers	8,385	Gardeners	3,110
Corn-chandlers	4,800	Fringe- and tape-makers	706
Porters	775	Farmers and saddlers	1,850
Masons	1,500	Cloth-brokers	1,430
Carpenters	2,995	Turners in wood	215
Sellers of betel-nut	365	Cloth-dressers	120
Butchers	21,750	Knife-makers	85
Cotton-carders	380	Painters	275
Blacksmiths	795	Basket-makers	180
Goldsmiths	992	Shoe-makers	550
Braziers	150	Grave-diggers	810
Dyers	3,450	Boatmen who carry stones	700
Sellers of woollen thread	2,829	Earth-cutters (peat)	40
Prostitutes	1,900	Wood-cutters	630
Cloth-merchants	1,250	Money-changers	716
Sellers of glass bangles	575	Cutters and polishers of precious stones	192
Menial Muhammadans (*halalkhor*)	11,965	Leather-sellers	160

Makers of woollen garments	165	Sellers of firewood	400
Bow-makers	475	Moongarees (makers of rice bread)	623
Cowherds	12,670	Paper-makers	775
Weavers	2,160	Miscellaneous	366
Friers of grain	111	Total	1,13,916
Leech sellers and dealers in medicine	913	or, Imperial Rs.	71,197
Comb-makers	30		

Taxation of Srinagar.

These direct taxes on shops and artificers have disappeared, but Srinagar is still liable to a certain amount of indirect taxation in the form of octroi. The exact revenue realized by the octroi cannot be given, as it is lumped up with the Kashmír import duties. Rice, the staple food of the city people, was exempted from octroi at the beginning of 1892, by my advice. I am strongly of opinion that direct taxation is advisable in Srinagar. The present system, under which municipal expenditure is met by a contribution from general revenues, is destructive of real municipal life and economy. A heavy outlay is now being incurred on the construction of a waterworks for Srinagar and on sanitary improvements. The citizens will pay nothing towards this; and the general revenues of the country, which should be devoted to communications and irrigation works, are diverted to purely municipal requirements.

The estimates of 1871–2 suggest that the land revenue amounted to Rs. 27,75,990. In this the revenue of Muzzafarabad district, which is now about Rs. 84,000, was included; but even after deducting this we obtain a land revenue demand for the valley which, I feel sure, could never have been collected. In 1887 the estimate of land revenue furnished to my predecessor amounted to Rs. 16,07,542; but, as I have shown elsewhere, this revenue existed only on paper; and the actual average of collections of land revenue from 1880 up to 1888 was only Rs. 12,68,280. I show below the actual collections of land revenue from 1888 to 1893 of the valley of Kashmír:—

	Rs.
1888-89	12,31,258
1889-90	12,55,734
1890-91	12,48,374
1891-92	12,49,614
1892-93	14,06,634
1893-94	14,79,839[1]

It is interesting to notice receipts from other heads, such as excise, court fees, courts and gaols, Posts and Telegraphs, and other miscellaneous sources, such as receipts from timber-depôts, gardens, Rakhs and farms of chob-i-kot, &c.:—

[1] Rs. 80,605 remitted for loss by flood included in this.

CHAP. IX.

	Rs.
1888-89	5,53,124
1889-90	5,72,440
1890-91	4,02,859
1891-92	5,93,441
1892-93	6,27,119
1893-94	9,15,265

I am chiefly concerned with the land revenue of the Kashmír valley, but the income from miscellaneous sources is of importance, and, like the land revenue, is increasing. I have shown in the chapter on the new Settlement that the result of my work has been to increase the land revenue by Rs. 1,85,103 per annum; but it should also be remembered that the large amount of waste land granted to applicants for cultivation will further swell the land revenue; and it may be said that the waste land granted up to the date of this Report, viz. 18,115 acres, will bring in a land revenue of Rs. 51,893 per annum. I look upon the valley of Kashmír as a very valuable and promising estate, if only it is wisely managed, and believe that if the rural population increases steadily it will be possible to enhance the revenue considerably at the end of ten years. So far as the statistics given can be trusted, it would appear that the present land revenue of the valley is rather higher than it was in the time of the Mughals:—

Period.	Revenue of Kashmír Valley.
Mughal	Rs. 12,69,381
Pathan	Unknown.
Sikh	13,00,000
Dogra—	
1861	15,00,000
1871 estimate	27,75,990
actual	Unknown.
1887 estimate	16,07,542
actual	Unknown.
1888 actual	12,31,258

In attempting any comparison between the present and the past, it should be remembered that a considerable item in the land revenue was alienated when Rájá Ram Singh, C.B., and Sir Amar Singh, K.C.S.I., received large tracts of cultivated land in the valley with a supposed land revenue of Rs. 74,607. Further, in the year 1872 fifty-seven villages, with a revenue of Rs. 59,490 per annum, were alienated to Mian Rajputs in the old Tahsils of Deosar and Shupiyon. Again, in 1891, land revenue amounting to Rs. 6,305 was alienated for religious endowments. These deductions, which involve a revenue of Rs. 1,40,402, should be borne in mind when we compare the land revenue of the valley of Kashmír as it now is and as it was in 1861.

The total area of land surveyed by my department amounts to 1,195,555 acres. Our practice was to survey up to the limit of cultivation. We have included the whole of the valley of Kashmír, saving the areas under lakes and hills—such as the Takht-i-Suliman and the Ahak Tung—and we have included all cultivated and culturable areas in the side valleys leading from the main valley. Forests and the sides of mountains have been excluded, and the boundaries of villages situated on the slopes of the mountains have been determined by the limit of cultivation. Where villages are situated in some distant nook of a mountain, separated from the plain by a long stretch of unculturable mountain land, we have not included in our statement of area these intervening stretches. Thus the Gurais valley is situated at a distance of 40 miles from the valley of Kashmír. The 6,054 acres of cultivated or culturable land contributed by Gurais to the total of 1,195,555 acres represents the area of the Gurais villages, and excludes mountain-sides, forests, and the long and intervening tract which separates Gurais from the Kashmír valley. It is quite possible that as population increases the margin of cultivation will ascend the mountain-sides, and already we have many applications for permission to break land up for cultivation in the forests and on the mountain-slopes, in tracts which lie beyond the limits of the village boundaries. The total area of 1,195,555 acres represents the land occupied by the Kashmíris for agricultural purposes. Much of the portion of this area which is returned as not available for cultivation is the swamp land, which will not be rendered available for cultivation until draining operations are undertaken. The villages situated around these swamps obtain excellent grazing from them for their cattle, and one or two dry years bring a large area on the edge of the swamps under cultivation. The swamps also yield a large amount of food to the people who live in their vicinity, and they may be considered as auxiliaries of cultivation. The area surveyed excludes the Jagir villages of Rájá Ram Singh, C.B., and Rájá Sir Amar Sing, K.C.S.I., and also a small number of villages held revenue-free by other persons.

The area with which I have had to deal is larger by 8,359 acres than the counties of Hereford, Hertford and Huntingdon, and supports a rural population of 646,654 or 267,840 more than the population of the three English counties. The area actually under crops is some 5,000 acres larger than the area of Oxfordshire.

The subjoined tables give the more important statistics regarding land in Kashmír.

CHAP. IX.

CLASSIFICATION OF AREA.

	Wazárat Khás.	Wazárat Anantnág.	Wazárat Kámráj.	Total.
	Acres.	Acres.	Acres.	Acres.
Area by village papers	398,945	408,036	388,574	1,195,555
Not available for cultivation	134,487	150,028	127,554	412,069
Culturable waste other than fallow	87,729	91,423	78,208	257,360
Current fallows	7,233	14,056	12,720	34 009
Net area cropped during the year	169,496	152,529	170,092	492,117
Irrigated from:				
Canals	93,461	93,757	57,235	244,453
Tanks	—	—	170	170
Other sources	2,306	284	1,531	4,121
Total area irrigated	95,767	94,041	58,936	248,744
Crops irrigated:				
Wheat	803	176	206	1,185
Other cereals and pulses	1,971	1,415	815	4,201
Miscellaneous food crops	88,894	89,463	56,846	235,203
Miscellaneous non-food crops	6,951	4,780	1,450	13,181

ACREAGE UNDER CROPS.

	Wazárat Khás.	Wazárat Anantnág.	Wazárat Kámráj.	Total.
Cereals and pulses:				
Rice	69,708	75,260	44,384	189,352
Wheat	13,421	7,324	9,095	29,840
Barley	8,699	6,258	15,146	30,103
Maize	35,524	27,088	68,032	130,644
Other food grains including pulses	10,111	14,130	19,629	43,870
Oil seeds:				
Linseed	12,653	6,560	2,272	21,485
Til or gingelly	725	1,250	1,752	3,727
Others	1,939	1,415	3,033	6,387
Condiments and spices	27	3	9	39
Fibres:				
Cotton	7,584	7,275	1,630	16,489
Drugs and narcotics:				
Opium	51	—	—	51
Tobacco	346	40	—	386
Others	78	132	85	295
Orchard and garden produce	11,722	7,801	5,956	25,479
Total	172,588	154,536	171,023	498,147
Area cropped more than once	3,092	2,007	931	6,030
Net area cropped during the year	169,496	152,529	170,092	492,117

STOCK, ETC.

	Wazárat Khás.	Wazárat Anantnág.	Wazárat Kámráj.	Total.
Bulls and bullocks	28,549	28,693	20,141	77,383
Cows	44,121	33,770	27,611	105,502
Male buffaloes	98	318	121	537
Cow buffaloes	2,891	3,437	5,174	11,502
Young stock (calves and buffalo calves)	14,270	19,365	15,685	49,320
Sheep	139,040	146,186	109,228	394,454
Goats	4,364	4,866	8,387	17,617
Horses and ponies	6,576	4,480	5,161	16,217
Mules and donkeys	457	294	149	900
Ploughs	13,948	13,301	9,990	37,239

Srinagar stands twenty-second in the order of magnitude among the towns of India. It is a struggling city, occupying an area of 3,795 acres. Of this area some portions are densely populated, others are sparsely inhabited or totally uninhabited. Including the suburbs lying between the slopes of the Takht-i-Suliman and the river Jhelum, and taking the village of Sonawar as forming a part of Srinagar, we find that the area of 3,795 acres contains a population of 139,410 persons, of whom 96,062 live on the right bank and 43,348 on the left bank of the river Jhelum. The most densely crowded parts of the city are close to the river banks. On the right bank, between the river and the Nalla-Már, we find a population of 160 per acre. On the left bank, between the Kut-kul and the river, there is a population of 100 per acre. The length of the river. from Sonawar to the last bridge (Safr Kadal), where the city population ends, is 6·66 miles; as the crow flies it is just under 3 miles. The distance from the first bridge (Amiran Kadal) to the last bridge, measured along the river, is 2·71 miles.

The greatest width of the city, measured as the crow flies from the Dud-Ganga river to the edge of the Dal lake, is just over 2 miles.

The real city population, as distinguished from the city and suburban population, is 118,960. These 118,960 persons are engaged in the following occupations :—

No.	Occupation.	No. of workers, with their dependants.
1.	Administration and defence	10,482
2.	Employed in connexion with live stock and agriculture	3.246
3.	Personal and household service	11,660
4.	Provision-sellers, artificers, &c.	65.395
5.	Commerce and transport	8.309
6.	Learned and artistic professions	8.371
7.	Indefinite occupations and persons independent of work	11.497

CHAP. IX. The most interesting of these divisions is No. 4, which includes most of the real workers of Srinagar. Among the callings which make up the total of 65,395 the wool industry alone accounts for 22,502 persons. Tailors and darners account for 13,117 persons, while the others follow crafts of that curiously minute and subdivided kind which are created by the requirements of a large oriental city.

Among the most important of these may be mentioned dairymen (2,601), butchers (1,432), grain-dealers (3,437), vegetable-sellers (2,059), fruit-sellers (1,348), tobacconists (945), sellers of fuel and grass (1,077), gold and silver workers (1,827), embroiderers (1,027), copper-workers (606), carpenters (1,316), chemists and druggists (557), boot and shoe makers (1,606).

Division 5 is necessarily small, for, as explained elsewhere, the trade of the country has hitherto been in the hands of the State, and it is to be hoped that many of the persons included in division 1 will disappear from administration, and will find their proper sphere in commerce. Of the total, 8.309, 3,582 persons are engaged in boat traffic, so that the commercial business of Srinagar, practically of Kashmír, is transacted by a population of 4,727 persons.

Division 6 shows that out of a total of 8,371, 6,519 persons depend on religion for their livelihood. Literature accounts for 206, law feeds 48 persons, while medicine and midwifery give occupation to 738 workers and dependants.

Division 7 shows that there are 1,254 mendicants. These persons must be lost to all sense of shame to be beggars, and to return themselves as beggars, in a city where food is so cheap, and wages so high and so easy to obtain, as in Srinagar.

Weights and measures. There are three different rupees in currency in Kashmír besides the British rupee. They are the—

Khám Rupee, value 8 British Annas, bearing the letters I.H.S.
Chilki Rupee, value 10 British Annas.
Nának Shahi Rupee, value from 12 to 16 British Annas.

The Nának Shahi rupee is passing out of circulation. and the British, or double rupee as it is called, is becoming more and more the coin of the country. The villagers, however, still make their calculations in Khám or Chilki rupees, and great confusion is caused, unless one carefully prefaces an inquiry into prices by a distinct understanding as to the value of the rupee. I have always found the Chilki rupee of 10 annas the best and easiest basis of calculation.

Weights. The kharwar, or ass's load, has been from centuries past the standard of weight in Kashmír. The word is usually abbreviated to khar.

CHAP. IX.

4 Khám Rupees	=	$3\frac{3}{5}$ tolas	=	1 Pal.		
30 Pals	=	108 tolas	=	1 Manwata	=	$2\frac{136}{175}$ lbs.
4 Manwatas			=	1 Trak	=	$11\frac{19}{175}$ lbs.
16 Traks			=	1 Kharwar [1]	=	$177\frac{129}{175}$ lbs.

Land measures are calculated not by length and breadth, but by the amount of seed required by certain areas of rice-cultivation. It has been found by our measurements that the kharwar of land—that is the rice area which is supposed to require a kharwar's weight of rice-seed—exactly corresponds to 4 British acres.

20 Pals	=	1 Seer.				
30 Pals	=	1 Manwata	=	10 Marlas.		
4 Manwatas	=	1 Trak	=	2 Kanals	=	1 Rood.
16 Traks	=	1 Kharwar	=	32 Kanals	=	4 Acres.

There are other local measures of land. The only one of these which need be noticed is—

25 Kurus	=	1 Trak.
16 Traks	=	1 Kharwar.

For rice-straw, the following measure is used—

6 Phulas	=	1 Gaddi.
2 Gaddis	=	1 Kuru.

For length, the following measure is used—

1 Gira	=	$2\frac{1}{4}$ inches.
16 Giras	=	1 Gaz.
20 Giras	=	1 Gaz, in measuring Pashmina cloth.

There is no sealed yard measure in Srinagar, but from frequent experiment I have found that the gaz of 16 giras is about $\frac{1}{2}$ in. longer than the British yard.

In his preliminary report, Mr. Wingate observed that in Kashmír prices were non-existent; and in 1889, when I commenced work, it might be said that money prices did not exist. Salaries were paid in grain, and I remember that in 1889 I was requested to take oil-seeds, in lieu of cash, in payment of the salary of myself and my department. Oil-seeds were looked upon as an appreciated currency, while maize and singhara nuts, with which many persons were paid, were regarded as a depreciated medium. Not only did the State pay its officials in grain, but private persons paid their servants in the same fashion, and 16 to 20 kharwars of shâli was the ordinary wage of a domestic servant. The currency was to a great extent shâli, Prices.

[1] By local custom a kharwar of shâli, maize, and barley consists of only 15 traks, or $166\frac{22}{35}$ lbs.

CHAP. IX. and silver played a subsidiary part in the business of the country. It is unfortunate, for the purpose of statistics, that the exact amount of coin minted by the State for use in Kashmír, as distinct from Jammu and other parts of H. H. the Mahárájá's territories, cannot be shown, but the following figures give the value, in British rupees, of the Chilki rupees coined since 1888 for the currency in Jammu and Kashmír. In the mint at Jammu, silver bullion is used as well as old uncurrent coin, and it may be taken that bullion forms one-third of the material used.

	Value in British Rupees of Chilki Rupees coined.
1888	2,88,521
1889	2 88,240
1890	1,50,442
1891	3,09,471
1892	3,81,171
1893	4,54,423

Beside the Chilki rupee, value 10 annas, a considerable number of British rupees are in circulation. These British rupees are brought into Kashmír by European visitors, and an examination of the currency in which the land revenue is paid shows that of late years a respectable part of payments made by the villagers has been in British coin. The number of European visitors is steadily increasing; and the number of permanent European residents, which in 1888 was practically represented by the Missionaries, is now considerable. Payments made by Europeans are necessarily made in cash, and though the amounts spent by them sink into insignificance when compared with the amount spent on public works, they are of importance, and have formed one among other causes leading to the substitution of a silver for a grain currency.

In 1889 the road from Kohala to Baramula was opened. Apart from the easier access given by this road to visitors and to trade, its construction has brought out Rs. 21,78,870 from the State hoards and has thrown this large amount of coin into circulation. Next, the road from Srinagar to Gilgit has similarly withdrawn from the State treasury a sum of Rs. 15,18,060, while Rs. 6,50,000 are annually spent on the purchase of grain, hire of carriage, and wages of labour in the valley of Kashmír for the supply of the Gilgit garrison.

The amount which will be spent on the Srinagar waterworks for wages will be about Rs. 3,05,000.

When it is remembered that all this coin has been suddenly thrown into circulation within the brief period of about five years, and when it is considered that the old system of paying the army and officials in grain has given place to regular cash payments, and that, in addition to the public works I have noticed, a large amount of money is being steadily expended on other works, it will be understood that the currency of Kashmír has been inflated. As a natural consequence money prices of commodities and labour have risen, but I am not sure that the rise in prices will be permanent. The great staple of Kashmír. *shálí*, has, partly by artificial means, partly by an extension of and improvement in cultivation, been kept down to its old price, and this year and last year (1893 and 1894) rice has been cheaper than it has been for some years. But other commodities over which the State has exercised no artificial checks, have shown a decided tendency to rise in price, and though the price of *shálí* might fairly be applied as a basis for wages it is obvious that it has ceased to be what it once was, the currency of the country, and the standard by which all commodities were valued. I have often been bitterly attacked by the Pandits of the city, and accused of raising the prices of agricultural produce. It is always hard for men on fixed incomes to find prices rising, but many of the most vehement opponents of the settlement in the city were themselves landowners, and they forgot the fact that, though they lost in wages of servants, they won in the higher prices that they obtained for their farm produce. It was no use my attempting to explain that the settlement had nothing to do with the rise in prices, or to quote Mill and Ricardo on the relation of prices to the currency. The rise in prices was contemporaneous with the operations of the Settlement, and that was sufficient argument for the Pandits of Srinagar. The amount of silver now in Srinagar is said, by competent observers, to be greater at the present time than it has ever been since the time of the Pathans. Briefly, the accumulated hoards of the State treasuries have passed into the circulation of Kashmír.

The following rise in prices of village commodities has practically taken place since 1887:—

Woollen Blankets have risen from Rs. 3 to 4.
Bullocks, prices have risen by Rs. 1 per annum since 1887.
Ghi used to sell at 4 seers per Rupee. Now sells at 3 or 2½ seers.
Ponies used to sell at Rs. 15 to 20 Now, owing to the great demand for ponies on the Gilgit road, the price ranges from Rs. 25 to 35.
Walnuts used to sell at Rs. 3 per kharwar. They now fetch Rs. 8 per kharwar.
Wool used to sell at 2 seers the Rupee. Now sells at 1½ seers.

Communications.

There are numerous passes leading from the valley. Abul Fazl mentions twenty-six, but the following table shows the passes chiefly used by travellers and traders:—

Situation.	Name.	Elevation (feet).	Destination.	Distance from Srinagar in miles.
North . . .	Razdiangan . .	11,800	Gurais . . .	73
	Burzil . . .	13,600	Gilgit . . .	230
South . . .	Marbal . . .	11,570	Kishtwar . . .	109
	Banihal . . .	9,200	Jammu . . .	147
			Sialkot . . .	174
	Pir Panjal . .	11,400	Bhimber . . .	148
			Gujrat . . .	176
East	Margan . . .	11,600	Wardwan . . .	
	Zogi La . . .	11,300	Ladákh (Leh) . .	252
	Kara Koran . .	18,317 }	Yarkand . . .	777
	Sugit Dawan . .	18,137 }		
West . . .	Tosh Maidan . .	10,500	Poonch . . .	69
			Jhelum . . .	173
North-west . .	Nattishannar . .	10,200	Karnáo (Titwal) .	88
			Muzzafarabad . .	119
			Abbottabad . .	163

I attach charts showing sections of the most interesting passes. Chart 1 shows the direct route to the Panjáb via the Banihal pass. On arrival at Kanabal (Islamabad) trade usually leaves the road and is carried in boats on the Jhelum river.

Chart 2 shows a short length of the well-known Pír Panjal route.

Chart 3 gives an excellent idea of the route to Gilgit, and is characteristic of the country. It shows how to the north of the valley trade must toil up mountain after mountain. It will explain better than words why, in this respect, such stress is laid on the importance of the new Gilgit road to the people of Kashmír. Before the present excellent road was made the difficulties of the journey to Gilgit were enormous, and men who had to carry loads to the distant garrison suffered heavily.

PLATE VI

To face page 246

A VIEW OF THE ZOGILA. THE PASS LEADING FROM KASHMIR INTO LITTLE TIBET

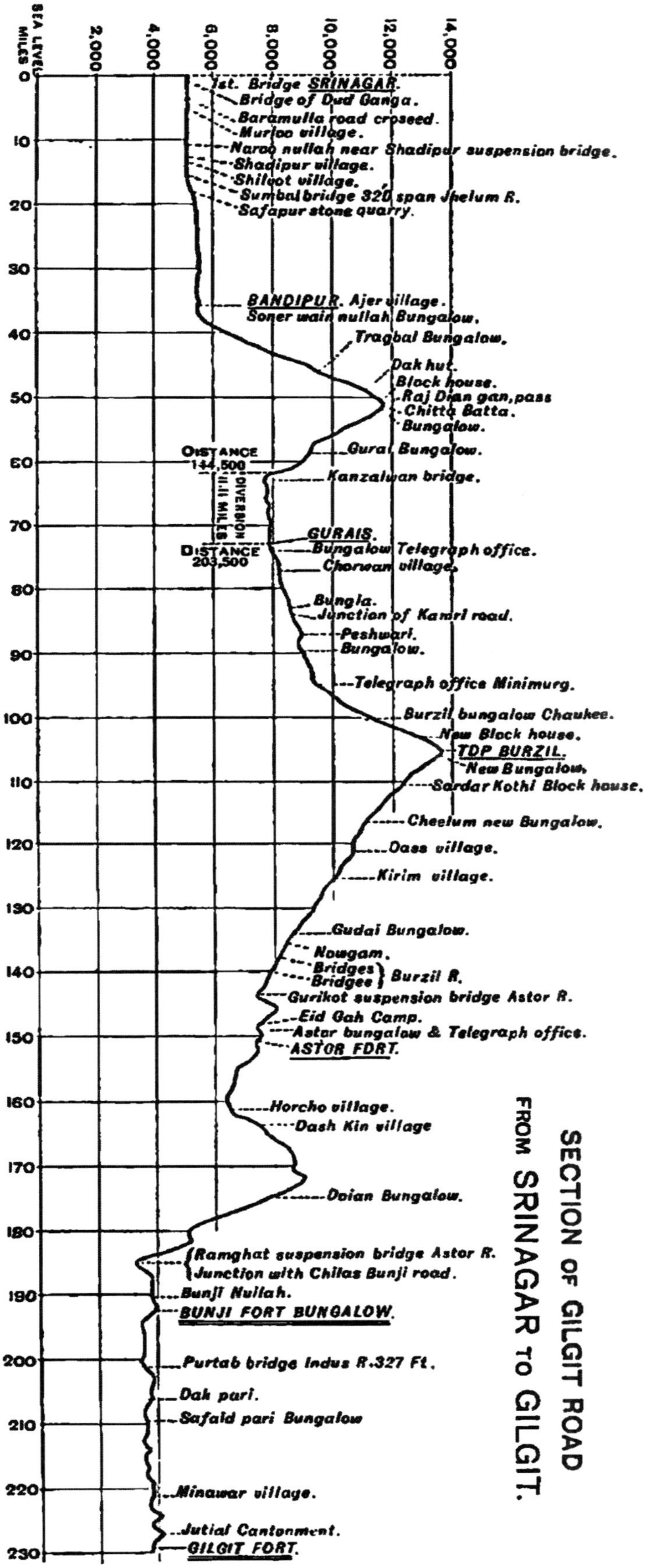
SECTION of GILGIT ROAD
FROM SRINAGAR to GILGIT.
SEA LEVEL
MILES
2,000
4,000
6,000
8,000
10,000
12,000
14,000
0
10
20
30
40
50
60
70
80
90
100
110
120
130
140
150
160
170
180
190
200
210
220
230
1st. Bridge SRINAGAR.
Bridge of Dud Ganga.
Baramulla road crossed.
Murloo village.
Naroo nullah near Shadipur suspension bridge.
Shadipur village.
Shilvot village.
Sumbal bridge 320 span Jhelum R.
Safapur stone quarry.
BANDIPUR. Ajer village.
Soner wain nullah Bungalow.
Tragbal Bungalow.
Dak hut.
Block house.
Raj Dian gan, pass
Chitta Batta.
Bungalow.
Gurai Bungalow.
DISTANCE 144,500
DIVERSION 11.11 MILES
Kanzalwan bridge.
GURAIS.
DISTANCE 203,500
Bungalow Telegraph office.
Chorwan village.
Bungla.
Junction of Kamri road.
Peshwari.
Bungalow.
Telegraph office Minimurg.
Burzil bungalow Chaukee.
New Block house.
TOP BURZIL.
New Bungalow.
Sardar Kothi Block house.
Cheelum new Bungalow.
Dass village.
Kirim village.
Gudai Bungalow.
Nowgam.
Bridges
Bridges } Burzil R.
Gurikot suspension bridge Astor R.
Eid Gah Camp.
Astor bungalow & Telegraph office.
ASTOR FORT.
Horcho village.
Dash Kin village
Doian Bungalow.
Ramghat suspension bridge Astor R.
Junction with Chilas Bunji road.
Bunji Nullah.
BUNJI FORT BUNGALOW.
Purtab bridge Indus R. 327 Ft.
Dak pari.
Safaid pari Bungalow
Minawar village.
Jutial Cantonment.
GILGIT FORT.

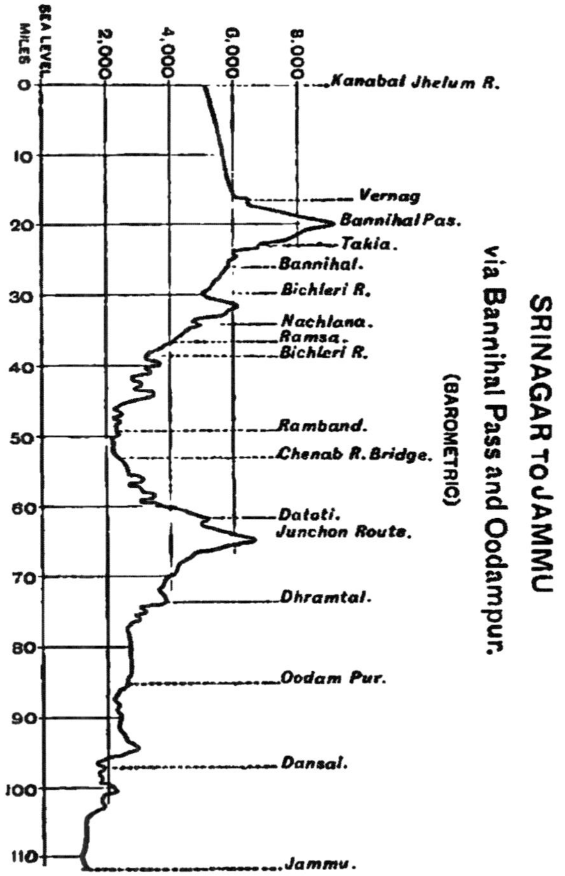
SRINAGAR TO JAMMU
via Bannihal Pass and Oodampur.
(BAROMETRIC)
SEA LEVEL
MILES
2,000
4,000
6,000
8,000
0
10
20
30
40
50
60
70
80
90
100
110
Kanabal Jhelum R.
Vernag
Bannihal Pas.
Takia.
Bannihal.
Bichleri R.
Nachlana.
Ramsa.
Bichleri R.
Ramband.
Chenab R. Bridge.
Datati.
Junchon Route.
Dhramtal.
Oodam Pur.
Dansal.
Jammu.

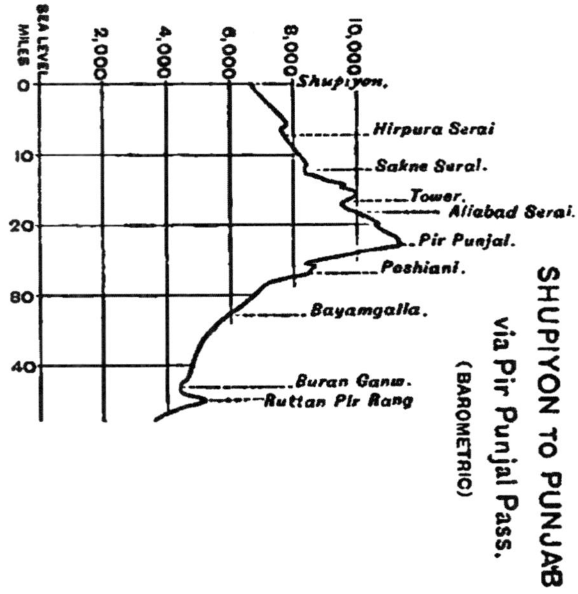
SHUPIYON TO PUNJAB
via Pir Punjal Pass.
(BAROMETRIC)
SEA LEVEL
MILES
2,000
4,000
6,000
8,000
10,000
0
10
20
30
40
Shupiyon.
Hirpura Serai
Sakne Serai.
Tower.
Aliabad Serai.
Pir Punjal.
Poshiani.
Bayamgalla.
Buran Ganw.
Ruttan Pir Rang

CHAPTER X.

SOCIAL LIFE.

'Hills, vales, woods, netted in a silver mist,
Farms, granges, doubled up among the hills,
And cattle grazing in the watered vales,
And cottage chimneys smoking from the woods,
And cottage gardens smelling everywhere
Confused with smell of orchards.'

Aurora Leigh.

CHAP. X.

The village.

THE Kashmíri village is beautiful in spite of itself. Shaded by the unrivalled plane-tree, by walnut, apple, and apricot, watered by a clear sparkling stream, the grass banks of which are streaked with the coral red of the willow rootlets, surrounded by the tender green of the young rice plant, or the dark, handsome fields of the *Imbrzal* and other rices of the black leaf, the Kashmíri village is rich in natural beauties. Later on the patches of rice-blooms look like a tesselated pavement, with colours running from red and russet green to copper. The rice-blooms are very varied, passing from deep bronze through olive, dark, and light green to pink and Indian red, all glowing like burnished metal under strong sunlight. Out through the luxuriant foliage peeps the cultivator's cottage, with its tumble-down, thatched gable roof. Each cottage has a garden plot well stocked with vegetables. Close to the cottage is the wooden granary, an erection like a huge sentry-box, in which the grain is stored, and from which it is taken out by a hole at the bottom. In the courtyard by the cottage the women are busy pounding the rice or maize, and the cotton-spinning wheel is for the time laid aside. Dogs are sleeping and little children rolling in the sun, while their elder brothers, also children, are away looking after the milch cows and cattle. On the stream is a quaint-looking bathing-house, where the villager leisurely performs his ablutions, and below the bathing-house the ducks are greedily eating. One of the prettiest objects in the village is the graveyard, shaded by the *Celtis Australis* and bright with iris, purple, white (*guli sosan*) and

PLATE VII

To face page 249]

Negative by Alam Chand, G.C.

AN ORDINARY PEASANT'S HUT. THE SENTRY-BOX TO THE LEFT IS THE GRANARY

yellow (*zambak*), which the people plant over their departed relatives. The village enjoys ample room. There is no crowding of houses, and each man's cottage stands within its ring fence of earth, stones or wattling. The earth walls around the garden plots are built in a very simple and ingenious manner. The earth is thrown into a mould formed by wooden planks, and on the top of the earthern slabs thorns are laid, over which more earth is placed. The thorn covering protects the walls against the rain, and the structure will last for some years. This kind of wall is known as *Dos*. CHAP. X.

Houses. The houses are made of unburnt bricks set in wooden frames, and of timber of cedar, pine and fir, the roofs being pointed to throw off snow. In the loft formed by the roof wood and grass are stored, and the ends are left open to allow these to be thrown out when fire occurs. The thatch is usually of straw. Rice straw is considered to be the best material, but in the vicinity of the lakes reeds are used. Near the forests the roofs are made of wooden shingles, and the houses are real log huts, the walls being formed of whole logs laid one upon another, like the cottages of the Russian peasantry. Further away from the forests the walls are of axe-cut planks fitted into grooved beams. Outside the first floor of the house is a balcony approached by a ladder, where the Kashmíri delights to sit in the summer weather. Later the balcony and the loft are festooned with ropes of dry turnips, apples, maize-cobs for seed, vegetable marrows and chilies, for winter use. Sometimes in the villages one finds the roofs of the larger houses and of the shrines (*ziárats*) made of birch bark with a layer of earth above it. This forms an excellent roof, and in the spring the housetops are covered with iris, purple, white, and yellow, with the red Turk's head and the Crown Imperial lilies. In the city nearly all the houses of well-to-do people are roofed with the birch bark and earth, so that looking down on Srinagar from the Hari-Parbat hill one sees miles of verdant roofing. In some of the larger and better houses there are pretty windows of lattice-work, open in the summer and closed by paper in the winter. As spring approaches the paper is torn down and the windows look ragged and untidy. On the ground floor the sheep and cattle are penned, and sometimes the sheep are crowded into a wooden locker known as the *dangij*, where the children sit in the winter and where the guest is made to sleep, for it is the warmest place in the house. One might imagine that the Kashmíri houses were neither comfortable nor healthy, but as a matter of fact they are warm enough. In the summer weather the houses are airy, and as winter comes on the chinks are stopped by thatch and grass and the dwelling is kept at a hot-house heat by the warm breath of the cattle and sheep, which comes up through openings from the ground floor to the first floor where the family lives. Some houses have fireplaces, but as a rule the villagers depend for warmth in

CHAP. X.

Kangars.

winter on their sheep. For lighting purposes they use oil, and in the higher villages *torches* made of pine wood are employed. The useful *kangar*, which forms so important a part of the Kashmíri's life, must not be left unnoticed. There is a proverb 'What Laili was on Majnun's bosom so is the *kangar* to a Kashmíri.' The *kangar* is a small earthenware bowl of a quaint shape, held in a frame of wicker-work. In the winter, and even in the summer when rains chill the air, hot embers are put into the *kangar* and it is slipped under the voluminous gown which all Kashmíris wear. Small children use the *kangar* day and night, and few of the people have escaped without burn-marks caused by carelessness at night. It is said that the *kangar* is often a cause of cancer. Sometimes the frequent fires which occur in the villages and in the city have been traced to the *kangar*. The *kangar* has been stated to have been introduced from Italy, but as there is mention of it in the Raja Tarangini it seems probable that it is indigenous. Much as the people owe to it they are wont to blame the *kangar* as the cause of their want of courage, and the 'goat heart' of the Kashmíri is always connected with its use. Among its other properties the *kangar* is said to aid digestion. A famous native physician was struck with the enormous meals of cold rice and singhára nut consumed by the Kashmíris, but when he saw the *kangar* he understood that the Kashmíris possessed a remedy against the evils caused by gorging. Among the most prized of the *Chhrar Sharif*[1] fairings is the pretty painted *kangar*. The best fuel for the *kangar* is '*hak*,' the small drift-wood which is collected at the mouth of the hill rivers by nets. Cowdung, and other dung mixed with dried chenar leaves, is also commonly used as fuel for the *kangar*. Some patriots go so far as to assert that the introduction of the *kangar*, and its necessary auxiliary the *gown*, was an act of statecraft on the part of the emperor Akbar, who wished to tame the brave Kashmíri of the period. But others say that the great king Zain-ul-abadin, in his effort to reduce the proud spirit of the Hindus, insisted on the use of the *kangar*, the gown, and *bási roti* (food cooked some hours before it is eaten).

Furniture.

The furniture of a Kashmíri house may be described briefly. There is none. In the villages and city alike the people sleep on mats and straw, bedsteads being unknown. A cotton-spinning wheel, a wooden pestle and mortar for husking rice, a few earthen vessels for cooking, and earthen jars for storing grain, complete the interior of a Kashmíri house. The useful *kilta* is found in all. This is a large creel, which the Kashmíri straps on his back, and in which heavy loads are carried. The *kilta* is usually made of the withies of willow, Cotoneaster or Parrotia.

Clothes.

The clothes of the villagers are simple and extremely mean in

[1] Chhrar Sharif is the place which holds the shrine of Kashmír's greatest saint, Nur Din. For illustration of a *kangar*, see p. 313.

appearance, and there is very little difference between the garb of a man and a woman, as they both wear the effeminate gown. Heavy and full it buttons at the neck and falls to the feet. Weight is given to the bottom of the gown by a deep hem, and sometimes this is artificially weighted, in order to exclude the air and to keep in the heat of the *kangar* when a man sits down on the ground. Underneath the gown the man wears drawers. In the winter these garments are made of wool, in the summer of cotton, either manufactured at home or imported from the Panjab. The ordinary headdress of the Kashmíri cultivator when he is at work is a cotton skullcap, but on State occasions he dons a white *pagri*. The fashionable Kashmíri likes to wear his *pagri* rather on the back of his head. and displays a large amount of forehead. The sleeves of the gown of the Musalmán cultivators are wide and loose, and it is a sign of respectability to wear the *cuffs turned* back. Leather shoes are worn by the well-to-do and by most people on holidays, but the ordinary covering of the foot in Kashmír is the leather or straw sandal, known as *tsapli* and *pulahru*, and the wooden patten for wet weather. Every Kashmíri can make his own *pulahru* from a wisp of rice straw. In the villages there is a strange absence of colour in the dress of the people, and the only thing which breaks the dull monotony of the dirty grey is the coloured skullcap of the children. The total absence of colour in the dress of the villagers is, from a picturesque point of view, much to be regretted. It is a relief to visit Jammu territory and to see again the bright oriental colours of the Rajput dress. The Kashmíris are by no means enamoured of their present fashion in dress, and have often told me that if an order is given they will adopt the Kishtwar fashion. But I am afraid that so long as the *kangar* is used so long will the effeminate gown remain in fashion. Out of the material of one gown a native of India could make two good coats. The Panditanis, however, wear dresses of dark maroon, known as *krimsi* (our cramasie), and blue, and fasten a girdle of white cloth around their waists. Their headdress is a kind of veil, which falls over the back of the head, and they and all Kashmíri women wear their hair in a peculiar arrangement of many plaits, in which black wool or silk is interwoven. Up to marriage these *plaits* are separate, but after marriage they are gathered together and fastened with a heavy *tassel*. Only the women of the wealthy veil themselves from the public gaze. The Kashmíris assert that their national dress is to be found in Kishtwar, and that it resembles the dress of a Kashmíri when he goes on a journey. The gown is then tucked up and bound around the waist by a cloth belt or tucked inside the drawers, and the drawers turn into manly knickerbockers, with leggings, which are simple and effective. *Bandages* of woollen cloth. the well-known puttie

CHAP. X.

of the Indian army, are wound around the calf of the leg and are said to give great support on long journeys. There is great art in binding the bandage and the Kashmíri knows the art. The Kashmíri villager spends little on show. His clothes are spun, woven, and made at home, and a reason often given for the absence of smartness is that any outward show was at once interpreted by the officials to mean hidden wealth, and domiciliary visits ensued. If the character of a people is reflected in its clothes, then the Kashmíris are mean and effeminate. There are certain peculiarities in dress which distinguish the Pandit from the Musalmán. The Pandit wears the *tuck* of his white turban on the right, the Musalmán on the left[1]. The Pandit fastens his gown on the left, the Musalmán on the right. The Pandit has long, narrow sleeves, the Musalmán short, full sleeves. It seems that the Musalmáns were enjoined to distinguish themselves from the Hindus, for I find that Musalmáns will invariably mount their ponies from the off side while the Pandits mount from the near side. And while the Pandit begins his ablutions from the left leg, the Musalmán invariably begins from the right leg. Other distinguishing peculiarities may be mentioned. The Pandits wear tight drawers, head-dresses of narrow white cloth, of twenty yards in length, and a smooth skullcap. They also retain a small lock of hair on their head, which is carefully guarded from the barber. Further, the Pandit uses his long narrow sleeve as a kind of glove, and though he may have put on his shoes with this glove he does not hesitate to eat food with the same sleeve. Musalmáns on the contrary wear loose drawers, *pagris* of broad white cloth, never more than ten yards in length, skullcaps with raised patterns; they shave their heads entirely, and they would regard food touched by the sleeve as impure. There are many differences between the Musalmáni and Panditani style of dress, and there are wide differences in their character. The Panditani wears a girdle, but no drawers. She has a white headdress, and has no embroidery except on her sleeves and around the collar. She never wears leather shoes but sticks to the old-fashioned grass sandal. She is more devoted to her husband than to her children, and will never mention her husband's name. The Musalmáni wears no girdle, but if she be of good position she will never stir out of the house without drawers. She wears a red headdress and has her tunic richly embroidered. She uses leather shoes. She is more devoted to her children than to her husband, and thinks it no shame to mention her husband's name. Finally, it is commonly said that the Pandit housewife is a far better and more economical manager than the Musalmáni. Both Hindu women and Musalmánis ride on ponies when occasion arises, man-fashion.

Distinctions in dress of Hindus and Musalmáns.

Hours and occupations.

The Kashmíri divides the day into thirty parts, and the night too has

[1] In India this is exactly reversed.

its thirty divisions. He is not an early riser, and does not begin any real work before 7 A.M., though he boasts that he rises at cockcrow when the weeding of the rice-fields commences. Still, when once he has commenced work, the Kashmíri cultivator will, when working for his own gain, exert himself, and during the season of rice-cultivation he thoroughly earns his night's rest when evening falls. When winter comes on many of the able-bodied men carry down apples and other loads to the Panjab, and work as porters in Lahore and elsewhere, returning to Kashmír in the spring. Those who stay in Kashmír are busy looking after their sheep and cattle, and pass the short days and the long winter nights in weaving woollen cloth and making baskets. Often the family works up to midnight, by the poor light of the pine torch or the oil dip, and it is no exaggeration to say that the villagers rarely sleep more than four to five hours in the winter months. As will be shown in the description of agriculture the Kashmíri cultivator has not much spare time. The land holdings are large, and up to quite recent times the cultivator spent a considerable part of his days on forced labour. Things have changed, but for some years to come the ordinary Kashmíri will have his days fully occupied. The *safed posh* class of villagers, that is the more affluent men, who wear white clothes, do not work, but look on while others toil. They have a better kind of house and often have excellent gardens and good orchards. They sometimes indulge in the luxury of a private cemetery. They ride the small ponies of the country and travel great distances, carrying their bedding with them. They pay frequent visits to the city, and are usually connected in marriage with Srinagar families. Their lives are fairly easy, and they have considerable influence in the villages. They have not much sympathy for the ordinary cultivators, and they are always spoken of in the country side as *Darbári* men, who side with the native officials.

Food. The Kashmíri cultivator is fond of eating, in fact is often a very gross feeder. When at work in the rice-fields a cultivator requires plenty of sustenance, the chief staples of food being rice and other grains cooked as porridge, or ground into flour and made into bread, vegetables, oil, salt and pepper, and unlimited milk. The ordinary meal of the Kashmíri indicates little of taste or culture. The boiled rice is made into balls and bolted; the sight of a villager at his food is not pleasant. But when the professional *cook* is called in some taste is displayed in the preparation and arrangement of viands, and the earthenware platters filled with brightly-coloured foods make a pretty show. The red rice in itself is bright to see. Clarified butter (*ghi*) is not much eaten, as the Kashmíri finds that it irritates his throat. Poultry (fowls, ducks and geese) is abundant, and the ordinary cultivator will eat fowls perhaps six times

CHAP. X.

a month, and mutton perhaps five times in the month. Whenever fish can be caught it is eaten. Hindus will not touch poultry or eggs, but they will eat wild fowl[1] and the eggs of the lake birds. Not long ago the villagers rarely obtained rice for their food, as it was always taken to the city, and maize, barley, millets, and buckwheat formed their diet. The more affluent villagers are very fond of tea[2] and sugar, and tea and snuff are both considered good for the cough which is very prevalent. The tea comes from three sources: Bombay tea from China, hill tea from Kangra in the Panjab, and green tea from China, via Lhassa and Ladákh. The Kashmíris like their tea very sweet or very salt: the former is known as *kahwa* and the latter as *shiri*, and is always mixed with milk. Both are made in the Russian samovar, which is a popular institution in Kashmír. It is the custom always to eat wheaten bread or biscuits with tea. Often spices, more especially cinnamon, are mixed with the tea. The sugar comes from the Panjab, and is either a cheap brown sugar known as *batás* or white loaf sugar known as *nabát*. Salt is an important article of diet both for men and for cattle and sheep. The Kashmíris like their food very salty. There are two kinds. The better comes from the Panjab, but salt of an inferior quality is brought from Ladákh. If rice is to be obtained a Kashmíri will not look at any other food, and the dish dearest to the people of the valley is *rice* coloured with turmeric. It must be confessed that the Kashmíri Musalmán is extravagant and greedy. He bolts his food, and sometimes eats more than is good for him. It is a curious fact that very few Pandits died in the great famine of 1877–79, whereas the mortality among the Musalmáns was enormous. Apart from the fact that the Pandits had great authority in the country and were better off than the Musalmáns, there is the further fact that the Pandits are the more dainty feeders, and that their religion accustoms them to abstinence from food, and thus perhaps they were better able to endure hunger. In the summer the abundant fruits of Kashmír sustain a large population, and there is a wealth of vegetable food. First come the mulberries, which feed not only the people but sheep, ponies, and even dogs; then the apricot and later apples and pears. So eager are the people to get fruit that most of the apples are eaten unripe. Later still come the walnuts, but walnuts are not esteemed as a food. Cucumbers, melons, and vegetable marrows supply abundant, if not wholesome, meals to the people when the cottage granaries begin to run low, and in the winter dried vegetables and dried fruits form an important article of diet. The Kashmíris consider that all kinds of grain are either hot or

[1] A curious fact has been brought to my notice, viz. that Hindus in Kashmír insist on having any birds they eat made *Haldl* in Musalmán fashion.

[2] Tea is said to have been introduced by Mirza Haidar from Yarkand.

cold, and are somewhat particular as to the way in which the various grains, vegetables and fruits should be mixed. Thus the dried apple, which is cold, is always boiled and eaten with the flour of the Amaranth, which is regarded as an extremely hot grain. This wealth of fruit and vegetables and the abundance of milk must be taken into consideration when an opinion is formed as to the condition of the rural classes. There is, however, no accumulation of wealth, and a failure of the autumn crop would at once be followed by considerable distress. If one looks to the purely material condition of the villagers I should say that the Kashmíri peasant is in every respect better off than his fellows in India. He has ample food, sufficient clothing, a comfortable house, and abundance of fuel, and he obtains these without much effort. There is general comfort but no luxury, and the process of distribution of wealth, by which a country is divided into the very poor and the very rich, has not yet commenced in Kashmír. There are professional beggars who are very well off, but there are no indigent poor.

Pastimes. When the day's work is done the Kashmíri seeks his home and after his food retires to rest. There is no place of meeting where the sociable pipe is passed around, and the use of the pipe seems to have passed out of fashion in the great famine of 1879. Now people have taken to snuff, which is brought over from Peshawar. There is no society in the villages, and the only gatherings are at weddings or at the fairs at the shrines of the saints. The women do not gather at the well, but there is gossip at the water-mill, from which the maize and wheat-flour is brought back in skins. There are no games for the young or old, and in the villages there is no leisure for games. Life is terribly earnest, and the child who can walk can work. Before the time of Mahárájá Guláb Singh the different wards of Srinagar city used to turn out with slings and stones, and played a very earnest and serious game. But Guláb Singh did not approve of this fighting spirit, and put a stop to the mimic warfare. *Tipcat*, which is common all over India, is played in Srinagar, and the loser has to give the winner a ride on his back. *Hop-scotch* is also a common game, and one of the seven compartments is known as 'hell.' Little girls have their rag dolls, and carry them in toy palankins, playing at marriage. And now cricket has found its way to Srinagar, and will spread. At fairs are seen aged men of religion jumping about with *single-sticks* [1], but the country-people never step into the ring; and although Kashmír was celebrated for its wrestlers I have never seen a wrestling-match. The men are splendid walkers and their physique is frequently admirable and athletic. I have tried to get up mountain races, but the people have no game

[1] The Kashmír Sikhs excel in single-stick.

instincts in them, and only cared about the money prizes. The Kashmíri may be said to have no idea of amusements, and probably he regards a seat in a balcony or a boat as the most perfect form of amusement. He is never so happy as when, at rest under the shade of a chenar tree, he issues orders to others who are working in the sun, and cries 'Shah Básh.' Perhaps, however, a love of game and of sport is latent in the Kashmíri, for many of the professional *shikáris* are good, keen sportsmen, and in saying that the Kashmíris have no game instincts, the boatmen, who will paddle till they drop rather than be beaten by a rival crew, should be omitted. It is probably due to the Kashmíri's inaptitude for active amusement that the strolling players, the *Band* or *Bhaggat*, have such a hold on the people. These players, who are well known in India, are enthusiastically received, and their wit and power of mimicry entitle them to a warm reception.

I have seen the best companies in Kashmír, though perhaps the best —the Bhaggats of Syebug—died off in the famine of 1877, and men now sigh: 'Alas! poor Yorick,' and speak of their excellent acting. The Bhaggats portray village life in a most vivid manner. Their dresses and make-up are excellent, and they represent most faithfully the internal working of a village community. It is said that Mahárájá Guláb Singh acquired a very intimate knowledge of village administration from the Bhaggats' performances, and I have picked up some hints from them as to the methods of the patwari, the village accountant. The plot is very much the same. The Rájá rides by, burning to redress injustice, and his Wazír seizes on the patwari and the lambardar and calls for the village accounts. The unfortunate villager who has brought his grievance to the Rájá's notice is at first very loud and noisy in his complaints, but as he sees the Wazír and the patwari laying their heads together he becomes silent and sits as one fascinated. The denouement is that the Wazír finds that the patwari is innocent, and the complainant receives a severe flogging. Other scenes of village life are depicted, and one of the most favourite representations with the country-people is the sowing, plucking and spinning of cotton. I shall have some more to say about these interesting Bhaggats later on. They relieve the sadness of village life in Kashmír. The Shairs must be distinguished from the Bhaggats for they never act. They are either minstrels who sing to the accompaniment of a guitar, or the village poets, who suddenly spring up in the midst of business and recite in a loud shrill tone the praises of the most influential person present. I knew many of these poets, and have spent many hours listening patiently to rhymes which seemed to have no end, and which jumbled up in a very curious manner oriental tropes with the most commonplace and technical terms of survey and revenue work. It is good to give these poets a few rupees, for they are often miserably poor. Many whom I have met are unfortunately not quite sane, and one, a Musalmán, who had formerly been a tutor to a high official, was hopelessly given to drinking, and justified his propensity by quotations from the Persian Poets. He reviled me in the strongest language when I declined to give him whiskey, and said that the 'iron age' of the Hindus had indeed arrived, and left my camp in tears.

In the city there is at any rate a crowd, and there is the sacred river with its floating life. The day can be passed somehow. The citizen can saunter down to the river *ghats* and bathe, he can do a little shopping or listen to the song-birds and the minstrels, or he can work his way up to the Amiran Kadal, the first bridge, and find out the latest rumour which has been concocted by the professionals who live by fabricating news. If he lives on the river or the Snake canal he can enjoy life from his latticed window.

> 'Ah, such a life, such a life as one leads at the window there.
>
> . . . .
>
> *Bang-whang-whang* goes the drum, *tootle-te-tootle* the fife,
> Oh, a day in the city square, there is no such pleasure in life.'

He can also lounge down to the palace and see what is going on. All are admitted, and all can have a public audience of His Highness the Mahárájá. Elsewhere I shall speak of the advantages of residing in Srinagar, but apart from the material advantages of getting food without exertion there is the further advantage of excitement and stir. The Kashmíris, like the Athenians of old, are greedy for news, and every day some new rumour is started for their edification. There are no representative institutions in Kashmír, but though the Kashmíri has no vote he can always affix his name to a monster petition got up by some official who is seeking office. A clever man of the city will affix several names to the petition, for the art of forging signatures is studied in Srinagar. One well-known professor would in his zeal stand in cold water in order to give a shaky turn to his handwriting.

Customs of birth, marriage and death.

The customs and ceremonies connected with birth, marriage and death in Kashmír are of some interest, and as they have not been described before it may be of use to enumerate them at some length. It must be explained that the customs vary according to the position and wealth of families, and that there is some difference between the observances of the city people and the villagers. But the chief incidents in birth, marriage and death are the same, and in the following description I have endeavoured to ascertain and describe the practices of the average Hindu and the average Musalmán. And inasmuch as the Musalmán villager and the Kashmíri Pandit are the most important and numerous

CHAP. X. classes in the valley, I have set forth their customs and ceremonies and have not attempted to give the special observances of the Hanji, Watal, and other tribes. Though these tribes have their special customs, the main ideas and ceremonies are practically the same as those which are found among the villagers. If a comparison be made between the customs of the Hindus and the Musalmáns, it will be seen that there are many points of resemblance, and the curious prominence of the walnut and salt, and the use of the *mendhi* dye, will be noticed. Besides the *mehnzrát*, or use of the *mendhi* dye, in both religions there is the *laganchir* or fixing of the marriage day; *phirsal*, the visit paid by the bridegroom to the bride's house after marriage; *gulimiut*, the giving of money and jewels; the dress and the title of the bridegroom as *mahárájá* and of the bride as *mahárání*; *chudsu*, the giving of presents on the fourth day after death, and the *wehrawari* and *barkhi*, the celebration respectively of the birthday and day of death. I give the customs as they are at present, but do not venture to speculate on their origin. The vernacular words must be given in the text, instead of relegating them to the glossary, for they have no English synonyms. They are words which one hears in daily intercourse with the people, and any one who has work in the valley will find that a knowledge of these words and customs will give him a hold over the Kashmíris.

Hindus' birth. A Hindu child is ushered into the world on a bed of soft straw of the darb (or koin) grass, which has been rendered holy by perfumes and by the utterance of Sanskrit *mantras*, and when the Musalmáni midwife has done her part the exact time of the birth is carefully noted by the family astrologer. The birth-bed is known as *hurru*, and near the bed is placed an earthen vessel known as *hurlij*. Close to the vessel the floor is carefully swept, and a mystic figure is traced on it in chalk, and on this figure is placed a stone pestle which is worshipped by some girl of the house. Around the stone and on all four sides of the bed boiled or uncooked rice is daily scattered (*rit*). The mother is known as *losa*, and if this is her first child she is called *sadh piai*. Often before the confinement a ram is brought into the room which the patient strokes three times. She then puts a handful of rice into a basket, her mother puts in a handful of flour, and her sister puts in some money. Then female relations come in, all bringing presents of figs, dates, almonds, rice and money. All these gifts are eventually given to the priest. Later the women scatter rice, flour, and money around the bed, and when the child is born, if it is a boy, the assembled relations shout and rejoice regardless of the effect of excitement on the patient. All food taken by the mother after her confinement has to be cooked on a fire worshipped by the girl and is placed in the *hurlij*, and the girl after the fire-worship anoints her forehead and the foreheads of the mother and child with *ghi*. For three days after childbirth the mother must eat but little, but on the fourth day a feast called *Panjiri*, composed of sesamum, walnuts, almonds and sugar fried in oil, is prepared and sent round to relatives and friends. On this day the mother eats some food from earthen vessels, and on the same day the mother's parents send her presents of roast meat and unleavened bread. On the ninth day after the birth (*sundar*) the mother and child are bathed in some auspicious hour and the child receives its name. On that day, too, the child is given clothes (*zafiru*), and the midwife throws away the old straw bed and makes a fresh one. After bathing, seven vessels, either of clay or of bronze, are filled with food. These vessels represent seven deities, and as some are flesh-eating deities and some vegetarian, the foods chosen have to be selected with care. Pulse, rice, walnuts and meat are the common selection, and they are worshipped. Seven women of the household must be present to represent the seven deities. After the food has been made holy, the midwife lights a torch of birch-bark and waves it around the heads of the mother and child and finally flings it into an earthen bowl filled with water. She then takes her leave, and in rich families is succeeded by a Musalmán wet nurse, and the holy food is distributed among relatives and neighbours. On this, the ninth day, the mother is allowed for the first time to eat from bronze vessels, and her parents send gifts of roast meats, bread, and cash. On the eleventh day the bed is again thrown away and the mother, no longer unclean, sallies forth to the courtyard, and with her child on her lap sits down on the same mystic figure mentioned above, and shows the sun to the infant. But if it happens that any woman of the *gotra* up to the seventh generation gives birth to a child, or any one of the *gotra* die during the eleven days, the weary days of purification must drag on for another eleven days. If the death or birth in the *gotra* be in families dating back to the eighth generation only four days more are added to the original term of eleven days. If beyond the eighth generation, only one day is added. Provided no such untoward birth or death has happened and the house is free from uncleanness (*sutak*) the *hons* or impurity is removed. The family Brahman is then summoned, and a curious ceremony known as *kah netar* is performed. The mother has to drink the five products of the cow. The seven vessels are again filled with food, of which relatives and friends partake. Among other details connected with the *kah netar* may be mentioned the tracing of a tree in chalk upon the wall. When the Brahman priest has discharged his functions, the astrologers of the father and the mother cast the child's horoscope (*zátuku*). On the day of the child's birth the parents send presents of walnuts to their relatives, and the mother's parents send a basket of sweetmeats and turmeric and ginger to their daughter. If the mother's recovery is slow the deities have to be appeased.

CHAP. X.

CHAP. X.

and the *kah netar* ceremony is repeated, and if the child wails or refuses nourishment the *sundar* rites are again performed. Sometimes on the eleventh day after birth, when the child takes its first look at the sun, a pen-box is placed before the child if a boy and a stone pestle if a girl. When the child is a month old (*mas netar*) he receives new clothes, and a feast of rice and milk is given to relatives and friends. These first clothes are made by the priest's wife, and she uses not a needle but a thorn of the wild rose. The needle is made by man, the thorn by God, and there is a superstition that the child whose first clothes are made with a thorn will never handle a sword, or hurt man or beast. When he reaches the age of six months he takes his first taste of rice boiled in milk (*ann prás*), and his ears are pierced. On this day food is distributed among relatives and friends, and in some families it is the custom to place before the child various articles, such as pen-boxes, grain, needles, &c. If the child touches the pen-box first, it is a sign that he will take to writing as a profession.

Shaving of head.

In the third year the ceremony of shaving the child's head (*zar kasa*) takes place, this being a very joyous occasion. The day before the ceremony the boy's hands and feet are coloured red with the dye of *mendhi* (Lawsonia inermis) or of a Lichen, and a great feast is prepared by the paternal aunt. The custom of dyeing the hands and feet with *mendhi* is known as *mehnzrát*, and is also observed on the occasions of assuming the sacred thread and of marriage. The food on this occasion is known as *wári*, and there are three kinds of *wári*. The first consists of rice, the fat of sheep or of goats, ginger, carraway seeds, salt and oil, and is known as *wári bat*. The second is made of turmeric, salt, carraway seed, assafoetida and pulse, and is known as *masáladár wári*, and the third, which is known as *wári*, consists of pulse and rice fried in oil. For her services the paternal aunt receives congratulatory gifts (*zang*) of rice, salt, and cash, and all the relatives and friends feast heartily on the *wáris*. In the case of a girl there is no shaving of the head. The boy's hair is carefully buried under a tree.

Investiture of the sacred thread.

When the boy has attained the age of seven years, and before he reaches his thirteenth year, he must don the sacred thread and become a true Brahman. An auspicious day is fixed by the astrologer, and five days before the date relatives are invited to the boy's house, and there is constant feasting, and the women sing and make merry. The maternal uncle presents gifts, and the day before the sacred thread is put on the rites of *deogun* are performed by the family priest. *Deogun* is a ceremony when the protection of sixty-four deities called *yognis* is invoked. Friends and relatives give the boy's father money (*awarah bal*), and sometimes considerable sums are received. On the day the boy is confirmed as a Brahman a small earthern dais is made in the courtyard on which a fire is lighted, and the boy throws almonds and pistachio nuts on to it. He is then shown a virgin and a heifer seven times, and the sacred thread of three strings (*janeo*) is placed on the boy. Later he stands on the mystic figure traced on the ground (*wegu*) while the women sing around him. Coins and shells are thrown over his head, and he is then carried in state down to the river, and performs his first *sandhia* or prayer ceremonies. Congratulations are offered, every one receives food, and the priests are given money. CHAP. X.

Marriage.

The next important event in the Hindu boy's life is his marriage. First the services of a professional match-maker (*manzim yor*), of whom there are some thirty in Srinagar, Musalmán and Hindu, are called in, and when he has marked down a likely bride the astrologers are called in and the horoscopes of the boy and girl are compared. If the horoscopes are favourable, and there is no hitch, the girl's parents send to the boy's parents a little salt and sugar, with sometimes a few rupees. As a rule the boy's mother has seen the girl, and has made up her mind, and the *manzim yor's* most lucrative work consists in bringing off matches between wealthy parvenus and old decayed families. Srinagar socially is an advanced plutocracy. A girl who has lost her mother is usually regarded as an undesirable wife. The astrologer fixes an auspicious day for the marriage, and information is sent to the bridegroom's parents of the number of guests who are to join in the marriage procession. Some days before the marriage the houses of the bride and bridegroom are swept and garnished, and the rites of *mehnzrát* and *deogun* are performed, and the bride's formal initiation into Brahmanism dates from this *deogun*. On the happy day the bridegroom, richly attired, decked with jewels, and brave with herons' plumes, sets out to the bride's house in a boat or on a horse. He is called on this day the Mahárájá and the bride is the Mahárání. Four Hindu attendants accompany him, three with yaks' tails and the fourth with a silver cup and shell, and a Musalmán, known as the *Shahgási*, holds an umbrella over the bridegroom's head. Decked out in the same brave fashion as the groom goes another boy, a near relative, who is known as the *Pot Mahárájá* or best man, and it is said that if some untoward event should happen to the bridegroom on this day the *Pot Mahárájá* would take his place. In the Pathan times it was not uncommon for the bridegroom to be seized as he went to his bride. As they approach the bride's house conches are blown, and a near relative or honoured guest of the bride's family comes down to meet the party. If the hour of marriage (*lagan*) falls in the daytime the wedding guests, after feasting, leave the bride's house, and return on the same day to escort the bride and bridegroom back to the bridegroom's house. If the hour falls in the night the party return in the morning. After the marriage ceremony, which sometimes

CHAP. X. takes place before the feast and sometimes after, the bride's father adds three more strings to the bridegroom's sacred thread. Before the bridegroom is allowed to enter his house with his bride, he must pay money to his maternal or paternal aunt or sister (*zámbránd*) who bars the door. The expenditure on marriages is very heavy, and food and fees are given to Brahmans and a host of attendants. After one or two days' sojourn in her new home the child-bride is taken back to her father's house for a day with *satrat* (brass and bronze utensils), and she shows her jewels, clothes and presents to her parents. She then goes back to her father-in-law's house, and after the marriage ceremony the girl can at any time visit her father's house, provided that his invitation to her is accompanied by the '*teth*' or sum of money which her father presents to his son-in-law on the marriage-day. This sum varies from 8 annas to 5 rupees, and as it has to be given by the bride's father whenever he invites his daughter to his house, and on all great holidays, anniversaries, domestic events, and birthdays, it is a severe tax on the Pandit who is blessed with daughters. As a rule cohabitation commences when the bride is about thirteen years old, and she then discards her anklets and wears a headdress known as *taranga*[1], and the *taranga* is a sign that the marriage has been consummated. The age of marriage, however, varies, and the richer the parents the earlier the age of the bride. The gifts to the bride from her father are numerous, consisting of gold and silver jewelry and valuable stuffs. The only ones which need be mentioned are the *dij haru*, and the *chandanhár*. The *dij haru* are ear-ornaments of pure gold, of the same mystic shape as the *wegu*; these are worn by the wife while her husband lives. The *chandanhár* is a gold ornament worn round the neck, and it should be mentioned as it is always given to the bride by her father-in-law. The bridegroom receives from his father-in-law gold ear-rings and gold armlets, also the terrible *teth* to which allusion has been made above. Before concluding this account of the marriage ceremonies, it should be noted that there is an absence of symbols denoting that the marriage is one of conquest. It is a decorous ceremony, there is little or no weeping when the bride leaves her home, and no abuse of the bridegroom by the women of the bride's house.

Death. From his marriage till his death the Hindu never again plays the chief part in ceremonials. When death draws nigh a straw bed of koin grass, if obtainable, is prepared for him on a clean spot, rice and salt and money are given to the poor and the *mantras* are recited to the dying man. When he has breathed his last his body is laid on the straw bed, and a lamp is kept lighted by his head whether it be night or day. Near it is placed a tray full of sesamum with a coin. Before the body is bathed it is

[1] The *taranga* is sometimes worn also by girls who have arrived at marriageable years.

covered with a sheet, woollen or linen, and after the performance of the Sradh ceremony the dead body is wrapped in what is called *kafan*. It consists of a loose toga, cap, and sranpat (a piece of cloth about two yards long and a quarter of a yard wide) wrapped round the stomach. The body is then placed on a wooden plank, and is either borne on the shoulders of four men or carried in a boat along the goblin-haunted track (*razbar*) to the burning-ground. The funeral pyre is lighted by the son of the deceased, but the work of cremation is done by Musalmáns known as *kawji*. For this they receive half of the shroud (*kafan*) and about Rs. 3 to Rs. 6. In return they have to supply wood for the funeral pyres. The other half of the shroud is burnt with the corpse. If the deceased is a woman one or two ornaments are left on the body, and these are recovered from the fire by the *kawji*. Two or three days after cremation a few bones of the corpse, which the fire has not consumed, are brought home, and are left in a hole of the wall of the house until the day of *Gang Ashtmi*, when they are taken to the holy lake under the mountain Haramukh. For ten days the house of the deceased is unclean and no one will eat food cooked in it, and for ten days, while the soul of the deceased is on its journey, rites for the dead (*kari karni*) are performed on the river bank. The son of the dead man shaves his head and beard, and when he has finished his ten days of active mourning he receives from his father-in-law a new dress, which he puts on. He then goes home accompanied by his relatives and friends. As they approach the house, the mourners draw themselves into two lines, the son enters the house and then immediately returns and passes down between the two lines. The mourners then take their leave. Meanwhile the women, who do not attend the ceremonies on the river bank, have been paying visits to the mourning family. On the eleventh day the *sharadh* service is performed for the deceased and for ancestors up to the seventh generation, and the family, which has abstained from flesh since the death, now eats meat. The Brahmans are feasted and are given clothes and cash in the name of the deceased. For the first three months after the death the *sharadh* service is performed every fifteenth day and thereafter monthly for the next nine months. A widow mourning for her husband, and the women of the family mourning for a relative, prolong their mourning for a year, and for some months do not change their clothes (*phir mal*). If, however, they are bidden to a marriage they are allowed to wear clean clothes and they resume the neck thread which was put on at marriage (*athful*).

Smallpox. It is a sad fact that the occurrence of smallpox has become one of the accepted customs of Kashmír, and the Hindus have regular ceremonies which must be observed when the disease attacks their families. When it appears that a child is sick with the smallpox, the first thing to be done is

CHAP. X. to sew rupees into his headdress. He is then placed in a separate room, and is surrounded by clay toys of horses, elephants, palankins, fans and sugar-cakes, water-chestnuts and shells. Until the pustules are developed the child is kept on rice and curd, and no salt may be given to the child or used by the mother or wet-nurse. A little fish or a piece of meat is always hung up in the sick room (*chhai ratan*), but while the smallpox lasts no meat may be eaten and no prayers may be repeated in the house. When the disease abates the rupees are taken out of the headdress, and are spent on rice boiled in milk, which is distributed to relations and friends. The room is cleaned and the toys and a plate full of rice are flung into the river. If the smallpox is very severe, Sitla Mata, the smallpox deity, must be propitiated, and offerings of sheep, goats, horses or donkeys, and eyes of gold or silver are made to her priests on Hari-Parbat. Forty days after the smallpox first makes its appearance (*chat jihun*), rice boiled in milk is again distributed to relations and neighbours.

Daily worship. These are the chief events in the life of the Kashmíri Pandit, but every day he must perform worship. When he arises in the morning he puts on wooden pattens, and with a water-jar in his hand he goes down to the sacred Jhelum, bathes and says his prayers (*sandhia*). If his father or mother is dead, he throws water in the air and utters the names of his ancestors back to seven generations. If he has an idol (*thakur*) in his house, he sprinkles it with river-water, placing flowers and rice before the image. Rich men keep Brahmans for this service. The *thakur* is a fossil from Nepal, the Narbadda, or from Shisha Nág in Kashmír. These *thakurs* are of very curious shape and often cost large sums. After this he dresses and puts the saffron mark (*tika*) on his forehead, and drinks some of the water with which the idol has been washed (*charan amrat*). He then goes to his work. Some Hindus, after bathing, make a *linga* of earth brought from the Takht-i-Suliman, and after worshipping the Phallic emblem cast it in the river. Others go daily to the temple of Sharka Devi or Hari-Parbat, and after service to the goddess walk round the hill barefoot. Others go to the different temples in the city. It is to be noticed that only the old Pandits bathe regularly through the winter and walk barefoot round Hari-Parbat. The younger generation is more delicate or perhaps less religious. Every month the strict Hindu will keep four fasts. Meat is prohibited on these days, but water-chestnuts and potatoes can be eaten on the eleventh day of the waxing and waning moon, and on the eighth day and fifteenth day of the full moon rice and vegetables are allowed once during twenty-four hours.

Holy days. There are many Hindu holy days in Kashmír, the chief of which may be mentioned briefly. It should be noted that, with the exception of State business, which is regulated by the solar months, all other transactions among Hindus in Kashmír proceed according to the lunar months. The holy days are calculated by the lunar months, whereas the worldly affairs of the Hindus are regulated by the solar months. The first day of solar Chetr is the Hindu spring day or *sont*. It is a great day with the villagers. In the early morning a basket, containing unhusked rice, curd, bread, salt, a pen-box, flowers and walnuts, is shown to every member of the family by a servant or a boy. Every one takes one or two walnuts, and after bathing the walnuts are thrown into the river. The unhusked rice is given to fishermen, who make a present of fish which is eaten in the evening of the spring day. On the fifth day of full moon in Baisakh a fair is held in honour of Rish Pir, a Hindu saint, at the Ali Kadal bridge. Rish Pir's funeral rites are performed, and every Hindu presents 14½ annas to the saint's representatives. and receives in return some fried rice, which is taken home and distributed among relations. The new moon of Chetr is celebrated by a festival known as *naurch*, and baskets are shown to the members of the house as on the *sont* day, but the chief article of importance in the basket is the almanack of the new year. Another festival is held on the third day of the *naurch* called *Trch*. A feast is given and sons-in-law are especially invited. *Chetr Nowmi*, or the ninth day of the waxing moon of Chetr, is sacred to Doorga, and from the fifth to the ninth day no meat must be eaten. Those that worship Ragyan (Khir Bhawáni) must not eat meat, some for eight, and some for five days; but those that worship Jwala or Sharka are at liberty to eat flesh. It is the custom to sow barley in some room in the house. The barley is covered with a dome in which a lamp is left burning night and day, and the seed is watered with milk. On the day of *Chetr Nowmi* the barley is cut and worn on the headdress for a few days and then flung into the river. Offerings of flesh and rice are taken to Sharka Devi on the Hari-Parbat. *Chetr Nowmi* is the birthday of Rama, and is considered one of the luckiest days in the year. *Jeth Ashtmi*, the eighth day of the waxing moon of the month Jeth, and *Hár Saptmi*, the seventh day of Hár, are days dedicated to the worship of Khir Bhawáni. *Hár Ashtmi*, the eighth day of the waxing moon of Hár, is sacred to Sharka Devi, and *Hár Chaturdashi*, the fourteenth day of the waxing moon of Hár, is the especial day of Jowala Mukhi, whose temple is at Krihu near Pámpur. *Shrawan Dvádashi*, or the twelfth day of the waxing moon of the month Sawan, is the day on which rites are performed for children who died before they received the sacred thread. and on this day the bereaved mothers flock to a spring called Kapál Mochan at Batpura in the Shupiyon Tahsil to intercede for their lost ones. *Puran Mashi*, the full moon of the month Sawan, is the day when pilgrims must reach the distant cave of Amarnáth and worship the snow *linga*, which gradually melts away after the Puran Mashi. Strict Hindus, both male and female, will discard their clothes and put on shirts of birch-bark before they enter the cave. *Janam Ashtmi*, the eighth day of the waning moon of Bhadron, is the birthday of Krishna, and a fast of three days is kept, of which one day is a complete fast. *Gang Ashtmi*, the eighth day of the waxing moon of Bhadron. is the day when Hindus take the bones (*astarak*) of their dead to the lake beneath Haramukh and perform the *sharadh* service for the departed. *Kambar Pach* is a period of fifteen days in the waning moon of the month Asuj, in which rites for the dead are performed in the houses of Hindus. *Maha Nowmi*, the ninth day of the waxing moon of Asuj, is attended with rites similar to those observed in *Chetr Nowmi*, and the next day is the Dussehra festival in honour of the conquest of Ceylon by Rama, but this festival is not observed by Kashmíri Hindus, nor is the Holi festival kept by them. *Khich Máwas* falls on the fifteenth day of the moon's waning in Poh, and is a day for the propitiation of evil spirits, who are conciliated by offerings of rice and pulse. *Bhimsan Ikádashi*, or eleventh day of the waxing moon of Magh, is observed as a fast. It is believed that the temperature of the earth changes on this date, and that the soil becomes warm. The last, and in some ways the most important, day in the Hindu calendar is the *Sheorátri*, or *Herat*, which falls on the thirteenth day of the declining moon of Magh. Offerings are made to an incarnation of Shiva, known as Bherow, and he is worshipped from sunset till midnight. At midnight the worshippers, who have fasted during the day, have a feast. Bherow is one of the Tantrik names. On the *Sheorátri*, Hindus are obliged to make their married daughters[1] presents according to the *teth*, and on this day every Hindu plays some game, but unlike the *Diwáli* festival in India there is no gambling. The women stand in rows advancing and retreating, singing the *Ru* song. On the Id the Musalmán women sing the same song. The song is pretty and the dance graceful.

Adoption and remarriage.

Before concluding this account of the ceremonies of the Kashmíri Hindus, it is necessary to allude to their customs of adoption and remarriage. Every Hindu can adopt a son either from his own *gotra* or from another *gotra*, and the only restriction on adoption is that the adopted son must not have been invested with the sacred thread. An adopted son cannot be disinherited, whereas a real son can be turned out by his father, and if a child is born after adoption, the adopted son is treated as the eldest son. Polygamy is practically unknown[2], but Hindus may remarry[3] and they often

[1] Daughters also receive presents on the Naureh, Hársatam, Vathtrwah, Janam Ashtmi, Khich Máwas, Shashar Sankrat, Navisál.

[2] I am speaking of the Hindus as a body. Many Hindus whom I have known remarried, and some have more than one wife. It is a satisfactory point to notice that where there is more than one wife the greatest tenderness is shown by the elder wife to the younger.

[3] A man will take more than one wife only when he has lost all hopes of having a child from

do take second wives on the death of their first. Remarriage is, however, regarded as a luxury, and many Pandits have assured me that it is not looked upon with favour in Kashmír. The child-widow, of perhaps seven years of age, can in no case make a second marriage, but she has the privilege of adopting a son, and it may be said that in a large percentage of adoptions the adopted son is taken from the wife's *gotra*. The widow lives, for the most part, in her deceased husband's family, but she is free to come and go between her father's and father-in-law's houses. The miseries caused by this unnatural system of child-widowhood, can be better imagined than described, and one of the saddest incidents of the cholera of 1892 is the number of girls who were left widows.

Musalmán marriage and *khána damádi*.

The Musalmáns, if possible, marry their daughters to some near relation, and if this is not possible, they ask some man of their own tribe, who has more sons than money, for a boy whom they take into their house (*khána damád*). The Kashmíri peasants have lately lowered the age at which their daughters are married, and it is not uncommon for a girl to be married at the age of seven. When a man's daughter is three years old, and he cannot arrange for her marriage with a near relative he will take a boy into his house (*khána damád*), and this boy, until he marries the daughter of the house, has to work like a drudge. The system of *khána damádi* is said to have become common in Sikh times, and if forced labour was wanted for transport the unfortunate *khána damád* was always sent. If he came back alive he won his bride. If he died it did not matter as the son of the house, at any rate, escaped. At present the custom of *khána damádi* is very popular. It has two advantages. In the first place, the father of the girl receives a drudge who works like a slave for seven years, and in the second place, the expenses on betrothal and marriage are very small. Some men are very unscrupulous in the matter of *khána damádi*, and turn boys out of their house on some small pretext and give their daughter to a stranger, but as a rule, the boy who has worked out his term of probation gets his bride. There is apparently no legal obligation, either on the part of the father or the *khána damád*, and the connexion can be broken at the will of either party. But there is a moral obligation on the part of the boy to work, and on the part of the father to give his daughter in marriage to the boy. It frequently happens that when a boy is taken into the house a deed of gift is executed, and in this case, if the boy leaves the house, the property covered by the deed of gift remains with the boy. Probably, if the boy brought an action to recover his bride he would succeed, but he would not be able to obtain any property with

the first wife, and even then the second marriage is performed with the sanction of his first wife. This is generally disliked, and may be considered very rare.

CHAP. X. her unless there was a deed of gift[1]. One of the reasons given for the popularity of *khána damádi* is that it enables a man to keep his daughter at home, and on the whole the system works well, and there are not many quarrels between the father and the *khána damád*. It is noticeable that the Musalmán father is very much attached to his daughter. Old men complain that the rising generation is becoming very independent, and that the *khána damád* is inclined to leave his father-in-law's house soon after the marriage. The *khána damád* adopts the Krám[2] name of his father-in-law.

If a marriage with a near relative cannot be arranged, the father of a son who has reached the years of puberty calls in the services of a go-between (*drál*, *miánji*, or *manzim yor*). This go-between is usually a man of great powers of persuasion, and he visits families with marriageable daughters, and tells highly-coloured stories of the magnificence and generosity of his client. He then suggests marriage and takes his leave. The girl is kept at home from that date, and is not allowed to play about in the village. A few days after, on one pretext or another, the fathers of the girl and the boy arrange an informal meeting, and settle a day for the betrothals (*nishán*). Shortly after, the boy's father goes with a small party of relatives and friends with presents (*bog*) to the girl's house, and the party is entertained by the girl's father. The presents, as a rule, consist of silver bracelets, cash, salt and sugar. After the feast, the betrothals are announced in the presence of the party, and a priest asks a blessing, and if there is no doubt about the faith of the contracting parties, he reduces the marriage contract to writing. If there is doubt, the contract is for the present merely oral. The party stay the night, and next morning the boy's father receives a blanket or a turban from the girl's father, and taking back half of the cash, sugar and salt sets off to his home. Afterwards, on the four chief Musalmán holidays, viz. *Id Ramzán*, *Id Kurbán*, *Mihráj Sharíf* and *Urs Nabi*, the boy's father sends presents to the girl. Then for six months visits follow, and at the end of this period the marriage day is fixed, and Rs. 20 to Rs. 50 are given as *Lagan chir* by the boy's father to the girl's father. Preliminaries are arranged, and invitations (*dapani*) are issued to relations and friends. For a week before the marriage, the bride sits indoors with her hair down (*malas behn*), and at both her house and the boy's house singing and drumming go on day and night. The day before the marriage, the boy's father sends a quantity of *mendhi* dye to the bride's house, and she stains her hands and feet with the red colour. On the marriage day the bridegroom, after a bath, dresses himself up like a Mahárájá, and decks himself out with all the jewelry he can borrow from

[1] In Gurais and Tilail, which now form part of Kashmír proper, the value of a wife is Rs. 100 and a pony. If a man is not rich enough to buy a bride he leaves his home and serves his future father-in-law twelve years. After twelve years' service he can claim his wife, but nothing more.

[2] Krám, see p. 304.

friends. His relatives give him presents of money, and then he and his party set off, riding or walking. First they visit some neighbouring shrine and say their prayers, then do reverence to the graves of the bridegroom's father or grandfather, and after that they make for the bride's house, sending on ahead the presents and the palanquin in which the bride will return. As they draw near the bride's house the women of the bride's party come out, singing the song of welcome (*wani wani*) and praising the bridegroom's beauty, and when they come to the door the village barber pours out a jar of water. Into the empty jar the bridegroom's representative tosses a rupee. This custom is known as *ábdul*, and is repeated when the bridegroom takes his bride back to his father's house. When the whole party are assembled the gorgeous groom sits on cushions and the feast commences, winding up with tea; when the guests can eat no more the Kázi proceeds to business, and if the marriage contract was not written before he writes it out, receiving a fee for his pains. Before this is done, however, the two fathers of the contracting parties commence a quarrel as to the amount of *mehr* or dower which should be fixed. *Mehr* is practically never claimed by the wife in Kashmír except in case of divorce. The quarrel is maintained with great spirit, but every one present knows that it is a mere form and that the amount of *mehr* will be settled according to custom. Then the headman of the village gets up and claims his dues, and the bride's father quarrels with him, and finally all the village officers, bearers and servants crowd in and demand their fees. Meanwhile the bride and her friends are examining the wedding presents, and when all is ready the bride, with her hair done up and in the best dress she has in her trousseau, is carried by her brother or maternal uncle to her palanquin. Inside the palanquin a sheep's heart and salt are placed, and the bride, followed by a crowd of singing women, departs with her husband. The bride's brother goes with her, and a female relative also accompanies the young girl (*dudh máj*) and instructs her in the formalities which have to be observed. As the party passes through a village all the women come out and insist on seeing the bride. When the bridegroom's house is reached the bride is lifted out of her palanquin and carried into a chamber set apart for her. She sits there with downcast head until her mother-in-law comes and raises her face. As the mother-in-law does this she abstracts from the bride's handkerchief some money which is her perquisite (*hash kant*). Then all the women of the bridegroom's family kiss the bride's hand and place rupees in it. A big feast is given on the marriage night (*tehl*) and the next day the guests depart. The bride remains seven days in her husband's house. Then, discarding her bridal dress, she puts on clothes given by her father-in-law (*tehl jor*) and sets off to her father's house. Sometimes her husband accompanies her, but he may not visit her again

CHAP. X. until he is invited by his father-in-law. The houses of the bride's father and the bridegroom's father are respectively known by the name of *huhur* and *Málun*. Three months, six months or a year after the bride's return to her father's house, the bridegroom and his friends are again bidden to the bride's house and a great feast is given. The bridegroom remains three days, and when he departs his father-in-law gives him a present of clothes. Thereafter, there is no restriction on the intercourse between bride and bridegroom. Cohabitation sometimes commences when the bride is nine years of age, but, as a rule, it may be said that the girl has intercourse with her husband at the age of twelve, and that she is a mother by fourteen[1].

Birth.

After two years from the last stage in the marriage ceremonies the young wife hopes for children, and if they are not forthcoming she goes to a religious man for a charm (*tawiz*) or visits a shrine, where she ties up a votive rag (*dush*) on the wall. Two months before her confinement she goes back to her father's house, and when the day arrives, if there be need, a wise woman (*warin*) is called in, and one of the family goes to the religious man for a charm. When the child is born the priest comes in, and taking the infant by the right ear, he whispers the *Azán*, welcoming the new arrival to this world of faith, and then he repeats in the left ear the *Takbir*, and adds as a warning that death is the end of all things. The young mother fasts for one or two days, and then has a meal of wheaten bread and eggs. The grass bed on which she lies is known as *hur* and is changed daily. On the seventh day, which is known as the *sundar* day, the mother bathes and the child is given its name. The name is given by the *Pir* of the family. He usually gives some name suggested by the month in which the child is born. Thus a boy born in the months of Ramzán, Sháhbán or Rajab will most likely be called Ramzán, Sháhbán or Rajab. A boy born in the month in which a great saint died is often named after the saint. Thus Sultán is probably the name of a boy who was born in the month in which the great saint Makhdúm Sahib died. The Krám name is of course added to the birth name—e.g. Rámzán Rahtor, Sháhbán Bat, Rajab Mir, Sultan Lon. Girls are never known by their Krám name. Among the more common names of girls may be mentioned Fazli, Máli, Mihri, Janu, Daulati, Rahmi, Kali, Pritsi, Sundri, Zuni (the moon maiden), Mukhti, Farzi, Ashumi. The richer people favour names like Taju, Sitáru, Begam and Ashu. The Shias will never call their sons Sultán, Sadik or Umr. On this seventh day the barber is called in and shaves the child's head, and a great feast is given. Two or three months

[1] Cf. Romeo and Juliet, Act i, scene 2:

'*Par.* Younger than she are happy mothers made.
Cap. And too soon marred are those so early made.'

PLATE VIII

To face page 271

Negative by Captain Godfrey

SHOWS A GRAVEYARD COVERED WITH IRIS FLOWERS, AND SHADED BY THE BRIMIJ (CELTIS AUSTRALIS) TO THE RIGHT IS THE VILLAGE MOSQUE

later the mother returns to her father-in-law's house, carrying with her presents, among which will be a cow with a calf or a pony mare with a foal.

Circumcision.

At the age of four or five the child will be circumcised, and this is an occasion of great rejoicing. Friends are invited, and the child's feet and hands are stained with the red *mendhi* dye, and he is decked out in brave apparel. For seven days before the ceremony there is nothing but singing and feasting, and on the day of the circumcision (*khutna*) the child is placed on a basket under which a cock[1] is cooped, the perquisite of the barber who performs the circumcision. All friends and relatives kiss the child's hand and give him money (*guli-myut*), after which the guests go off to a shrine with the boy and return to the house for a feast.

Death.

When a Musalmán approaches his end he is laid with his head towards the north or the east, and he is given as his last drink a *sharbat* made of honey. Those around call on the name of God, and break into weeping when he breathes his last. The corpse is then bathed and wrapped in a cotton cloth and placed in a wooden box (*tabut*), which is always in readiness at the mosque. The body is taken to the graveyard (*mazár*), and relatives and friends repeat the funeral service. Over the wooden box is flung a cotton pall, which is the perquisite of the gravedigger and the priest. The corpse is removed from the box and is buried in the cotton cloth. On the day of the funeral, and for three days after, the guests and priest are feasted by some relative of the deceased, as no food is eaten from the deceased's house. On the fourth day (*chaudas*) a big feast is given there, and on the Friday following the death all go to the graveyard, and some relative flings over the shoulder of the dead man's heir a coloured cloth. For forty days prayers are offered up for the deceased, and food is given to the priest and to the poor. For one year presents must be given every month to the priest, and hereafter on the anniversary of a man's death the priest receives a gift. The graveyard is planted over with many irises, narcissi, and other spring flowers, and some special trees, as the Celtis, all of which are sacred. In the spring the graveyards are gardens of lovely flowers.

There are many customs in the valley which would be of interest to the student of folk-lore, but space can only be found for two. These are similar in some ways to English customs. The first is the *Ánkút*, or harvest-home festival, which takes place on the second day of the Diwáli, when the city people are fed at the expense of the State on the first fruits of the autumn harvest. This custom was introduced by Mahárájá Gulab Singh, and has been kept up by his successors. Huge feasts of rice and other autumn cereals are prepared at six appointed places—for the better class Pandits, the common Pandits, the better class Musalmáns, the common Musalmáns, the Shias and the Dogras. The Dogra feast takes place in the

[1] In Russia the peasants believe that there is healing power in the hen-coop.

CHAP. X. Basant Bagh, to which the idol of the royal temple is carried in the morning. No flesh of any kind is eaten at the *Ánkút*. The feasts for the better class Pandits and Musalmáns are very prettily arranged. The guests sit down to their white rice and other dainties, salt and sweet. For the common herd there are platters of red rice with a portion of vegetables; but their feast is a scramble, and the hungry scavengers rush in and sweep up broken platters, dust and rice. The other custom is somewhat like our April Fools' Day. When the first snow falls every one tries to hand to his neighbour a piece of snow concealed in some clever manner. If he succeeds in deceiving his neighbour he can demand a forfeit.

Character and disposition of the people.

In trying to give an idea of the character and disposition of the people a distinction should be drawn between the villagers and the people of the city, the *shahr-básh*. There are certain characteristics which are common to all Kashmíris, whether Hindu or Musalmán, villager or *shahr-básh*: but in some respects a marked difference exists between the several classes.

The villagers.

It must be borne in mind that for a long time it has been the policy of the State to subordinate the interests of the cultivators to the welfare and ease of the city people, and allowances must be made for failings and faults in the character of the villagers which cannot be made for the pampered citizens of Srinagar. In my chapter on administration the relations of the city to the villages will be described at some length, but in order to make clear some of the remarks in this chapter I must allude briefly to the position held by the cultivators in the system of government in Kashmír. My predecessor, Mr. Wingate, in his preliminary report of settlement operations in Kashmír, writes in August, 1888:—

'The revenue system is such that, whether the Kashmíri cultivator works much or little, he is left with barely enough to get along on till next harvest. He is a machine to produce *shálí*[1] for a very large and mostly idle city population. The secret of the cheap *shálí* is because if the price were allowed to rise to its proper level the whole body of Pandits would compel the palace to yield to their demands.

'The Muhammadan cultivator is compelled to grow *shálí*, and in many years to part with it below its proper market rate, that the city may be content. If the harvest is too little for both, the city must be supplied, and is supplied, with any force that may be necessary, and the cultivator and his children must go without. That is the explanation of the angry discontent that filled the valley during the famine. The cultivator is considered to have rights neither to his land nor to his crops. The Pandits and the city population have a right to be well fed whether there is a famine or not at two Chilki rupees[2] per kharwar[3].'

[1] Shálí means unhusked rice.

[2] The Chilki rupee, known also in Kashmír as the Nawi and Pakka rupee, is equivalent to ten annas imperial.

[3] See Weights and Measures, pp. 242, 243.

It is unnecessary to dwell at length on the old system, but I can say that at the commencement of my work in Kashmír in 1889, the cultivators took no interest in their land, and had no belief in the land revenue settlement nor confidence nor hope in anything. It is not reasonable to look for virtues among an oppressed people, nor is it fair to descant on their vices. When one has been for some years living in the villages and seeing the Kashmíris as they are, one cannot help feeling pity for their lot and being a little blind to their faults. I have tried to make the best and not the worst of them, and it is possible that in the following remarks on the character and disposition of the Kashmíri cultivators I may not be expressing the views usually held on the subject. I can only urge that my work has given me opportunities, which no Europeans have previously enjoyed, of becoming acquainted with the people of the villages; but, in order to guard against special pleading, I shall conceal none of the faults of the Kashmíri, nor shall I keep back the views held by intelligent natives of the country or natives of the Panjáb. I would add, however, that many of the opinions regarding the Kashmíris are based on observations of the Srinagar people and the boatmen, and that the principle *ex uno disce omnes* is often at the bottom of the wholesale condemnation of the people of the valley.

The Kashmíri bears an evil reputation in the Panjáb, and indeed throughout Asia. Proverbs liken him to a snake in his morals and to a fowl in his manners, and men are warned against admitting a Kashmíri to their friendship. Moorcroft writes of the Kashmíri, 'Selfish, superstitious, ignorant, supple, intriguing, dishonest and false, he has great ingenuity as a mechanic and a decided genius for manufactures and commerce; but his transactions are always conducted in a fraudulent spirit, equalled only by the effrontery with which he faces detection;' and Drew admits that they are 'false-tongued, ready with a lie, and given to various forms of deceit.' Hugel has nothing good to say of the Kashmíris, and it is a matter of history that in the Mutiny the Kashmíris of Ludhiana turned against the English, and in the Settlement Report of the Kangra district the Kashmíris of Nurpur were spoken of unfavourably by Mr. Barnes. But it must be remembered that Moorcroft was speaking of the city people, and that the Kashmíris of Ludhiana and Kangra were the shawl-weavers, who are the lowest and meanest of the population, and it would not be fair to apply Moorcroft's epithets to the villagers as a body. He admits, too, that the vices of the Kashmíris are not innate, but are due to the government under which they lived. 'The natives of Kashmír have always been considered as amongst the most lively and ingenious people of Asia, and deservedly so. With a liberal and wise government they might assume an equally high scale as a moral and intellectual people, but at present a more degraded race does not exist.' . . . 'The vices of the Kashmíri I cannot help considering,

CHAP. X. however, as the effects of his political condition rather than his nature, and conceive that it would not be difficult to transform him into a very different being.' Knight (*Where Three Empires Meet*, p. 111) says, 'Whenever they saw a Kashmíri they would run up to him barking, whereupon in almost every instance that fine-looking, athletic, bearded disgrace to the human race would behave as a five-year-old English child would be ashamed to do, howling, weeping, and throwing himself down in the snow in deadly fear.' It is fair to add that even Indians show signs of fear when barked at by an English terrier. Perhaps the criticism which gives the true key-note to the national character is that of Victor Jacquemont, who wrote as follows in 1833:—'The Afghans having during the last century despoiled the Mughals of their conquest, and the Sikhs having expelled the Afghans in this century, a general pillage has ensued upon each conquest; and in the intervals of peace anarchy and oppression have done their utmost against labour and industry, so that the country is now completely ruined, and the poor Kashmíris appear to have thrown the handle after the hatchet, and to have become the most indolent of mankind. If one must fast, better do so with folded arms than bending beneath the weight of toil. In Kashmír there is hardly any better chance of a meal for the man who works, weaves, or plies the oar, than for him who in despair slumbers all day beneath the shade of the plane-tree.'

The theory held by the Kashmíris themselves is that they were once an honourable, brave people, and that they were reduced to their present abject state by continued foreign oppression. But some who have made a special study of the Raja Tarangini inform me that, long before the days of foreign conquest and oppression, the Kashmíris were noted for their cunning and dishonesty. It is useless, therefore, to speculate on what the Kashmíris once were. But when one reflects on what they now are one cannot help the thought that many races, had they lived through generations of oppression, like the Kashmíris, might have been more cunning and more dishonest. In a country where there was practically no justice, the only weapon in the hands of the weak was lying or subterfuge, and I must admit at once that the Kashmíris, in their dealings with officials, do not strictly adhere to the truth. They generally open a conversation by assuring one that they never tell untruths, and, indeed, cannot tell a lie. When detected they do not feel ashamed, and in the matter of speaking the truth they seem absolutely without any moral sense. Owing to the peculiar system of government, which encouraged a most elaborate scheme of espionage, the Kashmíris doubt and hate one another, and old men, when seeking causes for the present condition of Kashmír, attribute all its misery to two leading features of the national character—lying and *envy* or *malice*. A Kashmíri cannot bear to see any one getting on in life, and the elevation of a villager to office is by no means a popular measure in the country-side. The Kashmíri sticks at nothing, and has a great belief in the efficacy of a registered letter to the Darbar, in which he charges his rivals or enemies with a most detailed list of offences, chiefly untrue. He is very timid, and conducts himself in the most abject manner towards officials. I have often heard Kashmíris praise an official in his presence, and that very night the same men would come to my tent and revile the official, and bring the gravest charges against him. It is impossible to believe the Kashmíri when he is dealing with the officials of the country, or when he is presenting a petition in the city, but in his own village and in the presence of his fellow-villagers I have found it fairly easy to elicit the truth. It has been the custom for a Kashmíri to always overstate his case. He prepares his statement by heart, and directly he gets an opportunity he pours out a volley of words at the top of his voice. It is evident that in past times it was extremely difficult to obtain access to officials, and that it was necessary to attract the notice of the authorities by queer devices. A Kashmíri who wishes to show that he has been beaten by the officials or his neighbour will always produce a lock of hair, which he has carefully packed up in paper and stored away in his pocket. This is usually horsehair. To indicate his sad condition the Kashmíri will smear himself with the grey mud of the rice-fields, or will cover his naked body with dust. He frequently appears with a rope of rice straw around his neck, with a brick pendant. The brick signifies that he has been reduced to the condition of a clod; the rice-straw necklace means that his life has been practically destroyed. Men have frequently come out to meet me with their wives and children, flinging down their ploughs to indicate that husbandry has no further charms for them. In the sowing season scarcely a day passes without a petitioner appearing with sprouting grain or dried-up seedlings, to show that he cannot get water for irrigation. A common demonstration is a procession of two men and one woman. One man wears a shirt of matting, one carries a pan of embers on his head, and the woman bears a number of broken earthen pots. Sometimes the methods of venting a grievance are more elaborate. A man once came to me, carrying the corpse of an infant, and alleging that his enemies would not allow him even burying space. He had a land suit in his village, and this was his method of accentuating his grievance. Once a man came to me at Nagmarg, absolutely nude, and said his uncle had turned him naked into the world. It was very cold, so I gave him a suit of old clothes, and, by way of jest, told him that as he was now dressed like an Englishman he should assert his rights. He went home, and the uncle appeared next day bearing the marks of a severe castigation.

The Kashmíri is very loud and voluble. He is also very persistent.

CHAP. X. A Pandit, whose petition had been three times rejected, appeared a fourth time, and I told him that if he presented another petition I should have to report him to the local official. The next day the Pandit appeared with a paper in his hand; he was at once ordered to be removed, but explained that it was not a petition but a poem which he wished to present. The poem recited his grievances. Though loud in urging his worldly claims, the Kashmíri is extremely quiet under visitations, such as earthquake and cholera. Trustworthy eye-witnesses state that the Kashmíris sat silent in the earthquakes of 1885. And in the great cholera of 1892 I was in a badly-stricken part, and was much struck with the intense silence which prevailed in the villages. There was no wailing for the dead, and the people seemed to pass the day sitting quiet in the village graveyard. They wholly declined to attend me at my village inspections, and said that, as life was so uncertain, it seemed almost wicked to concern themselves with things of this world. In Srinagar there was the same absence of wailing or complaint, and a story was commonly told which accounted for this. A Panditani lost a son and mourned loudly. A spirit appeared and taunted her with wailing for one son, adding that before night-time she should have real reason to mourn. Before night came she had lost her husband and her other two sons. No one wailed after this.

In intellect the Kashmíris are perhaps the superior of the natives of India. They are very quick in argument, and they never abandon a case unless they are convinced that it is hopeless, and they always insist on knowing the grounds of a decision. Much of the quickness and readiness of wit in a Kashmíri may be attributed to the fact that he has usually travelled; though a native friend, a Kashmíri Pandit, whose family has been settled in India for some generations, says that the wit of the people is attributable to the climate. He writes, 'The Kashmíris that have settled down in the plains of the Panjab and other parts of India for a century or more have lost a great deal of this character, and as time passes on they will be just like all other natives of the plains.' Up to quite recent times the Kashmíri would quit his village on the slightest provocation, and would take up his abode in the easy city, or would seek a livelihood in the Panjab. Many have been as far as Calcutta and Bombay, and all are acquainted with legends of London and its power. Though London is frequently mentioned by the Kashmíris, I have found on inquiry that they have the vaguest ideas as to its locality. The usual answer is that London lies beyond Sukkur Bukkur on the Indus, which represents the *Ultima Thule* of rural Kashmíri thought. The commonest Kashmíri can talk intelligently on most subjects, and they have a great aptitude for sarcasm. The valley is so small that news of the palace and its doings quickly spreads, and the administration and its officials are discussed in a very critical and often very shrewd manner. They believe that every man has his price, but are quick to recognize ability in their rulers. Every Governor of Kashmír has his nickname, and it is a curious fact that the strong Governors who were hard to the people, have been given the most complimentary nicknames. Wazir Punnu, who did more work in Kashmír than any Governor, and who was hated in his time for his sternness, is known as 'the just.' Yet it was of Wazir Punnu that the proverb says—

'Wazir tsalih, Kashmír bali.'
When the Wazir goes, Kashmír will prosper.

The Kashmíri can turn his hand to anything. He is an excellent cultivator when he is working for himself. He is a good gardener, and has a considerable knowledge of horticulture. He can weave excellent woollen cloth, and can make first-rate baskets. He can build himself a house, can make his own sandals, and makes his own ropes. There is scarcely a thing which he cannot do, and as there are no middlemen like the Banyas of India, the Kashmíri is his own man of business. He understands profit and loss, and does not often make a bad bargain. He is, of course, like all orientals, conservative, and does not accept very readily crude suggestions regarding reforms in agriculture. I have at last induced them to cut down thistles, though the conservative party urged that the young thistles were an extremely pleasant vegetable in the spring. The Kashmíri can quote in support of his system of agriculture, and indeed in support of every act of his everyday life, some rhyming proverb, and he is essentially a man of routine. Everything in their lives, ploughing, sowing, sheep-shearing, &c., has its proper time, and the time is determined by the day on which the sun enters Aries and spring commences (the Nauroz) and the day on which the sun enters Libra (the Mezán) and autumn begins.

In his home life the Kashmíri cultivator is at his best. He is kind to his wife and children, and one rarely hears of divorce scandals or immorality among the villagers. A woman who has behaved badly is a marked character in the country, and public opinion is always against her. The husband sometimes chastises his wife, and the men talk somewhat boastfully of the necessity for maintaining discipline in their houses. But as a matter of fact the wife, both in Musalmán and Hindu houses, is all-powerful, and I believe that, as a rule, the Kashmíri lives in awe of his consort. The Kashmíri wife is a real helpmate, and joint work and joint interests give rise to a camaraderie between man and wife which is very healthy. I have often come across a woman in some deserted spot singing a wailing song for a husband dead long since. The cultivators look down upon the boatmen, and will not intermarry with them, as they consider them lax in the matter of morality. But, though kind to his own family, the Kashmíri is not always hospitable to his neighbours, and though generous enough to strangers, I have known many instances where he showed a lamentable want of charity. This arises in a great measure from the fact that there is no unity among the Musalmáns. Each man's house is a separate unit, and there have been no forces at work to bring these units together. The village is in no way a community, and if joint action is required to make a bridge or to repair the dams on the river, the villagers at once ask for the assistance of an official, who can compel all the villagers to co-operate. It is a curious and melancholy state of things, but the reasons are not far to seek, and will be explained in the chapter on Administration. Briefly, the Kashmíri cultivators have hitherto been treated as serfs, and have literally been forced to cultivate. They had no interest in their land, and were liable at any moment to be called away to work for officials or men of influence. They became absolutely hopeless and sullen, and each man played for his own hand. If they had combined their condition might have been happier. This sullen temper is one of the worst points in the Kashmíri character, and, joined to deep-rooted apathy, makes it very difficult to improve the condition of the people. It is said, and with some truth, that, even if bidden to a feast, the Kashmíri will not go unless he is forced; and when urgent work is necessary to prevent some disaster to the crops, the villagers themselves say, 'We do not want pay, but we want the slipper,' this being their phrase for compulsion. Crime is almost unknown in the villages. Property is absolutely safe, and I have never heard of such a thing as the theft of crops. Offences against the person are extremely rare, and when Kashmíris quarrel they call one another by bad names, and will occasionally go so far as to knock off a turban or seize an adversary by his effeminate gown. The sight of blood is abhorrent to them. But on occasions the Kashmíri will fight, and when the Sunnis and Shiahs fall out the dormant brute spirit of the Kashmíri wakes up. This absence of crime is due to the stern measures of repression taken by the rulers of Kashmír, more especially by Mahárájá Gulab Singh. The flaying alive of thieves has had its effect as a deterrent, and at the present time the only criminals of the valley are the Gulawáns, or horse-lifters. There are other reasons for the strange absence of crime. The duties of the village headman and the village watchman are very real, and they receive small mercy if they fail to report crime or to detect criminals; and further the old system of informers has made criminal pursuits unpopular and unprofitable. It may be truly said that the Kashmíri is afraid to commit crime.

The Kashmíris, like other artistic people, are very fond of exaggeration.

This is, of course, very noticeable in their suits for land, and in their dealings with officials. But in their private life also they like to exaggerate things. Everything which is unusual—wet weather, heavy snow, or very hot days—is spoken of by them as tyranny. They have three forms of address in conversation. In addressing a superior they call him *haz*, or saint. An equal is addressed as *sa*, a corruption of *sahib*, and an inferior is called *ba*, or brother. There are, similarly, three forms of address in speaking to women. Every Sikh is at once given brevet rank as 'Sirdar Sahib,' while a Panjabi Musalmán is at once elevated to the distinction of 'Khan Bahadur.' A faint reflection of the splendours of the old Mughal courts seems to survive in the valley, and one notices a formal politeness among the muddy-vestured peasants which has a tinge of burlesque about it.

In many respects the Kashmíri cultivator resembles the Irishman as described by Lever. He certainly possesses the quick wit which is so characteristic of the Irish, and has a deep-rooted objection to paying rent. There are many points of resemblance between Ireland and Kashmír. Both are small countries which have suffered or derived benefit from the rule and protection of more powerful nations, yet have never welcomed any change or improvement. Both Kashmíris and Irish love a joke, are fond of harmless deception, and are masters of good-humoured blarney. Both are kind to their children and the old folk. Both have the same disregard for the first principles of sanitation, though the interior of a Kashmíri hut is probably cleaner than that of a similar class of dwelling in Ireland. One day, while hearing petitions, I noticed an elderly Hindu villager standing on his head. He remained in that position for nearly half an hour before I asked him his business. He then explained that his affairs were in so confused a state that he did not know whether he was standing on his head or his heels. The boatmen are very ready in repartee. I asked some boatmen when they intended to take to agriculture. One old man at once replied, 'We shall take to agriculture when the river Jhelum dries up.' The boatmen, when questioned as to their origin, always say that they are descended from Noah. One characteristic of the Kashmíris, Musalmán and Hindu alike, is their conceit. One would not have expected that a down-trodden people would have much conceit left in them, but as a matter of fact the meanest Kashmíri always thinks that his way of doing things is the best. At first this conceit is amusing; but it sometimes has serious results, and one can never feel sure that a Kashmíri will not ruin some simple work by improving and modifying the instructions given to him.

The Kashmíris are fond of singing and of song-birds, and it is very pretty to hear them singing as they dibble in the young rice plants or

CHAP. X. break the clods with their wooden mallets. Some of the songs are full of poetical thought, and the airs are sweet and plaintive. They are fond of the beauties of nature, and the city people take their tea out to the almond gardens when they are in bloom, and sit rapt in delight for hours together. The almond gardens in the vicinity of Srinagar are most beautiful when they come into bloom in the early spring. The blossom is chiefly white, though pink flowers do occur. The Kashmíri is a very melancholy person. In the middle of a conversation he will sigh in the most irrelevant manner, and say that he sighs for his sins and for the curse that is on Kashmír. Hardly a day passes without reference being made to the curse and to the sin (*Páp*) which brought the curse. All misfortunes—oppression, failure of crops, and loss of cattle—are at once attributed to the curse. What the sin was which brought about the curse I have never discovered. The priests say that it was the sin of lying and malice. They rarely laugh or smile, but are easily moved to tears. When I first commenced the work of inspecting villages I was struck with the sight of grown-up men weeping like children, but I soon found that the tears were often feigned, and further discovered that one or two men were told off in each village to excite sympathy. They are perfect actors. One of the calamities which affects the rice crop is *rai*, and a plant affected by *rai* can at once be distinguished. At each village two or three men used to rush out with bundles of the damaged rice plant, but later, on making inquiries, I found that these bundles were sometimes carried from one village to another.

The Kashmíri is a weak-hearted, somewhat soft creature. He hates rain and cannot stand great heat. I have known men grumble at having to accompany me in the rain, and have seen others quite overcome with the sun when riding with me on village inspections. They possess great muscular strength and can carry enormous weights, but unless they are working for their own benefit they never exert themselves. They dawdle over work and are very fond of using only one hand. I have seen them on occasions, such as the repair of a shrine in cholera time, exert themselves in a surprising manner.

They are extremely dirty in their habits and person, and wash about once in ten days, and this, coupled with the fact that their clothes are equally dirty, makes them unpleasant companions in the warm weather. Soap is made in the valley, but is never used for personal ablutions. In the villages the barber shaves his clients with water. Soap is too valuable to be wasted on so trifling a matter as personal cleanliness, and is reserved for the purpose of softening the woollen cloth of Kashmír. It is a curious fact that, in spite of the dirty appearance of a Kashmíri's dress, great activity is shown in washing clothes, more especially in the city. It is true that the Kashmíris are a dirty people, but in many villages, especially in those which are not irrigated, there are latrines erected at some distance from the houses. So that the germ of sanitary ideas exists in the valley. CHAP. X

The city people.

The Musalmáns of the city are very similar in character and disposition to the Kashmíris of the villages, but the city man is more effeminate, more lazy, and more helpless. He will not work or try to improve his condition, for experience tells him that this is superfluous. It is, in his opinion, the duty of the State to feed him and to provide fuel cheap, but he himself is unfettered by any duties. When labour is wanted for carriage it must be obtained from the villages, as the city man is too delicate to work. He objects to any innovations, and when sanitary reforms are suggested the city howls with indignation. They soon forget the horrors of cholera and the ravages of fire, and they ridicule drainage and streets as wild ideas of another world. Like the villager, the city man likes to keep himself warm in the winter, and the home atmosphere in the winter months is neither healthy nor conducive to the development of energy. The *hammám* is a great institution, and there are four public baths in Srinagar. The men go to the bath in the day, the women at night, and they take their food with them. For half an anna a man can have a regular bath, while one-quarter of an anna entitles him to the privilege of standing under the tap of water. In the city the Musalmáns consider it necessary to resort to the *hammám* once a week, and there is a proverb which prescribes wine daily, the *hammám* every week, emetics once a month, and blood-letting once a year. I am sorry to say that drinking is increasing rapidly, both among the Hindus and the Musalmáns, the drink chiefly in use being the apple brandy made in the State distillery. The Hindus, being followers of Shiva, are justified in the use of meat and wine, but in the villages the Musalmáns still abstain from liquor, though I know one or two influential headmen who indulge. As in India, the sole object of drinking liquor is intoxication, and the fashionable youths of Srinagar back themselves to drink off a quart of apple brandy at a draught. Drinking brandy has replaced a worse habit, the indulgence in bhang mixed with almonds. As a rule Pandits do not take to opium before the age of forty. The city people are not satisfied with cheap food, but they must have their food brought to their very doors, and along their whole length the river banks are lined with boats containing State grain. When it was suggested that grain should be sold at a few places where supervision would be easy, the city people denounced the suggestion as a piece of tyranny. They are near the palace and can make themselves heard.

The city Hindu is in some respects very different to the Hindu of the villages. The latter is a man who works in his fields, and he is often

CHAP. X. a simple hard-working and healthy person. The Hindus of the city, who are said to get their living by—

'Nalam, kalam, ya halam,'
Lying, writing, or begging,

are men who have lived almost entirely upon State employment. They are a very intelligent and intellectual race of men, of excellent manners, and often very charming and amusing companions. They are fluent and ready writers. They can undergo great strain and fatigue when necessity arises, in spite of their soft, gentle appearance. They often amass great wealth in a short time, but they are very generous and lavish in their expenditure, and their money soon goes. It is to be regretted that they have not built any work of public utility in their beloved city. Musalmáns have built mosques and baths, but I cannot remember any institution bequeathed to the people by a Pandit. The expenditure on marriages is heavy, and the unfortunate head of a family has to support all the members, though many of them may be in good circumstances. They are very true to one another, and, owing to their unity and to the fact that they have monopolized all State offices, their power has been enormous. They used not to be very scrupulous in their methods of obtaining office and money, but they are bad managers, and have made very little out of the landed property acquired during their term of authority. In character, disposition, and ability they are, as private individuals, infinitely superior to the Musalmáns of Kashmír, but, as will be seen in the chapter on Administration, they have proved, as officials, rapacious, short-sighted, and cruel.

Conclusion. It is difficult to describe a people's character, but the account I have given of the Kashmíris is already too long, and there is no space for anecdotes which might perhaps give a better clue to character than general remarks. I would, however, add that the Kashmíris possess an individuality and national character which will cling to them wherever they go. I have seen men who have returned to Kashmír, whose ancestors left the country two or three generations ago. Their dress was changed and their manners had changed, yet they retained unmistakeable signs of a Kashmír origin, and their ways of thought and of speech showed their descent. The Kashmíris are fond of their own country, its food, its water, and its dress, and, though oppression has driven them out of the valley, many have come back and all are loth to leave. The Kashmíri proverb, '*Tsari chụ kand thari peth karar*,' which means that a bird is content when it is on its own branch, is often quoted by a Kashmíri when the advantages of service in the Panjab are pointed out to him. Finally, though the character of Kashmíris leaves much to be desired, I think that it is to their credit that it is not worse, considering the few chances they have had for becoming truthful, manly, and self-respecting. The word *izzat* is often on their lips, and they deplore the fact that they have no honour in the eyes of their rulers or of their fellows. A man who can be beaten and robbed by any one with a vestige of authority soon ceases to respect himself and his fellow-men, and it is useless to look for the virtues of a free people among the Kashmíris, and unfair to twit them with the absence of such virtues. The Kashmíri is what his rulers have made him, but I believe and hope that two generations of a just and strong rule will transform him into a useful, intelligent, and fairly honest man.

CHAPTER XI.

RELIGIONS.

Chap. XI.

Musalmáns.

Shiahs.

OUT of a population of 814,241, 52,576 are Hindus, 4,092 are Sikhs, and the rest are Musalmáns, who thus form over 93 per cent. of the total population of the valley. At the census of 1890 no distinction was made between Musalmáns of the Sunni and Shiah persuasions, but it may be roughly said that the Shiahs form only about 5 per cent. of the total Musalmán population. The Shiahs chiefly reside in the Zadi-Bal ward of Srinagar and in the Kámráj district, though they are found in other parts of the valley, where their presence can always be discovered by the appearance of the graves, which are level with the ground, whereas the Sunni graves have raised mounds above them. The Shiah system is said to have been introduced by Shams-ud-Din Iraki in A. D. 1450, but it has never, save during the short period of the Chaks, gained much hold on the valley, and from the first Shams-ud-Din Iraki met with great opposition. He was buried at Zadi-Bal, and his grave, which has several times been violated by the Sunnis, is held in great veneration by the Shiahs of Kashmír. The Shiahs are a most respectable community, and in Srinagar many of them are men of good position. They are true to one another, and are kind and helpful to poor members. From time to time fights, attended with great violence, take place between the Shiahs and Sunnis, and as late as 1872 there was a severe and prolonged conflict. The quarrel arose from the Shiahs commencing to build near the tomb of Madin Shah, who is claimed as a Sunni by the Sunnis and as a Shiah by the Shiahs. The Shiahs regard the Hindus with abhorrence, and will not even touch oil or use ink which has come into contact with a Pandit. The Sunnis, who are on friendly terms with the Kashmíri Hindus, look upon the Shiahs as outcasts, and will not speak of them as Musalmáns, but allude to them as *Ali Tashta*, or *Ráfiz*. They lay great stress on the fact that the Shiahs wash and drink from the same tank in the mosque, and they charge them with being an unclean people. There is only one ziárat in Kashmír, that of Alam Sahib, in the Narwara Mohalla of Srinagar, where Shiahs and Sunnis meet. Elsewhere their places of religion are wholly distinct. Zadi-Bal and Hassanabad in Srinagar, and Saidpura and Ahmadpura in the Kámráj district, contain the chief shrines of the Shiahs, but no Sunni would ever go to these places. In the city the Shiahs are chiefly shawl-weavers, and they practically monopolize the papier-maché industry. The Shiahs are famous physicians. A little experience enables one to tell a Shiah at once. They tie their turbans in a peculiar way, and trim their whiskers differently from the Sunnis.

Wahhábis. An attempt was made in recent times to introduce the Wahhábi doctrines into Kashmír, and about 200 families in the Shupiyon Tahsíl accepted the Wahhábi faith, but Mahárájá Ranbir Singh promptly stamped out the propagandists. The Wahhábi doctrines have again been preached during the last five years, and many Rishis of shrines, and others who speak with authority, declare that Wahhábi ideas are gaining ground. One idea commonly attributed by the orthodox Kashmíris to the Wahhábis is that they deny the individual and exclusive right of a husband in his wife.

Sunnis. The great majority of the Sunni Musalmáns of Kashmír belong to the Hanifi sect, but the Kubrawis, or followers of Mir Saiyad Ali of Hamadan, are of the Shafiai persuasion. The Sunni Musalmáns do not strike me as zealous or earnest in the profession of their faith, and, except in their quarrels with the Shiahs, they seem free from all forms of fanaticism. It is true that they observe very strictly the fast of Ramzán, but they do not keep Friday as a day of rest, and very few Kashmíris make the pilgrimage to Mecca, though the journey is now easy, and does not cost more than Rs. 340. In 1892 twenty-one Kashmíris went to Mecca, and this was an unusually large number. I do not base my ideas as to the laxness of Kashmíris in religious duties merely on my own observations. Holy men from Arabia have spoken to me with contempt of the feeble flame of Islám which burns in Kashmír, and the local Mullahs talk with indignation of the apathy of the people. In times of earthquake and cholera the Kashmíri falls to his prayers and displays a wonderful activity in repairing shrines and mosques, but in fair and easy times he allows the mosque and the shrine to fall into ruins and pays very little attention to the Mullah. The ordinary village mosque is no better than the meanest cultivator's cottage, and I have often seen a mosque without a thatch and a beautiful old shrine tumbling to pieces for want of some simple repairs. There is a want of system in the Musalmán religious administration. In quite small villages I have seen three miserable mosques, and when I have suggested that it would be better to have one good mosque and one respectable Mullah the villagers always urge the convenience of having a mosque close to their

CHAP. XI.

own houses, and these 'chapels of ease' are very frequent and very mean. The indifference shown in the matter of mosques and Mullahs may be accounted for by the fact that the Kashmíri Sunnis are only Musalmáns in name. In their hearts they are Hindus, and the religion of Islám is too abstract to satisfy their superstitious cravings, and they turn from the mean priest and the mean mosque to the pretty shrines of carved wood and roof bright with the iris flowers where the saints of past time lie buried. They like to gaze on the saint's old clothes and turban, and to examine the cave in which he spent his ascetic life. In connexion with the suggestion that the Kashmíris are at heart Hindus, it may be mentioned that certain places are held in reverence by Hindus and Musalmáns alike. As an instance, at Fattehpura in the Vernág Ilaka, and at Waripura in the Magam Ilaka, I have seen the imprint of a foot in a stone worshipped by the Musalmáns as Kadam-i-Rasul (the Prophet's footprint), and by the Hindus as Vishna pád (Vishnu's foot). And generally speaking it may be said that when one sees the Musalmán shrine with its shady chenárs and lofty poplars and elms, a little search will discover some old Hindu *Asthan*. It was only natural that the Musalmáns, when they were converted to Islam, should cling with tenderness to the old religious places [1], and should adopt sacred spots already familiar to the country-side. I have shown in my chapter on Customs how certain ideas are common to the Hindus and Musalmáns of Kashmír, but I attribute much of the delightful tolerance which exists between the followers of the two religions chiefly to the fact that the Kashmíri Musalmáns never really gave up the old Hindu religion of the country. There are two reasons for this tolerance which should be mentioned. In the first place, the strict prohibition of kine-killing removes one of the principal causes of ill feeling, and, in the second place, the strong rule under which the people have lived for generations would not brook any quarrelling between Hindus and Musalmáns. A government which maintained State Mullahs to celebrate marriages and farmed out the right of celebration was not likely to allow any signs of intolerance or fanaticism, and a revivalist in the old days would have met with short shrift.

Shrines.

Hindús at heart.

Saint-worship.

Every Kashmíri believes that 'the saints will aid if men will call,' and they think that a dead saint is more efficacious than a living priest. The Kashmíris are called by foreigners *Pir Parast*, that is saint-worshippers, and the epithet is well deserved. All the veneration in the Kashmíri character comes out as the Musalmáns approach a shrine. Lowly obeisances are made, and with bare feet the Kashmíri draws near the doorway and smears his throat and body with the holy dust of the sacred precincts. No man will dare to pass a shrine on horseback, and I once saw a striking example of the danger of neglecting this rule. A marriage party was crossing a stream

[1] The Kaaba stone at Mecca was sacred to other religions before the Musalmáns adopted it.

CHAP. XI.

above which stood the shrine of a saint. All of them dismounted and passed over the bridge, but the father of the bridegroom, with the bridegroom in his arms, rode boldly over. The bridge broke and the horse, father, and son were precipitated into the stream, where they lay struggling. I ran up and rebuked the crowd for not assisting the sufferers, but they looked on gloomily and said the man richly deserved his fate. After some trouble I induced some of my own people to disentangle the men from the horse, and then one of the attendants of the shrine explained to me that within the last ten years four men who had despised the saint and had ridden over the bridge had been killed. Though in many respects a lazy people, the Kashmíris think nothing of fatigue when a pilgrimage to a shrine has to be made, and I have often met families, who had come from distant places in the Panjab, trudging along leading a votive sheep gaily decked out with the lids of Tändstickor matchboxes. On the anniversary of a saint's death men will abstain from food, and Kashmíris far away in India observe these fasts.

Saint Nur Din, the patron saint of rural Kashmír.

Most of the best-known shrines may be traced back to the national saint, Shekh Nur Din. He and his ninety-nine followers, Khalifas, established themselves throughout the valley, and the ministers at the shrines of the Khalifas are still known as Rishis [1], though they do not lead the ascetic and celibate life of their famous predecessor. 'Plain living and high thinking are no more.' Among the most distinguished of Nur Din's Khalifas may be mentioned Shukr-ud-Din, whose shrine stands on the hill of Watlab, which looks over the Wular lake; Hanaf-ud-Din, whose shrine is built on a high detached hill known as Darrash, below the Tosh Maidan range; Zain-ud-Din, whose shrine stands like a castle on a mountain spur that looks over the Liddar valley; Lutf-ud-Din, whose shrine is on the pretty Pushkar hill; Nasir-ud-Din, whose shrine lies near that of his master at Chhrár Sharif; and Bam-ud-Din, whose shrine lies low at Bamzu. The well-known shrine below Gulmarg is sacred to Pa Imam Din, who was a Khalifa of Zain-ud-Din. The Rishis, the Babas, and the Makhdum Sahib Pirzadas are always looked upon as pure Kashmíri, and are called *Wami*, as distinguished from the Saiyads and the Saiyad Pirzadas, who found their way to the valley from foreign countries. All these are connected with shrine-worship, and I think that their influence is far greater than that exercised by Mullahs in the mosque. The shrines are associated with legends of self-denial and good works, they are pleasant places of meeting at fair-time, and the natural beauty of their position and surround-

His disciples.

[1] 'The most respectable people of this country are the Rishis, who, although they do not suffer themselves to be fettered by traditions, are doubtless true worshippers of God. They revile not any other sect, and ask nothing of any one; they plant the roads with fruit trees to furnish the traveller with refreshments; they abstain from flesh, and have no intercourse with the other sex. There are near two thousand of this sect in Kashmir.'—*Ain Akbari*.

CHAP. XI. ings may have an effect on the artistic temperature of the Kashmíris which the squalid mosques have not. Noble 'brotherhoods of venerable trees,' of chenars, elms, and the Kabuli poplar with its white bark and shimmer of silver leaves, give a pleasant shade, and there is always some spring of water for the thirsty. One exception must be made to this description, and that is the shrine of Shekh Nur Din at Chhrár Sharif. The shrine is perched on a dry bare hill, difficult of access and lacking in water. Srinagar has been often described by competent judges as the most filthy city in the East, but Chhrár Sharif is perhaps more filthy. There is a tank from which pilgrims drink, and I have never come across any tank so horrible in smell and colour. Musalmáns from all parts of the valley flock to Chhrár Sharif, and when scarcity is imminent, where calamities such as earthquake, cholera, and drought occur, thousands gather there and sit silent on the hills around, confessing their sins and begging for pardon. This impressive ceremony is known as *Nafl*. The great place for the confession of sins is the *Idgah*, a level grass plain lying between the city and the Anchar Dal, and it is here that the Musalmáns congregate on the Id-day. Among some of the more famous ziárats may be mentioned the beautiful shrine of Saiyad Mohammad Hussain Simanáni at Kulgám, with its exquisite wood carving and painted lattice, and the picturesque shrine of Zain Shah at Aishmakám in the Liddar valley. Zain Shah, or *Zain-ud-Din*, was a Khalifa of Shekh Nur Din, and the men of the shrine wear a peculiar headdress, with zigzag bars of colour. Once on a time one of the servants of the shrine, who had been sent out by Zain Shah for some work, was seized by the officials for forced labour. Zain Shah, in his anger, caused the Liddar river to dry up, thereby inflicting great loss on the rice crops. The king of Kashmír, on hearing of this, proceeded to Aishmakám, and in order to prevent similar mistakes occurring in future suggested that Zain Shah's followers should wear a distinctive headdress. This shrine is much respected by the boatmen of Kashmír, who take their children and cut off their first locks of hair. If this was done elsewhere the child would die or become blind. The votive offering of the boatmen is a fat ram. At Korwini is a famous shrine of Sadr Ded, the mother of the Shekh Nur Din, and here can be seen the turbans of Shekh Nur Din's father and son. Close to the shrine is the Mánch Nág (the honey spring), so called from the sweetness of its water. As a specimen of ancient work the shrine of Sada Baba Sahib at Pampur may be mentioned. Shah Wali's shrine at Andrháma in the Loláb is of great beauty, and the old trees near it are of great age and size. Shah Wali was a madman from Bukhara, and being mad he had no *murid* or followers. So he gave himself up to tree-planting, and having the miraculous power of animating dead things with life, he found little difficulty in arboriculture. Even the fish in the little pool by the shrine were brought dead to Andrháma, but Shah Wali restored them to life.

Another picturesque shrine is that of Khwaja Hassan Kari, which stands in the narrow ravine of Kulawaru, near Shewa (Zainagir). A spring of water known as the Makhdum Nág runs through the shrine, and it is said that the great saint Makhdum caused the water to flow from the hard dry rock. Khwája Hassan Kari was a disciple of Makhdum Sahib. Not far from this shrine is Tajar, the birthplace of the great Makhdum. He had no honour in his own village, and his companions laughed at his preaching and his prophecies, and insisted on his taking his share in the *corvée* of the village. Makhdum Sahib, or Hazrat Sultán as he is often called, left Tajar and cursed his people—they should want water not only for their crops, but even for their drink. The curse came true, for Tajar and Zainagir are dry to this day.

The organization of the shrine establishment is somewhat like that of a monastery. The abbot of the shrine is all-powerful. He regulates expenditure and apportions the daily tasks. In some cases his successor is chosen by lot; in others the office of abbot is hereditary. The finances of the shrine are based on the assumption that the offerings of the pious, which are chiefly made in kind, will be sufficient to defray all expenses, the chief of which is the giving of food to travellers.

At the larger shrines the attendants divide the offerings according as they are received on the days on which each attendant is on duty, and in the case of a shrine like Chhrár Sharif the income is considerable. Up to quite recent times every cultivator in Kashmír set apart a small share of his rice crop as an offering to the shrine, and one walnut tree in every village was devoted to some saint.

Fairs.

The annual fairs held at the various shrines are red letter days in the dull lives of the Kashmíri people. Thousands crowd together and spend the day eating and buying fairings, such as pretty *kángars*, wooden pattens, glass bangles, necklaces, and painted clay toys. Cobblers are hard at work repairing shoes, sweetmeat sellers drive a roaring trade, and alms flow into the shrine, where the many attendants (*Khadims*) fight vigorously over the offerings. Behind the shrine, wedged in by the crowd, are two rows of men bobbing up and down [1] and howling out songs in praise of the saint. In the middle of a dense circle of men two elderly, but very active faqirs are hard at work at *single-stick*. To the left of the tomb are thousands of women eating sweets, talking, and suckling their infants. The people believe that a visit to the shrines will secure the object of their wishes. Sick men will regain health, women will be vouchsafed children,

Efficacy of shrines.

[1] This religious exercise is known as *Dumali* or *Zikr*. It serves the same purpose as the dance of the Darwesh. The mind is thrown into a whirl, and the dancers fall into a religious ecstasy.

CHAP. XI. and the litigant will win his case, if a pilgrimage be made to Chhrár Sharif or any of the leading shrines. The white rags which are tied to the shrines are placed there by supplicants for offspring, and till a child is born the rag is left in its place.

The architecture of the shrines is always on the same plan[1]. The pagoda-like roof is surmounted by a curious *finial*, usually of pottery, and the four corners of the roof are finished by a kind of *gargoyle* with large wooden *tassels* attached. The wood carving and lattices of the hearse which covers the saint's tomb are often of beautiful design, and a very good specimen of modern work may be seen at the shrine of Baba Pa Imam Din Rishi near Gulmarg, commonly known as Baba Marishi. It has been suggested that the design of Musalmán shrines is borrowed from the aboriginal Hindu style, but the striking resemblance to the pagoda inclines one to think that the design owes its origin to Chinese influence, while the finial reminds one of the spires on the Buddhist *Chodtens* in Ladakh.

The mosques of the valley are mean in appearance, and the Mullah is ordinarily a man of no learning. In the Lal Tahsíl not one of the Mullahs can write. The mosque is often used as a village school, where children are taught to read the Koran, and it forms the only place where a stranger can find shelter and food at night. Even in the name of religion the hospitality shown to the stranger is of a meagre description, and the wayfarer is quickly passed on. Many of the mosques have a rude kind of *hammám*, where warmth and warm water can always be obtained in the winter. At Hazrat Bal, on the Dal lake, the *hammám* and the pilgrims' lodgings are substantial and good. This is due not to the efforts of the Kashmíris, but to the charity of a Nawab of Dacca.

The great mosque of Srinagar, the Jama Masjid, is a Saracenic building of some grandeur, with cloisters about 120 yards in length, supported by grand pillars of deodár-wood[2]. The spacious quadrangle is a pleasant place in the summer. There is the shade of trees, with green turf, and water is brought in a canal from the Sind river. The history of the Jama Masjid is of interest, and a casual examination of the building shows that it has passed through many vicissitudes. Verses on the door of the mosque state that the mosque was originally built by the great king Zain-ul-abadin, that it was again built by Sultan Hussan Shah, and that it was finally finished by Ibrahim and Ahmad Magre. In 909 A. H. the mosque was burnt down, and in 1029 A. H. it was again destroyed by fire. In 1082 A. H. the mosque was burnt down and rebuilt, and in 1232 A. H. it was repaired by Muhammad

[1] For illustration see frontispiece.

[2] These pillars are of great height, and are said by some to have been cut in the Tashwan forest, which lay on the left bank of the Jhelum, between Zaina and Fatteh bridges.

Azim Khan, the Pathán. In the time of the Sikhs the mosque was closed for twenty-three years, and was not opened until the time of Shekh Ghulam Muhi-ud-Din, the Musalmán Governor of the Sikhs.

Other accounts state that the ground on which the mosque stands was sacred to the Buddhists[1], and even now men from Ladákh visit the Jama Masjid and speak of it by its old name, Tsitsung Tsublak Kang. The site is also sacred to the Hindus, and there is a tradition that after the great persecution of the Hindus the Musalmáns tried in vain to erect a building on the ground, and that at last they were obliged to call in the aid of one of the Hindus who had remained in Kashmír. It is also stated that the present plan of the mosque was devised by the emperor Jehangir. It is much to be regretted that the Kashmíris cannot combine to keep this grand building in repair, but, as will often appear in this Report, combination for any public purpose has hitherto been impossible in this country. There are regular *preachers* in the Jama Masjid, and the most eloquent of these would never speak in any language but Kashmíri.

Preachers.

The leading Mullahs of the city, and occasionally a Mullah in the villages, exert some influence, but as a rule the ordinary Mullah is a man of no power. In some villages the curious duty of killing fowls is assigned to the Mullah, as the Kashmíri has a horror of blood.

Comparative sanctity of religious places and of Rishis, Babas, Saiyads, and Pirzádas.

It is extremely difficult to ascertain the views of the people as to the comparative sanctity of the various shrines and mosques, or to discover their ideas respecting the functions and position of the Rishis, the Babas, Saiyads, and Pirzádas. The general opinion seems to be that the Saiyads[2] stand first in the hierarchy of Kashmír, and that as regards the rest, influence depends on individuality and character. The Pirzádas are said to be descendants of Saiyad saints and of Makhdum Sahib. The descendants of the former have their clients in the Panjab, and proceed thither every second year to collect alms. The Makhdum Sahib Pirzádas have their clients in Kashmir. Formerly the Pirzádas held land which was cultivated for them by the Kashmíris, but now the villagers decline to work for their spiritual leaders, and the Pirzádas will either have to exert themselves or be thrown on the charity of their followers. The three great Saiyad names in the valley are Dastgir, Nakhsband, and Amir Kabir, the saint of Hamadán. Neither of the former ever visited Kashmír, but their fame was spread in the country, and hairs of Dastgir, which are said to cast no shadow and to hang in the air, are still to be seen in the ziárat

The great Saiyads.

Dastgir.

[1] 'The third time that the author followed the imperial stirrup to the delightful territory of Kashmír he met with some old men of this religion (Buddhist).'—*Ain Akbari*. Probably these were Buddhists from Ladákh.

[2] The Saiyads of Kashmír are regarded by foreigners with the greatest respect. I have been much impressed with this fact, and have received many letters from influential Musalmáns in India, asking me to assist Kashmíri Saiyads of little position and less power in their own country.

CHAP. XI.

at Khanyár. The followers of Dastgir are called Kádres, but all Musalmáns, whether followers of Dastgir or of other saints, reverence the saint of Khorasan, and his name is invoked by the boatmen, as they paddle up stream, in the cry, 'Ya Pir Dastgir.' Nakhsband spread his influence in Kashmír through a zealous disciple, Khwaja Moayan-ul-Din [1], and he has a few followers now in the valley, who call themselves Nakhsbandi. His shrine is also in Khanyár. But the saint who has exercised the most direct influence on the religion of Kashmír was Mir Saiyad Ali of Hamadán, who visited the valley in the time of Kutb-ud-Din, and practically established Islám in the valley. He is known as Amir-i-Kabir, Shah-i-Hamadán, and Ali Sani, and the Hindus say that he received his inspiration from a Hindu lady, Lalishri, who was an incarnation of a goddess. The Musalmáns deny this, but they hold her name in great respect, and speak of her as Lal Dedi [2]. Mir Saiyad Ali was poisoned on his way back to Hamadán, and the story is told that his coffin made miraculous marches to Khuttan in Persia. His mosque, the Shah-i-Hamadán in Srinagar, is one of the most sacred places in Kashmír, and is a worthy memorial of a man who in his time exerted an enormous influence over the country. His followers are known as Kúbrawé.

Nakhsband.

The saint of Hamadán.

The great Shekh saints.

Makhdum Sahib is always described as a Shekh, that is, a convert from Hinduism, and he is said to have been descended from a Rajput family of Nagrkot. He was a follower of Shekh Shahab-ul-Din Saherwardi of Baghdad, and was born in Kashmír. He rapidly acquired a large following. His followers are known as Saherwardi, and his shrine is on the Hari-Parbat hill. Both Makhdum Sahib and Shekh Nur Din are regarded as essentially Kashmíri, and they are probably more reverenced by the villagers than any of the foreign Saiyad saints, though, as before remarked, all Musalmáns in Kashmír hold Dastgir in veneration. Comparing many answers, I find that in sanctity the religious places of the Musalmáns take the following rank :—

The more famous religious places.

(1) Hazrat Bal.
(2) Shah-i-Hamadán mosque.
(3) Jama Masjid.
(4) Shrine of Nur Din at Chhrár Sharif.
(5) Ziárat of Dastgir, Khanyár.
(6) Ziárat of Makhdum Sahib, Hari-Parbat.

[1] Khwaja Khavand Mohmud, heir to Khwaja Bha-ud-Din Nakhsbandi, the great saint of Bukhara, came to Delhi in the reign of the emperor Shah Jehan. He was received with great honour, and his son, Khwaja Moayan-ul-Din, married the emperor's daughter. Shah Jehan sent them to Kashmír, and gave them the garden of Ynsaf Shah Chak as a place of residence. The Khangah of the Nakhsbandis is in this garden. It has recently been rebuilt, and is a beautiful specimen of Kashmír wood carving.

[2] Lal Dedi used to wander about naked till Mir Saiyad Ali came to Kashmír. She said that the

The shrine of Hazrat Bal is beautifully situated on the shores of the Dal lake, and a great fair is held there at the beginning of March, to which thousands resort from all parts of the valley, bringing with them the flags of renowned saints. The sanctity of Hazrat Bal is due to the presence of one of the Prophet's hairs, which was brought to Kashmír from Medina by Saiyad Abdullah in 1111 A.H. Saiyad Abdullah sold the hair to a merchant, Nur Din, for one lakh of rupees, and Nur Din exhibited the relic in Srinagar. The crowd was so great that many persons were crushed to death, and the ruler of the country wisely ordered that the hair should be kept in some open place. Four other shrines in Srinagar boast that they possess a hair of the Prophet—Kalashpura, Andarwara, Sowra and Dangarpura—and some believe that the hair shown at the shrine of Nabi Paighambr in Khirm by the Liddar valley is genuine. The hairs are exhibited six times in the year at the various shrines, but the villagers all go to the Hazrat Bal shrine.

CHAP. XI.

Hazrat Bal.

The Shah-i-Hamadán mosque was commenced in the reign of Sultan Kutb-ud-Din, and was built on the foundations of a Hindu temple, the priest of which had been convinced of his religious errors by the eloquence of Mir Saiyad Ali. Later on, Mir Muhammad Hamadán, with the assistance of Sultan Sikandar, increased the size of the building, and was given the revenue of three villages for its maintenance. The mosque has recently been repaired, and it forms one of the most striking objects in the city.

Shah-i-Hamadán mosque.

The outcome of this curious medley of saints and sects is an intense superstition and an unhappy and sullen fatalism. The saints can cure all kinds of illness, and a man has only to anoint himself with a kind of fuller's earth, found at Nur Din's shrine at Rishipura in the Kotahar valley, to become well. A *charm* from a holy man will arrest the spread of *rai*, which is so disastrous to the rice crop, and it is a saint who shuts in the cold wind on the Banihal and prevents it from destroying the rice plants in the valley below. The Kashmíris believe themselves to be under a curse. Some villages, like the six villages known as Charpatri in the Cherat Tahsíl, are under a special ban for insulting Shekh Nur Din, and have been afflicted with goitre and idiocy, but all are under the general curse. It is to this curse that they attribute the severity of their rulers, their sufferings in time of famine, earthquakes, and cholera, and the meanness and hopelessness of their condition. But they distinguish very quickly between temporary evils caused by man and inevitable evils caused by the curse. Under a visitation of cholera the Kashmíris are silent and submissive, but when an official or village headman oppresses them, they vent

Superstition and fatalism.

Kashmíris were not men, and that she had no reason to be ashamed. But in Mir Saiyad Ali she recognized a man, and forthwith wore clothes.

their grievances in loud language. Their favourite expression is that they will make themselves heard as far as London.

They believe in the sanctity of oaths taken in certain places, and there are certain trees of ordeal where a lying witness is sure to be overtaken with blindness. They believe in portents, and at the *Rozlu* spring in the Kond Ilaka curious signs have been seen. When the spring assumes its divining power the water is violently agitated for two days and finally disappears, giving place to a muddy bed. On this bed, if war is imminent, swords and guns appear. If famine is approaching, shapes of winnows, mills, and rice huskers are clearly shown, and when cholera is near the form of graves and spades is shown. Not many years ago great excitement was caused by the appearance of tents and helmets, and the late Mahárájá Ranbir Singh had horsemen posted along the road to Srinagar to report whether these signs again appeared. Men who are as intelligent on ordinary subjects as any in Kashmír have assured me that they have seen the portents, and it is extremely interesting to find Kashmíris with whom I have had daily intercourse for six years, and of whose abilities I hold a high opinion, believing absolutely in these old world tales. The whole valley is rich in superstitions, and there is not a mountain, river, or spring which has not some quaint legend attached to it—

> 'The fair humanities of old religions.
> The power, the beauty, the majesty,
> That had their haunts in dale or piny mountain
> Or forest, by slow stream or pebbly spring
> Or chasms and watery depths.'

On the great mountains are demons in the form of fair women, who sing sweet songs before they crush the passing traveller with an avalanche. On the Zogila offerings are still made to appease these cruel sirens. The vein of green emerald in the crest of Haramak, which no one but the gods has ever dared to approach, renders all snakes harmless, and so far as I have been able to discover no poisonous snakes occur in those parts of the valley whence Haramak can be seen.

The rivers are rich in legends, and there are mighty streams inside the mountains which are heard but never seen. The Pinglish Ilaka in the old Wular Tahsil once received irrigation through a subterraneous channel from the Liddar river. It is now dry because the people of Pinglish neglected to pay the annual tribute to the representative of the river god. The channel is closed, and the old men who knew the secret of the tunnel are dead. Pinglish looks sadly on its dry fields, which a few years ago were green with the rice plants. The mountain tarns are infested by dragons breathing fire, and strange tales are told of Konsa Nág, where monsters seize the unwary traveller and drown him in the depths of the lake. Fairies and pixies find a congenial home in the valley, and houses haunted by ghosts are not uncommon. The pretty springs of cold clear water so frequent throughout Kashmír are the abodes of the Nágs, the old deities who were worshipped in ancient times. When the Nág visits the world he leaves his home in the heart of some mountain, and creeping through sinuous passages like a snake emerges at the spring. Sometimes he comes with benevolent intent, sometimes on mischief bent, and all agree that he is powerful and to be propitiated. In all the village tales the serpent nature of the Nág is prominent. When the Nág assumes the human form he can be detected by the water that drips from his locks. If one has leisure to sit by a spring with the villagers, many curious legends[1] may be heard, often full of interest and beauty. There is a well-known spring, Vaishak Nág, the water of which is light and sweet. In the early part of May the wind blows violently for three days and water appears. In October the water dries up and departs to the Jammu side of the mountains for the winter. This happened in the following way. A holy man from the Jammu side, who deplored the absence of water, came to Vaishak Nág and by good fortune caught the snake, the lord of the spring, and put it in his gourd; while returning thanks he hung his gourd on a tree. Two women coming by thought the gourd might contain butter for anointing their hair, and took the gourd down, whereupon the snake escaped. The holy man returned and discovered his loss. As he stood weeping Mir Shah Baghdádi appeared and, moved by the holy man's distress, effected a compromise with the snake. So it comes to pass that Kashmír gets water for its rice crop, while the Jammu villages receive water for their spring crops. Every cave has its story, and quaint legends are told of religious recluses and their miracles. The legends of the greatest of these recluses, Shekh Nur Din, the national saint, who is said to have been a convert from Hinduism, point to the fact that he was a man of blameless life who taught simple lessons to the peasants, encouraging industry and repressing extravagance and quarrels. There are no such men nowadays, and their place seems to be taken by half-mad soothsayers, like Rasul Shah of the Sind valley. He is regarded with awe by the villagers, and Mahárájá Ranbir Singh used to consult him. When I saw him one of his fits of madness was on him, but he gave me good advice, perhaps not unmixed with sarcasm, namely, 'to read and learn.' In his sane hours he attends to secular business, and loses no opportunity of increasing his landed estate. Rasul Shah was originally a weaver, and there are other faqirs who are beginning to make a name for themselves in Kashmír. One of these was a Batal; another was a shepherd, and it is not at all necessary for a man to belong to a Saiyad family in order to gain a reputation for sanctity. Faqirs abound in the

Vaishak Nág.

[1] Many of these legends are given in the *Ain Akbari*.

CHAP. XI. valley, but, with the exception of the three to whom I have just alluded and a few others who have planted gardens and live simple harmless lives, they do not rise above the level of the ordinary religious mendicant of the East.

The Shara, or Muhammadan law. Before I finish my account of the religion of the Kashmíri Musalmáns I must allude to the working of the '*Shara*,' or Muhammadan law. The expounders of this law are the Kázis. There are four Kázis in Srinagar who decide the more intricate cases relating to inheritance and divorce. They jealously keep their knowledge to themselves and their sons, and the outside world is not allowed to learn the secrets of the *Shara*. In the villages the Mullah acts as a *Mufti* in small cases and gives a *decree*. Thus the village Mullah can decide petty questions relating to the lawfulness of food, and sometimes, if he is a man of some learning, he will give a decree regarding the division of land between members of a family. I have often read decrees given by the city Kázis. In one case which came before me the plaintiff produced one for possession of land. The defendant produced another for the possession of the same land, granted by the same Kázi. There was nothing strange in this, as the Kázi hears no evidence. He merely listens to the statement of his client, and assuming that that statement is correct he gives his opinion. The proverb, 'Tanha ba-Kázi,' is used to indicate *ex parte* proceedings. He is like a doctor who hears all that his patient has to say and then prescribes. My impression is that the city Kázis purposely avoid the introduction of local facts into their decrees, and eschew anything like secular knowledge of the people.

The Hindu religion. Of the 52,576 Hindus of Kashmír, 28,695 reside in Srinagar and the small towns, and the rural Hindus, who number 23,881, are scattered far and wide in the valley. Temples are rare in the villages, but nearly all the rural Hindus have an intimate connexion with Srinagar, and so far as their religion takes the form of public worship, it is observed in the city or in the temples of the small towns. Every Kashmíri Hindu, with the exception of the Khattri shop-keepers of Srinagar, who are known as Bohras, is called a Pandit or learned Brahman, a name which is in many cases given on the *lucus a non lucendo* principle. Though not all learned they are all Brahmans, and are chiefly followers of Shiva, the lord of the mountain and the god of the hill people. Khir Bhawáni is their favourite goddess, and perhaps the most sacred place in Kashmír is the spring of Khir Bhawáni at the mouth of the Sind valley. There are other springs sacred to this goddess, whose cult is said to have been introduced from Ceylon. At each there is the same curious superstition that the water of the springs changes colour. When I saw the great spring of Khir Bhawáni at Tula Mula, the water had a violet tinge, but when famine or cholera is imminent the water assumes a black hue. The peculiarity of

Shiva.

Khir Bhawáni.

PLATE IX

To face page 297] [Negative by Major Hepburn, R.A.

A VIEW OF A MODERN HINDU TEMPLE IN KASHMIR

Khir Bhawáni, the milk goddess, is that the Hindus must abstain from meat on the days when they visit her, and their offerings are sugar, milk, rice, and flowers. At Sharka Devi on Hari Parbat and at Jawala Mukhi in Krihu the livers and hearts of sheep are offered. There is hardly a river, spring, or hill-side in Kashmír that is not holy[1] to the Hindus, and it would require endless space if I were to attempt to give a list of places famous and dear to all Hindus. Generally speaking, and excluding the Tula Mula spring, which is badly situated in a swamp, it may be said that the Hindu in choosing his holy places had an eye for scenery, since most of the sacred Asthâns and Tiraths are surrounded by lovely objects. CHAP. XI.

A beautiful spring of clear water overshadowed by splendid shady trees and often teeming with sacred fish, a bold scarp of rock, a magnificent mountain torrent, or a sequestered glade are the accompaniments of the holy places where the Hindu bathes and offers his gifts of flowers and rice. In the temples the universal emblem is the phallic *linga* surrounded by a stone trench, around which the worshippers circle, sprinkling water and flowers, and at the hour of worship horrid music is made by the conch horns. Inside the temples are various emblems and relics, and outside are piled up old stone images of past ages, mostly smeared over with red paint. The temples are built of solid masonry and are approached by flights of stone steps. The roof is high and pointed, and in Srinagar is covered with tin plates. When the sun glints on these tin roofs and turns them into burnished silver the effect from a distance is very striking. Away from the haunts of men stand the old temples of ancient Hindu Kashmír silent and grand. Martand, stripped of its gold and cruelly maimed by the Iconoclast, stands on a high table-land and looks proudly down on the beautiful valley. The Wangat temples lie in a narrow ravine with lofty mountains overshadowing them. Payech nestles under a bluff and is far away from the high-road. Pandratan lies under a cliff and is almost hidden away by a dense grove of trees. But the oldest of all is Shankaracháraj, the temple on the Takht-i-Suliman[2], where worship is still performed. Thither every Monday the pious toil up the steep hill, and on the day of Sheorátri the Hindus swarm like ants up the picturesque hill, which looks over the city and the Dal lake on the one side and over the twisting course of the Jhelum on the other. The hill is a noble site for the guardian deities of Srinagar, and has at various times been sacred to the Buddhists[3] and Hindus. Its old name was Sandhimána Parvata, and the The temples.

[1] 'The Hindus regard all Kashmír as holy land. Forty-five places are dedicated to Mahadeo, and sixty-four to Bishen, three to Brahma, and twenty-two to Durga. In seven hundred places there are carved figures of snakes, which they worship.'—*Ain Akbari*.

[2] For an account of these old temples, see Chapter VI.

[3] A yellow Llama from Ladákh, who told me much about old Buddhist places in Kashmír,

CHAP. XI. common people say that though Sikandar the Iconoclast spared the temple he changed the name of the hill from Sandhiman to Suliman. Many of the villagers gravely assert that king Solomon once lived in the valley and that the hill was named after him. Across the city there rises another hill known as Hari Parbat, which is also very sacred to the Hindus. It was under this hill that the goddess Devi entombed the water-demon Jaldbo. Its old name was 'Pradimanpith,' but the Kashmíri Musalmáns call it the wicked hill, 'Kohi-Marán.' Devi of the eighteen hands (Sharka Devi) is worshipped there. Kashmír is the country of pilgrimages, and every detail of the various journeys is laid down with great precision. The most famous places are the Amarnáth cave, which lies far away up the Liddar valley, and the Ganga-Bal lake, which rests deep and still under the terrible snow-capped Haramukh. To Ganga-Bal the Hindus resort after the death of a parent, and fling the *knuckle-bones* which the funeral pyre has spared into the deep waters. The road is difficult, as early snow sometimes overtakes the pilgrims, and delicate women and children often perish from exposure. Amarnáth cave attracts pilgrims from all parts of Kashmír and India, and they swarm there in thousands. After a preliminary visit to Khir Bhawáni of Tula Mula, and after enjoying the free rations given by the State, the army of pilgrims musters in Srinagar and proceeds by appointed marches to Amarnáth, which must be reached on the full moon of Sawun (beginning of August). They must bathe at appointed places, and they pass through sacred Mach Bawan, which ranks next after Khir Bhawáni of Tula Mula in sanctity. At Mach Bawan the army is joined by the Pandits of that place, and further up the valley the Malik family of Batkot takes charge of the procession. These Maliks are bound to keep the difficult mountain path in order, to carry sick pilgrims, and to see that no property is stolen. But at the head of the procession goes Lal Gir Sádhu of Amritsar, and as each day's journey comes to an end Lal Gir Sádhu encamps in front. He must enter the sacred cave first. The offerings at the cave are divided into three parts—one goes to Lal Gir Sádhu, one to the Pandits of Mach Bawan, and one to the Maliks of Batkot. But as the Maliks are not allowed to enter the cave they do not receive their fair share of the offerings. The tale has been told to me by the Maliks of the late Mahárájá Ranbir Singh disguising himself as a villager and stealing a march on the Amritsar Sádhu. When the pilgrims arrived they found the Mahárájá seated in the cave, and though the Maliks enjoyed the incident the Hindus regarded it as a dangerous breach of precedent. When the pilgrims have bathed in the lake of Shisha Nág two marches have yet to be made before the sacred cave is reached. Then the pilgrims, covering their nakedness with strips of

Pilgrimages.

informed me that the Takht-i-Suliman is still regarded as sacred by Buddhists, and is known as Pus-Pahari.

birch bark, call on Shiva to appear, and if the god is propitious pigeons flutter out from the cave. Both the Amarnath and Haramukh pilgrimages satisfy the piety of the Hindus in being difficult and under certain circumstances dangerous, and I doubt whether they would like to have an easy road made to either place. Picturesque as these pilgrimages are, they have their ghastly side as cholera-conductors. Many of the pilgrims are weak and sick, and fall easy victims to an epidemic.

Worship of natural phenomena.

It is dangerous to discuss so great a mystery as the Hindu religion [1], yet I cannot help noticing the important part which *water-springs* and snakes play in the Kashmír mythology. Nor must I omit the fact that the Hindus seize with avidity on any abnormal display of the powers of nature. The intermittent springs in Ranbir Singh Pura, where the water rises and falls in an unaccountable manner at fixed periods; the Gangjetton hill-side in Donsu, dry all the year till September, when it becomes a waterfall; the subterraneous fire at Soiyam in Uttar Machipura, where people cook their food over the hot soil, attract numerous pilgrims and are ranked among the holy places of Kashmír. The Kashmír Hindu is always on the alert, and any manifestation of the powers of nature is seized upon and at once endowed with supernatural qualities. In connexion with this prevalence of animistic ideas in Kashmír it should be remembered that, previous to the introduction of Islám, the Hindu religion had gone through many phases, and that after the Buddhist schism had been stamped out the Hindus fell away from the strict observances of Shiva and became worshippers of fire, snakes, and the sun [2].

[1] During my six years' sojourn in Kashmír I have endeavoured to ascertain the religious ideas of the Hindus, but my conclusion is that religion, as understood in the West, exists only to a slight extent, and that its place is taken in Kashmír by an elaborate social code prescribing the conduct of daily life, the sanctions of which are social and not religious. Dr. Bühler, however, writes that Kashmíri Śaivism is a real separate religion, with peculiar ceremonies and sacrifices and transcendental doctrines. Dr. Bühler also refers to the existence of witchcraft, regarding which I have failed to elicit any facts. He says (*Tour in Search of Sanskrit MSS.*, 1875): 'In former days both the Kashmirian Sáktas and Śaivas were famous for their proficiency in the black art. The Raja Tarangini mentions this point more than once, and states that several kings, e.g. Chandrápída, were killed by means of sorcery (*abhichâra*). Now it is said that only few *Abhichrikas* exist, and that these carefully hide their art as the Maharája is much opposed to them and punishes them.' Dr. Bühler mentions the practice of driving pins into dolls, which recalls the leech of Folkestone in the *Ingoldsby Legends*. Dr. Bühler also writes: 'It may be that witchcraft is now not much practised in Kashmír, but the belief in its efficacy, in Yoginís, who celebrate their foul rites on the desert mountain-sides, and in Bhúts, is perhaps stronger and more universal in Kashmír than in India proper. The Kashmírian Pandits gave me the impression that they were a "gens religiosissima."'

[2] 'The religion in Kashmír has in like manner been Hindu from a very remote date. Originally, no doubt, it was Ophite or snake-worship, but this is part of the Hindu ritual, and the Nágas are included in the orthodox pantheon: the adoration of Śiva was soon engrafted upon this, even if the two rites were not originally identified.

'We have frequent occasions to notice the important figure which snakes and snake deities make in the worship and traditionary history of Kashmír. The extent and permanence of the superstition we may learn from Abul Fazal, who observes that in seven hundred places there are carved figures of snakes, which they worship.'—*An Essay on the Hindu History of Kashmír*, by H. H. Wilson.

CHAP. XI.

Laxness of Hindus.

Intelligent Hindus have often told me that a great laxness has crept into the Hindu religion within the last ten years. It used to be the custom to eat only the singhára (water-chestnut) on fast days, but ganhár, vegetable marrows, and red pepper are now freely eaten. People grumble at having to climb up the Takht-i-Suliman on the day of Sheorátri, and I could quote many instances of self-indulgence in religious observances. There are some curious facts about the Kashmír Brahmans which deserve mention. They are said to be extremely strict in following the rules of Brahmanism when they visit India, but in their own country they do things which would horrify the orthodox Hindus. They will drink water brought by a Musalmán; they will eat food cooked on a Musalmán boat; the foster-mother of Hindu children is usually a Musalmáni, while the foster-brother often obtains great power in a Hindu household. Mahárájá Gulab Singh did his utmost to stop the practice of drinking water brought by a Musalmán, and severely interdicted the eating of cheese. But it was all to no effect, and when it is remembered that there is no caste of water-carriers in Kashmír it is not to be wondered at that the Hindus failed to comply with Mahárájá Gulab Singh's edicts. Rational in this, it is odd that the Hindus of Kashmír should eschew some of the excellent vegetables of Kashmír because of their colour. Tomatoes, the red-fleshed kabuli vegetable marrow, carrots, and red beans are an abomination to the Hindu. Onions and leeks are avoided on other grounds. It is the more odd when it is remembered that they are flesh-eaters. An interesting fact about the Hindus of Kashmír is that they worship the likeness of Her Majesty the Queen Empress. This prevails not only among the Pandits of the city, but also among the village Hindus. It appears to be their custom to regard as divine the sovereign *de facto*, but in the case of the emperor Aurangzeb they made an exception, and his likeness was never worshipped, for he was a persecutor of the Hindus.

The Sikhs.

The Sikhs of Kashmír are few in number, and some doubt exists as to how they established themselves in the valley. Most people say that they came into Kashmír with the lieutenants of Ranjit Singh, but some state that there were Panjabi Brahmans already established in the country, and that they embraced Sikhism when the valley passed into the hands of Ranjit Singh. The Sikhs in Trahal assert that they came to Kashmír in the time of the Patháns[1], and they talk of a street in Kabul known as

[1] This is confirmed by Vigne, who states that the Sikhs came to Kashmír in the service of Rájá Sukhjewan, a Hindu of Shikarpur, who was sent as Governor of Kashmír by Timur Shah of Kabul, about A. D. 1775. Rájá Sukhjewan failed to pay tribute to Kabul, and tried to become independent, but, according to Vigne, he was defeated by Timur Shah and blinded. Other accounts fix the date of Rájá Sukhjewan earlier. Kashmíri histories say that he was crushed by Rájá Ranjit Deo, acting on behalf of the Mughals, and some say that Ahmad Shah Abdali was forced to coerce Rájá Sukhjewan for his contumacy in 1763. The Sikhs of Hamal always say that their ancestors came to Kashmír with Rájá Sukhjewan.

the Shekh Muhalla, so called by reason of its being occupied by converted Sikhs and Pandits taken away by force from the Dachanpara Tahsíl. In the history of Suraj Parkásh it is stated that there were Sikhs in Kashmír when Har Gobind was Guru, and this would show that the Sikh religion existed in Kashmír as far back as the time of Jehangir. Whatever their origin they are not a progressive people, and their places of religion show that there is neither money nor zeal among the Sikhs of Kashmír. The Dharmsala of Guru Har Gobind, near the Hari-Parbat, is in a ruined condition. The spiritual head of the Kashmíri Sikhs, Bhai Abtár Singh of Poonch, has just died, and the Rájá of Poonch will appoint a new head. Every second year this spiritual head visits Kashmír and collects his dues from the Sikhs. Judging from what I saw of Bhai Abtár Singh, and from the general appearance of the Sikhs of Kashmír, I should say that the Sikh community of the valley was feeble and effete. The Sikhs live by cultivation or service. They have few of the qualities which one associates with the Sikhs of the Panjab, and are neither brave nor brawny[1].

[1] Since writing the above I am glad to say that the Sikhs of Kashmír have taken up the question of their religious houses and endowments in a very practical manner, and considerable subscriptions have been raised.

CHAPTER XII.

RACES AND TRIBES.

CHAP. XII.

Hindus.

IT is a generally accepted fact that up to about the beginning of the fourteenth century the population of the valley was Hindu, and that about the middle and end of the century the mass of the people was converted to Islám, through the efforts of Shah-i-Hamadán and his followers and the violent bigotry and persecution of king Sikandar the Iconoclast. Tradition affirms that the persecution of the Hindus was so keen that only eleven families of Hindus remained in the valley. Their descendants are known by the name of Malmás, as distinguished from the fugitives and the Hindus of the Deccan, who came to Kashmír later on and are known as the Banamás. Some historians, however, state the Malmás Hindus to be the descendants of Kashaf, the saviour of the valley, and that the Banamás Brahmans were foreigners, who came from other countries. The Hindus who now live in Kashmír are, with a few exceptions, of the Brahman caste, and though tradition points to the fact that the Levite Brahmans were a powerful and numerous body, exerting great influence over the country and its rulers, there is frequent mention of the fighting class, and it is obvious that a large majority of the old Hindus must have been agricultural Jats of the Vaisya division. There are now no traces of the Jats among the Hindus of Kashmír. But there are still Khattris in Srinagar, known as Bohras and engaged in trade, who are cut off from communion with the Khattris of the Panjab, and there are certain Musalmán tribes who trace their origin to Khattri ancestors.

Brahmans.

The Brahmans of Kashmír, commonly known as Pandits, are 60,316 in number, of whom 28,695 live in Srinagar and the towns. The rest are scattered about in the villages and are for the most part engaged in agriculture. The Pandits divide themselves into three classes in Kashmír: the astrologer class (*Jotish*), the priest class (*Guru* or *Báchabat*), and the working class (*Kárkun*). The priest class do not intermarry with either of the other classes, partly because they are regarded as divine and cut off from mankind, and partly because the laity abhor their practice of accepting the apparel of deceased Hindus. But the Jotish and Kárkun Pandits intermarry. The Jotish Pandits are learned in the Shastras and expound them to the Hindus, and they draw up the *calendars* in which prophecies are made as to the events of the coming year. The priest class perform the rites and ceremonies of the Hindu religion. The vast majority of the Pandits belong to the *Kárkun* class and have usually made their livelihood in the employment of the State. But as State employment became harder to obtain and the numbers of the Pandits increased, the Brahmans of Kashmír sought other occupations, and many of them are in business, while others work as cooks, bakers, confectioners, and tailors. Briefly, it may be said that a Pandit may follow any trade or occupation except those of the cobbler, potter, corn-frier, porter, boatman, carpenter, mason, or fruit-seller. Pandits have been known to adopt the profession of acting and music, and a Pandit now in my employment was once a cavalry soldier in the army of His Highness the Maharana of Oodeypore. In 1894 many Pandits were working as daily labourers on the river embankments. As time goes on these intelligent and quick-witted people will no doubt take to new occupations. But at present the Kárkun Pandit regards the pen as his natural destiny, and though many have taken to agriculture and many more are looking to land as a means of employment and subsistence, they would infinitely prefer to spend their lives as clerks in some office. The Pandits of the villages consider it no degradation to follow the plough and to carry manure; but the city Pandit, who has not severed himself from the literary atmosphere of the capital, is inclined to look down upon the Brahman agriculturist, and though he will take a wife from the villages he will not, if a man of any position, permit his daughter to marry into a village family. At the present time no Pandit serving out of Srinagar would dream of taking his wife and family with him. In Kashmír, as in other countries, a man's occupation is the chief test of his social position, and it is quite possible that as agriculture becomes more profitable and popular, and as life in the city becomes harder and meaner, posterity may see the position reversed, and the Brahman of the village declining to give his daughter in marriage to the Srinagar Pandit. The future of the city Pandits is a matter of some anxiety. They have not the keen trading instinct of the natives of the Panjab, and may neglect the chances of commerce which easier communications with India should now offer. They are extremely conservative and short-sighted, and cannot believe that the old system, under which every adult Pandit had a finger in the collection of revenue, has passed away. They are deeply attached to their country, and though Kashmíri Pandits have risen to distinction in India, the large number of unemployed Brahmans of Srinagar will not seek service in the Panjab while it is possible to eke out a bare subsistence in the valley. Every city Pandit is sedulous for the education of his children, and in

CHAP. XII. Srinagar this, thanks to the free schools of the State and the Church of England Mission, can be easily acquired. I have had over 500 Pandits trained in mensuration, and the men who have taught them state that they are much quicker than the Panjabis. Their weak point is arithmetic. The Pandits are a handsome race of men, with fine, well-cut features, small hands and feet, and graceful figures. Their women are fairer than those of the Panjab, they are distinctly good-looking, and show more signs of refinement and breeding than the Musalmánis. The Hindu children are extremely pretty.

The Pandits are broken up into numerous *gôtras*, or tribal divisions, and though the name of the *gôtra* is repeated seven times by the Pandit as he performs his daily ablutions, the outside world rarely hears it mentioned, and the Pandits are known by their *Krám*[1], or family appellation. There are eighteen known *gôtras* among the Levite Brahmans and 103 among the other Brahmans in Kashmír. In one *gôtra* there may be many *Kráms*, as the following instances will show. Among the Malmás *gôtras* is one known as Paldeo Wasgargé, and this *gôtra* embraces families belonging to the following *Kráms*, or tribal subdivisions:—Sopuri-Pandit, Mála, Poot, Mirakhur, Kadlabaju, Kokru, Bangru, Bakáya, Khashu, Kichlu, Misri, Khar, and Mám. Marriage is forbidden within the *gôtra*, and a man of the Sopuri-Pandit subdivision cannot take a wife from the maidens of the Paldeo Wasgargé *gôtra*, nor can he marry into the *gôtras* of his mother, grandmother, or great-grandmother. Among the Banamás Pandits there is a *gôtra* known as the Dattatrye, and from this *gôtra* have sprung the great families of Kol and others less known, such as the Nagari, Jinse, Jalali, Watal, Neka, Sultan, Ogra, Amin, Moja, Bamjai, Dont, Tota, Sabin, Kissu, Manslal, Singári, Rafij, Balu, and Darabi. As will be afterwards shown when discussing the tribes of the Musalmáns, the *Krám* is often the relic of a nickname applied to the ancestor of the subdivision. Thus Sopuri-Pandit points to the fact that the ancestor came from Sopur; Kokru means fowl; Bakáya signifies that the ancestor formed one of a very numerous class in Kashmír, the revenue defaulter; Khár suggests that the ancestor was connected with the iron trade; Sultan, that the family had close relations with one of the first line of Musalmán kings, and so on.

Among the leading *Kráms* may be mentioned the following names:—Tikku, Razdán, Kák, Munshi, Mathu, Káchru, Pandit, Sipru, Bhán, Zitshu, Raina, Dar, Fotadar, Madan, Thusu, Wangnu, Muju, Hokhu, and Dulu. Of these the members of the Dár family have probably been the most influential, though proverbs[2] suggest that their influence has not been beneficial. The Kashmíri Pandits will not intermarry with the Brahmans

[1] See infra. [2] 'Dar na baiyad guzásht be zangir' = The Dárs like doors should be locked up.

of India. It is said that in Raja Seh Dev's time a Musalmán in the disguise of a Pandit mixed with the Kashmíri Brahmans and learnt their Sanskrit lore. On this being discovered the Pandits, in order to guard against similar frauds, decided to have no intercourse with foreign Brahmans. The village people always speak of the Pandits as 'Bat.' CHAP. XII.

Khattris. The other Hindus of the valley are not numerous. The Bohras or Khattris of Srinagar intermarry among themselves and are engaged in trade and shop-keeping. It is said that in former days some of them were admitted to caste among the Pandits, but at present, though they have adopted the customs and rites of the Brahmans. they enjoy no caste fellowship with them. With the two exceptions that the Bohra woman wears nose-rings and discards the girdle round her waist, a Bohra of either sex cannot be distinguished from the city Brahman.

Sikh Brahmans. The Sikhs of the valley, who were originally Brahmans from the Panjab, have been described in another chapter. They can be distinguished at once from the Brahmans of Kashmír by their method of wearing the hair, by the absence of the effeminate gown among the men, and by their accent, which always conveys the impression of being less refined and educated than that of the Pandits. The Sikhs are chiefly found in the Trahal pargana, Krihun, and Hamal. They are fair cultivators of dry crops, but are far behind the Kashmíri Musalmáns in rice cultivation. They look to service as their chief means of livelihood, and in former days were enlisted in the Nizámat regiment, which was maintained for the collection of revenue. At present they obtain service in the State as chaprasis, but they are likely to find the Pandits awkward rivals. They are men of slight build, not bad-looking, and often have light grey eyes. Very ignorant and troublesome tenants, they invariably quarrel with the Musalmán Kashmíris, and not infrequently among themselves.

Rajputs. The Mian Rajputs, to which tribe the rulers of Kashmír belong, are found chiefly in the Deosar Tahsíl, around the foot of the mountains to the south of the valley, where they have been granted *jágírs*, or land free of revenue. Formerly they rendered service to the State, but of late years they have remained idle, and this idleness is telling on their character and appearance. Though they still look smart and clean in comparison with the Kashmíri Musalmán, there is a great difference between the Mian Rajput of Deosar and his brethren in the Dogra country, and it is to be hoped that the State will find this fine race of men some congenial employment. It is doubtful whether they really like Kashmír, but they seem able to stand the rigour of the winter climate, and some of the Mians have attained to a great age. They have adopted the Kashmír style of architecture, but the house and courtyard are screened from the public view, as the Rajputs are very careful about the privacy of their women.

CHAP. XII.

Musalmans.

Of the 883,099 Musalmáns of Kashmír 93,575 reside in Srinagar. The rest may roughly be said to form the rural population of Kashmír, as the Musalmán inhabitants of the smaller towns are for the most part engaged in agriculture. The census of 1891 does not show the divisions into which the Musalmáns of the valley fall, but it may be stated that the great mass of the village people come under the head Shekh, and are descendants of the original Hindus, and that though the Saiyads are a numerous community, both they and the Mughals and Patháns are, when compared with the Shekhs, in a great minority.

Shekhs.

The Shekh Musalmáns of the valley may have retained, for some time after their conversion to Islam, some of the Hindu customs of endogamy within the caste and of exogamy outside the *gôtra*. But there is no trace now of these customs, and the different tribal names or *Kráms* are names and nothing more. There is no restriction on marriage, and a Musalmán of the Tántre Krám can either marry a Tántre girl or any other maiden of the villages, provided she be one of the agricultural families. The only line drawn is that one must not marry into Saiyad families on the one hand, nor into families of market-gardeners and menials on the other. It would be interesting to trace the origin of the *Krám* names, although by intermarriage the *Kráms* have ceased to have any individuality or distinction, and to inquire whether the various *Kráms* sprang from a Brahman, Khattri or Vaisya origin. It is supposed by many that Musalmáns of the Pandit, Kol, But, Aitu[1], Rishi, Mantu, and Ganai Kráms are descendants of Brahmans who were forcibly converted to Islam in the fourteenth century, and I have tried to trace in the features of the men of these *Kráms* something of the clean-cut physiognomy which is associated with the Brahman caste. But I find that the Musalmán of the Pandit Krám is exactly like the other Musalmáns. Other *Kráms* are believed to have sprung from Khattri origin, as ancient history mentions that the bearers of these names in Hindu times were a military and warlike people. Among these *Kráms* may be mentioned the Mágres, Tántres, Dárs, Dángars, Rainas, Rahtors, Thakurs, and Naiks. Only one *Krám*, the Lon[2], is generally assigned a Vaisya origin, and the Dámars are said to be descendants of Sudras, the lowest of the four Hindu castes.

The whole subject of the Kashmír *Kráms* is fraught with difficulty, and this is increased by the fact that men of low occupations are arrogating high-sounding names. Thus of late years the Dums of Kashmír have steadily assumed the *Krám* of Ganai, much to the annoyance of the original Ganais. To make matters worse, the gardeners and butchers have also taken a fancy to the *Krám* name Ganai. The boatmen of Kashmír have

[1] Some say that the Thakurs and Aitus came from Kishtwár.

[2] The villagers say that the Lons came from Chilás.

seized on the name Dár as a patent of respectability, and Musalmáns of the other *Kráms* are now annoying the Ganais and the Dárs by asserting that they were originally Dúms and boatmen. Some *Kráms* are, however, restricted to men of lowly pursuits, and the *Krám* name Sufi, which is said by some to be of Brahman origin, is chiefly found among market-gardeners, bakers, and servants. Pal is another such *Krám*. The barbers of the valley do not aim so high as the butchers and boatmen, and have contented themselves with appropriating the *Krám* of Thakur; but there is nothing to prevent Abdulla, the Dúm, calling himself Abdulla Pandit if he choose. At first the people would laugh, but after a time, if Abdulla Pandit prospered, his descendants would exhibit a lengthy pedigree table tracing their family back to one of the petty Rájás, lord of three villages and possessor of a fort, the ruins of which still stand in Abdulla Pandit's village. In making inquiries as to the descent of leading men of villages I have found several such cases, and in one instance went back generations until confronted with the inevitable Rájá. But the Rájá's descendant, in spite of his wealth and influence, puzzled me, as he was extremely dark-skinned, and it was some time after that I found that the pedigree table was fictitious, and that the man of royal descent was a Dúm, who had ingratiated himself with the authorities and had gradually established himself as an agriculturist of the bluest blood. The social system in Kashmír is delightfully plastic, and I know one or two instances of boatmen who have within recent times abandoned their boats and taken to agriculture. These men are now on an equality with the agricultural families and can intermarry with them. Similarly I know of an agriculturist who has degraded himself by taking up the work of a market-gardener, in which the use of *poudrette*[1] is essential. This man must now contract marriage alliances with other market-gardeners, for he is cut off from the families of the agricultural Musalmáns. Again new *Kráms* are springing up. In Zainigir I found a large number of families rejoicing in the *Krám* 'Chang.' Their ancestor was a man who played on the Jew's harp (*chang*). Azád, the Pathan tyrant, sliced off the ears of an old and faithful servant because he was slow, and banished him to the Loláb. His descendants are numerous, and their *Krám* is Kanachattu, the 'crop-eared.' In the Loláb a young *Krám* is arising known as Dogra. Two generations have been in the service of the Dogra rulers of the country.

Among the Shekhs must be mentioned the following classes who are more or less connected with the religion of Islam. The Pirzàdas, who are descendants of zealous converts to Islam, consider themselves equal to the

[1] The night-soil of the city and towns is at present deposited in the lanes and alleys. After a time it becomes mixed with dust and other refuse, and assumes a black colour. It is then applied as a manure to vegetable land, and is known as Kala Matti.

CHAP. XII. Saiyads and intermarry with them. The Babas, also descended from zealous converts, are now chiefly religious mendicants. The Rishis are the attendants at shrines established by the old ascetic recluses of Kashmír who were called Rishi, a corruption of the Sanskrit word Rikhi. The Mullahs or priesthood of Kashmír are Shekhs, and may be divided into two classes. The first class includes Mullahs learned in the law, and variously designated as Maulvi, Kazi, Akhund, or Mufti, and Mullahs less learned, who lead the prayers in the mosque, teach children the Koran, and live upon the offerings of the faithful. The second class consists of Mullahs who have fallen in social position and are known as Mals. These wash and prepare the bodies of the dead for burial and dig graves, and they are not allowed to intermarry with the Mullahs or with the villagers. Many Dúms and Hanjis have adopted the *Krám* 'Mal,' but the Hanjis regard the name as a corruption of the Panjabi word for boatmen (*Maláh*).

There is some doubt as to the origin of the Tsak or Chak tribe, which played so prominent a part in the history of Kashmír in the sixteenth century, and it is believed that they were not descendants of the Kashmír Hindus but Musalmán Dards from Chilás. There are many families in the valley of the Tsak Krám, but they are in no way distinguished from the other Musalmáns. The Kakru families, who are settled in Baramula, are said to be descendants of the Ghakkar tribe, and like the Tsak have no connexion with the original Hindus of Kashmír. The small Musalmán traders of the villages all belong to the Wáni Krám, and are said to be descendants of Khattri Hindus. About the origin of the Pare, Parar, Wár and Kambe Kráms, nothing is known. Their name is not mentioned in old histories, and inasmuch as *Krám* names are very easily manufactured, it is probable that these names were introduced after the conversion to Islam.

Saiyads. The Saiyads may be divided into those who follow the profession of religion (*Pir Muridi*) and those who have taken to agriculture and other pursuits. As compared with the Shekh Musalmáns they may be regarded as foreigners, though there is practically nothing in their appearance, manners or language which distinguishes them from other Kashmíri Musalmáns. Some Saiyad families are much looked up to in the villages, but those who have taken to agriculture are practically on a level with the other villagers, and intermarry with them. No villager would think of marrying into a Saiyad family of the Pir profession, as such presumption would bring bad luck.

Mír Kráms. Mír is the *Krám* name of the Saiyads. While he retains his saintly profession the Mír is prefixed to his name, when he takes to mundane pursuits the Mír is affixed to his name.

The Saiyad Makár fraternity are fraudulent *faqirs* who pretend to be Saiyads and wander about Kashmír and India cheating the public. Many have now taken to trade. They intermarry among themselves.

Mughals. The Mughals are not a numerous body in Kashmír, and have so intermarried with the ordinary Kashmíri Musalmáns that all trace of descent is lost. They came to Kashmír in the days of the early Musalmán kings, and in Mughal times. Their *Kráms* are Mír (a corruption of Mírza), Beg, Bandi, Bach, and Ashaye.

Patháns. The Patháns are more numerous than the Mughals, and are chiefly to be found in the Uttar Machipura Tahsíl, where Pathán colonies have from time to time been founded. The most interesting colony is that of the Kuki Kheyl Afridis of Dranghaiháma, who retain all the old Pathán customs, and still for the most part speak Pashtu. They wear a picturesque dress and carry swords and shields. They pride themselves on their bravery, and in the absence of a nobler foe engage the bear on foot with the sword, or spear him from their plucky little ponies. Another colony of Patháns is that of the Machipurias, but by intermarriage with Kashmíri women the Machipurias have lost most of the characteristics of the Pathán. The old men still talk Pashtu, but the younger generation resemble Kashmíris and speak their language. The Machipuria Patháns belong to the Yusufzai section, and are known as Marufkháni Patháns. The name Machipuria is erroneous, as they live in Hamal, which only adjoins Machipura. The Afridis, or Khyberis as they are called, furnish thirty-five men for service on the Gilgit road, and the Machipurias twenty-five. In payment for this they hold certain villages free of revenue. The majority of the Patháns came to Kashmír in the Durráni time, but many were introduced by the Mahárájá Guláb Singh, who granted them jágírs for service on the frontier. In Bhiru many villages are held by Swátis and Bonairwáls. Jugokharian belongs to a number of Khattak families. The Patháns are always given the title of Khan, and the snuff-sellers of Kashmír, who trade with Pesháwar, have now assumed Khan as a *Krám* name.

Bombas. The members of this interesting tribe are not numerous, and are chiefly found in the Machipura Tahsíl, where they hold land free of revenue. Originally a warlike tribe, they have degenerated into a feeble, ridiculous, and most pitiable condition. They are all poor, all quarrelsome, and are robbed by miserable parasites recruited from the slums of Indian bazaars. The Bombas say that they came from Turkey. They intermarry among themselves, and take wives from the Hatmal and Kahka families of the country below Baramula. They give daughters in marriage to Saiyads. Batkot is the old home of the Bombas in Kashmír, and when they die they are brought back to the beautiful burying-ground, still kept up in Batkot. The heads of Bomba families are addressed as Rájá, and the tract in which they live is known as Rájwara.

Faqirs. Several villages are held by Faqirs or professional beggars. They work as agriculturists during the summer and beg during the winter. They

CHAP. XII. regard the profession of beggar as most honourable, and maintain that great blame would attach to them if they left the path trodden by their fathers. They are not aggressive in their calling and are liked by the people. They intermarry with other beggar families or Bechanwols, and must be distinguished from the hordes of hungry rogues who visit the valley every summer. These foreign beggars are often thieves and are a curse to the country.

In the city the *Krám* name is purely a nickname. The old *Krám* names have for some reason been abandoned, and with the exception of Bandé Bach, Kanth, and Gán Kráms no respect is paid to descent. Wealth alone commands position, and poverty at once degrades a family. To obliterate all trace of a lowly origin, men have assumed surnames borrowed from familiar animals [1], insects [2], trades, occupations, and places.

One of the leading merchants of Srinagar is known by the name of Jackal. Another man, of considerable influence, has adopted the unpleasant word 'Latrine' as his family appellation. The Ashaye family, to which the well-known Haji Mukhtar Shah belonged, takes its name from the devoutness of its ancestors. It would serve no useful purpose to give a list of the city nicknames. Many are extremely coarse, and neither the giver nor the recipient of some of them is to be congratulated either for generosity or wit, and it is strange that men should have quietly allowed such names to be handed down in their families from generation to generation. The affix 'Ju,' which led old Bernier to imagine that the Kashmíris were of Jewish origin, is frequently given by way of respect or endearment. When a man has won the title 'Ju' he ceases to use his real *Krám* name. Thus, Habib Ju, the well-known silversmith, is properly Habib Gadah. Sulju, the cloth-merchant, is really Sultán Guzrbán. In the villages, too, the affix Ju sometimes displaces the *Krám* name. Thus Kádir Ghanai of Báwan is called Kádir Ju, and Ahd Dhár of Nail is always addressed as Ahd Ju. Ján is another affix given by way of respect to a colony of Kázis who settled in Khuihάma.

Inferior tribes. Just as the members of the various village *Kráms* possess no marked distinctive features, so they possess no distinctive localities and are scattered about in all parts of the valley. The only gradation in the social scale which is recognized among the agricultural families is that the 'zamíndárs' are superior to the 'taifidárs,' that is the market-gardeners, herdsmen, shepherds, boatmen, minstrels, leather-workers, and the menials of the villages. And this gradation is maintained by the fact that the agriculturist refuses to intermarry with these inferior castes. I have never heard any satisfactory account of the origin of the families who follow these various occupations, and can advance no theories as to whether the boatmen, for instance, were originally cultivators who lost social position by taking to river life or

[1] E.g. Gagru = rat; Dánd = bullock; Bror = cat.

[2] E.g. Pisu = flea.

whether they were a distinct caste originally. And it is all the more dangerous to advance theories, as within quite recent times certain cultivators have taken to boat-life. and others have taken to the profession of minstrels. But once a minstrel, always a minstrel, so far as customs and marriage are concerned, and great efforts have to be made before the minstrel's children can be received back into the pale of peasant respectability. There is nothing in their physiognomy to denote that the shepherds, minstrels, boatmen and the village menials are of a different race to the Kashmíri cultivators, though their clothes betray their occupation. but a Dúm, a Galawán or a Bátal can always be recognized by his face. The Dúm has a darker skin than the peasant, and the restless, furtive eye, which is characteristic of the thief. The Galawán and the Bátal can similarly be detected by the darkness of their skin.

Dúms.

The Dúms of Kashmír are an important tribe, and have up to quite recent times had great power in the villages. The village watchman was always a Dúm, and in addition to his police functions he was entrusted by the State with the duty of looking after the crops. The Dúms have undoubtedly the predatory instinct and are not to be trusted as private citizens, but it is to their credit that hitherto they have never stolen State treasure, although large amounts of silver are brought by them from the Tahsíl treasuries to Srinagar. In his position as village watchman the Dúm has endless opportunities of annoying and injuring the villagers. He is much dreaded and disliked and has to be propitiated. Of late Pandits have turned their attention to the work of village watchmen, but it is doubtful whether they will prove less tyrannical than the Dúms. Many fables are told by the Dúms about their origin [1], and they always claim descent from a Hindu king ,who, afraid of his numerous sons, scattered them all over the valley, but it is believed that they are of Sudra extraction.

Galawáns.

The Galawáns, or horse-keepers, of Kashmír are by some considered to be descendants of the Dúms, and their dark complexion suggests that they are not of the same race as the Kashmíri peasants. Others think that the Galawáns are the descendants of the Tsak tribe. But as far as I know there is no evidence to support the latter theory. Originally they earned their livelihood by grazing ponies, but as time went on they found it more remunerative to steal them, and they eventually developed into an established criminal tribe. They achieved notoriety in the days of Pathán rule, and when the Sikhs took over Kashmír the Galawáns were a terror to the country. They moved about in large parties, all mounted and armed with long, heavy clubs. They raided threshing-floors and frequently attacked a wedding-party and carried off the bride. Various stories are told of their daring, and Khaira Galawán is the hero of many

[1] Some say that the Dúms are descendants of the old Tsaks.

CHAP. XII. a legend. Colonel Mián Singh made great efforts to exterminate these marauders, and at last, with the assistance of accomplices, caught Khaira and hanged him, and succeeded in killing nearly half of the Galawáns. Mahárájá Guláb Singh continued the good work and imprisoned most of the tribe at Rughonáthpura, and Mahárájá Ranbir Singh finally sent them as colonists to Bunji. Many of the Galawáns have, however, returned to Kashmír, and pony-lifting frequently occurs. The ponies are carried off to Poonch, where they are disposed of with ease and safety. The term Galawán is now used to describe a man of violent and predatory habits, and it is said by the villagers that the Galawáns in their capacity of horse-keepers, often kill a young foal and eat it, returning the skin to the unfortunate owner.

Chaupáns. The shepherds of Kashmír are known as Chaupáns or Pohl, and though there is nothing in their physiognomy to distinguish them from the peasants of the valley they form a separate race, intermarrying sometimes with the Galawáns. An account of the Chaupán and his manner of life will be found in another chapter. He is a cheery, active man with a most characteristic whistle, and his healthy life in the high mountains makes him strong and robust. He has some knowledge of simples, and brings down medicinal herbs for the native doctors. The whole of the great mountain grazing-lands are partitioned among the various families of Chaupáns, and an intruder would very quickly be persuaded to retire. In the winter and early spring the Chaupán lives in the villages, where he sometimes possesses a little arable land. The Chaupáns and the Shírgujri or milk-sellers often bear the *Krám* name Waggi.

Bánd. The minstrels of Kashmír (*Bhaggat* or *Bánd*) can be recognized by their long black hair and stroller mien, and although they are practically a peculiar people so far as marriage goes, they sometimes recruit their companies by enlisting a villager. They combine the profession of singing and acting with that of begging, and are great wanderers, travelling down to the Panjab where they perform to Kashmíri audiences. With the curious exception of the Akangám company, which is formed of Pandits, the *Bhaggats* are all Musalmáns. They are much in request at marriage feasts, and at harvest time they move about the country, and in a year of good harvest will make a fair living on the presents of the villagers. Their orchestra usually consists of four fiddles with a drum in the centre, or of clarionets and drums, but the company often contains twenty members or more. Their wardrobe is frequently of great value, and several companies which I have met are said to have dresses and properties worth more than Rs. 2,000. Their acting is excellent and their songs are often very pretty. They are clever at improvisation and are fearless as to its results. They have songs in Kashmíri, Persian and Panjabi, but the Kashmíri songs are

PLATE X

To face page 313

[*Negative by Major Hepburn, R.A*

A GROUP OF HANJIS. THE BASKET IN FRONT IS THE KANGAR. THE POLES HELD BY THE TWO WOMEN ARE THE PESTLES WITH WHICH RICE IS HUSKED. THEY REST ON THE MORTAR

the only ones which I have heard. The story of the Akangám *Bhaggats* is peculiar. Brahmans considered acting to be degrading, and even now the Brahmans of Kashmír regard the Akangám players with contempt. But the Brahman players say that they took to the stage by the express order of the goddess Devi. The legend relates that many years ago Devi appeared to the ancestor of the Akangám Pandits, and, placing a fiddle in his hands, said, 'Play upon this fiddle.' He protested his inability, but on the goddess persisting, he took up the bow and played unearthly music. He was bidden by Devi to sit under the deodars of Akangám and play in her honour. For some years he and his sons obeyed the goddess' behest, but unable to withstand the prejudices of his caste, he finally declined to play any more. On this he was stricken with blindness and wandered away to the Liddar valley. In a dream Devi appeared to the Magistrate of the Liddar, and told him to take the old Pandit back to Akangám. On reaching Akangám the Pandit recovered his sight, and since that day he and his descendants fiddle away without further protest. These Pandits never send their children to school, as they believe that Devi would resent it and would kill the children. The *Bhaggats* are very pleasant people and their mirth and good humour form a cheerful contrast to the gloom of the Kashmíri peasant. They acknowledge two leaders or Sardars who arrange that the circuits shall not clash. They have a peculiar argot (*phirkat*)[1], which they employ in stage directions.

Hánjis.

The boatmen of Kashmír (Hánz or Hánji) are an important and prominent tribe, and according to the census of 1891 they number 33,870. It is impossible to obtain any information as to their origin, but the profession is very ancient, and history affirms that Rája Parbat Sen introduced boatmen from Sangaldip. They were of the Vaisya caste, and even now the Hánjis of Kashmír, when blaming one of the crew for his bad paddling, will say, 'You are a Sudra.' When questioned, the Hánjis claim Noah as their ancestor, but one account given to me by some representative Hánjis rather points to a gipsy origin. The father of the family is an autocrat, and while his sons and daughters remain on his boat all their earnings go to the father, who supplies them with food. When a son wishes to marry he must obtain his father's consent, which is often withheld, as there is little room for the young people in the Kashmíri boat. There are many divisions in the Hánji tribe. There are the half-amphibious paddlers of the Dal lake (Demb Hánz), who are really vegetable-gardeners, and the boatmen of the Wular lake, who gather the singhára nuts (Gári Hánz), and these two sections hold their heads high among the other Hánjis. Next in respectability come the boatmen, who live in the large barges known as *bahats* and *wár*, in which cargoes of 800 maunds of grain or wood are carried.

[1] Carpenters, goldsmiths, and the Wátals have also a slang of their own.

Then less respectable come the owners of the *dúngas* or passenger boats. These Dúnga Hánz prostitute their females, and, owing to the dependence of the city on the river, they have a footing in nearly every family of means. The worst of the Dúnga Hánz are the Már Hánz, or the boatmen who ply on the Nalla Már. Then there are the Gad Hánz, who net or angle for fish. These surpass even the Dúnga Hánz in their power of invective. Another small section of the tribe known as Hak Hánz make a livelihood by dredging for drift-wood in the rivers. The Dúnga and Gad Hánz are famous for their inventive powers and for their vocabulary of abuse, and when, as often happens, a quarrel arises between two boats, one woman stands up on the prow of her boat and commences a torrent of invective, to which one in the other boat promptly replies. The men remain seated listening with interest to the dialogue. If night sets in before the women are exhausted they invert their rice baskets (*paj*), which signifies that the quarrel is not ended but laid aside till morning, when the wordy warfare is recommenced with fresh vigour.

The Hánjis are a muscular, active people, and small children commence the work of towing or paddling at a very early age. The paddle is heart-shaped, and the Kashmíri boatmen by a turn of the wrist steer the small *shikár* boat without checking its way.

The Hánjis are a hardy people, and though the occupants of the large barges have warm cabins for the winter. the Dunga Hánjis, in spite of their mud fireplace on which their food is cooked, must find the matting walls of their boats a poor protection against the cold. If they are lax in morality it is little to be wondered at, as their cramped dwelling precludes decent privacy. But the Hánjis have no excuse for their quarrelsome and lying disposition. Half the tales about Kashmír and the Kashmíris can be traced to the imagination of the Hánji, who, after the manner of the Irish car-driver, tells travellers quaint stories of the valley and its rulers. They are clever people, and can do most things, from a big business in grain to cooking a visitor's dinner. The Hánji ashore is a great rascal, and Europeans would be wise if they left him in his boat. He rarely pays to the villagers the money entrusted to him for the purchase of supplies. Their favourite *Kráms* are Dangar, Dar, and Mal.

Wátals.

The Wátals have been called the gipsies of Kashmír, and are a peculiar people with a patois of their own. Socially they may be divided into two classes. Those who abstain from eating carrion, and are admitted to the mosques and to the Musalmán religion, belong to the first class, while those who eat the flesh of dead animals, and are excluded from the mosques, belong to the second. The Wátals are a wandering tribe, and though sometimes a family will settle down in a village, and will build a permanent hut, the roving instinct is too strong, and after a few years the family moves on. Their principal occupation is the manufacture of leather. The Wátals of the first class make boots and sandals, while the Wátals of the second class manufacture winnowing trays of leather and straw and perform the duties of scavengers. No Musalmán will have anything to do with the scavenger Wátals, and will not of his own freewill eat with a Wátal who has renounced carrion. The Wátals as a tribe are not considered very honest, and are much given to robbing hen-roosts. Their habitations, which are usually round, wattled huts, are always at some distance from the cottages of the peasants, and there the Wátal prepares the hides of dead cattle and buffaloes and the skins of sheep and goats, and rears poultry for sale. The Wátal women are fine and handsome, and often drift into the city, where they follow the profession of singing and dancing. About July the Wátals from all parts of the valley and the city assemble at Lala Bab's shrine near the Nasim Bagh, and many matters affecting the tribe are then settled and marriage alliances are made. The outcast Wátals have no religion, but they respect the shrines and often visit them, though they are not allowed to enter the holy precincts. There is no worship of Lal Beg, and the marriages and deaths of the outcast Wátals are not sanctified by the presence of the priest. The outcast has his remedy, for by the expenditure of a few rupees, and by the taking of an oath to renounce carrion, he can at once gain admittance to Islam. But the Wátal apparently does not think it worth while, for a large number are still outcasts, and one often hears of Wátals breaking their oath and lapsing into the old ways.

Nángár.

Besides these non-agricultural tribes there are the menials of the village, also outside the pale of peasant society. They are known in Kashmír by the name Nángár, and in a large village we find families of the following occupations who work for the villagers, either receiving a fixed share of the harvest or being paid according to the nature of the work :—carpenters, blacksmiths, potters, weavers, butchers, washermen, barbers, tailors, bakers, goldsmiths, carriers, oil-pressers, dyers, milkmen, cotton-cleaners, and snuff-makers. These menials have no hereditary land of their own, save the garden plots adjoining their houses, but as land is broken up the Nángár desert their old villages and become agriculturists. It is worthy of notice that the menials are extremely independent and make a point of refusing to attend their masters' houses. The most independent is the oil-presser, who is generally in very easy circumstances. The position of the Nángár is not defined in the same precise manner as that of the menials in the Indian village, and even the rate of remuneration is not always fixed Thus the carpenter and the barber are allowed so much grain per plough, but they always demand double that amount, and usually succeed in getting it. The carpenter, blacksmith, potter, barber, and washerman will always be

CHAP. XII. required in a large village, but with improved communication between the village and the towns it is quite possible that the other Nángár will disappear, and either repair to the town or take to agriculture. Many of them are already working on the land, and have proved to be fair farm labourers; and apparently the only non-agricultural classes which fail in agriculture are the miserable community of shawl-weavers—whose hands are too soft and knees too weak to cope with the rough work of husbandry—and the weavers of cotton cloth (*wawar*). Many of these shawl-weavers are scattered over the country, but they prefer their old, sedentary, unhealthy life to farm work, and sit at the looms from early morning to night, with only a short respite for food, on a wage of $1\frac{1}{4}$ annas per diem. They are useless as members of the village community, and will make no effort to earn better wages by carrying or working on the roads. In May and June the shawl-weavers subsist chiefly on mulberries and unripe apples. Their condition is bad and apparently hopeless, for there seems very little chance of a revival of the shawl industry, and the carpet industry is too small to employ all the poor wretches whose ill-paid toil once made Kashmír art renowned throughout the world.

With the exception of the shawl-weavers, whose weak frames and sallow faces reveal their calling, it is impossible to distinguish between the peasants proper and the menials of the villages, and there is nothing which suggests thât they were originally sprung from some inferior tribe. Nearly all the different occupations have some curious and peculiar customs, but in the main they conform to those described in Chapter X. and space would not allow of a separate enumeration of the customs of each small division of the people.

Gujars. The last tribe to be mentioned is that of the Gujars, who are not in any way Kashmíris, though they live on the fringe of the mountains of the valley. They are members of the semi-nomad tribe which grazes buffaloes and goats along the Himalayas and the Siwáliks. They have for some time past turned their attention to Kashmír, where they rapidly make clearings of the forest and build their flat-topped houses for themselves and their precious buffaloes. Their language, known as Parimu or Hindki, is wholly different from the Kashmíri language, and they rarely intermix with the Kashmíris, though, like them, they are Musalmáns by religion. They are a fine, tall race of men, with rather stupid faces and large, prominent teeth. Their one thought is the welfare of the buffalo, and when they take to cultivation they grow maize rather for the buffalo than for themselves They are an ignorant, inoffensive, and simple people, and in their relations with the State are infinitely more honest than the Kashmíris. Their good faith is proverbial, and they are a generous people, giving all the milk of Friday away in charity. Their women keep the accounts of

PLATE XI

To face page 316] [*Negative by Alam Chand, G.C*

A GROUP OF KASHMIRIS. NUMBERS 3 AND 4 IN THE BACK LINE FROM THE LEFT ARE GUJARS. NUMBERS 5 AND 6 IN THE BACK LINE FROM THE RIGHT ARE SIKHS. OF THE REST THOSE TO THE LEFT ARE MUSALMÁNS THOSE TO THE RIGHT COMMENCING WITH THE PANDIT BOY ARE HINDÚS (PANDITS)

the butter made over to the middleman by tying knots on a string. The favourite name of the Gujars is Muhammad, and a man of position among the herdsmen is always addressed as *Bhai* (brother). From the point of view of forestry their existence is to be regretted, but they serve a useful purpose as pioneers of cultivation, and the wise policy of the Kashmír State has been to encourage the Gujars.

Other tribes are scattered about in various Tahsíls. Some come from the Muzaffarabád district, like the Dúnds; others from the Hazára district, like the Turks; or from the Jhelum district, like the Bábas. These people are recent settlers, intermarry among themselves, and do not adopt the Kashmíri dress. There has of late been a considerable immigration from the Hazára district. There has also been a steady influx of families from Poonch and from the Hazáraját of Afghanistán. These Hazáras are excellent settlers.

Personal appearance.

Before concluding this account of the various tribes in Kashmír some attempt must be made to describe the appearance of the people. An eminent authority has said that the face of the Kashmíri is of the pure high Arian type, and Mr. Drew speaks of the peasantry as having a wide, straight-up and high forehead and a fine-shaped head, a well-cut square brow and eyes of a not very dark brown. 'With middle-aged and older people the nose acquires a decided hook of handsome outline, the mouth is often prettily curved with the young people, but it is apt to get straight and thin-lipped as they grow up. In figure they are of middle height, by our English standard, and not apt to run very much above it.' Moorcroft praises their muscles, and says that figures are to be found among the peasants which might have served for models of the Farnesan Hercules, and many other travellers have borne witness to the strength of the men and the beauty of the women.

That certain Kashmíris are strong and can carry enormous loads there can be no doubt. Mr. Drew quotes one case of a man carrying a weight of 240 lbs. for hundreds of miles over an uneven road, but judging from the hundreds of men whom I have seen, day by day, working almost naked in the rice-fields, I should be inclined to say that, omitting the muscular boatmen and perhaps the hillmen, models for the Farnesan Hercules were the exception and not the rule, and that the average Kashmíri would not excel the average Pathán in measurement, while he would be far behind the Panjab Ját in size, muscle and sinew. A friend, who knows Kashmír well, writes:—'I think that the finest physique is found among the boatmen, who often show a grand development of muscles in the arms, chest and back, though they are apt to fall off in the legs, which form the hillmen's strong point. The latter, as a race, possess great strength and endurance in carrying loads up steep hills and over dangerous scarps, when it is all an Englishman can do to get along unencumbered. They

CHAP. XII. perspire much less than an Englishman during a climb, and can probably outwalk him, but do not possess his power of jumping, and are weak in the arms. They are wonderfully sure-footed on bad ground, but on the flat a European can generally outpace them.' As regards beauty, I have met some striking faces among old men and children, always of a decided Jewish cast, but I should not describe the ordinary peasant as a good specimen of manly beauty, and I consider the Patháns handsomer than the Kashmíris. The mean and effeminate dress of the Kashmíris and its absence of colour detract from their personal appearance, but I have seen most of the heavy-footed villagers in a state of nature in the rice fields, and I have not been impressed with the idea that they were the handsome race of men suggested by travellers. The hooked nose is a prominent feature, and the prevailing type is distinctly Hebrew.

Beauty of the women.

As regards the beauty of the women it is difficult to speak, but I have seen thousands of women in the villages and cannot remember, save one or two exceptions, ever seeing a really beautiful face. They seem to age very quickly, and though the children are often lovely the average peasant woman is plain. Beauty, not 'beauty born of murmuring sound,' is perhaps more common among the Hánjis and the Wátals, but the old and prevailing idea among the natives of Hindustán, as to the beauty of the Kashmíri women, is probably due to the healthy, rosy cheeks that many of them have, so different from the wheaten hue of India. In the city there is the well-bred Panditáni, whose easier, more refined life makes beauty less difficult to inherit and keep than it is for her hard-worked and weather-worn sister of the villages, and I should say that if the fabled beauty of the Kashmíri woman really exists it is to be found in Srinagar and not in the villages of the valley. Apart from early marriage, hard work and exposure, the peasant women are often cruelly disfigured by smallpox, and though beauty may be found in the house of some affluent village headman, it does not show itself in the fields where the women sing and work. Bernier, in his *Journey to Kachemire, the Paradise of the Indies*, says, 'The women are very handsome, and it is from this country that nearly every individual, when first admitted to the Court of the Great Mogol, selects wives or concubines, that his children may be whiter than the Indians, and pass for genuine Mogols.' One ingenious writer suggests that the decadence of beauty in Kashmír is due to the fact that the fairest of Kashmír's women were taken away to India, and that the stock whence beauty might be bred has disappeared. Marco Polo, speaking of the women, says, 'Taking them as brunettes they are very beautiful.'

CHAPTER XIII.

AGRICULTURE AND CULTIVATION.

CHAP. XIII.

Soils.

OWING to its system of rivers Kashmír possesses a large area of alluvial soil. This alluvial soil may be divided into two classes: the new alluvial, which is found in the bays and deltas of the mountain rivers, and the old alluvial, which lies above the banks of the Jhelum river and extends as far as the Karéwa. The first is of great fertility, and every year is renewed and enriched by the silt of the mountain streams. Up to the present, in spite of the lax system of forest conservancy, the silt of the mountain streams is rich and of dark colour, but in the case of the Sind river there is an alarming increase of sand in the river deposit, which is partly due to the reckless felling of trees in the Sind valley. It behoves the State, in the interests of agriculture, to prevent the destruction of trees on the catchment areas which feed the mountain streams. The second class of alluvial soil is of less fertility, but in years of good and timely rains moderate tillage gives excellent dry crops. Rats abound in the old alluvial soil.

The Kashmíris, so far, have considered no crop worthy of attention save rice, and by irrigation and manuring an artificial soil has been obtained for the rice-fields, and it is rare to hear anything said about the original soil. But the Kashmíris recognize four classes of soil, which require peculiar treatment when under rice-cultivation. These classes are known as:—*Grutu*, *Bahil*, *Sekil*, *and Dazanlad*. *Grutu* soil contains a large proportion of clay. It holds water, and in years of scanty rainfall is the safest land for rice. But if the rains be heavy the soil cakes, and the outturn of rice is poor. *Bahil* is a rich loam of great natural strength, and there is always a danger that by over-manuring the soil will be too strong, and that the rice will run to leaf. The calamity known as *Rai*, to which allusion will be made below, frequently occurs in *Bahil* soil. *Sekil* is a light loam with

CHAP. XIII. a sandy subsoil, and if there be sufficient irrigation and good rains the outturn of rice will be always large in *Sekil* lands. *Dazanlad* soil is chiefly found in low-lying ground near the swamps, but it sometimes occurs in the higher villages. The soil is hot and feverish, and special precautions are taken to run off irrigation water when the rice plant shows signs of a too rapid growth. If these precautions are taken in time, the outturn of rice in *Dazanlad* land is sometimes very heavy. A peculiarity of *Dazanlad* soil is that the irrigation water turns red in colour. Near the banks of the river Jhelum, and in the vicinity of the Wular lake, is found the rich, peaty soil (*Nambal*), which in years of fair rain yields enormous crops of rape-seed and maize. This soil requires no manure and will not produce rice. It is the custom to burn standing weeds and the stubble of the last year's crop on this peaty land before ploughing.

The curious plateaus known as *Karéwa*[1], which form so striking an object in Kashmír scenery, are for the most part of *Grútú* soil, but there are varieties of this *Grútú*, and the varieties may be distinguished by colour. The most fertile of these varieties is the dark, blackish soil known as *Surh-*

[1] The soil of the Karewa is a question of great interest. At present, in this Tahsíl, as in all other Tahsils of Kashmír, the Karewa, unless it is irrigated and cultivated in rice, produces miserable crops. I have examined the soil of each Karewa. The soil varies in colour from a light yellowish hue, as on the Ompara Karewa, to the red-hued soil known as *Grutu* on the Bandgam Karewa and to the dark soil (*surhzamin*) of the Frekun Karewa. A description of the Karéwa soil will be found at page 45.

I have dug up soil on the Karewa, and the point which has always struck me is that the soil to a depth of three feet is coarse and does not bind. I have also noticed that where cotton is raised this coarse soil has been pulverized to a fine texture, and I have also noticed on the Frekun Karewa, where there are Panjabi cultivators, who excel in dry cultivation, that the soil is excellent, and the maize crops good. The conclusion which I have formed is that, in spite of the dryness of the ordinary Karewa, consequent on the rapid drainage into the ravines, the soil is fair, and only requires careful tilth. The crops of barley, wheat and linseed are usually poor, and the cultivation is so slovenly and dirty that it is to be wondered that any crop is produced; but where cotton is grown, and the land is carefully ploughed, the soil appears excellent, and when, as in the case of the Frekun Karewa, Panjabis cultivate, the dry crops are excellent. The Kashmíris are too few in number and too busily employed in their rice-fields to care for the Karewa, but as population increases the Karewa may become great producers of wheat, barley, and linseed. Karewa differ in many respects, but my opinion at present is that labour, with timely rains, will give excellent results on these now neglected tablelands of Kashmír. Wherever irrigation can be brought to the Karewa, fine crops of rice are raised, which would indicate that there is no inherent fault in the soil. For the first three years the outturn of rice on the Karewa is greater than that of the *maidani* villages. But after three years of rice it is necessary to give the Karewa land a rest, by means of rotation of crops. The *muru*, or dry cultivation, following rice on the Karewa gives a poor outturn, whereas the *muru* in *maidani* villages produces excellent crops of cotton. Still, if the Karewa rice-land is given rest by rotation, the outturn of rice is equal to, if not greater than, the outturn of rice in the *maidani* villages. The cultivators appeal to the fact that grass grows with difficulty on the Karewa, and that rain washes off the surface soil, but with the exception of cotton fields scattered here and there on the tablelands, I have never yet seen any attempt to cultivate the land decently.

zamin, the red *Grútú* is the next best, while the yellow, buff soil is esteemed the worst of all. Other classes of soil are recognized by the Kashmíris, and there are many local names. Thus land on the slope of the mountains, reclaimed from the forests, loses its pristine strength after from six to ten years of cultivation and is known as *Tand*. Land which is injured by percolation from irrigated fields is known as *Zabalzamin*. Sour soil, which sometimes occurs in the midst of most fertile areas, is known as *Kharzamin*, while soil which will not hold irrigation water is called *Tresh*. Land in which springs occur is known as *Limb*. *Ront* soil is a stiff, bad clay, which always cakes; *Sháth* is stony, sandy soil by the mountain rivers; *Tats* is soil which is rendered too warm by the presence of large stones, and is always liable to *Rai*. As regards comparative fertility, the new alluvial soil stands first, the mountain slopes and the reclaimed land on the edges of the swamps, rich in organic matter, second, the old alluvial third, and the Karewa soils fourth. The heaviest rice crops are obtained on lands near the deltas of the streams which have sufficient slope to allow of rapid drainage. CHAP. XIII.

Manures. The Kashmíris are fortunate in possessing ample *manure* for their fields, and are not compelled, like the natives of India, to use the greater part of the cattle-dung for fuel. The rule in Kashmír is that all dung, whether of sheep, cattle, or horses, dropped in the winter, when the animals are in the houses, is reserved for agriculture, while the summer dung is dried, and after being mixed with chenar leaves and willow twigs is kept for fuel. But the ashes are carefully stored and the fires are chiefly fed with wood, the dung aiding and regulating combustion. The dungheaps which one sees in early spring show that the Kashmíri wastes nothing which is useful in agriculture, but he has other resources. Firstly, the sheep, when the flocks commence to move towards the mountains, are folded on the fields, and secondly, the Kashmíri considers *turf clods* to be a far more effectual renovator of rice fields than farmyard manure. These clods are cut from the sides of watercourses and are rich in silt, and a dressing of clods will strengthen a field for three years, whereas farmyard manure must be applied every year. The strongest of the farmyard manure is that of poultry, and this is reserved for *onions*. The next best is the manure of sheep, which is always kept for the rice nurseries. Next comes cattle-dung, and last of all horse-dung[1]. The Kashmíri thoroughly appreciates the great importance of manure in cultivation, but his treatment of manure, though better than that obtaining in India, can be greatly improved. Litter is abundant in Kashmír, and a more liberal use of it, when cattle and

[1] In England, horse-dung ranks above cow-dung. Perhaps the reason that cow-dung is more efficacious in Kashmír is that cattle receive oilcake during the winter, while ponies get nothing but hay and straw.

CHAP. XIII. sheep are penned in the houses, would serve to prevent a waste of the valuable urine of live-stock. The Kashmíris have accepted this suggestion and will act upon it. Next, although the Kashmíris fully recognize the value of folding sheep on their fields in the spring, they neglect this in the autumn when the sheep return from the grazing-grounds, and for two months or more the sheep are allowed to wander about as they like. Oil-cake is given to all plough-cattle, and enriches the manure. The Kashmíris have not yet learnt the value of bones as a manure, and lime is never used in cultivation. Probably lime might be usefully applied to *Dazanlad* land, but I imagine that much of the irrigation water of Kashmír is rich in lime, and that it is unnecessary to apply lime to irrigated land. Green manuring is unconsciously practised by the Kashmíris, inasmuch as weeds, which grow very rapidly, are ploughed in when the land is prepared for the spring crops of wheat and barley. But unfortunately this green manuring does more harm than good, for the soil is already too loose, its pores are opened and it is light enough. If the Kashmíris would roll the soil after sowing I have no doubt that the green manuring would do good, but at present it is prejudicial to plant growth.

The value of night-soil is thoroughly understood. Near Srinagar and the towns the garden cultivation is excellent, and the one manure used is the *poudrette*, which is night-soil mixed with the dust of the city alleys and pulverized by the action of the sun. In the villages where there is no irrigation stream one sometimes finds latrines, and the night-soil is used in garden cultivation. In other villages land surrounding the cottages shows unmistakeable signs that man gives back to the soil what he has taken from it. Owing to the scattered nature of the houses of a Kashmír village the night-soil is more widely distributed than it is in the Indian village. With improved sanitation in Srinagar I hope that the night-soil will spread to some distance in the neighbourhood of the city, but at present the *maliárs*, or vegetable-gardeners, alone regard *poudrette* without prejudice.

In the chapter on Geology facts may be found which would suggest to the scientific agriculturist new and improved methods for fertilizing the soil in Kashmír, but in the present state of the population the one essential is good tillage. Good tillage, without any change in the present methods, will suffice for the new and old alluvial, and for the peaty soils. For the Karewá land, which occupies a large area, and which is practically neglected at present, I believe that much might be done by science if capital were forthcoming. But even on the Karewá land good tillage alone would make an enormous difference, and I have seen excellent results when labour has been expended on ploughing. The Kashmíris are very sceptical as to the potentialities of the Karewá, and say that land which will not grow grass will grow nothing. Yet they admit that in certain unknown cycles the Karewá lands yield astonishing crops of barley and wheat, and they also admit that Karewá land, to which irrigation is brought, rivals the new alluvial land in fertility. I shall notice the question of the Karewá at the end of this chapter. It is one of great importance, in view of the probability which now exists that there will be a large increase in population. CHAP. XIII.

Irrigation.

Up to the present agriculture in Kashmír practically depends on irrigation, and thanks to the formation of the country irrigation is easy, and in ordinary years abundant. If normal snows fall in the winter and the great mountains are well covered, the water supply for the rice will be sufficient. (The villagers always speak of the mountains as their treasuries, and in a year of good snowfall the treasuries are full.) The snows melt into various mountain streams, which lace the valley and rush down to the Jhelum river. From both sides of the Jhelum the country rises to the mountains in bold terraces, and the water passes quickly from one village to another in years of good snow. At convenient points on the mountain streams temporary weirs or projecting snags are erected, and the water is taken off in main channels, which pass into a network of small ducts and eventually empty themselves into the Jhelum, or into the large swamps which lie along the banks of the Jhelum. Lower down in the valley, where the streams flow gently, *dams* are erected. All villages which depend for their irrigation on a certain weir are obliged to assist in its construction and repair. The weir consists of wooden stakes and stones, with grasses and willow-branches twisted in between the stakes. The best grass for this purpose is the *fikal*. The channel often has to be taken over ravines and around the edges of the Karewá cliffs, and irrigation then becomes very difficult. In former days, when the State took a share of the crop, it was to the interest of the Darbar to look after irrigation and to assist in repairs. But since 1880, when the State tried to introduce a fixed assessment, the villagers have had to look after the repairs themselves, and when the channel passes through difficult ground the irrigation has become very uncertain. When a ravine has to be crossed, a flat-bottomed boat, similar to the boats in use in Kashmír, is erected on high trestles, and the water flows over in a quaint-looking aqueduct. When a Karewá has to be passed or skirted, a tunnel will sometimes be made, but as a rule the channel is cut along the face of the cliff, and great loss is caused by the frequent breaches. Stakes and wattles are used, and sometimes the flat-bottomed boat is called in. In old days over every main channel there was a *Miráb*—one of the villagers—whose duty was to see to repairs and to call out labour. These *Mirábs* had not received pay for years, and the channels had fallen into great disorder, but the useful office of *Miráb* has now been

CHAP. XIII. revived. The system of distribution is rough and simple, but it has the advantage that quarrels between villages rarely arise, and quarrels between cultivators of the same village never. The system is said to have been introduced by the emperor Jehángír. He laid down the rule that the upper villages which had no local spring and lower villages which received no overflow water from the upper villages were entitled to a share of irrigation from the main channel. These shares have been carefully recorded during settlement, with a view to obviating the disputes and claims regarding irrigation which are sure to arise as population extends and rice cultivation increases. Already the lower villages complain that upper villages, which formerly grew no rice, are now curtailing the water supply, but so far no serious diminution of the irrigation of the older rice villages has taken place, and the slope of the upper villages is so rapid that the water soon finds its way back to the main channels. As is always the case in irrigation by flow the cultivators take far more water than is necessary, and with proper distributaries and with some supervision the water service of Kashmír could be nearly doubled. Owing to the heights at which water can be taken off, there is scarcely any part of the valley which cannot be irrigated. Besides the irrigation which is derived from the mountain streams, there is an important auxiliary supply from the numerous springs of Kashmír. Some of these springs afford excellent irrigation, but there are two drawbacks. The spring water is always cold, and it does not carry with it the fertilizing silt which is brought down by the mountain streams, but in its place brings down a scum which is considered bad for rice. The Jhelum river, in its long, gentle course through the valley, gives no irrigation at present and its waters run to waste, but as population increases I imagine that its water will be lifted by the Persian wheel. The only lift-irrigation at present takes the form of the simple and inexpensive *dip well*, and in Srinagar and the small towns there is some splendid garden cultivation which depends wholly on the *dhenkli*. On some of the Karewá the spring levels are not very deep, and when all the irrigateable land of the valley has been taken up I hope that wells will be sunk on the Karewá. I think that the bucket and rope will be found more suitable than the Persian wheel, as the spring levels will be of more than eighteen feet in depth. In the north-west of the valley there are a few tanks, and I believe that tank irrigation might be introduced into many parts of Kashmír.

Implements. The agricultural implements of Kashmír are few and simple. The plough is of necessity light, as the cattle are small, and is made of various woods, the mulberry, the ash, and the apple being perhaps the most suitable material. The ploughshare is tipped with iron. For clod-breaking a wooden mallet is used and the work is done in gangs. Sometimes a *log*

PLATE XII

To face page 325]

Negative by Alam Chand, G.C.

A VIEW ILLUSTRATING AGRICULTURAL IMPLEMENTS. BEHIND THE PLOUGH TO THE LEFT IS THE MALLET FOR CLOD-CRUSHING—TO THE RIGHT IS THE SPADE. IN FRONT OF THE PLOUGH BULLOCKS ARE THE CREEL IN WHICH MANURE IS CARRIED AND THE HOE. THE GARDEN WALL TO THE RIGHT IS THE DOS OR EARTHEN FENCE OF KASHMÍR

of wood is drawn over the furrows by bullocks, the driver standing on the log. But as a rule, frost, snow, water, and the process known as *khushába*, are considered a sufficient agency for the disintegration of clods. The spade of Kashmír is made of wood, has a narrow face, and is tipped with iron. It is chiefly employed by the cultivator for digging out turf clods, and for arranging his fields for irrigation. For maize and cotton a small *hand hoe* is used to extract weeds and to loosen the soil. These are the implements of agriculture in Kashmír, but the universal *pestle* and *mortar*[1] for husking rice and pounding maize must be mentioned. The mortar is made of a hollowed-out bole of wood. The pestle is made of light, hard wood, and the best and hardest of woods for the purpose is the hawthorn. In some villages the rice is husked under a heavy log hammer, which works on a pivot, and is raised by men who step on and step off the end away from the hammer. The method of husking rice, though it affords a vigorous form of exercise for women and turns out a clean and polished grain, breaks and crushes much of the rice. I have tried to introduce a wooden hand-mill similar to those in use in the West Indies, but I am afraid that it also breaks the grain. It involves less labour, for only one pounding in the mortar is necessary after the grain has gone through the mill. With the mortar and pestle the grain must be husked three times before it is ready for use.

Agricultural operations.

Agricultural operations in Kashmír are carefully timed so as to fall within a certain period before or after the *Nauroz*, the spring day of the Musalmáns, and the *Mezan* or commencement of autumn. If the period is exceeded, there will be a certain failure in the crop, which is calculated in a most precise manner. The circumstance which interferes with punctuality in ploughing and sowing is the absence of irrigation water at the right time, and in the spring there is great excitement among the villagers if water is stopped by some natural cause, such as the late melting of snow or by other causes, such as the greediness of some privileged person who defies the local officials and takes more than his just share of water. Although the absence of water is the only circumstance which would delay operations in ordinary times, it often chanced, up to recent times, that the cultivator was seized for forced labour and could not plough or sow at the proper time. And though there is no doubt that rice ought to be sown within forty days after the *Nauroz*, sowing often continues up to the middle of June.

Inasmuch as the autumn crops are of chief importance in Kashmír, and as the year is held to begin in the spring, I will commence an account of agricultural operations from March, in which month ploughing for the

[1] For illustration see p. 313.

CHAP. XIII. autumn crops commences. A general idea of the cultivator's work may be obtained from the following calendar[1] :—

March and April . . .	Plough and manure for rice, plough for maize and other autumn crops.
April and May	Sow rice, maize, and other autumn crops.
May and June	Do. do. do. and plant out rice seedlings.
June and July	Harvest wheat and barley.
July and August	Weed rice, maize, and cotton, and harvest linseed.
August and September .	Do. do. and commence picking cotton.
September and October .	Harvest rice and maize, and other autumn crops. If timely rains fall, plough for wheat and barley, and sow wheat, barley, and rape-seed. Cut willows for sheep fodder.
October and November .	Harvest rice for first half of October, ploughing for wheat and barley.
November and December	Plough for wheat and barley.
December and January .	Thresh rice and maize, and other autumn crops. Attend to sheep and cattle, and weave woollen blankets.
January and February .	Do. do. do.
February and March . .	Do. do. do.

In March the rice fields, which have remained undisturbed since the last rice crop was cut, are hard and stiff. The soil has perhaps been worked by the frosts and snow, but if, as sometimes is the case, no snow has fallen, it will be difficult work for the plough bullocks, which are thin and poor after the long winter, to break up the soil. If rains do not fall, a plough watering must be given and ploughing then commences. In certain villages the soil is so damp that the ploughing has to be done perforce while the soil is wet, and the outturn is always poorer than that of fields where the soil is ploughed in a dry condition. All the litter of the village and the farmyard manure is carried out to the fields by women and ploughed in, or is heaped in a place through which the irrigation duct passes and so reaches the fields as liquid manure. Sometimes the manure is placed in heaps on the fields, and when the field is covered with water it is scattered about by hand. Later on in April, as the weather opens, turf clods are cut from the banks of streams and irrigation channels and

[1] The Kashmiris divide the year into six seasons, each of two months:—

1. *Sont*	March 15 to May 15.
2. *Grishm*	May 15 to July 15.
3. *Wairat*	July 15 to September 15.
4. *Hard*	September 15 to November 15.
5. *Wandh*	November 15 to January 15.
6. *Shishr*	January 15 to March 15.

It is useful to remember these names, as the Kashmiris are somewhat hazy as to months, and *grist* months, or months of agriculturists, are usually one month in advance of the official months. It is said that the *grist* calendar was introduced by Sultan Shamas Din, and the Kashmíri cultivators always talk of Vahek, Zeth, Shrawan, Bhodur, Ashud, Kartik, Mangor, and Tsitr, their equivalents for the Indian Bisakh, Jeth, Sawan, Bhadron, Asuj, Katik, Magar, and Chet.

PLATE XIII

To face page 327] [*Negative by Alam Chand, G C*

ILLUSTRATES THE MOST IMPORTANT WORK IN AGRICULTURE THE KHUSHÁBA OF RICE. THE MEN TO THE RIGHT WORK WITH THEIR FEET; THOSE TO THE LEFT WORK THE RICE-PLANTS WITH THEIR HANDS. IN THE CENTRE ARE THE BULLOCKS WHICH ARE DRIVEN UP AND DOWN THE RICE-FIELDS

flung broadcast over the wet fields. When four ploughings have been given and the clods have been crumbled with mallets, the soil is watered and sowing can commence in April. The rice seed, which has been carefully selected at threshing-time and has been stored away in grass bags, is again examined and tested by winnowing. It is then put back into the grass bag and immersed in water until germination commences. Sometimes the seed is placed in earthen vessels through which water is passed. Rice is grown up to an altitude of 7,000 feet, and in the higher villages it is convenient to sow earlier than in the lower villages, as the cold weather comes on quicker and it is essential to harvest the crop before snow falls. And I have noticed that in certain lower villages, where it is the custom to sow rice earlier than ordinary, the outturn is always heavy. The ploughing for maize and the autumn millets is not so careful as the ploughing for rice, and two or three ploughings are considered ample. A watering is sometimes given to maize fields to start the seed, but no manure is put in. Cotton alone receives manuring in the form of ashes mixed with the seed. All Kashmíris recognize that the greater the number of ploughings the greater will be the outturn of the crop, but the land holdings are large, and the cattle are small and weak. Great care is used in the selection of seed, and the seed grain is jealously put away after harvest in grass sacks. Nothing but the direst necessity would induce a Kashmíri to break in upon his seed store for food, and though there has been for many years a pleasant pretence of obtaining seed grain every year from the State, as a matter of fact the seed has been lying in the cultivator's house.

In June and July the barley and wheat are cut and threshed. The ears are trodden out by cattle or sometimes beaten by sticks. and when there is no wind a blanket is flapped to winnow the grain. Anything is good enough for the spring crops, which are regarded by the Kashmíris as a kind of lottery in which they generally lose their stakes. And at the same time there comes the real labour of rice weeding, the *khushába*, a word for which I know no English equivalent. It is not merely weeding, it is standing in the mud and water on all-fours, with a burning sun above and cold water below, scuffling with the mud, and kneading it as a baker kneads flour. It is placing the rice plants in their right places, and pressing the soft mud gently around the green seedling. No novice can do the work, as only an expert can detect the counterfeit grasses which pretend to be rice, and *khushába* must be learnt young. The Hindu boys, who are at school while their Musalmán contemporaries are at work with their fathers in the rice fields, never learn the mysteries of *khushába*, and one can tell a Hindu's rice field by its look. *Khushába* is best when done by hand, but it may be done by the feet (*Lat*), or it may be done, in a fashion, by cattle splashing up and down the wet fields of mud (*Gupan*

CHAP. XIII. *nind).* Though the Kashmíris know that this last method is a lazy substitute for the real *khushába*, they comfort themselves with the reflection that the cattle have cloven hoofs, and that the cleft may providentially come over the young rice plant. Sometimes when the rice is two feet high the whole crop is ploughed up (*sele*). While the men are working hard at the rice the women are more easily plying the hand hoe in the maize and cotton fields, weeding out the *pseudo-maize*, and loosening the soil around the roots. Day by day this goes on till the rice has bloomed and the grain has begun to form. Then the water is run off the fields, and a short time before harvest a final watering is given which swells the ears. Soon after the sickle is put in, and the golden rice falls on to the damp earth. Often while the rice is standing in its last watering, rape-seed is cast into the water. No ploughing is given and a crop of rape is thus lightly obtained. Before the harvest of the autumn crops commences, about the first half of September, rain may fall and it is very beneficial. It improves the rice crop and it also enables the cultivator to plough and sow for the spring crops. Such rain is known as *kámbar ká*, and there is great rejoicing when these timely rains fall. Before September, if rain has fallen, a large area of land will be ploughed up and sown with rape-seed, and both this and the early sowings for barley and wheat are of importance, as they come at a time when the cultivator and his cattle have some leisure, for then the *khushábas* are over and harvest has not commenced. When once harvest has commenced the cultivator has little time for anything but cutting and carrying. and he cuts in anxiety, as rain and sometimes snow may fall. As there are no carts in the valley, save in the flat plain around the Wular lake, where a primitive trolly is used ; and as the Kashmíris will not use their plough bullocks for carriage, the sheaves of rice and of other crops have to be slowly and laboriously carried by men from the fields to the threshing-floor. When the *rice ricks* are thoroughly dry threshing commences. Seizing a bundle [1] of rice plants in his two hands the cultivator beats them over a log of wood and detaches the rice ears from the stalk. The rice straw is carefully stored, as it is considered the best fodder and the best thatching straw of all. Threshing drags along all the winter. Rain and snow fall and stop operations, and threshing may last on till March. In one group of villages in the extreme

[1] In cutting rice the reaper takes as many plants as he can hold in his hand and cuts them close to the ground with a *sickle*. The handful of rice stalks is known as *Budu*.

2 Budus = 1 Tsap.
4 Tsap = 1 Phula.
96 Budus = 1 Kuru.

Near the river, where rice straw is sold for consumption in the city, the measurement is different. There the handful is spoken of as *Tsap*, and two *Tsap* make one *Phula*, and twelve *Phulas* one *Kuru*. One hundred *Kurus* of rice straw fetched Rs.2.1.0 in November, 1893.

north-west, where the rice plant is of stunted growth. threshing is done by cattle. When the weather is favourable, from October to December, the cultivator will be busy ploughing the huge areas of dry land for wheat and barley; but by the end of December ploughing must cease, and the Kashmíris occupy themselves with threshing and husking the rice and other crops and with domestic work. such as the tending of sheep and cattle and the weaving of blankets. It is difficult in mid-winter to tempt a Kashmíri out of his reeking house. The ploughings for wheat and barley are very few and very slovenly. I should estimate the ploughings for wheat to be three at the most, while for barley two ploughings are considered sufficient. There is no labour lost in weeding or manuring, and the standing crops of wheat and barley would shock a Panjábi farmer. The fields are choked with weeds, and it is wonderful that there should be any crops at all. Two years of barley or wheat would ruin any land, and the Kashmíris have the sense to follow a spring crop by an autumn crop. I hope that the day will come when the Kashmíris will pay more attention to their barley and wheat, but there are two facts which may prevent either of these crops being largely produced in the valley. The rainfall is scanty and very uncertain, and I imagine that if irrigation were attempted the water in the spring-time would prove too cold for plant growth. I have seen five spring harvests in Kashmír. The first was destroyed by heavy rains in the early spring, immediately followed by intense heat and dryness: the second was ruined by want of winter rains; the third was lost by the snows lying long into the spring, when they melted under a burst of hot weather which caked the soil and nipped the young wheat and barley plants; the fourth failed by the absence of either winter or spring rains; and the last was spoiled by the snow lying too late, and by excessive spring rains. The Kashmíris do not care for barley or wheat as a food, and if cultivation improves it will be with a view to trade.

Before describing the various crops of Kashmír I should first explain that the system of cultivation in Kashmír is what is known as *Ekfasli*, that is the land gives one crop in the year. Of course there are some exceptions to this rule. In the first place, the highly-cultivated garden lands in the neighbourhood of Srinagar and the towns give a number of crops in the year. A stolen crop of rape-seed is often obtained by sowing rape-seed in the ripening rice, and the *nurseries* in which the young rice is sown always give a crop of turnips in the autumn In certain villages along the Jhelum a new departure was made in 1892–3. Rape-seed was followed in the same year by rice and by *china*. The success which attended this new departure may encourage others to attempt double cropping. In the second place, there is some dry land which requires

CHAP. XIII. a year's fallow after a crop, but this class of land is not of great extent.

Following the order of the calendar, I will first notice the crops which ripen in the autumn, and next those which ripen in the summer. I have written at great length on rice cultivation in my fifteen Assessment Reports. Here I shall only allude to the more obvious points of rice cultivation. In the glossary will be found vernacular terms employed in rice-growing. The following table gives the crops of chief importance in Kashmír :—

AUTUMNAL CROPS.

English Name.	Botanical Name.	Kashmíri Name.
Rice	Oryza sativa	*Dhán.*
Maize	Zea Mays	*Makái*
Cotton	Gossypium herbaceum	*Kapás.*
Saffron crocus	Crocus sativus	*Kong.*
Tobacco	Nicotiana Tabacum	*Tamák.*
"	" rustica	*Tamák.*
Hop	Humulus Lupulus	*Hapis.*
Italian millet	Setaria italica	*Shol.*
Millet	Panicum miliaceum	*Ping.*
Amaranth	Amaranthus	*Ganhár.*
Buckwheat	Fagopyrum esculentum	*Trumbá.*
"	" tataricum.	
Pulse	Phaseolus Mungo	*Mung.*
"	" radiatus	*Máh.*
"	" aconitifolius	*Mothi.*
"	" vulgaris	*Razmáh.*
Sesame	Sesamum indicum	*Til.*

SPRING CROPS.

English Name.	Botanical Name.	Kashmíri Name.
Wheat	Triticum vulgare	*Kanak.*
Barley	Hordeum hexastichon	*Wiska.*
Tibet barley	" " var.	*Grim.*
Barley	" vulgare	*Wiska.*
Opium poppy	Papaver somniferum	*Afin.*
Rape	Brassica campestris	*Tilgoglu.*
"	" " sub-sp.	*Taruz* or *Sarshaf.*
"	" " sub-sp.	*Sandiji.*
Flax	Linum usitatissimum	*Alish.*
Pea	Pisum sativum	*Karré.*
Bean	Vicia faba	*Bágláh.*
"	Carum copticum	*Ajwáin.*

In every way the most important staple in Kashmír is rice, and the cultivator devotes all his energy to this crop. For rice he will terrace his fields, expend great labour in digging out irrigation channels, spend his nights out in the fields watching the flow of water, and will pass laborious days moving about like an amphibious animal in the wet deep mud. In the lower villages near the swamps there is an insect which irritates the skin, and to protect himself the cultivator smears his legs and arms with the pine pitch. He presents a curious appearance with his arms and legs black and his body splashed all over with grey mud. The soil of Kashmír is porous, and water must be kept running over the fields from the sowing time almost to harvest, for if once the land becomes hard and caked the stalks are pinched and the plant suffers, while the work of *khushába* is rendered impossible. At the most it is dangerous to leave the fields dry for more than seven days, and it is necessary that the cultivator should always be present to watch the water[1]. Next, the growth of weeds is very rapid, and once they get ahead of the rice it is extremely difficult to repair the injury caused and to eradicate the grasses, which none but an expert can distinguish from the real rice. Thus it follows that the old system, under which men were taken away for forced labour during the growth of the rice plant, was most prejudicial to good cultivation, and it may also be understood that the wage of four annas per diem would fail to induce a cultivator to leave his fields willingly when a day or two's absence might cause serious injury to the rice crop. The more that I see of rice cultivation in Kashmír the more am I convinced that small holdings mean a large outturn of grain, and I regard two acres of rice as the utmost that one man with a pair of bullocks can cultivate properly. There are two systems of cultivation. Under the first the rice is sown broadcast; under the second the rice is first sown in a nursery and then planted out. I have made frequent inquiries regarding the respective merits of the two systems, and though sometimes I have found a difference of opinion, the general result of my inquiries is to show that the broadcast system[2] gives the best outturn per acre. For successful broadcast cultivation the fields should be fairly large, and water must be available at the right time, and the supply must be ample. The labour entailed in broadcast cultivation is far heavier than that required in the nursery system. Two *khushábas* are sufficient for the latter, while four *khushábas* are essential in broadcast sowings. Provided the soil is good and irrigation is fairly abundant, the cultivator will choose the broadcast system, but in certain circumstances he will adopt the nursery method. If water comes late the rice plant can be kept alive in the nursery plots, and the young seedling need not be planted out till forty days after sowing.

[1] The cultivator also has to be on the look-out for *snails* and for *dádu*, a fish-like insect with hard scaly wings, both of which eat up the young rice plants. When the rice plant is a foot high the *dádu* does no harm, and is said to be of use, as it works the soil around the roots. *Leeches* also abound in the rice fields near the swamps. Allusions have been made in books to the fact that a weed known as *Prángos* is used by the rice cultivators as a preventive against insect pests. I have made careful inquiries and have never heard of the use of *Prángos* in Kashmír. In Poonch another umbelliferous plant is used to assist fermentation and germination.

[2] In Khuihâma the *Nihâli* or nursery system obtains, and is said to yield three to seven kh. per kharwar of land more than *Watrú* or the broadcast system. Every cultivator sows one or two fields broadcast, and keeps the produce for the seed of the next year's nursery, experience showing that broadcast rice gives the best seed.

CHAP. XIII. During this forty days' respite from drowning the land has enjoyed the benefit of sunshine and air, and it is about this time that the sheep of Kashmír are moving up from the villages to the great grazing tracts on the mountains, and as they pass up they enrich the land which is awaiting the nursery rice. The young grasses have come up and the food and strength of the sheep rapidly improve, and their manure is of greater value than it was a month before, when the broadcast lands were flooded for rice. Again, a man who has a large area of dry cultivation to attend to will often choose the nursery system, for this gives him breathing-time. Both systems have their advantages. The broadcast system gives the larger outturn, but it entails greater labour, and is frequently checked by cold wet weather in April. The nursery system requires less labour; it clears the ground of weeds, and it gives a softer rice than that given by the broadcast system. Still the Kashmíris understand their own business, and they look upon the nursery system as a *dernier ressort.*

Just as there are two methods of sowing the rice, so there are two methods of preparing the soil. The one is known as *tao,* the other as *kenalu.* There is an old proverb in Kashmír, 'Ya kezan ya dazan,' which means that for rice cultivation the land should be absolutely wet or absolutely dry. In *tao* cultivation the soil is ploughed dry, and when the clods are perfectly free from moisture and do not lose weight when placed over the fireplace at night, irrigation is given and the seed is sown. In *kenalu* cultivation the soil is ploughed wet, and when three ploughings are given and the soil is half water and half mud the outturn of *kenalu* is sometimes equal to that of *tao.* But as a rule it may be said that the *tao* system gives the best results and that *kenalu* involves the heavier labour. In low lands the cultivator has perforce to plough wet, but there are other circumstances which demand the *kenalu* system. If the snows on the mountains point to a short supply of water it is prudent to elect for *kenalu*; for in the spring water is always ample, and the soil can be so thoroughly soaked as to enable it to pass through the summer with a very scanty supply. *Tao,* on the other hand, requires ample water and a regular supply. There is certain hot sour soil which requires a rotation of the two systems, and after two years of *tao* it must be deluged with water and ploughed wet.

The rices of Kashmír are infinite in variety. In one tahsíl I have found fifty-three varieties. They may be roughly divided into two classes, the white and the red. As a food the white rice is the more esteemed, and the best of the white rices are the *básmati* and the *kanyun.* These varieties germinate very quickly and ripen more rapidly than any other rices. But they are very delicate plants and cannot stand exposure to cold winds. They give a small crop and require very careful husking. Certain villages are famous for their peculiar rices. Telbal on the Dal lake is noted for its soft white *chughal*, Kasba Lal for its *anzan*, Salora for its *gudh krihum*, while the following rhyme of a Kashmíri epicure selects Nipur near Islámabad as the place for good rice:— CHAP. XIII.

Mung az Khanpur,	Pulse from Khanpur,
Rogan az Lalipur,	Ghi from Lalipur,
Ság az Pampur,	Vegetables from Pampur,
Shir az Hirpur,	Milk from Hirpur,
Brinj az Nipur,	Rice from Nipur,
Barra az Nandpur,	Sheep from Nandpur,
Dach az Raipur.	Grapes from Raipur.

Nipur has now lost its reputation, and it is a sad fact that for many years the Kashmíris have done their utmost to avoid the notice of epicure officials, and have wilfully exterminated choice rices, melons, and fruit trees rather than submit to the requisitions of the dainty authorities in Srinagar.

The white rice. though esteemed as a food, is from a cultivator's point of view less popular than the red rice. In the first place, the white variety is a more delicate plant, and suffers more from changes in temperature than its hardier brother. It is said to exhaust the ground more quickly, though that is doubtful, and it certainly gives a smaller outturn than the red rices. And as, under the Kashmír administration, prices have hitherto been non-existent, and as the State gives the same commutation rate for white as for red rices [1], the cultivator had no motive for growing the choicer varieties, and his one thought has been to raise a large and fairly certain crop. Then too the red rice can be grown at higher elevations than the white varieties, and in certain parts where the crops are liable to the ravages of wild beasts it is found that the bear and the pig are fastidious and do not care for the red rice and its spiky *glumes*. Where the cold water from the mountains first enters the rice fields the red rice will always be grown, as the white rice cannot stand the chill of the irrigation. As one ascends the slopes of the valley the chief variety of rice is the *niwár*, a plant of short stout growth, which yields a hard red rice, very sweet and nourishing, but not esteemed by the city people. It is at first somewhat surprising to find how easily the Kashmíris identify the countless varieties of rice. They can recognize them in their various stages as seed, seedling, and plant, and after some time even a stranger can see the difference in the plant stage. There is the light green grass passing through countless shades of green into the dark bronze of the *imbrzal*, and when the rices are in flower the fields present a most brilliant collection of 'art' colours. It is well for the Kashmíri that nature helps him to identify the different varieties of his favourite crop, for otherwise he would not be able to detect the

[1] The State made an exception in favour of *basmati* and *kanyun* rices, giving 1 Chilki rupee more per kharwar than it gave for other kinds of rice.

CHAP. XIII. rogues and counterfeits which appear at weeding-time. The first and most difficult impostor with which the cultivator has to deal is the *kre*, or self-sown rice. If it is allowed to remain, or escapes the vigilance of the weeder, the *kre* will produce a blackish grain, which falls from the ear when the plant comes to maturity, and is again reproduced and again taxes the detective powers of the cultivator. To enable the villager to distinguish between the real rice and the *kre*, it is the custom to change every year the variety of rice sown. White rice may succeed red rice, or a green grass rice will succeed a dark grass variety, and in this way the careful cultivator will take out every *kre* plant in the field. Sometimes, but very rarely, the cultivator will grow red and white rice in the same field, and he says that they run a race and that the harvest comes more quickly. The next intruder is the *háma*, in which perhaps botanists might find the wild rice. Like the *kre*, and unlike the rice, it also sheds its seeds, but it is more easy to detect than the *kre*, as its leaf is slightly different from that of the cultivated rice. The *háma* grain is eaten by the people and is presented as an offering in the Hindu temples. But when the cultivator has done everything to keep his fields clean and his rice hearty and strong he has other dangers ahead. When the nights are warm and the mountains to the south and south-west of the valley are lit up by evening lightning, the rice plant seems to lose its vitality and the ears grow withered and white. The cultivator then knows that *rai* has set in, and that his crop has been destroyed. He will sometimes set to work and cut out the *rai*-stricken rice, for he believes that *rai* is contagious. He will also buy an amulet from some holy man and tie it to a post set up in the rice, or he will scatter holy dust over the field. Among other devices for arresting *rai* may be mentioned the setting up of poplar wands in the rice fields, and if a widow will walk through the *rai*-stricken plots with her head uncovered it is generally believed that the *rai* will be averted. There are two forms of *rai*. The common form is where the stem and ear are affected, and this is known as *Hil rai*. The other form is where the roots are attacked, and the plant withers from the root upwards. This is known as *Munj rai*. Maize is also liable to *rai*, especially in confined villages shut out from the breezes. I have sent specimens of rice plants attacked by *rai* to Calcutta, but no vegetable blight could be detected. The ears consisted of empty glumes, the ovary appearing either never to have fertilized or to have completely aborted subsequently to fertilization, and it was believed in Calcutta that the *rai* was due simply to unfavourable conditions of environment at the period of flowering. *Rai* is a very serious calamity in Kashmír, and certain localities are especially liable to its attacks. I have noticed that low-lying lands shut out from the evening breezes are especially liable, and that land of great natural strength is also more liable than land of ordinary fertility. Though it is of course necessary to give manure to land which bears rice year by year, the cultivator has to be very careful not to give too much manure, and when sheep are passing over the rice lands it is important to keep them moving, as if the soil is rendered too rich the rice will most likely be attacked by *rai*. For a good crop of rice the days should be sunny and hot and the nights cold, and warm muggy nights are the signal for the onset of *rai*. But though cold or rather cool nights are desirable, extreme cold will be almost as injurious as warm nights. Kashmír is surrounded by high mountains, and if early snow settles on the higher peaks the temperature of the side valleys falls very quickly. A cold breeze blows from off the peaks, and the forming grain is chilled and shrivelled. This is known as *handru*, and the rice plant is cut down and given as fodder to horses. An aggravated and more distressing form of *handru* sometimes occurs, known as *wohan*. When the rice is ready for harvesting snow will sometimes fall on the lower hills, and a cold blast strikes the crop. A crackling sound is heard, and the villagers say that the grain is twisted in the ear. When the time for husking comes the grain is not rice, but a useless white powder. So it may be seen that the cultivator has his troubles and anxieties even in fertile Kashmír, but the trouble which always haunts him is the fear of rain or snow at harvest-time. This is the event which brings famine, and when the Kashmíri prays that he may be delivered from *Hákim wa Hakím*—the ruler and the doctor—he also prays for fair weather at harvest-time. For a good rice harvest the following conditions are necessary:—Heavy snows in the winter on the mountains to fill the streams in the summer, good rains in March and the beginning of April, clear, bright, warm days and cool nights in May, June, July, and August, with an occasional shower and fine weather in September. In September the nights should be very cold. All Kashmíris assert that *sirdána*, or full grains, depend on cold *dew* penetrating the *outer husk* and swelling and hardening the *forming grain*.

I do not think that the Kashmíri has much to learn in rice cultivation, or that he can be fairly blamed for growing inferior varieties of rice. Up to the present his one object has been to secure quantity, and until trade springs up in Kashmír there will be no motive for aiming at quality. I have induced certain cultivators to plough up their rice lands where the soil is still damp after the harvest is reaped, and though they admit that the soil will receive the benefit of air and frost, they maintain that there will be greater difficulties in weeding the next year [1]. They also urge the

[1] Sometimes after the reaping of the rice crop the fields are again irrigated, and water is allowed to stand on them for two or three months. It is said that the water destroys weeds, and gives strength to exhausted soil. Opinions differ as to the benefits of this process, and it is by no means common.

CHAP. XIII. want of leisure for ploughing at harvest-time. As a rule, in answer to all suggestions, the Kashmíri has some sensible objection to make. But with all their conservative instincts there are signs of departure from the old strict rules based on the seasons, and old men deplore these innovations. So far as rice is concerned, it may be said that if a cultivator can obtain water and has manure he will continue to grow rice, and he will not dream of anything like rotation of crops. Where water is uncertain the rice land will be given a fallow [1], and sometimes I have found rice followed by four years of cotton, by maize, wheat, barley, and *máh* (pulse). There is no doubt that the rest from rice and the exposure to sunshine and air benefit the soil, but in average land which has sufficient irrigation the cultivator prefers, in spite of the benefits of rotation, to go on year by year growing rice.

It has been the fashion among officials and the non-agriculturists of the valley to exaggerate the yield of rice, and some of the figures quoted would surprise statisticians [2]. Thus it is stated that in Nihalpura, where the rice holdings were wisely limited to two acres, the harvest was a hundred-fold. There is no doubt that very heavy crops are sometimes raised in the homestead lands which are manured in a natural manner, but crop experiments made in fields of an ordinary description have justified me in taking 17 maunds of unhusked rice as the average outturn of an acre of rice land. In the higher villages the average has been taken as 15 maunds. I believe that as population increases in the villages and the land holdings become smaller and more workable the average production per acre will increase. I have not attempted to estimate the cost of production of rice, as such estimates in any country are vague and misleading, and in Kashmír they would be extremely so, as prices are in a fluid state. One fact should however be mentioned, namely, that the prices of plough bullocks are rising—an important item in cultivation.

Maize. The other crops can be dismissed more briefly. Next in importance to rice comes maize. The best soil for maize is reclaimed swamp, and enormous crops are raised in good years from the black peaty land which lies under the banks of the Jhelum. In the high villages occupied by the Gujar graziers very fine crops of maize are grown, and the large outturn is due to the heavy manuring given to the fields by the Gujars' buffaloes and

[1] Rice land requiring a fallow is known as *beth muru*. Rice followed by pulses or buckwheat is called *muru*.

[2] Nothing is more difficult than to ascertain the real facts regarding the outturn of rice. Officials exaggerate, cultivators under-estimate. Many say that the land is not so productive as it used to be, but land which yields under favourable conditions 48 traks of unhusked rice for every trak of seed cannot be regarded as unfertile. From inquiries I find that, though there has been no perceptible increase in the size of the *grain*, there is an increase in the number of the grains in each *spike*.

cattle. But with this exception maize receives no manure, and the system of harvesting renders manure unnecessary. A large part of the maize stalks is left on the fields, and in the winter the stalks rot with the snow and rain into the soil. Ordinarily two to three ploughings are given, and a final ploughing is done which covers over the seeds. A month after sowing, when the maize is about a foot high, women weed the fields with a small hand hoe and loosen the soil about the roots. As a rule. maize is grown on dry land, and it is rare to find the crop irrigated. For a really good crop of maize fortnightly rains are required, but in the swamp lands the natural moisture of the soil produces fair crops even if the rains are delayed. There are two varieties. The early maize has a white soft grain, and is sown at the same time as rice. It is usually grown in the naturally manured homestead fields. The ordinary maize has a red grain, and is sown in May and June. It is very sweet, and is preferred by the Kashmíris to the white maize. There is a small white maize, known as Poonch maize, which is grown in the higher villages on the west of the valley. The maize plant attains a great height, and as cultivation extends and grazing becomes scarce the maize stalks will afford an excellent fodder. At present the Gujars alone appreciate them as cattle food. As a diet maize ranks after rice, and the Kashmíri considers maize without milk unpalatable. The grain of maize is separated from the *core* by beating with sticks, and the *cores* are sent to the city and towns to be employed as fuel. Maize cobs, if properly dried, will keep good for three years, and it is calculated in Kashmír that 15 traks of cobs will give 12 traks of grain. Maize is liable to *rai*, and is also attacked by a disease known as *sás*, which is a kind of black smutty fungus, sometimes completely enveloping the cob. Enormous crops are sometimes raised in the rich soil of the reclaimed swamp, but our crop experiments have pointed to an average of 11 maunds in irrigated and dry swamp lands and 8 maunds in dry land per acre.

Kangni.

Kangni or *Shol* (Setaria italica) is an extremely useful plant, and when it is apparent from the look of the mountains that snow water will be scarce a large area of rice land is at once sown in *kangni*. The land, if a good crop is hoped for, must be carefully ploughed about four times, and the seed is sown in April and May about the same time as rice. Some weeding is done, but as a rule the hardy *kangni* is left to look after itself until it ripens in September. The grain, which is husked like rice, is not esteemed by the Kashmíris as a food, as it is considered to have heating properties. There are two varieties of *kangni*, the smaller and the greater, and the former is preferred as a food. The former is a red grain and the latter white. An average crop gives about three maunds to an acre.

China or *Ping* (Panicum miliaceum) is very like rice in appearance, but is

CHAP. XIII. grown in dry land. The field is ploughed three times, and after sowing cattle are turned on to the land and tread the soil down. The seed is sown in June and the crop is harvested in September. It is occasionally weeded, but like the *kangni*, with which it is always associated under the official name 'cheap food stuff,' the *china* does not receive much attention. As a food it is not considered either pleasant or nourishing, and whereas the *kangni* is abused for being hot, the *china* is denounced as being cold. It is a troublesome grain, as it is very hard and takes a very long time to cook. It is red or white in colour and is husked like rice in a mortar. An average crop would be about 4½ maunds per acre.

Amaranth. The most beautiful of all the crops is the *ganhár* (amaranth, Amaranthus) with its gold, coral, and crimson stalks and flowers. It is frequently sown in rows among the cotton fields or on the borders of maize plots, and the sulphur blooms of the cotton and the coral of the *ganhár* form a delightful combination of colour. *Ganhár* is sown in May after two or three ploughings. No manure or irrigation is given, and with timely rains a large outturn of minute grain is harvested in September. The grain is first parched, then ground and eaten with milk or water. It is considered a heating food by the people, and the Hindus eat it on their fast-days. The stalks of the *ganhár* are used by washermen, who extract an alkaline substance from the burnt ashes.

Buckwheat. The *trumba*, or buckwheat (Fagopyrum esculentum), is a most useful plant, as it can be sown late in almost any soil. and when the cultivator sees that there is no hope of water coming to his rice fields he will at once sow the sweet *trumba*. There are two varieties in Kashmír—the sweet *trumba*, which has white pinkish flowers, and is often grown as a substitute for rice where water is not forthcoming; it can be sown up to the middle of July, and with good rains it gives a fair crop. The bitter *trumba*, which has yellow flowers, is however not a mere makeshift, and in the higher villages it often forms the only food-grain of the people. The unhusked grain is black in colour, and is either ground in mills and made into bread or is eaten as porridge. The sweet *trumba* is said to be a good food for horses and for poultry. An average crop would be 4½ maunds per acre. In the higher villages the *trumba* crop is very precarious, as late frosts prevent the seed being sown in time, and, similarly, early snows may destroy the harvest. In the lower villages irrigation will sometimes be given, but in the high villages the crop is entirely dependent on rain, as the water is too cold for irrigation.

Pulses. Mung. The pulses of Kashmír are not considered of much importance by the people, and the Panjábis do not regard the Kashmír *dál* in a favourable light. *Gram* is unknown[1], and the best of the pulses is the *mung* (Pha-

[1] Dr. Aitchison informs me that he has seen *gram* (Cicer arietinum) between Sopur and

seolus Mungo). The land is ploughed three times and the seed is sown in May. No irrigation is given, and *mung* is often sown in rice lands which require a rest. The roots run deep and air the soil. No manure is given and the crop is not weeded, but, in spite of neglect, good crops of *mung* can be obtained if the soil is fair and the rains are timely. The crop ripens in September, and 2½ maunds to 3 maunds would be an average crop in Kashmír. CHAP. XIII.

Máh. *Máh* (Phaseolus radiatus) is cultivated in the same way as *mung*. It gives a heavier crop, but the pulse is more tasteless than the *mung*. An average crop would be 4 maunds per acre.

Mothi. *Mothi* (Phaseolus aconitifolius) is sown in April, and like *mung* is often grown in rice fields which are out of condition. The pulse is not esteemed as a food for men, but is an important sheep food in the winter.

Peas and delicious white beans (*razma*) are occasionally cultivated.

Oil-seeds. The oil-seeds of Kashmír are of some importance, and now that Kashmír is linked with the outer world they are assuming daily a greater importance as a trade staple. The Kashmíris do not use *ghi* (clarified butter) in their food, but they require vegetable oils, and at present they use these oils for lighting as well as for cooking purposes. Mineral oils are as yet too expensive for general use

Rape. The chief of the oil-seeds is the rape, of which there are three varieties in Kashmír. The first is the *tilgoglu*, which is sown in September and October on dry lands, and especially on the soft reclaimed swamp land. As a rule there is no weeding, but when, as happens in reclaimed swamp, the wild hemp is very vigorous, the cultivator has to weed. Timely rains from February to May are required, and the crop is harvested in May and June.

The second variety is known as *taruz* or *sarshaf*, and is sown in the spring. It ripens at the same time as the *tilgoglu*, but it gives a smaller amount of oil from its seed. Three maunds of seed to the acre would be an average for *tilgoglu*. The other varieties of rape give less. The third variety of the rape is known as *sandiji*, and is sown in the standing rice when the last watering is being given. It gives a small crop, but as no labour is expended the cultivator counts even the small crop as gain.

Flax. Flax is cultivated all over the valley, but the best fields I have seen have been on the lower slopes of the mountains. The land is ploughed twice, and a third ploughing is given when the seed is sown in April. The crop is harvested towards the end of July. Timely rains are required in May or the plant withers. The crop is said to exhaust the land. An average

Gulmarg. One old Panjabi official of the Kashmír State has told me that he once cultivated *gram* with success, but from inquiries I am of opinion that Kashmír is too cold for *gram*, and I have never seen a *field* of *gram*.

CHAP. XIII. crop would be 1½ to 2 maunds of linseed to an acre, but with proper cultivation the produce could be increased. No manure is given and the fields are not weeded, and as a rule the linseed crop has a very dirty and slovenly appearance. As one ascends the slopes of the mountains the plant has a long stem, and some time ago a fitful attempt was made to grow flax for fibre. Like all the other excellent schemes for introducing new staples and industries into Kashmír, the growing of this for fibre failed, as there was no one to supervise or to encourage the cultivators.

Sesame. *Til* (Sesamum indicum) is a very common crop, and is sown in April. The land is ploughed four times, and a fifth ploughing is given at sowing time. No manure is given, but *til* requires a rich soil, and requires also gentle and timely rains. The crop is weeded with the hand hoe, and is more carefully looked after than any of the other oil-seed plants. The *til* is a very delicate plant and is injured by cold winds. The crops ripen shortly after rice, and blankets are spread under the plants at harvest-time to catch the seeds, which fall out of the pods with the slightest movement. In Kashmír the oil, which is sweet, is valued as an ointment. An average crop would be about 1½ maunds of seed per acre.

Oil. This will be a convenient place to give a brief description of the oil production of Kashmír. Hitherto oil has been taken by the State in payment of revenue, but this practice has now ceased, and the cultivator either sells his oil-seed to Panjábi traders or expresses oil for his own consumption or for sale. There are *telis*, or professional oil-pressers, all over the valley, and they charge for their services a small amount of oil and keep the whole of the oil-cake, which they sell to the villagers for cattle-food. The oil-press is made of plane-wood, and is unlike any press which I have seen in India. It is worked by a single bullock, blindfolded, and the driver sits perched up at a great height on the beam which crushes the seed and is carried backwards. The press is fed with seed by a man who stands below. The Kashmíris say that rape-seed gives the best oil for lighting purposes, and linseed for eating, but as a matter of fact one never gets a pure oil from the press, as the various seeds are mixed by the oil-presser and further mixed with the kernels of the walnut and apricot. The natives give as a reason for mixing the various seeds in expressing the oil, that a much larger amount of oil is obtained by crushing together various sizes and kinds of seed than could be obtained from crushing separately each kind of seed. The walnut is an important oil-producer in Kashmír, but neither the walnut nor the apricot are considered good oils for lighting. Walnut oil is said to clog the throat, and does not give half the burning-power of other oil.

Cotton. *Cotton* is grown all over Kashmír up to a certain elevation, and as a rule I find that where the white rices cease to be cultivated owing to the coldness of the air, there too the cotton plant disappears. Cotton is cultivated on the karéwás and also in low-lying land which is irrigable, but requires a rest from rice. The soil should be frequently ploughed, and never less than three ploughings are given, and afterwards the clods are well pulverized by mallets. The seed is soaked in water and mixed with ashes before sowing, and beyond these ashes the plant receives no manure. Sowing takes place at the end of April and in May, and the fields are often watered at sowing-time. The supply of seed is liberal, and the Kashmíris say that one man's foot should cover at least seven seeds[1]. The cotton fields are well weeded, and worked by women with the hand hoe. The cotton plant of Kashmír is only about two feet high, and is an annual, as every year the plant rots away in the winter rains and snow. The cultivation of cotton used to be remunerative, but owing to the opening of the Jhelum valley road, and to the increased import of cotton cloth from India, the fibre is in a somewhat depressed condition. As a village staple for home use it will however live on, and the cotton spinning-wheel and the weavers' walk are familiar objects in every part of Kashmír. There are other reasons which will tend to keep up the cultivation of cotton. The villagers find that home-made cotton cloth is stronger and thicker than the cloth imported from the Panjab, and they look to the cotton plant, not only for its fibre, but for its seeds, from which they obtain oil and an excellent cattle food.

Spring crops. Barley.

Wheat and barley are the two spring crops of the valley, and of these the barley crop is the more important, if area alone be considered. The barley commonly grown in the valley is not of a good quality, and no pains are taken in its cultivation. One ploughing is given, and when the seed is sown, from October to December, the land is again ploughed. The fields are not weeded nor manured, and the barley lands of Kashmír probably have not their match for bad and slovenly cultivation in the world. It is sometimes difficult to distinguish the barley in the mass of *chirma* weed (Ranunculus sp.). The grain is not esteemed as a food, but is very often mixed by millers with wheat. In the higher villages, at an elevation of 7,000 feet, there is a peculiar kind of barley known as *grim*, or Tibet barley, which is an important food staple among the mountain people. The villagers always speak of it as bastard wheat. The grain has not the chaff scales adhering to it, but is naked like wheat. The people say that if this is cultivated at a lower altitude it takes on the type of ordinary barley. It is sown in May and June and ripens in August and September. Barley gives on an average $8\frac{1}{2}$ maunds per acre; *grim*, about 4 maunds.

Tibet barley.

Wheat.

Wheat receives better treatment than barley, but two ploughings, with

[1] In the Panjab the cultivator keeps his cotton plants wide apart, and the proverb, 'Dango dang kapah,' means that each plant should be at the distance of a long stick from its neighbour

CHAP. XIII. a covering ploughing at seed-time, are considered sufficient in Kashmír. The land is neither manured nor weeded, and as a rule no irrigation is ever given. It is sown in September and October and ripens in June. The common variety is a red wheat with a small hard grain, and the Panjábis consider Kashmír wheat-flour to be very inferior. I have, however, taken some pains to obtain clean wheat and to have it properly ground, and do not think that it is an inferior grain. I have sometimes found a small plot of a larger-grained white variety [1], introduced from the Panjáb in the great famine, but it has not succeeded in Kashmír and is not popular. We have taken as the average production of dry land 7 maunds per acre. At present it is difficult to say whether wheat or barley can ever become important staples of cultivation in Kashmír, but in spite of the uncertainty of the spring rains it is obvious that greater care in ploughing, manuring, and weeding would raise the average outturn, which is now almost exactly one-half the ordinary average obtained in India. Just as the grain of barley, and to a certain extent the grain of wheat, is looked down upon as a food by the rice-eating Kashmíris, so too the valuable straw of these cereals is neglected as a cattle-food, and it is common to see large ricks of wheat straw left to rot on the land. It is a peculiar fact that rice straw, which is used for fodder when all else fails in Northern India, is the most popular fodder in Kashmír. It may be that the high elevation of Kashmír renders the rice straw less flinty and more succulent than the rice straws of India. Wheat is liable to two diseases—one, known as *surma*, turns the grain into a black powder with an offensive smell; the other, known as *sás*, has been described under maize.

These are the chief crops of Kashmír, but it remains to describe certain special crops which are of importance and interest.

Saffron.

The *saffron* (Crocus sativus) of Kashmír is famous for its bouquet, and is in great request as a condiment and as a pigment for the *forehead marks* of the Hindus. Various substitutes, such as turmeric, are now used for the latter purpose by the Kashmiri Pandits, but if a man can afford it he will use the bright saffron colour, mixed with red lead and pounded with a piece of deodar wood. The cultivation of the saffron is peculiar, and the legend about its introduction into Kashmír shows at any rate that it is an ancient industry. In the time of king Lalta Dit there was a famous physician in Padampur, the city founded by Lalta Dit's minister, Wazir Padam. A *nág*, or water-god, fell sick of an eye complaint and went to the physician, who tried in vain to cure him. Baffled, the physician at last asked the water-god whether he was a man, and on finding out that he

[1] This white wheat never succeeded, and the Kashmíris assert that after two years' cultivation the white wheat became red.

was a *nág* he at once saw that the remedies applied to the *nág's* eyes were nullified by the poisonous vapours which issued from the water-god's mouth. He bound his eyes with a cloth and the *nág* was restored to health. In his gratitude the *nág* gave the physician a bulb of saffron, and the cultivation sprang up at Padampur, now known as Pámpur. The following facts, which I have verified on the spot, may suggest the idea that the system is unnecessarily slow and primitive, and the European methods of producing seed bulbs might increase the production of saffron in Kashmír. At present cultivation is extending as fast as the local method of seed production will allow. But that this method is slow may be inferred from the fact that at measurement of a total area of 4,527 acres of saffron land only 132 acres were actually cultivated with the crocus. In former days[1] the saffron cultivation was a large source of revenue to the State, but in the famine the people in their distress ate up the bulbs, and although seed has been imported from Kishtwár, and although every year land is set apart for the production of seed, the process of reproduction is slow. For seed purposes a particular aspect and *sloping ground* is required, and it takes three years before the bulbs can be planted out in the small square plots where the saffron is to be grown. These plots must remain fallow for eight years, and no manure can be given to them and no assistance given in the way of water. When once the bulb has been placed in the square it will live on for fourteen years without any help from the cultivator, new bulbs being produced and the old bulb rotting away. The time for planting out the bulbs is in July and August, and all that the cultivator has to do is to break up the surface gently a few times and to ensure the proper drainage of the plot by digging a neat trench on all four sides. The flowers appear about the middle of October, and the purple blooms and the delicious, though somewhat overpowering, scent of the saffron turn the dry, uninviting plateau above Pámpur into a rare and wonderful garden. Saffron is at present limited to the karéwás in the neighbourhood of Pámpur, but from inquiries I do not gather that there is any peculiar property in the Pámpur soil which does not exist in other karéwás. No one has ever confirmed the statement that the soil of the saffron fields was dug up from the Jhelum river, whereas many attest the fact that saffron has been grown on other karéwás. There is, however, no doubt that the soil above Pámpur is strong, for one sees excellent crops of wheat and barley.

Although cultivation has extended most satisfactorily during the last two years, I am afraid that the system of collection by farmers will prevent the industry from becoming popular, as during harvest-time the cultivators

[1] 'There are 10,000 or 12,000 bigahs of land covered with saffron, which . . . afford a prospect that would enchant those who are most difficult to please.'—*Aín Akbari*.

CHAP. XIII. are as carefully watched and supervised as diamond-diggers at Kimberley. In former days men came from all parts of Kashmír to cultivate saffron on the Pámpur karéwás, but now, with the exception of a few men from Srinagar, the cultivation is in the hands of local men. At harvest-time the whole flower is picked and put into bags and then taken to the farmer, who takes one bag for himself and gives the other bag to the cultivator. The bags are never opened, and it has been found by experience that the cultivator never attempts to foist a bad bag on the farmer. The cultivator then takes his bag to the left bank of the river, and makes his own arrangements for sale. When the flowers are collected the real work of extracting saffron commences. The flowers are dried in the sun, and the three long stigmata are picked out by the hand. The stigma has a red orange tip, and this tip forms the *shahi záfran*, the first quality saffron. The long white base of the stigma also makes saffron, but it is of inferior quality to the tips. The saffron thus collected in a dry condition is known to the trade as *mongla*, and fetches 1 rupee per tola. When the *mongla* saffron has been extracted the sun-dried flowers are beaten lightly with sticks and winnowed. Then the whole mass is thrown into water, when the petals swim and the essential parts of the flower sink. The parts which have sunk (*niwal*) are collected, and the parts which have risen to the top are dried and again beaten with sticks and then plunged into water. The process is repeated three times, and each time the *niwal* becomes poorer. One form of adulteration is to mix *niwal* of the third stage with *niwal* of the first process. The saffron obtained in this way is lighter in colour and of fainter scent than the *mongla*, and is known to the trade as *lacha*, and sells at 12 annas per tola. The saffron when made is sent to Amritsar and other trade centres by registered post. Another dye formerly cultivated in Kashmír was the madder (*majjit*). Up to the year S. 1923 it was largely grown in the Nagám Ilaka and at Pámpur, but apparently it was not a popular crop with the villagers. The roots from which the dye was extracted sold at 8 annas a seer. Indarkot was celebrated for its madder.

Cultivation of Dal lake.

Next to the saffron cultivation in interest come the floating gardens of the Dal lake, which resemble the 'chinampas' of old Mexico, and the whole cultivation and vegetation of the lake is full of interest and of great importance to the city people. The *rádh*, or floating gardens, are made of long strips of the lake reed, with a breadth of about six feet. These strips can be towed from place to place and are moored at the four corners by poles driven into the lake bed. When the *rádh* is sufficiently strong to bear the weight of a man heaps of weed and mud are extracted from the lake by poles, and these heaps are formed into cones and placed at intervals on the *rádh*. The cones are known as *pokar*, and each cone

PLATE XIV

To face page 345

Negative by Major Hepburn, R.A.

SHOWS THE FLOATING CULTIVATION OF THE DÁL LAKE. THE FLOATING RAFTS ARE MOORED BY POLES

accommodates two seedlings of melons or tomatoes, or four seedlings of water-melons or cucumbers. Everything that plant life requires is present. A rich soil and ample moisture, with the summer sun of Kashmír, help to produce vegetables in surprising abundance and of excellent quality. It is not an uncommon thing to gather thirty full-sized fruits from every plant, or from ninety to one hundred fruits from each receptacle. Not behind the floating gardens in fertility are the *demb* lands, which are formed along the sides and sometimes in the middle of the lake when the water is shallow. The cultivator selects his site, and plants willows and sometimes poplars along its four sides. Inside these willows he casts boat-loads of weed and mud until his land is above the flood level, and year by year he adds a new dressing of the rich lake weed and mud. Around the *demb* plot run little water-channels from the lake, so that moisture is always present, and on the *demb* a great variety of crops is raised. Rape-seed, maize, tobacco, melons and other cucurbitaceae, potatoes, onions, radishes, turnips, egg-plants, white beans, peaches, apricots, and quinces flourish on this rich soil, and if it were not for the constant liability to forced labour, and to the curious system under which revenue is collected daily from the half-amphibious dwellers on the Dal lake, the cultivators of the *demb* lands might have been the most prosperous people in Asia. The *demb* system is of importance, as it is not confined to the Dal lake, and all over Kashmír the people who live by the great swamps have begun to construct these curious oblong patches.

Wild products of the Dal lake.

But apart from the splendid produce of the *rádh* and *demb* lands, the cultivators of the Dal lake—the Mirbahri people, as they are called in Kashmír—have other sources of food which the lake yields them free of labour. The *singhara* nut affords an easy meal which is not to be despised; the *jewar* (Euryale ferox) gives a pleasant seed which is eaten raw or parched; the *bumbh*, with its long stem and white flower, provides a nourishing vegetable from the former and an agreeable *sharbat* from the latter; and then the glory of the lake, the noble pink lily, yields a sweet nut, and a warm, savoury vegetable in its leaf-stem, white, succulent. Lastly, and perhaps most useful of all, is the *pits*, the rush from which the matting of Kashmír is made; and this too gives a dainty food, known as the lake sweetmeat, which is made from a powder collected from the young rushes in the spring and boiled into the consistency of cheese. The roots, too, of the lake rush are eaten.

Tobacco.

Tobacco is cultivated in many parts of Kashmír, but it is chiefly grown in and around Srinagar and the smaller towns. The ordinary cultivator does not grow the plant, and it is almost entirely in the hands of the gardener class which exists in the city and the towns. The plant yielding the most esteemed tobacco grows in one part of Srinagar, and is known as

CHAP. XIII.

brewari (Nicotiana tabacum). It has pinkish flowers, and its product is of a bright yellow colour, and is extremely mild and less pungent than the *chilási* variety, which was introduced from the Panjáb. The *chilási* is Nicotiana rustica, a plant with green flowers. Tobacco is sown in April and is picked about the end of August. It requires very rich soil and is irrigated by the dip-wells of the country. Formerly the State took tobacco as revenue, and allowed a high commutation rate for the crop, but of late years tobacco is not accepted in payment of revenue, and my impression is that the cultivation of the plant is not increasing. The use of tobacco in Kashmír passed out of fashion at the great famine, and the narcotic is now chiefly taken in the form of snuff, which is imported from Peshāwar.

In the same rich land, black with *poudrette*, which the gardener class of the city and towns cultivate so carefully and well, the opium poppy is raised, and its dried capsules are used in medicine. *Ajwain* and *kalazíra* (Carum sp.) are both garden spring crops cultivated for local use as condiments for improving the condition of horses and other cattle. They are largely exported to India, Ladákh, and Afghanistan.

Vegetables.

Vegetables[1] are of great importance in Kashmír, and every villager has his small garden plot, where he raises a wealth of food with very small effort. In the neighbourhood of Srinagar some care is taken in the selection of seed, and the villager often buys his seed from the city; but in the remote corners of the valley very little attention is paid to garden cultivation, and the vegetables are poor, fibrous, and small. Though I have advanced the opinion that the Kashmíri has little to learn in the way of rice cultivation, I think that he has a great deal to learn as a grower of vegetables, and I look forward to the time when every village will purchase good seed and raise really good garden crops, and anticipate that Kashmír, like Afghanistan, will some day export seed to India.

[1] English Name.	Botanical Name.	Kashmíri Name.
Knol-kohl	Brassica oleracea, var. caulo-rapa	*Karm ság, karm hak*, or *kremi hák.*
Turnip	„ campestris, sub sp. rapa	*Gogji.*
Pumpkin (vegetable marrow)	Cucurbita Pepo	*Al.*
Cucumber	Cucumis sativus	*Lár.*
Tomato	Solanum lycopersicum	*Rudngan.*
Chili	Capsicum sp.	*Mirtswángan.*
Egg-plant	Solanum Melongena	*Wángan.*
Potato	„ tuberosum	*Alú.*
Asparagus	Asparagus officinalis.	
White bean	Phaseolus vulgaris (?)	*Rázmah.*
Endive	Cichorium Endivia.	
Lettuce	Lactuca sativa.	
Carrot	Daucus Carota	*Gázar.*
Onion	Allium sp.	*Prán.*

The national vegetable is the knol-kohl. It is a hardy plant, and in years of favourable rains large crops are raised without much labour. The green variety is the common one in Kashmír, and in the summer the leaves are eaten as spinach, while the root is kept for the winter. I have given out seeds of the purple variety and the villagers appreciate the plant. Next in importance is the turnip, which is largely cultivated. The root is cut into slices and dried for the winter. Vegetable marrows abound, and they too are dried in the sun and festooned on ropes for winter use. They are grown in raised cones of earth, through which the air passes easily to the roots. Tomatoes are a popular vegetable, but the plant is allowed to lie on the ground, and the fruit is small and ugly. It is cut into rings and dried in the sun for winter use. Chilies are chiefly grown by the regular gardening cultivators, and very large crops are raised in the neighbourhood of the city and the towns. Cucumbers of a large size are grown in abundance on the Dal lake, but they are not common in the districts. The egg-plant is well known in the valley, and last, but not least, the potato is gradually extending. On the hill slopes of the Trahal Ilaka, in Naubug and in one or two other places, excellent potatoes are raised, and now that the old fear that anything good would either be seized or would lead to an enhancement of revenue is passing away, I hope that they will be a common crop throughout the valley. The soil of the valley is well drained, friable, and loamy, and every condition requisite to successful potato cultivation is present. My inquiries lead me to believe that the Kashmíri knows nothing about the necessity for a change of seed and of soil for potatoes, and when the plant is grown in the vicinity of the city and the towns the tubers are very small. Nature is so bountiful to the Kashmíri that he cares little for vegetables in the spring or the summer, and his one idea is to grow something that will last him through the winter. His system of drying vegetables is simple and fairly effective, though the dried tomato in mid-winter has little but its colour to remind one of what it once was. Still, with oil, pepper, and salt it is not unpalatable, and I do not think the Kashmíri cares much about delicate flavours provided the food be filling.

Wild herbs.

It would be wearisome to enumerate the various herbs which the Kashmíris eat as vegetables in the spring and summer; thistles, nettles, the wild chicory, the dandelion—in fact, every plant which is not poisonous goes into the cooking-pot, and even the stalk of the walnut catkin is not despised. In the hills a dainty dish of the wild asparagus can be easily obtained, and the wild rhubarb cooked in honey has its charms. When one hears of the old saints of Kashmír who lived on the wild *wopal hák* (Dipsacus inermis) and the herbs of the forest, one need not picture an emaciated ascetic, for a man could live and live well on nature's products in Kashmír.

CHAP. XIII.

Fruits.

Kashmír is a country of fruits [1], and perhaps no country has greater facilities for horticulture, as the indigenous apple, pear, vine, mulberry, walnut, hazel, cherry, peach, apricot, raspberry, gooseberry, currant, and strawberry can be obtained without difficulty in most parts of the valley. The fruits of Kashmír are a great help to the people as a food, and they come in a pleasant and changing succession. When the first days of summer arrive the mulberry trees are surrounded by villagers with their outspread blankets, and cattle, ponies, and dogs, who all munch the sweet black or white fruit. There are grafted varieties, the best of which is *shah tút*, purple and juicy, and much esteemed as a preserve. With an eye to the winter the provident Kashmíri stores away the mulberries which he cannot eat, and they retain their sweetness long. The apricot ripens next, and they too are quickly eaten or stored away for the winter, but the Kashmíri looks on the apricot as intended to give oil rather than fruit. This fruit is used too by the silversmith for cleaning his metal, and by dyers as an astringent. The cherry is usually of the black morella variety, sour in taste, yet appreciated by the people, but in places the delicious whiteheart (an introduction from Europe via Arabia, Persia, and Afghanistan) is cultivated. Its Kashmíri name, *gilas*, is a corruption of Cerasus. People say that it is indigenous, and I have found it in places where one might almost imagine it was self-grown. The wild plums are excellent, and the cultivated plums are often very fine. The peach that has extended its area from cultivation is small but refreshing, and a wild raspberry is to my mind as good and as delicate in flavour as the cultivated raspberry of England. The gooseberry is small and flavourless, but the wild strawberry and black currant are excellent. Later in the season come the apples, pears, and walnuts, and as I believe that there is a great future

[1] English Name.	Botanical Name.	Kashmíri Name.
*Mulberry	Morus sp.	*Tul.*
†Apricot	Prunus Armeniaca	*Tser.*
Cherry	„ Cerasus.	
Sweet cherry	„ „ var. a.	*Gilás.*
*Bitter cherry	„ „ var. b.	*Aluchá.*
*Plum	„ communis	*Alúbukhárá* or *Ar.*
†Peach	„ Persica	*Tsunnan.*
Almond	„ Amygdalus	*Badám.*
*Apple	Pyrus Malus	*Tsunt.*
*Pear	„ communis	*Tang.*
Quince	„ Cydonia	*Bam Tsunt.*
*Vine	Vitis vinifera	*Dach.*
*Walnut	Juglans regia	*Dun.*
Melon	Cucumis Melo	*Kharbuz.*
Water-melon	Citrullus vulgaris	*Hindwand.*
*Pomegranate	Punica Granatum	*Dán.*

Of the above, those marked * are indigenous to the country; those marked † have spread from cultivation.

before Kashmír as a fruit-producing country, I shall deal with the subject of apples and pears at some length. The wild apple and pear can be obtained with ease from the forests on the slope of the hills surrounding the valley, and the Kashmíris have for generations brought down the wild stock from the hills and planted it in orchards. Their rule is to bring down trees of a good height and girth, and they plant them in the spring. In the State nursery we bring in young small trees with good roots, and always plant them before the winter snows arrive. Very little trouble is taken to ensure that the wild stock has good roots, and if half the orchard fails the Kashmíri is not surprised. The year after the wild stock is planted in the orchard, the tree is either grafted in the spring or budded later on, in July and August. The system of grafting is simple and on the whole effective. Three or four scions are affixed to the wild stock and clamped to it in mud wrapped around with birch bark. The mud is watered when the season is dry. The system of budding is also simple. The peel of the apple or pear which is to be reproduced is slipped off the young green shoot bearing a leaf and bud and is put into a saucer containing milk. This saucer is taken into the orchard of wild stock, and a shoot of the wild tree is stripped of its green bark and the new bud is slipped on to the wild stock. It is not tied by string, but it is left to take its chance, and the villagers say that the percentage of failures is small.

Apples.

The most popular apple in Kashmír is the *anbru* or *amri*, which has a large round red and white sweet fruit, ripening in October and keeping its condition for a long time. This is the apple which is exported in large quantities, and it finds favour with the natives of India for its sweetness and its handsome appearance. To an English taste it would seem woolly and flavourless. The *mohi amri* is like the *amri*, but is more acid and redder. It is largely exported. The *kuddu sari* apple is said to have been introduced from Kabul. It is in shape long, and is juicy and rather acid, ripening early and not keeping. But in my opinion the best of the Kashmír apples, so far as flavour goes, is the little *trel*[1], which abounds in the neighbourhood of Sopur. There are three common kinds—the *nabádi trel*, which is yellow; the *jambási trel*, which turns red; and the *sil trel*, which is rather larger than the *nabádi* and *jambási* and is of a deep red colour. When ripe these little apples have the most delicious taste, half sour, half sweet, and when they rot they are exactly like the medlar in flavour. From this apple, when picked at the right time, excellent cider has been made. A superior variety of the *trel* is the *khatoni trel*, which is larger, but possesses all the flavour of the smaller kind. There are many other varieties of apples, but the Kashmíri would give the palm to the *dud*

[1] The *lalbugi trel* is of a pale yellow colour and sweet. The *batpuri trel* is the wild *trel*.

CHAP. XIII. *amri*[1], which is the sweetest and finest of the *amri* kind. Many of the wild apples, e.g. the *tet shakr* and *malmu*, are very refreshing, and it is a curious fact that the greater part of the Kashmír orchards consist entirely of wild trees. About the beginning of September the people pick the wild apples and the *trel* apples, and, having cut them in half, dry them in the sun. These primitive pippins are very palatable and are eaten boiled up with the flour of amaranth.

The Kashmíris are conservative as regards their apples, and when I first came to the country they maintained that their methods of grafting and budding were the best, and that the *amri* apple was as good an apple as any in the world. It was sweet and would carry, and as a ready sale for the *amri* could be found in the Panjáb it seemed to the villagers absurd to introduce other kinds. But I took out into camp two men skilled in budding, and by degrees I overcame the prejudices of the people. They saw that the European method of budding was neater and safer than their own, and they admitted that our grafting material—pitch, mutton fat, and ashes—was more effective than their mud and birch bark. We have given out thousands of grafted trees from the State nurseries on the shores of the Dal lake, and we now have established orchards of good English and French apples in every corner of the valley. There is scarcely a nook in Kashmír where fruit-trees cannot be grown, and even on the dry plateau above Islamabád there is a nice orchard of French peaches sent out from the Dal lake nursery. Irrigation is not necessary, but pruning and fencing are necessities, and it is difficult to induce the Kashmíris to prune their trees or to keep cattle out of the orchards. The best horticulturists are the more affluent *lambardárs*, who are beginning to pride themselves on establishing orchards with high mud walls. Kuddus Mír of Rájpura has an excellent orchard, and many other *lambardárs* are following his example. But they like height in a tree and they do not yet believe in pruning back, and it will be years before they will manure their orchards or adopt any system of root-pruning.

Pears.

The pear[2] is as yet of secondary importance in Kashmír, as it does not form a large article of export. But there are several very good pears cultivated in the valley, the best of which are the *nák satarwati*, which has a beautiful shape and a sweet juicy flesh, and the *nák guldbi*, which

[1] The *dud amri* or *Samarkhand* ripens early and will not stand exportation. The *malmu* is a round, green, acid apple, will keep when dried, and is a good fruit for cooking. The *tet shakr* is acid in flavour.

[2] The *nak* is a large pear, gathered late in September, and keeps till the tree blossoms again in the spring. It is exported. The *gosh bág* is very sweet, but will not keep. The *harnak* is an early pear, ripening almost with the mulberries. The *waplnu* is a large pear, much used in the manufacture of brandy, and exported in a dry state to the Panjab. It is said to possess medical properties. Other varieties are the *kotenal*, *sirkatang*, *mamatang*, and the *jajiri tang*.

has a pretty red skin and is a very pleasant fruit. The Kashmíris, though they think it essential to peel an apple, never peel pears. They also hold that it is dangerous to eat pears in the winter. Cold in the head and the eyes is the result of such indulgence. The early pear of Kashmír is known as the *gosh búg* and is very refreshing, and the later fruit is called *tang*. None of these pears will keep for long, and late pears are required. From the State nurseries a splendid French pear has been sent out all over the valley, but unless these pears are most carefully packed and quickly transported they cannot reach India. The wild pear is found all over the valley, and it very often resembles the perry pear of Herefordshire. Besides the wild stock we have in quince cuttings an easy means of reproducing good varieties of English pears, and it is found that quince cuttings will flourish in damp soil unsuited to the wild pear.

Quinces.

The quinces, sour and sweet, are famous, and in the gardens of the Dal lake splendid specimens of this fruit are to be seen. The tree is grown for its seed, which is exported to the Panjáb. Pomegranates are common, but are not of any especial merit.

Pomegranates.

Grapes.

In old days Kashmír was celebrated for its grapes[1], but now, if a few vineyards at the mouth of the Sind valley be excluded, it is difficult to obtain a good dessert grape in the country. Everywhere one sees giant vines climbing up poplars and other trees, but they are often wild, and their fruit is poor and tasteless. The people say that they cut down their good vines in order to avoid the exactions of officials. The grapes, white and red, from the State vineyard at Raipur in the Sind valley are delicious, and efforts are being made to reproduce the Raipur vines in other parts of the valley. With the decline of the eating grape there has been an attempt to introduce the wine grape, and at present there are 389 acres of vineyards on the shore of the Dal lake. The vines were introduced from the Bordeaux district in Mahárájá Ranbir Singh's time, and no expense was spared to make the scheme a success. Perhaps the vines of Burgundy would have been more suitable to Kashmír. Costly distillery plant was imported and set up at Gupkar on the Dal lake, and wines of the Medoc and Barsac varieties, sometimes good, sometimes bad, have been manufactured year by year. But in spite of lavish expenditure the vineyards did not seem to flourish, and in 1890 it was evident that the vines were suffering from Phylloxera. American vines were at once imported, and are now gradually replacing the unhealthy Bordeaux plants. The vineyards are under the charge of an Italian, Signor Benvenuti, and the wine manufactory is worked

Wine grapes.

[1] Grapes were more plentiful in Akbar's time than they are now. 'In Kashmír 8 seers of grapes are bought for 1 dam, and the expense of transporting a maund is 2 rupees: the Kashmírians bring them on their backs in long baskets.'—*Ain Akbari*. A dam was one-fortieth of a rupee.

CHAP. XIII. by another Italian, Signor Bassi. Besides the Medoc and Barsac which are made at Gupkar, a large amount of apple brandy is distilled and finds a ready sale. It is rash to pronounce any opinion on the future of the wine trade of Kashmír. The vineyards are under the direct management of the State, and in spite of supervision the vines do not receive the sedulous cultivation which alone can give success. The cultivators of the country have not taken up viticulture, and although Rájá Sir Amar Singh, K.C.S.I., and Diwán Amar Nath maintain vineyards and send their produce to the wine factory, I do not think that the wine industry of Kashmír will ever attain real importance until the villagers engage in vine-growing. The only market at present for the wines is Srinagar, as the long road carriage and the duties levied at the frontier make it difficult to land Kashmír wine in India at a moderate price; and, briefly, the business in present circumstances does not pay.

Hops. But hops[1], also introduced by Mahárájá Ranbir Singh, do pay, and the hop-garden at Dubgam below Sopur has within the last few years been reclaimed from the wilderness into which it had passed and yields a handsome return to the State. Eighty-three acres were under hops in 1893, and the outturn amounted to 250 maunds. The soil of Dubgam is in no way superior to that of the country surrounding it, and there is nothing to prevent a large extension of the area now under hops. But as in the case of wine grapes so in the case of hops; the people have not taken up hop cultivation, and until some of the few wealthy landowners in Kashmír turn their attention to this most safe and profitable enterprise hop cultivation will remain in the hands of the State.

Walnuts. The walnut tree is indigenous to the country, and is known by the vernacular name *vont dun* (hard walnut), as under ordinary circumstances one is unable to break the shell. The fruit is useless, but the bark (*dandarsa*) used to be a large export to the Panjáb. The fruit of the cultivated tree is an important aid to the villager when the time comes to pay the revenue, and it is remarkable that the people seem to be somewhat indifferent to its reproduction. The tree is found all over the valley from an elevation of about 5,500 feet to 7,500 feet. The tree is propagated from seed, and although grafting is not uncommon, the general idea seems to be that the three varieties, the *kagazi*, the *burzal*, and the *wantu*, reproduce themselves from seed. I have asked why, if this is so, the people do not sow the *kagazi*, which has a shell like paper and a large excellent kernel, and commands as a nut a far higher price than the *burzal* or *wantu*. The answer is that hitherto walnuts have been grown for oil and not for eating,

[1] Hops were first introduced into Kashmír and Ladákh by Major Montgomery, of the Trigonometrical Survey, but not on any scale—merely as an experiment whether they would grow. These plants existed both in Srinagar and at Leh in 1872.

and that the *wantu*, in spite of its thick hard shell, is the largest fruiter and gives the most oil. The *burzal* stands halfway between the *kagazi* and the *wantu*, and is like the ordinary walnut of England. Some of the trees reach an enormous size, and the finest specimens are to be found as one ascends the mountain valleys. They give a pleasant shade, and when the time of fruit comes they are the resort of the black bear, which betrays its presence by the noisy manner in which it cracks the nuts. Up to the present the State has accepted walnut oil in payment of revenue, and it was more profitable to the villager to pay walnut oil as revenue than to sell the nuts to Panjabi traders [1]. In future no oil will be taken as revenue, and the export of walnuts is rapidly increasing. The Kashmíris do not care for the nut as a food, as it is heating, but it always forms part of the new year's presents among Hindús and Musalmáns. Not long ago the walnuts of Kashmír were exposed to a very serious danger. In Paris there was a demand for the huge warts which grow on the walnut stem, the wood of which is used by cabinet-makers for veneer work, and a Frenchman obtained from the State the right to saw off these warts. He found that in the south of the valley the warts were dark and valuable, but that in the north the wood was white and useless. Countless trees were destroyed, for life went with the wart. Another danger to which walnuts, like other fruit trees, are exposed is the occurrence of the *kut kushu*, an icy mist which settles over the valley in severe winters and freezes out the life of trees. The walnut may not be felled except with the permission of the State, and my impression is that walnut-planting will before long set in with activity, as many of the older trees are showing signs of decay. This year (1894) I have at last succeeded in inducing the villagers to sow walnuts, and in every village seed has been sown. Seeds

[1] '*Walnuts* form an important feature of the revenue of this tahsíl, and nearly every village pays something to the State on account of its walnuts. No care is bestowed on the cultivation of walnuts, and though the *kaghazi* walnuts find a ready market with the Panjab traders no effort is made to propagate the *kaghazi* variety. Similarly there is a great difference between the *wantu* and *burzal*; the latter has a thin shell and a large kernel. But the villagers are just as likely to plant a *wantu* as a *burzal* tree. According to the people a walnut tree commences to give fruit eight years after sowing, and it comes to maturity within fourteen years. A good tree will yield 4 traks of oil. To make 1 trak of oil 2 traks 3 manwatas of kernel (*goji*) without shell (*kandi*) are required. The assessment of walnuts was based on the assumption that the State would take three-quarters and the cultivator one-quarter of the produce. In the tahsils in which the new assessment has been introduced no walnut oil has been received as revenue, and no objection has been raised by the people to this change. But in Dachanpara the people urge that it was a great advantage to them to pay a part of their revenue in walnut oil, for which they receive a commutation rate of Rs. 2.2.0 per trak. They say that if they try to sell their walnut oil in the market the traders beat down prices, and will not give anything near Rs. 2.2.0 per trak. There is, no doubt, some truth in this, but it must be remembered that an increasing demand is springing up for walnuts, and that the people will be able to dispose of their walnuts at fair prices to the Panjab traders.'—*Dachanpara Tahsil*, para. 2.

CHAP. XIII. must be collected in the *gata pach*, the two dark weeks, and must be kept in a dry place till the day of Shevratri (March). They are then put into water and kept immersed for ten days. Sown in March the seed germinates in May. After two years the young trees are planted out. It is calculated that a walnut tree will yield half its bearing capacity in six years from sowing, and will be in full bearing in ten years. The system of picking the nuts is careless, and sticks and stones do much injury to the branches, though the mutilation of the tree may be justified on the English proverb which prescribes beating for a wife, a spaniel, and a walnut tree. It is a curious fact that I have seen many trees after the picking season with a quantity of nuts on them, and on inquiry have found that some villager had lost his life by falling from the tree in the previous year, and all were afraid to climb the fatal walnut. The tree is a capricious bearer, and two or three years of an excellent crop may be followed by two or three years of no fruit. The timber of the older trees is hard and of a darkish handsome grain. It is much in request for furniture and gunstocks.

Almonds.

There are large almond orchards scattered over the valley, and many of the hill-sides might easily be planted with this hardy and profitable tree. It is a somewhat uncertain crop, but very little attention is paid to its cultivation, and as a rule the almond orchards are unfenced. There are two kinds, the sweet and the bitter, and the former is worth double the latter in the market. Ruined almond gardens in all parts of the valley attest the fact that the State cannot succeed in horticulture. It is easy to give an order to plant a thousand orchards, but the almond gardens were not fenced in, and the trees were destroyed by cattle. Where private persons have planted almonds the results are very different. The same failure attended the efforts of the State to plant vines and to extend opium cultivation. No power in the world can coerce the Kashmíris into what they regard as fanciful cultivation.

Water-chestnut.

In another chapter I have attempted to enumerate some of the wild plants which are of economic value, but must include under the heading of agriculture the useful singhára, which gives an excellent food from its kernel and a welcome fuel from its shells. There are several varieties of the singhára, but all seem to have white flowers floating on the surface of the water on stems supported by air vessels. When the fruit ripens the nuts sink to the bottom of the lake. The singhára is found on the Dal lake and in other localities, but its home is the Wular lake. Of the chief varieties the best is called *basmati*, in honour of the rice of that name. The *basmati* is a small nut with a thin skin, and gives one-third of kernel for two-thirds of shell. The *dogru* is a larger nut with a thicker shell, and the *kangar* has a very thick shell with long projecting horns, and gives the least kernel of all. Attempts have been made to propagate the *basmati*, but it is found that after one year the inferior varieties assert themselves. The nuts are gathered in a very simple way. A boat is moored to a pole on the singhára ground, and two men rake the bottom of the lake with long poles to which are attached crescent-shaped *hoes*. They work in a circle around the pole by which the boat is moored, and scrape up a heap of nuts and mud. The mud is then beaten with a pole (*chokdan*), and a net (*khushabu*) is put down and the nuts are dragged into the boat. A good day's work will bring in about three maunds of nuts. The kernel is extracted by cutting the shells, and the shells are used for fuel. On and around the Wular lake an enormous weight of the water-chestnut is gathered year by year, and in the vicinity of the lake, wherever there is standing water, the singhára is found. From October to April, when the water is low, the waterside people are busy loading their small boats with the bountiful produce of the lake. Heavy floods and a high river usually mean a large crop, and in good years over 100,000[1] maunds of nuts are gathered. The kernel, which is white and mealy, is either ground into flour or parched and eaten as porridge and gruel, and one pound of kernel is sufficient for a day's food. It is not unpleasant to taste, and must be fairly nutritious, as many of the dwellers of the '*mahal singhára*,' or the villages whose only fields are the wide waters of the Wular lake, live entirely on the water-chestnut. The northern portion of the lake has always been '*Dharm*,' and every one and any one can gather the green singhára north of a line drawn from the promontory of Shukruddin to Garura. But when the nut ripens and sinks to the bed of the lake no one may touch it, as it is required for next year's seed.

Conclusion. To conclude, it may be said that almost all the vegetable products that exist in a temperate climate can be grown in the vale of Kashmír. As confidence springs up in the valley, and the cultivators find that land can be farmed for profit as well as for the bare means of existence, I believe that new staples can be successfully introduced. Oats have been cultivated with fair results, potatoes can be greatly extended, hops are an established success, all kinds of most delicate fruits and vegetables are raised, such as pears, peaches, apricots, greengages, and asparagus, and only await the advent of the canning industry to become famous, and there is no reason, except perhaps the dryness of the Kashmír climate, which would prevent the growth of beetroot for sugar. Excellent beetroot is already grown

[1] Moorcroft states that when he visited Kashmír, the Government was said to receive annually 96,000 kharwars of singhára nut. This would imply a total production of 384,000 maunds of nut. There is no doubt that the production of singhára has fallen off, and the people prefer agriculture. Many places in which singhára nuts used to be collected in large quantities are never resorted to now. In years like 1893, when the floods destroy the maize and other crops, the people turn their attention to the singhára nut, but in ordinary years I believe that the actual weight of nuts collected would not exceed 100,000 maunds.

CHAP. XIII. in the gardens of Europeans in Srinagar, and I have not been able to ascertain clearly whether a former attempt to cultivate beetroot as a field crop failed from climatic reasons or from neglect. Considering the demand for sugar in Kashmír, and its costliness, I should imagine that if capital and ability were forthcoming it would be worth while to attempt the cultivation of beetroot for sugar. And there can be no doubt that there are many parts of Kashmír in which the sugar maple could be introduced with success. Spanish chestnuts have been imported from Europe, but it is as yet too early to say whether they will form one of the food-products of Kashmír. The experience of the past clearly shows that no new staple will succeed unless the villagers take it up of their own accord, and the function of the State should be limited to the maintenance of a good botanical garden and an experimental farm. Neglected orchards, tumbled-down silk-houses in Kashmír, and ruined tea-gardens and indigo factories in Jammu, attest the hopelessness of schemes of merit and enterprise which were kept under the management of State officials. As regards existing cultivation in Kashmír, I believe that agriculture will improve rapidly as population increases. At present, owing to the large size of the holdings, the land is working at half pressure. The conditions of wheat, barley, and linseed are as bad as they can be, and with some expenditure of labour the outturn of these crops could be doubled. The land is never properly ploughed or manured and never weeded, and the fields are choked with wild indigo and other plants. As an instance of what dry land can do, I would mention the village of Lattapur near Pampur. There the soil receives five ploughings, the wheat crop is excellent and rarely fails. The land is always ploughed up after harvest. The introduction of seed drills would prove a great economy, and some form of wheeled carriage for the transport of the harvest and of manure would set free labour for other agricultural operations. Next it is quite possible that in many parts of Kashmír the cultivators will adopt a system of double cropping. This succeeded in 1892–3 in certain villages. In such directions the Kashmíri has many things to learn, but in the cultivation of the great staple rice it would be difficult to teach him much. The only suggestion which I have thought fit to make is that the rice fields, which are moist and soft when the crop is cut, should be at once ploughed up and exposed to the sun, air, frost, and snow, and I have urged that the plough-cattle are idle and in good condition at harvest-time, whereas they are thin and poor after the long winter; but the Kashmíri assures me that it is wiser to leave the fields alone until the spring, and that if they adopted my suggestions the labour of weeding would be doubled. He is probably right. As population increases, attention will be directed to the cultivation of the large *karéwa* lands and to the reclamation of the swamps. I have urged on the State the advisability of constructing earthen ridges along the edges of the karéwa. At present every heavy fall of rain washes away the surface soil of the karéwa, and I feel certain that if this were prevented, and if trees were planted on the edges of the karéwa, there would be a great improvement in the condition of the soil. As regards the swamps I believe that with capital an enormous area of rich peaty soil, excellent for maize and rape-seed, could be reclaimed, and I look forward to the time when steam pumps fed with peat will be at work. Irrigation can be greatly extended, and when the Sind and Liddar rivers have been forced to perform the irrigation work which can so easily be done, attention should be paid to the Jhelum itself as a source of irrigation. With the swamps to be drained, and the karéwa lands to be irrigated by channels and wells, there is a great future for agriculture in Kashmír, but the State should spend no money on such schemes until other available land has been taken up. This is now only a question of a few years.

CHAPTER XIV.

LIVE STOCK.

Chap. XIV.

Cattle.

The cattle of Kashmír are small but hardy, and for their size they do a fair tale of work. They are rather bigger than the Brittany cattle, have humps, and their prevailing colour is black or grey. In most villages cattle-breeding is carried on, but the Kashmíris as a rule do not pay any attention to the selection of sires. The *shir gujri*, or milksellers, have cows with a strain of Panjab blood, and gradually the *shir gujri* bulls are making their mark in the country. In the tracts around the Wular lake and in the north-west of the valley the cattle are distinctly finer than in the south, and I attribute this to the presence of the Panjab blood, known in Kashmír as *parimgao*. I measured some bullocks in the north-west of the valley. Two which I selected as average specimens of the bullocks employed in the hop-gardens weighed respectively 35 and 31 stone. Two average bullocks belonging to villagers weighed 22 and 22½ stone.

The Kashmír cattle are conservative in their habits. Thus a bullock bred in the low lands around the Wular lake will fall off in condition if taken to the higher villages, and the *Kandi* bullock bred in the hilly tracts will be of no use in the plains.

As summer approaches all the cattle save the requisite plough bullocks and the cows in milk are driven away to the high mountains, where they obtain excellent grazing, returning in the autumn to the stubbles. The Kashmíri will never use his plough bullocks for carriage, and while the harvest is being reaped and carried the bullocks stand by idle. The Kashmíri says that the bullocks must have rest, and that their feet split after working in the wet slush of the rice fields.

Every effort is made to collect fodder for the winter. Rice and maize straw is the chief fodder, but a large quantity of hay is also laid by. In the rice villages the boundaries of the fields give a grand crop of hay, which is carefully cut, dried, and twisted into ropes. These ropes are suspended from trees and remain dry and uninjured by the winter snows and rains. In

PLATE XV

To face page 358 [Negative by Alam Chand, G.C

AN ORDINARY PAIR OF PLOUGH BULLOCKS YOKED TO A CLOD-CRUSHER (MAJ)

the higher villages hay is made in the English fashion, and it remains sweet and fragrant. The best grasses are the *beran*, *jab*, *batakluit* (clover), and *methi*. Besides the grasses the leaves of many trees are carefully collected. The mountain willow and poplar, the cotoneaster and the hawthorn, all yield a valuable fodder, and as autumn draws on the trees of Kashmír wear a very maimed and desolate appearance. In the winter the plough bullocks and milch cows are given a little oilcake and cotton-seed, but the other cattle fare badly, and emerge in the spring from their hot, dark byres beneath their master's house, looking poor and thin. The Kashmíri certainly recognizes the fact that heat is food, but he is careless about ventilation. Plough bullocks have risen and are rising in price. A pair of ordinary plough bullocks can be bought for Rs. 25, and will begin hard regular work at the age of five. An average bullock will do good work for eight years, but diseases are prevalent, and a form of diarrhoea is very fatal.

The ordinary cow of the villagers is not a good milch animal, and a cow that gives 4 seers of milk a day is regarded as a treasure. The *shir gujri* of the city and the villages obtain better results, and by judicious feeding, and still more by judicious breeding, they have now cows which will yield 8 seers of milk per diem.

In the summer the swamp grass *nari*, and *khur*, are excellent fodder for milch cattle, and in the winter rice straw and rice husk mixed with starchy rice water are said to increase the yield of milk. Of course the Kashmíri has many proverbs about his cattle. One warns a man to try a plough bullock and to milk a cow before concluding his purchase—'Dánd wáyit gao chawit.' Another notices that a cow which lows loudly or has large udders rarely gives much milk.

Cows, like plough bullocks, have risen in price. Not many years ago a cow giving 4 seers of milk could be bought for Rs. 8; now it would be difficult to obtain such a cow for Rs. 15. Dairymen (*shir gujri*) pay a tax of 10 annas for every cow over three years of age.

Buffaloes.

Kashmír produces a large quantity of ghi (Kashmíri *rogan*), and though cows and goats furnish a part of this 'butter of India,' the great proportion of ghi is made from the milk of the buffalo. It has been the policy of the rulers of Kashmír to encourage the Gujars to take up their abode in the valley. Exemption from forced labour and an assessment in cash have induced these nomads to settle down, and all around the valley on the fringe of the forest the flat-topped Gujars' huts, hidden in maize crops, may be seen. The Gujar cares little for his hut or his fields. He calls himself the lord of the forests, and directly the snows have melted on the high mountains he and his family, putting on their best clothes, hurry off with the buffaloes to the heights. There they live a healthy gipsy life in

CHAP. XIV. wigwams, and make butter. This butter is bought up by Panjab traders, who convert the butter into ghi. In the summer months, when the grass is rich, 40 seers of butter will yield 32 seers of ghi. The middleman, of course, makes all the profit, and he increases his ghi by adulteration. Into 8 seers of ghi he will put 2 seers of walnut oil, but as walnut oil is now rising in price this form of adulteration will possibly cease. When the middleman receives the butter from the Gujar he salts it, and sometimes keeps it two months before he makes it into ghi. All Gujars are slaves of the middleman, by virtue of the *rekh*, or system of advances. I have often urged the Gujars to set themselves free and to participate in the rise in the price of ghi, but the Kashmíri Gujar is as stupid and slow as his friend and companion the buffalo. It is touching to notice how absolutely bound up in his buffalo the Gujar is. He thinks of nothing else and cares for nothing else.

Buffaloes give calves at five years, and after calving will yield milk for eighteen months. A buffalo will continue to give milk till she is fifteen years old.

For each buffalo giving milk a tax, known as *shákh shumári*, of Rs. 1.4.0 per annum is charged. Such a buffalo is known as *mesh*.

A barren buffalo (*phandri*) pays one-half of the tax, while a *naushikam*, or buffalo with her first calf, is exempt. A young heifer is known as *kati*, and the bull is called *jámús*. It is the custom to kill all the male calves of the herd except the one reserved for breeding purposes, and by this system of selection the breed of buffaloes in Kashmír is strong and fine. Opinions differ about the quality of the ghi of Kashmír, but good judges have told me that it is excellent. The most delicate ghi is made from cows' milk; buffalo ghi ranks next, while the ghi of goats, clear though it is in colour, is rank in taste.

The Gujars and the Patháns of the Loláb make a kind of cheese which they call milk-bread. Two English ladies have made cheeses for sale, and many people like them. There is little doubt that if an experienced cheese-maker with a little capital took up the business he would succeed. There is enough milk in the valley to supply all the garrisons of Upper India with cheese and butter.

Sheep. The sheep of Kashmír are numerous and of great importance to the villagers. They supply warmth, clothing, and manure. Like the pig in Ireland, they very often pay the rent, when they are sold to the city butchers for mutton. But the Kashmíri regards his sheep up to the age of four years as destined for wool-production, and it is only in time of dire necessity or on occasions of rejoicing that he will part with his ewes. Ewes drop their lambs in spring and in late autumn, but the spring lambs are the strongest, for they get the best food. Ewes commence lambing at two years, and breed till they are six years old. They then lose their teeth. In the spring and early summer the valley is green with grass, and the sheep find a rich, sweet food in the fallen mulberries. When the days become warm, and the sheep seek the shelter of the trees which abound in every village, the professional shepherd makes his appearance, and leads the village flocks away to the higher slopes of the valley. As he passes along with his flocks he folds the sheep on the rice fields as yet unsown, and in one night adds enormously to the fertility of the soil. For this service he is well paid, and as the shepherd passes up towards the mountains he is a very popular and jaunty person. But when once the shepherd is on the mountains popularity is followed by distrust, and at fixed intervals the villager takes long journeys to carry up salt for his sheep. It is amusing to watch the preoccupied air of the villager as he draws near the great grazing-grounds, and his delight, if he finds that only a small percentage of his sheep have fallen victim to the bear or panther. If a sheep is missing the shepherd must produce the head or skin, but as he never sells a sheep without stipulating that the skin is to be returned he is always able to silence the complaints of an importunate client. It is odd that the Kashmíri, usually so sharp in business, should submit to the robberies of the shepherd, or *chaupán*; but the *chaupán*, rascal as he is, understands his work, and takes good care that no other *chaupán* trespasses on his allotted pasture. The *chaupáns* are a distinct class, marrying among themselves, and they often protect a dishonest brother from punishment or loss of clients, so that the villager is practically at their mercy. Redress in the mountains is out of the question, for there the proverb holds good 'Koh Kotwál yár Subadár,' which means that the mountain is the magistrate, and the pine the policeman, and both are alike deaf to the complaints of the villager. I quote some remarks from my Assessment Report on Donsu Tahsíl, para. 2:—

'Cultivation has extended greatly, and there is little land for grazing. The villagers are therefore dependent on the mountain meadows, which lie to the west, and as summer advances, the cows not in milk, ponies, and flocks move to the Toshá Maidán mountain. In the month of Jeith the sheep gather towards Rayár, a fine pasture tract close to the place where the Suknág river leaves the mountains, towards Sondipura and towards Dragar. From Rayár to Dudpatri, the tract is known as *Hakakhal*, "the threshing-floor of sheep," and here the *Shumári*, or counting of the sheep, is effected by the contractors to whom the grazing tax is farmed. Each villager is obliged by custom to entrust his sheep to an appointed *chaupán*, or shepherd, and for each sheep the *chaupán* receives a fee, which varies from two to three manwatás[1] of shá li or maize. The fee varies according

[1] A manwatá = about 2¾ lbs.

CHAP. XIV. to the repute of the *chaupán*. If he has a character for honesty he will receive three manwatás. The villager is very helpless in the matter of choosing a *chaupán*. The office is practically hereditary, and as the *chaupáns* are a separate people, marrying among themselves, they often protect a dishonest brother from punishment or loss of clients. As a rule the *chaupán* eats or sells a considerable number of the sheep entrusted to his care. He is obliged to produce the head or skin of a missing sheep, or he is called upon to take an oath that the sheep was destroyed by a panther or some other wild beast. Failing this the *chaupán* pays eight annas for a missing sheep. In extreme cases the *chaupán* has to clear himself by ordeal at Habar, a village in the Birú Mágám Tahsíl. I was assured by several persons at Habar that a dishonest *chaupán*, some twenty years ago, passed under the elm tree of ordeal and came out blind. Three times in the grazing season the villager takes up salt to the *Ilák*, or grazing-mountains, and anxiously searches for his sheep.

'The *Ilák* are partitioned among the *chaupán*, and no newcomer would be admitted, unless with the consent of the *chaupán* brotherhood. Besides the fact that *chaupáns* help one another, and make it difficult for a villager to change his shepherd, there is also the fact that all cultivators regard it of the first importance to have the flocks of sheep penned on the rice fields previous to ploughing, and inconvenience arises if the *chaupán* has too many clients, as he cannot give each client a turn of the sheep droppings. The subject of grazing is one of great interest. Sheep often pay the revenue in bad years, and wool is an absolute necessity to the cultivator for his winter clothing. There are two shearings in the year, one six months after the *Nauroz*, and the second, from which only a small quantity of wool is obtained, three months later. A tax of two annas per sheep is taken by the State.'

The tax used to be farmed out to contractors, but is now collected by the State officials.

When autumn has arrived, and the sheep have eaten their fill of the sweet mountain grasses, the *chaupán*, with a dejected air, descends to the valley, where clamorous clients await him, and then Greek meets Greek, and haggling commences about the loss of sheep and the shepherd's wages, which take the form of grain[1]. Sometimes the villagers insist on the shepherd clearing himself by taking an oath at a shrine or beneath some tree of ordeal. The sheep then return to the village and find good grazing for some time, and eat with avidity the falling leaves of the mulberry.

[1] The *chaupán* receives grain and one pice per sheep. He also is entitled to the wool of one out of every thirty sheep. If the *chaupán* is honest, and brings back the full number of sheep, he is given one sheep out of every fifty. Among other perquisites of the *chaupán* is the butter which he makes from the sheep's milk.

Directly the sheep reach the valley washing begins, and as the sheep emerge from the river or lake they are roughly rubbed down with a hoop of iron, and shearing then commences. According to the old rule the shearing ought to be done when the sun enters Libra. Three months later a second shearing takes place, but little wool is obtained. This shearing enables the sheep to stand the heat of their crowded winter pen beneath the dwelling-rooms of the villagers. For the winter fodder of the sheep the Kashmíri depends on leaves of the willow, and on the sweet dried leaves of the Flag (*Iris*). Occasionally a pulse (*Mothi*) is given, and once a month salt must be mixed in the sheep's food. In the close, confined atmosphere many sheep die during the winter, and when the villager sees that recovery is hopeless he cuts the throat of the patient and eats the braxy mutton.

The wool of Kashmír varies in quality in the several districts, and seems to depend on the character of the grasses of the different mountains on which the sheep feed in the summer. Thus the grasses of the southern pastures are rank and strong, and the wool of that part of the valley is long and rather coarse, and the blankets are not so valuable as those of Shupiyon, whose mountain pastures are sweet and good. The best and softest wool comes from the country to the west of the Wular lake, and the people say that the excellent quality is due to the abundance of mulberry leaves. Wethers (*bála*) up to the age of five years give the largest amount of wool. The choicest mutton in Kashmír is raised in the village of Nandpur on the Dal lake, where the sheep graze on the tender grasses of the artificially-made land known as *Demb*. But the mutton of Kashmír is throughout excellent, and the sheep of the valley have been pronounced by a competent authority to be as good as the Southdowns. The Kashmíri considers two-year-old wether mutton as the best. In spite of the number of sheep in Kashmír it is often difficult to obtain mutton in the villages, for the people want wool and warmth in the winter, and the man who has plenty of sheep on his ground floor can keep his family warm in the most bitter weather. A tax of thirteen Chilki rupees is levied per hundred sheep. This tax (*zar-i-chaupán*) is collected as the flocks (*ramba*) pass up to the mountain pastures. Up to quite recent times the State exercised the privilege of selecting one in every thousand sheep as the flocks passed up the mountains, and one out of every hundred in a flock. The first was known as Hazári or Khilkat, the second as Barrá. The Khilkat would compare favourably in size and weight with a Cotswold. Now the shepherd is liable to no such feudal services. The only return which he makes for his privileges is the present, for use in the temples. of the *Dhup* roots which are employed as incense.

The Kashmíri believes that salt improves and increases the growth

CHAP. XIV. of wool, and has a proverb to that effect: 'Nun che mun,' Salt means wool.

Goats. Goats are not numerous in the valley, but every year enormous flocks are brought up to the Kashmír mountains by the Bakarwáls and Gujars of Hazárá, Poonch, and the lower hills of Jammu. The goats of the Gujars are very fine animals and are valuable property, as they supply ghi, meat, and skins for carrying ghi. The skin of a goat will fetch one rupee in the mountains. In the city goats are kept for the sustenance of infants, and the milch goat goes round every morning to its customers, and having fed one child passes on to another. The milk of the goat is considered to be very strengthening. The hair of the goat is used for making grain-bags, but is not employed in the manufacture of finer fabrics. An attempt was made to introduce the shawl-goat into Kashmír, but it failed, as the climate is not sufficiently severe to induce the undergrowth of wool which nature provides in Tarfán for the protection of goats and other animals from the keen winds of that country. The annual inroad of goats into Kashmír, though it brings in a certain amount of revenue in the form of a grazing-tax, is to be regretted, as they and their masters cause wanton injury to the forests. The tax on goats for the summer-grazing in Kashmír is only Rs. 5 per hundred head.

Ponies. The ponies of Kashmír are small in size, but wiry, and of great endurance. Nearly every village has its pony mares, and they breed very fast. It is not an unusual thing to see a mare accompanied by three of her offspring. The most prolific breeding-grounds lie towards the shores of the Wular, where the ponies pass the days up to their bellies in the deep water of the swamps grazing the rich succulent grasses. The State formerly maintained large grass Rakhs for pony-breeding, and of the few which now exist the largest are in the neighbourhood of the Wular, and much of the stock has a strain of Panjáb blood in it. But in spite of this the ponies of the swamp country are not so good as the indigenous breeds of the Liddar valley and the stony country of Deosar. The swamp ponies have soft feet, and though they can amble along at a good pace, carrying a fat Kashmíri and his bedding, they are useless when they leave the easy valley tracks and reach the mountain paths. In the absence of cart roads, pony carriage is of great importance in Kashmír, and is in the hands of a special class, the *Markhbáns*. These men do not breed ponies, but buy them from the villages, where the conditions are favourable to muscle and hard feet. Some few years ago pony breeding became very unpopular, as villages with ponies were liable to constant requisitions for carriage to Gilgit and Jammu. Things have happily changed, and in the last three years there has been great activity in pony breeding. Prices have nearly doubled, and a good animal cannot now be bought under 60 rupees. Kashmír has every facility for pony or horse breeding, and it is hoped that before long the more intelligent of the villagers will adopt some simple system of rational breeding and selection of sires. When a *Markhbán* buys a pony he at once gelds him, but the villagers allow their mares to be indiscriminately covered by the numerous stallions on the pastures, and make no attempt to segregate the mares. I speak from some experience, as for three years I tried to introduce mule breeding into the valley, and I found that the one obstacle to success was the fact that the people would not segregate the mares after they had been covered by the donkey. They urged as an excuse that they could not afford the time to cut grass for the mares, and said that if mule breeding involved tying up the mares in a stable they would find it more profitable to keep to pony breeding. Just as the sheep are entrusted to the professional *chaupán*, so the ponies of Kashmír are made over to the charge of the *galawáns*, who look after long strings of them on the mountain pastures, and while the *chaupán* is not noted for his honesty, the *galawán* has made such a name for himself that the words thief and *galawán* are synonymous. The *galawán* charges four annas per pony. In the winter ponies are fed on rice straw, and barley and maize are the chief kinds of grain given to them. In the villages the ponies are always shackled by the fore-legs, and this, combined with the fact that they have to carry great weights when they are young, tends to make them knock-kneed and cow-hocked. An ordinary pony will carry 2½ maunds for a stage.

I do not think that there need be any anxiety about the future of pony breeding in Kashmír, provided that the arrangements for Gilgit transport are maintained on something like their present footing, but if the old system is revived, under which every man who had a pony could be sent off at a minute's notice to Gilgit, the villagers will sell off their mares and pony breeding will again languish.

Much can be done by the State to improve the breed in Kashmír, and a few Salutris armed with authority to geld all ponies not required for breeding purposes, would in a short time effect a marked improvement in the country. The measure would not be unpopular, but it must be by order.

Poultry. Poultry is abundant in Kashmír, and excellent fowls are to be found in every village. Wherever there is water ducks are kept, and in the neighbourhood of the Wular lake geese are plentiful. There is a large export of ducks to the Panjáb. The best breed of fowls is found in the Loláb valley, where the practice of making capons is common. This practice is said to have been introduced by the Patháns. Formerly

CHAP. XIV. capons were only found in the village of Lálpur, but now every village in the Loláb has its capons, which are sold at prices varying from eight to twelve annas, or are kept as a choice offering to the shrines. Fowls are made capons at the age of six months. Poultry and eggs are a source of considerable income to the villagers, and the fowl cholera (*kokar-kun*), which sometimes visits Kashmír, causes great loss. This disease was very fatal in the winter of 1892. Apparently the higher villages on the slopes of the mountains are less liable to the disease than the villages lower down. Turkeys have not as yet succeeded in the valley, and the people say that the climate disagrees with them. Pigeons are common in Srinagar. Tame rabbits thrive, but they have not been introduced into the villages. The Musalmáns of the valley are partial to all kinds of poultry and eggs, but the Hindus eschew them.

Honey. Honey is cultivated in the higher villages of the valley, and used to form an item of taxation. One house will often contain many hives, and in a good year a hive will give eight seers of honeycomb. The system of apiculture is very simple, and though bee-masters in England would smile at the primitive methods of the Kashmíri, it must be remembered that it is all gain to the latter, and that he is rarely at the expense of feeding his bees in a bad summer or in the winter. In a bad year vegetable marrow and *kangni*, a millet, are given to the bees. The hive consists of two large concave clay plates let into the wall of the house, and in the outer plate there is a small hole through which the bees enter. In October the bee-master removes the inner plate, and with a small torch of rice straw fumigates the hive, driving the bees out through the entrance hole. He leaves half the honey for the bees' winter food. It might be expected that in this operation the bee-master would be badly stung, but the little bees of Kashmír are neither fierce nor very venomous, and though they do sting, the pain is slight and very quickly passes away. Honey is much esteemed in a country where sugar is expensive, and it is used in cooking and for making preserves. The wax is sold to the cobblers and goldsmiths of the city and towns, and commands a good price. The honey is usually clear and excellent, but the whitest and best specimens of honeycomb which I have seen come from the Liddar valley. Machil, in Uttar Machipura Tahsíl, is said by the people to produce the best honey in Kashmír. Kuli Nárwáo, in the south, also produces good honey, and it is thought that the best villages for apiculture are those which receive the early morning sun. There is the old west country superstition that the bees come to the lucky man, and it is esteemed a bad omen when bees leave a house. The superstitions of letting the bees know of a death in the house, or of avoiding bad language in their hearing, do not exist in Kashmír. Honeycomb sells at about four to five annas per seer.

Sericulture.

The history of sericulture in Kashmír has been fitful and desultory. The silk industry is of ancient standing, for Mirza Haidar, in his history (A.D. 1536), alludes to the abundance of mulberry trees in Kashmír, and to the fact that the people would not allow the leaves to be used for any purpose other than that of food for silkworms. Mr. N. G. Mukerji, the expert on silk under the Government of Bengal, writes:—

'Before 1869 the silk industry of Kashmír had existed in the unorganized, crude state in which it had probably existed for centuries. from the days when Bactrian silk was exported to Damascus and other centres of manufacture. There is little doubt that Kashmír formed a part of the ancient kingdom of Bactria before the Christian era, and that some of the raw silk that found its way to the west came from Kashmír also. Nothing, however, is known in Kashmír about the origin of its silk industry, beyond the fact that it is very ancient, and that it is intimately connected with that of Bukhara, with which it has always had interchange of seed and silk.'

Mr. Thomas Wardle says, 'that India learned the art from China is generally understood, although at what period is not known.'

It is said by the people that sericulture existed in the times of king Zain-ul-Ab-ul-din, that it had fallen into disuse in the Pathán times, and that the Patháns restored the industry. In later times the important date is the year 1869, when Mahárájá Ranbir Singh. an enthusiast in new industries, revived the silk production on a large scale. No expense was spared, and 127 fine rearing-houses were built in all parts of the valley. Reeling appliances and machinery were imported from Europe, and a large Department was formed for the purpose of developing a business in silk. It is easy to be wise after the event, but the idea suggests itself that the system of revival was not wise. A guild of silk-rearers known as *Kirm kash* (literally worm-killers) was created, and these men were given certain privileges, such as exemption from forced labour. They were also allowed to annex the houses of villagers for silk-breeding purposes, and they were further appointed as informers regarding damage done to mulberry trees. In a short time the name *Kirm kash* became hateful to the villagers, and there is no doubt that the silk-rearers abused their position and oppressed the people. The whole business was too official, and the general public looked upon it with hatred or disgust. Next it may be said that the revival was too ambitious. The cost of buildings and plant was enormous, and the rearing-houses being scattered in all parts of the valley could not be properly supervised. Unfortunately there was no one possessing any technical knowledge to supervise, and though great improvements were made in reeling. there was no man in Kashmír who could avert the calamity which befell the industry in 1878, when nearly the whole of the silkworms

CHAP. XIV. were carried off by disease. Every credit is due to Babu Nilamber Mukerji, the chief justice of Kashmír, for his efforts, and his success in improving the reeling of silk is attested by the favourable reports received from Europe, all speaking highly of the quality of the fibre. The industry lingered on until 1882, and from that time to 1890 the State left it to the silk-rearers. The quantity of seed rapidly diminished, and sericulture was virtually at an end. The fine buildings had fallen down, and out of the 127 houses built in 1869 only two remain, one at Raghnáthpura and the other at Cherpur. It is generally understood that the disease which proved so fatal was brought into Kashmír with the imported seeds of highly domesticated, though superior, foreign cocoons, from Europe, China, and Japan. The silk-rearers declare that the Japan seeds were the cause of the calamity.

In 1889, on the advice of Sir Edward Buck, C.S.I., Secretary to the Government of India, it was decided to follow the example set by Bengal, and to adopt the Pasteur system of microscopical examination. The services of a trained Bengali were obtained, and a Kashmíri was deputed to Bengal to learn the system of microscopical examination. Good seed was imported from Italy and France, and an excellent crop of cocoons was obtained. In 1891 the success achieved was nullified by the neglect of the subordinates, who were unfortunately left in charge at a critical time, and progress was temporarily arrested. The operations from 1889 to the beginning of 1894 were under the charge of Babu Rishibar Mukerji, the chief judge of Kashmír, a brother of Babu Nilamber Mukerji. Though I was associated with him in the work, he deserves all the credit for having achieved the chief object of securing healthy local seed. This year, 1894, while imported seeds have in many cases bred diseased worms, the worms from our examined seeds have done splendidly, and there is no disease among them. Owing to financial reasons, at the beginning of 1894 Babu Rishibar Mukerji's connexion with sericulture terminated, and I was placed in charge. My object since I was associated with sericulture in 1889 has been to avoid expense, and to limit our efforts to obtaining healthy seed. Knowing that the Kotahár valley contained a number of old silk-rearers, I have this year given all our seed to the Kotahár people. Supervision is thus rendered possible. I have further raised the price paid by the State for cocoons so as to give some profit to the rearers. Our expenditure has been covered by our income, and unless some unforeseen calamity occurs we shall have seed sufficient to supply all the old silk-rearers in 1895. I have only kept the Raghnáthpura and Cherpur houses in repair, and I hold strongly that the ordinary Kashmíri house is fairly suited to sericulture. It is well ventilated, and the Kashmíri knows well how to regulate the temperature. Signor Bassi, the Italian in charge of the wine manufactory, has a thorough knowledge of sericulture, and visited Kotahár, in 1894, with me. He sees much that is hopeful, and agrees with me in thinking that the Kashmíri house is suited to the requirements of silk-rearing. He has instructed us in the art of pruning mulberry trees, and orders have now been issued which will, it is hoped, stop the reckless lopping which formerly prevailed. Everywhere I find the villagers eager to take up sericulture as a cottage industry, and from all parts of the valley men have this year implored me to give them seed. I am of opinion that the State should confine itself to the production of healthy seed, and should give up silk-rearing and silk-reeling. I further hold that it would be wise to lease out the right to use mulberry leaves to capitalists. It is impossible to exaggerate the potentialities of silk in Kashmír, but I am certain that these potentialities will never be realized while the industry remains in the hands of the State.

The wild mulberry silkworm is found in Kashmír, and up to 1894 the State farmed out the right to collect the wild cocoons. The silk is of the purest white.

The diseases with which the silkworm is attacked in the valley are Pebrine and Flacherie. Other diseases are so far unknown.

Dogs of the Pariah description swarm in the city and the villages, and are rather bigger and more aggressive than their brethren in India. The shepherds have a breed of Ladákh dogs, which are brave and intelligent. Dogs.

Cats are also very common, but are rarely domesticated. They are small and of a grey colour. Cats.

CHAPTER XV.

INDUSTRIES AND OCCUPATIONS.

CHAP. XV.

Village manufactures.

Weavers.

THE Kashmíris have won a great reputation as artisans, and were celebrated in the old days for their skill in art manufactures. The chief centre of Kashmíri industries is of course Srinagar, but other localities are famous for their special manufactures. Thus Islamabad turns out excellent embroideries. Kulgám is famous for its lacquered woodwork. Bijbihára has a reputation for its excellence in wood-carving, while the villagers of the Zainagir circle are famed for their soft woollen cloth. Every Kashmíri seems to excel as a weaver, and the homespun cloth woven by the villagers in the winter is highly appreciated both by Europeans and visitors. The homespun (*pattu*) is often the well-worn blanket of the villager, who sells it to the Srinagar merchants.

The best wool in Kashmír is found in the north where the grasses are good; the best weavers are found in the south. The Shupiyon wide blankets (*ekbari*) are sold according to quality and fineness, and the *khudrang*[1] blankets, made at Turk Wangam, 12 yards long and 1½ yards broad, command prices of Rs. 24 and Rs. 25. The *dobari* blanket, which consists of two breadths sewn together (the two pieces being 1½ yards broad, with a length of 10 yards), commands a lower price and used to be sold by weight, 1 seer fetching Rs. 2. A good *khudrang dobari* blanket now fetches Rs. 6 or Rs. 7, while a white blanket can be bought for Rs. 5 or Rs. 5.8. Considering the great amount of labour which is expended by the Kashmíris on the production of a blanket, the prices are still very low.

Carpenters.

The carpenters of the villages are extremely adroit, and do excellent work when they are in the right mood. Some of the *lattice-work* and carving of the shrines is very beautiful, and argues a strong artistic instinct. The skill of the carpenter is the more to be admired when one considers the rude and primitive tools which he carries in his leathern apron. With a kind of half hammer, half adze (*túr*), and a chisel (*túrats*), the rural carpenter will execute any work which his clients may require. Unfortu-

[1] *Khudrang* means natural colour. The brown wool is picked out carefully.

nately, like all Kashmíris, the carpenter only works when it suits his inclination. A very few hours' work will provide food for the week, and unless there be some special incentive, such as the repairs of a shrine in cholera time, the ordinary carpenter will sit sunning himself in his verandah, thanking fate that he is not a husbandman.

The following note, written by Mr. C. Tickell, Director of the Kashmír P. W. D., will be of interest:—

'The Kashmíri is an indifferent carpenter and a bad joiner. His carpentry has much improved in late years, since he has learned to use more civilized kinds of tools than the few primitive implements which till recently formed his stock-in-trade. But his joinery continues to be of the worst. He seems too dishonest by nature to make a formal joint, and in this respect his work forms a strange contrast to that of his Panjábi neighbour, in whose sight a tenon which does not completely fill the mortise into which it is driven is an abomination. A door or window made by a Kashmíri requires to constantly have pieces cut away from the bottom and added to the top, owing to its sagging in its frame.

'Both the Kashmíri and Panjábi have a great natural talent for floral and geometric design, which the carpenters apply with great effect as surface decoration or as perforated work, but the Kashmíri's joinery is so abominably bad that, as a rule, any article of furniture made by him is nearly useless for the purpose for which it is primarily intended, however beautifully its surface may be carved.

'There is a method of joining in use amongst the Kashmíri carpenters which appears to be peculiar to them, or which at any rate is applied by them to a variety of purposes for which other means would be employed elsewhere. It is really a rough form of panelling. To take the commonest example, many Kashmíri houses are constructed of wood. First a framework of round or roughly-squared vertical and horizontal posts is erected, each post having previously had a groove about 1 inch wide and 1½ inches deep cut along its edges by means of a chisel, the back of an adze (nearly the only other tool used for such rough work) being used in place of a mallet. Roughly-split planks are then fitted into the grooves, and mud plaster is applied to one or both sides of them, and the result is a kind of lath and mud-plaster wall. The building is of course entirely dependent on the posts for stability, and as diagonal bracing is usually omitted the houses are after a year or two often anything but perpendicular. Such work is known as *pachar bandi.*

'The apparently insuperable difficulty of inserting the planks into grooves round a rectangular opening, after all the posts enclosing it have been filled, is got over in a way as simple and at the same time as effective as that adopted by Columbus in balancing the egg; a portion of the side

CHAP. XV. of a groove is cut or torn away and afterwards repaired by a couple of nails or wooden pegs.

'By another application of the same principle an excellent panelled wall is made. Grooves having been made in the horizontals and verticals forming the framework (say of the sides of a houseboat), a plank is first inserted and slid up to the end of the opening and into the vertical groove. Then a small post is inserted, which besides engaging in the grooves of the top and bottom post is itself grooved on both its sides. By thus alternating planks and double-grooved posts a panelled wall is formed, each panel of which is held in a groove on every side. The so-called Kashmíri ceilings (*khatamband*) are a most ingenious extension of exactly the same principle. Thin panels of soft wood, generally *Picea Webbiana*, are cut into various geometric forms, and are held together by being placed in the grooves of small double-grooved battens. To this kind of work, which is a speciality of a limited number of workmen in Srinagar and Islámábád, the above strictures on the joinery of the Kashmíri do not apply. The fitting of the numerous small pieces of wood forming a well-executed Kashmíri ceiling is most accurately done, but this is doubtless due to the fact that there are only a certain number of *different* pieces forming each pattern, which have each to be repeated many hundreds of times, and (as in the *Pinjara* work) a special contrivance is made use of to ensure all the similar pieces being exactly alike and interchangeable with each other.'

Axemen and sawyers.

Allied with the carpenter are the axemen and sawyers. The saw is a recent innovation, but the sawing industry now furnishes employment to many, and even the fine-fingered shawl-weavers of the city are taking to sawing. The Kashmíri prefers axe-cut timber both for houses and boats, and a boat made of axe-cut timber fetches more than one made of sawn timber.

Basket-makers.

The basket industry is of importance, and most villages have their artisan who makes the necessary basket for the *kángar*, and baskets for agricultural purposes, and the *kiltas* used for the transport of apples and for rough village work. The superior *kiltas*, covered with leather, so familiar to the European traveller, are made in the city.

Blacksmiths.

The blacksmith is found in most villages of importance. He is a more industrious worker than the carpenter. His chief work is the manufacture of agricultural implements and domestic requirements, such as chains, padlocks, and *shovels*. Some of the blacksmiths in the city are possessed of extraordinary skill. One man, who has been employed in connexion with silk-reeling, can imitate the most intricate machinery. Excellent surgical instruments are made, and many instruments now in use in the Hospital are locally manufactured. The well-known gunsmiths, Amira and Usmana, can turn out good guns and rifles, and replace parts of weapons in so clever a manner that it is difficult to detect the difference between the Kashmíri and English workmanship. Swords are largely manufactured in Srinagar, and are much appreciated at Jammu. CHAP. XV.

Potters. Potters exist in sufficient numbers to supply the wants of the rural population. Their work at present is limited to the useful, and the ornamental side of pottery is neglected. The village potters have a market for their wares in the city, for it is found by experience that the vessels made in the villages last longer than those made in the city. In Srinagar the best and most durable pottery is manufactured in Rainawari.

These are the most important of the village industries. The artisans are skilful but unambitious. If a demand for better work arose the village artisans would no doubt rise to the occasion, but I think that for some time to come the Kashmíri peasant will be content with his present style of house, dress, and cooking-utensils, and that there is not likely to be any change of importance in the village handicrafts.

It is different in the city. There the manufactures depend considerably on the tastes and fashions of people less conservative than the Kashmíris, and I am afraid that the influence of the outside world on the art wares of Srinagar has not on the whole proved salutary. The citizens of Srinagar have a common saying[1] to the effect that when the taxation went the prosperity of the city went also, and they explain this by the fact that the removal of taxation led to the breaking up of what were practically guilds sanctioned and protected by the State. When the taxation was removed outsiders rushed in and competition at once reduced prices of art wares. Copper-work which sold at seven rupees per seer in the days of taxation now sells at three rupees, and this is the case with many other art wares. But in arguing that the prosperity of the city has departed, the citizens omit sometimes to explain that in the days of taxation the State exercised a vigorous supervision over the quality of the raw material and of the manufactured article. In the good days of the shawl-trade no spurious wool was brought in from Amritsar to be mixed with the real shawl-wool of Central Asia, and woe betide the weaver who did bad work or the silversmith who was too liberal with his alloy.

There is no such supervision nowadays. Competition has lowered prices, and the real masters of weaving, silver, papier-maché and copper-work have to bend to the times and supply their customers with cheap, inferior work. Ask an old artist in papier-maché to show the work which formerly went to Kabul, and he will show something very different from the miserable trash which is now sold. But the Patháns of Kabul

[1] 'Yeli báj gao teli barkat gae.'

CHAP. XV. paid the price of good work; the visitors to the valley want cheap work and they get it. It is very difficult to arrest the deterioration of art work. The Kashmíris have the artistic instinct, but artists must live, and their livelihood depends on the market for art wares. I think, however, that something might be done both towards improving the existing condition of art manufacturers and towards introducing new arts. I have advocated the institution of a Technical School with an Art Department, and believe that such a school would do much for the people of Srinagar. As regards improvements in the existing condition of art manufactures, I think that something like prohibitive duties on the import of aniline dyes, and the introduction of a system of *prix fixée*, to be worked by a committee of experts, might prove beneficial. One of the chief causes of the degradation of Kashmíri art work is the fact that every one suspects the Srinagar middleman of being an ultra-oriental rogue. If he asks a rupee it is at once obvious to most persons that one-half a rupee would be an exorbitant price to pay. But the Kashmíri artist will never flourish under the present system of sweating—and in my opinion the system would to a great extent break down if the State allowed grain to be sold at market rates. Wages would then rise, and it is possible that the slaves of the middlemen would gain emancipation. If they are to remain slaves it is better that they should be slaves of the State as in old times, and pay in taxation for the cheap grain. No one save the sweater benefits from the present system. The principle of co-operation is sadly lacking in Kashmír. If one excepts the shawl and carpet trades, where men are necessarily congregated, it may be said that the journeymen of other trades work apart and independently of one another, but dependent on the middleman who always holds them in his debt. No artisan in Srinagar will do work unless he first receives an advance for food, and having obtained this advance he will idle over his work until hunger urges him to action. The dilatory manner in which orders are executed is one of the worst features in the art manufactures of Srinagar. With the exception of the shawl-merchants the shopkeepers keep no stock, and would-be purchasers are obliged to wait for months if they order any special pattern. This is partly due to a want of capital, but the chief cause of the unbusiness-like methods of the dealers and artisans of Srinagar is the utter absence of enterprise and energy.

I do not propose to give the details of each manufacture of Srinagar. The surroundings of the artisans are miserable and squalid, and it is sad to contrast the beauty of the art work with the ugliness of the workmen's lives. They are, however, a difficult people to help, for they will make no effort to help themselves.

Shawls.

The shawl industry is now unfortunately a tradition—a memory of the past. The trade received its deathblow when war broke out between Germany and France in 1870, and I have been told by an eye-witness of the intense excitement and interest with which the Kashmíri shawl-weavers watched the fate of France in that great struggle—bursting into tears and loud lamentations when the news of Germany's victories reached them. If there had been any hope that the industry would revive, and that shawls would again become fashionable, this hope was dashed when the famine of 1877–79 visited the valley. None suffered more heavily in that calamity than the poor weakly shawl-weavers. Some of the survivors migrated to the villages, where they still work for starvation wages in heated, unhealthy rooms, hermetically sealed in the winter. The city census of 1891 states that there were 5,148 shawl-weavers, but of these some 800 to 900 are employed in the manufacture of carpets. It is commonly reported that the fine wool of the Central Asian goats no longer finds its way to Kashmír, and the scarcity of the raw material, combined with the smallness of the demand, has reduced the shawl-trade to the smallest dimensions. All the facts connected with this interesting and once most important industry will be found in Moorcroft's *Travels*, vol. ii. ch. iii. Though it was a lucrative industry to the State, which took Rs. 30 per annum from employers of shawl-weavers per head, an impost of 20 per cent. on the manufactured article, and an export duty of Rs. 7.15 on a long shawl, and Rs. 5.13 on a square shawl, it was a poor industry for the weavers. In 1871 one or two annas per diem was the ordinary wage for a weaver, and Moorcroft noticed that the general earnings of an industrious and expert spinner were Rs. 1.8.0 per mensem, and probably less. M. Henri Dauvergne, who has been intimately connected with the shawl-trade for many years, and who has done much to improve the art manufactures of Srinagar, gives me much valuable information regarding shawls. According to M. Dauvergne the Kashmíri shawl dates back to the times of the emperor Babar. The Mughal emperors wore on their turbans a jewelled ornament known as *jigha*, in shape like an almond. On the top of the *jigha* was an aigrette of feathers. An Andijáni weaver imitated the design of the *jigha* in a scarf made for the emperor Babar, and was so successful that the *jigha* became the fashionable design in all scarves and shawls. Many Andijáni weavers were brought down to India and Kashmír by the Mughal emperors, and the *jigha* design was adopted in art centres in India and also in Persia. Many of the small carpets of Persia represent the *jigha*, and at the present time there is a class of shawls and *butadárs* made in Srinagar entirely for the Persian market.

CHAP. XV.

In the *jamawárs* the *jigha* design can always be found interlaced with strips of various colours covered with small flowers.

Both *butadárs* and *jamawárs* are still exported, via Bombay, to Persia, where they are used for the edging of chogas and other robes.

The first shawls which reached Europe were brought by Napoleon, at the time of the campaign in Egypt, as a present to the empress Josephine, and from that time shawls became fashionable. In those days the *jigha* varied from 1 foot in depth to 18 inches, but later on General Ventura—then in Mahárájá Ranjit Singh's service—sent to France shawls in which the *jigha* had attained large proportions. These shawls were known as Palms. They were 10 to 11 feet long by 4½ feet wide. The centre was plain, usually black in colour, the borders were covered with elongated *jighas* or palms in parallel rows. The shawl was made of the finest Pashm material, obtained from the goats of the Tibetan mountains, but the best material came from the Tian Shan (Celestial Mountains) and Ush Tarfan. It was brought by caravans via Yarkand and Ladákh, and it passed on to Amritsar, Lahore, and Ludhianá, where it was woven in various textures of plain *alwand* or in shawls. The weavers of Amritsar used to adulterate the real Pashm with the hair taken from the lower part of the neck of the Bactrian camel. This adulteration gave a heaviness and coarseness to the shawls, which lacked the suppleness of the Kashmír article made of pure Tarfáni Pashm.

The best shawls ever made in Kashmír were manufactured in the time of Mahárájá Ranbir Singh, between the years 1865–72. They were very fine in texture, very soft in colour, and of the most elaborate and graceful patterns, of a purely Eastern style of decoration. About this time aniline dyes made their appearance. Every effort was made to persuade the shawl-manufacturers to avoid these pernicious colours, and the French agents, by refusing to purchase shawls in which aniline dyes were present, succeeded in stamping out the abomination. But their labours in the interests of art were in vain, for the shawl industry perished when war broke out between France and Germany. It is well to remember the services of the French purchasing-agents in fighting against aniline dyes, for it has been stated that the popularity of shawls in Europe declined owing to the employment of these dyes in Kashmír.

Prices of shawls ranged from 150 to 5,000 British rupees. The Islamabad shawls, which represented one-fifth of the total production of Kashmír, were inferior, and never fetched more than Rs. 450 per pair. They were made from the commonest Pashm of Chang Thang in Tibet. From 1862–70 the export of shawls averaged 25 to 28 lakhs of rupees per annum, and when the trade was at its zenith 25,000 to 28,000 persons were engaged in the manufacture of shawls[1]. Those of the shawl-weavers who have not taken to boating and other occupations are now engaged in weaving *akvand*, or plain Pashmina, or *jamawárs* and *butadárs* for the Persian market. There is no export to Europe. *Amlikár*, or hand-embroidered shawls, were also largely manufactured. They were made entirely by the needle on a plain piece of *alwand*. Some of the designs were very effective, being in bold relief, and it was possible to secure colour effects which would have been almost impossible in a woven shawl. They were cheaper than the *binoet*, or loom-woven shawl, and never fetched more than 200 rupees. Other shawls, embroidered with silk and gold thread, were known as *chiknikár*, *katankár*, and *morsakár*. The last was very striking, having the appearance of jewellery, like the Delhi embroideries. A class of work which is still sold is the *dorikár*, which is silk embroidery on a plain Pashmina *alwand*.

Carpets.

Many of the survivors of the famine of 1877–79 have now found occupation in the manufacture of carpets. Three Europeans carry on business in Srinagar as manufacturers of carpets. Their work is of good quality, and apparently they can with difficulty keep pace with the orders which they receive from India and Europe. There is now, I believe, no attempt to manufacture the costly, though superb, rugs in which the shawl-wool was used, and the Srinagar looms consume wool imported from India or wool locally produced. Srinagar has a formidable rival in Amritsar, where a large colony of Kashmíri weavers is settled, and considerable capital is employed in the manufacture of carpets. The same curious system is followed in the manufacture of carpets as obtained in the weaving of shawls. The pattern of the shawl or of the carpet, after being designed by the *artist*, is committed to paper. This *paper* contains a series of hieroglyphics, intelligible to the craft, indicating numbers and colours. The man who reads these hieroglyphics calls out to the rows of sickly men and boys who sit at the loom, 'lift five and use red,' or 'lift one and use green,' but neither he nor the weavers have any idea as to what the pattern of the fabric will be. This is known to the *nakásh*, and the pattern never goes into the factory.

The carpet industry has given employment to a considerable number of the shawl-weavers, and many are employed in embroidering felts or *numdahs*. The best felts are imported from Yarkand, but felts of a somewhat inferior description are manufactured in Kashmír. The coloured felts embroidered in Srinagar are perhaps the most artistic of the Kashmíri textiles. Calico printing is extensively carried on in Srinagar; coarse, locally-manufactured cloth is used, and the patterns are similar to the shawl

[1] The export of shawls in 1893-94 only amounted to Rs. 22,850.

CHAP. XV. designs. The dyes employed are indigo, safflower, madder, red and yellow.

Papier-maché. The lacquered work, or papier-maché, of Srinagar once had a great reputation, but at present the industry is in a somewhat reduced condition. The amount of real papier-maché which is made from the pulp of paper is small, and the *nakásh* or lacquer-workers chiefly apply their beautiful designs to smooth wood. These designs are very intricate, and the drawing is all freehand, for the workmen do not possess mathematical instruments. The skill shown by the *nakásh* in sketching and designing is remarkable. The papier-maché work is known as *kar-i-kalamdáni*, as the best specimens of the old work were the pen-boxes (*kalamdán*), but a variety of articles such as tables, cabinets and trays are now made, and the richer classes call in the *nakásh* for the decoration of their ceilings and walls. Papier-maché has perhaps suffered more than any other industry from the taste of foreign purchasers.

Silver-work. The silver-work of Kashmír is extremely beautiful, and some of the indigenous patterns, the chenar and lotus leaf, are of exquisite design. The silversmith works with a hammer and chisel, and will faithfully copy any design which may be given to him. Up to recent years, the silver-work of Kashmír had a peculiar white sheen, very beautiful at first sight, but apt to tarnish after a short time. This whiteness is said to be due to the practice of boiling the silver work in apricot juice. Complaints are very common regarding the quality of the silver put into the work. and some simple system of assay would be a boon, not only to the purchaser but also to the manufacturers. The metal is either imported in ingots via Yarkand or is rupee silver.

Copper-work. Perhaps the most effective and certainly the best value for the money is the copper-work of Srinagar. The coppersmith works with a hammer and chisels, and many of the present coppersmiths are men who used once to work in silver. They also work in brass. Their designs are very quaint and bold, and they are very ready to adopt any new pattern that may be offered to them. The copper-work of Srinagar is admirably adapted for electro-plating, and some smiths now turn out a finer kind of article specially for electro-plating. A large demand has arisen for the beautiful copper trays framed as tables in carved walnut-wood, and the carpenter is now the close ally of the coppersmith. Of the enamel work, the enamels on brass are, I think, the best, though the enamelled silver-work is very pretty. Copper does not lend itself to enamel.

Woodwork. The woodwork of Srinagar lacks the finish of the Panjab carving, but the Kashmíri carver is perhaps second to none in his skill as a designer. He works with a hammer and chisels, and a great deal of the roughness and inequality of his pieces is due to the difficulty of obtaining seasoned walnut-wood. A speciality in Kashmír woodwork deserves mention: beautiful ceilings of perfect design, cheap and effective, are made by a few carpenters, who with marvellous skill piece together thin slices of pine-wood. This is known as *khatamband*. The result is a charming ceiling, in which the various shades of the pine-slips blend together in perfect harmony. A great impetus has been given to this industry by the builders of houseboats, and the darker colours of the walnut-wood have been mixed with the lighter shades of the pine. Any one who wishes to see a good specimen of modern Kashmíri woodwork and Kashmíri ceilings should visit the well-known shrine of Nakshbandi, not far from the Jama Masjid of Srinagar. A few of the *khatamband* ceilings have been introduced into England. They are cheap and extremely effective. I thought that the work was peculiar to Kashmír, but M. Dauvergne informs me that ceilings of the same construction and design are found in Samarkand, Bukhara, Persia, Constantinople, Algiers and Morocco.

Leather. There is a large trade in leather in Kashmír; hides are prepared in the villages by the Wátals and are then brought to Srinagar, where they undergo a refining process. Skins are brought in raw, and are prepared in the city. Moorcroft spoke in high praise of the leather of Kashmír, and there is no doubt that there is abundance of raw material, and that the tanners of the country can turn out an excellent leather if they choose. If one is to judge from one's own experience, one must admit that the leather of the chappli sandals is apt to stretch in wet weather, but, on the other hand, the leather portmanteaux and valises made in Srinagar stand an amount of rough usage which few English solid leather bags would survive. It is claimed for the leather of Srinagar that the *saddles* last for ever, and my impression is that the man who knows what good leather is can get it in Srinagar, if he is prepared to pay a fair price and to wait for an inordinate time.

Furs. The furriers of Srinagar chiefly depend for their livelihood on the business given to them by sportsmen, who send in skins to be cured. The recent law for the protection of game, under which the sale of skins and horns is prohibited, has curtailed the business of the furriers.

Lapidaries. The lapidaries of Srinagar possess very great skill, and are especially proficient as seal-cutters. The lapidaries are not a prosperous people, but if the seal-cutters were to seek work in India they could command high wages.

Paper. Kashmír was once famous for its paper, which was much in request in India for manuscripts, and was used by all who wished to impart dignity to their correspondence. The pulp from which the paper is made is a mixture of rags and hemp fibre, obtained by pounding these materials under a lever mill worked by water-power. Lime and some kind of soda

CHAP. XV. are used to whiten the pulp, which is taken from the mills in the Sind valley and the Dáchigám Nullah to the factory in the city. The pulp is then placed in stone troughs or baths and mixed with water, and from this mixture a layer of the pulp is extracted on a light frame of reeds. This layer is the paper, which is pressed and dried in the sun. Next it is polished with pumice stone, and then its surface is glazed with rice water. A final polishing with onyx stone is given, and the paper is then ready for use. I have used the paper of Kashmír to a large extent. It is durable and in many ways excellent, but it cannot compete with the cheap mill paper of India. Its high glaze is dangerous, as entries can be obliterated by water. The industry is declining, and the recent order of the State, that paper made in the Srinagar gaol is to be used by all offices, will hasten the extinction of what once was an important and renowned manufacture. Korans are still written on paper made from hemp fibre, but printing has destroyed those men of beautiful penmanship, the *khushnavis* of Srinagar, just as the Indian paper-mills have destroyed the once famous handmade foolscap of Kashmír. It is said that the industry of paper-making, as well as of bookbinding, was introduced by the great king Zain-ul-Ab-ul-din from Samarkand, and that the paper-workers were settled in the Nawa Shahr district of Srinagar. There are still some thirty-six families in Nawa Shahr, and each family to work efficiently should have fourteen members. An average family will make five *dastas* of good, or seven *dastas* of rough paper in a day, a *dasta* containing twenty-four sheets. There are three qualities:—

1. *Farmáshi*, also called Maharáji or Royal. This is a fine paper, highly glazed, made of a pulp containing two parts of hemp fibre to every sixteen parts of rags.

2. *Dahmashti*, made from a pulp containing three parts of hemp fibre to every 177 parts of rags.

3. *Kalamdáni*, the paper now chiefly manufactured, contains no hemp fibre.

Hemp fibre is rising in price, and fetches Rs. 5 to Rs. 8 per kharwar, and the poor paper-makers often have to use old gunny-bags.

Even the *Lata farosh*, or rag-sellers, charge Rs. 3 per kharwar for rags, so that materials are expensive. It is sad to think of the old days when literature was honoured by a paper composed of one part of silk to twenty-two parts of rags.

Ranga maz is a coloured paper used for packing purposes.

Boats. The boating industry of Kashmír is one of great importance. The Hánz or Hánji, as the boatmen are called, are 33,870 in number, and their avocations bring them into contact with all classes of the population. The boating industry is an old one in Kashmír, and we learn from the *Ain*

PLATE XVI

To face page 381.] [*Negative by Major Hepburn, R.A.*

SHOWS CHENÁR-TREES. THE BOAT TO THE RIGHT IS THE DUNGA OR PASSENGER-BOAT THAT TO THE LEFT IS THE COMMON CARGO-BOAT OF KASHMÍR

Akbari that boats were the centre upon which all commerce moved, and that 'in Kashmír there was made a model of a ship that astonished every one who saw it.' There are many kinds of boats, all flat-bottomed, but, with the exception of the *parinda*, none of them would cause much astonishment in the present day. Excluding boats owned by private persons, and used for private purposes, there are about 2,417 boats employed in trade and passenger traffic. Of these, 1,066 are boats of the larger size. The greater portion of the grain and wood imported into Srinagar by the river is brought in large barges not unlike canal barges. These are towed or poled up stream and drop down the river with the current. There are two kinds of barge. The larger is known as *bahats*, and has a high prow and stern. Aft is a cabin with two rooms, in which the boatman and his family live, and the hold in which the grain is stored is roofed in with thatch. The *bahats* will carry a cargo of 800 to 1,000 maunds. The smaller barge is known as *wár*, and it has a low prow. The *wár* will carry a cargo of 400 maunds. One of the most common form of boats is the *dúnga*. This is a flat-bottomed boat, about 50 to 60 feet in length and about 6 feet in width, and draws about 2 feet of water. It has a sloping roof of matting, and side walls of a similar material. The boatmen live in the aft of the *dúnga*, and have their kitchen made of dried clay. The passenger lives in the front part of the boat, and in warm weather life in a *dúnga* is very pleasant. In the winter, when the passenger traffic is at a standstill, the *dúngas* are employed in carrying grain. A good *dúnga* will carry up to 200 maunds. The *dúnga* boatmen used, like all other classes, to be subject to a tax, and the older mariners complain that when the tax was remitted an inferior race of men came into the profession. There is no doubt that many of the present *dúnga*-men are unsatisfactory, but then their charge, Rs. 15 per mensem for a boat and four paddlers, is very small. The great impetus lately given to the building of houseboats may before long impair the profits of the *dúnga*-men, and I imagine that the opening of the cart-road from Baramula to Srinagar will also affect injuriously the passenger traffic of the boats. Few will care to cross the Wular lake in the helpless *dúnga*, and to submit to the delays caused by that uncertain and treacherous lake, when a three hours' drive will carry them from Baramula to Srinagar. The *shikára* is a small edition of the *dúnga*, very useful for short journeys. It is propelled by paddles. The *kuchu* is a heavy, clumsy boat without any roof, and is used for the transport of stone and rough goods which are not injured by the rain. The *dembnáo* is a tiny dugout, in which vegetables are brought to market. The amphibious denizens of the Dal lake almost live in the *dembnáo*. The *tsatawar* is a small boat without a roof, only used on the Wular. There are two rows of paddlers, and they will cross

CHAP. XV. the lake in all weather. The *tsalawar* boatmen are more courageous than the ordinary *hánjis*, and sometimes discharge the functions of a lifeboat.

The *parinda, larindo* and *chakwari* are not for the common herd, but are the dignified vehicles of the rulers of Kashmír. The *parinda*, or 'flyer,' is a long, light boat with forty or fifty paddlers. In the front is a raised seat covered with a canopy in which four persons can sit. The *parinda* is the fastest craft on the Jhelum, and it is a pretty sight to see fifty paddlers, all keeping excellent time, racing up the river. The *parinda* paddlers indulge in fancy strokes which are known as *kirpardmi chappr*, in honour of the pleasure-loving Sikh Governor Kirpa Rám. The *larindo* is not unlike a college barge, while the *chakwari* has a great length from the stern to the saloon.

When the river is high navigation is a simple matter, but in the winter, when the Jhelum is low, it is very difficult to bring the heavy barges past the shoals, and the boatmen have to work hard, often digging out a channel with their heart-shaped paddles. Even when there is sufficient water, the absence of a tow-path causes delay and trouble. The river has frequently to be waded by the towers, and every side creek has to be forded. The tow-rope must be passed around trees, jutting out on the river, and a journey up stream is calculated to try the temper of any one to whom time is a consideration. I have often advocated the construction of a tow-path. It is especially necessary in the city itself, as the current of the river through the bridges is sufficiently strong to render the passage of big boats difficult.

I fear that evil days are in store for the boatmen of Kashmír. Forest conservancy will make it difficult to obtain the long planks of cedar of which the boats used to be made, and the deodar punt-pole, so precious to the bargeman, will be a thing of the past. When cart traffic is established between Srinagar and Baramula, and its advantages are recognized, it will not be long before cart-roads are made in other parts of the valley. River carriage is cheap in most countries, but in Kashmír it is expensive, as the boatmen not only steal a portion of the cargo, but they often spoil the whole of their grain consignments by wanton adulteration. No one will trust his grain to a boatman if he can procure any other carrier. I should add that the boatmen of Kámráj, the northern end of the valley, are more honest than the *hánjis* of the rest of Kashmír.

PLATE XVII

To face page 383

[*Negative by Alam Chand, G.C.*

GROUP OF KASHMIRI PORTERS RESTING ON MARCH

CHAPTER XVI.

TRADE.

Chap. XVI.

THE Kashmír valley, owing to its remoteness from the railway and to its difficult approaches, has been thrown on its own resources, and is to a great extent a self-supporting country. In normal years the food supply of the valley is ample for its inhabitants; for clothing the people have wool and a certain amount of locally-produced cotton of a fair quality. There is a wealth of fibres, ample timber, and with the single exception of salt there is no necessity of life which need be imported. Iron locally produced used to suffice for agricultural implements, and clay vessels serve all the purposes of copper and brass in domestic life. But in spite of difficulties of communication with the Panjab, and of the fact that Kashmír is practically a self-supporting country, inhabited by a people who are singularly free from extravagant tastes, a trade has sprung up which will probably increase largely. The genesis of this trade lay in the circumstance that a certain proportion of the able-bodied men of Kashmír went down to the Panjab every year after the autumn harvest was reaped, carrying with them local produce for sale, and these men never returned empty-handed. Many used to go down to work as coolies in the Panjab during the winter, and their wages were always spent on the purchase of commodities which were light to carry and which would either be used by their families or sold to others. Besides this trade, which was carried on the backs of the Kashmíris, there was the trade carried by the professional muleteers or *Markhbán*, a class which has always existed in Kashmír, and the trade which Panjab bullock-drivers transacted.

Routes.

Three routes were followed by trade. Of these the most direct was the road which crossed the Banihal pass and ran to Jammu; the most popular with the pony men was the old imperial road which ran over the Pír Pánjál and reached the railway at Gujrat, and the third was the route known as the Jhelum valley road, which ran along the river Jhelum from Baramula to Kohala.

CHAP. XVI.

Jhelum valley cart-road.

In September, 1890, the road from Baramula to Kohala was opened to cart traffic, and the immediate result was that trade deserted to a certain extent the Banihal and Pir Pánjál routes. But as a trade route the Jhelum valley road has up to the present disappointed expectations. It is frequently closed for months together, owing to heavy landslips, and carriers find that the cost of fodder along the line is a serious obstacle to their business. The heavy expenses entailed by the construction of the Jhelum valley road and its maintenance have prevented the Durbar from keeping the Banihal and Pir Pánjál routes in good order, and it is quite possible that until the Jhelum valley road hardens into a permanent and safe thoroughfare, with bridges capable of carrying heavy carts, its construction will not lead to an appreciable or steady increase of trade. Further, unless the alternative routes are kept in good repair, it is possible that the trade between Kashmír and the Punjab may diminish.

Total trade.

The following table shows the exports from Kashmír to the Panjab, and the imports from the Panjab to Kashmír. The figures are taken from the Panjab trade reports, and as railway communication between Kashmír and the Panjab has been much discussed of late, I have added statistics showing the trade between Ladákh and the Panjab, surmising that if Srinagar is linked with the railway all the trade with Ladákh and Yarkand will pass through Kashmír, or at any rate through Gilgit. The figures given by the Panjab trade reports deal not only with the valley of Kashmír, but include the trade of Jammu territory. It has been calculated that Kashmír proper accounts for half the trade shown in the table, but if one looks to the population of the various divisions of the Kashmír State, it would seem that Kashmír proper is given a larger share than would be justified by census statistics. The population of Jammu territory, according to the census of 1891, amounted to 1,439,543. The population of Kashmír proper amounted to only 814,241. Even if the through trade to Skardu and Gilgit be included, and their population of 127,094 be added, we should then have a population of 941,335, which is still less than half. It is unfortunate that exact figures cannot be given for the Kashmír valley, as distinguished from the rest of the territories of His Highness the Mahárájá of Jammu and Kashmír, but a fairly accurate idea can be formed of the trade of the valley, based partly on the figures shown in the statement and partly on local information obtained in Kashmír.

TABLE I.—TOTAL TRADE.

CHAP. XVI.

	EXPORTS.		IMPORTS.		TOTAL.	
	Maunds.	Value. Rs.	Maunds.	Value. Rs.	Maunds.	Value. Rs.
1884-85.						
Kashmír	Logs. 29,741 864,474	54,59,130	340,766	38,49,991	Logs. 26,741 1,205,240	93,09,121
Ladakh	15,915	3,78,321	6,069	3,39,746	21,984	7,18,067
1885-86.						
Kashmír	Logs. 44,586 792,030	51,34,913	353,262	37,77,822	Logs. 44,586 1,145,292	89,12,735
Ladakh	16,802	4,57,746	7,000	3,44,087	23,802	8,01,833
1886-87.						
Kashmír	Logs. 2,300 8,432,399	53,86,572	398,987	42,68,043	Logs. 23,030 1,242,286	96,54,615
Ladakh	7,596	2,23,067	5,797	2,24,748	13,393	4,47,815
1887-88.						
Kashmír	Logs. 25,172 1,007,498	69,31,738	478,790	53,10,303	Logs. 25,172 1,486,183	1,22,42,041
Ladakh	7,742	3,45,380	6,854	3,17,115	14,596	6,62,495
1888-89.						
Kashmír	Logs. 20,986 976,421	81,23,443	456,476	49,57,047	Logs. 20,986 1,432,897	1,30,80,499
Ladakh	8,417	3,03,624	6,112	2,99,297	14,529	6,02,921
1889-90.						
Kashmír	Logs. 9,097 1,050,057	66,40,851	540,062	56,41,947	Logs. 9,097 1,590,119	1,22,82,828
Ladakh	8,706	2,48,746	5,945	2,26,682	14,651	4,75,428
1890-91.						
Kashmír	Logs. 5,702 978,089	55,99,542	473,068	56,61,734	Logs. 5,702 1,451,157	1,12,61,276
Ladakh	7,743	3,41,908	5,820	2,85,211	13,563	6,27,119
1891-92.						
Kashmír	Logs. 20,289 1,289,249	65,05,088	565,314	66,16,145	Logs. 20,289 1,854,563	1,31,21,233
Ladakh	7,963	3,07,789	4,010	2,22,378	11,973	5,30,167
1892-93.						
Kashmír	Logs. 6,684 1,818,825	53,33,092	498,867	48,68,247	Logs. 6,684 1,317,692	1,02,01,339
Ladakh	8,938	3,22,413	4,155	2,16,141	13,093	5,38,554

CHAP. XVI. If one looks at the figures of the year 1891–92 it would appear that the opening of the Jhelum valley road had caused a large increase in trade. The value of the imports into Kashmír amounted to Rs. 66,16,145, and of the exports to Rs. 65,05,088, and the total value of the trade was greater than that of any preceding years, exceeding that of 1888–89, the next best year, by Rs. 40,734. But in 1892–93 the trade falls to an import value of Rs. 48,68,247, and an export value of Rs. 53.33,092, giving a total value of Rs. 1,02,01,339. In 1883–84, the year preceding the period covered by the table, the exports to the Panjab amounted to Rs. 52,90,127, and the imports from the Panjab amounted to Rs. 37,25,914, giving a total value of Rs. 90,16,031, so that if the trade of 1892–93 be regarded as normal there has only been an increase of Rs. 11,85,308 in ten years. But there were special causes for a falling off in trade in the year 1892–93. The harvest was bad, owing to the small amount of snow on the mountains; Srinagar was visited by a serious conflagration; and a severe epidemic of cholera paralyzed all trade in the city and the valley.

On the whole the figures given in the table need cause no despondency as to the future of the Kashmír trade. At present the country is in a transition state. Cart traffic on the Jhelum valley road has disturbed the old method of carriage, but owing to the imperfections of the road it has not yet supplanted it. Meanwhile the old method has to a certain extent fallen into abeyance. The cultivators, who were formerly obliged to work as carriers in the cold weather in order to acquire money for the payment of the land revenue, are now able to pay the revenue from the proceeds of agriculture, and they do not go down in the same numbers as in former times to the Panjab. The pony carriers of Kashmír have found a more lucrative field for carriage in the direction of Gilgit, and in 1893 some 10,000 ponies of Kashmír were employed on the Gilgit road. And lastly, owing to the costliness of the Jhelum valley road, it has been impossible to keep the other two routes in order. The outward signs of these changes are the decadence of Islamábád on the Banihal route and of Shupiyon on the Pír-Pánjál route, and the sudden growth and prosperity of Báránúlá on the Jhelum valley route and of Bạndipura on the Gilgit road. Just as trade is in a transition state owing to the change in the routes, so it is in a transition state owing to the change in the condition of the people.

I think it may be said that the agricultural classes of Kashmír are more prosperous now than they were in 1889–90. Apart from changes made in the revenue system, all tending to the betterment of the cultivators, there has been a great influx of money into Kashmír, caused by large public works, by transport operations on the Gilgit road, and by the steady increase in the number of visitors to Kashmír, who spend considerable sums in Srinagar and the valley. But this sudden increase in money does not at once lead to an increase in trade, and indeed it may for a time tend to a diminution in the export trade. Men who formerly were obliged to look to carriage and to the state of produce in the Panjab as a means of earning sufficient money to pay the land revenue have been able to earn wages locally. The Kashmíris are perhaps more improvident than any of the races of India, and if they can acquire sufficient to keep themselves and their families in comfort for the year they will make no effort to lay by money for bad times. It is therefore quite possible that an increase in prosperity among the agricultural classes may for a time tend to decrease the amount of the export trade, and it is also possible that until prosperity creates new needs and new tastes there will be no marked increase in the imports.

Dépôts of trade. In Kashmír there are certain dépôts of trade, the chief being Srinagar, Bárámúlá, Islamábád, Shupiyon, and Bandipur. Latterly Panjabi traders have opened business in these places, importing manufactured cotton and piece goods, brass, copper, and iron, salt, sugar, tea, tobacco, and a certain amount, and that an increasing amount, of petroleum. These traders export to the Panjab non-intoxicating drugs, fibres, fruits, hides and skins, ghi, linseed, rape-seed and *jingli*, wool raw and manufactured. The exports of timber and of shawls are in other hands and need not for the present be considered.

The Wáni. The Banya of India is practically unknown in Kashmír, but in all the larger villages there is found a *Wáni* or *Bakal*, who is a Musalmán huckster, with a stock-in-trade amounting to about Rs. 20 to 30 worth of salt, oil, spices, snuff, sugar, tea, and sometimes a few rolls of European or Indian cotton piece goods. When these have been disposed of the *Wáni* sets off to the nearest dépôt and replenishes his stock. The *Wáni* sometimes lends money to his customers under the system known as *wád*, to which allusion has been made in Chapter I. Although both lender and borrower repudiate the idea of interest passing, as a matter of fact the profit made by the *Wáni* represents a rate of interest varying from 24 to 36 per cent. He is a man of no enterprise, and he allows the export trade to pass entirely into the hands of the Panjabi traders of the city and the towns, who have their agents busily buying up by the system of advances all articles of the export trade. **Export trade.** The following table presents some of the most interesting facts of the export trade:—

TABLE II.—KASHMÍR TRADE.

EXPORTS. VALUE IN RUPEES.

	1886–87.	1887–88.	1888–89.	1889–90.	1890–91.	1891–92.	1892–93.
Drugs, other sorts, not intoxicating	1,78,843	2,47,016	2,61,130	2,09,571	3,40,672	4,07,969	1,60,625
Dyes	31,712	12,332	12,204	77,366	55,389	1,65,251	2,74,826
Fibres, raw	6,279	14,861	13,466	10,245	10,435	11,570	8,919
Fibres, manufactured	12,951	25,698	23,118	34,165	57,665	41,626	32,812
Fruits, other kinds	1,41,485	2,57,542	2,43,501	3,01,068	2,27,782	2,22,245	2,38,683
Hides	1,13,504	77,535	97,236	1,31,260	2,32,143	2,77,594	1,86,594
Skins	71,443	85,319	1,16,994	1,91,048	2,02,211	1,78,931	1,39,386
Leather, unmanufactured	38,430	45,100	32,407	20,190	7,430	25,920	10,218
Oilcakes	1,609	2,782	2,072	1,603	378	2,869	965
Ghi	9,19,219	11,99,048	13,15,862	15,49,774	14,55,813	15,79,640	16,58,172
Linseed	1,766	660	627	6,201	18,528	5,479	1,335
Mustard and rape	9,114	13,893	35,673	81,189	1,34,191	99,624	59,769
Til	12,140	35,283	16,000	47,160	82,941	49,644	1,07,024
Logs	1,85,914	2,89,333	2,53,765	48,282	43,890	2,02,124	49,696
Other timber	6,65,569	6,35,803	7,98,820	9,33,124	7,63,143	12,33,323	6,02,368
Wool, raw	10,386	5,697	4,880	17,602	50,795	20,001	18,149
Manufactured piece goods, Indian	5,93,257	5,49,463	6,00,729	7,17,721	6,37,522	5,11,235	5,91,439
Shawls	12,10,012	12,68,500	6,07,510	7,08,300	1,96,250	85,250	2,19,275

Drugs.

So far as the agricultural classes are concerned, drugs, fibres, fruits, oil-seeds, wool, and woollen piece goods are of the chief importance. It is the custom to send all sheep to distant grazing-grounds on the high mountains in the summer in charge of professional shepherds. Twice or three times in the season the villagers go themselves to the mountains, taking with them salt for their sheep, and they bring back various drugs and roots which have a commercial value. Of these the chief are the root of Saussurea Lappa (*chob-i-kot*)—the sale of which is a State monopoly—the leaves of *gáo zabán* (Macrotomia Benthami), and the leaves and seeds of Hyoscyamus niger, the henbane. Many other drugs are collected and sold by the villagers, and a reference to the chapter on indigenous plants yielding economic products will show the numerous articles which swell the trade heading of non-intoxicating drugs. Violets are collected, and the seeds of the quince, *bihdána*, are exported in large quantities to the Panjab. Morels bring in considerable income to the hill-villages, and are readily bought by Panjabi traders for export. The export of fibres is still in its infancy, but the valley possesses a great quantity of valuable fibres, and it is possible that if attention were paid to the abutilon a large profit could be made by its export.

Fibres.

Fruits.

The trade in fruits has reached some magnitude, and improvements in horticulture lead to the hope that there will be considerable extension in the fruit business of Kashmír. Walnuts, which used to be employed merely for the manufacture of oil, are now exported in large quantities. while apples and, to a less extent, pears find a ready market with the Panjabi traders.

Oil-seeds.

The trade in oil-seeds is at present small, but both the traders and the agriculturists are beginning to turn their attention to linseed, rape-seed, and sesame as objects of export. The soil and climate of Kashmír are eminently suited to the growth of these staples, and from an agricultural point of view it seems likely that in future years the oil-seed trade will occupy the first place. It must, however, be remembered that the Kashmíris eschew *ghi* and consume large quantities of oil in their food, so that there will always be a considerable local demand for oil. Still, if petroleum takes the place of vegetable oils as an illuminant, there will be a large quantity of oil-seeds available for export. The demand for mineral oil will vary inversely with its price, and follow the present tendency to increase with the security and cheapness of transport.

Wool.

The wool of Kashmír is of good quality, and in my opinion its production is increasing. But, in spite of the excellent fodders which can be obtained with little expense for the winter food of the sheep, and in spite of the grand grazing-grounds furnished by the mountains which encircle the valley, it is very doubtful whether sheep-farming on a large scale would

CHAP. XVI. pay. It is profitable to individuals who own small flocks of twenty to fifty sheep. Penned in the winter on the ground floor of the dwelling-house they give warmth to the house, manure to the fields, and wool for sale or use. Every cultivator has his willow trees, the leaves of which are one of the best of sheep fodders; but if any one attempted sheep-farming on big lines he would find it difficult to obtain winter fodder, and still more difficult to procure undisturbed grazing on the mountains. Every Kashmíri is a weaver, and in the winter months, all day and all night, the women spin the wool, and the men weave it into the light excellent blankets which, when worn out, are remanufactured into the *pattu* or homespun cloth so appreciated by European visitors. Kashmíri blankets form a great article of export to India, reaching in 1889–90 to a value of Rs. 7,17,721. A large amount of woollen piece goods exported from Kashmír probably escapes registration, as the Kashmíris all carry down blankets for their personal use, and these are sold in the Panjab when they set out on their return journey to Kashmír.

Fewness of indigenous traders.

The introduction of capital and foreign enterprise would lend a great stimulus to the export trade of Kashmír. The Kashmíris are lacking both in enterprise and in capital, and it will be long before a class of men arises in the valley who will engage in large trade operations. The few Panjabi traders who are found in the city and the towns have not sufficient agents to exploit the resources of the valley, while the local *Wánis* have not the means or the enterprise to take up the position of collecting-agents. The reason for this absence of enterprise will be found in the chapter on Administration, but a brief reference may be made to it in this place. The development of local trade has been utterly checked by the system under which the State itself monopolized all trade. The great staple of Kashmír, rice, has been practically kept in the hands of the Durbar, and the system of holding enormous stocks of unhusked rice and of selling the grain at very cheap rates has prevented the growth of indigenous grain merchants. Trade, like all other occupations, calls for special knowledge and special qualifications, and the result of the system of State monopolies has been that every Kashmíri villager is his own shopkeeper, and that no class corresponding to the Banyas of India exists in Kashmír. It has been the policy of the settlement to gradually set the State free from the ruinous business of storing grain and selling it at unprofitable rates, and many monopolies have been given up. The change has, however, to be made gradually, owing to the helplessness and the pauperization of the Srinagar population, and the State cannot abandon its position of sole grain-dealer until a new agency of private grain-dealers springs up. But it is clear that with every reduction of the amount of revenue taken by the State in kind there will be a corresponding expansion of private trade. The following figures will give some idea as to the extent to which the State has interfered with private trade:— CHAP. XVI.

Year.	Value of revenue taken in kind.	Value of revenue taken in cash.
	Chilki rupees.	Chilki rupees.
1862	16,93.077	9,62,057
1871	29,44,844	14,96,741
1880–81	9,87,000	5,56,000
1881–82	10,48,000	5,60,000
1882–83	8,84,000	5,99,000
1883–84	8,57,000	4,67,000
1884–85	14,05,000	5,55,000
1885–86	9,27,000	3,90,000
1886–87	9,45,000	5,61,000
1887–88	10,00,000	6,35,000
1888–89	10,04,000	5,69,000
1889–90	13,78,326	10,29,131
1890–91	12,70,882	8,76,362
1891–92	6,02,748	15,59,533
1892–93	9,50,921	14,35,377
1893–94	6,00,000	

The Rs. 6,00,000 worth of grain taken as revenue in 1893–94 will be sold to the inhabitants of Srinagar, and the State has wisely abandoned the former custom of selling grain at prices below the market rates to the people of the towns, and of providing supplies at the various staging places in the valley. Private enterprise has stepped in, and it is hoped that its success will induce the Durbar to abandon the business of selling grain to the people of Srinagar. This digression on the position held by the State in regard to the trade of Kashmír is necessary in order to explain the curious absence of local commerce, and though I am sanguine that the trade of Kashmír will increase, it will be well not to expect any rapid expansion from the improvements made in communications and from the amelioration of the condition of the agricultural classes. Briefly speaking, the Kashmír villagers, who in the absence of any class of enterprising traders were compelled to trade for themselves, are now abandoning barter and are devoting themselves to agriculture. In the interval private enterprise is springing up slowly but steadily, and if the State will withdraw from competition in the grain trade there will be a large number of merchants trading on a rational system unfettered by monopolies and by an arbitrary regulation of prices. Until this happens it is doubtful whether Kashmír trade will ever be placed on a sound footing. If one looks to India one finds that grain is the foundation of trade and of the Banya class, and until the *Wánis* of Kashmír sell necessities as well as luxuries, and become the middlemen of the producers, trade will continue to be fitful and insignificant. Perhaps the present

CHAP. XVI. condition of the rural population, unnatural though it is from a Western point of view, is in some ways to be admired. The villager produces all his necessities save salt, and does not waste his money on luxuries or run into debt. But as population increases, as it will do very rapidly if famines are averted and the ravages of cholera and smallpox are mitigated, the land of Kashmír will be fully occupied. and a landless class will arise dependent for their welfare on the existence of shops and shopkeepers. From the point of view of the urban population, the organization of trade on a healthy and rational basis is much to be desired, and it is to be hoped that the citizens of Srinagar will seize on trade as an occupation, and will not stand by idle and allow foreigners to capture the commerce of the valley. And, further, as the land-holdings in Kashmír, which are now too large for proper cultivation, become subdivided, and as the available waste becomes cultivated, the agricultural classes will have to look to export trade as a means of supplementing the resources drawn from agriculture. Rice, the great staple of agriculture, is never likely to be exported in large quantities, but there is, as above stated, probably a great future for oil-seeds. The wheat and barley of Kashmír at present do not give much promise of becoming articles of export, but oats, which have been recently introduced, and succeed in Kashmír, will probably be exported to a certain extent, and there should be a great expansion in the export of dyes, fibres, fruits, and wool, which are produced so lavishly and easily in the congenial climate of Kashmír.

Hides and skins.

Hides and skins are at present in the hands of the Watal class, and the quantity of the live stock is so great and increases so steadily that there must always be a considerable export.

Ghi.

Ghi is by far the most important article of the export trade of Kashmír, and is made chiefly by the pastoral Gujars and the nomad goatherds, who find the mountains of Kashmir a convenient and cheap resort, as the forests of India become more and more closed to the destructive buffalo and goat. The trade in ghi is entirely in the hands of middlemen, chiefly Panjabis, and the producer is at their mercy. There is still room for the expansion of this trade, and forest conservancy need not in Kashmír cause any serious diminution in the area of grazing-land. There can be no doubt that the Gujars with their buffaloes and the Bakkrwals with their goats cause great and wanton injury to the forests, nor that the grazing tax of Rs. 1.4.0 per milk buffalo and Rs. 5 per hundred head of goats is an inadequate payment for the grazing and the damage caused thereby to trees. But Kashmír is a favourite haunt of the graziers, and even if forest conservancy be made stricter and grazing fees be enhanced. buffaloes and goats will still be brought.

CHAP. XVI.

Timber.

The timber trade is practically in the hands of the State, and it is impossible to say whether the export trade is likely to expand or shrink. The general opinion is that the forests of Kashmír have been overworked, and that they will not recover for many years. It seems probable that the growing demand for timber and fuel in Kashmír itself, and the decreasing demand for logs in India, will lead to a diminution in the timber trade. The figures given in the export table point to a large decrease.

Imports.

If cotton piece goods and salt, and perhaps petroleum, be excepted from the table giving the imports into Kashmír, it will be seen that nearly all articles brought into Kashmír would fall under the head luxuries. And so far as the agricultural population is concerned, European cloth with the stamp ostentatiously displayed in a conspicuous part of the dress is looked upon as an excess of fashion and as a symptom of foppishness. My impression is that the greater part of the European and Indian piece goods imported is consumed in the city and the towns, and that only a small portion of it finds its way to the villages. The State has considered the question of starting cotton manufactures in Kashmír, and in view of the large value of the imports and of the facilities for growing cotton in the valley there is no reason why the manufacture of cotton piece goods locally should not succeed.

Piece goods.

Metals.

Metals—brass and copper—do not show any steady increase, and in the villages the excellent clay of the country affords a cheap and efficient material for cooking utensils. Copper and brass will always be required in some quantity by the coppersmiths of Srinagar, but the villagers will in all probability not take to metal cooking-utensils for a long time.

Iron.

As regards iron, the import might fall off at any moment if the State would allow the excellent iron ore of the valley to be worked. Up to quite recent times the iron of Sof furnished material for agricultural implements, and this iron, which has been described as a mild 'steel,' is even now more popular than the metal imported from India.

Salt.

Salt is of great importance, and the imports have risen rapidly since 1888-9. A certain amount of earth salt is still imported from Ladákh as food for cattle[1], but the figures given in the table refer to Panjab salt. Taking the population of the Kashmír State as 2,515,678, including Ladákh, and taking the average quantity of salt imported as 168,265 maunds, the amount of salt available for each person is somewhat over 5 lbs. per annum, but it must be remembered that from the 168,265 maunds cattle and sheep have to be fed. In India, where the consumption of salt is by no means lavish, the general average of consumption is

[1] The average quantity of salt annually imported from Ladákh is about 812 maunds, valued at Rs. 2,233.

CHAP. XVI.

TABLE III.—KASHMÍR TRADE.

IMPORTS. VALUE IN RUPEES.

	1886–87.	1887–88.	1888–89.	1889–90.	1890–91.	1891–92.	1892–93.
Cotton, raw	20,064	25,501	26,240	27,074	14,942	82,304	67,335
Cotton, manufactured, twist & yarn:							
European	49,323	66,067	31,296	49,840	70,234	64,065	76,688
Indian	24,073	45,160	32,330	24,100	21,679	25,293	21,572
Piece goods:							
European	16,63,436	22,27,436	20,62,692	23,75,700	21,30,595	22,43,390	17,06,378
Indian	3,94,075	4,60,159	4,92,196	5,84,674	4,79,234	4,67,571	3,71,893
Metals:							
Brass and copper	1,50,897	1,96,360	1,31,611	1,83,309	2,50,152	2,10,836	1,33,143
Iron	82,179	94,668	81,739	1,23,141	1,20,857	1,07,481	1,31,270
Salt	3,15,834	3,34,072	3,36,066	5,25,388	4,96,417	5,31,463	4,83,293
Sugar:							
Refined	2,83,272	2,96,874	2,82,307	2,61,379	4,85,437	3,97,945	4,82,584
Unrefined	81,934	1,04,585	89,587	88,441	1,13,147	1,78,217	1,15,433
Tea:							
Indian	2,17,677	1,99,795	1,82,122	2,07,050	1,98,995	1,05,550	1,73,730
Foreign	6,500	31,410	9,850	16,150	65,130	31,340	2,030
Tobacco	54,496	62,659	49,135	56,788	85,929	1,31,802	1,01,253
Petroleum	—	—	2,987	31,405	35,188	63,792	56,112

10 lbs. per head of population, so that it is obvious that the Kashmíris do not obtain a sufficiency. As salt is a necessity both for men and cattle, it is to be hoped that the State will use every endeavour to encourage the salt trade, and the two methods by which encouragement can be given are the improvement of communications and the reduction or abolition of the heavy duty on salt. CHAP. XVI.

Sugar.

The import of sugar, like salt, shows signs of a steady increase. But it is regarded by the agricultural classes of Kashmír as a luxury pure and simple. The Kashmíris are, however, very fond of sugar with their food and in their tea, and it is probable that as prosperity increases there will be a large and steady increase in its consumption. Schemes for the introduction of beetroot sugar manufacture, and for the propagation of the sugar maple, may some day supply the demand of the valley locally. But it seems likely that the import of sugar from India will always remain an important item in the trade of Kashmír, and if, as it is hoped, the industry of preserving and canning fruits springs up, the sugar trade will receive a further impetus.

Tea.

Tea is passing from the rank of a luxury to that of a necessity in Kashmír, and every villager of any pretension to affluence drinks his tea, while in the city and towns the public flock to the tea-shop, where, in china cups, tea mixed with milk and salt is dispensed at cheap rates. The figures given in the table would indicate a falling off in the import of Indian tea for the years 1890 to 1892-93, but as a matter of fact, though the value has decreased[1], the weight of tea imported has increased from 4806 maunds to 5238 maunds. Foreign tea is apparently liable to great fluctuations, but the general public are, I think, here as in Ladákh and Yarkand, in favour of the cheaper kinds of Indian tea. A people who used to employ yew bark and strawberry roots as a substitute for tea are not likely to be very fastidious about quality, and from experiments made to introduce certain kinds of Assam tea into the valley, I am of opinion that there is a large trade to be done in Kashmír in cheap but wholesome teas. The retail agency is present in the *Wánis*, but the merchants of Srinagar are lacking in energy and make no effort to push the sale of tea.

Tobacco and snuff.

The Kashmíris do not indulge in smoking to any extent, but men and women alike are inveterate snuff-takers, and the great bulk of the tobacco imported into Kashmír comes in that form. The best snuff comes from Peshawar. Many of the snuff-makers in that city are Kashmíris, who return to the valley in the summer bringing back part of their wages in snuff. Every *Wáni's* shop has a row of bottles containing snuff, which is sold in small packets made of birch bark.

Petroleum.

Petroleum has been included in the table, not because it is at present

[1] In 1893-94 the import of tea rose by more than one lakh of rupees.

CHAP. XVI. a large item of trade, but because I believe that the process by which petroleum has displaced vegetable oils as an illuminant in India will be repeated in Kashmír. In the hill-villages, however, near the pine forests, the villagers light their houses by torches of pine-wood. So I doubt whether petroleum will find its way to the higher tracts of the valley for many years, unless indeed the Forest Department prohibits the ancient custom of destroying pine trees for the sake of light.

Future of Kashmir trade.

It would be rash to attempt to predict the future of the trade of Kashmír. Its expansion depends rather on the development and tastes of the agricultural community than on the industries and wants of the people of the city and towns. The shawls for which Kashmír was once so famous are practically extinct, and the manufacture of carpets and embroideries occupies a certain portion of the fine-fingered weavers only. Various art manufactures flourish in a fitful and unbusiness-like fashion, but the profits are made by the middlemen, who are 'sweaters' of the most pronounced type. The poor workmen derive from their labour hardly sufficient to keep themselves alive, and wages are kept down because the State sells the staple grain at cheap rates below the real market prices. In short the art manufactures of Srinagar are bringing profit to a few middlemen, but no wealth to the working-classes, and the people of Srinagar will not, until things are radically changed, be in a position to take imported articles. If the State were to abandon the present ruinous system of providing the city people with cheap rice, the middlemen would have to content themselves with a profit less than 50 per cent., and would be obliged to raise wages. I do not believe that the industries of Srinagar will ever be healthy or vigorous until the Darbar gives up this semi-bounty, which brings nothing to the revenue. Nor do I see anything in the present condition of the art manufactures of Srinagar which points to an increase of wealth in the working-classes. The aristocracy is rapidly becoming poorer and less able to indulge in luxuries. Their perquisites have ceased and are now divided between the State and the agricultural classes. Up to quite recent times the agricultural classes cultivated merely for subsistence, and were happy if they struggled through the year with a minimum of hungry days. Profits from agriculture were taken by official middlemen, and the cultivator made no effort to improve or extend cultivation, or to obtain a surplus which would be available for the purchase of comforts or luxuries. But this has changed, and at the present time the agricultural population does secure a balance after supplying the needs of life and meeting the State's revenue demand. This balance must find its way into trade before long, but the Kashmíris are somewhat slow in grasping the changed position, and in realizing that their life is not bounded by the reaping and division of the autumn harvest. They are also slow in acquiring new tastes. So the increase in the prosperity of the agricultural classes will probably manifest itself in an enhanced consumption of salt, sugar, tea, and tobacco. But it will be long before they adopt expensive fashions of dress or more durable material for their household utensils They are frugal in their expenditure and do not lavish money on marriage feasts or extravagances of a similar nature, as is the case in India. This unhappily may change, and the Kashmíri will be driven to furnish staples for export in order to supply himself with the luxuries offered by the import trade.

Internal trade.

I have said little regarding the internal trade of Kashmír, and it may be dismissed in a few words. There are grain merchants in Srinagar and the towns who import grain from the villages to supplement that provided by the State. Their position has hitherto been precarious, as they never knew how much grain the State would bring to the city, and they never felt certain whether the State would not at the last moment issue some regulation altering the prices of grain and thus upsetting their calculations. Since the State has withdrawn from dealing in any commodity save unhusked rice and maize, the grain merchants have extended their operations, but, as shown above, want of capital, absence of enterprise, and the fact that most Kashmíri citizens of any position make their own arrangements for purchasing grain direct from the villages, have prevented the local dealers in Srinagar from securing their proper position of middlemen between the village producers and the city consumers. The city and the towns import village produce, and export to the villages salt, sugar, tea, and tobacco, and a small amount of cotton piece goods.

Through cart-road to Srinagar.

The cart-road from Báráműlá to Srinagar will probably give a great impetus to internal trade. The boatmen of Kashmír bear a bad reputation, and the grain-dealers in Srinagar restrict their operations to the immediate neighbourhood of the city, bringing in grain and other village produce by pony or coolie carriage. The new road will enable them to extend their purchases to more distant villages, and trade will no longer be hampered by the frauds and adulteration in which the boatmen are so expert. It is impossible to correctly forecast the future of Kashmír trade, but the two important dépôts for the country may be Muzaffarabad for the Jhelum valley road and Rámbhan for the Banihal road. If a railway is made through the Hazara district, Muzaffarabad will only be two stages from the railroad, and carts will quickly carry goods from Muzaffarabad to Srinagar. The heavy work entailed by the ascent to Murree will be avoided, and in ordinary winters traffic might continue unchecked by the snow which usually blocks the road through Murree. As regards Rámbhan, a very slight expenditure would make the road from the railway station at Jammu to Rámbhan passable for camels. From Rámbhan it is only three stages to Kashmír, and Kashmír ponies

CHAP. XVI. and coolies could throw an immense quantity of supplies into the valley if there was a well-stocked dépôt at Rámbhan. Grass and water are abundant on the Banihal route, and it is the most direct line to the Punjab. It is in many ways to be regretted that the State did not bring the cart-road via the Banihal instead of via Báràmúlá, and it is to be hoped that before long the Durbar will add to the prosperity of Kashmír by constructing a cart-road from Jammu to Srinagar. There are no serious engineering difficulties.

CHAPTER XVII.

THE OLD ADMINISTRATION.

Chap. XVII.

Land revenue.

It is usual under the head of administration to treat at length the various branches, executive and judicial, criminal, police and gaols, revenue taxation and registration, education and medical staff, and dispensaries [1]; and though all these branches of administration are to be found in Kashmír, I shall only discuss in this chapter the working of the Land Revenue Department, which is by far the most difficult and the most important branch of the administration of Kashmír. Happily hitherto there has been very little litigation in the valley, so that the Judicial Department has not had much effect on the people; crime is almost unknown, thus the police and gaols do not concern the great mass of the population; while education and dispensaries are still in their infancy. I imagine that in Kashmír, as in other Native States, where civilization is not so far advanced as it is in British India, the happiness and welfare of the people depend almost entirely on the revenue system and the methods of taxation. Perhaps owing to the peculiarities of the administration in Kashmír the revenue system has had a more momentous effect on the character and development of the people than it has had in any other Native State. Before discussing the revenue system as it stood when the settlement of Kashmír was commenced, I would remark that in a country where there were no records or maps to indicate what a man's holding in land amounted to, or to show what his revenue liabilities were, it is surprising, not that full justice was not done in cases of land disputes and in matters relating to taxation, but that any kind of justice was meted out to litigants, and it is probable that the helplessness and ignorance of the revenue officials was one of the chief causes why litigation has not hitherto possessed the same charm for the Kashmíris as it possesses for the Indians. The next point I would notice is that there has never been continuity in the administration

[1] Details on these subjects will be found in Chapter IX.

CHAP. XVII.

of Kashmír. Even since the commencement of the Dogra rule, there has been the annual interregnum when the Mahárájá leaves the valley at the end of the summer for his winter capital at Jammu, and it is during this interval that officialdom worked its own will on the people unchecked by the Darbar. The Kashmíri people are clever and voluble conversationists, and during the years which I have spent in camp I can never remember any man speaking in other than terms of affection and admiration of the Mahárájás, and they invariably attribute all their wrongs to officials who have kept their masters in ignorance of the real facts of the revenue administration. There have of course been good and active officials in Kashmír who inspected the villages and kept their subordinates under strict control, but these men, whose names are still well remembered and respected in the valley, were not of the Pandit class, but came from the Jammu country. They may have been harsh and stern, but they knew the country and did their best to encourage cultivation and to prevent petty peculation. They were loyal to their master, and were wise enough to see that in most points the interests of the Mahárájá and the people were identical. But unfortunately these vigorous and loyal officials were few in number, and the desperate condition into which Kashmír had fallen when the present Mahárájá decided to carry out a settlement was due to the fact that revenue officials from the highest to the lowest combined to rob their master and to despoil the people. It was no new thing, for peculation and oppression had been equally common in the times of the Patháns and Sikhs, but peculation was placed on a safe and intelligent basis when the administration was practically vested in the hands of the Pandits of Kashmír. In revenue matters in the East it is always right to trace effects to their first causes, and in Kashmír the revenue administration proceeds from the *patwari*, the village accountant, and he is a Pandit. On cramped pieces of paper or birch bark which he hides away in the deep pocket of his ample gown he enters the area of the holding of each villager. It has been pointed out that the *patwari* keeps three editions of this statement of holding, 'one for himself, which may be supposed to be near the truth, one for the *tahsíldar*, and another for the villagers, the two latter being prepared with a view to convincing each side of the excellent bargain he has secured.' The area of the holdings was not ascertained by measurement, but was calculated by the amount of seed required for each field, and experience gained during survey operations shows that the headmen and influential villagers were apparently able to cultivate with far less seed than their poorer brethren, and in consequence their holdings were, according to the *patwaris'* papers, much smaller and their land revenue much lighter than that of men who in reality held only a fraction of the areas possessed by the powerful members of the village. Over the *patwaris* was a small

Old officialdom.

The old *patwari*.

band of Pandits, who were employed in the tahsíl in various revenue capacities, but they did not condescend to manipulate the taxation of individuals, and dealt with villages as a whole. Over the *patwari* and the tahsíl Pandits was a *tahsíldar* and one or two *naib-tahsíldars*, mostly Pandits. There were fifteen tahsíls, and these tahsíls were divided into three districts or *wazárats*, which were presided over by officers known as *wazir wazárats*, all of whom were Pandits. These *wazirs* were subordinate to the *Hakim-i-Ala* or Governor of Kashmír, and his revenue establishment, known as the *Daftar-i-Diwáni*, was composed entirely of Pandits. CHAP. XVII.

In a country where education has not yet made much progress it is only natural that the State should employ the Pandits, who at any rate can read and write with ease. They are a local agency, and as they have depended on office as a means of existence for many generations, it is just and expedient to employ them. Still it is to be regretted that the interests of the State and of the people should have been entrusted to one class of men, and still more to be regretted that these men, the Pandits, should have systematically combined to defraud the State and to rob the people. The Pandits are loyal to one another, and the village *patwari* knows that when awkward questions are asked he has friends at the tahsíl, at the head-quarters of the *wazir wazárat*, and in the *Daftar-i-Diwáni*. It was a powerful ring of iron, inside which the village taxpayer lay fascinated, and if he were wise, silent. It is frequently remarked that a Native State does little for the people, and spends but a small amount of its revenue on the material development of the country by public works, or on the moral development of the people by education, but in defence of the system of Native States it should be remembered that the State is most liberal in its expenditure on offices. In recent times there were few Pandits who were not in receipt of pay from the State, and the number of offices was legion. But though this generosity in the matter of official establishments was an enormous boon to the Pandit class, it was a curse and misfortune to the Musalmáns of Kashmír; for the Pandit does not value a post for its pay, but rather for its perquisites, and every post in the valley was quickly made a source of perquisites. I have no wish to condemn the Pandits, and have always recognized that any other class of men, given the same opportunities for peculation which the Pandits have enjoyed, would have been equally lax in official morality, and I have strong hopes that when honesty and industry are properly encouraged, and laziness and dishonesty are fittingly discouraged, the Pandits will prove themselves worthy and efficient servants of the State. But in order to understand the remarks I shall have to make on the revenue administration of Kashmír, it is necessary to grasp the fact that official morality has, generally speaking, been non-existent.

CHAP. XVII.

Old systems of revenue.

As in other parts of India, the chief revenue of the country is drawn from the land, and there have been various systems under which this revenue was collected. In the early Hindu period the State was contented with one-sixth of the produce of the land. In the time of the Sultáns the State took one-half. Their Mughal successors, who found the valley in a ruined condition, considered that one-half the produce of the country would not suffice for the wants of the city population, and accordingly decreed that the cultivating classes should dispense with grain for three months and should live on fruits, and the State's share was from that time three-quarters of the produce of the land[1]. The land in those days was apparently regarded as the absolute property of the State, and every year allotments were made to the cultivators. Coming down to later times we find in A. D. 1859 the country parcelled out among *kárdárs*, who were land agents of the State, with very large powers. The *kárdár* divided his charge into three belts. In the lower belt he would allow nothing to be grown but rice, in the middle belt he allowed some rice to be grown, and in the highest belt he permitted no rice. It was the *kárdár's* duty to get the largest possible amount of grain for the State, and he knew that rice cultivation at a high altitude was on the whole unprofitable.

Every year the *kárdár* would arrange for the cultivation of the estate. The unit was known as '*nafre*,' which consisted of a man and his wife and one adult son. To the *nafre* was given four acres of irrigated land. The *nim nafre*, or half unit, consisted of a man and his wife, and they were given two acres of irrigated land. The *pao nafre*, or quarter unit, was a bachelor, and he only received one-and-a-half acres of irrigated land. After the *kárdár* had made his annual distribution of the land the village passed into the hands of a person known as *shakdár*, whose duty was to sit in the village and watch the crops. In a large village there would be several *shakdárs*, one to each threshing-floor. The *shakdár* received 8 kharwars of *shali* from the State, and took as his perquisite about 12 kharwars from the village. Over the *shakdárs* was an official known as *sazawol*, who received for ten months in the year Rs. 2½ per mensem. When the harvest-time came a regiment known as the *nizámat paltan*[2] moved out into the villages to enforce the State's claim, and this regiment was always supplemented by sepoys from the regular army.

The State took three-quarters of rice, maize, millets, and buckwheat, and

[1] *Ain Akbari.* Sultan Shams-ud-Din (Shah Mir) 'exacted from the husbandman only a fourth of the produce of the soil,' but cf. *ibid.*

'Although formerly Government was said to take only a third of the produce of the soil, yet in fact the husbandman was not left in the enjoyment of near one-half, but His Majesty (Akbar) has now commanded that the crops shall be divided equally between the husbandman and the State.'

[2] In 1884 the Nizámat regiments consisted of 7,429 men Of these the greater part were stationed in Kashmír.

of oil-seeds, pulses, and cotton the share taken was nine-sixteenths. This system lasted till A.D. 1860, when the State reduced its share to a little over one-half, but this liberality was more than discounted by the unfortunate devices which were adopted for the collection of revenue. Speculating contractors, known as *chakladárs*, came in, who robbed the State and the cultivators, and where the *chakladárs* did not see their way to making large profits the land was held *amáni*, that is, the State took its share of the actual produce of a village. The system of farming out groups of villages to *chakladárs* continued till 1873, when an attempt was made to introduce a three years' raiyatwari settlement. This was of course unpopular with the contractors and the swarms of middlemen who had lived at their ease on the old system, and even if the great famine of 1877–79 had not thrown the whole country into confusion, the officials would have nullified all the benevolent intentions of the scheme introduced in 1873.

System in 1880.

In 1880 an assessment supposed to be on holdings, but really an assessment on villages, was made, known as the *assámiwár khewat*, and the basis of this assessment was supposed to have been the average of the collections of the three previous years. This is still known as the cash assessment, but it was only a cash assessment in name, and it rested with the *Hakim-i-Ala* to say, year by year, how much of the assessment he would take in cash and how much in kind. This assessment of 1880 is practically the only financial foundation upon which I have had to work, and the cultivators whose names were entered in the papers of 1880 are regarded as having stronger claim to the occupancy right in land than those who left their villages in the great famine and have since returned. In the Assessment Reports which I have submitted for the 15 tahsíls of Kashmír various details are given as to the assessment of 1880 and its subsequent modifications, and the remarks which I now make are general, and apply to the whole of the valley. In 1880 the work of assessment was done in a very brief and expeditious manner. A few picked officials went to the various centres of Kashmír and announced the assessments which would be taken from the villages. No attempt was made to inspect villages or to ascertain the condition of the cultivators and the state of irrigation or of cultivation. The average of the previous year's collections was taken, and to this a considerable percentage, never less than 30 per cent., was added in order to guard the State against loss. Thus it happened that villages which by some chance had held together and tided over the famine were called upon to pay heavily, while villages which had broken down and had not recovered before 1880 got off lightly. This is one of the causes of the unequal incidence of taxation, but as the assessing officers did not think it necessary to examine the villages or to obtain statistics of population this inequality is not to be wondered at. But there were other causes at

CHAP. XVII. work which caused irregularity. An influential headman of a village knew how to propitiate the assessing officers and how to throw the burden of taxation from his village on to the smaller and weaker villages. As a matter of form each village was asked whether it accepted the new assessment. Some accepted, but those who refused were soon brought to their senses, and each assessing officer vied with another in his zeal to secure a fine revenue for the State. In many instances these zealous officials actually told the villagers that the revenue was nominal and would not be collected. Often they told the villagers that at least half of the assessment would be given back in the form of seed grain, but in spite of their blandishments there was little inclination on the part of the majority of the villages to accept the assessment of 1880. Then, after one or two days' work, the assessing officers hurried back in their boats to Srinagar and proudly laid the results of their operations before the authorities *on paper*. The Kashmíri, in spite of his abject condition, is a very obstinate and determined person, and in cases where he considered that the assessment was too high he has steadily declined to pay the excess. An active and severe official has occasionally realized the revenue assessed in 1880 in full by selling up the sheep and cattle of a village, but the next year the village was fallow and the cultivators had emigrated to other villages more fairly assessed, or had taken service as farm labourers under some privileged landholder. No attempt was made by the assessing officers in 1880 to distribute the land revenue of a village over the holdings, and this most difficult and delicate work was left to the *patwari* and *lambardár*, with the natural result that very little of the revenue fell on the holdings of the *patwari* and *lambardár* and very much fell on the holdings of their enemies. The Kashmíris, when talking of the revenue administration, constantly observe that faith has never been kept with them, and certainly if they expected, as they affirm, that the assessment of 1880 would be allowed to stand, they have reason to be doubtful about the faith of officials. It is, however, fair to remark that it was impossible to make a just assessment in 1880, as the country had only just passed through the miseries of the famine, and villagers were wandering about and cultivation was in an unsettled condition. But it is to be regretted that more breathing-time was not given to the men who were present at the assessment of 1880, and still more to be regretted that the arrangements made for enhancement were carried out with so little consideration for the people or for the prosperity of the country.

Izád boli. In 1882 the device of auctioning villages (*izád boli*) was adopted, with very disastrous results. Officials paid a hurried visit to the various tahsíls, accompanied by a string of needy Pandits, boatmen, snuff-sellers, and other adventurous spirits from the city, and the greater part of the villages of

Kashmír were formally auctioned. The auctioneers seem to have been men of some humour, for they laid great stress on the fact that certain villages possessed charming and shady plane trees, and that the cultivators were an extremely amenable people who would gladly pay the revenue to the highest bidder at the auction. The whole business was conducted in a jocose spirit, and the only parties who had reason to be sorry were the State and the villagers. The Pandits, boatmen, &c., who bid for villages knew nothing of the capacity of the village and cared less, for they were speculating on the year's crops, and in Kashmír no man seems to look beyond the twelve months. As it happened that the year's crops were not very good, nearly all the speculating bidders (*mustájír*), after taking all they could wring from the villagers, absconded without paying the State a single rupee. I have given many instances of the results of the auction sales in my Assessment Reports. In one tahsíl a group of eight villages had been managed by an influential headman who paid the State Rs. 5,500 per annum. At the auction sales an ignorant boatman bid Rs. 13,000 for these villages, but after one month's experience he absconded and these eight villages were saddled with a revenue of Rs. 13,000. Of course this has never been paid; but, what is worse, the original Rs. 5,500 has never been realized since the auction sale. The worst part of the auction sales was that, although the men who had run up the revenue of the villages were not to be found when the time for payment came, and although it was obvious to the meanest intellect that the sums offered at the auction could never be squeezed out of the wretched villagers, and that the whole business was a farce, still the sums offered were regarded as the future revenue demand of the village, and every effort has been made to realize an impossible and fictitious revenue demand year by year.

Kasr-i-nirkh.

One would have thought that the auction scheme was enough for one year, but a further blow was struck by the revenue officials, and a change in the commutation rate sanctioned in 1880 was made. In 1880 it was decided that the villagers should receive a credit of Rs. 1-4-0 per kharwar of *shálí* and maize, paid by them as revenue to the State. In 1880 the value of *shálí* and maize in the city was about equal. But soon after maize began to depreciate, and it was resolved to alter the commutation rate. It was also discovered that something had to be paid by the State for the transport of grain taken as revenue to the city, and it struck the officials that the cost might very well be borne by the villagers. So the commutation rate was altered, and the villagers, instead of receiving Rs. 1-4-0 for maize, were only allowed a commutation rate of 15 annas, while for *shálí* they received 16 or 17 annas. Inasmuch as a large proportion of the revenue was taken in kind, this alteration in the commutation rate (*kasr-i-nirkh*) caused great loss to the villagers. Various other devices were from

CHAP. XVII. time to time introduced by the officials to screw up the revenue, but they were on a small scale, and chiefly took the simple form of abstracting land from the assessed area of a village and making it over to some influential Pandit or assigning it to the Land Improvement Department (*tarakiát*). There are very few villages in which there is not a *takrári jama*, or item of revenue disputed by the villagers, and this item is as a rule cast into the limbo of arrears. In order to show the working of the revenue system in Kashmír between the years 1880 and 1887, when the settlement commenced, I will try to describe an ordinary village. Its revenue in 1880 was assessed on the basis that the State took ten-sixteenths of the gross produce of the autumn crops and nine-sixteenths of the spring crops. To the revenue thus obtained an addition of over 30 per cent. was made. Two years later the village was put up to auction, and in the same year the commutation rate for revenue in kind was lowered from 20 to 16 annas. The revenue demand in 1880 was about Rs. 2,000, but by 1882 it had been raised to Rs. 2,939. The *patwari* and *lambardár* settled between themselves how this Rs. 2,939 was to be distributed over the cultivators of the village, but they made up their minds that the assessment was too high by Rs. 600, and every year this village has paid up a nominal revenue of Rs. 2,339, and every year Rs. 600 has been entered as arrears. I say the nominal revenue, for by the system under which the *Hakim-i-Ala* year by year settled the amount of cash and of kind to be taken, the revenue could be greatly modified and manipulated. For under the old system the State did not merely take *shâli* and maize in payment of revenue, but accepted cotton, oil-seed, and pulses (*ghalat kimiti*), and for some mysterious reason the commutation rate allowed for these commodities was sometimes double the rate at which these articles could be bought in the bazaar. So the preoccupation of the village was to induce the officials to take as much of the revenue of Rs. 2,339 in cotton, oil-seeds, and pulses as possible, and as little in *shâli* and maize, which they wanted for the support of themselves and their children. If they were complaisant, quiet people, ready to oblige every official from the tahsíldar down to the village watchman with 'loans,' at least Rs. 1,000 would be taken in cotton and oil-seeds; for although neither oil-seeds nor cotton were grown in the village, they could be easily bought from the State stores. If they were unusually complaisant, the greater part of the balance, Rs. 1,339, would be taken in cash, and the happy village would have enough *shâli* or maize for their year's food. But one year the people were foolish and demurred to 'lending,' their excuse being that there had been three changes of tahsíldars in the year, and the third tahsíldar in his wrath made an example of them, and instead of taking cotton and oil-seeds pounced on the *shâli*. That year the village dispersed, and at the time of survey it could not have paid a revenue of

Rs. 1,000. The greater part of the land was out of cultivation, and though the old cultivators have now come back, it will be some years before the village will be able to pay a revenue of Rs. 2,339. This system of annually settling the demand in kind and in cash was known as the *mujawaza*. It has been a source of enormous profit to the officials, of great loss to the State, and of misery and demoralization to the people.

Mujawaza.

Seed grain advances.

Before the settlement commenced it was necessary to force the people to cultivate, and as sufficient grain had not been left for the purposes of the winter's food and the spring sowings, it was the custom to allot to each village a certain amount of grain for seed. This advance was known as *tukm musáda*, but, as I have shown in the chapter on Agriculture, every cultivator saves his own seed grain, and would never use the mixed and adulterated grain which came from the State storehouses. Sometimes in cases of great emergency the people would take State grain to save themselves from starvation, but as a rule the advances of seed grain were merely an instrument of peculation. The grain never reached the cultivators, but was divided between the officials, the village headman, and the *patwari*, and the value of the grain was gravely entered every year as an arrear against the village.

Arrears.

When the officials have exhausted the resources of the *mujawaza* and *musáda* they have an equally fertile source of perquisites in arrears (*báki*), and until the settlement commenced it was in the power of the tahsíldar to decide year by year how much of the revenue demand should stand over as an arrear. It was an understood thing that in any tahsíl certain villages should be regarded as poor and unable to pay the revenue, and each new tahsíldar would add a few villages to the list (*sakim-ul-hal*[1]. But when I commenced the inspection of villages, I soon found that the *sakim-ul-hal* villages were often in far better condition than others not on the list, and I have discovered that the whole system of arrears was a conspiracy between the headmen of the villages and the officials to defraud the State. The fraud was a very simple one. A village has to pay Rs. 1,000 per annum as revenue, and in all probability could easily pay that amount. But having got on the list of *sakim-ul-hal* it would never pay more than

[1] *Sakim-ul-hal* signifies 'infirm condition.' I quote remarks made by me in the Assessment Report of the Chirat Tahsíl, para. 6:—'As it is in these two villages, so it is in the other thirty-eight villages which are entered in the tahsíldar's list of *sakim-ul hal*. They know that their nominal revenue is absurd, and that it cannot be collected. Some villages, owing to slack supervision, are able to conceal their crops; others bribe the tahsíl authorities, and pay about one-half of what they could with ease pay and with justice be called on to pay. I have frequently heard lambardars and villagers of honest revenue-paying villages complain that it is unfair that they should have to pay their revenue in full, while a neighbouring village of equal advantages only has to pay about one-half of its proper revenue, because it is entered in the *sakim-ul-hal* list. The system is a very bad and dangerous one, and it spreads very quickly. If it is not at once checked by the introduction of fair assessments, the greater part of the Chirat villages will become *sakim-ul-hal*.'

CHAP. XVII. Rs. 700. Of the balance, Rs. 150 would go to the officials, and Rs. 50 would be divided between the headman and *patwari* of the village, and the remaining Rs. 100 would be divided among the cultivators. A sum of Rs. 300 would be entered as arrears, but both the villagers and the officials knew perfectly well that the arrears would never be collected. In such a case as this it will be observed that there was a certain amount of honourable dealing, and the cultivators were allowed to share in the robbery. But more often the whole revenue would be collected from the villagers, and the amount of Rs. 300 which was entered by the officials as arrears would be divided among officials, with perhaps a small present for the headman of the village and the *patwari*.

In nearly every village there are huge arrears of revenue, the greater part of which was absolutely fictitious. The famine of 1877–79 naturally caused heavy arrears which could not and ought not to have been realized. Then came the auction sales of 1882, by which the revenue was run up by men who were mere speculators, and had no intention of paying the amounts which they had bid for the farm of the villages. The increase offered by these farmers (*mustájir*), but never paid by them, was considered as part of the revenue demand, and has been solemnly entered year by year as an arrear against the villages.

I have shown in my Assessment Reports how the enormous arrear statement has been swelled by items which in justice could never have been demanded from the villagers. Land was often taken from the assessed area for public purposes, or rather for the private purposes of officials, but no revenue was remitted on this account. Grants of revenue to be collected in kind were often made to individuals for services in no way connected with the villages, and the amounts realized by these persons were shown every year as an arrear against the villages, although they had paid up their full revenue. Many other instances have been noticed in the Assessment Reports, and the probable reason why the Darbar has not been beset by the howls of the people is, that there was a tacit understanding between the villagers and the officials that arrears would do no one any harm, except of course the State. But this system, ruinous as it has been from a financial point of view, has been equally disastrous as a means of corrupting the people. An honest village which paid its revenue would soon lose heart when it saw its neighbours waxing fat under the designation of *sakim-ul-hal*, while a straightforward and difficult endeavour to discharge its revenue liabilities met with very little encouragement on the part of the officials. If a village stood out too long and declined to join in the conspiracy to rob the State, the officials could soon make it see the error and folly of its ways, and if in such a village arrears occurred from floods or drought or some calamity of the season, no mercy would be shown when the time of collecting the revenue came. Under the name *giriftani* the *tahsíldar* every year would decide how much should be collected on account of arrears, and pressure in the matter of *giriftani* for arrears which were fictitious would soon ruin a village. In short, when one considers the past system of the revenue administration, one wonders that any village should have remained honest in the midst of so much corruption, and wonders too, not that the land revenue rapidly decreased, but that any revenue should have found its way to the State Treasury. It should be remembered here that the system of accounts was so intricate and dark, that a real falling off in revenue could be explained away to the Darbar by some elaborate statement which obscured the real facts. No official from the *patwari* upwards would ever admit that there was a falling off in the revenue, and it was for that reason that land taken up for public purposes was still retained on the revenue roll, and that revenue alienated under the order of the Darbar for services and collected by the grantee was shown each year as an arrear against the village. In my Assessment Report on the Ich-Nagam tahsíl, I quoted the case of Mahanur as an instance of the way in which revenue accounts were kept in the Daftar-i-Diwani. At the time of assessing Mahanur I found that the Daftar-i-Diwani had a bill of arrears amounting to Rs. 8,139 against it for the years 1880–89. The annual revenue demand for these years was Rs. 821, and I found from the *patwari's* accounts that the annual collections had amounted to Rs. 873, so that instead of being in arrears Mahanur had paid up Rs. 52 per annum in excess of its revenue. On pursuing my inquiries I found that the village had been held by a revenue-farmer, who paid in the revenue to the Treasury in full, but took from the Treasury an equivalent sum in the form of *musáda*. The farmer has, like all the other revenue-farmers in Kashmír, disappeared from the revenue system, after holding Mahanur free of revenue for nine years.

Giriftani.

It would be interesting from an historical point of view to mention numerous other devices for defrauding the State which were practised by the officials, but as they and the abuses mentioned above have now been stopped and cannot very easily be revived I will devote my space to dealing with other abuses which, although greatly reduced, still linger on.

Collections in kind.

The city of Srinagar contains a population of 118,960, mostly paupers, in the sense that they could not exist unless they were fed with grain at State rates, which at the time I now write are exactly one-half of the real or market rates. A great part of the city population consists of shawl-weavers, who in the days when Kashmír shawls were in demand, contributed a large revenue to the State, amounting, it is said, to Rs. 6,00,000 or 7,00,000 per annum. In those days, from a financial point of view, it paid the State to give the shawl-weavers cheap grain, in spite of the fact that the

CHAP. XVII. system of realizing the greater part of the land revenue in kind checked cultivation and utterly impeded the development of the agricultural resources of Kashmír, and that this cheap grain and the exemption from *begár* granted to all shawl-weavers resulted in large numbers abandoning cultivation and flocking to the city to take up the work of weaving. But the shawl trade received its deathblow in 1870, when war broke out between Germany and France, and the shawl-weavers no longer contribute to the revenue of the State. Yet though the only financial reason for taking revenue in kind and selling grain at rates far lower than the real rates to the city people has disappeared, the influential Pandits and others who reside in Srinagar have brought such pressure to bear upon the Darbar that the old system continues, and the State still accepts the difficult and ruinous responsibility of feeding 130,000[1] persons at pauper rates[2]. I shall deal with the question in another chapter, and here shall only discuss the effects of the system of collecting revenue in kind from the point of view of the cultivator and of the revenue officials. Many authorities maintain that the old system, under which oriental governments took a share of the crops, possessed at any rate the virtue of elasticity, and that the State and the people suffered alike and gained alike in bad and good seasons. But it will have been seen that in Kashmír there was no such elasticity, for the revenue demand was fixed irrespective of the vicissitudes of the season, but instead of paying the revenue in hard cash, as they do in India, the Kashmíris paid a part in cash and a part in kind, and it rested with the *Hakim-i-Ala* of the year to say how much should be taken in kind, and whether the State would take the great food staples from the people or cotton, oil-seeds, and pulses.

In my settlement I have endeavoured to remove as many opportunities for peculation as possible, and have limited the demand in kind to *shâli* and maize, and have taken the greater bulk of the revenue in cash. I am of opinion that it would have been just to have taken the whole of the revenue in cash, and the cultivators would have gladly paid the land revenue in cash, but the Darbar had to consider the interests of the people of the city as well as those of the cultivators. Accordingly in 1892 I was directed to provide for the collection of 3,500,000 kharwars of *shâli* and maize for the purpose of feeding the city people, and though I consider it is a mistake to take so large a share of the revenue in kind, I admit that the helplessness of the city, caused by long years of pauperization and the backwardness of private enterprise and trade, furnished good argument for the decision

[1] The city proper contains a population of 118,960. The State, however, gives grain at favoured rates to some of the outlying villages.

[2] Burke's words should be remembered: 'And having looked to Government for bread, on the very first scarcity they will turn and bite the hand that fed them.'

arrived at by the State. My chief objection to the realization of any part of the State's revenue in kind is that it gives opportunities for endless peculation, and that whereas it is possible to check exactions when the revenue is taken in cash, and to prove cases of illegal exaction against the officials, it is almost impossible to prevent excessive collections of grain. By the settlement record it has been feasible to decide exactly how much grain each holding should pay to the State, and each cultivator has documents showing the amount of cash and of kind he has to pay at each of the four instalments of revenue. But a clever weighman (*tarazudár*) can by a turn of the wrist add a considerable amount to the weighment, and the officials have to be propitiated if a bad sample of grain is to be palmed off on the State. When the time comes for the collection of *sháli* or maize the cultivator's heap looks big enough to last him through the year, and it would be churlish to grudge a few handfuls to the officials and their followers. But many handfuls soon arouse the unfortunate revenue-payer to the fact that for every fifteen traks of *sháli* or maize which he has to pay to the State he has paid seventeen traks. He then comes to me with a complaint, but when an investigation is made no proof is forthcoming. I have attempted to introduce grain measures in order to do away with the weighman, but am met with the difficulty that the different kinds of *sháli* vary in bulk and weight, and I am of opinion that so long as the State takes any of its revenue in kind, so long will peculation flourish. And it is necessary to bear in mind that as one by one the various methods of peculation are removed, the officials naturally turn their attention to the one opportunity that now remains for making money, and the system of collections in kind affords that opportunity.

Kár begár.

The power enjoyed by the officials under the system of *mujawaza*, in virtue of which they could deprive a village of its year's food stocks, was great, but not so great as the power wielded by them in the levy of *begár*, or forced labour. A man could sometimes hide his grain in secret pits (*zusu*), and could save enough food to keep him and his children alive till the fruits and vegetables came, but it was more difficult to hide himself when the officials were on the look-out for human carriage, and the Kashmír pressgang would watch and wait if a reluctant villager fled to the mountains. *Begár* means to the Kashmíris far more than the mere impressment of labour, for under its comprehensive name every kind of demand for labour or property taken but not paid for by the officials was included. I will first deal with the labour side of *begár*.

It is an unfortunate fact that in Kashmír there is no special labouring class. The agricultural population is not yet sufficient for the full and proper cultivation of the soil, and their chief staple, rice, is a crop of so exacting a nature that great damage is caused if the cultivators are kept

CHAP. XVII. away too long from the villages. The labouring class under other administrations would have long ago been found in the city, but it has been the custom to exempt the people of Srinagar from *begár* and to throw the whole demand for labour on the villagers, who have no leisure for such labour. Other exemptions have been made, and Pandits, Sikhs, Pirzádas, Gujars, and cultivators working on the land grants of officials and others are free from all fear of being seized for *begár*, and, in consequence of these exemptions, out of a total population of 814,241, 52,216 men are free because they are Hindus, 4,092 because they are Sikhs, and 114,170 because they are Musalmáns residing in the city and the towns. I cannot give the number of the Pirzádas, or of the very numerous Musalmáns who cultivate under privileged landholders and jágirdárs, but according to the census in two jágirs alone there is a population of 24,334 which is wholly exempt from State *begár*. At the very lowest computation, I should think that, out of a total population of 814,241, 350,000 persons are exempt from *begár* by rule, and that another 50,000 are exempt by favour. It follows that the incidence of *begár* falls with intense severity on the remaining 414,241. Considering the area of Kashmír, it might be supposed a population of 414,241, or, excluding women and children, about 138,080 men, would be sufficient to perform all the transport work of the valley, without difficulty or hardship, and this supposition would be correct if the arrangements made for the levy of *begár* had been fair and honest. But the officials have regarded the system of *begár* as one peculiarly devised to fill their purses, and nothing has done more to ruin Kashmír than the corrupt and cruel manipulation of the *corvée*. I have often been present when a requisition for carriage arrives in a village, and the following account of the system is a simple statement of what used to be an everyday occurrence. Some one in Srinagar wants ten coolies or porters to carry his baggage for a stage, or for one or more stages. The official to whom the requisition is made passes on the order of the district officer, and in order to make sure that there will be no deficiency in the number of the coolies writes that twenty men are wanted. The district officer writes to the *tahsíldar* and, acting on the same prudent calculation, orders forty coolies. The *tahsíldar* then seizes eighty coolies from the villages. Nearly all these eighty men are engaged, perhaps, in weeding or watering their rice, and as they do not know how long they may be kept waiting in Srinagar, and as they dread that in their absence their fields will run dry or will be choked with weeds, they are not allured by the idea of a wage of four annas a day which they may or may not receive. Bargaining begins, and if the official in charge of the business is a smart man he will take seventy four-annas from the seventy villagers whom he exempts, and will send in ten men to Srinagar. If he is a very smart man he will take eighty four-annas from the eighty villagers, and will still send in ten men to Srinagar. No arrangements were made to distribute the *begár* according to population, or to take it by turns from villages, and as a rule the unfortunate people who lived near the city or the towns, or who lived near the tahsíl head-quarters or along the line of communications, were harassed daily, while more remote villages, whose inhabitants could flee to the mountains when the news came that coolies were wanted, had a comparatively speaking easy time. The instance I have given above refers to the modest demand for carriage made by a European visitor, and in such instances the wage of four annas per stage was invariably paid, but when the requisition for coolies was on account of State work no wage would be paid. Among many reforms made during the reign of the present Mahárájá, I hold that the construction of the road to Gilgit is perhaps one of the most important. Gilgit to the Kashmíri is a constant terror, and when it was rumoured that transport was wanted to convey the baggage of the troops going to or coming from Gilgit there was a general stampede among the villagers. I have seen whole villages bivouacking on the mountains when the agents for the collection of transport arrived in their tahsíl, and I have seen inhuman punishment dealt out to men who demurred to leaving their homes for two or three months with the prospect of death from cold or starvation. I have seen villagers maimed from frostbite or shrivelled and paralyzed from exposure to cold, and it is no marvel that the Kashmíris should loathe the very name of Gilgit[1]. It may be added that if men would pay four annas in order to avoid carrying a load for one easy stage, they would very gladly pay much larger sums to escape a journey to Gilgit, and I know that since I have been in Kashmír villagers have paid from Rs. 70 to Rs. 90 per head in order to purchase their exemption. The construction of the Gilgit road, along which ponies and mules can now travel, has removed the dread of Gilgit and the necessity of paying huge bribes to the officials, but *begár* in a modified form will linger on until good roads are made through the valley and until population

[1] 'In May, 1888, I was on cholera duty in Islámábád. Just as the epidemic was reaching its height, and hundreds were dying every day in all the districts around, a levy of 5,000 or more coolies was called for. The villagers were almost distracted with fear. Who would do all their agricultural work? What would happen during their long absence to their wives and children? To what perils of pestilence and inclemency of weather would they themselves be exposed, in the crowded bivouacs and snowy passes of that deadly Gilgit district? I was present at a sort of farewell service on a maidan outside Islámábád, when nearly 1,000 men were starting, and when they took leave of the friends who had accompanied them so far, loud was the sobbing of some, fervid the demeanour of all, as, led by the mullah, they intoned their prayers and chanted some of their special Ramzán penitential psalms. Braver men might well have been agitated at such a time. It is certain that cholera clung to the camp, and that the unburied corpses of hundreds of these poor *begáris* marked the whole line of march from Srinagar to Bunji.'—Note on departure of *begáris* to Gilgit, by Dr. A. Neve, Medical Mission.

CHAP. XVII. and the increasing difficulty of living idly in the city bring a labouring class into existence. 'Honest labour wears a lovely face' cannot be said to hold good in Kashmír, and, apart from the fact that carrying burdens is not the most useful or ennobling task to which men can be set, there is a deep-rooted distaste to the work, which is not unnatural when all the facts connected with the 'carrying industry' are considered. Even under the most favourable circumstances the wage of four annas per stage is not enticing when it is remembered that the coolie is called, perhaps, from a long distance, a day or two days previous to the date fixed by his hirer, and that when he has done his day's stage he has to find his way back to his village, where he probably finds that his neighbour has cut off the water from his rice fields or that his maize field is being grazed down by strangers' cattle.

The other side of *begár* is also a great trouble to the villagers, but it has been easier to abolish. It consists of requisitions for village produce, and is a form of purveyance on behalf of officials. Under this system officials would obtain wood, grass, milk, poultry and grain, blankets and an occasional pony, cows and sheep free of cost, and higher officials would build houses in the city or cultivate waste land through the unpaid labour of the villagers. When I commenced work in Kashmír I came across numerous instances of this kind of *begár*, and in one tahsíl I found that three villages had been sold to a recent *Hakim-i-Ala* for very trivial amounts, giving an average of about Rs. 40 per village. On making inquiries I found that the villagers were only too glad to part with their then shadowy rights in the land, as the purchaser had given them a written order exempting them from all kinds of *begár*, and the flourishing condition of the villages and the sleek appearance of the cultivators showed that they had made a good though illegal bargain. Many other villages were similarly sold, all for nominal sums, the real consideration being that the villages were to be freed from *begár*. In one instance a *tahsíldar* bought a fine village for Rs. 130, but he did not even go through the form of paying this sum, but excused the villagers Rs. 130 from their revenue and entered it as an arrear. All these sales have been cancelled, but they show in a simple way the enormous influence worked on the country by the *begár* system. In the same way officials who obtained waste land on privileged terms (*chakdár*) were able to entice away cultivators from their original holdings, where *begár* was in full force, and no *chakdár* ever found difficulty in obtaining farm labourers, as directly men took service under him they were at once exempted from the *corvée*. The object of the State in making grants of waste land was to increase cultivation, but the officials frustrated this object. Every man taken away from a revenue-paying village for work on a *chakdár's* estate meant a shrinking in cultivation in that village and a loss of revenue to the State. Briefly speaking, the man liable to *begár* was an 'outlaw' without rights of any description, and *begár* was looked upon by the officials as an incident of serfdom which entitled them to take all things, either labour or commodities, free of payment, from the villagers. Such a system took all heart out of the people, and many villages, formerly famous for special kinds of rice or for fruits, rather than expose themselves to the constant exactions of the officials, took to cultivating more common kinds of rice and cut down their fruit trees. CHAP. XVII.

Rasum.

Apart from the opportunities for peculation afforded by the recognized methods of the revenue system, the officials enjoyed other perquisites which are known by the name *rasum*. The *patwari* keeps a list of these perquisites, and when he is pressed or when it suits his purpose he will often show these lists to me. I take at random a list of the perquisites taken in one year from an average village.

Its legitimate revenue was Rs. 1,332.6.0 Chilki, made up of the following items:—

	Chilki. Rs.	a.	p.
Half-share of kharif and rabi crops	520	0	0
Item on account of walnut trees	63	12	0
Lump sum paid for land cultivated by shawl-weavers and for land under vegetables	138	12	0
An advance on the original assessment made by a Pandit. The Pandit failed to pay, but the State insisted on the village paying the advance (*izád boli*)	300	0	0
Item for jungle produce	7	0	0
Item for grass and village officers	9	0	0
Total	1,038	8	0

These items are supposed to be permanent, and are known as *kaul*, but in 1883 the State levied in addition the following taxes:—

	Chilki. Rs.	a.	p.
Tax of 2 per cent. (*Do kharwari*)	18	13	0
Sala, *Jalus*. (*Sala* is a tax on account of a Sanskrit school. *Jalus* is a tax on account of expenses of English visitors)	18	13	0
Kanungo tax	3	14	0
Patwari tax	3	14	0
Tax on account of Mahárájá's temple	2	8	0
Khitmatgars	1	4	0
Tax on account of establishment	77	3	0
Tax on account of land granted to chakdár[1]. The chakdár did not cultivate, so the village was called upon to pay the amount assessed on the chakdár's land	58	9	0

[1] This was a very common incident in Kashmír villages. A Pandit obtained a grant of waste land in a village, but neglected to cultivate it. The State then insisted on the village paying the assessment fixed on the grant, whether the land was cultivated or not.

CHAP. XVII.

	Chilki. Rs.	a.	p.
Tax on account of apricot trees (it is worthy of notice that there are no apricot trees)	10	0	0
Various taxes—(1) loss on ponies seized by the State and paid for at prices far below market price, (2) Nazrana, (3) tax for support of temples, (4) tax on occasion of marriage in Royal House, (5) tax for dispensary	99	0	0
Total	293	14	0

The perquisites (*rasum*) taken in one year in addition to this revenue were as follows:—

	Amount. Rs.	a.	p.	Chilki.
Tahsíldars	12	0	0	
Tahsíldar's Assistant	8	0	0	
Naib-tahsíldar	8	0	0	
Naib-tahsíldar's Assistant	5	0	0	
Parcha Navis	5	0	0	
Mir Chaudhri	13	0	0	
Ahd Ghanai, Assistant to Mir Chaudhri	11	0	0	
Mir Zilladar	5	0	0	
Zilladar	10	0	0	
Rassad-Talabana	25	0	0	
Blankets taken	4	0	0	Price was Rs. 10. Price given by officials was Rs. 6.
Ponies	22	0	0	Price was Rs. 40. Officials gave Rs. 18.
Item for permission to pay as revenue 1 kharwar of cotton[1]	5	0	0	
Ghi taken	12	0	0	
Sheep taken	6	0	0	
Violets, Zira and Guchis	4	0	0	
Chob-i-kot	21	0	0	
Wool	12	0	0	
Grass	8	0	0	
Share of crop taken by Zilladar	9	0	0	
Share of crop taken by Mir Chaudhri	7	0	0	
Share of crop taken by Patwari and Lambardár	7	0	0	
Item taken by Police	6	0	0	
Tahsíl Establishment	7	0	0	
Wasil Báki Navis	10	0	0	

[1] This item is of great importance. Under the old system, the State accepted a certain portion of its revenue in cotton, oil-seeds, and pulses, and gave for these articles a commutation rate considerably higher than the market price. The villages would buy cotton from the bazaar at Rs. 8, and pay it in to Government at Rs. 14, and it was worth their while to bribe the *tahsíldar* for the privilege of paying their revenue in highly-priced commodities. The village in question never grows cotton.

	Amount. Rs.	a.	p.	Chilki.
Sihaya Navis	3	0	0	
Tahsil Treasurer	2	0	0	
Tahsil Kanungo	4	0	0	
Twenty fowls taken for officials .	5	0	0	
Tahsildars' fine not credited to the State	10	0	0	
Miscellaneous	4	0	0	
Total . .	270	0	0	

When one considers that each tahsíl has on an average from 150 to 200 villages, it will be seen that the *tahsíldar* and his subordinates could make a very fair living out of perquisites, and it is not therefore surprising that they never grumbled at their low pay, and never complained if their pay was greatly in arrears.

Other forms of taxation.

In the list of *rasum* there are certain items which call for notice, and which throw a light on the old system of taxation in Kashmír. It has been pointed out by many writers on the subject that nearly everything in the valley was brought under taxation. The usual method was to make each product a State monopoly, and to farm out the monopoly to some contractor[1]. Silk, saffron, *chob-i-kot*, violets, various kinds of forest products, hemp, tobacco, water-nuts, and paper have at various times formed the subject of a State monopoly. The right to legalize marriages was farmed out, and it is said that the office of grave-digger was also taxed. Prostitutes were taxed, and, without going into details, it may be said that nearly everything save air and water was brought under taxation. The system of farming out taxes to contractors was bad for the people and bad for the State, as the Kashmíri 'publican' was usually a man of straw, who had to pay large fees to the officials before he obtained a farm, and invariably proved a defaulter when called upon to pay the State's dues. This was injurious to the State, and it may be imagined that it was equally injurious to the people, inasmuch as the publican had small mercy for them when he began collecting the article for which he had purchased the farm. In the list of *rasum* given above will be noticed violets and *chob-i-kot*. A publican would offer a certain sum for the right to collect violets for the year. Having obtained a written order to the effect that he was contractor of violets, he would get together a number of able-bodied loafers, and charge them with the duty of collecting the State's share of the violets of Kashmír, which in theory is two-thirds. But the villagers at violet-time are busy in their fields, and have little leisure or inclination to gather flowers. The publican's man would wait till the violets were withered and then claim

Farms.

[1] Cf. Dr. Johnson's definition of Excise: 'A hateful tax levied upon commodities, and adjudged not by the common judges of property, but wretches hired by those to whom excise is paid.'

CHAP. XVII. a weight of violets probably double the amount produced in the village. After a great deal of violence and trouble, and in order to get rid at any cost of the publican's man, who was living free in the village, the cultivators would pay up a lump sum in cash. For all practical purposes it would have been equally convenient, from the publican's point of view, to have obtained a farm of butterflies. He did not want violets, and in many villages there were no violets, and provided the cultivators would pay him a round sum in cash, he did not care. I have come across many instances of the results of these curious forms of taxes. The *watals* of the villages used to be taxed so many hides of cattle per annum, and the tax was of course farmed out. In one village in which I was camped the publican's man came for three hides, which he said was the annual demand from the village. The *watals* came to me, and explained that as no cattle had died during the year they were unable to comply with the publican's demand. Eventually the matter was settled by the payment of money, and then I ascertained that the *watals* were making capital of my ignorance, and that they always paid money and rarely ever hides. The tax on *chob-i-kot*, the aromatic root of the Saussurea, was often worked in the same way, but a large amount of the root is extracted and is exported at considerable profit. The incidence of the tax was most unequal, and the publican often realized the State's supposed share of *chob-i-kot* in cash and not in kind. The plant is found on the high mountains, but villages many marches distant from the mountains were liable to contribution. Every year a sum of money (*dádani*) was supposed to be advanced to the villagers, but, like all transactions in which cash played a part, the money never reached the cultivators. Taking one tahsíl as an example: in 1889 the villagers of the Phák tahsíl supplied 48 kharwars of *chob-i-kot*, for which they received a credit of Rs. 4 per kharwar. In most instances the villagers did not extract the root themselves, but purchased it at Rs. 6 per kharwar from mountain villagers or from shepherds. They lost Rs. 96 on the transaction, and besides had to carry the root from a long distance to the State Dépôt. In 1890, 141 kharwars of *chob-i-kot* were demanded from the Phák tahsíl, and it was in the power of the *Hakim-i-Ala* to vary the demand, irrespective of the season or of the powers of the villagers to obtain the root.

The same system was followed in regard to birch bark (*bhoj pattr*), which is so much in demand for roofing houses. In the Phák tahsíl the State used to demand from 18 to 29 kharwars of birch bark per annum. The villagers, who live at a great distance from the high mountains on which the birch tree grows, had to buy the bark at Rs. 3.2.0 per kharwar, and when they had carried it to Srinagar they received a credit of Rs. 2 per kharwar. In 1889, suddenly and without any reason being given, the district officer demanded 200 kharwars of birch bark from the Phák tahsíl.

No attempt was ever made to base the demand for *chob-i-kot* or birch bark on a consideration of local facts. In 1889 a demand was made on the village of Shadipur, which is situated at the junction of the Sind and Jhelum rivers, for a large amount of birch bark to be delivered at Gulmarg. To comply with this demand the Shadipur men had to go several marches up the Sind valley, for by old custom each tahsíl is restricted to certain mountains. Having obtained the birch bark they had to march back to Shadipur, and thence they had to carry the birch bark two more marches to Gulmarg. It has always struck me that in these numerous and vexatious impositions the officials used every device in order to make the demand burdensome and costly to the people, and it seems to have been the aim of every servant of the State to display his zeal and his administrative ability by discovering some new product which could be made the subject of a tax. It was always forgotten that there are limitations to taxation even in Kashmír, and while some zealous official was busily developing the resources of violets, the authorities omitted to notice that for every Rs. 10 gained from violets, there was a falling off of Rs. 10 or perhaps Rs. 20 in the land revenue. A formidable list of taxes might have given satisfaction to the authorities in Srinagar, and no doubt assured them that the fiscal resources of the State had been fully exploited, but land, which alone can be relied upon for revenue purposes, became with every new imposition less productive to the State and to the cultivator, and every year saw a real diminution in revenue which was carefully concealed from the Mahárájá.

As will be seen in the chapter which describes the settlement operations, most of these miscellaneous sources of revenue have now disappeared. Many of them were very curious, and it is easy to understand that the State would be reluctant to give up any source of taxation, when it had once become established as a part of the *Ain* or system of Kashmír.

The old revenue staff.

It is necessary to give some idea of the men who collected the land revenue, the permanent revenue establishment, who must be distinguished from those soldiers of fortune, the tax-farmers, publicans, who usually disappeared after the year's speculation. The valley of Kashmír at the time when the work of settlement commenced was divided into fifteen tahsíls, but in many cases the tahsíls were not demarcated by clear boundaries, and villages of one tahsíl would be scattered within the limits of another tahsíl. This confusion lent itself to the system of defrauding the State, for at harvest-time it was easy for a village to hide its crops in another village under the jurisdiction of another *tahsíldar*. The *tahsíldar* was a man on small pay, but as has been explained pay was no object, and a *tahsíldar* of moderate ideas drawing a nominal salary of Rs. 30 would live at the rate of Rs. 300 to Rs. 500 per mensem. His tahsíl building was of the most squalid description—a rambling house, built of unburnt bricks, with a grass

CHAP. XVII. thatch, kept in precarious repair by the villagers. But as the *tahsîldar* held his office on uncertain tenure, and as his one idea was to be transferred directly the collections for the autumn harvest were finished, and before any unpleasant questions regarding arrears could be raised, he did not care much about the tahsîl buildings, and he left them in the same ruined condition as he found them. The *tahsîldar* never lacked society. Apart from the fact that he could run into Srinagar whenever he wished, he always kept with him in the tahsîl a number of relatives and friends, known as *mutabir*, to whom he delegated the duties of his office. As these men received no pay from the State, they took it from the villagers, and the more friends and relatives the *tahsîldar* had, the worse was it for the villagers. This system of *mutabir* obtained in all ranks of the service, and I have known instances of the *chaukidar* delegating his duties to friends. There were no fixed instalments of revenue, and in consequence emissaries from the tahsîl, known as *sipahi*, were always in the villages, living free on the forced hospitality of the people. The *tahsîldar* rarely moved out, except at the time of ploughing for the autumn crops, when it was necessary to urge the villagers to cultivate, and at the time of the ripening of the rice and maize, when he appraised the crop and calculated by a rapid scrutiny (*nazardîd*) how much grain could be taken for himself and how much for the State. One of the preoccupations of the *tahsîldar* was to entice back runaways who had fled in the time of his predecessor, and fierce official altercations would often arise between *tahsîldars*, one demanding back the cultivators and the other declining to give them. The coercive processes for recovering the land revenue may be described as measures of personal violence, and one *tahsîldar* not long ago distinguished himself by the use of nettle scourges in the summer, and by plunging recusant taxpayers into cold water in the winter. The cultivator, when life became too hard, had his remedy in flight. He could not leave the valley without a pass, but he could abscond to villages under a more lenient assessment and a less rigorous *tahsîldar*, or he could, if he were wise, seek a shelter in the city, where he added to the population of paupers fed by the help of the State. It must be remembered that the ordinary villager possessed little but his clothes and his sheep, and it was very easy to find a house, which with a little repair could be made fit for habitation. He left nothing dear behind him but his vegetable plot. Of course when flight became universal the *tahsîldar* stood revealed as a bad revenue officer, and he would be removed from office or transferred to another tahsîl, where he would celebrate his arrival by taking large contributions as accession fees (*nazardna*).

The *tahsîldar*, in spite of his large powers, enjoyed very little dignity or respect. The villagers despised him for his apathy and dishonesty, and they despised him because the higher officials treated him as though he

Chap. XVII.

were dirt under their feet. I have seen a *tahsildar* abused like a dog in the presence of the villagers by the district officer (*wazir wazárat*), and I have seen a *wazir wazárat* waiting on the Governor (*Hakim-i-Ala*) like a menial servant, also in the presence of the villagers. All this is subversive of a good strong Government, and I have made every effort to insist on all officials being treated with the respect due to their office. I have known many cases of men of fair ability and good family, who had no means of subsistence, declining the post of *tahsildar* because it carried with it no respect or dignity. On behalf of the *tahsildars* of Kashmír it is fair to remark that the small pay of their office, the uncertainty of its tenure, the absence of any system of pensions for old age (*inglishi*), and the want of honour attaching to the post, form some excuse for the peculation which used to be carried on.

Espionage.

It has always been the policy of the Kashmír State to have small revenue divisions. Before the fifteen tahsíls, which were in existence at the time settlement commenced, there were thirty-four tahsíls, and before this the country was parcelled out into small blocks, over which revenue collectors, sometimes known as *chakladárs*, sometimes as *kárdárs*, were appointed, the idea being that with a small charge an official's opportunities for peculation would be restricted, and that one revenue agent would spy upon another and bring cases of peculation to the notice of the Darbar. In one respect this idea was justified, for there was and is still a most elaborate system of espionage; but, as in former days there was no one who could make an honest and independent investigation into cases of peculation, no useful purpose was served by the host of informers (*mukhbir*) who pervaded the valley. The profession of a spy is not regarded with the same contempt in Kashmír as it is in other countries, and the spy always speaks of his occupation as *khair khwáhi*, or wishing well to the State. If he was an active man, with a detective turn of mind, he could very soon obtain sufficient information for blackmailing the officials, and his income from blackmail was considerable. The number of spies has largely decreased and the profession is now in very reduced circumstances, but the system still remains, and many officials are still regularly watched by recognized spies. The facilities afforded by the Postal Department struck a severe blow at the professional informers, and the people now act as informers through the medium of the registered letter. They have great faith in the efficacy of the registered letter, and it behoves the authorities of Kashmír to put an end to the evil and undignified system of espionage by ignoring all registered letters in which vague complaints are made of officials. The *tahsildars* are extremely nervous on the subject, and an old official put the former position of affairs concisely by saying that four annas spent on a registered letter could turn a *tahsildar* out of office.

CHAP. XVII. I am of opinion that in no country does custom die so hard as in Kashmír, and it will take many years to uproot the system of espionage and to remove the evils which have resulted from it. At present no man trusts another. The villagers suspect one another, and the officials, although they are loyal and united in their treatment of the land revenue, always fear betrayal when their interests clash. I can say with truth that I have never heard one official say a good word for another, and their usual method of discussing their brother officers is that of damning by faint praise or clever innuendo. If it were not for the pickings and the perquisites, I cannot understand how any man could have served as a *tahsíldar* in former days. He could take no interest in his tahsíl, for he was a bird of passage, and he lived in a state of constant terror, caused partly by the rough way in which he was treated by his superiors and partly by the knowledge that he was assailed on all sides by charges, some true and some false. Of course there were bright exceptions to this general picture which I have given of the Kashmíri *tahsíldars*, and there are several old officials who were active, just, not outrageous in the matter of perquisites, and above all loyal to the Darbar and its financial interests. These men were respected by the Kashmíris, and on the whole their abilities have been appreciated by the State, but the average *tahsíldar* was corrupt, lazy, and disloyal. One curious fact must be mentioned regarding the old revenue service of Kashmír, and that is the absence of any system of promotion by merit or seniority, and it is not an uncommon thing to find a man serving as a *tahsíldar* who ten or twenty years ago was officer of a district.

Conclusion.

All this is changing, but the change will be slow. The State has a fine recruiting-ground for its services in the clever, quick Pandits of Srinagar, the active and loyal Dogras of the Jammu territory, and in the Musalmáns of the hills and the Jhelum valley. A beginning has been made, and some youths who have passed examinations from the State schools have been trained in the Settlement Department and have been entered in the list of the *naib-tahsíldars*. Some of these will succeed, and will hereafter form a healthy leaven in the old officialdom, which must for many reasons linger on for another generation. It is impossible to ignore the fact that in Kashmír consideration has been and will be given to the services of old official families, and for some time to come men will be appointed to office not for their abilities, but rather on account of their family claims. I have often advocated the establishment of a school for the education of the children of the upper classes in Kashmír, as I hold that in a Native State like Kashmír there must be an officer caste and a rank-and-file caste, and the officer caste must be sought for among the families of the old officials. The difficulty is that the sons of the higher families have hitherto looked upon the office of *naib-tahsildar* with contempt, and expect to at once attain to the position of a district officer.

In considering the character of the *tahsildars* and of the *patwaris* it must always be remembered that the old system of farming out the revenue of villages was in itself enough to destroy all zeal and interest in their work. A *tahsildar*, when he saw his tahsil divided into blocks and farmed out to men who ignored his office, naturally ceased to take any interest in cultivation or in irrigation, and the *patwari*, when he saw that the revenue farmer ignored the primitive village records and seized the crops regardless of the size of holdings and of the old revenue demand, very soon realized that his office was superfluous, gave up all idea of acting as the village accountant, and devoted himself to securing his prescribed share of the crop. If he could, he would side with the villagers, and both he and the *tahsildar*, recognizing the fact that the system of farming the revenue caused loss to all parties and merely brought profit to an unworthy body of men—the publicans—gave up all attempt to improve and maintain the landed property of the State. When the system of farming was abolished the *tahsildar* and *patwaris* found the country demoralized and the revenue accounts in a chaotic state, and the object of the settlement is to evoke order out of this chaos, to restore the office and to insist on the responsibilities of the *tahsildar* and *patwaris*, to provide them with village records defining the rights of the cultivators and their revenue liabilities, and lastly to secure those rights and to limit those liabilities in such a manner as to create a feeling of confidence in the country, and to make the title in the land valuable and an object of desire. The operations and results of the settlement will be described in the next chapter, but the foregoing remarks on the revenue administration as it was at the time when the settlement commenced must be borne in mind, and it must never be forgotten that the settlement has clashed with the interests of the officials and middlemen who gorged themselves on the spoils of the vanishing land revenue. They must have anticipated that an end would come, and that the country and the Darbar would turn and rend them, and it was this anticipation which made them reckless and determined to take as much as they could in the short time remaining. But they did not give up their methods of making money without a fierce and prolonged struggle, and they watch with hope for the smallest opening through which they may again enter on the easy path to wealth.

CHAPTER XVIII.

THE NEW SETTLEMENT.

CHAP. XVIII.

Commencement.

THE settlement of the Kashmír valley was commenced by Mr. Wingate, I.C.S., C.I.E., in 1887, and when I was appointed as his *locum tenens* in April, 1889, two tahsíls, Lal and Phak, had been surveyed, an excellent system of accounts for the settlement establishment had been introduced, and rulings on all important points had been carefully recorded. Mr. Wingate, in his Preliminary Report, has described the difficulties with which he and his Panjabi subordinates had to contend, and has clearly pointed out the chief abuses of the old system, indicating the lines on which reform should proceed. By following these lines, as Mr. Wingate's *locum tenens*, and by adhering to them, when I was appointed permanently as Settlement Officer in 1890, I have been enabled to avoid many mistakes and to carry the work through to completion.

Opposition.

Opposition lingered on during 1889 and 1890, but, thanks to the unfailing support given to me by the State Council, this opposition caused only temporary delays and annoyançe. The Settlement Department by the year 1891 had become so recognized as a part of the administration that it is now almost impossible to realize how, in 1889, a *tahsíldar* peremptorily stopped survey operations, and ordered all my subordinates to leave his jurisdiction. It was only natural that the officials should oppose the settlement, and that they should boycott my subordinates, but the serious impediment to work was the fact that the villagers themselves distrusted the settlement.

Attitude of the villagers.

For many years preceding 1887, surveys of the villages had been in progress, but nothing came of them. The people were harassed by the presence of hungry *Amins*, but beyond a fictitious survey there was no result. The Kashmíris believed that the survey commenced by Mr. Wingate in 1887 would lead to the same results, and the officials spared no pains to convince them that the laborious chaining of the rice fields would end in nothing. In 1889 I at once commenced inspecting the Lal Tahsíl in order to frame assessments.

The *tahsíldar* not only remained absent himself, but succeeded in preventing the villagers from communicating with me. I managed, however, to become acquainted with certain of the villagers, and through them informed the countryside that I meant to introduce a new assessment based on the survey records by the end of 1889; that though there were many local facts, only known to the agriculturists, which might enable me to avoid mistakes in assessment, I must, in the absence of the villagers, value the land unaided by local experience. The villagers still distrusted the settlement, and it was not until I announced the new assessments in November, 1889, that they believed that the survey was not, like its predecessors, a sham. From November, 1889, everything changed. The villagers who had regarded our work with indifference, not condescending to attend when their fields were being measured, now showed some interest in our operations, and land began to acquire a value. Wanderers in the valley and fugitives from the Panjab returned to their villages, and the work of survey and assessment progressed steadily, evoking the keenest interest among the Kashmíris. Shortly after taking over charge of the settlement, rules were framed by the State Council regarding the disposal of waste land, and the allotment of waste land was entrusted to me. Next, it was decided that all suits in any way connected with land should be removed from the ordinary Revenue Courts, and be made over to the Settlement Department. So our work increased, and with it our influence extended, and the *tahsíldars* and others, who had formerly done their utmost to thwart and decry the work of the settlement, now showed signs of truce. Every effort was made to employ Kashmíris in the Settlement Department, and the suspicions of the *tahsíldars* and others were allayed when they saw that no Panjábis were brought in to supplant them. In fifteen Assessment Reports I have placed before the Council the facts connected with my settlement and the valuation of land, and here it will be sufficient to give a brief sketch of the most salient points. When I commenced work I found that the people distrusted everything and everybody, and that they placed no value on the occupancy of land. When they saw that the assessment of the Lál Tahsíl limited the State demand for ten years, that it took only a small part of the revenue in kind, leaving them an ample supply of food, that it removed from the villages the ever-present sepoy, that it insisted on the needs of agriculture being considered of greater importance than the demands for *begár*, the Kashmíris began to realize that some good, even though temporary, might arise from the settlement. Ruined houses and desolate gardens were restored, absentees returned, and applications for waste land came in faster than was convenient.

CHAP. XVIII.

Changes.

Chief points of the settlement.

The simple rule laid down by Mr. Wingate on the subject of entries of the occupancy of land was to the effect that Musalmáns in the undisputed

Entries regarding land.

CHAP. XVIII. possession of land were to be entered as *assámis*. In case of a dispute, evidence was to be recorded on the spot, and the case was to be decided by the settlement officer. In the case of Hindus or Sikhs, no final entry could be made until the orders of the settlement officer were obtained.

Privileged holders. Besides the ordinary *assámi*, or occupant of village land, there were many privileged holders of land variously known as *chakdar* or *mukararidar*—men who had acquired landed property under deeds granted by the State. A careful inquiry was made in all such cases, and the following rule has been applied:—The land assigned by the deed has been confirmed to the holder for the term of settlement at the privileged rates mentioned in the deed. Land held in excess of the deed has been, in the absence of dispute, made over to the privileged holder, but at the ordinary rates obtaining in the village or the assessment circle. Most of these grants are formed of parcels of land taken from several villages, and the privileged classes made a strong effort to have their grant separated off as a distinct estate. We have, however, avoided this, and the *chakdar* or *mukararidar* is now an *assámi* of the several villages in which his estates lie. Although there is nothing in the deeds which entitles these persons to privileged rates, I think that the State made a wise concession in continuing the privileged rates for the ten years during which the assessment will run, but at the end of that period the land should be all assessed at the ordinary rates of agricultural land, and the *chakdars* will become *assámis* of the villages in which their holdings are situated.

Waste land. From time immemorial the Kashmíri village has possessed no rights in the waste, and the only right recognized by the villagers is that a man who plants trees on the waste is owner of such trees. But he has no right to the waste land on which the trees stand. Mr. Wingate described the land system of Kashmír as raiyatwari in ruins, and if it be necessary to apply Indian terms to Kashmíri tenures, perhaps ruined raiyatwari will be the most appropriate description of the plastic system of Kashmír. Before the Mughal times I believe that a pure raiyatwari system existed, but Tondar, as the people style the great Todar Mal, introduced the offices of *lambardár* and *patwari*, and with them has crept in some ideas of joint responsibility for the land revenue. At any rate, though in theory the Kashmír *assámi* may hold land on the raiyatwari system, he only suffers from its disabilities and does not profit from its benefits. If an *assámi* absconds or defaults, the *lambardár* promptly throws the revenue liabilities of the absconder on to the other *assámis*, thus enforcing the joint responsibility of the village. But the system is raiyatwari, in that the *assámi* possesses no rights in the waste lands. Accordingly, at survey, we have entered only cultivated land as in the occupancy of the *assámis*, and we have entered all waste and old fallow as *khalsa*, that is, State land unburdened with individual *assámi* rights. It will thus be seen that the management of waste land forms an important part of our work, and vitally affects the future administration of land revenue. In disposing of waste land we have recognized that the *assámis* of the village in which it is situated have a prior claim to outsiders. If the *assámis* neglect to acquire the waste land under the waste land rules, the State can then make it over to an outsider[1]. At first, when I considered the importance of village grazing in India, I thought it would be advisable to demarcate grazing-grounds in each village which should under no circumstances be broken up for cultivation. But further experience has taught me that the mountains are the natural grazing-grounds for the cattle and sheep of Kashmír, that fodder is abundant, and that it is unnecessary to lay down any hard-and-fast rules for 'village stint.' The only rule observed in the allotment of waste lands is that waste to the extent of 10 per cent. on the cultivated area recorded at survey must be left for village uses. I have pointed out in Assessment Reports that the land revenue taken from the villages really includes rights enjoyed from time immemorial in the forests which surround the valley. Up to the present the agricultural classes have been allowed timber for their houses and farm implements. and fuel free of charge. I would urge most strongly that no restriction should be placed upon these old rights of user in the forests. If, hereafter, forest conservancy does impair those rights, it will be necessary to reconsider the rates put upon the land by me, for I would never have taken so high a revenue had I known that timber and fuel would be charged for by the State[2]. Any drastic

Rights to user in forests.

[1] *Assessment Report, Donsu Tahsil*, paragraph 25: 'The culturable waste land amounts to some 5,900 acres. Much of this land, though entered as culturable at measurement, will hardly repay cultivation for some time. It lies on the sides of ravines or on the dryest of karéwas, and until population increases, will hardly come within the margin of cultivation. Some of it, however, will be rapidly broken up, either by the *assámis* or by *chakdars*, who will take up the land under the rules. The operation of the waste land rules is very simple, and enables the State to dispose of the waste land without difficulty to itself or hardship to the village. The waste land is wholly State property, and, saving some small pieces of waste which have been entered at measurement in the names of individual *assámis*, and which will come under assessment, it is absolutely at the disposal of the Darbár. The village pays nothing for the waste, and, provided the State leaves enough land for the cattle, the cultivators cannot complain if the waste land is made over to outsiders. The State gives the village the first refusal. If the village decides to take up the land itself, and to pay the rates prescribed by the rules, the outside applicant has to go elsewhere; but if the village declines to take up the land, there is no hardship if an outsider is admitted. It is impossible for me to include the waste land in assessment. The village boundaries are extremely capricious, and one village has an enormous extent of waste land, while another has very little. Any rate, however light, assessed on the waste land would bear heavily on most villages, and I think that the system sanctioned for Lál and Phák, and suggested here, will work well for the next ten years. It is a self-adjusting system. If the villagers really require the waste land, they can get it at easy rates under the rules. If they do not require the land, then the outsider comes in.'

[2] *Dachanpára Assessment Report*, paragraph 1: 'The custom hitherto has been that the villagers obtain wood for their houses and agricultural implements free of cost. This year the

CHAP. XVIII. measures which would tend to curtail the privileges hitherto enjoyed in the forests may lead to serious difficulties in the collection of the land revenue. I am of opinion that in a small country like Kashmír the right policy is to encourage cultivation, and I believe that if the whole of the village area, which includes all land up to the slopes of the mountains and the borders of the forests, were brought under cultivation, grass, timber, and fuel sufficient for agricultural requirements could be supplied without injury to the State forests. A Forest Department has been in existence for some years, but at the time of writing no rules have been issued on the subject of protection, and it is of the highest importance that when protection commences the agricultural needs of the country should be carefully considered.

The *assámi*. It is necessary to define the word *assámi*, so often used in this Report. It is a word of old standing in Kashmír. The *assámi* may be defined as a man recognized by the State as the lawful occupant of land in Kashmír, and in the Mughal times and thereafter, from the point of view of the State, the status of *assámi* in theory meant nothing more than a tenant-at-will. But in the village the *assámi* was a man in whom vested the *mirás* or hereditary right to certain plots of good and irrigated land within the boundaries of the village. In the many disputes which I have had to decide as to rights in land the decision always rested on the existence of *mirás*, and in the village it was never difficult to ascertain on the spot whether a claimant were a *mirásdár* or not. Changes of dynasty and changes of system, earthquakes, floods, and famines, have alike failed to obliterate the hereditary principle in land tenures in Kashmír, and while Mughals, Patháns, Sikhs, and Dogras have steadily ignored the existence of hereditary occupancy rights, these rights have been kept alive by the village.

The disastrous famine of 1877–79, which is said by some to have swept off three-fifths of the population of the valley, threw the country into utter confusion, but the sturdy survivors of the calamity held to their *mirás* lands, and when the settlement of 1880 was made these men were entered as *assámis* of the village. In my settlement these men have been regarded as possessing superior claims to the *assámi* right, and though every effort has been made to accommodate fugitives who have returned to their villages, no man who can prove that he accepted the assessment of certain

Forest Department, or rather the contractor to whom forests have been farmed, has without any proper authority refused to give timber for building purposes except on payment. This action of the Forest Department has given rise to serious inconvenience and discontent, and I would point out to the Darbar that if the old custom of giving wood free to the cultivators is stopped, a corresponding reduction must be made in the land revenue. One of the reasons why the present heavy rates of land revenue can be paid is, that the people have hitherto enjoyed considerable advantages of forest and grazing practically untaxed. I would strongly recommend that the old system be allowed to continue.'

land in 1880 has been turned out. In very many cases the *assámi* of 1880 has of his free will given up fields to returned fugitives, and, as before stated, I have never found it difficult to ascertain whether the fugitive was a *mirásdár* or not. The Kashmíris have a bad name for dishonesty, but their conduct in the matter of admitting fugitive *mirásdárs* is worthy of praise and admiration [1]. At survey each person in undisputed occupancy of cultivated land was registered as *assámi* of that land, but at survey and later, when the new village assessment was distributed over the several holdings of *assámis*, permission was freely given to those who wished to relinquish a part of their holdings. When the revenue assessed on the holding was accepted by the *assámi* the registration was fixed. The words used in each Assessment Report which was submitted for the sanction of the Darbar were as follows:—'Permanent hereditary occupancy rights will be bestowed on every person who, at the time of assessment or at the time when the distribution of assessments is effected, agrees to pay the assessment fixed on the fields entered in his or her name in the settlement

[1] *Donsu Assessment Report*, paragraph 10: 'It may appear to the Council that it is hard to refuse possession to men who were driven away by famine, and who now, thanks to the liberal and enlightened policy of the Darbar, wish to return to their villages. But it must be remembered that it is much harder on the men who kept a good heart in the famine, and who resolved to remain in Kashmír in spite of everything—men who by their courage saved Kashmír from becoming a desert, who undertook to pay the assessment fixed in Sambat 1937, and who have cultivated and improved their lands—if now they are to be ejected from their holdings which have been registered in their names at measurement. For the men who now return to Kashmír, and who seek to obtain the lands they held many years ago, one of two things can be done. First, by the consent and free will of the registered *assámis* of their old village, these men can obtain their own land, and can have their names entered in our papers. To validate this transaction we should require a document signed by the registered *assámi*, who was resigning his holding or part of his holding, by the *lambardár*, and by the *patwari*, and a second document signed by the returned cultivator, in which he would undertake to pay the revenue assessed on the land. Second, the Settlement Department, which knows where the holdings are too large for the registered *assámis*, could offer to the returned cultivators land with hereditary occupancy right in other villages, in cases where the registered *assámis* of their old village refused them their original land.

'. . . By appealing to the sentiments of brotherhood by pointing out that the holdings of the village were still too large for careful cultivation, and by convincing the assembled villagers that another worker would lessen their revenue burdens, I have in every case succeeded in obtaining the consent of the village to the readmission of the returned fugitive to his ancestral land, or to such portion of his ancestral land as will ensure a maintenance to the *assámi* and his family. This settlement of *assámis* who have returned from the Panjab or from other tahsíls can only be effected on the spot, and I have made it a rule never to *compel* the villagers to readmit an old *assámi*. The readmission of an old *assámi* and the entry of his name in the settlement papers is conditional on certain acts. The returned *assámi* must settle in the village, and must engage not to leave the village permanently during the period of settlement, viz. ten years. This precludes a contingency feared by the villagers, namely, that Kashmíris will return from the Panjab merely for the purpose of registering their names as *assámis*, and will then leave the village. I have also, in considering the claims of returned fugitives, paid first attention to the size of holdings. It is a generally accepted fact that one *assámi* can cultivate at the utmost 6 acres, of which 2 acres will be irrigated and 4 acres dry. Thus, when returned fugitives claim land in excess of this limit of 6 acres, and the village is unwilling to give up so much land, I have never pressed the claim, and have always advised both the claimant and the village that 6 acres was ample.'

CHAP. XVIII.

The *assámi* right inalienable.

papers. So long as the assessment is paid, such occupant will not be liable to ejection.' This right of occupancy is hereditary, but it is not alienable either by sale or mortgage.

An old Musalmán gentleman, resident in the city and unconnected with land, who had always worked hard in the interests of the Musalmáns of Kashmír, frequently urged that the Kashmíris were entitled to the same rights in land as they would have enjoyed if the country had not been made over by the British Government to Mahárájá Guláb Singh. He also warned me that anything short of full proprietary rights would be refused by the Kashmíris, and that general disappointment would be caused if I adhered to my views that the rights should be rights of hereditary occupancy, not alienable by sale or mortgage. As the question is of importance I quote my remarks when I referred the point for the orders of the State:—

'I feel great diffidence in proposing rules regarding the rights to be conferred on cultivators in the land which they now cultivate, inasmuch as Mr. Wingate has already submitted an elaborate draft of rules dealing with the question.

'Mr. Wingate, previous to submitting this draft of rules, had expressed his opinion on the subject of the rights in land which should be given to the cultivators of Kashmír. In paragraph 52 of his Preliminary Report he wrote: "The Darbar cannot protect itself without the assistance of the cultivators, nor is any land settlement likely to last which does not engage the active sympathies of the agricultural population in support of the State policy. This assistance and this sympathy can only be won by conferring upon the cultivators possession of the land they till." In paragraph 57 he gives still more powerful reasons for conferring this right. In paragraph 72 of the same Report Mr. Wingate writes: "I have considered if leases for the time of settlement, or for some longer periods, would not suffice to give that stability to the cultivator without which settlement is impossible. If he is to sell his produce, buy cattle and seed, enter into banking arrangements, who is going to contract or to open accounts with a day labourer, a man who, when he is turned out, wanders about with a petition in his hand for months?"

'In the draft rules[1] Mr. Wingate, in Rule 10, defines occupancy right. I agree with him that permanent occupancy rights should be bestowed on every man who at settlement agrees to pay the assessment fixed on the fields entered in his name in our settlement papers, and that so long as the assessment is paid such occupant should not be liable to ejection. I also agree that the occupancy rights should be hereditary.

'But I venture to suggest that at present the second sentence of

[1] These rules were not sanctioned by the State Council

Mr. Wingate's rule, No. 10, "the occupant, under conditions hereinafter provided, will have the right of sale, mortgage, or transfer," would be dangerous, even when restricted by the conditions of Rule 34.

'In the first place, it must be remembered that the proposal to confer the rights of sale or mortgage on occupants is an innovation; and that, although many cases have come to light where land has been sold, the right to sell has never been recognized by the State or claimed by the cultivators. I have myself come across cases where whole villages have been sold for paltry sums of Rs. 50 and Rs. 60, and have formed a strong opinion that the Kashmíri cultivators do not yet understand the value of land or rights in land. I fear, therefore, that the right to sell or to mortgage land would be the signal for extensive alienations; and that in a few years large properties would be acquired either by officials, or by the more influential Musalmán *lambardárs*. I hold strongly that the State should avoid, as far as possible, the creation of middlemen, and I regard the proposal to give the rights of sale and mortgage to ignorant and inexperienced cultivators as the surest way towards the creation of middlemen.

'In Rule 34 Mr. Wingate has restricted the right to sell, mortgage, or transfer. "Persons holding land at full settlement rates, and upon the occupancy tenure, may sell, mortgage, or transfer the land to any person who belongs to the cultivating class, i.e. who is a bona fide cultivator, without sanction."

'By Rule 35, sale, mortgage, or transfer to non-cultivators is null and void without the sanction of the Darbar, to be obtained through an officer specially constituted for this purpose.

'It occurs to me, first, that, even with the restrictions of Rule 34, we should have energetic and clever *lambardárs* buying up land in all directions for most inadequate sums, and that city Pandits would soon appoint cultivators as their agents, to buy up land for them. This has already been done to my knowledge.

'Second, I would ask what officer specially constituted for this purpose could deal satisfactorily with sales, mortgages, or transfers, under Rule 35? Such an officer would have to be intimately acquainted with all the villages of Kashmír, and would have to be paid so highly as to remove him from all temptations of bribes.

'I have quoted paragraph 72 of Mr. Wingate's Preliminary Report, for it gives a strong reason for granting the right to sell and mortgage. This paragraph implies that the cultivator, in order to carry on agriculture properly, ought to be able to raise money by sale or mortgage, or, in other words, ought to possess some credit, "if he is to sell his produce, buy cattle and seed, and enter into banking arrangements."

'There is great truth in this, but at present the cultivator, somehow or other. manages to cultivate his land without going to the money-lender, and, considering *begár* and other facts, the cultivation is fair, the number of cattle sufficient, the houses comfortable, and the clothes and domestic contrivances adequate. I cannot, therefore, accept the theory that the cultivation will be below the proper standard until the cultivator has, by selling or mortgaging his land, borrowed capital at his back to help him; and I believe that if a fair settlement is made, the occupant will be able to gain sufficient credit in the market on the strength of his year's crops.

'I write with far less experience than Mr. Wingate, but my short tour in Kashmír has given me the idea that the Kashmíri is extremely improvident. and that if opportunities were given to him, he would surpass other Musalmán tribes in their love for borrowing for extravagant expenses. To give one instance. The State now advances *sháli* and other grains as seed (*musáda*). The cultivator, as a rule, has already put by his seed; but he takes the *musáda* for his food, and if the State or any other agency will lend, the Kashmíri will borrow whether he really requires the loan or not. I need hardly remind the Council of what has happened in India from the grant to the cultivators of the right to sell and mortgage their land, and of the fact that every year Musalmán proprietors are becoming the servants of Hindu Banias.

'Knowing, as I do, that the right to sell and mortgage land in India has been attended with ruin to many Musalmán communities, I would counsel the Darbar to consider carefully whether it is necessary to confer the right on the Musalmáns of Kashmír. They are ignorant and very short-sighted. They are poor, and would most certainly squander the wealth which would at once be handed over to them, if the State now gives the right to sell and mortgage the occupancy right. And as I believe that the right to sell and mortgage would in the end injure the Musalmáns of Kashmír, so do I believe that it would also injure the State, by the introduction of a large class of powerful middlemen, who would intercept the land revenue due to the Darbar.

'Owing to the construction of the road to Kohala, it is probable that the value of land in Kashmír will rise considerably, and speculators in land will at once come forward, if the right to sell and mortgage the occupancy right in land is now conferred by the State. I would therefore advise that the Darbar should not bestow the right to sell, mortgage, or transfer until it is satisfied that the occupants are capable of properly using this right, and until population has so increased as to make transfer of land necessary. For the present, I believe that the Kashmíri cultivators will be quite satisfied if a permanent and hereditary occupancy right is given to them.'

I may add that so far no Kashmíri villager has ever demanded rights beyond those conferred by the State, and all are agreed that the right to sell and mortgage land would have been attended with disastrous results. The rights conferred by the State upon the *assámis* have proved sufficient to inspire confidence in the villages, and the evidence of this is the return of fugitives, the increase in cultivation, the greater care bestowed on cultivation, and the eagerness to obtain the *assámi* right or even the right of a permanent tenant holding under the *assámi*. CHAP. XVIII.

Settling wanderers.

The work of settling the *assámis* of Kashmír was somewhat like that of placing men upon a chess-board. Not only had fugitives to the Panjab to be replaced in their villages, but men who had left their ancestral lands for other villages in which the assessment was light and the headmen influential had to be coaxed back. The work has been done, and in most villages the *assámis* are sufficient, not for high cultivation, but for cultivation which will produce harvests from which the cultivator can live in comfort and pay the State's revenue. The agricultural population is no longer at the low ebb which I found when I began work, and, though there was heavy mortality from cholera in 1892, the revenue was collected in full.

The assessment.

Having settled the *assámis* in their villages, the next step was to decide what revenue should be assessed upon the villages, and for how long a period the assessment should be fixed. After due consideration, I thought it wise to suggest that the assessment should be fixed for ten years. I considered that it would be unfair to tie the hands of the State by fixing a longer period. The population of Kashmír is not yet sufficient for the adequate cultivation of the land. When population increases, as it will if unchecked by famine, cholera, and smallpox, when the holdings diminish in size and high cultivation becomes the rule instead of the exception, then the real value of land in Kashmír can be ascertained. I had also to bear in mind that the State was laying out capital on the cart-road to India and on the road to Gilgit, and to remember that the former would before many years work a change in prices, while the latter would improve the condition of the agricultural classes by freeing them from the dreaded Gilgit *begár*. I believe that in the ten years for which the new assessments have been sanctioned, the agricultural classes will develop the resources of the land, that they will become attached to their holdings, and that if the assessment is enhanced at the end of the ten years they will, from their attachment to their land, accept the enhancement rather than relinquish the holding.

This belief may be too sanguine, but in the few years during which the new assessments have been in force, the change in the attitude of the *assámis* has been so marked that I feel confident that land in Kashmír

CHAP. XVIII.

will be regarded, as it is in India, with a tenacious and superstitious affection. I have explained elsewhere how readily an *assámi* would leave his land and wander to other villages, and have shown that the limit of endurance in a Kashmíri was very defined. Once this limit was passed and the exactions proved too heavy, the Kashmíri would set off with his family or sheep, leaving behind him nothing that he regretted, save perhaps the vegetable plot[1]. This wandering disposition is hard to change, and when I was too high in my assessment the village always threatened me with instant migration[2]. Happily, however, there have been no such migrations, and the *tahsíldar* no longer pursues fugitives and haggles with a brother *tahsíldar* as to rights over the runaway. The sacredness of the hereditary right in land exists, but mismanagement and exactions scattered the *assámis* and turned them into vagabonds. The great object to be achieved is to inspire such confidence in the villages that the *assámis* will cling to their lands. I am of opinion that this has been achieved, but any breach of faith or non-fulfilment of the promises made at settlement may again cause wandering and throw the country into confusion.

Basis of assessment.

In the Assessment Reports I have tried to explain the method in which I arrived at the assessment of the villages. It was responsible and anxious work. The curious, almost inexplicable, differences in the fertility of adjoining villages of apparently the same soil and of the same advantages as regards irrigation, configuration, &c., were such that at first I never knew until I had announced the new assessments in the presence of the assembled *assámis*, whether I was right or wrong. We employed the same devices as are used elsewhere for the valuation of land, we had estimates of the net produce of each village based on crop experiments made in the circle in which the village was situated, and we had rough and ready revenue rates deduced from the existing revenue. But these rates were only useful to me as 'danger signals,' and my chief guide at first in assessment was the frequent inspection of the villages. My experience is, that the people will accept an assessment perhaps slightly too high if their land has been carefully inspected and their numerous complaints patiently heard. In Kashmír there are many men who have in former days farmed the land revenue of Kashmír. These men are valuation experts, and if they could

[1] Cf. *Dachanpara Assessment Report*: 'I cannot impress too clearly on the Council the fact that the cultivators of Kashmir do not deem it a strange or very inconvenient thing to leave their village at a moment's notice, and this is especially the case in the Dachanpara tahsil. A man who leaves his village, where the revenue is heavy, will with ease find land, a house, garden plot, and welcome in a village within a ten miles' radius in some other tahsil. I know very few villages in which at the present moment a fugitive could not find an empty house and ample land for the asking.'

[2] A favourite device of *assámis* who thought that they had been over-assessed was to follow me asking for *rahdari*, or permission to leave Kashmír. The necessity for *rahdari* was abolished in the famine, and all are now free to leave the valley when they wish.

be trusted, could tell one to a fraction the exact produce of a village. Though I could not trust these men to give a fair opinion as to the revenue to be placed on an individual village, I soon found that they could give me an excellent opinion as to the comparative value of villages, and their assistance has been of the greatest help to me.

In a State where the revenue accounts have been manipulated in such a way as they have in Kashmír, little dependence could be placed on the statement of collections since 1880, furnished to me by the Central Revenue Office in Srinagar. But by comparing these figures with the figures given by the *patwaris* and *lambardárs* in the villages I arrived at some idea of the average revenue actually paid by a village, and I could see from the appearance of the villagers, the cultivation, and the district, whether this average revenue was too high. Another clue was the fact that over and above the revenue of the village an extra sum was collected in some instances on account of arrears. When this sum, '*giriftani*,' was regularly collected it could be inferred that the actual assessment on the village was not too high. The great fact in the revenue history of a village was the flight of *assámis*. If many *assámis* had fled since 1880, they had fled either because the revenue was too heavy or the *begár* too severe. These were all useful guides, but there were other points to be ascertained most vital to a correct valuation of the villages. In the first place, the facts of irrigation had to be carefully inquired into, and with irrigation the question of elevation was connected. The rice crop of Kashmír is by far the most important factor in the cultivation of the valley. In the high villages water is abundant, but it is cold, and only inferior kinds of rice can be grown. The crop is always precarious, as the fall of early snow on the mountains chills and kills the rice just before harvest. Lower down there is still abundant water, the temperature of which is warm enough for the rice crop, but still lower down there comes a point where the water becomes scanty in years when there has been little snow on the mountains. It is very important to distinguish between the lower, or *paiáb*, and the upper, or *siráb*, villages, and to distinguish between the high villages where inferior and precarious rices are grown, and villages which, though high, are warm enough for the superior rices. It does not suffice to draw a line across a map, but it is necessary to see every village, and to see it several times. The shadow of the mountains makes a great difference in the production of rice, and I have often pondered over the division made by the Kashmíris, in virtue of which certain lengths of country are placed on the right hand and others placed on the left hand of the sun's course. I often found this division very mysterious, but a *dachan* village, as the right-hand villages are called, was undoubtedly better for rice cultivation than a *khowar*, or left-hand village. A *khowar* village might be lower in elevation than a *dachan*

CHAP. XVIII. village, but in the latter good rices could be sown and harvested, while in the former only inferior rices could be grown. Again, a village might geographically be *paiáb*, but by the configuration of the country all the overflow water from the upper villages would find its way thither. Such a village could stand as high, and sometimes a higher, assessment than an upper or *siráb* village. Many watercourses pass over difficult ground, where wooden aqueducts are necessary and where constant breaches occur, necessitating frequent repairs. Villages irrigated from such watercourses are of course much worse off than villages enjoying an easy and constant supply of water. Sometimes, owing to a fault in the bed of the channel, the water would disappear altogether when the supply from the mountain ran low. The configuration of the country must always be of importance in the valuation of land, but it possesses a peculiar importance in a country like Kashmír, perched on the mountains and seamed by ravines and karéwa bluffs. If one finds a tract of land shut out from the breezes by mountain spurs, one can predicate that the rice and maize crops will be liable to *rai*[1]. Again, in the hilly country known as the *kandi*, one side of a hill will produce excellent maize while the other hardly gives back the seed. Then, as one approached the sides of the Jhelum river, floods and water-logged swamp land had to be taken into consideration. Vicinity to the forests, where bears and pigs abounded, was often attended by loss to the crops. Villages lying along the funnel-like ravines, down which the cold breezes blow from some well-known mountain-peak, are always liable to loss when the crop fails to ripen. Numerous instances have been given by me in the Assessment Reports to account for differences existing between neighbouring villages, and I mention some of them here in order to show that the system of grouping villages together for assessment purposes, though useful, had to be supplemented by frequent inspection and local knowledge. I would add that for assessment purposes in Kashmír the village itself is a large and dangerous generalization. If I had had time and an establishment which could be entrusted with such work, I should have treated the holding and not the village as the unit to be valued.

In order to ascertain what revenue a village could pay it was of great importance to find out all the facts connected with irrigation, but it was of equal importance to note the number of *assámis*, or rather of the actual workers in the village, and to remark the size of the holdings. After many inquiries, and after personal observation, I am of opinion that one *assámi* with a pair of bullocks cannot cultivate thoroughly more than two acres of rice land and four acres of dry land. As a matter of fact, in the best rice tahsíl[2]

[1] *Rai*—cf. chapter on Agriculture.

[2] *Donsu Assessment Report*, paragraph 13: 'After excluding the *shalput* and *nangar*, who only hold vegetable plots and do not cultivate, I find that the average size of holdings in the Donsu

the average size of the rice holding is greater than this, and in other parts of Kashmír it is considerably greater. Sometimes the *assámis* of a village were so few and the holdings so large as to preclude the possibility of adequate cultivation, and in such cases it was impossible to assess upon the land actually under cultivation. The assessment in such villages was something in the nature of a poll-tax modified by rates and local knowledge. At the end of ten years it will be possible to assess such villages according to acreage rates. I could not do so, and had to consider, not the amount of land, but the amount of labour available for the land. Many such villages had to be dealt with by me when I commenced the work of assessment, but as the *assámis* flocked back to their villages, the question of population ceased to embarrass me. But I always found that a village with a heavy population could pay a higher revenue than a similar village with a lighter population.

Besides the actual cultivated land the village possessed other assets which have always been liable to taxation, such as walnut trees, fruit-trees, apricots. and apricot oil, and honey. These items have now been included in my land revenue, which includes all agricultural taxes, save the pony and sheep taxes, and save the *patwári* cess of 2 per cent. on revenue collections and the *lambardár* cess of 5 per cent. on revenue. Walnut trees are in many villages an important source of wealth. Formerly the nuts were converted into oil, and the oil was paid as part of the revenue. By my settlement no oil is received as revenue, but oil is still made, and a large quantity of nuts are sold annually for export to the Panjab. Grafted apple trees also furnish a welcome addition to the income of the village. Apples, and to a less extent pears, are sold to Panjabi traders for export. Mulberry and apricot trees provide a pleasant food to the people, and the kernels of the apricot furnish an oil. Honey is not much sold, but is a valued luxury in a country where sugar is so expensive. I have not paid any attention to the honey production of the villages, but in assessing I have always remembered the fact that certain villages were rich in walnut and grafted

tahsíl is 5 ghumaos 7 kanals 11 marlas. Of this, 3 ghumaos 5 kanals 16 marlas is *abi*, and 2 ghumaos 1 kanal 15 marlas is dry, that is to say, the *assámis* hold more than the ideal amount of *abi* land, and less than the ideal amount of dry land. In Donsu the average of holdings is perhaps misleading, as the heavy population of villages like Ichgam, Bhimna, Ompura, and Pitmakahama lowers the average of the size of the holdings. We have to deal in this tahsíl with two extremes. In the one case we have several villages with a large population and small holdings. The rice cultivation is in this case excellent, and the fact shows that there is ample room in most villages of Kashmír for a very largely increased population. In the other case we have small struggling villages which have, since Sambat 1937, broken up an excessive amount of land. Their revenue is, comparatively speaking, light, but their cultivation is slovenly, and the outturn much smaller than that of the more densely populated villages. Such villages would gladly receive new *assámis*, and I trust that if the flow of returned fugitives continues, this department will be able to arrange for the proper complement of *assámis* in villages where the land is now beyond the strength of the cultivators.'

CHAP. XVIII. fruit-trees. One of the great sources of wealth in Kashmír is sheep-farming. An *assámi* who has a good flock of sheep can keep his house warm in the winter, has ample wool for house use and for sale, and has sufficient manure for his rice fields when the spring comes. He pays the State two annas per sheep for the privilege of grazing on the mountain pastures, but he pays nothing for the willow branches and the iris leaves which form the sheep fodder in the winter. A man with sheep will not only weave woollen cloth for himself and his family, but will often be able to sell one or two blankets at fair prices, which have a rising tendency. I think it is only fair to consider in assessment that certain villages possess a large number of willow trees and have a large area of iris within their boundaries. I have never made the presence of walnut and fruit-trees, or of sheep and willow trees, a reason for enhancing revenue, but I have frequently considered their presence as a sufficient reason for not decreasing revenue.

Announcing the new assessment.

Having finally determined the revenue of a village for ten years, and having obtained the sanction of the State to the proposed revenue, my next duty was to announce the new revenue to the assembled villages. At first the revenue officials, the leading *lambardárs* and the *patwaris*, canvassed the country and urged people to refuse the new revenue, and some few villages declined to accept my assessment. But within six months from the time when the new assessments were distributed over the holdings and the new system of quarterly instalments was introduced, the recusant villagers came in and begged for admission to the benefits of the settlement. The work of announcing assessments was always fraught with anxiety, as powerful interests were brought to bear upon the people, but after assessing five tahsíls I had but little trouble. I could then appeal to the condition of the tahsíls which had been assessed.

Fixing the amount in cash and in kind.

The next point in the assessment was to decide how much should be taken in cash and how much in kind. I had always held that the assessment should be wholly in cash, and my idea was that as each tahsíl came under assessment and the amount of revenue taken in kind by the State was decreased, the city people who have hitherto fed on the cheap grain sold by the State would make arrangements to buy grain in the open market, and that private trade would spring up. I was however told that the villagers themselves could not pay the whole revenue in cash, and great pressure was brought to bear in order to induce me to abandon the idea of a purely cash payment. This story that the people could not or did not wish to pay the revenue in cash has been told to others.

Sir Richard Temple was told this in 1871 [1], and the officials of Kashmír

[1] 'As regards the revenue, there really seemed to be money assessments of the land tax in all the districts of the Mahárájá's kingdom save Kashmír itself; even here the landholders had the option of one if they chose to avail themselves of it, which they seldom appeared to do. The taking

have never lost an opportunity of asserting that a cash arrangement would be unpopular with the people. In 1847 it was arranged between Mahárájá Gulab Singh and Lieutenant Reynell Taylor that the districts in the neighbourhood of Srinagar should pay their revenue in cash, and that the sale of rice should be left entirely to the will and option of the zamindárs. It was added that any man selling at a higher rate than 1 rupee per kharwar would be answerable to Government for it. No embargo was to be placed on the export of grain to the Panjab. In 1873 it was reported that a cash assessment had been made, and that the zamindárs were at liberty to sell grain at what prices they pleased.

There can be no doubt that Mahárájá Ranbir Singh wished to introduce a cash assessment, and that he was fully alive to the fact that collections in kind caused loss to the State and injury to the villagers. An effort was made in 1873 to make a cash assessment, but the officials and the middlemen prevented it. The old system, under which it lay within the power of the Governor of Kashmír to decide at his will how much cash and how much grain should be collected year by year, remained in full force until it was modified by my new assessment.

Reasons for opposition to cash assessment.

There are two reasons which have compelled the official and influential classes in Kashmír to fiercely oppose a cash assessment. The first reason is that the collection of revenue in kind gives employment to a large number of city Pandits, and also gives them great opportunities for perquisites and peculation. It may be stated that the real or market price of unhusked rice is in ordinary years about double the price at which the State sells the grain, and it is natural that every one should wish to handle a commodity in which there is so large a margin of profit. The men who obtain employment in the collection of grain make their first gains in the village, where they take sometimes as much as one-fifth in excess of the legal State demand. They make a further gain when they adulterate the grain on its way to Srinagar. Each *assámi* is ready to pay considerable sums if bad samples of grain are received as revenue and the good grain is left, but the simplest way of making money in revenue collections is to boldly sell the grain for Rs. 4 and to credit the State with Rs. 2, the State rate. When the grain reached the city, the officials in charge of the grain boats would make over to their friends and relatives a boat-load of good grain. Bad or suspicious grain would be sold to the city people at State rates.

The second reason is that the city of Srinagar undoubtedly contains a

of the Government share of the staple rice crop of Kashmír in kind no doubt leads to abuses; on the other hand, the authorities, who virtually regulated prices, seemed to keep them very cheap, vastly cheaper than in the surrounding territories. This may have been convenient to the people at the time, but it really retarded the progress of the valley.'—Sir R. Temple, *Journals kept in Hyderabad, Kashmír, Sikkim, and Nepál*, vol. ii. p. 141.

CHAP. XVIII. large number of persons who are extremely poor. To these people, receiving starvation wages from middlemen 'sweaters,' unhusked rice at the low rates prescribed by the State is at present essential. They are the remnants of the once flourishing shawl-trade men, who used to earn from one to two annas per diem. In 1871 there were some 24,000 persons employed in the manufacture of shawls. In that year the value of the revenue taken in kind was Rs. 16,93,077, and the revenue taken in cash was only Rs. 9,62,057. But the State derived a revenue of Rs. 6,00,000 from taxation on shawls and Rs. 1,13,916 from taxes on city shopkeepers. From a financial point of view there was some excuse for taking a large proportion of the land revenue in kind. The losses attending collections in kind were more than balanced by the handsome income so easily collected from the shawl-workers. But this excuse no longer existed in 1873, when the shawl trade was dead, and Mahárájá Ranbir Singh had strong financial as well as other reasons for wishing to introduce a cash assessment. He was not allowed to do so. I have explained that my idea was to gradually substitute a cash assessment for an assessment which was chiefly collected in kind, and in the first seven tahsíls which I assessed I acted on the following plan:—I limited the revenue to be taken in kind to the two most important staples, viz. rice and maize, and I declined to take oil-seeds, cotton, and pulses [1]. At the time of announcing the assessment I gave each village the option as to the amount which should be paid in cash and in kind, and I further gave each village the power of commuting the amount of kind agreed upon by cash payments.

[1] *Lál Assessment Report*, paragraph 16: 'I propose, however, to make a change in the present system of collection, which, even if the existing revenue demand remains as it is at present, will in some villages make that demand considerably heavier than it has been hitherto. Although a glance at the table showing the proportion borne by the several crops to the cultivated area will indicate that rice and maize are of chief importance, many villages have hitherto derived considerable advantage from paying a part of their revenue in such crops as *tilgoglu*, *mung*, cotton, &c., the Government rates for which are much higher than the real or market price. Thus at the present moment for every kharwar of *tilgoglu* a cultivator will get a credit of Rs. 9 from Government, whereas if he sold it in the market he would only get Rs. 5, and for every kharwar of *mung* he would get a credit from Government of Rs. 7.14.0, whereas if he sold it in the city he would only get Rs. 4. The present system of revenue collection involves considerable loss to the State, and at the same time places a most dangerous power in the hands of the subordinate officials, for the object of each individual *assámi* is to retain his rice and maize, and to pay his revenue in articles for which he receives a high credit, and he is ready to bribe in order to gain this object. The original intention of the Darbar when it decided to receive a part of its revenue in *tilgoglu*, cotton, *mung*, &c., may have been to encourage variety in cultivation, or it may have been that the State actually wanted these articles for its army and for other purposes. The former purpose has, however, been frustrated, for to my knowledge many villages buy *tilgoglu*, cotton, &c., from the city at the market price and pay it as revenue at the higher Government rate, while as regards the necessities of the army it is safe to say that the supply of these staples will always be equal to the demand. The proposal which I have to make is that in future the revenue of the Lál Tahsíl be entirely taken in rice, maize, or in cash. I have in each village inquired what proportion of cash could be paid, and I would suggest that cash to that amount be taken, and that the balance of the revenue be accepted in rice or maize.'

My scheme of gradually introducing a cash assessment worked without difficulty until I had finished the settlement of seven tahsíls, but in my absence in the winter of 1891 the Governor of Kashmír brought about a crisis by taking the greater part of the revenue of the eight unassessed tahsíls in cash. The consequence was that very little State grain came into the city. The Governor of Kashmír had given no warning of his intentions to the State, but the enormous quantity of grain imported by private persons showed that others had an inkling of the Governor's purposes. The time chosen by the Governor for this sudden change was unfortunate. There was no snow on the mountains, and the Kashmíris always predict a short rice crop when the snowfall is deficient. In 1892 a disastrous fire broke out in the city, destroying enormous stocks of grain. This was followed by the severe epidemic of cholera. Business was paralyzed, shops were closed, and the villagers brought in no grain or other supplies to the infected city. Prices of grain rose rapidly, and though prompt measures prevented a famine in the city, it was obvious that the sudden substitution of cash for kind collections would cause difficulties in Srinagar[1].

CHAP. XVIII.

Sardár Rup Singh's action.

[1] *Note by Rai Bahadur Pandit Suraj Kaul, C.I.E., Revenue Member of the State Council, on the causes of the scarcity of grain in Srinagar and the arrangements made for the relief of the population:—*

'The late distress in Srinagar is too well known to require any detailed description. Complaints of scarcity of food poured in from all sides. The so-called distress was not due to unfavourable or bad harvest, but had been brought about by a combination of untoward circumstances, the principal of which were the following:—

'From time immemorial, the State invariably kept a reserve stock of grain for the town of Srinagar, making supplies at rates far below the market price of staples. The result was a dead loss to the State on the one hand, and on the other the annihilation of free trade on mercantile principles.

'Depending on the bounty of the State, the people naturally neglected to avail themselves of the blessings of self-help, and their happiness was centred in the fullness of the State godowns and the readiness with which supplies were issued from them.

'The state of affairs during the incumbency of Sardár Rup Singh, Governor of Kashmír, was extremely unsatisfactory. The books showed a nominal reserve of 6 lakhs' worth of grain, though the granaries were practically empty and their emptiness no longer remained a secret.

'In consequence of the ingenious frauds practised by local officials, the prevailing system of collecting the State revenue in kind was found to result in a dead loss to the State, and advantage was accordingly taken of the recent settlement to introduce a system of cash assessments; this system was not, however, extended to the whole province of Kashmír, a portion of the land revenue still continuing to be collected in kind from the unassessed tahsils, to meet the immediate requirements of the city of Srinagar—but for some unaccountable reason, and in spite of strict orders, the grain collections were so badly managed that people were actually forced to make payments in cash instead of kind, while the little that had been collected in kind was most dishonestly sold at enhanced prices which simply went to fill the pockets of the Sadr Treasurer and his *tahvildars*, and curiously enough the chief revenue authority, viz. the Governor, did not take the least notice of these occurrences.

'The consequence was that the former tahvil under the Governor, and the latter under the Sadr Treasurer and his son, participated largely in the peculation of State *shali* and the disorganization of the recognized system of collection, and the people naturally suspected the ruinous condition of

CHAP. XVIII.

The Settlement Department takes up the question of collections in kind.

Up to that time I had declined to take any part in the collection of grain or in its storage, but when the State, alarmed by the occurrences of 1892, decided that some part of the revenue should be collected in kind, I agreed to assist in the distribution of the demand for kind over the unassessed tahsíls, and to watch the arrangements made for collection, storage, and sale. My reason for holding aloof from the business of collections in kind was that I believed that it would die a natural death, and from the first I have endeavoured to avoid interference in matters which were within the province of the Governor. But when the State intimated that for some time to come an appreciable part of the revenue would be taken in kind, I deemed it necessary in the interests of my settlement to take an active part in the collection and disposal of the revenue taken in kind.

Arrangements for collections in kind.

For the first year the demand in kind was fixed at 360,000 kharwárs. The advocates of a revenue in kind urged that this was too small, and that 700,000 kharwárs was the lowest amount that could be taken with safety. We found, however, that after selling freely to the people of Srinagar, and after meeting all State requirements for the army and other departments, we had a balance of 68,315 kharwárs at the end of the year. Prices were low in the grain markets, and not a complaint was heard from the city. Steps were taken to introduce some system into the collections, boats were properly caulked, and boatmen found guilty of adulteration were punished. The State granaries were repaired, and it appeared that there was not space in the whole of the granaries for more than 100,000 kharwárs of grain, a clear proof that the limit of 700,000 kharwárs suggested by the Pandits was fictitious. If 700,000 kharwárs were collected, its grain was never sold to the city people. The old practice of making over boat-loads of grain to influential persons who retailed rice at a profit of cent. per cent. was stopped, and if any one wanted State grain he had to go down to the river-side, where he obtained at the monthly sales 21 seers of unhusked rice or maize for each member of his family. It would take too long to describe the difficulties which attended reforms in the collection, storage, and sale of State grain. Though the rich and influential opposed every change, it is satisfactory to know that the poor people in Srinagar were enabled to buy clean, unadulterated grain at State rates. The policy which should guide the State in future is to reduce the demand every year. In 1893 the

the granaries. To add to their misfortunes, the scarcity of grain was followed by the destructive fires which burnt down as many as 1,500 houses in a densely populated part of the city, and with them several thousands of kharwárs of the *shálí* stored in them. To give an idea of the magnitude of this conflagration, and of the havoc which followed in its train, it will be sufficient to mention that more than 7,000 persons were rendered homeless, without any kind of shelter against the severity of a Kashmír winter; coupled with this the appearance of cholera, which eventually developed into a very severe epidemic, caused a mortality fearful to describe, the deaths averaging up to nearly 500 per diem.'

demand was reduced to 300,000 kharwárs, and I believe that it would be right to reduce it to 100,000[1]. With every reduction in the demand made by the State, there will be a corresponding expansion in the private grain trade. But until the trade of Kashmír is on a more healthy footing, and prices are ruled by the same considerations as obtain in other countries, it may be wise to maintain a State reserve of 100,000 kharwárs. This reserve would act partly to prevent a ring being formed among the grain-dealers, partly as a seed supply in case of a total failure of the rice crop. Among other needless and injurious practices I abolished the old system by which a large part of the State grain was set apart for the consumption of the small towns and staging-places in the valley. Sixty thousand kharwárs were loudly demanded for the towns and about 20,000 kharwárs for the staging-places. I was enabled to show that the grain never reached the towns, but was a perquisite of the officials. As regards the staging-places I induced private traders to undertake the supply of grain and other necessaries. The arrangement worked smoothly, and the officials of Kashmír, saving those in Srinagar, are now relieved from the duty of retailing provisions. They are at the same time deprived of a valuable perquisite. This has, however, been made up to them by a substantial increase in pay. CHAP. XVIII.

One argument against the sudden substitution of cash for kind collections is furnished by the existing condition of trade in Kashmír. It has often been asserted that the Kashmíri villager will not sell his surplus grain. It is forgotten that up to the time when the settlement commenced, and even later, a Kashmíri cultivator who sold unhusked rice would have been summarily punished. The officials knew too well the value of the monopoly in grain to allow the producers to compete, and even now the old-fashioned villager sells his grain by stealth. This is rapidly changing, and I believe that in a few years there will be no reluctance on the part of the cultivators as regards sale. The Kashmíri is intelligent, and he knows that grain deteriorates after two years. It is quite possible that he will keep a year's supply in reserve, but he will not keep more.

As regards the amount to which the demand in kind has been reduced, I do not think that the collection of 300,000 kharwárs of grain seriously injures agricultural interests. But it causes loss to the State in many ways, and throws a large and unnecessary burden on the Revenue officials. Owing to large public works, and to the steady increase in the number of visitors to Kashmír, money is more plentiful than it was, and I believe that the whole revenue could be paid in cash. Judging from the numerous petitions which I receive for permission to pay the whole assessment in cash, I should say that there were few *assámis* in the valley who would not welcome a cash assessment.

[1] Since this was written the demand has been reduced to 175,000 kharwárs for ten years.

CHAP. XVIII. Apart from the pilfering which must always attend collections in kind, however well supervised, the State has to pay the carriage of the grain from the threshing-floor to the city, and has to maintain granaries and an agency for the storage and sale of the grain. All this is absolute loss to the State, and it is obvious that, if middlemen and sweaters who are making enormous profits in artware and the pauperized citizens of Srinagar be excepted, all will benefit from the steady reduction in the amount of grain taken as revenue. The middlemen who formerly lived on the perquisites attending collections in grain would find a more healthy and equally lucrative sphere in legitimate trade, and the old feeling of the agriculturists that they were merely serfs cultivating in the interests of the city would disappear [1].

[1] Mr. Wingate, in his Preliminary Report, dated August 1, 1888, deals fully with this subject. I quote extracts from paragraphs 28 and 29:—

'I saw mobs struggling and fighting to secure a chance of getting a few seers of the Government *shálí*, in a way that I have not witnessed since the great famine of Southern India.

'Shortly after Mahárájá Guláb Singh assumed the control, the present system of collecting *shálí* in large granaries in the city, and selling it by retail through Government officials, appears to have been introduced, and the price of *shálí*, with a brief interval about A.D. 1879 when it was raised to Rs. 1½, has remained stationary at Rs. 1¼ per kharwár of 15 traks, = 2 maunds and 1 seer of standard weight at 80 tolas per seer. For over forty years the system has been sufficiently profitable to support a large body of the Pandit population of the city in idleness, and the Government has gradually become on the one side a farmer working with coolies under a management closely approximating to forced labour, and on the other side a gigantic banniá's shop doling out food to poor in exchange for their coppers, and keeping with every cultivator an account showing what is taken from him, whether in the way of grain, oil, wool, ponies, cows, &c., and what is given to him in the shape of seed, plough, cattle, cotton or wool to spin and weave, and a hundred other petty details.

'There are neither grain shops in the bazaar nor banniás nor bankers anywhere *. I do not know whether it is an offence to sell *shálí*, but I do know that the cultivators are afraid to do so, and in tahsíls nominally under a cash settlement and with an abundant harvest my establishment have once and again been literally starving, and the only way they can get food is by having it sent out, rice, atta, dal, &c. &c., from the Government storehouses in Srinagar to the *tahsíldars*, who thereupon sell to my men for cash. My men still find difficulty in procuring the necessaries of life, and only very urgent representations at head-quarters have secured the supplies necessary to stop the angry and to me humiliating clamour of my subordinates to be allowed to buy food for ready money. Doubtless this annoyance has been partly due to the feeling of hostility with which my department is regarded by every official from the highest to the lowest †, but the scenes I have described in the city convinced me that the widow and the orphan, the weak and the sickly, must fare badly when it comes to physical wrestling for the daily bread. In Kashmír the *tahsíldar* is the banniá, and he is a branch of the great official firm in Srinagar where the chief business is conducted.

Profits on the sale of cleaned rice.

'29. The system is so intricate and so constantly changing that I do not attempt to explain how the State treasury on the one hand and the poor on the other suffer. I merely confine myself to one or two facts. The amount of cleaned rice to be got out of *shálí* varies with the quality and with the degree of cleanness thought necessary by the consumer. Compiling, however, a good many answers, I gather that the quantity is never less than half for the cleanest rice of the well-to-do, and not greater than two-thirds for the dirtiest eaten by the poor. The quantity of cleaned rice may thus vary between 48 and 64 seers per kharwár, and the ordinary proportion for the mass of the people may

* Cultivators, however, do get advances from people in the city.

† This season several of the circles are able to supply themselves in the villages by paying rather more than the fixed price.

Among other results of the unfortunate action taken by the Governor at the end of 1891 was the strict prohibition of the export of rice from Kashmír. The prohibition has not yet affected prices, and there has never been any appreciable export of rice. But with new land coming under cultivation, and with improvements in existing cultivation, the production of rice will undoubtedly increase, and it is possible that with increase of good harvests a kharwár of unhusked rice might fall to Rs. 1.8.0 or even to Rs. 1.4.0, the State rate. I have advised the State to permit export when the price of unhusked rice falls to Rs. 1.8.0 per kharwár.

Internal distribution of the revenue.

Having settled the revenue of each village, and the amount which should be paid in cash and in kind, and having fixed the proportion of the revenue which should be collected at each of the four instalments, the next step was to distribute the revenue over the various holdings. Formerly the *lambardár* and other influential persons in the village paid only a nominal revenue, and the State's dues were paid by the weaker and voiceless *assámis*. My distribution was made according to the area of the holding,

be taken at three of cleaned rice to two of husk. Three and a half seers of rice per trak of *shάli* is not an uncommon reply, and that gives 56 seers of cleaned rice per kharwár, and as that amount is near enough to the proportion of three to two I shall adopt it. The kharwár spoken of has only 15 traks, but that is a detail. The State sells *shάli* at Rs. 1¼ per kharwár, or 10 annas per one maund and half a seer standard weight, and *shάli* is not allowed to be sold openly at any other price. But if *shάli* cannot be sold, rice can, though the State officials are supposed to sell white rice at 28 Kashmiri seers and red rice at 32 Kashmíri seers per rupee. Except to the followers of the British visitors or to persons of influence, rice was however not procurable at these rates, and was admittedly sold in the city last year for 16 to 20 Kashmíri seers per rupee, though I was informed by Panjabis that the price ran as high as 10 to 12 Kashmíri seers per rupee. A 15-trak kharwár of *shάli*, or 90 local seers, was sold for Rs. 1¼. Half a seer per trak is ordinarily paid for husking. Deducting therefore 7½ seers from 90, the balance is 82½ seers, from which about 48 seers of cleaned rice would be got. It was possible, therefore, for a man to secure rice at a cost of about 38 seers per rupee, and to sell it at 19 or 20 seers per rupee, or about double the price he paid for it. The State do their cleaning expensively, but even they can profitably sell at 32 seers per rupee, even supposing the rice is cleaned for the most fastidious. For 90 seers $-7\frac{1}{2} = 82\frac{1}{2}$ seers $\div 2 = 41\frac{1}{4}$ seers of cleaned rice for Rs. 1¼ or 33 seers per rupee. Now if the cheapest rice was not procurable under 20 seers per rupee, and the dearest ran up to 10 seers, it requires no argument to show that *shάli* was not distributed last year at Rs. 1¼ per kharwár, except in very limited and insufficient quantity. The places of sale were few, the days of sale fewer, the officers appointed insufficient. Every expedient was resorted to that admitted of the smallest public sale with the maintenance of the farce of selling freely. Large sales were, however, reported to the State treasury, and the money duly paid in at Rs. 1¼ per kharwár. The profit was divided between the officials who made over the *shάli* and the favoured recipient; the poor paid twice as much for their rice as the State intended, and the State got nothing but their maledictions. Influential people were always able to get their *shάli* at Rs. 1¼, and these included the larger proportion of the Pandits. All these facts I explained in public Darbar, with the satisfaction of being informed that I was the first who had brought to notice that the poor could not get *shάli* at the Government price. This year, the *shάli* is being distributed freely at 7½ traks of *shάli* per head per mensem, or 6 kharwárs per annum, and consequently rice is to be had at its proper price and the city is quiet. But it is obvious this cannot last, even if the traditions of former years are finally at an end. The price of *shάli* must rise and fall with the outturn of the harvest. With a fixed price, the moment it gets scarce or is made scarce, enormous profits are made on the rice, and the mendicancy which prevails throughout the valley is only one of the signs that for years back the staple grain has been dealt out by measure to the people.'

CHAP. XVIII. its quality, and the position as regards irrigation. The result was that the burden of the *assámis* was lightened, while the *lambardárs*, *patwáris*, and other influential persons were suddenly called upon to pay their share of the revenue. Opposition was aroused, but was overcome. When it was possible, the distribution of the revenue was made in accordance with the wishes and opinion of the village and of the majority of the *assámis*. When there seemed to be no hope of agreement, the revenue was distributed according to the various rates which I had suggested for each class of soil. The holding of a Kashmír village contains every class of soil, and though in some few instances certain holdings were over-assessed while others were under-assessed, on the whole, thanks to the fact that the holding is scattered over the village, the distribution of the revenue has brought about a fair, though perhaps not perfect, incidence of taxation.

The *patwáris*. The *lambardárs* were to a certain extent appeased by the fact that they would receive 5 per cent. on collections, but for the *patwáris* and others I had no consolation to offer. The *patwáris*, whatever they may have been in the Mughal times, had practically ceased to be an agency of any importance under the system of farming out the land revenue. When the settlement commenced, Mr. Wingate made an effort to utilize the *patwáris* in the survey, but he found that it was hopeless. I started *patwári* schools, from which I obtained some excellent surveyors, but experience in the villages soon showed me that the old *patwári* system of Kashmír would have to be greatly modified. The *patwári* was appointed and dismissed by the villagers, and the tahsíl authorities neither knew nor cared about the *patwári* agency. The old idea that the office of *patwári* was hereditary had died out, and not only would a village turn out a *patwári* once every two years, but factions would arise in a village and each faction would elect its own *patwári*. The papers kept up by the *patwári* were meagre in the extreme and lacked continuity. The office was practically unrecognized by the local authorities, though the central officials in Srinagar fostered the belief that a real *patwári's* agency was in existence, and that real revenue accounts were kept up. The number of *patwáris* was legion, and their pay was what they could get from the villagers. We have had to cut down the number very considerably, and have divided the new *patwáris* of Kashmír into three classes. In the first two classes, Kashmíris who have worked in the settlement, and who can maintain the records and revenue accounts of a village, are appointed. Villages liable to floods and villages of large revenue are made over to the *patwáris* of the first and second class. In the third class the more efficient and deserving of the old *patwáris* are appointed. Hill-villages, in which the revenue is not considerable and is not likely to expand, are made over to the *patwáris* of the third class. Much as one regrets any radical change which involves loss to a large number of persons, a great reduction in the *patwáris* was necessary, and it must be remembered that before the settlement the *patwáris* were only temporary office-holders on the sufferance of the villages, and that most of them have land which forms their chief means of subsistence. To keep up the records and maps made at settlement a trained agency is necessary and the new *patwáris* who have been appointed are all Kashmíris, and many of them sons or relatives of the old *patwáris*. The experience of the past thirteen years shows that *patwáris* who held office at the will of the villagers did not protect the revenue interest of the State. It is therefore essential, both in the interests of the State revenue and for the sake of keeping the village records alive, that the new *patwáris* should be trained men and servants, not of the villagers, but of the Government.

The *lambardárs*.

Just as the *patwáris* were appointed and dismissed by the villagers, so too the *lambardárs* were liable to removal if they displeased a powerful faction or showed too great zeal in collecting the land revenue. *Lambardárs* have been finally appointed, and they hold office under direct appointment of His Highness the Maháráíá. The office will be hereditary. I have often considered the question whether it would be possible to introduce the system under which the *assámis* of a village would be jointly responsible for the revenue, but I do not think that the conditions of the Kashmír village are such as to allow of the system. There is no unity or co-operation between the *assámis* of a village. Every man distrusts his neighbour, and no one would willingly become security for an insolvent or improvident member of the village. The *lambardár*, who receives a salary from the State of 5 per cent. on the revenue, is held responsible for the payment of the land revenue. It is his duty to prevent *assámis* from absconding, and in the event of the death or flight of an *assámi* he is bound to arrange for the cultivation of his holding and the payment of the revenue on that holding. In ordinary cases the *lambardár* can easily accomplish this. But when, as may happen, a village is overtaken by some great calamity, such as an earthquake or cholera, the *lambardár* cannot be held responsible for the non-payment of the revenue, and any holdings for which cultivators cannot be obtained will be removed from the rent roll. In short, the old system has been retained, but the office of *lambardár* has been placed on a sound footing, and its duties have been defined and will be enforced. A great deal will depend on the *lambardárs* in the future. The *assámis* of a village now know the exact extent of their revenue liabilities, and are very quick to protest if the *lambardár* or any one else attempts to take more than the amount fixed at settlement. In the past the more influential *lambardárs* have proved a great curse to the people, but their powers and opportunities for robbery and peculation have been largely curtailed. The *lambardár* will still take his perquisites, as he does

Perquisites.

in other oriental countries, but he will no longer act as a collecting agent of corrupt officials. I do not say that all the officials will become honest in a few years, but I am confident that the old system of official perquisites (*rasum*) is defunct. The *assámis* of Kashmír have grasped the fact that they need not pay *rasum* unless they wish, and the Kashmíri pays nothing for nothing.

The considerations for *rasum* were the exemption from the Gilgit *begár* and other impressments of a serious nature, the collection of the revenue in cotton, oil-seeds, &c., by which the villagers obtained not only pecuniary benefits, but also retained rice and grains sufficient for their subsistence, and the permission to keep back a certain proportion of the State's revenue as arrears. The *tahsíldar* no longer has these considerations to offer. Serious *begár* has disappeared; each *assámi* pays the cash or the kind, rice and maize, assessed by me; and arrears are not allowed to stand over until competent authorities are satisfied that the revenue cannot be paid in full.

Arrears.

The question of arrears has been discussed by me at some length in the various Assessment Reports. It is an old tradition of the State that a man is more amenable when he is a debtor to the treasury, a *bákidár*. Most officials have been *bákidárs*, and all villages have been entered in the list of arrears. Allusion to the widespread system of arrears has been made in my chapter on Administration. I will quote from the Assessment Report which led His Highness the Mahárájá to declare before the assembled *lambardárs* and their sons that the arrears of the land revenue were remitted. It was a wise and generous act on the part of the State. The old officials opposed the measure, for if my view on the subject of arrears were correct, they stood condemned of fraud and disloyalty; old tradition urged that it was a dangerous departure to give up this hold over the villagers, and the financial position of the State demanded that every effort should be made to realize assets, however doubtful. But for this measure, as for all other measures which have been sanctioned by His Highness the Mahárájá and his Council, all that was required was proof, and ample proof was given that the villagers had derived no benefit from the huge system of frauds which had been perpetrated under the name 'arrears.'

Assessment Report of Ranbir Singhpura Tahsíl, paragraph 6: 'Briefly speaking, the policy of the revenue officials in Kashmír has been to exaggerate the revenue capacity of the country and to deceive the Darbar as to its real income. They thought that if they could show an increase of revenue on paper they would be well thought of at head-quarters, and the consequence of this policy is that the nominal revenue of the tahsíl is absurd, while the fictitious arrears are enormous. I could quote numerous instances in this tahsíl to show how false and misleading the nominal revenue is. In Naupura the nominal revenue is Rs. 2,141. In Sambat 1948 the arrears amounted to Rs. 1,561. In Sambat 1947 only Rs. 7 were realized. It is absurd to suppose that in a large village like Naupura, the *tahsíldar*, if he had made an effort, could only realize Rs. 7; but the revenue arrangements are so bad in Ranbir Singhpura, owing to mistakes made in Sambat 1937, that the villagers do not consider themselves bound to pay any revenue, and they know that the nominal revenue was a sham, merely calculated to deceive the Darbar. This state of things makes it extremely difficult to introduce a fair settlement, as it is easy to understand that a village like Naupura would be far better off under a system where the *tahsíldar* is content with a payment of Rs. 7 for the whole year, than under a system where the failure to pay a fair revenue would be followed by coercive processes. Walnuts and fruit alone in this village are worth over Rs. 100, but the State only receives Rs. 7 for walnuts, fruit, and 195 acres of cultivated land. I need hardly remark that the twenty-nine *assámis* of Naupura, although they paid far less than the proper revenue in Sambat 1947, probably paid considerably more than Rs. 7, but the balance did not reach the State treasury.

'It is difficult to understand how this system of darkening and confusing the revenue accounts was allowed to commence, and how it has so long escaped detection. When, for instance, His Highness Mahárájá Guláb Singh granted a *guzárish* of Rs. 710 from the revenue of Naugam, it might have been supposed that he intended this to be an alienation of revenue. And it has been an alienation of revenue, but the Daftar-i-Diwáni, in order to make it appear that the revenue had not been diminished, showed the Rs. 710 year by year as an arrear against the Naugam village. The arrears entered against Naugam now amount to Rs. 9,749. The same system of exaggerating the revenue obtains throughout the tahsíl, and the total arrears of Ranbir Singhpura up to Sambat 1947 amount to Rs. 5,96,644. As in the other tahsíls for which I have submitted Assessment Reports, I consider that these arrears are nearly entirely fictitious, and I urge most strongly that it would be unwise to attempt to realize anything on account of these arrears. I shall, as in all the tahsíls which I have assessed, propose a very full assessment, and I maintain that the villagers for some years to come will not be able to pay anything in addition to their new assessment. If the Council remembers the manner in which the revenue accounts have been kept—how a *guzárish* granted by the Mahárájá himself is entered as an arrear against the village; if it remembers that large amounts were practically remitted on the very day that the assessments of Sambat 1937 were announced, and that other large amounts were also practically remitted under the system of *Takrári Jama*; and if it finally remembers that the nominal revenue fixed in Sambat 1937 has never been acted upon either

CHAP. XVIII. by the *tahsíldar* or the villagers, it will, I hope, consent to the wiping off of all arrears before the new assessments are announced. This was the course taken by the Council when the Assessment Reports of Lál and Phák Tahsíls were sanctioned, but for some reason no definite orders have been passed regarding the arrears in other tahsíls. To put the case briefly, I would say that nothing will be realized if an attempt is made to recover arrears, and next that the work of the settlement will be rendered practically worthless. One of the chief objects of the settlement is to fix a fair and full assessment, and to place in the hands of the Darbar and its revenue officials clear records showing what each *assámi* in Kashmír has to pay. By these records the power of the *tahsíldar* and his subordinates for peculation will be removed, and prosperity to the country will be assured. But if arrears are still held over the heads of the villagers, the *tahsíldar* will have it in his power to confuse all accounts again, and the old fraudulent system of the *tahsíldar's majawaza*, of the *musáda* and the *giriftáni*, will again flourish, to the loss and bad name of the Darbar, and to the ruin and corruption of the cultivators. If I thought that it was possible to distinguish between real and fictitious arrears, or possible to find out the real defaulters and to recover something from them, I would not hesitate to recommend an attempt to realize some part of the arrears; but the *mustájirs*, the defaulters, have disappeared; *tahsíldars* have been transferred or have left the service; and the *lambardárs* and *patwáris*, who have enjoyed a share of the spoil, have no property worth seizing. Any attempt to collect arrears would be the signal for the general flight of the *assámis*, and I advise on every ground, and I speak with an experience of eleven out of the fifteen tahsíls of Kashmír, that all arrears should be written off before the new assessments are announced. I do not include in arrears the *musáda* which has been granted during the year previous to assessment.'

Conclusion. These are the main points of the settlement. The State by its justice and moderation has won the confidence of the agricultural classes, and Kashmír is now more prosperous and more fully cultivated than it has been in the memory of man. The deadly cholera of 1892 and the disastrous floods of 1893 have done their worst, but the affected villages survive, damaged but not broken, and the rent roll remains unimpaired. The agriculturists, who used to wander from one village to another in quest of the fair treatment and security which they never found, are now settled down on their lands and permanently attached to their ancestral villages. The revenue is often paid up before the date on which it falls due, and whereas in 1884 it was necessary to maintain a force of 7,429 soldiers for the collection of the revenue, now the tahsíl *chaprasi* rarely visits a village. The publican has disappeared from the scene, and the villagers have now to deal with *tahsíldars* whose pay enables them to live respectably. Every *assámi* knows his revenue liabilities in cash and in kind, and he quickly and successfully resists any attempt to extort more than the amount entered in his revenue-book. The more serious evils of *begár* have been removed, and the cultivator has ample time to look after his fields. The annual dread that sufficient food-grain would not be left for the support of himself and his family has ceased, and the agricultural classes of Kashmír are, I believe, at the present time as well off in the matter of food and clothing as any agriculturists in the world. CHAP. XVIII.

If the conditions of the settlement are faithfully observed confidence will increase, and there will be a great change not only in the cultivation and development of the country, but also in the character and honesty of the people. Faith has never yet been kept with them. Other measures have been taken since the settlement commenced, which will have an important effect on the agricultural prosperity of the country. Sanitary reforms in Srinagar may mitigate the ravages of cholera, and so save the agricultural population from recurring losses, while the zeal shown in vaccination at the end of 1893, if it be continued, will certainly work an important change in vital statistics. Only two things are wanted to make Kashmír one of the most fertile and prosperous countries in the world. The first is an honest and strong administration, the second is a steady increase in population.

Time occupied in settlement.

The work of survey was commenced in the summer of 1887; it was finished in September, 1893. The field season in Kashmír may be said to last from May to October, but delays were caused by the fact that our establishment had to survey not only Kashmír but also certain tahsíls in the Jammu territory. Great dislocation was caused by the movements between Jammu and Kashmír. In 1890, and again in 1892, I remained during the winter in Kashmír. Apart from the delay caused by these moves, the rice fields in Kashmír are small and the work of survey is intricate and difficult. If I had largely increased my survey establishment I could have finished the work of survey more rapidly, but for several reasons I considered it best to proceed gradually. The assessment work in all its details I retained entirely in my own hands, and it was with extreme difficulty and effort that I kept pace with the survey. Again, my position in Kashmír was not that of an ordinary settlement officer. I was consulted by the State on all subjects connected with the revenue administration; all suits regarding land were removed from the ordinary courts and placed under my jurisdiction, and many duties which in ordinary times would have been discharged by the Governor and his subordinates were relegated to me. The work of superintending the collections in kind alone occupied a large part of my time in 1892, while the work of inspecting the villages which suffered from the great flood of 1893 forced me for

CHAP. XVIII. a time to lay aside my work of settlement. In the same year a journey to Gilgit and back occupied a month of my time. The work of allotting waste lands throws considerable labour on my office, while the duties of superintending the vineyards, hop-garden, and horticulture, and in a lesser degree my connexion with sericulture, have tended to prevent the rapid completion of the settlement. But the experience gained leads me to think that it would have been a great mistake to have hurried through the work of the settlement. Every year brought greater knowledge and power over the officials and the people, and at first our work was very much in the nature of an experiment, and we were not certain of our ground. I doubt whether haste would have been economical; I know that it would have been fatal to accuracy or permanency.

Looking at our settlement operations from a financial point of view; considering merely the immediate financial result and ignoring the large increase of revenue which will be gained from the amount of waste land which has been cultivated, and will year by year be added to the revenue roll; ignoring, too, the fact that the revenue demand is now a reality and not, as it was before, a sham, that regiments are no longer required for the realization of the revenue, and that the collections come to the State treasury instead of going into the pockets of middlemen, we find that the account is as follows:—

	Rs.
Total expenditure on settlement	3,37,010
Annual increase in revenue resulting from settlement .	1,85,103

That is to say, the expenditure on the settlement will be recouped within less than two years.

Notice of officers employed in settlement.

In another Report I have set forth the technical details of our work, and in this chapter I have only attended to matters which may possess a general interest. But a chapter on the new settlement would be incomplete if I omitted to mention the men who did the work. My three assistants were Mr. H. L. Rivett, Lala Narsingh Das, and Saiyad Alam Shah. Mr. H. L. Rivett joined me in the summer of 1891 as Irrigation and General Assistant. His knowledge of the people and his kindness to them quickly won the confidence of the Kashmíris, while his industry and ability have saved me much work. Narsingh Das joined at the commencement of the work, and left Kashmír at the beginning of 1893, to take up the appointment of Settlement Officer of the Jammu district. A man of ripe experience, great tact, and extraordinary industry, he did as much as any of us to carry through the Kashmír settlement. He has left behind him an excellent name in Kashmír, and I can never sufficiently express my obligations to Lala Narsingh Das. Saiyad Alam Shah joined the settlement in 1890, and remained till the survey was completed in 1893. He worked with the greatest industry, and with intense sympathy, and he has done much to encourage and re-settle fugitive Kashmíris. He passed two severe winters in Kashmír, and his health and eyesight suffered. But he never lost heart, and throughout opposition and abuse heaped on his head by the Hindus of Kashmír, he did his duty. To all these I am much indebted. The lower grades in the settlement contained many excellent workers. The Kashmíris have found employment in their own country, but the Panjabis worked with the full knowledge that their services would win them no appointments in Kashmír when the settlement was finished. Many of these men deserve high praise, but I can only mention here Deputy Superintendents Gursahi Mal and Amir Singh. Gursahi Mal was the best of the Deputy Superintendents, and died in harness in 1891. His zeal and industry made the *Patwári* School a success, and all his work was good and careful. His death was caused by devotion to his work. Amir Singh was appointed to the Gilgit settlement in June, 1893. His work in Kashmír was thorough and satisfactory. The settlement establishment of Kashmír is now dispersed. The State owes them its gratitude, and will remember that the establishment was formed by Mr. Wingate, and recruited by the late Lieutenant-Colonel Wace, Financial Commissioner of the Panjab.

CHAPTER XIX.

LANGUAGE AND GLOSSARY.

I. LANGUAGE.

CHAP. XIX.

KÁSHUR, the language of the Kashmíris, is said to be a Prákrit[1] of the pure and original Sanskrit, and some say that it was in former times a written language in Shárada characters, Shárada being a brother form of the Devanágari. There are doubts, however, as to whether it was ever written, and at present any one who wishes to write in the Káshur language employs Persian letters, to which certain sibilants not known in the Persian alphabet have to be added. *Ch* is used by Kashmíris to represent *ts*, a letter very common but most difficult to pronounce; final *l*, *m* *n*, *r* are usually pronounced as though they had a vowel added to them; *w* and *b* are sometimes convertible. The town we know as Bárámúlá is known to most Kashmíris as *Wáramula*.

Most of the learned Kashmíris state that the Káshur vocabulary is a polyglot, and that out of every hundred words 25 will be Sanskrit, 40 Persian, 15 Hindustáni, and 10 Arabic. The remaining 10 will be Tibetan, Turki, Dogri, and Panjabi. Káshur has a grammar of its own, which distinctly recalls one's faint efforts in Sanskrit grammar. It is highly inflectional, and offers not only forms of reduplication, but also makes changes within the root. My knowledge of Káshur is chiefly limited to a colloquial acquaintance with terms in common use in village and agricultural life. What else I have learnt I owe to Pir Hassan Shah, a learned Kashmíri, whose work lies entirely among the villagers. It is an interesting fact that Kashmíri emigrants in distant parts of India retain their old language, though generations have passed since they left the valley.

I have alluded elsewhere to the curious hieroglyphs of the shawl-weavers, known as Tálim. This is a writing purely for loom purposes,

[1] Dr. Bühler writes, 'I feel therefore not certain that the Shárada alphabet is not one of the ancient literary alphabets, dating perhaps from the times of the Guptas or earlier . . . . . . Kashmíri is a Prakrit, one of the languages descended from the Sanskrit, or rather from one of the dialects out of which the classical Sanskrit was formed. It differs, however, very considerably from all its Indian sister-tongues. Nearest to it comes Sindhî.'

and the shawl-weavers in everyday life speak the ordinary Káshur. At first sight the Tálim reminds one of the notation used in music. CHAP. XIX.

In the glossary I have given the more common words in use among the villagers, excluding all words which are obviously Persian or Hindustáni. Kashmíri names of plants, trees, and economic products will be found in the body of the Report. The curious use of sibilants and nasals in Káshur almost defies transliteration, but I hope that the Kashmíri words which I have given will be intelligible to those who understand the difference between *a* and *á* and *u* and *ú*. In every case, before transliteration, I have first had the word written in the Persian character. The glossary may prove useful to those who have business with the villagers. Small as Kashmír is, it is large enough to boast of two or three dialects [1], and there is a great difference between the language of the Srinagar people and that of the agriculturists. It is natural that the language of the citizens of Srinagar should have been more affected by the various foreign dynasties which have ruled in Kashmír than the language of the villagers. In Srinagar nearly every Kashmíri word has its Persian synonym. In the villages real Kashmíri is spoken, and though *lambardárs* and other persons of position can converse in Urdu, the ordinary peasant will speak Kashmíri. It is a common thing to hear the villagers remonstrating with one of their number who is speaking a mixture of bad Urdu, Panjabi, and Dogri, and exhorting him to speak in Kashmíri—*Káshur pat.*

The Kashmíri language has never been considered worthy of study by the foreigners who have ruled the country for so many generations, and, with the exception of the Pandits, there are practically no officials who can do more than give simple orders in Kashmíri. This is to be regretted, as apart from the fact that the language would repay study [2], the people are extremely proud and pleased to find any one who can understand their mother-tongue. The language of Srinagar has been studied by the missionaries, and a grammar and small dictionary have been written, which are of great help to the beginner. But the language of the valley has yet to be investigated, and the philologist would find a delightful task in preparing a grammar and dictionary of the Kashmíri language. My brief and imperfect study convinces me that the vocabulary is rich, that the phrases are direct and unambiguous, and that many terms are full of poetic thought. A collection of proverbs has been made, and many in use among the villagers argue shrewdness and wit. The songs of the Kashmíris are chiefly erotic, and have the same turns of thought as are

[1] The dialect of Kámraj, the northern portion of Kashmír, differs from the dialect of Maráj, the southern portion, and both differ from that of Yamráj, Srinagar.

[2] Dr. Bühler remarks, 'It has the greatest importance for the comparative grammar of the Indian vernaculars, because, for instance, it so clearly reveals the manner in which the new cases of the declension have been formed from the old bases, a point which in other languages is exceedingly difficult.'

CHAP. XIX. found in Persian poetry. The accent of the language is curiously like the English, and I have often, when listening to Kashmíris, imagined that an Englishman was speaking. Among the expressions which strike me as poetical is the use of the word *shongan*, to fall asleep, to signify death; and among the many proverbs which the villagers quote so freely I mention the following:—

Tsarin katan na sud;
Tsarin gagrain na rud;
Tsarin tongan na dudh.

'In many words there is no profit;
With much thunder there is no rain;
With much lowing there is no milk.'

Yeli piyi rúd
Teli wati rab.

'When rain falls
Then comes mud.'

'There is no smoke without fire.'

Many of the proverbs commenting on the agricultural classes would appear to have been written by dwellers in the city. The agriculturist is, according to the proverbs, an elephant, devoid of taste, a false friend, and a cowardly foe:—

Grustụ hastu.

'The agriculturist is an elephant.'

Grust yár kayur nár.

'The friendship of the peasant is like pine fuel,' i.e. it is soon burnt out.'

The *grust*, or agriculturists, respond in kind, and the proverbs regarding the city Pandits are not complimentary. According to the proverbs the Pandit is your friend while he wants something; he is dark in his ways and cruel:—

Bata yár be rozgár.

'The Pandit is your friend when he is out of employment.'

Bata kár gatá kár.

'Pandit's work—dark work.'

Bata chuh gratah.

'The Pandit is like a mill.'

The proverb—

Gabih buthih ramahhún

exactly corresponds to our—

'Wolf in sheep's clothing.'

Alan chuh phal, nendan chuh dánih.

'Ploughing gives harvest, weeding gives rice,'

is an obvious proposition, but it is often necessary to remind careless cultivators of it. CHAP. XIX.

Many proverbs give a fair idea of the former condition of the country.

Kanh mat ditam
Kantil nitam.

'Don't give me wages, but give me access to your ear,'

recalls days not long distant when influence with a person in power could be turned into money.

Khuda sanz khar
Tah naid sanz chep.

'God gives the scaldhead, and
The barber aggravates matters by gashing your head.'

This proverb, as an old and experienced official told me, was frequently applied to a woman who, having lost a child in the river, is arrested by the police on a trumped-up charge of murder.

Aram kad na muj
Fakiran daras kisht.

'The market-gardener has not pulled a radish, but the beggar pushes forward his bowl.'

The beggars with their bowls (*kisht*) are very common in Kashmír, and they spare no man, however small his possessions may be.

Raomut pula har sheht mohur.

'He has lost his grass shoes, and claims seven gold mohurs as compensation.'

The Kashmíris, like other orientals, are inclined to exaggerate their losses, though they always under-estimate their possessions.

Mulan drot tah patran sag.

'He cuts the roots and waters the leaves.'

This proverb is used of a treacherous, intriguing man.

Yak chat sum ta sas gau kulih.

'One man cuts the bridge and a thousand are drowned.'

The names of villages strike one as peculiar, and it is possible that any one with a knowledge of Sanskrit might be able to trace the meaning of the names. The Kashmíri of course denies that there is any meaning in them. Among common affixes in village names may be mentioned—*Búg-*, *Háma-*, *Shistr-*, *Mula-*, *Littar-*, *Nagri-*, *Ingu-*, *Hal-*, *Nur-*, *Gund-*, *Bal-*, *Patri-*, *Wáma-*, *Gul-*, *Gu-*, *Than-*, *Yera-*, *Waji-*, *Zu-*, and *Zar-*. It is said that the present quaint, often unspellable, names are old Sanskrit words corrupted by Todar Mal when he drew up a list of the villages of Kashmír for his master Akbar.

CHAP. XIX.

II. GLOSSARY.

ENGLISH.	KASHMÍRI.
A.	
Abdomen	*Yad.*
Abutilon	*Yechkár.*
Accusation	*Háts.*
Actors	*Bánd.*
Adieu	*Hawalat khuda.*
Affluent	*Diárwol.*
Aged	*Piri mard.*
Agricultural association	*Kumak.*
Agriculture	*Grist.*
Ague	*Tab.*
Alive, to be	*Lasan.*
All	*Soré.*
Alloy	*Kut.*
Almonds	*Badám.*
— sweet	*— shirin.*
— bitter	*— talkh.*
Alone	*Kuni.*
Amidst	*Manz-bágh.*
Amulet	*Táwiz.*
Anecdote	*Kat.*
Angling	*Wol.*
Appetite, to have	*Shrapun.*
Apple	Tsu*nt.*
Aqueduct	*Nahritár.*
Arrange	*Sherun.*
Artist	*Nakásh.*
Ass	*Khar.*
Aunt, paternal	*Pop.*
— maternal	*Más.*
Avalanche	*Mán.*
Awake	*Hushár.*
Axeman	*Tabadár.*
B.	
Baby	*Shur.*
Bachelor	*Anhor.*
Baker	*Kándr.*
Ball	*Pind.*
Bandage for leg	*Patawa* (corrupted into *Patti*).
Bank	*Sut.*
Bara-singh	*Hángal.*
Barber	*Naid.*
Barges, large, with raised prow, carrying 800 maunds	*Bahats.*
— smaller, with low prow	*Wár.*
Barley	*Wiska.*
Basket-maker	*Shákzas* or *Kainyal.*
Baskets for rice	*Paj.*
Beams	*Kháda.*
Bean	*Bákla.*
Bear	*Hápat.*
— red	*— koin.*
— black	*— bombur.*
Bed	*Wathran.*
Bees	*Mánchtilr.*
Beggar	*Bechan-wol.*
Beggar's bowl	*Kisht.*
Behind	*Pat.*
Big	*Bod.*
Birds	*Jánawár.*
Blacksmith	*Khár.*
Blanket	*Lohi.*
Blood	*Rat.*
Boat	*Náo.*
Boil, a	*Fafar.*
— to	*Kárun.*
Both	*Dushwai.*
Boundary	*And.*
Brass	*Sártal.*
Bread	*Tsut* or *Tsacha.*
Breakfast	*Nipari.*
Brick	*Sír.*
Bride	*Nush.*
Bride's house	*Málun.*
Bridegroom's house	*Wáreo.*
Bridge	*Kadal.*
Bring, to	*Annun.*
Budding	*Pirth paiwand* or *Barg paiwand.*
Bullock	*Dánd.*
Burn, to	*Dazun.*
Bush	*Thara.*
Butter	*Than.*

ENGLISH.	KASHMÍRI.

C.

Calendar	*Jantri.*
Call, to	*Nád diun.*
Cap	*Kal posh.*
Capon	*Kas kokar.*
Carnation	*Neaó posh.*
Carpenter	*Chán.*
Carrier-pony	*Markhbán.*
— donkey	*Kharwála.*
Cat	*Bror.*
Caterpillar	*Moru.*
Cattle	*Dánd.*
— diseases—	
Diarrhoea	*Chirágh beg.*
Pox—remedy for this is slitting of ears	*Hul haji.*
Swelled mouth and feet	*Asnur.*
Swelling in throat	*Kafgan.*
Change of air, one who has changed his mode of living (used of sheep and cattle)	*Pánporad.*
Clematis	*Wan alach.*
Cold, to be	*Túrun.*
— to make	*Shaelun.*
Colour—	
Green	*Sabz.*
Yellow	*Zarnak.*
Light yellow	*Gandak.*
Purple	*Sosni.*
Chocolate	*Hirmaji.*
Crimson	*Shingrafi* or *Krimsi.*
Red	*Wozul.*
White	*Chut.*
Black	*Kruhun.*
Comb, to	*Páran.*
Come, to	*Yiun.*
Cook	*Waza.*
— to	*Ranun.*
Copper	*Tram.*
Core of maize	*Kashri.*
Cost, to	*Laiun.*
Cotton seed	*Tudth.*
Cough	*Nazla.*
Counting	*Ganzarak.*
Courtyard	*Angun.*
Credit	*Pats.*
Cross	*Tarun.*
Cuckoo	*Shakúk.*
Cuffs of sleeves turned up	*Nur phirit.*
Cut, to, crops	*Lonun.*
— trees	*Tsatun.*

D.

Dam	*Gand.*
Dance, to	*Natsun.*
— at shrine in honour of saint	*Dumáli.*
Daphne	*Ganda linu.*
Dark	*Anigat.*
Daughter	*Kur.*
Day	*Doh.*
Daylight	*Gásh.*
Dear	*Drúg.*
Debt, to discharge	*Horun nak walun.*
Deceive, to	*Tambláwan.*
Decree given by mufti or Kázi	*Fatwah.*
Deep	*Sun.*
Destroy, to	*Gálun.*
Dew	*Lawa* or *Shabnam.*
Dibble in, to (used of rice plants)	*Runun.*
Dig, to	*Khanun.*
Dinner	*Battakheu.*
Dip well	*Dhenkli.*
Dish	*Bána.*
— of food	*Sun.*
Dog	*Hun.*
Dog-rose	*Krir.*
Door of house	*Baran.*
Drag, to	*Lamun.*
Drink, to	*Cheun.*
Drum	*Nagára.*
Dry	*Huk.*
Dung, of horses	*Lid.*
— cattle	*Gu.*
— sheep	*Mengan.*

CHAP. XIX.

E.

ENGLISH.	KASHMÍRI.
Early	*Sulih.*
Earthquake	*Bunyal.*
Edge, on the	*Andáand.*
Eggs	*Tul.*
Elm	*Bren.*
Enter, to	*Atsun.*
Envy, malice	*Hassad.*
Eye	*Ach.*
Eyebrow	*Bomb.*
Eyelash	*Achawál.*

F.

ENGLISH.	KASHMÍRI.
Face	*But.*
Fall, to	*Piun.*
Fallow of rice	*Muru.*
Famine	*Drág.*
Fat	*Viot.*
Father	*Mol* or *Bab.*
Fear	*Bim.*
Feast	*Sawálá.*
— marriage	*Yera.*
Feather	*Tir.*
Fetch, to	*Hiyun.*
Field, irrigated or vegetable land	*Dúr.*
— dry	*Daj.*
Fight—	
Words	*Harahar.*
Blows	*Lahilahi.*
Fill, to	*Barun.*
Fine (of weather)	*Dur.*
Finial of shrine	*Prang.*
Fire	*Tungal.*
— (conflagration)	*Nár.*
Fish	*Gád.*
Flag	*Alam.*
Floating	*Yéra.*
Flood	*Yúp.*
Flower	*Posh.*
Followers or disciples	*Murid.*
Food	*Khen.*
Foot	*Khor.*
— to go on	*Pathar pakun.*
Forest	*Wan.*
Forget, to	*Mashráwun.*
Fowl	*Kukar.*
Frog	*Ningi mundak.*
Front, in	*Bont.*
Frost	*Sur.*
Fuel—	
Cowdung cake	*But* or *Lubr.*
Grass and briars	*Thathri.*
Shells of singhara nuts	*Kanga.*

G.

ENGLISH.	KASHMÍRI.
Gargoyle of shrine	*Lewach.*
Glade	*Patri.*
Glumes of rice	*Kesar.*
Glutton	*Yadal.*
Goat	*Tsáwaj.*
Goitre	*Gadaru.*
Graft	*Arrahpaiwand.*
Grain, swelling	*Máyah.*
— ripe (of rice)	*Phul.*
Granary, wooden	*Kuthár.*
— made of clay	*Lopanu.*
Grandfather	*Budibab.*
Grazing-ground	*Núr;* the Gujars use the word *Dok.*
Great, to grow	*Badun.*
Grind, to	*Pihun.*
Guest	*Puts.*
Guitar	*Rabab.*

H.

ENGLISH.	KASHMÍRI.
Hail	*Dont.*
Hair	*Mast.*
Hammer	*Dokar.*
Handkerchief	*Daj.*
Hatchet	*Túr.*
Hawthorn	*Ring.*
Hay	*Láo.*
Hazel nut	*Virin.*
Head	*Kal.*
Heron	*Breg.*
Heron's feathers, plume of	*Gund.*
Hide, to	*Khattun.*
Hive	*Mánchgan.*
Hoe, hand	*Tongru.*

ENGLISH.	KASHMÍRI.
Hoes on long poles for gathering singhara nuts	*Kamkhuru.*
Hole	*Gud.*
Honey	*Mánch.*
Honey-bees	*Mánch tilr.*
Honeysuckle	*Pakhr Phul.*
Horse	*Gur.*
Horse-keepers	*Galwán.*
House	*Lar.*
— ground floor	*Gán.*
— first floor	*Kutphor.*
— loft	*Kuinphor.*
— apertures through which heated breath of cattle and sheep passes from ground floor to first floor	*Wúg.*
Husk (outer husk of rice)	*Toh.*
— to	*Munnun.*
Husked	*Mun.*
Husking, result of	*Mántr.*

I.

ENGLISH.	KASHMÍRI.
Ibex	*Kel.*
Ice	*Tulr katr.*
Icicle	*Shishr-gánt.*
Indigo, wild	*Kats.*
Ink	*Míl.*
Irrigation	*Ábpáshi.*
— system by which villagers are bound to repair and clean irregular channels	*Atilkulwán.*
Ivy	*Kirmil.*

J.

ENGLISH.	KASHMÍRI.
Jasmine	*Hé.*
Join, to	*Wútun.*

K.

ENGLISH.	KASHMÍRI.
Karéwa	*Udar.*
Kernel of walnut	*Gojh.*
Knife	*Sharák.*
— pocket	*Sharák poch.*
Knot of a tree	*Ag.*
Knuckle bones and other bones which are left after a Hindu is burnt	*Astarak.*

L.

ENGLISH.	KASHMÍRI.
Lake	*Dal* (said to be a Tibetan word meaning 'still').
Land near houses	*Gámdu.*
Last watch of day	*Patim.*
Lattice-work	*Pinjara.*
Leaf	*Panwatr.*
Leaf-stem of Nilumbium speciosum	*Nadru.*
Leech	*Drik.*
Left side	*Khowar.*
Leopard, snow	*Rámahun.*
Lift, to	*Tulun.*
Lightning	*Wuza mal.*
Lilac	*Yosmun.*
Lime	*Ahak.*
Little	*Lokat.*
Loan	*Wazam.*
Locker in which sheep are penned	*Dangij.*
Locust	*Hálu.*
Log harrow	*Maj.*
— over which rice is threshed	*Wana munda.*
Lost, to be	*Ráwun.*
Lunatics	*Múdt.*
Lunch	*Mimus.*

M.

ENGLISH.	KASHMÍRI.
Man	*Mániyu.*
— who reads hieroglyphics of Tálim	*Gadanwol.*
Manal pheasant	*Sonar chickur.*
Manure	*Hel.*
— basket-load of	*Yethi.*
Marks on foreheads of Hindus	*Tika.*
Marriage	*Khándr.*
Meat	*Máz.*
Meet, to	*Samkhun.*

CHAP. XIX.

English.	Kashmíri.
Melon	*Kharbuz.*
— water	*Hindawand.*
Menials	*Nángár.*
Middle-aged	*Adwár.*
Midwife	*Wárin.*
Milk	*Dodh.*
— skim	*Guras.*
— curdled	*Zamat.*
Milk-seller	*Gaogujri.*
Mill	*Grát.*
Minstrels	*Shàir.*
Mist	*Zánd.*
Mix, to	*Ádrun.*
Moon	*Zun.*
Morels	*Guchi.*
Mortar	*Kanz.*
Mother	*Mojh.*
Mother-in-law	*Hash.*
Mountain	*Pántsál.*
Much, excessive	*Wárujáh.*
Mud	*Rab.*
Musk-bag	*Nafa.*
— deer	*Kastura.*

N.

English.	Kashmíri.
Nail, human	*Nam.*
— metal	*Kuil.*
Naked	*Netnun.*
Name	*Nao.*
Needle	*Satzan.*
Nephew	*Báptar.*
Net	*Zál.*
Nettles	*Soi.*
Niece	*Bawaza.*
Nose	*Nast.*
Nursery for rice	*Thajnár.*

O.

English.	Kashmíri.
Oath	*Dre.*
Oil cake	*Kaj.*
Old, to grow	*Budun.*
Onion	*Prán.*
Open, to	*Mutsaráwun.*

P.

English.	Kashmíri.
Paddle, a	*Kúr.*
Paddle, to	*Waiun.* (This verb is also used of ringing coins to see if they are genuine.)
Pain	*Dod.*
Panther	*Ser.*
Paper on which design of carpet or shawl is written	*Tálim.*
Parrot	*Shogh.*
Passage leading to a house	*Kocha.*
Pattens	*Karawahar.*
Pattu, the woollen homespun of Kashmír	*Put.*
Peace	*Rahat.*
Peach	Tsannan.
Pestle	*Mohl.*
Piece	*Fal.*
Pieces of money	*Diár.*
Pigeon	*Kotar.*
Pipe	*Jajir.*
Pit used for concealing grain from officials	*Zús.*
Pitch	*Kilam.*
Plaits of hair	*Wank.*
— gathered into a knot and fastened by a tassel	*Wankopan.*
Plank	*Latawat.*
Plant, to	*Runun.*
Play, to	*Gindun.*
Pony	*Gúr.*
Poppy, red	*Gulála.*
Population of a village including agriculturists and menials	*Janaját.*
Porridge	*Wogur.*
Potter	*Král.*
Poudrette	*Kála mitti.*
Powder-gun	*Shora.*
Preacher	*Wáz khwán.*
Prop	*Tham.*

Q.

English.	Kashmíri.
Quickly	*Wudan* or *Tikán.*

ENGLISH.	KASHMÍRI.
R.	
Radish	*Mujh.*
Rain	*Rud.*
Rainbow	*Rám Rám badrin dún*, lit. the bow of Ram Chandr.
Rat	*Gagar.*
Razor	*Khúr.*
Report	*Shhurat.*
Rice, red	*Zag.*
— white	*Prun.*
— plants	*Thal.*
— husker	*Kanz ta mohl.*
— lever mill	*Indr mohl.*
— coloured with turmeric	*Tahar.*
— ricks of	*Guni.*
— fields, large	*Bad wattru.*
— „ small	*Lar wattru.*
— „ terraced	*Ach karu* or *Dulwushu.*
— final watering of	*Popasag.*
— kinds of—	
good white	*Básmati.*
„	*Kanyun.*
„	*Dud krir.*
„	*Brez.*
„	*Reban.*
„	*Katchán.*
„	*Imbrzal.*
„	*Watihal.*
„	*Babar.*
„	*Mughal biol.*
„	*Mushk budji.*
— good croppers—	
red	*Kai zag.*
„	*Maiwan.*
„	*Mawar.*
— hardy growing—	
at high elevation	*Niwar.*
„	*Shiwar.*
„	*Shalkyun.*
— ploughing—dry	*Táo.*
„ wet	*Kenalu.*
— sowing—broadcast	*Wattru.*
„ nursery	*Niháli.*
„ seedlings	*Thal.*
Rice, sowing season	*Wap* or *Ziyut.*
— seedlings, planting of	*Trupai.*
— weeds in fields	*Kach.*
— weeding and working—	
by hand	*Khushába.*
by feet	*Lat.*
by cattle	*Haji, gupannind* or *Hillu.*
— 1st Khushába	*Watai, aree-tsar pangrai* or *Kachnind.*
— 2nd „	*Srond* or *Mahznind.*
— 3rd „	*Motnind.*
— 4th „	*Trowanind, dalnind* or *Basta phuráo.*
Right side	*Dachan.*
Ring finger	*Waj.*
Road	*Wat.*
Roasted	*Buzit.*
Robbery	*Sau.*
Roof	*Pash.*
Rope of vegetables	*Tsaráh.*
Rosary	*Tasbih.*
Rub, to	*Guhun.*
Run, to	*Takun.*
S.	
Sacks of grass in which seeds are kept	*Vetran.*
Sad, to be	*Diyan.*
Saddle	*Káthi.*
Salt	*Nún.*
Sand	*Sek.*
Sawyer	*Arikash.*
School	Ts*átahál.*
Scissors	*Dakúr.*
Scratch, to	*Kashun.*
Scum on water	*Shil.*
Search, to	*Gárun, tsándun.*
Seed	*Biol.*
Sew, to	*Sivun.*
Shawl-weavers	*Shálpút.*
Sheep, a flock	*Tir.*
— female	*Gab.*
— male	*Kat.*
— ram	*Wur.*

CHAP. XIX.

ENGLISH.	KASHMÍRI.
Sheep tax	*Dánai.*
— wether	*Bála.*
Shepherd	*Pohl.*
Shingle	*Pachi.*
Shop	*Wán.*
Shopkeeper	*Wáni.*
Shovel	*Krúts.*
Shrine	*Ziárat.*
Sickle	*Dátri.*
Sieve	*Párun.*
Sift or divide	*Tsárun.*
Silk	*Pot.*
Silkworm	*Potkium.*
Single-stick	*Gatka.*
Sky	*Nab.*
Slants of a roof	*Cheháru.*
Sleep, to	*Shongan.*
— to put to	*Sawun.*
Smooth	*Pishal.*
Snail	*Hángi.*
Snake	*Saraf.*
Snow	*Shin.*
Snuff	*Nást.*
— a pinch of	*Nást mushk.*
Son	*Nechu.*
Son-in-law	*Zamtur.*
Sorry, to be	*Pashun.*
Sow, to	*Wáwun.*
Spade	*Lewan.*
Spike of rice	*Huil.*
Spring day	*Sont.*
— of water	*Nág.*
Stem of a tree	*Godah.*
Stick	*Lúr.*
Stone	*Kánah.*
Strawberry	*Ingrach.*
Suit, to	*Waiun.*
Sunshine	*Táp.*
Swamp	*Nambal.*
Sweet	*Mudrer.*

T.

ENGLISH.	KASHMÍRI.
Tailor	*Suts.*
Take off	*Kadun.*
Tassels of wood attached to gargoyles of shrine	*Kanadur.*
Tea with sugar	*Kahwa.*
Thin	*Shust.*
Thistle	*Mitsai kundu.*
Threshing	*Chúmba.*
Throw, to	*Tsunnun.*
Thunder	*Gagrain.*
Tipcat	*Lat kinch lut.*
Torch	*Lashi.*
Torture, tyranny	*Azáb.*
Trolly	*Hagru.*
True	*Poz.*
Tuck of turban	*But.*
Tunic worn by all Kashmíris	*Pheran.*
Tunnel	*Hodahgulu.*
Turf clods	*Chak.*

U.

ENGLISH.	KASHMÍRI.
Uncle	*Pitr.*
Untrue	*Apoz.*

V.

ENGLISH.	KASHMÍRI.
Vegetables	*Hák.*
Violets	*Nuna posh*, lit. the salt flower, as villagers exchange violets for salt.

W.

ENGLISH.	KASHMÍRI.
Wait, to	*Parárun.*
Wall	*Lab, dos.*
Walnuts	*Dun.*
Warm, to	*Táwan.*
— to be	*Tatun.*
Wash, to	*Ehhalun.*
Washerman	*Dhób.*
Water	*Áb.*
Watercourse for irrigation	*Kul.*
— repairs	*Kulwán.*
Weave, to	*Wanun.*
Weaver	*Wáwar.*
— of shawls	*Shálpút.*
Weeding	*Ninda.*
Well	*Krur.*
Wet	*Adur.*
Why?	*Kyáza.*

ENGLISH.	KASHMÍRI.
Widow	*Mund.*
Wind	*Wawa.*

[The '*Wawa mal*' blows from the Banihal and is good for the crops.
The '*Bada Dabár*' blows from Bárámúlá and drives away malaria.
The '*Bada shál*' or '*Kamrázi*' is a violent wind blowing from Karnao.]

ENGLISH.	KASHMÍRI.
Woman	*Zandna.*
Wool	*Yer.*
— from Central Asian goats	*Fand* (pronounced in Kashmír, '*pamb*').
Wrap, to	*Walun.*

INDEX

C.

G.

H.

I.

R.

T.

U.

V.

W.

KASHMIR.

Compiled and drawn by Messrs R. L. Sinclair, E. C. Dowling, and S. C. Watson

Photo., S. I. O., Calcutta.

No. 423-S. 94.

REFERENCES

Tahsil Bd^y	—·—·—
do H^d Qr^s	•
Tablelands	(outline)

TAHSILS

NO	NAME
1	Lal Phak
2	Shahr Khas
3	Awantpura
4	Anantnág
5	Sri Ranbir Singhp^ra
6	Hampur
7	Naggám
8	Sri Partab Singhp^ra
9	Pattan
10	Uttar Machip^ra
11	Sopur